Maximizing MS-DOS 5

David Solomon
Jim Boyce
Michael O. Coulter
Jerry W. Ellis
Danny R. Kusnierz
Mark Marchi
Stuart Stuple
David Trout
Brian Underdahl
Karen Lynn White

NRP
NEW RIDERS
PUBLISHING

New Riders Publishing, Carmel, Indiana

Maximizing MS-DOS 5

By David Solomon
Jim Boyce
Michael O. Coulter
Jerry W. Ellis
Danny R. Kusnierz
Mark Marchi
Stuart Stuple
David Trout
Brian Underdahl
Karen Lynn White

Published by:
New Riders Publishing
11711 N. College Ave., Suite 140
Carmel, IN 46032 USA

Printed in the United States of America 1 2 3 4 5 6 7 8 9 0

Library of Congress Cataloging-in-Publication Data
Maximizing MS-DOS 5 / David W. Solomon ... [et al.].
        p.   cm.
    Includes index.
    ISBN 1-56205-013-3
    1. Operating systems (Computers 2. MS-DOS.   I. Solomon, David W.
QA76.76.083M372 199
005.4'4—DC20   91-19867
                                                         CIP

Publisher
David P. Ewing

Acquisitions Editor
Brad Koch

Product Director
David Solomon

Production Editors
Tim Huddleston
Nancy Sixsmith

Technical Editors
Brad Koch
Daniel Kusnierz
John Little
Dan Schultz
Stuart Stuple

Editors
Peter Kuhns
Richard Limacher
Mark Montieth
Robert Tidrow

Editorial Secretary
Karen Opal

Book Design and Production
William Hartman, Hartman Publishing

Proofreader
Nancy Sixsmith

Indexed by
Jill Bomaster

Composed in Bookman, Helvetica, and Courier by
William Hartman, Hartman Publishing

About the Authors

David W. Solomon, Director of Product Development for New Riders Publishing, is also a staff writer who specializes in operating systems, database management, and programming. Since 1978, he has worked with a variety of operating systems on both minicomputers and microcomputers, and has developed and written custom software for scientific and business applications on a worldwide basis. Mr. Solomon has authored or co-authored more than ten books about microcomputer software.

Jim Boyce has been involved with computers since the late 1970s as a user, system administrator, programmer, and college educator. He was a full-time member of the faculty of Texas State Technical Institute for six years. He is currently a free-lance author whose work has appeared regularly in a number of CAD- and computer-related magazines, including *CADalyst, CADENCE, MicroCAD News,* and *PC Magazine*. Mr. Boyce was author of *Maximizing Windows 3*, and a contributor to *Inside AutoCAD*, Sixth Edition, both of which are published by New Riders Publishing. He is a full press member of the Computer Press Association.

Michael O. Coulter is a professional computer consultant and writer. He holds a bachelor of arts degree, majoring in English from Indiana University. He has worked in the computer industry for more than 12 years, specializing in insurance and restaurant business applications. He has a wide background in formal writing, as well as fiction.

Jerry W. Ellis is a product development specialist for Que Corporation. Mr. Ellis has provided technical support on a wide variety of best-selling Que books. He has worked with a variety of microcomputers and minicomputer systems since the early 1980s. Mr. Ellis is the former owner and operator of Ellis & Associates, a computer consulting firm. He designed and set up statewide computer networks, specializing in communications and applications development.

Danny R. Kusnierz is a Novell-Certified Netware engineer with more than 13 years in the personal computer industry. He is currently working as a computer consultant with an emphasis on LANS. His past experience includes computer sales, end-user training, programming and systems engineering.

Mark Pio Marchi holds an Associate Degree in Computer Science from Indiana Vocational and Technical College. He has been employed since 1984 as a computer programmer and systems analyst for Fourway Computer Products.

Stuart J. Stuple is a Project Editor for New Riders Publishing, focusing on operating systems, user interfaces and network technology. He lives in the Portland, Oregon area and, in addition to his work for NRP, teaches computer science and psychology at several local colleges. Mr. Stuple has worked with computer technology for more than ten years and has extensive experience with DOS, UNIX, and Macintosh applications and operating systems. He holds degrees from Reed College and Lewis and Clark College.

David Trout attended Indiana University and is currently finishing a degree in computer science at Vincennes University. He is presently employed at Heath Zenith Computers as a Systems Engineer and is a Certified NetWare Engineer. Mr. Trout has worked professionally in the computer industry for the past five years.

Brian Underdahl is an independent consultant based in Reno, Nevada. He has authored, co-authored, or has been technical editor of a number of books for Macmillan Computer Publishing. His background in both engineering and business gives him the ability to accurately present complex topics in an effective, understandable style.

Karen Lynn White is the senior technical programmer for the Medical Sciences Program at Indiana University in Bloomington, Indiana. She holds a Master of Science degree in computer science from Indiana University and a Bachelor of Arts degree in Mathematics. She has worked in the field for five years, doing everything from technical design to consulting. Although she has written several technical papers, this is the first time she has written for the popular market.

Acknowledgments

New Riders Publishing would like to express its sincere thanks to the following people and companies, for their valuable contributions to this book:

Tom Lennon, of Microsoft's MS-DOS 5 Programming Team, for input early in the DOS 5 Beta cycle.

Christy Gersich, Public Relations Coordinator of Microsoft Corporation, for coordinating Beta software for the authors.

Tanya D. van Dam, Public Relations Specialist, Advanced Operating Systems, for assistance with LAN Manager information.

Brad Koch, for assembling the authoring team for *Maximizing MS-DOS 5*.

NRP Production Editors Nancy Sixsmith and Tim Huddleston, for their expert management of the editing and preproduction preparation of the text.

Copy Editors Peter Kuhns, Robert Tidrow, Richard Limacher, and Mark Montieth, for cheerfully learning DOS conventions and working at an exhausting pace.

Bill Hartman of Hartman Publishing, for the design effort and expeditious handling of materials.

Karen Opal, for editorial assistance wherever needed.

Special thanks to Microsoft Corporation, for providing the material that appears in Appendix C.

Trademark Acknowledgments

Warning and Disclaimer

Contents at a Glance

Table of Contents

Part One

Part Two

Part Three

10 Configuring DOS for Optimal Memory Usage 297

Part Four

A   B   C

Introduction

MS-DOS is the operating system that more people use than any other operating system. Since its introduction in 1981, MS-DOS has evolved through five major revisions and numerous minor revisions. Each revision brought new features and benefits to PC users and programmers. Version 5.0 represents the latest and most useful version of MS-DOS to date. Version 5.0 offers users of MS-DOS V3 and V4 enhancements that make daily computing more efficient and powerful.

Maximizing MS-DOS 5 is written to the new MS-DOS 5 standard and provides DOS users with a practical, example-oriented text that maximizes the user's existing knowledge and then expands that knowledge even further. The Product Development team at New Riders Publishing recognizes that PC users have to budget their DOS learning time sparingly in order to concentrate their efforts on gaining skill in the areas of their primary applications software. Still, nearly every PC user can improve his or her computing experience by investing learning time in the effective use of MS-DOS.

This book presents countless examples of DOS commands and configurations in action. You can see the DOS syntax screen dialog in running examples. You learn tips and techniques for using the trusted "core" DOS commands and increase your DOS prowess through the task-oriented examples of the less frequently used commands. If networking connections and Microsoft Windows are parts of your computing regimen, you will find plenty of notes that elaborate on DOS' kinship with these important areas. If you need a trusted reference guide to DOS, you have found it in *Maximizing MS-DOS 5*. You can flip to the Command Reference section and appendixes to get quick, accurate answers to your questions.

1

As a bonus, you receive the accompanying disk, which contains numerous macros, batch files, QBASIC utilities, and source code. You can use these macros, batch files, and utilities as they come on the disk, or you can modify them to suit your own unique needs. In either case, you will find that the disk's contents add another learning dimension to the book.

Who Should Read this Book?

Maximizing MS-DOS 5 is written for PC users who need a practical, task-oriented reference to DOS. This book explains the key concepts of DOS that provide an understanding of DOS beyond the introductory level. Yet *Maximizing MS-DOS 5* is not a highly technical or intimidating treatment of DOS. For example, the authors of the text assume that you know how to insert disks into drives and use your keyboard and mouse. At the same time, the authors assume that you may not be sure of how the file allocation table and directory structure are important to many commands. You may know how to copy a group of files using COPY, but do you know how to copy a branch of the directory structure with XCOPY? If XCOPY and other intermediate-level commands such as FDISK, REPLACE, and RESTORE are not in your DOS repertoire, then you (and your computing efficiency) will benefit from reading *Maximizing MS-DOS 5*.

What Versions of MS-DOS are Covered?

Maximizing MS-DOS 5 covers MS-DOS V5.0 (the text generally refers to the software as simply "DOS 5"). Users of previous versions of DOS will find that many of the tasks outlined in the text are compatible with their versions of DOS. To get the most from this book (and your PC), however, you should be using V5.0. Various original equipment manufacturers offer V5.0 in their customized form, but the customized DOS is still anchored to Microsoft's V5.0.

What Hardware is Covered?

Virtually all personal computers that support MS-DOS comply with the information presented in this book. Because the book shows you how to configure systems with various memory sizes and processors, you can use *Maximizing MS-DOS 5* to help you get the most from your 286 notebook machine, your old 8088 XT clone, or your new 486. The hardware coverage includes IBM Personal System /2 machines.

What Topics are not Covered?

Maximizing MS-DOS 5 does not cover the DOS programming environment or DEBUG. EDLIN and the LINK utility are not covered. EDLIN and DEBUG subcommands, however, are included in this book's Command Reference.

The Details of this Book

You can flip quickly through this book to get a feel for its organization. The beginning of the book lays a conceptual foundation for DOS and the PC. The text then builds on that conceptual information through topical chapters that present a practical view of DOS commands and capabilities. The book then presents a syntax-based command reference and appendixes. You can read the chapters in order, or pick and choose the order you that want to use. Wherever possible, an example that builds on another example or concept includes a reference to the location of the text that presents the referenced concept. You will notice that individual authors cover some important topics that another author has covered. This feature enables you to see commands and concepts from more than one perspective or in more than one context. The book is sectioned into four distinct parts. Each part carries a main theme through its chapters. Each theme is designed to approach your learning DOS in the same manner that you approach DOS work.

Part One—Getting up to Speed

Part One is a tutorial review of important DOS concepts. Before you can become fully effective with the many commands, directives, and configurations that DOS offers, you need a solid foundation in basic DOS concepts. Through the information presented in Part One, you will be equipped to get the most from the rest of the book.

Chapter 1, "Understanding Hardware and Software," presents the PC's hardware and fundamental software components. You will learn about system and peripheral hardware. You also will see that a working PC is not a single computing entity, but rather a system of interdependent layers that divides the computing activity into areas of responsibility.

Chapter 2, "Understanding DOS Data Structures," looks under the surface of the DOS command line to show you the "invisible" parts of DOS that shoulder the bulk of DOS' assigned file system duties. While you can use DOS commands without this inside knowledge, you will use many commands in an informed manner after you read this chapter. Parts Two and Three reference and elaborate on the facts and concepts presented in this chapter.

Chapter 3, "The Command Processor," presents COMMAND.COM and related topics. In this chapter, you will see the DOS command line processor and its enhancements, such as DOSKEY. If you have been issuing DOS commands by rote, this chapter will help you use general rules of syntax that enable you to be in control of DOS commands' actions. You will learn easy and efficient ways to issue, edit, and re-use command lines. With the information presented in this chapter and the previous two chapters, you will be ready to move to Part Two.

Part Two—Using Commands Productively

The DOS activity that most PC users do most frequently is issue commands at the DOS command line. The chapters in Part Two concentrate on DOS commands that make your computing work easier and ensure your data's integrity. Commands are presented in tasks that you are likely to perform as a proficient PC user. Part Two focuses on a category of commands that enable you to manage your PC.

Chapter 4, "Staying in Control of Disks," covers the commands offered by DOS for disk-level management. You will learn how to prepare and manipulate hard-disk partitions, format disks using various options, copy and compare disks, and more.

Chapter 5, "Navigating Directories," includes tasks that illustrate the important directory-management commands, as well as file management commands with directory-level options. If you want to maintain good organization of your hard disk directories, this chapter is a good beginning.

Chapter 6, "Keeping in Control of Files," presents DOS' file management and file-processing commands. Here, you will learn to use some of DOS' intermediate file commands to make your file maintenance tasks more efficient.

Chapter 7, "Using Filters, Pipes, and Redirection for Productivity," explains these important DOS provisions and shows you how to take advantage of their power. You will see tasks that use pipes and filters to build custom commands. You also will learn how redirection offers many powerful possibilities to the DOS user.

Chapter 8, "Ensuring Data Integrity," focuses on the commands and techniques that you use to minimize or eliminate the loss of disk information. This chapter reviews some DOS commands in the context of data integrity as it introduces new commands that are useful for recovering data.

Chapter 9, "Building on Your DOS Repertoire," discusses a variety of DOS commands that you may have occasion to use, but have used very little or taken for granted.

Part Three—Maximizing the Power of DOS 5

While understanding the usefulness of DOS commands is important to effective computing, so too is taking maximum advantage of your hardware resources. Part Three gives you the information you need to make the most of your memory and devices. In addition, Part Two presents practical tutorials on batch-file and macro programming as well as the new QBASIC programming language. The new DOS Shell is presented as an alternative user interface for conducting DOS-level work and providing a task-switched environment. After reading Part Two, you will have mastered some enhanced techniques for tackling DOS-level problems.

Chapter 10, "Configuring DOS for Optimal Memory Usage," guides you through the concepts and actions necessary to maximize the basic power of your memory configuration. You will learn how DOS 5 uses extended and expanded memory, and you will come to appreciate the gains in performance from fine-tuning files and buffer directives. You will learn to take advantage of disk- and directory-caching and you will find configuration tips for the 8088, 80286, 80386, and 80486 processors.

Chapter 11, "Controlling Devices," is your information resource for establishing devices in CONFIG.SYS and managing devices through DOS' device-control commands. You will be in control of your PC using the knowledge you gain in this chapter.

Chapter 12, "The DOS Shell," presents the DOS Shell. Chapter 12 gives serious consideration to your using the DOS Shell as an effective alternative to the DOS command line. If you are a Windows user, you will appreciate the many comparisons of the Windows environment with the DOS Shell.

Chapter 13, "Tapping the Power of Macros and Batch Files," is an informative, practical tutorial for anyone who wants to simplify complicated DOS tasks. Chapter 13 steps you through batch file and DOSKEY macro concepts as you follow usable examples.

Chapter 14, "Programming with QBasic," introduces Microsoft's new BASIC language to DOS users. While Chapter 14 is not intended to be a complete QBASIC tutorial, most DOS users will find that the chapter presents QBASIC in a manner that puts the language in perspective. QBASIC is an attractive alternative in many cases to batch-file programming. This chapter uses DOS utility programs as examples.

Part Four—Command Reference

Part Four is a complete presentation of DOS 5 commands and their syntax. You will find the Command Reference a valuable asset while using this book and while using DOS commands at your PC. The Command Reference describes each command, explaining the command's purpose and syntax, and offering examples of the command at work. You will learn when to use a command and find notes that clarify issues of the command's use or actions. You will want to keep this book close to your PC for easy access to the Command Reference.

Appendixes

At the end of the text are four appendixes that round out the contents of the book. Appendix A, "DOS 5 and Windows 3," gives attention to the use of DOS 5 with Windows 3. Appendix B, "NetWare Considerations," addresses topics that users and administrators of Novell NetWare will find helpful in installing, configuring, and using DOS 5. Appendix C, "LAN Manager Considerations," offers a similar discussion of the use of DOS 5 with LAN Manager. The final appendix, "Menu Map of the DOS 5 Editor," shows you the menu structure of the new DOS Editor. You can refer to the menu map while learning the editor or accessing new editing features for the first time.

Learning More about Operating Systems

Unfortunately, a single book can not concentrate at the same time on DOS, networking, Windows, and other operating systems. If you have a greater need for information in one or more of these areas, you will find that NRP offers a variety of books that suit your needs.

If you are an experienced PC user who is making the transition to Windows 3, NRP's *Inside Windows* is an ideal book to use as a fast-track learning aid. *Inside Windows* teaches you about the Windows-based features common to the majority of Windows-capable applications. With *Inside Windows*, you will reach the power curve of Windows computing.

If you have been using Windows 3, or if you are just beginning but are a fast study, then NRP's *Maximizing Windows 3* has content tailored for your needs. *Maximizing Windows 3* is the inside track to power Windows use.

If you are a Novell Netware user, NRP's *Inside Novell Netware* deserves a spot on your bookshelf. *Inside Novell Netware* is written to an end user's perspective of network computing. The book provides content that end users can readily use and appreciate. The book avoids "high-powered" networking concepts while concentrating on issues that cause ordinary users to lose comput-ing efficiency. Yet coverage of Netware is sufficient for supervisors of small Netware installations.

If Microsoft's LAN Manager is your network operating system, then you may select NRP's *Inside LAN Manager* as a resource for understanding LAN Man-ager and being proficient in a LAN Manager setting. For in-depth coverage of LAN Manager, NRP offers *Maximizing LAN Manager. Maximizing LAN Manager* approaches the network as an extension of the desktop in an enterprise com-puting model.

If you work with SCO UNIX or Xenix, or if UNIX or Xenix is in your future, then you will benefit from NRP's *Inside SCO UNIX. Inside SCO UNIX* guides you through this powerful operating system so that you can concentrate on the many applications that are now available for UNIX.

Conventions Used in this Book

Certain conventions are used in this book to help you more easily understand the discussions. The conventions are explained again at appropriate places in the book.

Special Typefaces

This section describes the special typefaces used in *Maximizing MS-DOS 5*.

Typeface	Meaning
Special font	This font is used for DOS commands, the names of files and directories, and system output, such as prompt signs and screen messages.
Bold, special font	This font is used for user input, such as commands, options to commands, and names of directories and files used as arguments.
Italic, special font	This font is used for names of variable elements to which values are given by the user.
ALL CAPS, SPECIAL FONT	This font is used for screen output.
ALL CAPS, BOLD, SPECIAL FONT	This font is used for user input.

Windows Notes

The Windows Notes provide information about the advantages of the Windows environment when combined with DOS 5. These notes provide tips, recommendations, and insights about using the Windows graphical user interface to perform a wide variety of tasks. Windows configuration issues are discussed in Appendix A.

DOS Shell Notes

DOS 5 features a greatly enhanced DOS Shell, which provides a graphical user interface for file and program management. The DOS Shell Notes provide guidelines for performing common command line tasks using the new DOS Shell environment. Chapter 12 guides you through the components of the DOS Shell and presents an overview of its use.

Novell Netware Notes

The Novell Netware Notes provide advice to network users who use Novell products and DOS 5. Specific recommendations are provided for getting the best performance by selecting the appropriate tool for many common tasks. Appendix C provides information about proper installation of DOS 5 in a NetWare environment.

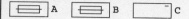
Part One

Understanding Hardware and Software

Understanding DOS Data Structures

The Command Processor

1

Understanding Hardware and Software

Today's computers bear little resemblance to their forerunners. The computing power found in many of today's personal computers would have filled an entire room scarcely fifteen years ago. These computers were not only huge, but also very expensive. The type of computing power in today's typical $5,000 PC cost hundreds of thousands of dollars just over a decade ago.

As computers have evolved during the past decade, they have become more powerful and simpler to use. Improvements in speed and capability have made it possible to make the computer perform more work for the user, while at the same time performing an even greater amount of work "behind the scenes." A large portion of that work is increasingly geared toward interacting with the user. Fortunately, personal computers have become powerful enough not only to do their jobs, but also to provide a much higher level of interaction with the user.

Typically, interaction with a computer occurs through an *operating system* and a *user interface*. DOS 5 serves as both. In this chapter, you begin to learn what operating systems and user interfaces are, how they interact with you as a user, how they interact with your hardware, and how you can begin to use the many complexities of DOS to your advantage.

The chapter starts with an overview of software and hardware, examining the roles that each one plays in the overall system. Then, you examine DOS in

11

greater detail, learning what it is, how it interacts with you and your hardware, and how it is used to manage information and run applications.

This chapter also gives you a basic understanding of each of the hardware components in your computer system. You learn, for example, about the CPU, memory, and data storage devices, such as hard disks. Although it is not meant to be a comprehensive guide to PC hardware, the latter sections in this chapter help you understand DOS from a hardware standpoint.

Comparing Software and Hardware

Most computer users, even those who have little experience with PCs, have some concept of what computer hardware is. After all, the word *hardware* carries a connotation of something physical, sturdy, and heavy. Computer hardware is definitely physical and occasionally sturdy, and fortunately is rapidly becoming lighter and smaller.

New users can understand that *hardware* means the physical computer—the monitor on the desk, the keyboard in front of it, and the system unit on or beside the desk. *Software*, on the other hand, is something that many new users have a little more difficulty understanding. That is not surprising because software can take many forms.

Software, in the loosest sense of the word, usually is a set of instructions that directs computer hardware to operate according to some plan. Word processing programs are a form of software, as are databases, spreadsheets, graphics programs, and those ever-present computer games. But software also comes in other forms. DOS itself is software. It includes commands that are much like the business programs you use every day, with the exception that those DOS command programs generally are very small when compared to programs such as Microsoft Word and Lotus 1-2-3.

DOS also includes mini-programs called *device drivers* that help it interact with the various hardware components in your system. These device drivers serve as control programs between DOS and the computer hardware. DOS is a control program (actually a group of programs) between you, the hardware, and your applications. But if DOS is doing all of those things, just what *is* DOS?

Understanding the Role of DOS

"DOS" is an acronym for *Disk Operating System*. The term "DOS" is a generic term that many computer manufacturers and systems use to describe the program or group of programs that form the interface between a user and the computer hardware. It is called an operating system because it forms the structure under which the computer and applications operate. Operating systems often are called *disk operating systems* because part of the operating system's responsibility is to manage information stored on a disk, either floppy or hard.

Although the term "DOS" sometimes is used generically, the term *MS-DOS* is not generic. MS-DOS, which stands for *Microsoft Disk Operating System*, is a registered trademark of Microsoft Corporation, the developers of MS-DOS. Other operating systems that are functionally equivalent to MS-DOS are available, including PC DOS, DR-DOS, and COMPAQ DOS. Although *Maximizing MS-DOS 5* covers MS-DOS, many of the commands and concepts are shared with the other, compatible operating systems. When you see the term DOS used throughout this book, it refers specifically to MS-DOS 5. You will find that the majority of commands and concepts discussed apply to versions of MS-DOS prior to version 5.

As with other operating systems, DOS is a group of programs that control your personal computer. First, DOS serves as a control facility between you and your system's hardware. By using the various commands that DOS includes, you can run applications, create files, erase files, use the system's printer, and perform other common tasks. In addition to acting as an interface layer between you and the computer system, DOS also acts as an intermediary between the computer and the applications you run on it. Just as DOS lets you access each of the components in your system, it also lets your applications access those components.

Examining the Different Flavors of DOS

In the early 1980s, IBM Corporation developed the IBM Personal Computer, which has come to be known simply as the PC. It used a *microprocessor* (also called a central processing unit, or CPU) manufactured by Intel Corporation. Along with these developments, Microsoft developed an operating system for the IBM PC, which was named MS-DOS.

Over the next decade, scores of competing systems were developed that eventually had one thing in common—they all ran software written for the IBM PC running the MS-DOS operating system (or an operating system compatible with MS-DOS). Because IBM was first in the marketplace, these competing systems became known as *IBM compatibles*. As these competing systems have garnered larger and larger shares of the PC market, the emphasis has shifted from hardware compatibility to software compatibility. Today, it is more logical to call these systems *MS-DOS compatible*, meaning that they run the MS-DOS operating system and the applications that are designed to run on top of MS-DOS.

PCs have changed dramatically from the original IBM PC. As Intel has developed new microprocessors, such as the 8086, 80286, 80386, and 80486, these new CPUs have been used in PCs. As these new CPUs have been implemented, DOS has been updated to keep pace and take advantage of the new CPUs' capabilities. DOS began as IBM's PC-DOS with release 1.0 and has progressed through four major revisions, and numerous minor ones, to today's MS-DOS 5.0.

Looking at MS-DOS as a Software Product

Just like the business or personal applications you use, such as spreadsheets, word processors, and games, DOS is a software product. And, like most software products, DOS is *licensed*. When you license a program, you do not buy it. Instead, you pay a one-time fee to use the program. You usually have the right to make a backup copy of a program you have licensed, but you cannot make duplicate copies to use on more than one machine at a time or resell the product.

The same is true for DOS. When you purchase a PC, you must choose an operating system for it. If you decide to choose DOS, you should purchase a license for it. You can think of DOS as just another program, but one that is required for your other programs to work. DOS comes packaged in a box just like your other applications. It includes distribution diskettes containing the DOS files, a software manual, and other supporting documentation. If you purchased a computer that did not include a packaged version of DOS complete with manuals and disks, but DOS is installed on the system's hard disk, you probably have not paid the license fee for DOS. The manufacturer or dealer simply placed a copy of the DOS programs on the hard disk. DOS is not particular—it functions perfectly whether you have purchased a license or not. You should, however, purchase a DOS package if for no other reason than to have a legal copy and to have the benefit of the manual and distribution diskettes.

Booting up with DOS

Without an operating system, a PC is basically lifeless. When you turn it on, the computer has just enough built-in capability to run a few diagnostic checks. After it performs those system checks, the PC begins looking around for an operating system. If it does not find one, it stops dead in its tracks. If it does find a suitable operating system, the computer *boots* that operating system. Essentially, that means it loads a small portion of the operating system into memory, then instructs the operating system to take over. From that point on, the operating system (DOS) is the boss.

The area where the computer looks for DOS depends primarily on the configuration of the system. In any case, however, it looks for two *hidden* files. The files, IO.SYS and MSDOS.SYS, are called hidden files because they do not show up in a directory listing of the boot disk or in the disk from which DOS is loaded.

If the system has a diskette drive, the computer's boot routine first checks the first floppy drive (drive A) to see if a disk is in the drive. If a disk is present, the boot routine checks for the existence of the DOS system files, IO.SYS and MSDOS.SYS, on the disk. If it finds them and a third file called COMMAND.COM, the boot routine loads the operating system from the disk.

If no disk drive exists, or a disk is not in the drive, the boot routine looks for the same files in the main directory, called the *root* directory, of drive C. Drive C is the designation given to the first hard drive in the system (types of hard drives are discussed later in this chapter and in Chapter 2). If the boot routine does not find DOS either in drive A or on drive C, the system cannot continue, so it issues an error message and locks up.

Some systems, called *diskless workstations*, do not have a floppy disk drive or a hard drive. In fact, they have no local storage at all. Diskless workstations are connected to a network of other computers. The diskless workstation contains a *boot ROM* that either contains just enough of the operating system to get the computer up and running, or directs the boot routine to look somewhere on the network for the operating system.

Hard drives are so common today that it is unlikely that you do not have one in your system. When you install DOS, you typically install it on the hard drive. The DOS distribution diskettes include an installation program that installs DOS on the hard drive if that is where you want it stored. This installation process copies the DOS files, both hidden and otherwise, to the boot disk (which can be a floppy or a hard drive). After DOS has been installed, the disk is *bootable*, meaning that the computer can boot DOS from it.

Whether you boot from a floppy or a hard disk, you should have a backup bootable diskette. This backup diskette is used in the event your primary boot diskette is damaged or lost, your hard drive fails, or important files, such as COMMAND.COM, are erased accidentally from the disk.

To create a bootable DOS diskette after you have installed DOS, place a new, unused diskette in drive A and type the following:

```
FORMAT A: /S
```

DOS formats the diskette, then transfers the operating system and command processor files to it. You also may want to copy all of the other DOS files to the backup diskette to ensure that they are available if you must boot the system from the backup.

Reaching the System Prompt

After DOS boots, you receive a *system prompt*. What you see as a system prompt depends on whether your prompt has been customized. By default, you see a *drive ID* followed by the symbol **>**, as in the following prompt:

```
C>
```

The C in the preceding example indicates that drive C, the hard drive, is the current drive. Any DOS commands you type that affect the drive are carried out on drive C unless you direct otherwise. The > symbol is used to separate the drive ID prompt from any commands that you type. If you boot from a floppy disk in drive A, the prompt looks like the following:

```
A>
```

The only difference between this prompt and any other drive prompt, such as the hard drive prompt, is the drive ID.

When you see the system prompt, you are "in DOS"; that is, DOS is loaded and is waiting for you to give it a command. The system prompt is a product of the file COMMAND.COM, which was mentioned earlier in this chapter and is covered in greater detail in Chapter 3.

When DOS finishes booting, it runs the program COMMAND.COM. COMMAND.COM is a *command interpreter*, meaning that it interprets commands. When you type something on the keyboard and press Enter, that input is directed to the COMMAND.COM program. COMMAND.COM examines what you typed and then checks to see if it is a valid DOS command. If it is a valid DOS command, COMMAND.COM executes the command. If it does not recognize the command, DOS looks on the current drive (or other drive you specify) for an executable file (program) that matches the name you have typed. If it finds such a file, COMMAND.COM loads and executes the program. If it does not find a matching file, COMMAND.COM returns a short and relatively uninformative message:

```
Bad command or filename
```

This means you have asked COMMAND.COM to do something it does not know how to do.

When you see the system prompt, you are at the DOS *system level*; that is, you are at the system command level and COMMAND.COM is waiting for its next instruction from you. Many applications, such as spreadsheets and databases, give you an option to "exit to the DOS prompt" or "return to DOS." This means that you have the option of exiting from the program and returning to the system level, where you can enter new commands or start other programs.

Looking behind the DOS Prompt

Although the DOS prompt, or command prompt, is the most visible aspect of DOS, it is only a small amount of what constitutes DOS. COMMAND.COM, which is essentially the DOS prompt, is but one of many DOS commands. COMMAND.COM simply provides a vehicle for accessing the rest of DOS' many commands.

Another aspect of DOS is system configuration. After the system completes its hardware diagnostics, called the POST (Power On Self Test), it looks for and boots the operating system (DOS). Once its core is installed, DOS takes over. This DOS core then begins the task of configuring the system to make it ready to run applications. DOS first looks for a file called CONFIG.SYS, which contains instructions that direct DOS to set up the system's hardware configuration. CONFIG.SYS does not have to be in your system, nor does it need to be executed by DOS for your system to operate. Most systems, however, include a CONFIG.SYS file. DOS 5, for example, creates by default a CONFIG.SYS file when it is installed.

Once the CONFIG.SYS file has been executed, DOS searches for a file called AUTOEXEC.BAT. Whereas CONFIG.SYS primarily controls the hardware configuration of the system, AUTOEXEC.BAT is used primarily to control the software environment. Like CONFIG.SYS, an AUTOEXEC.BAT file does not need to exist or to be executed in your system; however, most systems have one.

You can see that with all its capabilities and responsibilities, DOS is not a single entity. It consists of many programs, procedures, and routines. It comprises the hidden files IO.SYS and MSDOS.SYS, COMMAND.COM, the configuration files CONFIG.SYS and AUTOEXEC.BAT, and many other commands. DOS is built in layers, each relying on the layer below. To understand what the layers are and how they relate to one another, you must dive to the deepest level—the system's hardware.

The Hardware

Later sections in this chapter examine a typical PC's hardware in depth. This section only touches on some of the aspects of your PC's hardware to provide a basis for understanding how the different layers of DOS interact with the system's hardware.

A computer is not a computer without a *CPU*, or *Central Processing Unit*. The CPU is the true "brain" of the computer and is where nearly all of the actual computations take place. Everything else in the system is geared to serve the CPU in some manner. All MS-DOS-compatible systems currently use a CPU originally developed by Intel. Most common CPU types are the Intel 80286, 80386, and 80486 microprocessors. Earlier and now less-common CPUs include the 8088 and 8086 microprocessors. The 80586 is in development and surely will find its way into production systems relatively soon. Until only a few years ago, Intel was the sole designer and manufacturer of these types of CPUs. Now, however, other manufacturers are designing and manufacturing compatible CPUs.

A CPU is relatively useless without memory in which to store data and program code, so PCs include varying amounts of memory. A PC's memory is segregated into *addresses*. The address serves much the same purpose as does a house address—the operating system locates a given memory location by its address.

You can view memory addresses as pigeonholes, each one capable of storing an electrical charge. Information is stored in the memory addresses in different patterns of charges. A particular pattern might represent the letter A or the number 65. You might think this is a cumbersome way to store information, but computers excel at managing these bits of data.

A *bit* is the smallest possible amount of data and represents the presence of a charge (on) or the absence of a charge (off). A bit is equal to just one-eighth of a character. Eight bits make up one *byte*, which is the amount of data required to store a single character, such as the letter A. A *kilobyte* (1K) is equal to a little more than a thousand bytes (1024 bytes). Just over a thousand kilobytes (1024K or one million bytes) is called a *megabyte* and is abbreviated as M. That means 1,048,576 bytes (characters) are in one megabyte.

The various CPUs can address different amounts of memory. This is done with the number of physical pins each one has to connect it to the rest of the computer system. The original 8088 and 8086 CPUs (as in the original IBM PC), can address 1024K memory addresses, or 1M. The 80286, because it has more address pins, can address up to 16M of memory. The 80386 and 80486 CPUs can address up to 4 gigabytes (4096 megabytes).

In addition to the CPU and memory, computer systems include *peripheral devices*, such as parallel and serial communication ports, a keyboard, a display, one or more printers, and other devices. As mentioned earlier, all of these other devices serve the CPU in some way, either to gather input or to display output.

The hardware items are electrical devices. They use *binary states*, which are on or off states, to store and manage information. The operating system's primary function is to serve as a glue that binds all of these devices together, letting them communicate back and forth, as well as letting the user communicate with the devices. One component of DOS—the BIOS, or Basic Input/Output System—takes care of much of the interaction between devices.

The BIOS

The BIOS consists of a number of software routines (very small programs) that control access to each of the system's components. You can consider the BIOS to be the lowest level of the operating system. The majority of the BIOS routines are contained in a *read-only memory* (ROM) chip located on the computer's main circuit board. ROM chips are the PC's main storage chips that are designed to retain their contents even when the system is turned off. Other BIOS routines are sometimes contained on adapter cards, which are additional control circuit cards that are installed in the computer.

In addition to these ROM-based BIOS routines, DOS includes extensions and additional routines of its own. DOS stores these additional routines in the IO.SYS file, mentioned earlier in this chapter. When the system is booted, these BIOS routines are *mapped* into different areas in memory. Mapping means that DOS sets up the BIOS routines to appear at a given memory address. This lets DOS locate a specific BIOS routine by its address.

The BIOS routines are mapped into various sections of memory, some within the first 640K of memory, and some in the *reserved I/O address space*—memory addresses from 640K to 1024K. These BIOS routines serve as fundamental tools that DOS uses to control hardware. BIOS routines act as tools for DOS because the routines perform work on DOS' behalf. BIOS routines free DOS from dealing with repetitive, low-level work. When DOS requires access to specific hardware, it calls upon appropriate BIOS "tool" routines to do the work. Thanks to the BIOS, DOS does not have to be programmed to manipulate the disk hardware, the display hardware, or other hardware. The BIOS performs these tasks at the machine level and DOS uses the BIOS routines as its tools.

The DOS Kernel

The BIOS is the lowest level in the operating system. The next level above it is the DOS *kernel*. An operating system kernel is a set of software routines and data tables that provide access to the BIOS, as well as perform system-level tasks, such as gathering input, directing output, allocating memory, and managing the file system. The kernel takes the tools provided by the BIOS, puts them together with its own set of tools, and provides those basic system services to other entities, such as COMMAND.COM, other DOS commands, and applications, that are above it in the operating environment.

Similar to DOS' BIOS file, IO.SYS, the DOS kernel file is a hidden system file called MSDOS.SYS. After the system boots and loads IO.SYS into memory, MSDOS.SYS is loaded and parceled out into various locations in memory. As with the BIOS, you do not deal directly with the DOS kernel. Instead, another layer of program routines, COMMAND.COM, is laid on top of the kernel for you to use to access the system.

The DOS Command Processor

After the BIOS and kernel are installed, the command processor is installed. COMMAND.COM, in some ways like the BIOS and kernel, is a collection of program routines. Its primary purpose is to provide a meaningful interface between the user and the kernel, which controls the BIOS and in turn, controls the hardware. You may think that this is a round-about way to do things, but COMMAND.COM provides a much more understandable way of control than the hardware interrupts and binary world that the BIOS sees. COMMAND.COM responds to a form of interaction that makes sense to a human being—typed commands.

When you type a command at the DOS prompt, COMMAND.COM interprets that command. It first checks to see if the command is one that is defined as a program routine within COMMAND.COM itself. If it is, COMMAND.COM executes that portion of itself to perform the requested task. If the command is not an internal DOS command, COMMAND.COM checks the current disk (or specified disk) for a file name that matches the command name. COMMAND.COM can load COM and EXE files, which are executable program files. The majority of DOS commands actually are external programs that reside in the DOS directory. If it finds the requested file, COMMAND.COM loads the file into memory, then turns execution over to the command. When the command finishes executing, it returns control to COMMAND.COM.

COMMAND.COM also can execute one other type of file—a *batch* file. Batch files are files containing DOS commands and program statements. COMMAND.COM executes the statements in a batch file one at a time. Batch files are discussed in depth in Chapter 13.

The DOS Shell

The DOS command interpreter, COMMAND.COM, provides quite a bit of control over the computer system. With it, you can manage the file system, create files, print, and perform many other tasks. Similar to many command line interfaces, however, COMMAND.COM often is difficult for many users to work with. Some commands are easy to use, whereas others are impossibly cryptic. DOS offers a solution to the sometimes enigmatic nature of COMMAND.COM—the *MS-DOS Shell.*

The DOS Shell is a DOS program that runs much like any other application (its executable file is DOSSHELL.EXE). The DOS Shell provides an insulating layer of control between the user and COMMAND.COM. It collects the commands and features of COMMAND.COM into a menu-driven program. To format a disk, for example, you select an option from a menu, rather than issuing the FORMAT command from the DOS command line.

The DOS Shell also provides functions not directly available from COMMAND.COM. *Program groups*, for example, can be defined in the DOS Shell. Program groups are logical collections of applications. If you use three different word processors, for example, you might include all three in one group. The DOS Shell also provides a Task Switcher that lets you start a program running, then switch back to the Shell to start another without terminating the first application. While one application is active, others are suspended. By using the Task Switcher, you can run a number of different programs available for activation with a few keystrokes. The program that you activate will be waiting just where it left off.

The DOS Environment

Although the DOS Shell and COMMAND.COM are programs, you can use them to run other programs. These other programs, also called *applications*, are the ones you probably use every day—Excel, Word, Lotus 1-2-3, Ami, WordPerfect, as well as many others. These applications can run directly on top of COMMAND.COM (by loading the application from the DOS command line), or they can run on top of the DOS Shell (by selecting them from within the Shell). If you choose to run an application from the DOS Shell, you do not see the DOS Shell once the program is running. At that point, you are dealing directly with the application. If you exit the application or switch out of it, you return to the DOS Shell.

Not only can COMMAND.COM and the DOS Shell run other programs, but they can run other *operating environments* as well. An operating environment is a program that provides a common interface for a group of applications. The DOS Shell is itself an operating environment in some respects. Other operating environments are Microsoft Windows and Quarterdeck's DESQview that provide common interfaces under which to run other applications.

All the DOS components serve applications in some manner. The application communicates with COMMAND.COM, which in turn communicates with the kernel. The kernel communicates with the BIOS, providing access to the hardware. At times, the application communicates directly with the BIOS and the hardware.

You can see from this that DOS has a hierarchical or layered structure. By starting at the foundation, which is the system's hardware, and working your way up through it, DOS has the following layers: BIOS, DOS kernel, COMMAND.COM, DOS Shell, other operating environments, and applications. This layered approach may seem inefficient, but it has definite advantages, particularly when you want to upgrade the operating system. The BIOS, for example, needs to know only how to communicate with the hardware and to service requests from the kernel. The kernel does not have to understand how the BIOS handles hardware—that is the BIOS' job. COMMAND.COM does not know how the kernel or the BIOS works. This lets COMMAND.COM do its job more quickly and efficently. When any one of these key elements in the system needs to be modified, it can be updated almost independently of the rest of the system.

Understanding the System's Hardware

Regardless of the layer at which you interact with DOS—whether it is at the COMMAND.COM level, at the DOS Shell level, or via an application—all the layers of DOS are at work translating your actions into something the hardware can use. Most users have little concept of what goes on inside the computer, and even less how each component in the system functions. You do not have to know how the system operates to be able to use it, just as you do not have to know how internal combustion engines work in order to drive a car. The more you understand about the system, however, the better off you will be if something goes wrong.

The following sections of this chapter introduce the main components in your system and explain in general terms how they work. It is not meant to give you an in-depth knowledge of how PCs function, but it will give you a good overview. Not all of the system's components are examined, obviously, because that would require much more than one chapter. Instead, the chapter focuses on the CPU, memory, data bus, and disk storage.

The CPU

At the heart of every computer is a *microprocessor*, also called a CPU. The CPU is not only the heart of the system, but the brain as well. Nearly all of the computations are performed by the CPU and it runs programs, controls access to devices, and performs virtually every other task. In general, every operation is supervised by the CPU. In a sense, the CPU *is* the computer because the other devices and peripherals act as extensions of the CPU.

The BIOS and the DOS kernel communicate with the CPU to move data back and forth, as well as to perform other tasks that collectively make up computing. An application's use of the CPU is requested through, and controlled by, the BIOS and kernel.

CPUs found in MS-DOS-compatible systems (or IBM-compatible systems) are based on the Intel line of microprocessors. The original IBM PC used the Intel 8088 CPU, which is an 8-bit microprocessor capable of working with data that is eight bits wide. Actually, the 8088's internal registers are sixteen bits wide, but its data bus, which is the path it uses to communicate with the rest of the system, can transfer only eight bits at a time. The 8088, therefore, is often referred to as an 8-bit CPU.

The Intel 8086 came into use after the 8088. The 8088 and 8086 CPUs are compatible with one another, the primary difference being that the 8086 is a true 16-bit CPU. The 8086's internal data registers are 16 bits wide and its data bus can transfer 16 bits of data at a time. Because it can transfer more data in the same amount of time, the 8086 provides faster performance than the 8088. Both the 8088 and 8086 CPUs can address a maximum of 1M of memory.

The first IBM AT-class systems used the Intel 80286 CPU, which also is a 16-bit CPU but can address up to 16M of memory. Although the differences between the 80286 and its predecessors are many, the 80286 is fully upward-compatible with the 8088 and 8086 CPUs; that is, it can run applications written for the two earlier microprocessors. The 80286 operates at a higher speed than the earlier CPUs and includes other operating modes that the others do not. These new operating modes let the 80286 take advantage of more memory and make better use of the system's resources. CPU operating modes are discussed a little later in this chapter.

The 80386DX is a 32-bit CPU that was introduced after the 80286. It includes yet another operating mode that the 80286 does not have and can access a great deal more memory than the earlier models—up to 4G (4 gigabytes, equal to 4096M). The 80386DX also offers better memory management and higher operating speeds than the 80286. The 80386DX can manipulate and transfer 32 bits of data at a time, allowing it to transfer twice as much data in the same amount of time as the 80286 model.

The 80386SX is a stripped-down, lower-priced alternative to the DX version. The SX version is functionally equivalent to the DX version, but it uses a 16-bit data path as opposed to the DX's 32-bit data path. The SX version of the 80386 uses all of the same operating modes and can run all the software that the DX version can run. The SX version is just slower than the DX version.

The 80486DX was the next CPU introduced by Intel. It was generally equivalent to the 80386DX, except that the 80486 contained an on-board math coprocessor (also called FPU for Floating Point Unit because math coprocessors excel at floating point math operations). The 80486 is able to perform math operations that require the FPU more quickly because the math chip is part of the CPU, not located elsewhere in the system. The SX version of the 80486 is the same CPU as the DX version, but with the FPU disabled. This makes the 80486SX a lower-cost alternative to the 80486DX.

Other CPUs are in development by Intel and other microprocessor manufacturers. Although your system may contain a CPU designed and manufactured by Intel or some other company, such as Advanced Micro Devices, MS-DOS is designed to run on it.

Understanding Processor Operating Modes

The last section briefly discussed operating modes. This section examines processor operating modes in a little more detail, starting with the operating mode supported by all of the Intel CPUs—*real mode.*

The 8088 and 8086 CPUs operate in what is now known as real mode. Actually, real mode was introduced on the 80286, which came after the 8088 and 8086 CPUs. Real mode, however, was designed to imitate the 8086 environment on the 80286 so the 8088 and 8086 actually operated in real mode.

DOS originally was written to run under real mode because that was the only mode available at the time DOS was first developed. When operating in real mode, the CPU can address only 1M of memory. This limited application programmers, so they wrote standard DOS programs that accessed only 1M of memory.

The introduction of the 80286 changed that when it introduced a new operating mode called *protected mode.* Protected mode does just what the name implies—it protects memory addresses above 1M from conflicts between applications requesting memory. Address conflict protection makes the 80286 suitable for multitasking operations.

The 80386 microprocessor introduced yet another mode—*virtual mode*. Virtual mode lets the 80386 set up *virtual machines* using protected areas of memory. Each virtual machine functions as a separate 8086 computer, complete with its own memory addresses, video memory, and other resources. It is analogous to having multiple computers inside your system, each capable of running its own program. Applications such as Quarterdeck DESQview and Microsoft Windows use virtual mode on an 80386 (and 80486) to run multiple DOS applications at the same time.

Each of the three possible operating modes uses the system's memory in a different way. Real mode, for example, only uses the memory from 0K to 1024K (the first megabyte). Protected mode and virtual mode both use memory above 1M. You will learn a little later in this chapter the way in which the different types of memory are structured in the PC. First, however, you will examine how the CPU communicates with the rest of the system, including its memory.

Examining the Motherboard and Bus

The main assembly that makes up the typical PC is called the *motherboard*. The motherboard is a large printed circuit board that contains the CPU, support circuitry, some or all of the system's RAM, the BIOS ROM, and special sockets to connect additional *adapter cards* to the motherboard. Adapter cards, which will be discussed in more detail later, are additional circuit boards that plug into the motherboard. These adapter cards generally perform the function of controlling devices, such as the system's monitor, printer, disk drives, and other devices.

Although the CPU is where all of the computational work goes on, the CPU would be similar to a disembodied brain if it had no way to communicate with the rest of the system. The support circuitry built into the motherboard—which includes timing devices, hardware controllers, and circuits to convert signals coming from and going to the CPU—serves as the network that the CPU uses to communicate with and control the various devices in the system. If the CPU is the brain, the support circuitry serves as the first part of its nervous system.

Another part of that nervous system is the *bus*, which serves as a pipeline between the CPU and other devices in the system. The adapter cards connect to the system's bus. Adapter cards often include their own BIOS, which provide a set of low-level instructions that the DOS kernel can use to control devices connected to the adapter.

Adapter cards need their own BIOS because of the restricted scope of the standard BIOS. For DOS to support all of the disk drives, tape drives, CD-ROM devices, and countless other devices available for the PC, DOS' standard BIOS would have to be extremely large and complex. In addition, the system BIOS would have to be updated each time a new type of peripheral is made available. There would literally be no end to the BIOS revisions to keep up with new devices. Instead, each adapter includes its own BIOS when the standard BIOS does not have the appropriate functions to control the attached device.

When the system boots, the primary BIOS on the motherboard and the BIOS extensions contained in the IO.SYS file are mapped into memory. Any BIOS routines contained on adapter cards that are installed in the system also are mapped into memory. Once the routines are in memory, they are accessible by the DOS kernel and by any application that is written to access the BIOS directly. This is why today's PC BIOS is called *extensible*—its capabilities can be extended by adding new BIOS routines or replacing existing ones.

The motherboard's bus plays a very important role in the CPU's communication with the system's devices. The data travels from the CPU, out along the bus, to the adapter card connected to the bus, and through the adapter to the peripheral itself (such as a disk drive or monitor). The operating system is an integral component in that data transfer. The CPU communicates along the bus with the BIOS, which converts the CPU's instructions into instructions the adapter card can understand. The adapter card then translates the instructions into control signals the device can understand.

When information from the device returns to the CPU, it first goes through the adapter card and is converted into instructions the kernel can understand. The kernel then translates the instructions to the BIOS, which translates the information to the CPU. This multi-layered marriage of hardware and software is what makes the system so flexible. For it to work properly, the CPU does not need to know how the rest of the system works. All it needs to know is how to ask the BIOS for the information it needs.

Although virtually all system communication takes place on the bus, the bus is actually split into two, with parallel data paths to the adapter expansion bus and to memory. The reason a single set of data paths will not work in today's fast systems is that memory operates much faster than the adapter cards and the peripherals attached to the system. Consequently, a high-speed bus is needed for memory, and a lower-speed bus is needed for the expansion bus.

Taking a Closer Look at Memory

The memory in your system is its most important resource. Almost invariably, more memory translates into better performance. In addition, the way DOS uses the memory in your system has a great deal to do with performance.

Earlier in this chapter you saw that memory is really nothing but a collection of storage locations. As a simplistic view of memory and to help you understand how memory works, you can view these storage locations, which are located and accessed by their numeric *address*, as containing electrical charges. These charges are interpreted by the computer as data.

Two primary types of memory exist—Dynamic Random Access Memory (DRAM) and Static Random Access Memory (SRAM). Dynamic RAM and static RAM both store data using electrical charges. They just use different methods to do it.

In dynamic RAM, a charge placed in a memory location leaks out, or dissipates, very quickly. To maintain the data, the memory must be *refreshed* periodically to keep the charges (and the data they represent) in place. This dynamic manipulation and refreshing of memory is the way dynamic RAM gets its name.

Static RAM is a little different. Whereas DRAM loses its charge and must be regularly refreshed to maintain its state, static RAM does not. Once a static RAM memory register is *latched* (has assumed an on or off state), it retains that information as long as a source of power is going to the chip to maintain the state. If the power to the SRAM chip is shut off, the SRAM reverts to its original state. The end result is not any different from DRAM—you still have just a collection of places to store information. Only the method you use to actually store the information is different.

Most PCs use both DRAM and SRAM to some degree, but DRAM is used for primary data and application code storage because it is cheaper to manufacture. SRAM is used when a relatively small amount of memory is required, such as for a *memory cache*. A memory cache is a small, temporary storage location for often-used data and code.

The first megabyte of memory, which is the range of memory addresses from 0K to 1024K, is called *conventional* memory. Conventional memory is the only type of memory that the core functions of DOS recognize. As you saw earlier, this is because the original implementation of DOS was designed for systems with only 1M of RAM. Standard DOS applications, therefore, can access memory addresses only within that first 1M of RAM.

If the PC has more than 1M of RAM installed, the memory in excess of 1024K (1M) is called either *expanded* or *extended* memory, depending on how it is configured and used. Extended memory (sometimes referred to as XMS) is the more straightforward of the two. Extended memory begins at address 1024K and extends through the full range of available addresses. The 80286 and later CPUs can access extended memory in linear fashion, much like they access conventional memory.

Plain DOS cannot use extended memory directly because DOS is not aware of any memory addresses over 1024K. A software module called a *DOS extender* is used to let DOS applications use extended memory. The DOS extender is a program that manages access to the extended memory and serves as a middleman between DOS and memory addresses above 1024K. Standard DOS applications, therefore, must be written specifically to take advantage of extended memory.

Although expanded memory (also called EMS) works much differently from extended memory, it also requires a memory manager. The memory manager takes a portion of the system's conventional memory and sets it up as a *page frame*. The expanded-memory manager then takes a section of expanded memory and maps its addresses into the page frame, much like placing a slide into a frame. The page frame is located in conventional memory and DOS and DOS applications can see the "slide" of memory. When a different section of expanded memory is required, the expanded-memory manager simply maps the new section into the page frame where DOS can see it.

The low-level routines that enable this page-frame swapping to occur are part of the expanded-memory manager, not part of standard DOS. Here again, applications must be specifically written to take advantage of expanded memory.

Whether the system is addressing memory in real mode, protected mode, or virtual mode, access to memory by DOS and DOS applications is handled through the kernel and the BIOS. An application requests a block of memory, and that request filters through the layers of the operating system to the CPU, which services the request.

Memory is just one of the data storage devices in your PC. The next section explains the most common type of data storage device—disk drives.

Understanding Data Storage Devices

Memory is volatile. Turn off the machine, reset it, or experience a power outage, and the contents of the system's memory are lost. Also, the amount of physical memory in a PC is significantly less than the total amount of data that most users require. If you use a large number of common applications or create many large data files, you need 40M to 100M of storage—ten to twenty-five times the amount of memory in a common PC. The system's memory cannot do the whole job so some form of permanent storage is required.

Most often, that storage is a disk drive. Most PCs contain a hard drive and at least one floppy drive. Both use the same general technology to store data, but the hard drive is much faster. Disk storage is an important system resource and is second only to memory.

Emphasizing the "Disk" in Disk Operating System

The importance of disk storage is evident in DOS's name—*Disk* Operating System. The word disk is used to describe both *floppy disks* and *hard disks*, and generally describes the part of the device on which data is stored. The disk drive is the part of the device that rotates the disk. In the case of a floppy disk, the disk itself is removable from the drive. In a hard disk, it is not. For a hard disk, therefore, the term *disk* generally refers to the entire disk assembly (the drive, the disks, and the read/write heads), not just the disk itself.

Many similarities exist between the two types of disks because they use the same basic technology. In both cases, the data-storing disk is a circular platter that is coated by a metal oxide. In the case of a floppy disk, the platter is a very thin sheet of Mylar. In a hard drive, the platter usually is made of aluminum. The oxide coating on both, which is built up in very fine, smooth layers, can store magnetic charges. The disk drive uses two or more read/write heads that record magnetic patterns on the disk. These patterns of magnetic charges can be later read by the heads and interpreted as data. Disk drives store information by translating electrical charges, which can dissipate and be lost, into magnetic charges that can last for years if need be.

Magnetic data recording is not new—audio tape recorders have been using the technology for decades. The main difference between audio recording and data recording on a disk drive is that the audio recorder records an analog signal (fluctuation of charge) and a disk drive records data in digital form (charges represent on and off patterns).

The quality of reproduction for digital data on a disk is much more critical than for an audio recording. The data *must* be exact for digitally stored data, whereas the audio data can suffer distortions and loss without any great effect, except the loss of sound quality. That is not to say that disk drives function flawlessly, always faithfully reading and writing data without error.

Occasionally, the drive is unable to read the data back from the disk because the charge has been altered by wearing of the oxide coating, exposure to an external magnetic field, or a trip through an airport metal detector. When the drive fails to read the disk, a *read error* occurs. If, for some reason, the drive fails to write to the disk, a *write error* occurs.

Floppy drives and hard drives, because they use much of the same technology, have many internal components in common. Both, for example, use a motor to spin the disk, have read/write heads that record and read back data, and use a positioning system to move the heads across the disk. The next two sections explain the two types of disks and point out some of the differences.

Floppy Disks

A floppy disk gets its name from the fact that the disk itself is flexible. If you remove the oxide-coated disk from its protective plastic jacket, the disk almost is as limp as a piece of paper. The protective jacket holds the disk rigid enough for the floppy drive's motor to spin it, which allows the head to read the data passing underneath it.

The first floppy disks measured eight inches in diameter and could store a relatively small amount of data compared to today's floppy disks. The low-density 5 1/4-inch floppy appeared next, followed by higher density 5 1/4-inch floppies. (Disk-data density is discussed a little later in this section.) Today's double-sided, double-density 5 1/4-inch disks hold 360K after DOS formatting, slightly more than the larger and obsolete 8-inch floppies. High-density 5 1/4-inch floppies hold 1.2M—roughly three and a half times as much data as the earlier floppies. All three types of floppies use the same basic technology. The gain in storage space and decrease in size of the 5 1/4-inch disks is due primarily to improvements in oxide coating and head sensitivity.

The 3 1/2-inch floppy appeared next. The low-density 3 1/2-inch versions hold 720K of data, whereas the high-density versions hold 1.44M. Quad-density 3 1/2-inch floppies that can store 2.88M of data are now becoming available. All 3 1/2-inch floppies are encased in a rigid plastic case, instead of the flexible plastic jacket that the larger types use. The disk inside the case, however, is virtually the same as in the larger floppies, only smaller. The decrease in size and increase in storage capacity are due mainly to the use of a rigid hub instead of a flexible one. This lets the drive spin the floppy faster and more accurately, with less distortion and flutter. More data can be safely packed into a smaller area when less distortion is presented to the media.

Floppies of any size are referred to as *diskettes*. 5 1/4-inch diskettes often are referred to as *minifloppies*, whereas 3 1/2-inch diskettes are referred to as *microfloppies*. The term *disk* generally is used to refer to all types of disks, both floppy and hard. Whenever you read instructions that refer to removing or inserting a disk in a drive, you should assume they mean a floppy disk.

Hard Disk Drives

Hard disk drives get their name from the fact that the disk platter is rigid, or hard, rather than flexible. They also are called *fixed disks*. Usually, these types of disks are referred to as hard disks or hard drives.

Hard disks work much the same as floppy disks. The main difference is that floppy disks consists of a single disk platter, whereas hard disks consist of multiple platters, each spinning on a common shaft. Also, floppy drives employ two heads—one on top and one on the bottom—and hard drives employ multiple heads for each platter. Hard disk platters are coated with metal oxide, as are floppy disk platters.

The rigid hard disk platters can spin much faster than floppy disks, providing much faster access time (the time required to read and write to the disk). The platters' rigidity also means less distortion of the disk, allowing an even greater amount of data to be packed into a smaller area than on floppy disks. For that reason, hard disks hold a much larger quantity of data than floppy disks.

Hard disks provide greater storage capacity and greater speed, but they lack the portability of floppy disks. It is not practical to remove a hard drive from one computer in order to access its data on another computer. This requires opening the system's case, disconnecting data and power cables, and reversing the process to install it in the second system. Hard disks, therefore, serve as high-capacity, long-term local storage, whereas floppy disks serve as a means of data archival and portability.

Read/Write Heads

All disk drives use read/write heads to read information from the disk and to write information to it. The head reads information from the disk by sensing the presence or absence of magnetic charges passing underneath it. The pattern of these magnetic charges are converted to electrical signals that are translated up a wire, through the drive electronics to the adapter card that controls the drive, down the data bus, and eventually to the CPU. Writing data to the disk happens in reverse—a signal travels from the CPU through the various layers of the operating system and hardware to the heads, which write data by changing the polarity of the magnetic field of very small areas on the disk.

Early floppy drives used a head on only one side of the disk. Today's floppy drives use heads on both sides. Hard drives, on the other hand, use heads on both sides of their multiple platters.

Disk Tracks

A disk, whether it consists of a single platter or multiple platters, spins in order to move data past the read/write heads. Floppy disks spin at roughly 360 RPM (revolutions per minute) and hard disks spin at approximately 3,600 RPM. The higher speed of a hard disk is one of the major reasons that data can be read from and written to a hard disk much more quickly than a floppy disk.

A floppy drive's heads actually rest on the surface of the disk. A hard drive's heads fly on a cushion of air very close above the surface of the disk. In order to read data across the entire width of the disk, the heads move radially from near the center of the disk to near the edge. The heads move in *steps*; that is, they move in fixed increments that are controlled by a motor, called a *stepper motor*.

As a disk spins, the heads traverse a circular path over the surface of the disk. This circular pattern at each step of the heads is called a disk *track*. When a drive is formatted, a special magnetic pattern is written to the disk at each step of the heads to magnetically mark the boundaries of each track. The tracks then serve as logically defined concentric areas in which to store data.

Disk Cylinders, Sectors, and Seek Time

You now know that hard disks often have multiple platters, each with a head on top and a head on the bottom of the platter. With the platters stacked one above the other, the tracks on each platter line up with one another. This alignment of tracks is called a *cylinder*.

Imagine a cylinder made up of tracks stacked one on top of the other. Each track is further divided radially into pie-shaped areas called *sectors*. The number of sectors a track can physically hold varies theoretically because tracks near the outside rim of the disk have a larger diameter, and therefore, more possible space. The number of sectors per track is held constant, however, as they are laid out radially from the center of the platter.

Data is located by its track and sector number. A given piece of information, for example, might be located at track 10, sector 5. Whenever possible, the data is stored in contiguous (side-by-side) sectors to make accessing the data much faster.

The least efficient aspect of disk reading and writing is head movement because it takes time to accelerate the head, move it to a new position, and stop it. The drive, therefore, writes to each track in the cylinder before moving to another track. If the drive has four platters, for example, eight tracks can be read or written before the head must move again.

The time that it takes for the heads to move from the current track to any other specified track is called the *seek time* of the disk. Most common seek times for today's hard disks are from 14 milliseconds to approximately 28 milliseconds. Older disk drives typically have seek times of around 65 milliseconds. Floppy drives have seek times that are much longer than those of hard drives. A typical floppy's seek time is over 250 milliseconds.

Seek time has a significant impact on disk performance. To retrieve or store data on the disk, the system usually must locate the data on more than one track and cylinder. The data is parceled out across the disk as space permits. The drive attempts to locate the data in contiguous sectors, but as the drive is used more and more, fewer contiguous sectors are available on the disk. The data, therefore, is scattered across the disk. This breaking up of files across the disk is called *fragmentation*.

You can undo file fragmentation. The files must be read from the disk and written back in contiguous sectors. Utility programs are available that perform just that task. They read files into memory or to a temporary location on disk to make contiguous space available, then place the file back on the disk in those contiguous sectors. A file that is not fragmented can be retrieved much more quickly because the heads do not have to be repositioned as much. Defragmenting the hard disk, therefore, can significantly increase the drive's performance.

Data Density

The number of tracks on a disk helps determine its capacity. The more tracks that can be placed on the disk, the more data you can store on it. You will recall that tracks are concentric rings that are magnetically arranged on the disk. By making the tracks smaller (narrower), you can increase the amount of data that can be stored on the disk. If you cut the track width in half, you double the capacity of the disk.

This may sound like a terrific way to boost disk capacity, but it does have it limits. Because data is stored magnetically on the disk, making tracks narrower means that the data on one track is closer to the data on its adjacent tracks. With the data closer together, the head must be more sensitive in order to pick up only the current track and not the adjacent tracks as well. If the tracks are put too close together, the data in one track will interfere magnetically with the adjacent tracks.

The tracks can successfully be brought closer together in one of two ways: the disk's surface can be made using finer coatings that are less susceptible to cross-track interference, or more sensitive heads can be used. Both, of course, have physical and economical limits. The physical limits vary depending on the type of disk. A hard disk's platter is fixed in one place so the position of the tracks underneath the heads can be closely controlled. A floppy disk drive, on the other hand, must contend with disks that are moved in and out of the drive, resulting in a greater possible variation in head/track positioning and requiring a greater tolerance for misalignment. Floppy drives, therefore, are much more limited in the amount of data that they can store safely.

Disk Capacity

Earlier in the chapter you learned that the smallest amount of data that a computer recognizes is called a bit. PCs store data in groups of eight bits, which are called bytes. A byte is the amount of data needed to store one character, such as a letter or number.

When data is stored on a disk, it is written in magnetic pulses, each of which represents a bit. The bits must be located in a pattern so the drive's heads can read the bits and recognize groups of bits as bytes. The drive, therefore, writes a fixed number of bytes in each sector in a fixed pattern. The combination of this fixed pattern and number of bytes per sector is referred to as the disk's *format*. When you format a disk, the tracks and sectors are laid out according to the required format.

Because the tracks and sectors are laid out magnetically rather than physically, the head needs some means of locating a given track and sector. That is, the head needs something to tell it where the track begins. On a 5 1/4-inch floppy disk, a light sensor is used to scan for an index hole that is punched in the disk. Each time the hole passes under the sensor, a signal is transmitted through the drive's circuitry to be used as an index, or point of reference. Based on the location of the hole, the drive can locate any track and sector on the disk.

3 1/2-inch floppy disks use a special index pulse located at track one, sector one, instead of using an index hole. After the drive has identified the index pulse at track one, sector one, it can use that position to locate any other track and sector.

Disk Format

The arrangement and number of tracks and sectors on a disk are referred to as the disk's format. A 360K 5 1/4-inch floppy disk uses 40 tracks, with 9 sectors per track. The 1.2M 5 1/4-inch floppy uses 80 tracks with 15 sectors per track. 720K 3 1/2-inch floppy disks use 80 tracks with 9 sectors per track. 1.44M 3 1/2-inch floppy disks use 80 tracks with 18 sectors per track. In each case, a sector contains 512 bytes and two sectors are needed to hold 1K of data (1024 bytes).

A Note on Disk Capacity

You can find the capacity of the disk by knowing the number of sectors on the disk. The 3 1/2-inch high-density disk, for example, has 18 sectors in each of its 80 tracks. By multiplying those two numbers, you get a total of 2880 sectors in which to store data. Because each sector holds 1/2K, divide the 2880 sectors by two to get the total capacity of 1440K, or 1.44M.

Hard disks are a bit different when it comes to formats. The number of tracks varies from one drive type to another, as well as the number of platters in the drive. Most hard drives use 17 or 34 sectors per track, depending on the drive type. Some disks use a completely different number. The same concept for disk capacity still applies, however. The total number of sectors (which also have a 512-byte capacity) is based on the number of tracks, heads, and sectors per track. By dividing the number of total sectors by two, you have the capacity of the disk.

A wealth of other information about disks is available, particularly regarding the way they store and retrieve data, that has not been examined in this chapter. Chapter 2 goes into detail about DOS data structures and how the drive stores data. In addition, other chapters discuss other peripheral devices in your system as they relate to each chapter's topic.

Using Device Drivers To Talk to Devices

You learned earlier in this chapter that PCs contain adapter cards that plug into the system's bus to provide an interface between the system and the device to which the adapter card is attached. Adapter cards also are referred to as *controllers* because they are used by the system to control peripheral devices.

Although the controller is responsible for controlling the device, the controller still requires something to handle the communication between it and the PC. A *device driver* serves that purpose. A device driver is a mini-program that acts as a middleman between the DOS kernel and the controller. As you read earlier, instructions are translated up through the layers of the operating system to the device driver, which converts the instructions into a form the controller can use. The controller then directs the device according to those instructions.

Generally, two classes of device drivers are available—*character* device drivers and *block* device drivers. The type of driver a device uses depends on the way the device functions.

Character Device Drivers

All device drivers move information and instructions between the operating system and the controller. Character device drivers perform that function one byte at a time, or one *character* at a time. Devices that use character device drivers include the keyboard, serial ports, and the display. The device driver supplies DOS with a name of one to eight characters that DOS uses as a reference by which to access the device (such as COM1). Applications treat the character device much like a file, referencing it by its name.

The data is sent by the DOS kernel to a storage buffer, where it remains until the system is able to send it through the device driver and to the device. Depending on the type of device, the kernel routines may check the data stream for control characters, such as Ctrl-C, and take appropriate action if the control character is found (such as terminating communication). With other devices, the data is not scanned, but instead sent to the device.

Character device drivers are perfect for devices that process data one byte at a time. They are too slow, however, for devices that work with larger amounts of data at one time. Disk drives are a prime example of such a device. These devices use *block device drivers*.

Block Device Drivers

A block device driver performs the same function as a character device driver; that is, it transfers information and instructions between the DOS kernel and a device. The difference is in how it sends the data to the device. Block device drivers transfer data in *blocks*, which are larger units of data than a single byte. The amount of data in a block depends on the type of device. For a disk drive, for example, a block contains one disk sector.

Whereas character devices are assigned a one- to eight-character name, block devices receive a single letter designation. You already are familiar with this letter assignment in disk drives—the first floppy is A, the first hard drive is C, and so on.

DOS treats block devices as logical disks (as opposed to character devices that are treated as *files*.) Block device drivers even let one device be referenced by multiple ID letters. Chapter 11 teaches you how to do that with the drives in your system, assigning more than one drive ID to the same drive. In addition, block device drivers can be used to reference a block device that does not exist as a physical device. RAM drives, for example, are areas of memory that are set up to function as a disk drive. Once set up and controlled by an appropriate block device driver, DOS treats the RAM drive just like any physical disk drive. The separation of the operating system into layers provides this flexibility.

Installing Device Drivers

You now know that device drivers are special purpose mini-programs used to translate data between the lower levels of the operating system and a device (typically to the device's controller). Device drivers come in two forms—*resident* device drivers and *installable* device drivers. The following sections discuss the similarities and differences between the two types.

Resident Device Drivers

An abundance of devices are available for PCs, partly because you can easily add devices to the DOS environment through the BIOS and device drivers. DOS, however, cannot possibly provide for all possible devices. Device diversity makes it necessary, therefore, for other device drivers to be built to control devices that DOS is not specifically written to address.

DOS, however, does have built-in support for some standard devices. The DOS hidden system file IO.SYS contains device drivers for standard system devices. These device drivers are installed automatically as part of the DOS environment when DOS boots. They are called *resident device drivers* because they are part of the default DOS environment. This eliminates the need for you to install them yourself.

The standard MS-DOS IO.SYS file contains a particular set of device drivers. Your IO.SYS file, however, may contain a slightly different set of device drivers. Many PC manufacturers customize the IO.SYS file so that DOS automatically takes advantage of special hardware capabilities built into their systems. Table 1.1 lists the standard devices supported by the device drivers in IO.SYS.

Table 1.1
DOS 5 Resident Device Drivers

Driver	Explanation
CLOCK$	System clock.
CON	Combination of keyboard and display for input and output.
AUX or COM1	Primary serial communications port.
COMn	Serial communications ports COM2, COM3, and COM4.
LPT1 or PRN	Primary parallel communications port.
LPTn	Parallel communications ports LPT2 and LPT3.
NUL	Null (dummy) device used to discard unwanted output, such as command responses generated within a batch file. Standard output can be redirected to the NUL device.

The standard resident device drivers cover many possible devices, particularly devices that use the parallel and serial communications ports. The resident drivers, however, do not cover all potential devices so DOS uses a second type of device driver.

Installable Device Drivers

A browse through your DOS directory will reveal a number of files with SYS file extensions. These are *installable device drivers* that are included as part of the standard DOS distribution package. They are called installable device drivers because, instead of being incorporated as part of the DOS BIOS and kernel, they must be installed by the user.

This type of device driver is installed by the system's CONFIG.SYS file. CONFIG.SYS, which was discussed earlier in this chapter, contains command statements that set up the system's hardware configuration. Because device drivers are designed to manage hardware, they also are installed in CONFIG.SYS. Installing device drivers via CONFIG.SYS is discussed a little later in this chapter. Table 1.2 shows the SYS installable device drivers that are included as part of the standard DOS 5 distribution.

Table 1.2
DOS 5 Installable Device Drivers

Driver	Explanation
ANSI.SYS	Provides extended control of the keyboard and display, including redefining characters and controlling display text attributes.
DISPLAY.SYS	Provides for code-pages switching for the console.
DRIVER.SYS	Creates logical drives for physical floppy disk drives. DRIVER.SYS is used to add a new external floppy drive to the system, or to add more than one logical drive ID to a single physical drive.
EGA.SYS	Saves and restores the display on EGA systems when the Task Switcher is used to switch between applications.
EMM386.SYS	Microsoft's expanded-memory manager. EMM386.SYS simulates expanded memory using physical extended memory on 80386 or newer systems.
HIMEM.SYS	Microsoft's extended-memory manager for 80286, 80386, and newer processors.
PRINTER.SYS	Provides for code-page switching on printers.
RAMDRIVE.SYS	Creates a virtual disk in the system's RAM. The RAM drive can then be accessed and used like a physical drive.
SMARTDRV.SYS	Disk-caching driver that can be set up in extended or expanded memory.

Not all of the installable drivers are required by the typical user. In fact, many installations do not require any of the drivers for the system to function, although using many of the standard DOS installable drivers increases system performance and provides functions not otherwise possible.

Installing a Device Driver in CONFIG.SYS

Your system may also include one or more third-party installable device drivers to drive devices supplied by those companies. Microsoft and Logitech mouse drivers are two examples of third-party devices that DOS can use. Both of these devices are named MOUSE.SYS. Many device drivers are supplied, not by hardware manufacturers, but by software developers. They include special utility programs, disk-cache programs, and other system enhancement software modules.

Installing a device driver in CONFIG.SYS, whether it is a third-party driver or one of the standard MS-DOS installable drivers, is a relatively simple task. The following are examples of commands that are used to install them:

```
DEVICE=C:\MOUSE\MOUSE.SYS /2

DEVICEHIGH=C:\ANSI.SYS
```

The first command loads a specified driver into conventional memory (memory below 640K). The command parameters after the DEVICE= command include the name of the device-driver file and any necessary command line switches.

The second command loads the device driver into the reserved I/O space between 640K and 1024K, freeing memory below 640K for application use. The capability to load a particular driver into reserved RAM depends on the system/RAM combination and the driver itself. If you are unsure whether one of your drivers can be loaded in reserved RAM, check its documentation to be sure.

The DOS configuration files, CONFIG.SYS and AUTOEXEC.BAT, are two of the most important files in your system. Without proper configuration, your system will not operate optimally. Chapters 10 and 13 examine the CONFIG.SYS and AUTOEXEC.BAT files, and give you information to fine-tune your system's configuration.

Installing Other Device Drivers

In addition to SYS- type device drivers, many third-party vendors provide a second type of device driver with a COM file extension. Instead of installing via the CONFIG.SYS file automatically during startup, these device drivers install by running the device driver program (COM files are executable by DOS). COM-type device drivers are useful because they do not have to be loaded until you actually need them. If, for example, you use the mouse only with a particular program, you can load the mouse driver before executing the application.

To install this type of device driver, you simply type its name followed by any necessary switches. The following command, for example, loads the Logitech mouse driver, MOUSE.COM, and assigns it to COM2:

```
C:\>C:\MOUSE\MOUSE /2
```

DOS searches the \MOUSE directory for a file called MOUSE, finds the file named MOUSE.COM, and executes it.

Summary

MS-DOS is a complex, multi-layered environment. The many facets of DOS may make it seem overwhelming to understand, but fortunately, the average user needs to understand only how to use the commands that DOS provides. She does not need to understand how the BIOS and kernel function, how device drivers control devices, or any of the other low-level functions carried out by DOS.

By having at least a basic understanding of how those low-level functions operate, however, you can exercise a finer control of your system and perform functions that you might otherwise not be able to perform.

If you are not familiar already with the components in your system, take the time to find out the type of CPU it uses, the type of memory installed in it, the types of drives installed, and as much other information as you can gather about the system. Much of that information is contained in the system's manuals.

You should now have a good, basic understanding of the role DOS plays in controlling your system. This chapter has explained the different levels of the operating system, the main hardware components, and how the operating system and the hardware interact with one another.

The next chapter examines DOS data structures, providing you with an understanding of how DOS maintains the data you create. You will learn about DOS's important data structures, such as directories and subdirectories. You also will see what DOS is doing behind the scenes as you do your computing.

2

Understanding DOS Data Structures

You learned in Chapter 1 that DOS is a collection of multilayered programs and software routines that provide basic services and access to the computer system's hardware. One of the main functions of any operating system, including DOS, is to provide a means for storing and retrieving data. The primary type of storage used in PCs is a hard disk; floppy disks provide temporary, backup, and distribution storage. Although other types of data storage are available for PCs, disks are the leading storage devices and will continue to be for many years.

You also learned in Chapter 1 that floppy disks and hard disks are very similar in some ways because they use the same basic technology to store and retrieve data. This chapter examines disk drives in more detail, but from the point of view of the user and operating environment rather than focusing on the hardware. Data storage on disk is so much a part of DOS that you should have an understanding of how DOS goes about managing that data.

This chapter teaches you about the DOS *data structure*, which is essentially the form DOS uses to store data on a disk. You learn first about files and the file system that represent the highest order in the data structure. Once you have a good overview, you examine the lower levels in the structure to learn how DOS stores and retrieves data from a disk. This chapter does not teach you how to use the many commands available for working with data stored on disk. Those commands are examined in depth in other chapters. Instead, this chapter teaches you the underlying concepts behind data storage and retrieval that are necessary for you to use DOS' disk and disk-related commands effectively.

Before you can learn how DOS stores information, you must first learn *what* it stores. The best place to begin is with a look at files and file systems.

Understanding the DOS File System

By now, you probably can appreciate the reasons why DOS is a layered operating system. The lowest layers of the operating system, the BIOS and kernel, perform the complex tasks of accessing the system's hardware. You do not need to know how a block of memory is read or written to in order to load an application. Nor do you have to know how to direct the system's hardware to save and retrieve data. Just as it provides a higher-order layer to the operating system (COMMAND.COM) for working with applications and performing other computing tasks, DOS also imposes a higher-order structure to the data stored on disk. This structured order is called the *file system*.

A file system is simply a logically ordered group of files. The extent of the file system's organization depends primarily on you as a data manager. DOS provides a minimal level of order to the file system, but it is up to you to further refine and manage that order. DOS provides a foundation and set of tools, and you must use those tools to shape the file system into something that best serves the type of work you do.

The file system is made up not just of files, but of other data that DOS uses to manage the file system. Although you usually have no control over this extra "control" data, it is important to know what it is and how DOS uses it. First, however, take a look at the part of the file system you will work with most often—files.

Exploring Files

A *file* is a collection of data grouped in a logical format on the disk. The file can be any length (within the physical limits imposed by the disk capacity) and can contain virtually any type of information. A file may contain program code, portions of a program (called *overlays*), data, or a combination of program code and data. Regardless of the contents of the file, the file itself consists of groups of magnetic fields on the disk. Some of the techniques and hardware involved in storing and reading those magnetic fields were examined in Chapter 1.

The actual contents and format for any particular file can vary widely from the contents and format of another file. A spreadsheet file, for example, is considerably different in content and format from a simple ASCII text file or drawing file. With very few exceptions, DOS does not require specific formats or impose restrictions for files. The data file, for example, generated by one spreadsheet application may be (and probably is) quite different in format from another spreadsheet application's data file. By the same token, two word processing applications usually will implement two different file formats. This makes data portability between applications a difficult task in many cases, but the lack of restrictions and standard formats in many ways allows for greater flexibility within the application itself.

Although DOS does not impose restrictions on the content or logical structure of a file, it does impose some form of order to make the file system usable. Files are referenced by file names, which consist of a root name and an optional extension. The root name (usually referred to simply as the *name*) can include up to eight characters. A period (.) and an extension, which can have up to three characters, follow the name. The following are examples of valid DOS file names:

WORD.EXE	COMMAND.COM	1991SALE.XLS
FIG12-22.PCX	QRXY53AB.$AC	NOEXTENS
NO.GO		

DOS imposes only a few restrictions on file names, namely certain characters that are special punctuation marks or other symbols. Besides these characters, you have few limitations when you name your files. DOS does not demand that the file name always have an extension. Some applications, however, expect data files to have specific extensions. Executable files, for instance, must have an extension of BAT, COM, or EXE, but the *name* portion of the file name can literally be anything—as long as it consists of valid characters. In short, DOS provides a general structure for file names, but it is up to you to fill in that structure with something meaningful.

Chapter 6 discusses files and file names in more detail. Also, Chapter 3 provides suggestions for file naming that will make managing files in groups much easier.

Exploring the File System

A *file system* is a collection of files that have been grouped together in a logical way. Although the DOS file system may seem confusing at first, it is really quite simple once you understand its basic concepts.

In DOS, each disk has its own file system. Generally, common files are grouped together into *directories*. A directory is a logical area of the disk that can be accessed by name. Directories can contain files, other directories (called subdirectories), or a combination of the two. Directories provide you with a means of grouping your files together in a way that makes sense to you and to your applications. Directories are examined in more detail later in this chapter.

Multi-user operating environments, such as UNIX, require that a file system be *mounted* before it can be accessed. Mounting means that a disk's logical structure is added to the existing file system to make it appear as an integral part of that file system. All of the disks in a UNIX installation are usually recognized as being part of the same structure, with each disk appearing as a collection of files stored in a directory. Whether you add a new hard disk to the system or you simply want to display the directory listing of a floppy disk, the disk must be mounted under the file system before you can access it. In the case of a floppy, it must be *unmounted* (break the logical association) before you remove the floppy disk from the disk drive.

DOS file systems are different. Although a DOS command (JOIN) simulates the UNIX *mount* command, each disk in a DOS environment generally is recognized as a separate file system. You may have two hard disks, for example, but you see them as two separate entities, such as drive C and drive D. They are not gathered together into one logical entity as they would be with an operating system such as UNIX.

When you format a disk with DOS (discussed in detail in Chapter 4), you create an empty file system. DOS lays down a physical structure on the disk—the tracks and sectors discussed in Chapter 1. In addition to that physical structure, DOS also adds logical structure to a disk when it is formatted. The next section examines part of the process DOS uses to build that logical structure—formatting and partitioning.

Looking at Formatting and Disk Partitioning

Before it can be used, a new disk must be formatted. By formatting a disk, you create the "template" on the disk that DOS uses to store information. Floppy disks and hard disks must both be formatted before they can be used, although slight differences occur when they are formatted.

Floppy disks are formatted using the FORMAT command. FORMAT lays out the tracks and sectors on the floppy disk, and creates other logical structures on the disk (discussed later) that are needed for DOS to store information on it. Once formatted, a floppy disk does not need to be formatted again unless an area on the disk becomes unusable for some reason, or you want to remove all data on the disk completely without the possibility of later retrieving it.

Low-Level Formatting

Hard disks require a preliminary step before they are formatted with the FORMAT command. This preliminary step is called *low-level formatting*. By comparison, the type of format executed by the FORMAT command is called a *high-level format*. A low-level format is usually performed on a hard disk at the factory or by the computer system vendor. A low-level format creates the physical track and sector structure on the hard disk. The FORMAT command performs that task for floppy disks. On a hard drive, the FORMAT command simply cleans up the existing tracks and sectors, makes them ready to hold information, and sets up the control data mentioned previously. The FORMAT command automatically performs the correct operation depending on the disk type. You do not need to specify a different form of the command to format either a floppy disk or a hard disk.

Low-level formatting is not a standard part of the DOS command set. Low-level format routines are often built into the hard disk controller's hardware, or are available as separate DOS programs that are supplied with the disk drive's controller or with the drive itself. Most users, however, will not have to low-level format a hard disk—the low-level format will have been done by the manufacturer or vendor.

Partitioning

In addition to a low-level format, a hard disk requires *partitioning*. Partitioning allows a disk to be broken up into different storage areas. A partition is a group of disk sectors that have organized into a logical structure. Three types of partitions are supported by DOS:

❑ **Primary DOS Partition**. The primary DOS partition contains the IO.SYS, MSDOS.SYS, and COMMAND.COM system files. The primary DOS partition is generally the partition from which DOS is booted. The primary DOS partition is identified as drive C. If desired, the primary DOS partition can encompass the entire drive; that is, the entire drive can be recognized as drive C.

❑ **Extended DOS Partition**. The extended DOS partition is optional and can be used to set up *logical drives*. Although logical drives are located on a single physical drive, they appear to the operating system as separate drives. The extended DOS partition can be divided into as many as 23 logical drives, using drive indicators D through Z (A and B are reserved for floppy drives, and C is reserved for the primary DOS partition).

❏ **Non-DOS Partition**. In addition to DOS partitions, a disk can include non-DOS partitions that contain operating systems other than DOS. A single hard disk, for example, can contain both DOS and a PC version of UNIX. The UNIX operating system would be located in a non-DOS partition.

The first sector on a hard disk is called the *boot sector*. The boot sector contains a *partition table* and a *bootstrap program*. The partition table lists all the partitions currently on the disk, the type of each partition, the sector number where each partition starts, a flag to signify which partition is active, and other information about the partitions.

The bootstrap program located in the first sector of the drive is executed automatically when the system is turned on or reset. The bootstrap program is a very small, low-level program that the computer boot ROM can execute to get the system up and running. The bootstrap program checks the partition table to determine which partition is active and whether it is a bootable partition (meaning that an operating system can be loaded from it).

Each bootable partition also includes in its first sector its own boot program. The system bootstrap program (in the first sector of the drive) loads the boot program from the first sector of the active partition and turns control over to it. This second partition boot program is what loads into memory the operating system contained in the partition. Once the operating system is loaded, the boot program relinquishes control to the operating system.

Fortunately, DOS keeps much of the inner workings of the partitions and partition table isolated from the user. All you must do to boot an operating system from any bootable partition is use the FDISK command to make the partition active and then reset the system. Everything else happens automatically. You do not need to know where the boot program is or how it works, just as you do not need to know where the starter is in your car or how it works before you can start your car.

If DOS is your only operating system, you do not have to worry about setting an active partition—the primary DOS partition will be active by default. All you have to do is turn on the computer to make it boot (assuming you boot from a hard drive or you have inserted a boot diskette in drive A).

Understanding the Way DOS Manages the File System

You now know that you store information on disk in files and that a logical ordering of files is called a file system. You also know that a disk must be formatted before it can be used, and in the case of a hard disk, it also must be partitioned. You probably have realized that the DOS file system is layered like the DOS operating system itself—lower levels represent fundamental units of data, and upper levels represent much more organized relationships between data.

To begin to put these different file system layers into perspective, you must travel back to the lower levels and take a closer look at such things as tracks and sectors.

Exploring Cylinders, Tracks, Sectors, and Clusters

You learned in Chapter 1 that disk drives use electromagnetic read/write heads to align areas on a disk magnetically (write data) or to sense the magnetic alignment that already exists on a disk (read data). The disk may actually consist of multiple disks (platters) with a head for each side of each platter. The platters spin underneath the heads, which read and write information in circular rings called *tracks*. The heads move radially across the disk (center to edge and back) in steps. A track is defined at each step of the heads.

Each track is divided into a fixed number of sectors, providing a fixed number of storage places in each track in which to store data. The tracks that are aligned with each other from one platter to another form a cylinder. The outer-most track on each platter, for example, forms one cylinder. If the disk consists of five platters (a hard disk), and each platter has two read/write heads, a total of ten tracks are in each cylinder—five platters multiplied by two heads per platter.

You can see that there is a logical structure to a disk drive. Cylinders are made up of a certain numbers of tracks, and tracks are made up of a certain number of sectors. Sectors are the smallest logical unit of organized storage area on a disk. One other logical collection of space is on a disk, however, and it fits in between sectors and tracks. It is called a *cluster*.

When DOS allocates space on the disk, it does so in clusters. A cluster is simply a group of a fixed number of adjacent sectors that are collectively identified by a *cluster number*. Depending on the type of disk, a cluster may consist of one, two, four, eight, or more sectors. Regardless of the number of sectors used per cluster, the logical collection is referred to as a single cluster. Any particular drive has a fixed number of sectors in one cluster, a fixed number of clusters in one track, a fixed number of tracks in one cylinder, and a fixed number of cylinders on the disk.

Examining the Four Disk Control Areas

You can see that the file system, even at its lower levels, is complex. DOS needs a way to keep track of data as it is stored on the disk. It does that by creating four common control areas and index tables on each disk it formats, whether it is a hard disk or floppy disk. The first area is called the *reserve area* and consists of one or more sectors, depending on the disk type and format. The first sector in the reserve area is the boot sector, which is always located at logical sector 0. As you read earlier in this chapter, the boot sector contains the partition table and bootstrap program.

The second control area on the disk is called the *FAT*, which stands for *File Allocation Table*. The FAT (discussed in detail later in this chapter) is used by DOS to keep track of clusters in use (those that contain data), clusters that are not in use (those that do not contain data), and clusters that are unusable because of disk defects or formatting errors. DOS references the FAT each time data is stored or removed from the disk. The FAT varies in size depending on the disk type and format.

The third control area is called the *root directory*. The root directory area contains information about the files in the disk's root directory. The information includes each file's name, size, starting cluster number, as well as other information.

The final area on a disk is called the *files area*. The files area takes up the bulk of the disk and is used to store files and subdirectory entries.

Keeping Track with the FAT

The File Allocation Table on a disk really is not much more than a reference table of all of the clusters on the disk. As mentioned previously, the FAT keeps track of available clusters, clusters in use, and clusters that are unavailable because they contain one or more bad sectors. The FAT keeps track of cluster information using a single entry for each cluster. The value of the entry defines the status of the cluster, as you will see a little later in the chapter.

DOS allocates clusters whenever data is stored on the disk. DOS uses a complex set of rules to determine cluster allocation, but in general, it allocates the clusters by starting at the top of the FAT's cluster list and working down, allocating available clusters as it finds them. Adjacent clusters are allocated to a file whenever possible.

If the disk has been formatted recently, or no files have been removed from the disk, the used clusters will be at the top of the list. Unused clusters will be available in a single contiguous block starting from the last used cluster and working down to the bottom of the list, which is the last possible cluster. When a new file is added, DOS allocates the next available cluster and as many clusters following it as are needed.

But what happens if you erase a file? Assume, for example, that all clusters from 1 through 20 are used by three files. The second file, called FILE2.TXT, uses clusters 10, 11, and 12. If you erase FILE2.TXT, those three clusters will become available because they will no longer be in use by the FILE2.TXT file. DOS alters the entries in the FAT to reflect that clusters 10, 11, and 12 are now available for use.

Next, you create a new file called FILE4.TXT that requires five clusters to contain the entire file. DOS searches through the FAT starting at cluster 1, and finds clusters 10, 11, and 12 available. DOS stores the first part of FILE4.TXT in cluster 10, then uses clusters 11 and 12. It still must store two more clusters-worth of data so DOS continues scanning the FAT for available clusters. The next available cluster it finds is cluster 21, so DOS allocates clusters 21 and 22 to FILE4.TXT. The entire file has been stored, but not in adjacent clusters—it is located in clusters 10, 11, 12, 21, and 22. A gap exists from cluster 13 to cluster 20, and the clusters in that "gap" are all in use by another file.

This allocation of files into noncontiguous clusters is called *fragmentation*. More gaps arise in the FAT when you erase files from and add new files to the disk, resulting in a more fragmented file system. The files are safe and intact, but are located in adjacent clusters. This means that more time is needed for the drive's heads to scan across the disk to read each of the clusters in the file. Utility programs that defragment the disk scan the FAT and safely reallocate clusters, moving all of each file's data into adjacent clusters. Eventually, the entire disk is reordered and all of the files on the disk have their data located in adjacent clusters. Then, when you start writing to your disk again, the process of fragmentation begins all over again.

Even if files do not become fragmented, DOS still needs some means of determining the following:

❏ Which clusters belong to a file

❏ Where the first cluster in a file is located

❏ How to move from the first cluster in the files to the last cluster

❏ How to know when it has reached the last cluster

For many of the preceding items, DOS stores the information in the FAT. The location of the starting cluster for a file, however, is not stored as part of the FAT. Instead, it is stored in the file's directory entry. You will see how DOS locates the beginning cluster of a file later in this chapter. Once it has located the first cluster, DOS uses information in the FAT to help it move from one cluster to the next until it has located all of a given file (or as much as it was directed to find).

Earlier in this section, you learned that each cluster is referenced in the FAT with an entry indicating whether it is in use or free. This entry is how DOS allocates clusters when they are needed. This entry, however, is the only entry a cluster has in the FAT.

DOS uses this one entry for more than indicating the used/free status of a cluster. Table 2.1 lists the possible values for each cluster's entry in the FAT. Note that the actual hexidecimal values representing each entry are given as a reference. In addition, two types of FATs are listed—12-bit FATs and 16-bit FATs—which indicate the type of number used to store the value of each entry. An explanation of the differences between 12-bit and 16-bit FATs goes beyond the scope of this book, but for the purposes of this chapter, the two are functionally equivalent. Table 2.1 simply illustrates that each FAT entry can take on more than one value and that fixed values are used to represent cluster status.

Table 2.1
16-bit FAT Values

16-bit Value	Meaning
0	Unused cluster
FFF0-FFF6H	Reserved cluster
FFF7H	Bad cluster
FFF8-FFFFH	Last cluster in a file
<other values>	Next cluster in a file

Each possible value is represented by a specific number. The *unused cluster* value is self-explanatory. If the entry has the value of *reserved cluster*, the cluster has been set aside by DOS and cannot be used for file storage. A *bad cluster* value indicates that one or more bad sectors are present in the cluster, or the cluster cannot be accessed for some similar reason. The *last clus-*

ter in a file and *next cluster in a file* entries, however, demand a bit more explanation.

You first must understand that even though the clusters allocated to a file may not be adjacent and their entries in the FAT may not be sequential, DOS accesses the FAT sequentially when searching for a file. Once DOS knows the starting cluster for a file, it jumps to the corresponding entry in the FAT and reads the value of that cluster entry. If the entry has the value of *last cluster in a file*, the end of the file has been reached and DOS does not continue to search for additional clusters.

If the entry does not mark the cluster as either unused, reserved, bad, or last cluster, the entry contains the number of the next cluster of the file. DOS reads from the disk the cluster that is referenced by the current FAT entry, then uses the value of the entry to jump to the next cluster entry in the FAT. It reads from the disk *that* cluster, then checks the value of the FAT entry to determine its next course of action. If it finds a *last cluster* value, DOS stops checking for additional clusters. Otherwise, the value represents the next cluster in the file and DOS continues searching until it finds a *last cluster* value.

How does that concept translate into actual file storage from a user's point of view? Up to this point in the chapter, you have seen that DOS allocates disk space in clusters. The clusters are located in the disk's file storage area, which is one of the four disk areas discussed earlier in this chapter. The only data that is stored in the file storage area is the file's contents, not its name or other information. Information defining the clusters in use by a file is stored in the FAT. You have examined, therefore, how DOS uses two of the four disk areas—the reserved area and the FAT. The next area is the *root directory*.

Exploring the Root Directory Area

The root directory contains a directory data table similar to the FAT. Instead of keeping track of clusters, however, the root directory table maintains a log of the files stored in the root, or uppermost level, of the file system. A disk's root directory table contains the following information about each entry in the root directory:

❏ **File name**. The name of the file, which is stored as ASCII characters.

❏ **File extension**. The file's extension, also stored as ASCII characters.

❏ **Attribute**. A value that represents the type of file. The attribute can be set to include the following: read-only, hidden, system, volume label, subdirectory, or archive.

❏ **Reserved**. Each directory entry contains one entry that is currently not used by DOS. This reserved entry may be implemented in future releases of the DOS operating system.

❏ **Time**. Stores the time the file is created or last revised.

❏ **Date**. Stores the date the file is created or last revised.

❏ **Starting cluster number**. This field contains the cluster number for the first cluster in a file. DOS uses this value to access a file's data via the FAT. Files that have no space allocated (a size of 0) have a starting cluster number of 0. Volume label entries also have a starting cluster number of 0.

❏ **File size**. The exact size of the file in bytes. Because a file may use only a portion of its last cluster (only some of the sectors in the cluster), the actual file size may be smaller than the total cluster space used by the file.

Root directory tables are sized according to disk capacity, which varies according to disk size. The more storage space that is available on a disk, the more entries a root directory table can contain. Table 2.2 lists the number of directory entries in the root directory table of standard disk formats.

Table 2.2
Number of Entries in Root Directory Table

Disk Format	Capacity	Directory Entries
5 1/4-inch	360K	112
	1.2M	224
3 1/2-inch	720K	112
	1.44M	224
	2.88M	448
Most hard disks	Varies	512

For the purposes of this chapter, the *file name*, *file extension*, and *starting cluster number* are the most important aspects to consider of the root directory table. To understand how DOS uses the directory table and the FAT together to access a file, consider one example—erasing a file by using the ERASE command.

The Inner Workings of ERASE

When you erase a file by using the ERASE command (discussed in Chapters 5 and 8), DOS removes the specified file from the file system. DOS does not remove the file physically—it only removes the file's logical association in the disk's control areas.

First, DOS checks the directory table for the file name specified with the ERASE command. If it does not find the specified file, DOS generates an error message and returns to the DOS command prompt. If it finds the file, however, the ERASE command uses the starting cluster number for the file to jump to the FAT and read the value for the cluster's entry. If the value for the cluster entry represents that the cluster is the last one in the file, the ERASE command's action results in a 0 (zero) being stored in the cluster entry, indicating that the cluster is unused. DOS then removes the file's entry from the directory table.

If the file consists of more than one cluster, the ERASE command jumps through the FAT, seeking and resetting each of the file's cluster entries to 0 until it reaches the *last cluster* entry. ERASE then removes the file's entry from the directory table. When the file(s) has been removed, ERASE returns control to COMMAND.COM. The actual mechanics of the ERASE operation are somewhat different (only part of the directory entry is actually removed, for example), but the general concept fits and will give you a good idea of DOS commands' effects on the file-storing mechanisms.

You can see that the directory table is used as pointer reference to the FAT. DOS checks the directory table for the starting cluster of the file, then jumps to the FAT to begin locating the data clusters used by the file.

But what about the data itself? This is where the file storage area comes into the picture.

Exploring the File Storage Area

The fourth and last area that DOS reserves on a disk is the file storage area. The file storage area takes up the vast majority of a disk. For any given disk format, the size of the reserved area, the directory table, and the FAT are fixed. The file storage area, therefore, starts in the same cluster for each disk of a given format.

Taken by itself, the file storage area is useless. Based on the data stored solely in the file storage area, there is no way to reconstruct a file. To find the pieces of a file scattered within the file storage area, DOS requires both the directory table and the FAT. Each of the clusters in the file storage area is like a numbered hole in a pegboard. You can store information in any given cluster (place a peg in a hole), but without some type of map to navigate from one linked cluster to the next, the information stored in the file storage area is a jumble of data (unrelated pegs in unrelated holes).

The leap from unrelated clusters to the logical structure of a file system is a fairly large one. You have seen the part that the boot sector, directory table, FAT, and file storage area play in managing data on the disk. You now are ready to take a brief look to see the way in which the hardware and operating system fit together in the process.

Examining the Controller and Device Driver

The functions of allocating and accessing clusters are relatively high-level when compared to the actual process of moving the drive's head to a particular sector and reading or writing the information in it. To access the disk, DOS simply requests information from the disk's FAT using information found in the directory table. The requests go through the BIOS, which communicates with the disk controller. The disk controller converts the request into head movements and other machine-level tasks necessary to retrieve the requested information. The information comes back up the chain in reverse order.

Once DOS has the information on a file it has requested from the FAT, it requests specific actions (read or write) on the applicable clusters. Again, the request passes through the BIOS to the disk drive controller, where it is translated into machine-level instructions. These insulating layers (BIOS and controller) allow DOS to access virtually any disk drive. It does not matter that one drive has five heads and another ten, or that one drive has twice as many clusters as another. DOS simply checks the FAT for the locations of the desired file (or available storage locations) and passes its instructions to the BIOS based on the information it finds in the FAT. DOS does not have to be able to make the drive's heads move to a specific track or read from a specific sector. The controller takes care of locating data in a specific sector based on instructions it receives from the BIOS.

Looking at the Beginnings of Structure

You can see that the same type of structure found in the DOS operating system exists in the DOS file system. Sectors represent the smallest logical collection of disk organization (disregarding bytes and bits). Sectors are organized into clusters, which are organized into tracks. Each disk has a fixed number of tracks.

The way the disk is formatted also plays a part in imposing a sense of order on the disk's data. When you format a disk, you set up the tracks and sectors on the disk, as well as the four control areas on the disk. The directory table is used to access the FAT, and the FAT is used to access the data that makes up a file.

Understanding the DOS Directory Structure

The topics discussed so far in this chapter represent relatively low-level structures in the DOS file system. This section steps up a level to examine directories from the viewpoint of the user rather than the operating system. The following pages will show you not how DOS structures data, but how *you* can structure data.

If you think of a disk as a file cabinet, you can think of the directories as the drawers. With a file cabinet, you can open each drawer and pull out a file folder. With a disk, you can open a directory and pull out a file. The main difference conceptually between a physical file cabinet and a disk is that a file cabinet's drawers cannot contain other drawers. Each cabinet has a fixed number of drawers and the drawers can contain only files. A disk, on the other hand, can have a variable number of directories (drawers) and each directory can contain other directories (other drawers), files, or a combination of the two.

Looking at the Root Directory

If you consider the disk to be a file cabinet, the collection of file drawers can collectively be called the root directory. Each DOS disk contains a reserved area called the root directory, which was discussed earlier in this chapter. You learned that the root directory of a disk contains a fixed number of entries, or a fixed number of places in which to store files. A directory is simply a logical grouping of data within the scope of the file system. Directories provide a means of effectively creating named compartments (drawers) in which to store data.

The root directory itself is a data table on the disk, but is presented to you as a list of files and subdirectories. The root directory potentially can contain any file and any number of subdirectories, up to the limit on the number of entries imposed by the disk format.

The root directory is the master directory under which everything else is stored. You can consider it to be the highest order in the DOS data structure. Although the limitation of entries that DOS imposes in a directory may at first seem a disadvantage, it really is not. Generally, the root directory should contain as few files as possible, to make finding files and directories easier. Many experienced users keep only the files COMMAND.COM, CONFIG.SYS, and AUTOEXEC.BAT in the root directory.

To illustrate this point, assume that you are storing files on a hard disk and have used all 512 possible directory entries in the root directory. You now need to locate a file and you have only a vague recollection of what the file's name is. You must then search through a listing of 512 files to find it, which could take a considerable amount of time. It makes much better sense to segregate your files into different areas to make them easier to find. These areas are called *subdirectories*.

Looking at Subdirectories

A disk has only one root directory, but that one root directory can be divided into other storage areas called subdirectories. You can consider a subdirectory to be a secondary storage area located within another directory— something like a box in a box. You can store files in the main box (the root directory), or open up one of the other boxes in it (a subdirectory) and store the file in the secondary box. Subdirectories are often referred to simply as *directories*, while the root directory is always referred to as the root directory.

The root directory is a data table stored in the reserved root directory area on the disk, but subdirectories are actually files that are stored in the file storage area, similar to data files. Subdirectories also have file names like files. In fact, a subdirectory's name is no different from a data file's name and can even include an extension. Generally, however, file-name extensions are not used for directories. The root directory is in a fixed location with a fixed size, so it does not require or allow a directory name to be assigned to it.

Subdirectories are located in the file storage area and are not limited as to the number of entries they can contain. A subdirectory can grow to include as many files as necessary, within the physical space limitation imposed by the size of the file storage area. You can actually place 1000 files (or any other number) in a subdirectory—as long as you have enough disk space to do so.

Looking at DOS' Tree Structure

The DOS data structure is a hierarchy of files and directories that make up the file system. At the uppermost level in the DOS data structure is the disk itself, which represents the entire file system. The next layer is the root directory. Below the root directory are subdirectories and files.

The file system can be pictured somewhat like an inverted tree. The root directory, representing the root of the tree, is located at the top. Subdirectory branches grow from the root, with each of those subdirectories branching further into other subdirectories'. You can think of files as the individual leaves on each branch.

This tree analogy even carries over into the DOS command set. DOS provides a command called TREE that displays a top-down representation of the branches in the file system. It starts with the root directory at the top and graphically shows the branching subdirectories underneath the root.

This hierarchical structure—coupled with the ability to create and name your own directories and place as many files as you desire in a subdirectory—provides nearly unlimited control over the structure of the file system. DOS includes a number of commands for creating and removing directories, copying files between directories, and other file system management commands. DOS' directory structure and directory management commands are discussed in detail in Chapter 5. To understand how to use those commands, however, you must understand a little bit about how to navigate through DOS' tree structure. The next section will help you do just that.

Understanding Directory Defaults

You know that when you turn the computer on or reboot it, the operating system is booted from the disk. The process involves the boot ROM, the boot sector of the disk, the active partition, the bootstrap program, and a number of other factors. Fortunately, you do not have to consider any of that—you simply turn the system on. When the boot process is complete and COMMAND.COM is running, the DOS command prompt appears on the screen.

When you first receive the command prompt after the system has booted, the boot disk will be the current (active) drive and the root directory of the boot disk will be the current directory. Only one drive and directory can be current at a time. Any file operations are always carried out on the current directory unless you specify otherwise. Consider the following command:

```
ERASE MYFILE.TXT
```

This command instructs DOS to erase a file called MYFILE.TXT. No information is supplied other than the file name. By default, DOS searches the current directory of the current drive for the file. If it finds the file in the current directory, DOS erases it. If it does not find it in the current directory, DOS displays an error message telling you that it cannot find the file.

The current drive and directory are called the *default* drive and directory. If you do not specify any other drive or directory for DOS to use for the requested file operation, DOS *defaults* to the current drive and directory.

If you need to access a file that is not located in the current directory, you can make the file's directory current. Then, because the new directory is current, DOS defaults to it when you specify a file operation. The command that allows you to make another directory current is the CD command, which stands for Change Directory. Assume, for example, that you have just booted the system from the hard disk. The current drive is C and the root directory of drive C is the current directory. To change to a subdirectory called DOCU-MENT that is located under the root, type the following command:

    CD \DOCUMENT

You have not changed active drives, only the active directory. Consequently, the active directory is now C:\DOCUMENT.

Note that the current drive/directory combination is referenced by the current drive ID (C:), a backslash (\), and the name of the directory. This combination of drive and directory specification is called the *path name*.

Understanding Path Names

When a file is located in the root directory and you direct DOS to perform some type of action on the file, DOS has little trouble finding it. It simply looks in the root directory area on the disk, locates the first cluster for the file, then examines the FAT to find the rest of the clusters.

Finding a file located in a subdirectory, however, is not so easy. Suppose, for example, that you want to access a file called FILE1.TXT that is located in a directory called LETTERS, which is a subdirectory of the DOCUMENT directory. The DOCUMENT directory is a subdirectory of the root directory of drive C. In this example, FILE1.TXT is buried two levels deep in the file system.

DOS cannot simply access the root directory area on the disk to locate the file's starting cluster because the file does not exist in the root directory. No entry for the file exists in the root directory. You must explicitly tell DOS where to find the file. To do this, give it a path to follow to find the file. The path consists of the names of directories DOS must consecutively examine to locate the file. This path of directory names, combined with the drive ID and the file name itself, is called a *path name*. The following is the path name for the file FILE1.TXT from the previous example:

    C:\DOCUMENT\LETTERS\FILE1.TXT

Each of the items in the path name is separated by a backslash (\). The path name is structured in descending order, starting with the drive ID and working down through the directory structure to the file itself. By passing the preceding path name to DOS, you are requesting DOS to access the file

FILE1.TXT in the C:\DOCUMENT\LETTERS subdirectory. DOS locates the DOCUMENT subdirectory entry (its name and starting cluster) in the root directory of C: that tells DOS where to access the DOCUMENT subdirectory. DOS searches in C:\DOCUMENT to find the location of the subdirectory LETTERS. DOS, then accesses the LETTERS subdirectory and finds the entry for FILE1.TXT. The entry for FILE1.TXT references the first cluster location of FILE1.TXT's contents in the file storage area. With the starting cluster number, DOS can finally read the file.

You actually string file names together to form a path name. DOS subdirectories are files from a directory entry and storage allocation point of view. You can consider, however, only the final part of a path name to be a file. Directory entries, even though they are file names, are considered by the average user to be simply a logical structure rather than a physical file.

Path names allow you to access virtually any file from any drive or directory. If the required file is not in the current directory, you can direct DOS to find it by passing it the full path name for the file.

Summary

The DOS file system is nearly as complex as the DOS operating system. Like the operating system, the file system is structured in varying levels of association. The file system's layering provides the same benefits to you as a user as does the operating system's layers—you are isolated from the lowest levels of the data structure by intermediate levels.

At the bottom layer is the disk itself, controlled by the drive's controller. The next logical level above that is the disk's sectors. Sectors are then grouped logically into clusters, with a fixed number of clusters in a track. As a DOS user, you generally are not concerned with these lower layers in the data structure. You do not have to know how DOS accesses a cluster, for example, in order to create and manipulate files.

Files represent the next layer in the DOS data structure. Files, which are stored as a collection of disk clusters, represent the level in the DOS data structure that you most often access. You also can impose another layer of order on the file system by grouping files into directories. Effective use of DOS' directory capability ensures that your data is easy to manage.

In this chapter, you have learned about the structure of DOS' file system, but you have not learned how to manipulate the file system. Other chapters will show you how to create directories, remove them, copy files, rename files, and perform other disk management tasks.

3

The Command Processor

So far, you have read in Part One about the layers of DOS and the PC on which it is operating. Most of the activities of DOS, as you have seen, occur behind the scenes. You have to learn about DOS' underlying services and data structures by reading about them. In contrast, the DOS command processor, COMMAND.COM, is a highly visible layer of DOS. If you ask DOS users to describe the operation of DOS, they will most likely tell you about the operation of COMMAND.COM and its related topics.

It is easy to see how users relate the command processor to the term DOS. Most PC users manage their disks, files, directories, and devices at the DOS command line. The most familiar computer prompt in the world is the > character presented by COMMAND.COM. For all practical purposes, doing DOS work is equivalent to issuing DOS commands at the command line. Most other operating systems have their equivalent to COMMAND.COM as a command processor. UNIX has its Bourne, Korn, and C shells as command processors. Digital Equipment Corporation minicomputers have their Monitor Console Routines. Not surprisingly, the operation of these command processors include common actions and responses.

The DOS command processor is DOS' primary shell program. COMMAND.COM is a shell from a layered-DOS point of view. As a shell surrounding the internal components of DOS, the command processor "hides" DOS' internal details while it provides a smooth interface between DOS and you, the user. You should not, however, confuse COMMAND.COM as the primary shell with DOSSHELL. DOSSHELL is a higher-level program that accesses the surfaces of COMMAND.COM to perform many functions. COMMAND.COM is the first program that appears after the operating system is loaded by the boot program. Without this primary shell, the booted computer has no way of taking your instructions in the form of DOS commands.

When COMMAND.COM loads into your system's memory and presents you with the system prompt, you are placed in control of your machine. You issue command lines to run DOS commands or application programs. If you form the command line properly, COMMAND.COM arranges for the execution of the command or program you indicate. If you form the command line improperly, COMMAND.COM presents you with an error message indicating the nature of the problem. You can even form a proper command line that COMMAND.COM will execute that does something other than you intended. Just ask someone who used DEL with an inappropriate wild card!

This chapter presents the command interpreter along with related issues that you will want to be clear about before moving to Part Two. Whereas individual commands require individual considerations, many general principles exist that affect all command lines. You will learn about these considerations in this chapter. If you feel comfortable with your general knowledge of commands, you still should review this chapter to reinforce your knowledge.

Understanding the Command Processor's Role

In an operating system setting, the terms "command processor," "command interpreter," and "shell" mean the same thing. You may hear COMMAND.COM referred to by any (or all) of these three terms. Yet, each of these terms implies a slightly different type of action. "Command processor" implies carrying out some command action. Indeed, COMMAND.COM incorporates several built-in commands that carry out DOS management actions. "Command interpreter" implies translating information into a form that can be used or understood. In this context, COMMAND.COM incorporates the capability to accept your typed command line, interpret the line's meaning, and carry out (or arrange for some other command to carry out) an understood action. "Shell" implies an impenetrable layer that divides the outside from the inside. COMMAND.COM certainly acts as a layer between the programmatic, algorithmic internals of DOS and the abstraction of a user's typing "English-like" DOS commands on a keyboard. Each of the three terms is correct when used to describe COMMAND.COM, but their combined meaning is perhaps the most accurate description of COMMAND.COM's role on a working PC. In the next sections, you will get a more concrete understanding of the role of COMMAND.COM, ranging from reporting error messages to executing internal commands. Because you associate DOS work with the command line, a good place to start with your understanding is at the command line.

Interpreting Commands

You type command names and other items at the DOS prompt to form command lines. To make terminology more streamlined, you can think of the complete command line as the DOS command. Each DOS command consists of at least a command name, as well as optional parameters. The command name and the parameters are the elements of the command. The command name is the first element of the command. If you examine the elements of a typical DOS command, you will find something like the following:

```
COMMAND_NAME parameter parameter. . . switch switch. . .
```

COMMAND_NAME is the name of a DOS command that describes the command's action. Parameter, sometimes called argument or specifier, indicates the element(s) that are acted upon by the command. Switch initiates a modification or further clarification of the command's action. A switch is preceded by a slash (/) character. The ellipsis (. . .) following an element shows that more than one of the element may appear in the command. One or more spaces or tab characters separate the elements of the command line.

As an example, the following simple command gives DIR as the command name, BUDGET.WKS as a file name parameter, and /W as a switch:

```
DIR BUDGET.WKS /W
```

The minimum number of parameters and switches varies from command to command. Some elements are mandatory, or required. The command name, for instance, obviously is required for COMMAND.COM to know what action to take. The drive parameter for a FORMAT command is mandatory. Other elements, such as a file name parameter in a DIR command, are optional. You do not have to include optional elements of a command when you type a command line. Switches, for instance, are optional.

Understanding Syntax

For each command, the arrangement of the command name, parameters, and switches is called command syntax. Syntax is the proper inclusion and arrangement of command elements. Syntax rules are the statement of syntax. You will see sample syntaxes for commands in the remaining parts of the book. The Command Reference includes the syntax for each command. By using correct syntax for a command, you enable the command interpreter to process your command. COMMAND.COM relies on proper syntax of a command as it breaks the command into components during interpretation of the command. COMMAND.COM's act of breaking the command line is called *parsing.* COMMAND.COM parses every command, even if the command consists of only a command name. Before COMMAND.COM executes a command, it must satisfactorily parse the command to determine your intention. COMMAND.COM considers any command that it cannot parse to be a syntax error. Remember that DOS is not case-sensitive. You can enter commands in uppercase letters or in lowercase letters. DOS responds to the command in the same way in either case.

Editing Command Lines

Although you know one or two people who never make a mistake, most people make them. In keeping with this tradition, DOS users sometimes make mistakes when entering commands. Several methods for correcting command line mistakes are available. Just remember that you must correct a mistake *before* you press Enter. The Enter key is the signal to COMMAND.COM that you are ready for the command line to be executed. Prior to pressing Enter, you can correct a line or start over again.

If the line you are typing is completely botched and you want to start the line fresh, press Esc. The cursor will back up on the line to the prompt and await your input. After you press Esc, COMMAND.COM discards everything you have typed on the line.

You can correct a line by pressing Backspace to erase errant text. Unfortunately, you will erase every character that you backspace over. Still, you can back up to an error, correct the error, and then retype the rest of the line.

Sometimes you can re-use most of the command line that you just issued. Perhaps your current COPY command's destination file name has changed by one character in the extension from the last command. In this case, you can recall and edit the previous command line. COMMAND.COM enables you to recall the previous command line in two ways—a character at a time and a line at a time.

Press F1 once for each character you want to recall from the previous line. At points in the current line where you want to change the next character, type it at the keyboard. If you want to insert an additional character between the last character and the next character to be recalled, press Ins and type the character. If you want to delete the next character that would be recalled, press Del and then F1. The recall action skips one character. You should experiment with F1, Ins, and Del using sample DIR command lines. You will get a sense of the usefulness of recalling the previous command line a character at a time.

To recall the last command line in its entirety, simply press F3. When you press F3, the previously executed command line is presented at the prompt and your cursor sits in the next character position after the last character of the line. From there, you can use Backspace to modify the line or simply issue the line again by pressing Enter.

Whichever method you use to edit command lines, be sure that you take a moment to read what you have typed before pressing Enter. DOS has no universal UNDO command like many application programs offer.

Using DOSKEY To Edit and Recall Commands

DOSKEY is a program new in DOS 5. DOSKEY provides services pertaining to keyboard entry. One area of service, macros, is discussed later in this chapter and again in detail in Chapter 13. The other area of service provided by DOSKEY is command-line editing and recall. The Command Reference details the various switches and options used with DOSKEY. For simple recall and editing of commands, you can issue the DOSKEY command with no parameters, as follows:

```
C:/DOS> DOSKEY
```

DOSKEY loads and remains resident in memory. DOSKEY intercepts your keystrokes before they are given to COMMAND.COM. When DOSKEY finds a keystroke that is associated with a DOSKEY feature, DOSKEY substitutes its own text for the keystroke before passing the text on to COMMAND.COM.

When you press the down-arrow key, DOSKEY recalls the command you just finished. Pressing the up-arrow key recalls the command before that. You can press up arrow many times and move backward through the list of commands that you issued previously.

The down-arrow key reverses your progress through the list of previous commands. You move from older commands to more recently issued ones.

The PgUp key recalls the oldest command that you used in the current session. The number of commands that DOSKEY remembers is limited to the size of memory buffer that is associated with DOSKEY. The default size holds about 512 characters.

The PgDn key recalls the most recent command you entered. Press PgDn to move to the end of the command list after you have moved several commands toward the beginning of the list.

To edit a command line while DOSKEY is active, use the right- and left-arrow keys to move the cursor to the desired position. At that position, you can insert and delete characters as though you were using a text editor. When your editing is finished, you do not have to move the cursor to the end of the line before pressing Enter. DOS will accept the entire command line in any event.

Although other useful features of DOSKEY for recall and editing are available, the features described here give you some distinct advantages over the standard command-line editing and recall provisions.

Stopping and Pausing Commands

You occasionally may want to stop a DOS command while it is executing. You may have seen enough output and do not need to see the rest. You may have issued a command that you did not intend to issue. You can stop executing commands by pressing Ctrl-C or Ctrl-Break. When you press Ctrl-C or Ctrl-Break in the middle of most commands, the command stops quickly. Other commands continue running for a brief period before they stop. Be forewarned, however, that any processing that the command has done before stopping will remain. You can Ctrl-C while FORMAT is formatting your disk, but you cannot stop FORMAT fast enough to save the disk's data from being lost. You simply end up with a partially formatted (and unusable) disk.

You can pause screen output by pressing the Pause key or Crtl-S. Pausing a screen is handy when screen output is scrolling off of the top of the screen. To restart screen output, press any key. If you have a situation in which DOS seems to "clip" off the first character you type on a line, you might suspect that you have inadvertently paused the screen. The first key after the pause is taken as a "resume" indicator, not a literal key.

Understanding Internal and External Commands

Each DOS command is a program or routine that performs some useful operating-system-level work. Commands are either internal to COMMAND.COM or external, self-sufficient programs. COMMAND.COM checks the command name that it parses from your command line and determines whether the command name is one of COMMAND.COM's built-in or internal commands. If the command is internal, COMMAND.COM consults its own internal routine for the command and executes the command process. COMMAND.COM remains in memory while processing internal commands. If the name in the command-name position of the command is not an internal command, then COMMAND.COM assumes that the command is an executable file or batch file located on a disk. COMMAND.COM initiates access to the disk containing the external command file and loads the command into memory. The PC's control is handed over from COMMAND.COM to the external program. When the external program completes execution, COMMAND.COM retakes control of the PC and awaits more keyboard input.

You will learn later about a third type of command name, called a *macro*. Macros are defined through the DOSKEY command to do a sequence of other commands. COMMAND.COM cooperates with DOSKEY to make macros appear as internal programs.

A Note on the Transient and Resident Portions of COMMAND.COM

Often, an external program is of such a size that the program requires memory space occupied by COMMAND.COM. When external programs require this space, only a small portion of COMMAND.COM remains in memory while DOS allocates much of COMMAND.COM's memory space for loading the external program. The portion of COMMAND.COM that remains in memory is called the *resident portion*, while the part that is available for needed allocation is called the *transient portion*.

COMMAND.COM is unique in this "split personality" operation. By keeping its essential routines in memory at all times, COMMAND.COM ensures that error message processing is intact. The resident portion also enables the transient portion to reload when the displacing external command is finished. The only time that you might be aware of COMMAND.COM's shuffling routine is when you boot from a floppy disk and then remove the disk. Before you do much computing, you will see a message asking you to place the floppy containing COMMAND.COM back into the drive. The transient portion wants to be reloaded.

Internal Commands

The commands that COMMAND.COM itself handles are very basic commands. These internal commands provide fundamental DOS services. Internal commands are not elaborate commands compared to many external commands. There are two reasons why. First, more elaborate commands (programs) require more memory. One of the design goals for a command processor is to keep the memory requirements of the command processor at a minimum. The conservative size enables the command processor to run on a PC with very little memory.

The second reason to avoid elaborate internal commands is to accommodate change. In the DOS environment, external commands can change from version to version. Making a change requires adding or modifying an external command program. The change is limited to a single program. Changing an internal command, however, requires modifying the command processor. For compatibility reasons, the command processor should remain fairly stable from version to version. A good example of an elaborate external command that works in much the same way as its internal counterpart is XCOPY. The external XCOPY (eXtended COPY) is a much more powerful command than the internal COPY. Yet, in the DOS world, each has its place. COPY is internal, and therefore is always available. XCOPY is powerful, though it must be loaded before it can work.

Any time that you see the DOS prompt, you can issue an internal command. In some circumstances, such as when you boot from a bootable but otherwise empty floppy, internal commands are the *only* commands immediately accessible to you. Internal commands give you the basic survival capability to do DOS work. You change the default drive to your hard disk with no aid from an external command. You use the internal CD to log to a new directory. You use the internal DIR command to see your files and programs. You can even use the internal COPY command to create an AUTOEXEC.BAT and a CONFIG.SYS file.

Because internal commands are imbedded in the COMMAND.COM program itself, you cannot see the internal command names in a file listing. These internal commands are so basic that most DOS users remember them with no problem. The following is a list of the internal commands that you use at the DOS prompt.

BREAK	CHCP	CD (CHDIR)	CLS	COMMAND
COPY	CTTY	DATE	DEL (ERASE)	DIR
ECHO	EXIT	FOR	LOADHIGH (LH)	MD (MKDIR)
PATH	PAUSE	PROMPT	RENAME (REN)	RD (RMDIR)
SET	TIME	TREE	TYPE	VER
VOL				

External Commands

External commands are external in the sense that they are not contained within COMMAND.COM. Each external DOS command is a stand-alone program in its own right. In fact, the primary claim that external commands have to being part of DOS is that they come on the DOS distribution disks and do "DOS-like" work. Otherwise, external commands are the same as any "outside" program that you run on your machine.

External commands, like other programs, reside as a disk file until they are loaded into memory for execution. Like other executable files, external commands have COM or EXE extensions. You do not have to type the extension on the command line unless you want to differentiate a command name that has both a COM and also an EXE extension.

The exact directory location of the external DOS commands can vary from PC to PC. Most DOS users copy the external commands into a \DOS or a \BIN directory of their bootable DOS partition of the hard disk. While a \DOS location for external commands is the leading convention, it is by no means chiseled in stone. Although COMMAND.COM is responsible for loading external programs into memory for execution, it has no preprogrammed indication of any external program's exact drive and directory location. To successfully run an external program, you have to "help" COMMAND.COM find the file in one of the following three ways:

1. Precede the command's name with the drive and directory in which it resides.
2. Log to the external command's drive and directory.
3. Establish a path specification for DOS to use as a search guide when the external command is not in the current directory.

Preceding the command name with a drive and directory specification is an absolute way to access the command. By using the drive and directory specification, you are assured of pointing DOS to the correct file, regardless of your current drive and directory. To access the FORMAT command located in the A:\DOS directory to format the disk in drive B, for example, issue the following command:

```
C:\DOS> A:\DOS\FORMAT B:
```

In this instance, DOS loads FORMAT from the \DOS directory of drive A even if FORMAT is present in the default \DOS directory or the default drive C. Remember, input that you type is shown in bold text. Output that DOS supplies is shown in nonbold text.

By changing to the disk and directory that contains the desired external program, you take advantage of the fact that DOS searches the current directory for a file to execute any time that a drive or directory does not precede the command name. To use this method while following the preceding example, change to drive A and CD to the \DOS directory. Finally, issue the FORMAT command. The sequence appears on screen as the following:

```
C:\DOS> A:

A:\> CD \DOS

A:\DOS> FORMAT B:
```

Perhaps the most useful method of accessing external programs is establishing a search path to the directory containing the desired file. As a tool for establishing the search path, COMMAND.COM provides the internal PATH command. Nearly every DOS user includes a PATH command within his or her AUTOEXEC.BAT file. As you recall, AUTOEXEC.BAT is executed by COMMAND.COM at the end of the boot process. You can issue the PATH command from the command prompt at any time, too. For accessing external DOS commands in the \DOS directory of drive C, you issue the PATH command as follows:

```
C:\> PATH=C:\DOS
```

DOS stores the search directory in an internal location of memory. If you want DOS to search in additional directories, you include additional drives and directories separated in the command with a semicolon (;). If your command name is not in the current directory, or is not an absolute location name, DOS searches the directories of the search path in the order you give them until the desired file is found or the PATH is exhausted.

Batch Files

Another type of external file that DOS executes is the *batch file*. Batch files are named with a BAT extension and contain DOS commands, but appear as ordinary text files in all other ways. You can read about batch files in detail in Chapter 13. Part Two includes many batch file examples as well. For now, you should understand that COMMAND.COM interprets and executes the commands contained in a batch file.

Nearly all batch files are created by users or software vendors and are not supplied with the DOS product. The disk that comes with this book contains several batch files. One noteworthy batch file that DOS 5 includes in the installation process is AUTOEXEC.BAT. As you have read, AUTOEXEC.BAT is automatically executed (if it is present) at the end of the boot operation.

To execute a batch file, you enter its name as a command. COMMAND.COM locates the file on the disk and loads it for execution. The same principles for finding and loading COM and EXE files are followed for batch files. You must set an appropriate path, change to the batch file's current directory, or give the full path name on the command line for the batch file. Be aware that you can have, for example, the files GO.COM, GO.EXE, and GO.BAT in the same directory. They each have the root file name of GO. Because you type the root file name as the command name, DOS must prioritize the loading preference for the duplicated root name. In case of root file name duplication, DOS executes the COM file. If no COM file exists, DOS loads the EXE file. If no COM or EXE file exists, DOS loads the BAT file. Of course, you can include the desired extension with the command name to ensure that the appropriate file is executed.

COMMAND.COM remains in memory to execute a batch file. In most respects, COMMAND.COM interprets the individual lines of a batch file as though a user entered the lines from the keyboard. COMMAND.COM, however, provides special processing of batch commands. You will read about differences between batch and command line interpretation a bit later in this chapter. For now, you need only to understand that COMMAND.COM is responsible for executing batch files.

Macros

DOS 5 introduced a feature that provides many of the benefits of batch file operation, but requires no batch file. The feature is called the *keyboard macros* or simply *macro*. A macro, in the DOS sense, is a series of recorded DOS commands that are stored in memory under an assigned name. COMMAND.COM does not contain the macro feature, but an external program called DOSKEY does. If you execute DOSKEY, you can define macros. COMMAND.COM cooperates with DOSKEY by consulting the macro name list for a match to the command name that you type on the command line. If a match is found, COMMAND.COM executes the command sequence assigned to the macro name.

The macro execution is much the same as batch file execution, with a few differences. Batch file commands are stored in files, whereas macro commands are stored in memory. When you shut down your PC or reboot, the macro assignments you have made will be lost. The batch files, of course, remain intact on the disk after power down or reboot. Whereas batch files have the lowest priority for execution in root name conflict situations, macros have the highest. Batch files can contain thousands of DOS commands because the batch file size is limited only by available disk space. Macros can contain relatively few commands because they are stored in memory. You will see more in Chapter 13 about macros and how to use them. What is important to remember now is that COMMAND.COM, through DOSKEY, is responsible for parsing and executing a named macro.

Understanding the Environment

In DOS, the *environment* is a small portion of system memory set aside to contain values and their names. The names are called environment *variables* because they exist in the environment and their values can vary. DOS places automatically a few variable names and their values (contents) in the environment. Users can add variables to the environment through an assignment command. Every program that executes receives a copy of the environment. A program may contain instructions that look at certain environment variables to obtain operational information, such as directory names, color settings, and modes of operation. A program may modify the contents of its copy of the environment, too. Not all programs consult or modify their copy of the environment. As a DOS user, you will be interested in environment variables created automatically and created through command line assignment.

Assigning Variables Automatically

Certain commands, such as PATH and PROMPT, establish or change values that DOS uses to access programs and display the command prompt. You will learn about these commands' operations in Part Two. In this section, you will see how the PATH command assigns a value to the PATH environment variable.

To view the current environment settings, issue the SET command with no parameters, as in the following:

    C:\DOS> **SET**

DOS reports the current settings in a screen report similar to the following one:

    COMSPEC=C:\DOS\COMMAND.COM

    PATH=C:\DOS;C:\;C:\DOS\UTIL;C:\DBASE

    PROMPT=PG

This screen output shows variable names on the left followed by an equal sign. To the right of the equal sign is each variable's assigned value. Notice the middle variable, PATH. The current PATH variable contains several alternative search directories. If you issue a PATH command with a new path parameter, DOS will automatically update the PATH environment variable. You will not want to try this next command because your path would be changed, but follow the command in the text. The command is the following:

    C:\DOS> **PATH C:\TEMP**

The new DOS path is now C:\TEMP. When the SET command is issued again, DOS reports the following:

```
COMSPEC=C:\DOS\COMMAND.COM

PROMPT=$P$G

PATH=C:\TEMP
```

Notice that the PATH environment variable is now last in the list. DOS deleted the previous PATH variable and established a new one. Notice too that the value of the PATH variable is now C:\TEMP. The PATH command has not only updated the path, but it also updated the PATH environment variable.

Assigning Variables Manually

You have seen the SET command used to display the environment. You also use the SET command to change the environment by adding, removing, or modifying variables. To illustrate the assignment of a variable with the SET command, you will see an example that assigns the DIRCMD variable. DIRCMD is a variable that the DOS 5 DIR command uses to present its output in a predefined format. You assign a desired switch to the DIRCMD variable. When you issue the DIR command, DIR consults the DIRCMD variable and appends the switch to the command line. If you often use a particular DIR switch or set of switches, you can "program" the DIR command to provide the desired output format by default.

To assign an environment variable, you type the SET command and the variable's name, followed by an equal sign. Following the equal sign, you type the value. Do not type spaces on either side of the equal sign. A leading space becomes part of the variable. To set the DIRCMD variable to the value of /W, issue the following command:

```
C:\DOS> SET DIRCMD=/W
```

To see the new variable, enter the SET command with no arguments. SET will report something like the following:

```
COMSPEC=C:\DOS\COMMAND.COM

PATH=C:\DOS;C:\;C:\DOS\UTIL;C:\DBASE

PROMPT=$P$G

DIRCMD=/W
```

You see the new DIRCMD variable at the end of the list. To see how the DIR command uses the variable's contents, issue a DIR command with no switches as in the following command:

```
C:\DOS> DIR *.CPI
```

DIR, through the DIRCMD variable, incorporates the /W switch and produces the following screen:

```
Volume in drive C is LAP TOP
Volume Serial Number is 1691-78CA
Directory of C:\DOS
EGA.CPI      4201.CPI      4208.CPI      5202.CPI      LCD.CPI
         5 file(s)       77145 bytes
                        802816 bytes free
```

You see that DIR produces a /W (wide) output format. You will see other examples of environment variables in Part Two, but for now, understand that COMMAND.COM, external commands, and programs all have access to the environment and can use the values contained in the variables.

Using File Name Generation

Anyone who has used DOS for more than a few days realizes that he or she often uses file names as parameters in commands. The frequency of use of file-name parameters is not surprising considering the number of file-management and processing commands that DOS offers. COMMAND.COM parses a command to extract parameters. If the command name is that of an internal command, COMMAND.COM uses file parameters directly as it processes the command. If the command is an external command, COMMAND.COM passes to the external command all command parameters and switches that it has parsed. File-name parameters are included in the passed parameters.

Through parsing and parameter passing, both COMMAND.COM, while executing an internal command, and external commands have all necessary parameters and switches to execute the command. When a file-name parameter is a literal file name, such as MYFILE.DOC, COMMAND.COM or an external file command can use the file name immediately. When you want to use a command to manage or manipulate one file, then a literal file name for the file parameter is adequate.

Many file-related commands are capable of operating on more than one file per execution. Commands get this enhanced operating capability by translating two characters from a literal meaning to new meaning. The two characters are the * and the ? characters. When a component of DOS, such as

COMMAND.COM or an external program, operate with a character in some non-literal way, the character is known as a *meta-character*. In file-name parameters, the two meta-characters commonly are called wild-card characters. Wild-card characters enable commands to operate on file names that are "close" to being the same as the file-name parameter. Literal character patterns in the file names match the literal characters patterns given in the parameters. Any character(s) in file names match wild-card characters in parameters when the positions of the wild cards are the same as the file-name characters. You will see how position is important to wild-card pattern matching in a moment.

Most file-capable commands accept wild cards in file-name parameters. The TYPE command, for instance, does not. For now, consider the commands that do. Before a command begins to process files, the command performs pattern matching on file names using wild cards from the file-name parameter(s) as the pattern to match. In effect, the command is generating a list of files to be operated on during the current running of the command. From your vantage point, the command somehow knows which files you want to include in the command's scope. Internally, the command is consulting file names in the appropriate directory and performing pattern-matching on each name.

Because DOS file names consist of an eight-position root file name and a three-position extension, DOS gives wild-card capability to both root names, as well as extensions. As a result, you can form wild card patterns in the root name of a file-name parameter while the extension remains literal. DOS generates a file list of file names matching the root-name pattern as long as the parameter's extension is exactly the same. On the other hand, you can form a wild-card pattern in an extension of a file-name parameter and the command performs pattern-matching based on the extension. You can form wild-card patterns, of course, in both the root name and also the extension. The command performs pattern-matching on both as it generates a file list.

Now that you have read about file-name generation and wild-card pattern matching from an overview perspective, it's time to see wild cards in action.

Matching File Names with *

The * wild card is the "match the rest" character. When you type a * character in a root file name parameter, commands will match any root file-name pattern from the position of the * to the beginning of the extension. Likewise, when the * character appears in an extension, commands will match any characters from the position of the wild card to the end of the extension. Any characters you use that follow * in parameters are ignored. The * instructs the command to match the rest of the file name or extension, so your literal characters following the * are not considered. In other words, the parameter *xyz is interpreted as *. The following are some examples of pattern matching and not matching using * characters.

File-Name Parameter	Matches	Does not Match
BUDGET.*	BUDGET.WKS BUDGET.OLD	BUDGET1.WKS BUDG.WKS
*.WKS	BUDGET.WKS SALES.WKS	BUDGET.OLD SALES.DOC
PARTS.D*	PARTS.DBF PARTS.DOC	PARTS.MDX PRICES.DBF
P*.DBF	PURCHACE.DBF PROFITS.DBF	L_PRICE.DBF PROFITS.DBT
.	Any Name	N/A

As you see in the examples, the * wild card used in the root name or the extension applies only to the root name or the extension. If you are creating numerous files that share a common theme, you should consider naming the files with a consistent root name. If all of your files for projects, for instance, begin with PRJ, you can easily manipulate them as a group with a PRJ*.* wild-card parameter. If you name with a common extension all of your files of the same general type, you can manipulate those files using a wild-card root file name in commands, while supplying a literal extension. If you name all of your casual letters to friends using a LET extension, for example, you can easily copy all of your letters to a floppy disk using COPY with a *.LET source file parameter.

One command that "bends the rules" concerning the * wild card is the DIR command. When you supply a root name as a parameter to the DIR command, but supply no . and extension, DIR generates its file list as though you supplied a .* extension. The following example shows the DIR command's handling of a root file-name parameter and no extension.

```
C:\DOS> DIR QBASIC
 Volume in drive C is LAP TOP
 Volume Serial Number is 1691-78CA
 Directory of C:\DOS
QBASIC   HLP    130810 03-08-91   5:05a
QBASIC   EXE    254847 03-08-91   5:05a
QBASIC   INI        48 04-17-91   3:57p
         3 file(s)     385705 bytes
                       827392 bytes free
```

Notice that DIR located three files in the current directory that match the root name and have extensions. Although no extension was supplied with the parameter in the command, DIR automatically supplied a .* extension. The same extension principle works when DIR is given a wild card in the root name, but still no extension. The following example illustrates the case.

```
C:\DOS> DIR Q*

 Volume in drive C is LAP TOP
 Volume Serial Number is 1691-78CA
 Directory of C:\DOS

QBASIC   HLP    130810 03-08-91  5:05a
QBASIC   EXE    254847 03-08-91  5:05a
QBASIC   INI        48 04-17-91  3:57p
       3 file(s)     385705 bytes
                     827392 bytes free
```

You see that DIR found all the files that have Q as the first letter regardless of their extensions. Although it may be handy to have DIR show file names with a default * as an extension, you need to be able to match files exactly in some cases. Using the DIR command, you can remove the default * wild-card extension by typing the . separator as part of the file parameter. DIR sees the . in the file parameter and takes the extension as being blank. In other words, the desired files have no extensions. The same command as the previous example is given, but this time the . is included after the root file-name parameter.

```
C:\DOS> DIR Q*.
 Volume in drive C is LAP TOP
 Volume Serial Number is 1691-78CA
 Directory of C:\DOS

 File not found
```

The presence of the . in the Q*. parameter removed the default * as the extension of the parameter and DIR found no files to match. You may use the root name plus . to find directories with the DIR command. Although directory names may have extensions, most users do not include an extension with a directory name. This example shows the subdirectory names of C:\DOS as found on the example disk.

```
C:\DOS> DIR *.

 Volume in drive C is LAP TOP
 Volume Serial Number is 1691-78CA
 Directory of C:\DOS
```

```
    .           <DIR>      12-27-88  12:30p
    ..          <DIR>      12-27-88  12:30p
   UTIL         <DIR>      11-07-90  10:02p
   DRIVERS      <DIR>      11-07-90  10:00p
   BASIC        <DIR>      05-13-91   3:34p
         5 file(s)            0 bytes
                      827392 bytes free
```

The command reports the subdirectories of C:\DOS. Of course, the command would report any file that was named without an extension. You should note that only DIR includes this default extension provision. Other commands that process files look for pattern formations in root file parameters and extensions and do not assume a * extension if you do not provide an extension.

Matching File Names with ?

The ? wild card matches a single character. In a file-name parameter, ? wild cards enable you to select files whose names vary by a few characters. As with the * wild card, the position of the ? wild card is important to the meaning of the pattern. Again, the root name and the extension are treated separately in pattern matching using ? characters. The following are some examples of pattern matching using ? wild cards.

File-Name Parameter	Matches	Doesn't Match
MEM?OLD.DOC	MEM1OLD.DOC MEM3OLD.DOC	MEM12OLD.DOC MEMOLD.DOC
PROJECT.D?C	PROJECT.DOC PROJECT.DAC	PROJECT.DBF PROJECT.
COMMAND.C??	COMMAND.COM COMMAND.CMD	COMMAND.DAT COMM.COM
????????.??? Same as *.*	Anything	N/A

The single-character ? wild card is useful for manipulating files that are named in a similar, but not exact manner. A person word processing a operator's manual, for instance, might use the common OPMAN part of a file name for all sections of the manual. Following OPMAN, the writer might number sections from 01 to 99, resulting in root file names such as OPMAN06 and OPMAN77. By including an appropriate extension, the file name OPMAN23.FIN conveys the meaning, "Section 23 of the Operator's Manual—Final Draft." The writer can copy all files associated with sections 20 through

29 by using the file-name parameter OPMAN2?.*. When you choose file names, remember that * and ? wild cards are most useful when your file names have some underlying logic to their character patterns.

? wild-card matching between parameters and file names is positional, with one exception. Fortunately, the exception is easy to remember. When you give a file-name parameter with ? wild-card characters as the last characters in either the root or the extension, DOS matches any characters in the corresponding positions, including spaces. You will recall that a root file name consists of up to eight characters and an extension consists of up to three characters. In directory storage, file names that do not use all of the positions for characters contain spaces in the trailing positions of directory storage. You do not include the spaces in parameters, but the spaces are present in the directory. If a ? wild card matches the position of one of the trailing spaces, then DOS' pattern-matching mechanism considers it a valid match. As a result, you cannot use ? wild cards to represent file names that contain exactly a given number of characters. The following example illustrates the point.

A directory contains some text files as shown in the DIR command:

```
C:\DOS> DIR

    Volume in drive C is LAP TOP
    Volume Serial Number is 1691-78CA
    Directory of C:\DOS

    .           <DIR>      05-20-91  11:39a
    ..          <DIR>      05-20-91  11:39a
    1     TXT       297 05-20-91  10:58a
    12    TXT       297 05-20-91  10:58a
    123   TXT        97 05-20-91  10:59a
    1234  TXT       297 05-20-91  10:58a
    12345 TXT       379 05-20-91  11:33a
           7 file(s)      1367 bytes
                     802816 bytes free
```

Notice that the root file names in this directory contain from one to five characters. After the final character in each root name, you see the spaces until DOS reports the extension. If you want to match a file name that is one character long, you issue the command:

```
C:\DOS> DIR ?.TXT
```

The DIR command generates its file list that consists of the one file that pattern matches a single ? character, as shown by the following:

```
Volume in drive C is LAP TOP
Volume Serial Number is 1691-78CA
Directory of C:\DOS

1        TXT        297 05-20-91  10:58a
        1 file(s)         297 bytes
                     802816 bytes free
```

Note, by consulting the full directory listing, 1.TXT is the only file that matches the ?.TXT parameter. Now try the DIR command with two ? wildcards to see what matches, as in the following.

```
C:\DOS> DIR ??.TXT

Volume in drive C is LAP TOP
Volume Serial Number is 1691-78CA
Directory of C:\DOS

1        TXT        297 05-20-91  10:58a
12       TXT        297 05-20-91  10:58a
        2 file(s)         594 bytes
                     802816 bytes free
```

The DIR command's pattern-matching found the file with a two-character root file name as you would expect. The same command, however, reports the 1.TXT file too. The 1.TXT file is reported because the second ? in the ??.TXT parameter matches the space following 1 in the directory. The command is unable to isolate the files containing exactly two characters. As long as trailing spaces to match exist, ? wild cards cause their inclusion in the generated file list. As a final example on this topic, the following command uses five ? wild card characters:

```
C:\DOS> DIR ?????.TXT

Volume in drive C is LAP TOP
Volume Serial Number is 1691-78CA
Directory of C:\DOS

1        TXT        297 05-20-91  10:58a
12       TXT        297 05-20-91  10:58a
123      TXT         97 05-20-91  10:59a
1234     TXT        297 05-20-91  10:58a
12345    TXT        379 05-20-91  11:33a
        5 file(s)        1367 bytes
                     802816 bytes free
```

In this example, all the files in the directory match because they all have between one and five characters in their root-file names. If the file parameter consists of eight ? wild cards as the root file-name parameter, and three ? characters as the extension, then all files in the directory match. A ? wild card in every position of a file-name parameter means the same as *.*.

These examples of wild cards and file manipulation illustrate some of the file naming and processing activities that take place at the command prompt. You will read about other considerations for file processing, naming, and manipulation when you read the tasks and concepts presented in Parts Two and Three.

Understanding Variable Name Substitution

You recall from earlier discussion in this chapter that COMMAND.COM is responsible for executing the commands contained in batch files. In most respects, COMMAND.COM processes the commands contained in batch file lines as though you had typed the commands on your keyboard. Although you will learn batch file execution in detail in Chapter 13, you should note here the one difference between batch processing and command line processing. The difference is in the way that references to environment variables are handled by COMMAND.COM.

As you learned before, DOS provides the environment as a storage area for named values called variables. You or your programs assign variables. Some DOS commands, such as PATH, assign variables. Regardless of the source of assignment, variables are available to programs that need to access one or more of them.

While COMMAND.COM is executing a batch file, it can identify a variable by special delimiting characters. Variable names contained within a pair of % characters are taken symbolically rather than literally. COMMAND.COM substitutes the *value* of the variable for the *name* of the variable. Variable substitution is part of the parsing process. COMMAND.COM does not execute the command until all variable substitution is complete. You should note that COMMAND.COM does not do variable substitution on commands that you enter from the command line. Variable substitution is a feature of batch file processing.

The following example illustrates variable substitution and the difference between variables. First, the variable named PARAM is created and assigned with the SET command.

```
C:\DOS> SET PARAM=Q*.*
```

PARAM is now stored in the environment and contains the characters Q*.*. Now a batch file called TEST.BAT is created using the following COPY command.

```
C:\DOS> COPY CON TEST.BAT
```

As soon as the user presses Enter, the cursor drops to the next line and awaits user input. The user input becomes the content of TEST.BAT. This COPY command takes keyboard input (from the CON device) and holds it in a memory buffer until the user presses F6 or Ctrl-Z. Copy then writes the buffer's contents to the TEST.BAT file. The following line is entered:

```
DIR %PARAM%
```

The F6 is the DOS end-of-file indicator that signals COPY that no more input follows. COPY writes the file to disk. At this point, the PARAM variable has been assigned and the TEST.BAT that references PARAM has been created. Before running the batch file, the user can attempt to reference PARAM through the keyboard at the command prompt using the same command contained in TEST.BAT, such as the following:

```
C:\DOS> DIR %PARAM%
```

COMMAND.COM processes the internal DIR command. DIR looks in the directory for the literal file name %PARAM%.

```
Volume in drive C is LAP TOP
Volume Serial Number is 1691-78CA
Directory of C:\DOS

File not found
```

DIR reports `File not found` because no file here is named %PARAM%.

Now, the batch file is executed. Remember that the batch file contains the exact same command text as was entered at the keyboard previously, as in the following command:

```
C:\DOS> TEST
```

Assuming that DOS's ECHO setting is on, DOS echoes the command as COMMAND.COM processes the line in the batch file. Due to variable substitution, the command is displayed as follows:

```
C:\DOS> DIR Q*.*
```

COMMAND.COM first substituted the contents of PARAM in the command, echoed the command, and executed the expanded command line, producing the following:

```
Volume in drive C is LAP TOP
Volume Serial Number is 1691-78CA
Directory of C:\DOS

QBASIC    HLP      130810 03-08-91    5:05a
QBASIC    EXE      254847 03-08-91    5:05a
QBASIC    INI          48 04-17-91    3:57p
        3 file(s)      385705 bytes
                       800768 bytes free
```

The batch file's output is the same as if you had entered DIR Q*.* on the command line. Later in the book, you will see examples using variable substitution to add search alternatives to your PATH variable. For now, just be aware that COMMAND.COM substitutes variables when executing batch files.

Using Special Characters

You have seen that COMMAND.COM uses spaces or tabs to separate parameters. You also know that drive specifiers are the drive letter followed by a colon. The wild-card characters * and ? are given special treatment in file names. You have just seen an example in which % characters were used to indicate a variable substitution in a batch file. All of these characters have special meanings to COMMAND.COM. When COMMAND.COM parses the command line, it looks for special characters to ascertain the command line's full meaning.

COMMAND.COM looks for three other special characters as it parses the command. The first two characters indicate to COMMAND.COM that input or output of a command is to be redirected. The > character signals output redirection to a file or device. Two > characters together (>>) signals output redirection to the end of an existing file. The third special character, the | or *pipe* character, signals that the output of a command should be provided as the input for another command. Connecting two commands together with a pipe character is called command *pipelining*. Redirection and pipelining (or simply piping) are covered in detail in Chapter 7, but because the special characters affect COMMAND.COM's parsing, these topic are worth mentioning here.

Using Redirection Characters

DOS commands most often get their inputs from the CON device or keyboard. CON is called the *standard input device*. You type responses to commands' prompts on the keyboard because commands expect their inputs to come from the keyboard. Commands send their outputs to the CON device or display screen as well as files in some cases. Command output consists of the actual result of the command and of the messages and prompt the command outputs for your information or response. The actual output of the command is called *standard output*. The information messages, error messages, and some prompts are called *standard error*. DOS enables the redirection of standard input through the < character. Standard output redirection is enabled through the > and the >> characters. DOS does not provide a way to redirect standard error output. Commands route standard error message to the screen. To illustrate the difference between standard output and standard error, consider the following example.

An ordinary DIR command sequence looks like the following:

```
C:\DOS> DIR *.TXT

    Volume in drive C is LAP TOP
    Volume Serial Number is 1691-78CA
    Directory of C:\DOS

1         TXT        297 05-20-91  10:58a
12        TXT        297 05-20-91  10:58a
123       TXT         97 05-20-91  10:59a
1234      TXT        297 05-20-91  10:58a
12345     TXT        379 05-20-91  11:33a
          5 file(s)       1367 bytes
                        802816 bytes free
```

By default, the DIR command's output appears on the screen (CON). You can redirect the same command's standard output to a file named KEEP.ASC using the redirection character as in the following:

```
C:\DOS> DIR *.TXT > KEEP.ASC
```

When you issue this command, the disk light flashes, but nothing appears on the screen until the DOS prompt returns. The output from the DIR command is redirected to the KEEP.ASC file. You can see the contents of KEEP.ASC using the TYPE command as in the following:

```
C:\DOS> TYPE KEEP.ASC
```

The TYPE command sends the output of KEEP.ASC to the screen. The output is exactly the same as if you had issued the DIR *.TXT command instead of the TYPE command. There is a good reason for this similarity. The content of KEEP.ASC *is* the output of DIR *.TXT.

This exercise illustrates the redirection of standard output, but another example is in order to show what happens to standard error output. Assume that no files with DOC extensions are in the current directory when you issue the following redirection command:

```
C:\DOS> DIR *.DOC >KEEP.ASC
```

You immediately see the following error message on your screen:

```
File not found
```

Because there are no DOC files to report, DIR issues the `File not found` message on the standard error, which is always your screen. If you use the TYPE command to view the new contents of KEEP.ASC, you will see the following:

```
Volume in drive C is LAP TOP
Volume Serial Number is 1691-78CA
Directory of C:\DOS
```

The DIR command produced at least this much standard output before reporting through standard error that no files were found.

What you should carry from these output redirection examples is that not all screen output is redirected when you use > or >> characters and a file name. If you are not sure what you are redirecting, examine the redirection output file after the redirection command to see if you got what you intended. You will see useful ways to use redirection in Part Two.

Using Pipe Characters

Now that you have read about redirection characters, you should understand pipe characters a bit more easily. Piping is very similar to redirection. Whereas redirection characters redirect input or output from a command and a file or device, pipe characters redirect output from a command to another command. Not many DOS commands are capable of accepting as input the output of another command. DOS, however, includes a few commands suitable for piping. You will read about them in detail in Chapter 7. For now, you should understand how pipes affect command syntax.

Some of the programs supplied with DOS that users pipe to are called *filter* programs. Filter programs accept input, manipulate it in some way, and send the manipulated output to the standard output. A good example filter program is the SORT command. SORT is designed to get input characters from the keyboard as standard input. You can pipe the output of a command to SORT, however, and the pipe provides the redirected input. Even though the pipe operation involves the redirection of standard input, you do not use the < input redirection character. The | pipe character implies that the operation involves redirection. SORT in a pipeline simply alphabetizes lines that it receives as input and presents them as output. An example pipelined SORT command using DIR looks like the following:

```
C:\DOS> DIR *.EXE | SORT
```

This command line invokes SORT to alphabetize the output of the DIR command. The resulting screen output looks like the following:

```
                  800768 bytes free
          35 file(s)    1181146 bytes
      Directory of C:\DOS
      Volume in drive C is LAP TOP
      Volume Serial Number is 1691-78CA
      APPEND   EXE     10774 03-08-91    5:05a
      ATTRIB   EXE     15796 03-08-91    5:05a
      BACKUP   EXE     36092 03-08-91    5:05a
      CHKDSK   EXE     16200 03-08-91    5:05a
      CLEANUP  EXE     43946 12-13-90    4:09a
      COMP     EXE     14282 03-08-91    5:05a
      DEBUG    EXE     20634 03-08-91    5:05a
      DELOLDOS EXE     17660 03-08-91    5:05a
      DOSSHELL EXE    235380 03-08-91    5:05a
      DOSSWAP  EXE     18724 03-08-91    5:05a
      EDLIN    EXE     12642 03-08-91    5:05a
      EMM386   EXE     91742 03-08-91    5:05a
      EXE2BIN  EXE      8424 03-08-91    5:05a
      EXPAND   EXE     14563 03-08-91    5:05a
      FASTOPEN EXE     12050 03-08-91    5:05a
      FC       EXE     18650 03-08-91    5:05a
      FDISK    EXE     57224 03-08-91    5:05a
      FIND     EXE      6770 03-08-91    5:05a
      HELP     EXE     11473 03-08-91    5:05a
      JOIN     EXE     17870 03-08-91    5:05a
      LABEL    EXE      9390 03-08-91    5:05a
      MEM      EXE     39818 03-08-91    5:05a
      NLSFUNC  EXE      7052 03-08-91    5:05a
      PRINT    EXE     15656 03-08-91    5:05a
      QBASIC   EXE    254847 03-08-91    5:05a
      RECOVER  EXE      9146 03-08-91    5:05a
```

```
REDIR    EXE    27822 08-15-90  3:33a
REPLACE  EXE    20226 03-08-91  5:05a
RESTORE  EXE    38294 03-08-91  5:05a
SETVER   EXE    12007 03-08-91  5:05a
SHARE    EXE    10912 03-08-91  5:05a
SORT     EXE     6938 03-08-91  5:05a
SUBST    EXE    18478 03-08-91  5:05a
UNDELETE EXE    13860 03-08-91  5:05a
XCOPY    EXE    15804 03-08-91  5:05a
```

Notice that the list of files is in alphabetical order. The first five lines look jumbled, however. SORT counts leading spaces and tabs as characters to be alphabetized, so the first few lines of the DIR report get jumbled as they get alphabetized. Of course, DOS 5 offers the /N switch, which alphabetizes the output of the DIR command automatically. Yet this SORT example illustrates that the output of one command can indeed be piped to the input of another.

Accessing Help

If you can learn and retain all the concepts and syntax for every DOS command, you are indeed a talented individual. Most DOS users, however, need help from time to time. DOS 5 introduced on-line help capabilities to lessen the burden of memorizing commands. DOS help comes in two basic forms—the /? (Help) switch on the command line and the HELP command. You may want to use one or both of these help mechanisms.

Getting Command Line Help for Commands

When you are using DOS 5, help with syntax, parameters, and switches is never far away. In fact, you need only issue the command name followed by a /? switch to view help information. You can access help information for any DOS command using the /? switch. The process is simple. If you want to see the switches available for the COPY command, for instance, you issue the following command:

```
C:\DOS> COPY /?
```

DOS displays the following text:

```
Copies one or more files to another location.
COPY [/A | /B] source [/A | /B] [+ source [/A | /B] [+ ...]] [destination
  [/A | /B]] [/V]
  source       Specifies the file or files to be copied.
  /A           Indicates an ASCII text file.
  /B           Indicates a binary file.
```

```
destination  Specifies the directory and/or filename for the new file(s).
  /V              Verifies that new files are written correctly.
To append files, specify a single file for destination, but multiple files
for source (using wildcards or file1+file2+file3 format).
```

As you can see, DOS offers a good syntax reference for COPY. In DOS' syntax diagrams, elements that are optional appear within square brackets. When you must choose one element or another, the two choices are separated by a | character. Items in which you supply actual values are indicated by lower-case words.

Command line help is not intended to be a comprehensive tutorial for every command. It is intended to refresh you on elements you need to issue commands.

Using the HELP Command

The external HELP command provides help similar to issuing a command with the /? switch. HELP provides you with a way to view all command names, however. To view an alphabetical listing of command names, issue the HELP command alone as follows:

```
C:\DOS> HELP
```

HELP lists a screen of commands and waits for you to press a key before displaying more. The first screen looks like the following:

```
For more information on a specific command, type HELP command-name
APPEND    Allows programs to open data files in specified directories as if
          they were in the current directory.
ASSIGN    Redirects requests for disk operations on one drive to a different
          drive.
ATTRIB    Displays or changes file attributes.
BACKUP    Backs up one or more files from one disk to another.
BREAK     Sets or clears extended CTRL+C checking.
CALL      Calls one batch program from another.
CD        Displays the name of or changes the current directory.
CHCP      Displays or sets the active code page number.
CHDIR     Displays the name of or changes the current directory.
CHKDSK    Checks a disk and displays a status report.
CLS       Clears the screen.
COMMAND   Starts a new instance of the MS-DOS command interpreter.
COMP      Compares the contents of two files or sets of files.
COPY      Copies one or more files to another location.
CTTY      Changes the terminal device used to control your system.
DATE      Displays or sets the date.
```

```
DEBUG      Runs Debug, a program testing and editing tool.
DEL        Deletes one or more files.
DIR        Displays a list of files and subdirectories in a directory.
--More--
```

You see the command names and a brief description of each. To see another screen of commands, press any key. If you do not need to see any more commands, press Ctrl-C or Ctrl-Break to terminate the command.

For help concerning a specific command, issue the HELP command with the desired command name as a parameter. You will see syntax information about the command similar to what appears when you use a /? switch with a command.

Summary

This chapter concludes Part One of the book. This chapter focused on COMMAND.COM and related issues. You have learned about the role of COMMAND.COM. Commands are internal or external. Command lines may contain parameters and switches. Syntax is the correct arrangement of a command, its parameters, and its switches. COMMAND.COM parses command lines to extract the command name and parameters. You edit a command line through the standard DOS editing keys or by running DOSKEY and using its editing capabilities. All these topics pertain to all DOS command line work.

You were introduced to wild cards, pipes, filters, variables, and their basic uses. These items are represented or delimited using special characters in commands.

Batch files are sequences of commands that are stored in a text file and executed by COMMAND.COM. Macros are sequences of commands stored in memory through DOSKEY and executed by COMMAND.COM. Both batch files and macros extend the basic power of commands. Finally, you have learned how to access help for DOS commands. With this knowledge, and the knowledge you gained in Chapters 1 and 2, you are ready to move to Part Two. In the next chapter, you will see how to deal with your disks through disk-related commands.

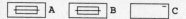

Part Two

Staying in Control of Disks

Navigating Directories

Keeping in Control of Files

Using Filters, Pipes, and Redirection for Productivity

Ensuring Data Integrity

Building on Your DOS Repertoire

4

Staying in Control of Disks

In previous chapters, you learned about your PC's hardware, took a look at the basics of DOS 5, and were shown how to use the DOS command processor, COMMAND.COM. You now should have enough knowledge about the file allocation table (FAT), hierarchical-directory structures, and disk features, such as tracks and sectors, to understand the tasks presented in this chapter.

In this chapter, you are shown how to tackle tasks that let you prepare and access disks—both hard disks and floppy disks. The concentration is on disk-level DOS commands, although some non-disk-level commands, such as ATTRIB, are mentioned in specific tasks.

Disk-level DOS commands are used to prepare and to directly access disks. File commands, on the other hand, are used to access and maintain files. You probably are more familiar with file commands than disk commands. Because of this and the power of disk-level commands, you should exercise caution when practicing the exercises in this chapter. Disk-level commands can quickly destroy entire disks that are full of valuable data if used incorrectly. Be sure you understand what a command does before trying it.

Windows

The additional security that is built into the DOS Shell and Windows environments makes it more difficult to cause such devastation. By default, each disk command prompts with a list of what will be changed by the command. You can then confirm before your file structure is changed. For more information about the benefits of DOS Shell, see Chapter 12.

95

As a starting point, you will learn about applying and reading disk volume labels. You will see that labels are important because they help you, as well as some programs, keep track of disks. You will examine your hard disk's partition table and see how to change the size of the logical structures on the disk, or how to create a structure that lets two or more disk operating systems (compatible or not) reside on a single hard disk.

The discussion shows how to create several different types of boot floppies that allows you to configure your system for special purposes. You will see how to add the files needed to make a non-bootable disk into a system, or boot, disk. Options for sharing data between PCs with different capacity disk drives are discussed, as well as creating of accurate duplicate disks in a minimum of time.

Finally, you will learn what to do when disk errors occur. When you are armed with the knowledge that you may be able to recover lost or damaged files, you should have greater confidence in your ability to handle situations which might otherwise cause panic.

Disk-Level Commands Covered in Chapter 4

This chapter covers the following major DOS commands:

- ❏ **LABEL**. Assigns or removes a disk's volume label.
- ❏ **VOL**. Displays the volume label assigned to a disk.
- ❏ **FDISK**. Prepares a hard disk for formatting, creates partitions, and displays partition data.
- ❏ **FORMAT**. Prepares a disk for use.
- ❏ **UNFORMAT**. Recovers data from a disk that was formatted in error and displays hard disk partition data.
- ❏ **SYS**. Transfers system files to a disk to create a boot disk.
- ❏ **DISKCOPY**. Creates an exact copy of a floppy disk.
- ❏ **DISKCOMP**. Verifies that floppy disks are identical.
- ❏ **CHKDSK**. Checks for and repairs certain types of logical disk errors.
- ❏ **RECOVER**. Rebuilds files or disks when severe errors prevent normal access.

Reviewing Disk Concepts

You may find several concepts presented earlier in this book that will be useful in understanding the tasks presented here. To understand the operation of the FDISK command, for example, you should know a little about the physical structure of a hard disk as well as logical partitions. To understand the FORMAT examples, on the other hand, you should have a grasp of subjects such as tracks, sectors, clusters, file allocation tables (FATs), and the boot record. These same subjects are equally important in considering tasks that use the UNFORMAT command. Also, tree structured directories and file attributes play a role in recovering files "lost" to disk errors.

If you are not comfortable with these concepts, you are encouraged to take the time now to review the earlier sections in this book in which they are presented. The more you know about these subjects, the better will be your understanding of these tasks. Remember, you should take the time to understand your disk before you execute a command beause disk-level commands can be dangerous to your data.

Managing Disks Using Volume Labels

Volume labels are not stick-on, paper labels that you apply to the plastic outer shell of a floppy disk. They are, rather, labels that you apply electronically that help you manage your disks. These electronic labels have an advantage that the stick-on labels lack: they appear on-screen (or on your printer if you redirect output, as discussed in Chapter 7) when you issue one of the commands that display disk volume labels, such as DIR, VOL, or CHKDSK. Some programs, such as the DOS 5 SETUP program, also can read the volume label to determine if you have inserted the proper disk.

Consider the directory listings for the following two floppy disks:

```
Volume in drive A has no label
Volume Serial Number is 17E7-2202
Directory of A:\

SCREEN00 TXT      255 05-30-91  12:25p
        1 file(s)         255 bytes
                     361472 bytes free

Volume in drive A has no label
Volume Serial Number is 3E23-15DA
Directory of A:\
```

```
SCREEN00 TXT        255 04-30-91  12:58p
     1 file(s)           255 bytes
                    361472 bytes free
```

You may have difficulty determining which disk is which in the preceding example because neither disk has a volume label. Both of the disk's Volume Serial Numbers are different, but you may find that remembering Volume Serial Numbers is not an easy task. After all, which data disk is 17E7-2202 and which is 3E23-15DA? One method of making your disks easier to identify is to apply a volume label, such as the following:

```
Volume in drive A is BACKUP 01
Volume Serial Number is 3E23-15DA
Directory of A:\

SCREEN00 TXT        255 04-30-91  12:58p
          1 file(s)           255 bytes
                    361472 bytes free
```

A Note on Volume Labels

DOS automatically supplies a unique Volume Serial Number whenever you format a disk or copy a disk. You have no control over the Volume Serial Number and only a few programs make use of it. The SHARE file locking and access control utility is one of the rare programs that keeps track of Volume Serial Numbers.

Another reason why you should use a volume label on your disk is that it does not use up disk space. In the preceding two directory listings, the disk with Volume Serial Number 3E23-15DA has the same number of bytes, 361,472, whether or not it has the volume label, BACKUP 01. You can add a volume label without consuming any of the disk's available space.

Applying Volume Labels

Two different DOS commands apply volume labels to disks. The FORMAT command, which is examined in detail later in this chapter, automatically requests a volume label once it finishes formatting a disk. The following prompts are presented when the formatting process is complete:

```
Format complete.
Volume label (11 characters, ENTER for none)?
```

You can respond to this prompt or you can use the LABEL command to apply a volume label. The LABEL command also lets you change or delete a volume label. You are not given these two options when you apply a volume label as part of formatting a disk. Regardless of the method you choose, the following rules apply to the label you apply:

❏ Volume labels can contain 0 to 11 characters.

❏ You can use any combination of upper- and lowercase letters; however, both FORMAT and LABEL translate all characters to uppercase before applying the label.

❏ You cannot use the following characters in a volume label: ? / \ | . , ; : + = [ ] ( ) & ^ Esc Tab.

❏ ASCII characters between 128 and 255 can be entered by pressing the Alt key, entering the ASCII number code using the keypad (not the number keys at the top of the keyboard), and releasing the Alt key.

❏ Control characters (ASCII 31 and lower) cannot be used for either FORMAT or LABEL.

❏ LABEL cannot apply, change, or delete a volume label on a drive created with the ASSIGN, JOIN, or SUBST commands.

A volume label can be applied easily with the LABEL command. You either can specify the volume label as an argument following the command, or you can use the optional command form that prompts you to supply a volume label. To specify the label as an argument, enter the following command:

```
LABEL A: WEEK 30 91
```

In the preceding command, the floppy disk in drive A will be labeled as WEEK 30 91. No message is displayed telling you that this is occurs.

If you wish to see the existing volume label before adding a new one, changing the existing one, or removing the current one, enter the LABEL command without specifying a label argument, such as the following:

```
LABEL A:
```

When you issue the command in this format, the existing volume label is displayed and you are prompted to enter a new one:

```
Volume in drive A is WEEK 30 91
Volume Serial Number is 1B09-0FFE
Volume label (11 characters, ENTER for none)?
```

If you wish to change to a new volume label, enter up to eleven characters (keeping in mind the rules about which characters are acceptable). As you are deciding what to use as the volume label, consider the type of data you will be storing on the disk. If you are storing accounting data, for example, a label similar to WEEK 30 91 can be used to indicate that the disk contains reports for the 30th week of 1991.

To leave the current label unchanged or to remove the existing label, press Enter without making another entry on the line. The LABEL command then lets you delete the current label or leave it unchanged with the following prompt:

```
Delete current volume label (Y/N)?
```

If you respond N to the preceding prompt, the label is left unchanged. If you want to delete the current label, enter Y.

Windows

The Windows' File Manager File command does not prompt you for a label. You must use the Label command in File Manager's Disk menu instead.

Viewing Volume Labels

Several DOS commands can display the volume label, including CHKDSK, DIR, TREE, and VOL. CHKDSK is discussed later in this chapter. DIR and TREE are covered in detail in later chapters. VOL, which has the single purpose of displaying volume label information, is covered in the following section.

The VOL command has two major advantages over the other three commands when you want to know a disk's volume label. VOL is much faster than the CHKDSK, DIR, or TREE commands. In addition, because it displays only two lines of information, the volume label line will not scroll off the screen as it might with the CHKDSK, DIR, or TREE commands.

The VOL command makes no changes to the volume label. Because of this, you can use this command without fear of changing or destroying the existing label. You can enter the VOL command using the following command:

```
VOL A:
```

DOS responds by displaying the volume label and volume serial number similar to the following message:

```
Volume in drive A is WEEK 30 91
Volume Serial Number is 1B09-0FFE
```

Developing a Standard for Volume Labels

Now that you know how to set and display disk volume labels, you should consider methods that will make these labels work for you. In an earlier example, you saw that floppy disks used, to hold weekly accounting reports,can be labeled to reflect the data they are storing. Several other possibilities for disk volume labels exist as well, such as the following:

❑ Different categories of graphics images.

❑ Letters to specific groups or types of customers.

❑ Program revision levels.

Regardless of your specific needs, you should make use of volume labels to help maintain your disks. As an example of how the volume label can help you do this, place a disk in drive A and enter the following command:

```
DIR A: >> FILEFIND.TXT
```

If you use tree structured directories on your floppy disks, use either one of the following commands:

```
DIR A:/S >> FILEFIND.TXT
TREE A:/ F >> FILEFIND.TXT
```

This command redirects and appends the output of the DIR command to a file called FILEFIND.TXT on the current drive (for more information on redirecting commands, see Chapter 7). After the command is finished and the DOS prompt returns, replace the disk in drive A with another disk and repeat the command. Continue replacing disks and repeating the command until you've logged several disk directories into the FILEFIND.TXT file.

FILEFIND.TXT is an ASCII text file that can be loaded into most word processors or even the DOS 5 screen editor, EDIT. Once you have created the file and have loaded it into your word processor or editor, you can use the word processor's or editor's Search function to find the location of any file contained on one of the logged disks. When you find a file's listing, the disk volume label of the disk containing the file is the last volume label preceding the file's listing.

This example demonstrates one way you can use disk volume labels to help manage your disks. Although this method might not be practical if the contents of your disks change quite often, you will find that method useful in cataloging disks containing seldom changed archival data. In addition, you might even decide to include the log file (FILEFIND.TXT) on a master disk that you store along with your data disks.

Now that you have used some of the simpler disk-level commands, you will examine some that are more powerful and require more care to prevent damage to your system.

Managing Disk Partitions with FDISK

FDISK is an external DOS program that provides high-level access to the partition table on PCs. FDISK enters into the partition table the basic information needed by DOS to find the physical space it has been allocated on a hard disk. FDISK also can be used to change the amount of space allocated to DOS, thus allowing another non-compatible disk operating system to share the hard disk. Finally, FDISK can be used to create logical partitions that make a single hard disk appear to be several smaller ones.

Overcoming the 32M Hard Disk Limit

DOS versions 2.x and 3.x were unable to access hard disks larger than 32M in a single volume. Two reasons for this limitation exist. First, the FAT could hold no more than 65,536 entries (64K). Second, because the FAT entries were sectors, and DOS uses 512 byte sectors, no more than 32M of storage (or 65,536 times 512 bytes) could be tracked by the FAT.

DOS versions 4 and 5 use a slightly different method of tracking disk space usage. Instead of keeping track of sectors, space is allocated in multiple sector units called *clusters*. When you prepare a disk, the number of sectors per cluster is adjusted automatically to allow access to the entire partition. Thus, a hard disk using four-sector (2048 byte) clusters and the same 65,536 entries can contain 128M of storage.

Changing Partition Sizes

Because many DOS 5 users are upgrading from DOS versions prior to DOS 4, changing to DOS 5 gives them their first opportunity to bypass the 32M disk size limit. This requires that they use FDISK to change the hard disk's partition size. The following sections show how to use FDISK to examine and, if desired, change the size of your hard disk partitions. Before changing your hard disk partition sizes, however, several potential problems exist that you should consider.

FDISK Can be Dangerous to Your Data

All space on a hard disk is allocated based on the entries in the partition table. If an existing partition is deleted or changed in size, all data contained in that partition is lost. **FDISK**, the command used to modify the partition table, can be an extremely dangerous command. If used improperly, the command can destroy data or even make it impossible to access a disk at all. **FDISK** presents warnings before proceeding with actions that can cause damage—be sure to heed those warnings.

Larger Cluster Sizes May Waste Space

Although changing your hard disk's partition size can let you access a large hard disk as a single drive instead of as a number of smaller ones, a tradeoff does exist. The smallest unit of space that can be allocated for storage on a disk is equal to its cluster size. This means that every file, no matter how small, will always use at least one cluster. A 20-byte batch file, for example, will use 512 bytes of space on a floppy disk, but 2048 bytes on a hard disk with four sector clusters. If the disk used 16 sector clusters, that same 20-byte file would require 8192 bytes of hard disk storage space.

Generally, you can count on wasting about one half of a cluster for each file stored on a disk. This figure assumes that the typical file's size will not be an exact multiple of the disk's cluster size. If a file is even one byte too large to fit in a cluster, another cluster must be allocated to finish storing the file. For a large number of average files, this extra storage typically works out to about one half of a cluster per file. On a floppy disk with one sector (512 byte) clusters, approximately 256 bytes are wasted for each file stored. Hard disks with larger cluster sizes waste even more space. With four sector clusters, for example, an average of 1024 bytes are wasted per file.

You may want to consider if the advantages of having your entire hard disk available as a single volume offset the space that will be wasted. In most cases, the answer is yes. But if your hard disk is full of a large number of very small files, you may want to use the preceding figures to calculate if the change will be worthwhile on your system.

Larger Partitions May Complicate Operations

Another point to consider before changing to larger partition sizes is the method you use to back up your hard disk. If, for example, you use a tape backup unit that has a 40M capacity, increasing your hard disk's partition size may complicate your backup procedure. Instead of the unattended backups you may be used to, larger partition sizes may force you to swap tapes in the middle of the backup.

If your hard disk is partitioned as several logical drives, you probably will have to adjust the configuration files for any of your programs that use a drive other than C. If your program and data directories were on a logical drive that no longer exists, you will likely encounter error messages when you try to load these programs. Any batch files that change drives will also require adjustment, as will the PATH command included in your AUTOEXEC.BAT, file if it refers to directories on drives that have been deleted.

Windows

If you change to a single partition on the hard disk, the Windows' Swapfile is destroyed (it is not backed up). If you use a 386 or 486 system, you should re-create a permanent Swapfile after you partition again.

To create a permanent swap file, run Windows in real mode (WIN/R) and use the Run command to execute SWAPFILE.EXE (with all applications closed, not just minimized). Remember that the space used for Swapfile is unavailable for file storage.

Preparing Hard Disks with FDISK

The following sections show you how to use the FDISK command to perform several tasks, including the following:

❑ Creating primary and extended DOS partitions.

❑ Creating logical DOS drives in extended DOS partitions.

❑ Setting a partition's status as active.

❑ Deleting partitions.

❑ Displaying partition table information.

You also will learn to use the DOS 5 UNFORMAT command to display partition table information without using FDISK. In addition, you will learn steps that are necessary following the use of FDISK to prepare a new hard disk or one that has had its partition table data changed.

Backing Up Before You Proceed

FDISK can be used to examine the partition table without making a backup, as long as you do not make any changes with FDISK. If, however, you make any changes using FDISK, you must first make a complete backup of the entire physical hard disk. If your hard disk was partitioned into a C, D, and E drive using DOS 3.3, for example, all three logical drives must be backed up before you change to a single DOS 5 partition.

Although the BACKUP command is covered in more detail in Chapter 6, you can use the following syntax to back up your files for now:

```
BACKUP source destination-drive: /S /F:size
```

In the preceding syntax, *source* specifies the drive to back up, and *destination-drive* specifies the drive onto which to save the backup copies. The /S switch tells DOS to back up contents of subdirectories and the /F:size variable specifies that floppy disks should be formatted in a specific size. To back up the D drive to 720K floppy disks in a 1.44M B drive, for example, enter the following command:

```
BACKUP D:\*.* B: /S /F:720
```

When your backup is complete, or if you are installing a new hard disk, you are ready to continue. If you merely intend to examine the partition table information, you can continue, but be certain to heed the warnings FDISK provides and do not make any changes.

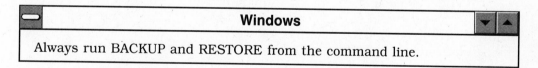

Windows

Always run BACKUP and RESTORE from the command line.

Making a Boot Disk for Emergencies

In addition to backing up the files on your hard disk, and before using FDISK, you should create a floppy disk that can be used to boot your system. Later in this chapter, you will examine this process in detail and create several different types of boot floppies. For now, however, place a new floppy disk in drive A and enter the following command:

```
FORMAT A: /S
```

When you see the following message, answer N:

```
Format another (Y/N)?
```

Enter the following command to copy the external commands RESTORE, FDISK, SYS, and FORMAT to the boot floppy:

COPY C:\DOS\RESTORE.EXE A:

If your DOS files are in another directory, substitute the correct directory for C:\DOS

Next, enter the following commands to finish copying RESTORE, FDISK, SYS, and FORMAT:

COPY C:\DOS\FORMAT.COM A:
COPY C:\DOS\FDISK.EXE A:
COPY C:\DOS\SYS.COM A:

You now have a floppy disk that can both boot your system and restore the backed up files to the hard disk. You may want to copy additional files to make the process of restoring your hard disk a little easier, but the floppy disk you just created will perform the minimum necessary tasks.

Starting FDISK

FDISK is an external DOS command and must be in the current directory or in a directory listed in the PATH environment variable. This book assumes that your DOS commands are located in C:\DOS and that the C:\DOS directory is on the command search path specified by PATH. You cannot use FDISK on a networked drive or with a network loaded. You must be logged off any network and have FDISK on a local drive before you begin. Enter the following command to start the FDISK program:

```
FDISK
```

The following screen is displayed:

```
                MS-DOS Version 5.00
            Fixed Disk Setup Program
       (C)Copyright Microsoft Corp. 1983 - 1991


                FDISK Options

Current fixed disk drive: 1
Choose one of the following:

1. Create DOS partition or Logical DOS Drive
2. Set active partition
```

```
3. Delete partition or Logical DOS Drive
4. Display partition information

Enter choice: [1]

Press Esc to exit FDISK
```

If you have more than one hard disk installed in your system, the following additional main menu selection appears:

```
5. Change current fixed disk drive
```

In the preceding FDISK screen, the default option is to create a DOS partition or a logical DOS drive. If you are preparing a new hard disk drive for use, this is the first choice you should make. If, on the other hand, you are changing partition table settings for an existing drive, one of the other options should be your first choice.

In every case, FDISK requires you to press Enter after typing your choice in the `Enter choice: [ ]` selection box. Also, the Esc key is always used to back out of a menu without making a choice. In the preceding display, you can see that Esc is used to exit FDISK.

Creating DOS Partitions with FDISK

FDISK lets you create a single, *primary* DOS partition and one *extended* DOS partition (which can contain up to 23 logical drives) on a hard disk. You can have a maximum of 26 disk drives in a system. Drive letters A and B are reserved for floppy disk drives and drive letter C is reserved for the first primary DOS partition. Drive letters D through Z are available for any additional drives—physical or logical.

You cannot use FDISK to create non-DOS partitions. If you are sharing your hard disk between DOS and another operating system, such as XENIX, you must use the other operating system's disk-partitioning program to create its own partition.

| | | **NetWare** | | |

Most Novell NetWare installations assume that drive F will be the first available network drive. If you have a large hard drive, DOS 3.X may have forced you to go beyond three DOS partitions, making your system the exception to the rule. You can now take advantage of the greater than 32M partition support in FDISK to configure your hard drive(s) as C, D and E, leaving drive F available for the first network drive.

To create a DOS partition, enter a 1 in the `Enter choice:` [ ] selection box and press Enter. FDISK displays the following screen:

```
        Create DOS Partition or Logical DOS Drive

Current fixed disk drive: 1

Choose one of the following:

1. Create Primary DOS Partition
2. Create Extended DOS Partition
3. Create Logical DOS Drive(s) in the Extended DOS Partition

Enter choice: [1]

Press Esc to return to FDISK Options
```

You must create a primary DOS partition (and, as you will see later, make it active) if you intend to boot DOS from your hard drive. Even if you wish to create logical drives in the extended DOS partition, you must first create a primary partition. FDISK recognizes this and displays the following default choice:

```
1. Create Primary DOS Partition
```

Press Enter to accept this selection and FDISK displays a screen similar to the following one:

```
        Create Primary DOS Partition

Current fixed disk drive: 1

Do you wish to use the maximum available size for a Primary DOS
Partition and make the partition active (Y/N)?
```

If a primary DOS partition already exists, a screen similar to the following will be displayed instead:

```
        Create Primary DOS Partition

Current fixed disk drive: 1

Partition Status Type    Volume Label Mbytes   System Usage
C: 1      A      PRI DOS Fixed   C      65 FAT16 100%

   Primary DOS Partition already exists.

   Press Esc to continue
```

Because you can create only a single primary DOS partition, press Esc to clear this screen and return to the previous menu.

If you answer Y to the `Do you wish to use the maximum available size for a Primary DOS Partition and make the partition active (Y/N)?` prompt, FDISK uses the entire available space for a primary DOS partition and will mark it as active. If your system contains only a single hard disk, FDISK displays the following message:

```
System will now restart

Insert DOS system diskette in drive A:
Press any key when ready
```

Place your boot floppy in drive A and press Enter. You now will have to use the FORMAT command to continue the preparation of your hard disk. The FORMAT command is covered in more detail following the discussion of FDISK.

If you are creating a primary DOS partition on a second hard disk, the FDISK prompt will not include the phrase: `and make the partition active`.

If you answer N to the preceding prompt, FDISK displays a message similar to the following:

```
Total disk space is 65 Mbytes (1 Mbyte = 1048576 bytes)
Maximum space available for partition is 65 Mbytes
Enter partition size in Mbytes or percent of disk space (%) to create a
Primary DOS Partition
```

The total disk space and maximum space available for the primary partition normally will be the same. The preceding example prompt shows a common hard disk size of 65M.

Enter the size in either megabytes or as a percentage of the available space that you want to allocate to the primary partition. To create a 20M primary partition, for example, you can enter 20 or 30%.(If you are entering the partition size as a percentage, you must include the percent sign (%).)

Once you have created a primary DOS partition, you can create an extended DOS partition using the space remaining on the hard disk. Select 1 from the main FDISK menu and FDISK displays following message:

```
Create DOS Partition or Logical DOS Drive

Current fixed disk drive: 1

Choose one of the following:
```

```
1. Create Primary DOS Partition
2. Create Extended DOS Partition
3. Create Logical DOS Drive(s) in the Extended DOS Partition

Enter choice: [1]

Press Esc to return to FDISK Options
```

Select choice 2 and FDISK displays the following prompt:

```
Create Extended DOS Partition

Maximum space available for partition is 45 Mbytes

Enter partition size in Mbytes or percent of disk space (%) to create an
Extended DOS Partition
```

Unless you are allocating disk space to another operating system, press Enter
to allocate the entire remaining disk space as the size of the extended DOS
partition. If you do not allocate all of the disk's space to the primary and extended DOS partitions, any remaining space will be unavailable to DOS.

Next, select choice 3 from the preceding menu. Before you can store data in
the extended DOS partition, you must use this selection to create logical
drives in the partition. FDISK will display a screen similar to the following:

```
Create Logical DOS Drive(s) in the Extended DOS Partition

Drv Volume Label  Mbytes  System  Usage

Total Extended DOS Partition size is 45 Mbytes (1 MByte = 1048576 bytes)
Maximum space available for logical drive is 45 Mbytes
Enter logical drive size in Mbytes or percent of disk space (%)
```

Press Enter to allocate the entire extended DOS partition to a single logical
drive, or enter the size for each logical drive until the entire extended DOS
partition is allocated. Once the entire extended DOS partition has been allocated, the main FDISK menu will reappear on the screen.

Setting the Active Partition with FDISK

Before a PC can boot from a hard disk, one of the partitions must be marked
as the active partition. DOS can boot only from an active, primary partition.
When booting from a hard disk, your system determines which disk operating
system should be used by examining the disk partition table to see which
operating system owns the active partition.

Unless your hard disk is shared among two or more operating systems, the
primary DOS partition should always be marked as active. In fact, if you have

two hard disks in your system, the primary partition in each should be marked as active. If your C drive should fail, your D drive then would become the replacement C drive and could boot your system.

To set the primary DOS partition as active, select 2 from the main FDISK menu. A screen similar to the following appears:

```
        Set Active Partition

    Current fixed disk drive: 1

    Partition  Status  Type    Volume  Label  Mbytes   System Usage
       C: 1      PRI    DOS     Fixed    C      65 FAT16  100%

  Enter the number of the partition you want to make active
```

If your hard disk contains only one partition and it is already marked as active, FDISK displays the following message:

```
    The only startable partition on Drive 1 is already set active.

    Press Esc to continue
```

The active partition will show A in its status field to indicate that it is active.

Deleting a Partition with FDISK

Once you have created a partition, you cannot change its size. The only way to change partition size is to delete one or more existing partitions and then create new ones of the desired size. Remember, though, that if you delete a partition, any data it contains will be lost. You cannot change partition sizes without losing all existing data.

To delete one or more existing partitions, select 3 from the main FDISK menu. The following screen displays:

```
        Delete DOS Partition or Logical DOS Drive

    Current fixed disk drive: 1

    Choose one of the following:

    1. Delete Primary DOS Partition
    2. Delete Extended DOS Partition
    3. Delete Logical DOS Drive(s) in the Extended DOS Partition
    4. Delete Non-DOS Partition

    Enter choice: [ ]

    Press Esc to return to FDISK Options
```

FDISK does not provide a default selection on this menu. This prevents you from accidently deleting a partition should you press Enter. FDISK lets you remove any partition that exists; it does not have to be one created by FDISK.

If you choose 1, a screen similar to the following appears:

```
     Delete Primary DOS Partition

Current fixed disk drive: 1

Partition Status Type    Volume Label Mbytes   System Usage
C: 1       A      PRI DOS Fixed    C       65 FAT16  100%

Total disk space is   65 Mbytes (1 Mbyte = 1048576 bytes)

WARNING! Data in the deleted Primary DOS Partition will be lost.
What primary partition do you want to delete..? [1]

Press Esc to return to FDISK Options
```

If you do not want to delete your primary partition and lose any data it contains, press Esc. If you press Enter, FDISK asks you for the volume label with the following prompt:

```
Enter Volume Label
```

FDISK gives you the following warning:

```
Do you wish to continue (Y/N)
```

This is the last warning FDISK provides before deleting the primary DOS partition. Be certain you heed the warning!

If you want to delete the extended DOS partition, select 2 at the preceding menu prompt. FDISK displays the following prompt:

```
     Delete Extended DOS Partition

Current fixed disk drive: 1

Partition Status Type    Volume Label Mbytes   System Usage
C: 1              EXT DOS Fixed    C       65 FAT16  100%

Total disk space is   65 Mbytes (1 Mbyte = 1048576 bytes)

WARNING! Data in the deleted Extended DOS Partition will be lost.
Do you wish to continue? (Y/N)

Press Esc to return to FDISK Options
```

Again, be certain that you want to delete the extended DOS partition before proceeding.

FDISK gives you another option relating to the extended DOS partition. The following choice is slightly different from the other options on the preceding menu:

3. Delete Logical DOS Drive(s) in the Extended DOS Partition

Although deleting a logical drive destroys any data that it may contain, other logical drives are not affected. If, for example, your extended DOS partition contains four logical drives, D, E, F, and G, you can delete drives F and G without affecting drives D and E. You then can create a new drive F that uses the space formerly used by drives F and G.

If you do select choice 3, FDISK gives you the following warning:

WARNING! Data in a deleted Logical DOS Drive will be lost.

FDISK prompts you for the drive with the following:

What drive do you want to delete?

After you enter the drive number, FDISK prompts you to enter the volume label with the following:

Enter Volume Label

You are given the following confirmation prompt. This is your last chance to keep the data on your drive.

Are you sure? (Y/N)

If you delete logical drives, the letters assigned to any later logical drives will adjust automatically. DOS does not allow any gaps to exist in the assigned drive letters. If, in the above example, you deleted logical drive E, your logical drives would be reassigned. Your old drive F becomes E, and your old G drive becomes F.

Finally, if you select 4 from the preceding menu, FDISK gives you the option of removing any partitions assigned to another disk operating system. Like the other choices on this menu, this selection has the potential to destroy data. It is especially dangerous because FDISK cannot be used to add a non-DOS partition. If you do select this option, FDISK displays the following series of prompts:

Delete Non-DOS Partition

WARNING! Data in the deleted Non-DOS Partition will be lost.

What Non-DOS partition do you want to delete..?

If you have used any of the `Delete DOS Partition or Logical DOS Drive` menu selections to delete a partition, you must create new partitions before you can use the space that the deleted partition or partitions occupied. Refer to the earlier section on creating partitions with FDISK for information.

Displaying Partition Information with FDISK and UNFORMAT

If the previous FDISK examples have left you with the idea that FDISK must be used with extreme caution, you have learned one of the most important points about this program. In fact, you may want to follow the example of many experienced PC users and remove the FDISK program from your hard disk to prevent accidental use.

FDISK does have one main menu option, `4. Display partition information`, that cannot damage or destroy data. If you select this option, FDISK shows you how your hard disk is currently partitioned with a message similar to the following:

```
     Display Partition Information

Current fixed disk drive: 1

Partition Status Type    Volume Label Mbytes    System Usage
C: 1      A       PRI DOS Fixed   C     65 FAT16 100%

Total disk space is  65 Mbytes (1 Mbyte = 1048576 bytes)

Press Esc to continue
```

If you decide to remove FDISK to the safety of an emergency floppy disk, you still can see your hard disk's partition information using the UNFORMAT command with two switches. Enter the following command line:

UNFORMAT /PARTN /L

DOS responds by displaying a screen similar to the following:

```
Hard Disk Partition Table display.

Drive # 80h has 1022 cylinders, 5 heads, 26 sectors (from BIOS).

The following table is from drive 80h, cylinder 0, head 0, sector 1:
```

```
              Total_size  Start_partition    End_partition

Type      Bytes  Sectors  Cyl Head Sector  Cyl  Head Sector  Rel#
--------  -------------  ---------------  ----------------  ----
HUGE Boot  65M    132834   0   1    1    1021   4    26      26
```

Although not presented in quite the same format as the FDISK command displays, the partition table information shown by UNFORMAT actually is more complete. Also, because UNFORMAT is safer than FDISK, you may prefer to use it instead of keeping FDISK on your hard disk.

Rebuilding the Partition Table

Prior to DOS 5, a corrupted hard disk partition table resulted in the complete loss of all data on the affected drive. Later you will see how the UNFORMAT and MIRROR commands can be used to recover from such a severe problem.

Creating Disks for Different Purposes

If you have created any DOS partitions on your hard disk, your next step is to use the FORMAT command to format the drives that were created. In this section, you will use the FORMAT command to create different types of floppy disks. The discussion of bootable floppies applies to your hard disk as well. In addition, Chapter 5 discusses tree structured directories—a subject that has even more importance if you have changed your hard disk from several small volumes to a single large one spanning the entire disk.

Bootable versus Non-Bootable Disks

Before a PC can boot (or load and run) DOS, it must be able to access a disk that contains three files: IO.SYS, MSDOS.SYS, and COMMAND.COM. You cannot just copy these files to a disk, though, because the first two of them have specific requirements regarding where they must be located, both physically and in the root directory listing. DOS 5 is slightly more tolerant of where they are located than earlier versions of DOS, but DOS 5 still has fairly strict conditions that must be considered.

Because a bootable disk must contain the three system files, less room is available for data storage. In fact, the current version of these three files uses about 116K of disk storage. Obviously, you do not want to waste this much space on disks used simply for data storage. Because most floppy disks are used for data storage as opposed to booting the system, most floppy disks should be formatted without adding the system files. Even so, floppy disks that can be used for booting the system are important.

Considering Different Types of Bootable Floppy Disks

Just as you probably use several different types of programs to perform different jobs on your PC, you may need several different types of bootable floppy disks. The following are some possibilities that you might want to consider:

❑ Boot floppies for emergencies such as hard disk failures.

❑ Boot floppies used to access a DOS partition on a hard disk if another disk operating system owns the active partition.

❑ Boot floppies that use the DOS files on your hard disk but configure your system for special purposes.

Preparing Emergency Boot Floppy Disks

Hard disks can and do fail. Of course, many levels of failure exist, but when you are faced with a PC screen that displays one of the error messages in the following list, you will be glad you had an emergency boot floppy disk.

```
File allocation table bad
Invalid COMMAND.COM
Cannot load COMMAND, system halted
Not ready
Invalid device request
Seek error
Invalid media type
Sector not found
Read fault error
General failure
Invalid drive specification
Current drive is no longer valid
Invalid drive in search path
```

Once you see one of these messages and have not made an emergency boot floppy disk, you are too late to wish you had created one. These messages can happen while you are trying to boot from your hard disk, while you are trying to load a program, or while you are in any other operation that accesses your hard disk. Do not wait for trouble to strike. Get out some new floppy disks and create a boot floppy now.

The following are some rules for bootable floppy disk creation:

❑ Always create boot floppies in the A drive. DOS cannot be booted from the B drive—you must use a disk compatible with the A drive.

❑ Clearly label the boot floppy. Include both the DOS version used to create the disk and the date it was created.

❏ Write-protect and store the emergency boot floppy in a safe place. In an emergency you need to find the boot floppy quickly.

NetWare

Not only is it wise to create an emergency boot floppy for stand-alone DOS machines, but you should also make an emergency workstation boot floppy for each of your NetWare workstations. Because each workstation may have its own set of switch and jumper settings for the installed network interface card, each workstation requires a different IPX.COM file. If all of your workstations' network interface cards are configured in the same way, you can get by with only one emergency workstation boot floppy. To check the configuration of each workstation without removing the cover, you can change to the current directory on each workstation that contains the IPX.COM file and type: **IPX I**. This reports the type of adapter card that is installed, as well as the current interrupt, DMA, memory address, and so forth. Use this information to decide how many different emergency disks to make.

Creating an Emergency Boot Floppy Disk

If possible, use a new floppy disk that matches the highest capacity your A drive can format. When you format a disk at a drive's highest capacity, you not only get more disk space, but you also get a more reliable disk. Use high-quality disks; when dealing with a hard disk emergency you do not want to worry about a floppy disk failure as well.

The first step in creating an emergency boot floppy disk is to use the FORMAT command with the /S option. This creates a minimum level bootable disk containing the following three system files: IO.SYS, MSDOS.SYS, and COMMAND.COM. Place the disk that will become your emergency boot floppy in drive A and enter the following command:

```
FORMAT A: /U /S
```

Notice that both the /U and /S switches are used. The DOS 5 FORMAT command uses the /U switch to force an unconditional format. By using this format mode, the FORMAT command writes over the entire disk. This is the default mode for new, unformatted disks and should always be used when creating an emergency boot floppy.

The /S switch causes the three system files to be transferred to the disk after the format is completed. The SYS command, which is discussed later in this chapter, also can be used to transfer these three files.

The preceding syntax attempts to format the floppy disk at the A drive's highest capacity. If you do not have a high-capacity disk available, you can use the /F:size switch to force the drive to format a lower-density disk. To format a 360K floppy disk in a 1.2M drive, for example, use the following syntax:

```
FORMAT A: /U /S /F:360
```

To format a 720K disk in a 1.44M drive, for example, insert the following:

```
FORMAT A: /U /S /F:720
```

Choosing Files for the Emergency Boot Disk

If you have an emergency, such as a hard disk failure, you want as much function as possible. You certainly should have any DOS utilities that might help you restore your hard disk or at least allow you to correct as many errors as possible. When determining which files should be on your emergency disk, remember that you may not be able to access any files on the hard disk—everything you will need should be on the floppy disk.

The capacity of your emergency boot floppy determines largely which DOS utility programs you should select. The higher its capacity, the greater the functionality you can obtain through a more complete collection of program files. The following lists show recommended sets of files that system disks of different capacities can hold.

Copying Files to 360K Emergency Boot Disks

If your A drive is a 5 1/4-inch and you are limited to double-density, 360K disks, you will have room only for a small number of essential program files in addition to the system files. Once you have formatted your emergency boot disk, enter the following commands to copy these files to the emergency boot disk:

```
COPY C:\DOS\BACKUP.EXE A:
COPY C:\DOS\CHKDSK.EXE A:
COPY C:\DOS\EDLIN.EXE A:
COPY C:\DOS\FDISK.EXE A:
COPY C:\DOS\FORMAT.COM A:
COPY C:\DOS\RESTORE.EXE A:
COPY C:\DOS\SYS.COM A:
COPY C:\DOS\UNFORMAT.COM A:
COPY C:\AUTOEXEC.BAT A:\ AUTOEXEC.HD
COPY C:\CONFIG.SYS A:\ CONFIG.HD
```

Copying Files to 720K Emergency Boot Disks

If your A drive is a 3 1/2-inch and you are limited to 720K disks, you have room for a larger number of essential program files in addition to the system files. Once you have formatted your emergency boot disk, enter the following commands to copy these files to the emergency boot disk:

```
COPY C:\DOS\ATTRIB.EXE A:
COPY C:\DOS\BACKUP.EXE A:
COPY C:\DOS\CHKDSK.EXE A:
COPY C:\DOS\DEBUG.EXE A:
COPY C:\DOS\DISKCOMP.COM A:
COPY C:\DOS\DISKCOPY.COM A:
COPY C:\DOS\DOSHELP.HLP A:
COPY C:\DOS\DOSKEY.COM A:
COPY C:\DOS\DRIVER.SYS A:
COPY C:\DOS\EDLIN.EXE A:
COPY C:\DOS\FDISK.EXE A:
COPY C:\DOS\FORMAT.COM A:
COPY C:\DOS\HIMEM.SYS A:
COPY C:\DOS\LABEL.EXE A:
COPY C:\DOS\LOADFIX.COM A:
COPY C:\DOS\MEM.EXE A:
COPY C:\DOS\MIRROR.COM A:
COPY C:\DOS\MODE.COM A:
COPY C:\DOS\MORE.COM A:
COPY C:\DOS\REPLACE.EXE A:
COPY C:\DOS\RESTORE.EXE A:
COPY C:\DOS\SETVER.EXE A:
COPY C:\DOS\SMARTDRV.SYS A:
COPY C:\DOS\SYS.COM A:
COPY C:\DOS\UNDELETE.EXE A:
COPY C:\DOS\UNFORMAT.COM A:
COPY C:\DOS\XCOPY.EXE A:
```

Copying Files to 1.2M Emergency Boot Disks

If your A drive is a high density 5 1/4-inch and you can use 1.2M disks, you have room for a much larger number of essential program files in addition to the system files. Once you have formatted your emergency boot disk, enter the following commands to copy these files to the emergency boot disk:

```
COPY C:\DOS\APPEND.EXE A:
COPY C:\DOS\ASSIGN.COM A:
COPY C:\DOS\ATTRIB.EXE A:
```

```
COPY C:\DOS\BACKUP.EXE A:
COPY C:\DOS\CHKDSK.EXE A:
COPY C:\DOS\COMP.EXE A:
COPY C:\DOS\DEBUG.EXE A:
COPY C:\DOS\DISKCOMP.COM A:
COPY C:\DOS\DISKCOPY.COM A:
COPY C:\DOS\DOSHELP.HLP A:
COPY C:\DOS\DOSKEY.COM A:
COPY C:\DOS\DRIVER.SYS A:
COPY C:\DOS\EDIT.COM A:
COPY C:\DOS\EDIT.HLP A:
COPY C:\DOS\EMM386.EXE A:
COPY C:\DOS\FC.EXE A:
COPY C:\DOS\FDISK.EXE A:
COPY C:\DOS\FIND.EXE A:
COPY C:\DOS\FORMAT.COM A:
COPY C:\DOS\HIMEM.SYS A:
COPY C:\DOS\JOIN.EXE A:
COPY C:\DOS\LABEL.EXE A:
COPY C:\DOS\LOADFIX.COM A:
COPY C:\DOS\MEM.EXE A:
COPY C:\DOS\MIRROR.COM A:
COPY C:\DOS\MODE.COM A:
COPY C:\DOS\MORE.COM A:
COPY C:\DOS\QBASIC.EXE A:
COPY C:\DOS\QBASIC.HLP A:
COPY C:\DOS\REPLACE.EXE A:
COPY C:\DOS\RESTORE.EXE A:
COPY C:\DOS\SETVER.EXE A:
COPY C:\DOS\SHARE.EXE A:
COPY C:\DOS\SMARTDRV.SYS A:
COPY C:\DOS\SUBST.EXE A:
COPY C:\DOS\SYS.COM A:
COPY C:\DOS\TREE.COM A:
COPY C:\DOS\UNDELETE.EXE A:
COPY C:\DOS\UNFORMAT.COM A:
COPY C:\DOS\XCOPY.EXE A:
COPY C:\AUTOEXEC BAT A:\ AUTOEXEC.HD
COPY C:\CONFIG.SYS A:\ CONFIG.HD
```

Copying Files to 1.44M Emergency Boot Disks

If your A drive is a high density 3 1/2-inch and you can use 1.44M disks,
you have room for a much larger number of essential program files in addition to the system files. Once you have formatted your emergency boot disk,
enter the following commands to copy these files to the emergency boot disk:

```
COPY C:\DOS\APPEND.EXE A:
COPY C:\DOS\ASSIGN.COM A:
COPY C:\DOS\ATTRIB.EXE A:
COPY C:\DOS\BACKUP.EXE A:
COPY C:\DOS\CHKDSK.EXE A:
COPY C:\DOS\COMP.EXE A:
COPY C:\DOS\COUNTRY.SYS A:
COPY C:\DOS\DEBUG.EXE A:
COPY C:\DOS\DISKCOMP.COM A:
COPY C:\DOS\DISKCOPY.COM A:
COPY C:\DOS\DISPLAY.SYS A:
COPY C:\DOS\DOSHELP.HLP A:
COPY C:\DOS\DOSKEY.COM A:
COPY C:\DOS\DRIVER.SYS A:
COPY C:\DOS\EDIT.COM A:
COPY C:\DOS\EDIT.HLP A:
COPY C:\DOS\EMM386.EXE A:
COPY C:\DOS\FASTOPEN.EXE A:
COPY C:\DOS\FC.EXE A:
COPY C:\DOS\FDISK.EXE A:
COPY C:\DOS\FIND.EXE A:
COPY C:\DOS\FORMAT.COM A:
COPY C:\DOS\HELP.EXE A:
COPY C:\DOS\HIMEM.SYS A:
COPY C:\DOS\JOIN.EXE A:
COPY C:\DOS\LABEL.EXE A:
COPY C:\DOS\LOADFIX.COM A:
COPY C:\DOS\MEM.EXE A:
COPY C:\DOS\MIRROR.COM A:
COPY C:\DOS\MODE.COM A:
COPY C:\DOS\MORE.COM A:
COPY C:\DOS\PRINTER.SYS A:
COPY C:\DOS\PRINT.EXE A:
COPY C:\DOS\QBASIC.EXE A:
COPY C:\DOS\QBASIC.HLP A:
COPY C:\DOS\RAMDRIVE.SYS A:
COPY C:\DOS\RECOVER.EXE A:
COPY C:\DOS\REPLACE.EXE A:
COPY C:\DOS\RESTORE.EXE A:
COPY C:\DOS\SETVER.EXE A:
COPY C:\DOS\SHARE.EXE A:
COPY C:\DOS\SMARTDRV.SYS A:
COPY C:\DOS\SORT.EXE A:
COPY C:\DOS\SUBST.EXE A:
COPY C:\DOS\SYS.COM A:
```

```
COPY C:\DOS\TREE.COM A:
COPY C:\DOS\UNDELETE.EXE A:
COPY C:\DOS\UNFORMAT.COM A:
COPY C:\DOS\XCOPY.EXE A:
COPY C:\AUTOEXEC.BAT A:\AUTOEXEC.HD
COPY C:\CONFIG.SYS A:\ CONFIG.HD
```

Windows ▼ ▲

It is a good idea to create an emergency disk and make sure you can start Windows when you use it. If space permits, copy the *.INI and *.GRP files from your Windows directory onto the emergency disk.

Alternatives to the Emergency Boot Disk

If you are using DOS 5, two alternatives to an emergency boot disks may have been created when you installed it. If you installed DOS 5 on floppy disks, one of the disks you created should be labeled STARTUP (if you are using 5 1/4-inch disks) or STARTUP/SUPPORT (if you are using 3 1/2-inch disks). The following files should be on these disks:

Files on STARTUP disk (5 1/4-inch)

AUTOEXEC.BAT	COMMAND.COM	CONFIG.SYS	COUNTRY.SYS
DISPLAY.SYS	EGA.CPI	EGA.SYS	FORMAT.COM
HIMEM.SYS	IO.SYS	KEYBOARD.SYS	KEYB.COM
MODE.COM	MSDOS.SYS	NLSFUNC.EXE	SETVER.EXE

Files on STARTUP/SUPPORT disk (3 1/2-inch)

ANSI.SYS	AUTOEXEC.BAT	COMMAND.COM	CONFIG.SYS
COUNTRY.SYS	DEBUG.EXE	DISPLAY.SYS	DOSKEY.COM
EDLIN.EXE	EGA.CPI	EGA.SYS	EMM386.EXE
FASTOPEN.EXE	FDISK.EXE	FORMAT.COM	HIMEM.SYS
IO.SYS	KEYBOARD.SYS	KEYB.COM	MEM.EXE
MIRROR.COM	MODE.COM	MSDOS.SYS	NLSFUNC.EXE
RAMDRIVE.SYS	SETVER.EXE	SHARE.EXE	SMARTDRV.SYS
SYS.COM	UNDELETE.EXE	UNFORMAT.COM	XCOPY.EXE

Neither the STARTUP nor the STARTUP/SUPPORT disk are set up with maximum utility in mind. If you rely on either of these disks for emergencies, you will find it necessary to swap disks to use some of the important DOS utility programs.

If you installed DOS 5 directly to your hard disk, you created either one or two UNINSTALL disks. The first uninstall disk also can be used to boot your PC, but it does not contain any of the utilities you will need in an emergency.

Creating Boot Floppies To Access Partitions on Hard Disk

Compared to the task of creating an emergency boot floppy, creating a boot floppy that allows your hard disk's active partition to belong to another disk operating system is quite simple. In fact, because the floppy disk is not used after the system has been booted, only two files, AUTOEXEC.BAT and CONFIG.SYS, in addition to the system files, are needed.

Recall from the discussion of FDISK that a PC can boot only from an active partition. If you have another disk operating system, such as XENIX, installed on your hard disk, you may decide to use DOS as a secondary disk operating system.

Formatting the Boot Floppy

The only way you can use a disk operating system that is in a hard-disk partition not marked as active is to boot from the A drive. You should start, therefore, by formatting a system boot disk. Enter the following command:

```
FORMAT A: /S /U
```

As in the preceding example, both the /S and /U switches are used. Once the disk has been formatted and the message System transferred is displayed, you are ready to continue.

Creating COMSPEC with CONFIG.SYS

DOS uses an environment variable, COMSPEC, to tell programs where to find the command processor (normally COMMAND.COM). Unless you specify a value for the COMSPEC variable, the value is set to the root directory of the boot disk. If you boot from a floppy disk, programs normally will look for COMMAND.COM in the root directory of the A drive. If you remove the boot disk and replace it with a disk that does not contain COMMAND.COM, when

DOS needs to find the command processor it will display a message similar to the following:

```
Insert disk with \COMMAND.COM in drive A
and press any key when ready
```

By setting the COMSPEC variable to access COMMAND.COM on your C drive, you can eliminate this problem. The way to do this is to include a SHELL directive in CONFIG.SYS. CONFIG.SYS contains system-configuration commands that are executed when your PC boots. The SHELL directive is one of the commands that can be included in CONFIG.SYS. DEVICE, DEVICEHIGH, DOS, FILES, BUFFERS, and BREAK are some other common CONFIG.SYS directives.

To create a simple CONFIG.SYS file on the boot floppy, you first need to make the A drive current by entering A:. Next, enter the following command to begin creating CONFIG.SYS:

```
COPY CON CONFIG.SYS
```

After you enter the command, the cursor drops down to the start of the next line. Any text you type is copied into a new file called CONFIG.SYS until you indicate you have reached the end of the file by entering Ctrl-Z. Enter the SHELL directive into the CONFIG.SYS file by typing the following line (do not press Enter after typing this line):

```
SHELL=C:\DOS\COMMAND.COM C:\DOS\ /E:512 /P
```

The first part of the command, SHELL=C:\DOS\COMMAND.COM, specifies that you want DOS to use the copy of COMMAND.COM located in the \DOS directory on the C drive as the command processor. The second part of the command, C:\DOS\, specifies where the command processor should look for COMMAND.COM when its transient part must be reloaded. This argument is used to set the COMSPEC variable.

The next part of the command, /E:512, increases the size of the DOS environment space from the default 256 bytes to 512 bytes. By increasing the size of this space, more room for items such as the PATH and PROMPT variables is provided. The last part of the command, /P, makes the changes permanent for the current DOS session.

After you type the preceding line, press Space and then the F6 function key (^Z will appear). Now you can press Enter to create your CONFIG.SYS file. DOS responds with the following message:

```
1 file(s) copied
```

Although this CONFIG.SYS file accomplishes the task of ensuring that
C:\DOS\COMMAND.COM is used instead of A:\COMMAND.COM, it does not
include any of the other commands that commonly are used in CONFIG.SYS.
Because CONFIG.SYS commands are executed only when the system is
booted, you may need to include other items in your CONFIG.SYS file. The
following sample file shows some other commands you may wish to include:

```
REM The next line installs the DOS 5 SETVER device driver
DEVICE=C:\DOS\SETVER.EXE
REM HIMEM.SYS is the DOS extended memory manager.
REM It must be included if you wish to load DOS into the High Memory
Area (HMA)
REM HIMEM.SYS is for 80286, 80386, and 80486 PCs only
DEVICE=C:\DOS\HIMEM.SYS
REM The DOS directive is used to load DOS into the HMA
REM and provide Upper Memory Block (UMB) support
DOS=HIGH,UMB
REM EMM386.EXE provides expanded memory support and
REM UMB support for 80386 and 80486 PCs
REM Use the NOEMS argument to provide UMBs only, or the RAM
REM argument to provide expanded memory support at the cost of
REM some UMB space
DEVICE=C:\DOS\EMM386.EXE NOEMS
REM Set the FILES value to 60 for use with DOS 5 and Windows 3
FILES=30
REM Set the BUFFERS value to 3 when using a disk cache like SMARTDRV.SYS
BUFFERS = 3
REM Set BREAK=ON to force DOS to respond to the BREAK key
BREAK=ON
REM SMARTDRV.SYS is a disk cache program
DEVICEHIGH=C:\DOS\SMARTDRV.SYS 2048 512
REM The SHELL command specifies the command processor
SHELL=C:\DOS\COMMAND.COM C:\DOS\ /E:512 /p
```

Windows

See Appendix A for more information about configuring DOS for Windows.

If you decide to include any of the commands from the preceding sample
CONFIG.SYS file in the file you create on the boot floppy, press Enter after
you type each line. After the last line, press F6.

Setting the PATH with AUTOEXEC.BAT

Although the boot floppy now can be used to make the non-active DOS partition seem as if it were the active partition, adding a PATH command to an AUTOEXEC.BAT file adds further refinement. A PATH command ensures that the other DOS programs, such as FORMAT and BACKUP, are found when you want to use them.

You can create the AUTOEXEC.BAT file similar to the way you created the CONFIG.SYS file. First, make sure the A drive is the current drive (enter **A:** if necessary). Then enter the following commands:

```
COPY CON AUTOEXEC.BAT
@ECHO OFF
PATH C:\DOS
```

If you also wish to change the DOS prompt, enter a line similar to the following:

```
PROMPT Current Directory is - $P$_Your command? -
```

After typing the preceding line, press Space, the F6 function key, and Enter. DOS responds with the following message:

```
1 file(s) copied
```

Your boot floppy now is ready to use. If you reboot your system without a disk in drive A, your PC boots using the disk operating system whose hard disk partition is marked active. If you reboot using your new boot floppy, your PC will act as though the DOS partition is active.

Creating Boot Disks for Special Purposes

In the preceding example, you examined a method of running DOS in cases in which another disk operating system (instead of DOS) was the active one. The example showed you how to boot from a floppy disk, but then operate as if your PC had been booted directly from the hard disk. Next, you will see a more general example of the same idea: creating boot floppy disks that configure your system for special purposes.

You may use several different pieces of software in the course of operating your PC. In many cases, each piece of software requires its own, unique system configuration for optimum operation. If you run several different Windows applications, for example, some may work best in 386-enhanced mode, some in standard mode, and some older program versions may require real mode. In addition, you may also use DOS programs that require your system to be configured differently than what is ideal for Windows. One solution to this chaos is to create specialized boot floppies that you can use when you need to change your configuration. Your standard hard disk configuration remains unchanged, but you easily can boot up a new configuration as needed.

Creating the Basic Boot Floppy Disk

The following are the steps in creating special boot floppy disks.

❑ Each specialized boot floppy begins as a basic boot floppy.

❑ CONFIG.SYS and AUTOEXEC.BAT files are created that access system files on the hard disk.

❑ CONFIG.SYS and AUTOEXEC.BAT files are modified to create the unique configurations for each special purpose.

As in previous examples, you start creating your boot floppy disks by formatting a system boot disk. Because the specialized boot floppy contains only a small number of files, you can safely use a 360K or 720K disk even if your A drive is a high-capacity drive. Enter the following command:

```
FORMAT A: /S /U
```

Once the disk has been formatted and the message System transferred is displayed, you are ready to continue. Be sure to add a stick-on label indicating the special configuration that this disk will boot. You might label, for example, the disk "Windows Real Mode Boot Disk."

Creating COMSPEC with CONFIG.SYS

Next, you must create the environment variable COMSPEC to tell programs where to find COMMAND.COM. Unless you specify a value for the COMSPEC variable, it is set to the root directory of the boot disk. In this case, the root directory would be the root directory of the A drive. To eliminate this problem, set the COMSPEC variable to access COMMAND.COM on your C drive. When you create the CONFIG.SYS file on the specialized boot floppy, include a SHELL directive in CONFIG.SYS, which lets you set COMSPEC.

Determining the Contents of the Specialized Boot Disk

Often the best software for one purpose is a poor choice for another use. One example of this is evident in the area of disk-caching software. DOS 5 includes a disk-cache program called SMARTDRV.SYS. This program was designed to work well with Windows 3 by adjusting its memory usage to share extended memory when necessary. If you are already using another disk-caching program (many are available on the market), you may find that your current program offers higher performance with the database software you use, but does not share memory with Windows. Rather than choosing between lower performance and compatibility with Windows, why not create a specialized boot disk that lets you use the best configuration for each situation?

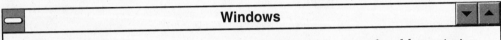

Windows

If you use Windows as your primary environment, you should maximize Windows' performance to improve the performance of applications in DOS windows.

By running disk-optimizing software, such as the SD (Speed Disk) program in the Norton Utilities, you can improve the performance of your hard disk by reducing file fragmentation. Some PC users feel the improvement is great enough that they include a command to run their disk-optimizing software from their AUTOEXEC.BAT file every time they boot their system. Unfortunately, running disk-optimizing software, because it moves files around on the disk, makes it impossible to recover accidently deleted files. If you automatically run disk-optimizing software from your AUTOEXEC.BAT file, why not create a specialized boot floppy that boots your system in its standard configuration without the command for the disk-optimizing software?

You may have many other reasons for creating specialized boot floppies. The following examples should give you a strong foundation on which you can create exactly what you need.

Creating a Boot Floppy Disk To Change Caching Programs

Suppose, for example, that the CONFIG.SYS file on your hard disk looks similar to the following example, which is the same example presented earlier in the chapter:

```
REM The next line installs the MS-DOS 5 SETVER device driver
DEVICE=C:\DOS\SETVER.EXE
REM HIMEM.SYS is the DOS extended memory manager.
REM It must be included if you wish to load DOS into the High Memory
Area (HMA)
REM HIMEM.SYS is for 80286, 80386, and 80486 PCs only
DEVICE=C:\DOS\HIMEM.SYS
REM The DOS directive is used to load DOS into the HMA
REM and provide Upper Memory Block (UMB) support
DOS=HIGH,UMB
REM EMM386.EXE provides expanded memory support and
REM UMB support for 80386 and 80486 PCs
REM Use the NOEMS argument to provide UMBs only, or the RAM
```

```
REM argument to provide expanded memory support at the cost of
REM some UMB space
DEVICE=C:\DOS\EMM386.EXE NOEMS
REM Set the FILES value to 60 for use with MS-DOS 5 and Windows 3
FILES= 60
REM Set the BUFFERS value to 3 when using a disk cache like SMARTDRV.SYS
BUFFERS = 3
REM Set BREAK=ON to force DOS to respond to the BREAK key
BREAK=ON
REM SMARTDRV.SYS is a disk cache program
DEVICEHIGH=C:\DOS\SMARTDRV.SYS 2048 512
REM The SHELL command specifies the command processor
SHELL=C:\DOS\COMMAND.COM C:\DOS\ /E:512 /p
```

You may find that, although the configuration set up by this file works fine with Windows 3, your database manager works better with another disk-caching program called DISKCACH.SYS, for example. Through experimentation, you find that by using DISKCACH.SYS instead of SMARTDRV.SYS, you can update 25,000 records in your sales database in one hour instead of three. On the other hand, using DISKCACH.SYS makes it impossible to run your Windows-based communications program that runs in the background downloading sales data from your field offices while you are writing your reports in Word for Windows. Instead of constantly changing the CONFIG.SYS file on your hard disk or putting up with the problems, you should create a new CONFIG.SYS file on your specialized boot floppy.

Because the rest of the commands in CONFIG.SYS work fine in either case, all you will have to do is change the command that loads the disk-caching software. Begin by copying CONFIG.SYS from the hard disk to the specialized boot floppy with the following command:

```
COPY C:\CONFIG.SYS A:
```

DOS responds with the following message:

```
1 file(s) copied
```

Next, edit the CONFIG.SYS file on the specialized boot floppy. In this case, use the DOS 5 full-screen editor, EDIT, to make the changes. Enter the following command to load EDIT and CONFIG.SYS:

```
EDIT A:CONFIG.SYS
```

When CONFIG.SYS appears on the screen, move the cursor down to the beginning of the line that says the following:

```
DEVICEHIGH=C:\DOS\SMARTDRV.SYS 2048 512
```

Change the line into a remark line by adding REM to the beginning of the line. Remark lines in CONFIG.SYS are not executed. The line should now look like the following:

```
REM DEVICEHIGH=C:\DOS\SMARTDRV.SYS 2048 512
```

Add the line that loads DISKCACH.SYS and supplies any optional parameters it may require. Move the cursor to the end of the line and press Enter. EDIT inserts a blank line that you use to add the new command. Enter the following line:

```
DEVICE=C:\DOS\DISKCACH.SYS 2048 /E
```

In the preceding syntax, 2048 and /E are the optional parameters needed by DISKCACH.SYS.

Because no other changes are needed, write the new CONFIG.SYS file to the floppy disk and exit from the EDIT program. Use the following steps to save and exit: press Alt, File, Exit, and then Yes.

Next, copy your existing AUTOEXEC.BAT to the specialized boot floppy with the following command:

```
COPY C:\AUTOEXEC.BAT A:
```

Once you have completed these steps, the boot floppy is ready to use. If you boot from the hard disk, SMARTDRV.SYS is used as your disk-caching program. If you boot from the floppy disk, DISKCACH.SYS is used. All other areas of system operation are identical, regardless of which disk you boot from.

You should note that all device driver directives in the sample CONFIG.SYS file include an explicit reference to the C drive. CONFIG.SYS directives do not specifically require you to include the drive reference if the referenced files are on the boot drive. If you are booting your system from the C drive, therefore, the following two lines have the same effect:

```
DEVICEHIGH=C:\DOS\SMARTDRV.SYS 2048 512
```

```
DEVICEHIGH=\DOS\SMARTDRV.SYS 2048 512
```

On the other hand, when CONFIG.SYS is copied to a floppy disk and the system is booted from the A drive, the two lines are quite different. In that case, the first line loads SMARTDRV.SYS from the C drive and the second line attempts to load it from A:\DOS. You should always include the optional drive designator in both CONFIG.SYS directives and AUTOEXEC.BAT commands, such as the PATH command.

Creating a Boot Floppy to Bypass Hard Disk Optimizing

In the previous example, booting from the floppy disk required changing a CONFIG.SYS directive but keeping the same AUTOEXEC.BAT file. Disk-optimizing software, however, is executed from the DOS command line. A specialized boot disk that prevents disk-optimizing software from automatically running uses the same CONFIG.SYS file as on the hard disk, but includes a change in the AUTOEXEC.BAT file.

As before, begin by formatting a boot disk using the command:

```
FORMAT A: /S /U
```

Then copy CONFIG.SYS and AUTOEXEC.BAT from the C drive to the A drive using the following commands:

```
COPY C:\CONFIG.SYS A:
COPY C:\AUTOEXEC.BAT A:
```

Next, use EDIT to change the copy of AUTOEXEC.BAT in the A drive so that the line that runs the disk-optimizing software is changed to a remark. Suppose, for example, that the line that runs the disk-optimizing software looks similar to the following line:

```
SD C: /U
```

Make the A drive current and load EDIT and AUTOEXEC.BAT by entering the following command:

```
EDIT AUTOEXEC.BAT
```

Move the cursor to the beginning of the line that runs the disk-optimizing software and change it to a remark line by typing REM. The line should now look like the following:

```
REM SD C: /U
```

Write the new AUTOEXEC.BAT file to the floppy disk and exit from the EDIT program. Use the following steps to save and exit: press Alt, File, Exit, and then Yes.

Label the floppy disk, "Standard DOS Boot Without Disk Optimization." If you need to reboot your system but want to bypass disk optimization so you can recover files deleted in error, you can use this new specialized boot disk.

Creating Disks To Share Data between Systems

You may have access to a modern, powerful system at the office and an older, less powerful system that you use to work with at home in the evenings or on weekends. You also may have a need to share data between different PCs in your office. Regardless of the reason, you probably will use floppy disks to carry data from one system to another. Several disk-related commands, including FORMAT, DISKCOPY, and DISKCOMP, may be used to help create these disks.

Copying Disks Successfully

To make copies of disks that can be shared between systems, you need to know how to do the following:

- ❏ Use DISKCOPY to make exact duplicates of disks.
- ❏ Use DISKCOMP to verify that two disks are identical.
- ❏ Save time by using the DISKCOPY /V switch.
- ❏ Prevent problems caused by creating low-density disks in high-capacity drives.

Windows	▼ ▲
Never use a command to copy data while within a DOS window. Either use File Manager or exit to DOS.	

Using DISKCOPY

The DISKCOPY and DISKCOMP commands are exclusively floppy disk commands; they cannot be used to copy or compare hard disks. Both commands work at the track and sector level; that is, they do not use the DOS file system, but instead copy or compare disks as complete units.

Both the source and target disks must be capable of being formatted identically. That is, you cannot use DISKCOPY to copy a 3 1/2-inch disk to a 5 1/4-inch disk or to copy a 5 1/4-inch disk to a 3 1/2-inch disk. If your PC has two floppy disk drives, you can make a DISKCOPY copy between the drives only if they are the same size drives. This does not mean, however, that you cannot use DISKCOPY to duplicate a disk if your drives are not the same—just that the source disk and the target disk must end up identically. If, for example, your A drive is a 1.2M 5-1/4 inch drive and your B drive is a 360K

5 1/4-inch drive, you can DISKCOPY 360K disks using both drives. To DISKCOPY a 1.2M drive, you need to use the A drive for both the source and target by swapping disks.

Reviewing Source and Target

Many DOS commands work with two parameters—the source and the target. The source is the origin, or, in the case of DISKCOPY, the disk that you want to copy. The target is the destination; that is, the disk you want to create.

When you use a command like DISKCOPY and a single disk drive, it is easy to confuse the two, especially if the phone rings while you are trying to keep track of which disk is which. One easy trick that may help prevent errors is to always write-protect the source disk; DISKCOPY never has to write to the source disk.

To write-protect a 5 1/4-inch floppy disk, cover the cutout notch in the side of the disk with a write-protect tab—those little stick-on tabs that are always packed with the disk labels. Make sure the tab will not come off in the drive.

To write-protect 3 1/2-inch disks, move the plastic tab located in the corner of the disk so you can see through the hole. Move the tab back to cover the hole when you want to write to the disk. Incidentally, if you want to reuse a 3 1/2-inch disk that lacks the plastic tab (such as the disks used to distribute some software), simply place a write-protect tab from a 5 1/4-inch disk on the bottom of the 3 1/2-inch disk so it covers the hole. Do not allow the tab to hang over the side of the disk, however, because it jams the disk in the drive.

Windows ▼ ▲

The Disk Copy command in File Manager uses the DOS DISKCOPY. It is a good idea to always write-protect your source floppy.

Copying a Disk with DISKCOPY

To use DISKCOPY on a system with identical floppy disk drives, write-protect the source disk and place it in drive A. Place a new disk, or one that you do not mind losing any files from, in drive B and enter the following command:

```
DISKCOPY A: B:
```

If the two disk drives are the same physical size but have different capacities, you can DISKCOPY a disk that has the capacity of the lower-density drive.

Place the source disk in the higher-capacity drive and the target disk in the lower-capacity drive. Be sure to specify the source and target drives correctly when you issue the DISKCOPY command.

To copy a disk using a single drive, specify the same drive as both the source and the target. To copy a disk using only the A drive, for example, you need to enter the following command:

```
DISKCOPY A: A:
```

DISKCOPY prompts you first to place the source disk in drive A with the following message:

```
Insert SOURCE diskette in drive A:
```

DISKCOPY reads the disk's format and as much of the data as will fit in available memory. Next, DISKCOPY prompts you with the following:

```
Insert TARGET diskette in drive A:
```

If necessary, DISKCOPY prompts you to replace the source disk in drive A so more of the disk's data can be read. If so, after reading additional data, it again prompts you to replace the target disk. This will continue until the disk has been copied completely. When the copy is complete, DISKCOPY will display the target disk's new volume serial number in the following format:

```
Volume Serial Number is xxxx-xxxx
```

DISKCOPY asks if you wish to copy another disk:

```
Copy another diskette (Y/N)?
```

DISKCOPY makes a single copy of a disk. If you answer **Y** to the Copy another diskette (Y/N)? prompt, DISKCOPY prompts you to insert the source disk in the drive.

Comparing Disks with DISKCOMP

Although DISKCOPY makes an exact copy of a disk, you may want to verify that the target disk is an exact duplicate. The DISKCOMP command was designed to compare two floppy disks to make sure no differences exist. DISKCOMP is related closely to DISKCOPY and has the identical restrictions noted for DISKCOPY.

To compare disks using two disk drives, place one disk in drive A, the other in drive B, and enter the following command:

```
DISKCOMP A: B:
```

To compare disks using a single drive, place the first disk in the drive (A in this example) and enter the following command:

```
DISKCOMP A: A:
```

DISKCOMP prompts with the following:

```
Insert FIRST diskette in drive A:
```

Press Enter to begin. DISKCOMP reads the disk's format and reports with a message similar to the following:

```
Comparing x tracks y sectors per track, z side(s)
```

It reads as much of the disk's data as will fit in memory and prompts the following:

```
Insert SECOND diskette in drive A:
```

Like the DISKCOPY command, DISKCOMP prompts you to replace disks if necessary. When it is finished, DISKCOMP reports with the following message if no differences between the disks are found:

```
Compare OK
```

If there are differences, DISKCOMP reports with a similar message as the following one:

```
Compare error on side x, track y
Compare process ended
```

In either case, DISKCOMP asks if you wish to compare more disks:

```
Compare another diskette (Y/N) ?
```

Answer **N** to end the DISKCOMP process.

Comparing Disks Faster with DISKCOPY /V

Copying disks with DISKCOPY and then verifying them with DISKCOMP requires that the source disk be read completely twice and the target disk be read completely once. The DISKCOPY /V switch streamlines the process by eliminating the second read of the source disk. It also reduces the number of times you have to swap disks. Because of this, if you use DISKCOPY with the /V switch, the process of copying and verifying the copy will take only about two-thirds as long as using both DISKCOPY and DISKCOMP.

To copy a disk and verify the copy in a single process, use the following command for dual drives:

```
DISKCOPY A: B: /V
```

To copy a disk and verify the copy in a single process, use the following command for a single drive:

```
DISKCOPY A: A: /V
```

Preventing Problems between High- and Low-Capacity Drives

Although you can format low-capacity floppy disks in high-capacity disk drives, you can experience problems. Usually, disks being read on a 360K drive that were formatted at 360K on a 1.2M drive have problems. This is not a problem, however, with 720K disks that were formatted in 1.44M drive. The reason for this relates directly to a major difference between 5 1/4-inch and 3 1/2-inch disk drives. Table 4.1 shows why.

Table 4.1
Disk-Formatting Specifications

Size	Capacity	Tracks	Sectors
3 1/2-inch	720K	80	9
3 1/2-inch	1.44M	80	18
5 1/4-inch	360K	40	9
5 1/4-inch	1.2M	80	15

Both 3 1/2-inch disk capacities use the same number of tracks—80. The two 5 1/4-inch disk capacities, however, are formatted using two different track counts. If a 1.2M drive is used to format a 360K disk, it does so by formatting every other track. If the disk has existing data from previous use, only half of the old data is overwritten. You can see why the 360K drive, which reads a wider track (equal to two tracks in the 1.2M drive), gets confused.

One way to reduce or eliminate the problem of exchanging data between 1.2M and 360K disk drives is always to format the disk in the 360K drive. The 1.2M drive can then both read and write to the disk without error. Most likely the 360K drive will not have any problem reading the data written by the 1.2M drive, either.

Finding and Correcting Disk Errors

Modern PCs are quite reliable. You probably can use a system for years and never have a single hardware-caused disk problem. Unfortunately, other factors can cause disk problems. Software that crashes can scramble disks so you cannot access them; power failures can do the same. You can even be the cause of disk problems if you think rebooting your system is a shortcut method of exiting programs. Similarly, formatting a disk that contains data you still need can fall under the heading of disk errors.

Using UNFORMAT To Recover from Formatting Errors

UNFORMAT is a command that is new to DOS 5. It is designed to assist when you have accidently formatted a disk. When you format a disk, you do not necessarily destroy all the data on the disk. In versions prior to DOS 5, the FORMAT command wrote over the entire disk, destroying any existing data. With the introduction of DOS 5, however, the operation of the FORMAT command has been modified. FORMAT now has three modes of operation, as described in table 4.2.

Table 4.2
DOS 5 FORMAT Modes

Mode	Switch	Description
Unconditional	/U	Writes over entire disk.
Safe Format	None (default)	Overwrites FAT and root directory, verifies disk.
Quick Format	/Q	Overwrites FAT and root directory, does not verify disk.

If you use either the default Safe Format mode or the Quick Format mode to format disks, none of the data on the disk is overwritten. The UNFORMAT command can then be used to recover any data that was not overwritten by files saved to the disk after formatting.

Suppose you have a data disk that shows the following when you enter the DIR command:

```
C:\>DIR A:

Volume in drive A is DATA 01
Volume Serial Number is 3E23-15DA
```

```
Directory of A:\

NEWP      BAT        37 04-30-91  12:55p
OLDP      BAT        20 04-30-91  12:55p
SCREEN00 TXT       255 04-30-91  12:58p
         3 file(s)           312 bytes
                          359424 bytes free


C:\>
```

Using the new Quick Format mode, you can format the disk using the following command:

FORMAT A: /Q

DOS responds with the following:

```
Insert new diskette for drive A:
and press ENTER when ready...

Checking existing disk format.
Saving UNFORMAT information.
QuickFormatting 360K
Format complete.

Volume label (11 characters, ENTER for none)? OLD DATA

   362496 bytes total disk space
   362496 bytes available on disk

     1024 bytes in each allocation unit.
      354 allocation units available on disk.

Volume Serial Number is 091E-0FE1

QuickFormat another (Y/N)?
```

Answer **N**. Now, to verify that the files that were on the disk are gone, enter the following:

DIR A:

DOS displays the disk directory:

```
Volume in drive A is OLD DATA
Volume Serial Number is 091E-0FE1
Directory of A:\

File not found
```

This indicates that the disk is ready to use and no files are listed in its root directory. To unformat the disk and recover the files, enter the following:

UNFORMAT A:

DOS responds with the following prompt:

```
Insert disk to rebuild in drive A:
and press ENTER when ready.

Restores the system area of your disk by using the image file created
by the MIRROR command.

    WARNING !!        WARNING !!

This command should be used only to recover from the inadvertent use of
the FORMAT command or the RECOVER command. Any other use of the UNFORMAT
command may cause you to lose data!  Files modified since the MIRROR
image
file was created may be lost.

Searching disk for MIRROR image.

The last time the MIRROR or FORMAT command was used was at 08:26 on 05-
06-91.

The MIRROR image file has been validated.

Are you sure you want to update the system area of your drive A (Y/N)?
```

Enter **Y** to continue. The disk will be restored and DOS informs you of the following:

```
The system area of drive A has been rebuilt.

You may need to restart the system.
```

Although DOS tells you that you may need to restart the system, you only need to reboot after using the UNFORMAT command if you have unformatted the disk that contains the active copy of COMMAND.COM (the disk indicated by COMSPEC).

Windows ▼ ▲

UNFORMAT is not yet part of the Windows environment. You can access it by using a DOS window and executing it at the command line. The File Manager's FORMAT command performs a safe copy and creates the file necessary to UNFORMAT the disk.

A Note on the UNFORMAT command

UNFORMAT uses the mirror file—a hidden file that is created by both FORMAT and MIRROR. If the mirror file does not exist, UNFORMAT still attempts to recover the files that existed before the disk was formatted. This method is less reliable, however, because fragmented files are truncated or deleted.

Using CHKDSK To Find and Correct Disk Errors

CHKDSK finds errors in the FAT and the directory structure. The types of errors found by CHKDSK often are related to program crashes, power failures, and rebooting your system instead of properly exiting programs. These "logical" errors result in disk space that is improperly allocated. This is usually a result of the FAT or a directory entry not being correctly updated.

One of the most common problems reported by CHKDSK is *lost clusters*. This term refers to disk clusters that are shown in the FAT as allocated, but in reality are not in use. Other errors found by CHKDSK include *cross-linked files* (the same disk clusters are allocated to more than one file), invalid cluster numbers, defective FAT sectors, and damage to directories.

Windows

Never run CHKDSK from within Windows. It does not recognize Windows' swap files and reports them as lost clusters. If Windows attempts to "fix" these lost clusters, it crashes.

To find disk errors using CHKDSK, you always should first issue the command without the /F (fix errors) switch. This gives you the opportunity to copy files to another disk before allowing CHKDSK to attempt repairs if it does report errors. Enter **CHKDSK** without the /F switch to check for disk errors. You receive a message similar to the following:

```
Volume DATA 01    created 05-06-1991 8:24a
Volume Serial Number is 3E23-15DA
Errors found, F parameter not specified
Corrections will not be written to disk

    1 lost allocation units found in 1 chains.
      1024 bytes disk space would be freed
```

```
362496 bytes total disk space
  3072 bytes in 3 user files
358400 bytes available on disk

  1024 bytes in each allocation unit
   354 total allocation units on disk
   350 available allocation units on disk

651264 total bytes memory
505216 bytes free
```

Notice that CHKDSK reports the following:

```
Errors found, F parameter not specified
Corrections will not be written to disk.
```

This is your cue to take further action. Next, it reports the number and type of errors that were found:

```
1 lost allocation units found in 1 chains.
  1024 bytes disk space would be freed
```

This message indicates that the FAT has an error showing that one disk cluster is marked as allocated to a file, but no directory entry points to the FAT entry. Thus the cluster currently is unavailable for use even though it is not really being used. To correct this error, enter the following:

CHKDSK /F

Each chain of lost clusters are either converted to a file or freed, depending on your response to the following prompt:

```
Convert lost chains to files (Y/N) ?
```

If you answer **N**, the FAT is corrected and the disk space is made available for use. If you answer **Y**, however, each chain is converted to a file, placed in the root directory, and named FILEnnnn.CHK (in which nnnn is a number starting with 0000 and incremented for each additional chain).

The files created by CHKDSK usually are of little use. Unless such a file is a text file (you can examine the files with EDIT), an application program probably will be unable to use the FILEnnnn.CHK file even if you rename it.

You also should note that the number of files allowed in the root directory is limited. Depending on the size and type of disk, between 112 and 512 files are allowed in the root directory. If your disk already contains many files, you may not have room for many FILEnnnn.CHK files. If CHKDSK reports that the root directory is full, you have to copy the FILEnnnn.CHK files to another disk, delete them from the root directory, and restart CHKDSK.

In the preceding example, only one chain of lost clusters existed. Enter the following command:

```
DIR A:
```

This results in the following message:

```
Volume in drive A is DATA 01
Volume Serial Number is 3E23-15DA
Directory of A:\

NEWP     BAT      37 04-30-91  12:55p
OLDP     BAT      20 04-30-91  12:55p
SCREEN00 TXT     255 04-30-91  12:58p
FILE0000 CHK    1024 05-06-91   9:45a
        4 file(s)        1336 bytes
                      358400 bytes free
```

Another type of error CHKDSK can correct is an allocation size error. This type of error results if the size shown in the directory does not match the FAT entry. If, for example, you enter DIR A:, the following display tells you that the file OLDP.BAT probably is not a zero byte file.

```
Volume in drive A is DATA 01
Volume Serial Number is 3E23-15DA
Directory of A:\

NEWP     BAT      37 04-30-91  12:55p
OLDP     BAT       0 04-30-91  12:55p
DATA         <DIR>    05-06-91   9:47a
        3 file(s)          37 bytes
                      356352 bytes free
```

To correct this problem, use the CHKDSK A: /F command. The allocation size for OLDP.BAT is adjusted to match the number of clusters allocated to the file in the FAT, as in the following display:

```
Volume DATA 01    created 05-06-1991 8:24a
Volume Serial Number is 3E23-15DA
A:\OLDP.BAT
   Allocation error, size adjusted

   362496 bytes total disk space
     1024 bytes in 1 directories
```

```
   5120 bytes in 5 user files
 356352 bytes available on disk
   1024 bytes in each allocation unit
    354 total allocation units on disk
    348 available allocation units on disk

 655360 total bytes memory
 527680 bytes free
```

When you issue the DIR A: command, CHKDSK displays the following:

```
Volume in drive A is DATA 01
Volume Serial Number is 3E23-15DA
Directory of A:\

NEWP     BAT       37 04-30-91  12:55p
OLDP     BAT     1024 04-30-91  12:55p
DATA          <DIR>      05-06-91   9:47a
        3 file(s)       1061 bytes
                      356352 bytes free
```

Even though OLDP.BAT originally was listed as 20 bytes, an entire 1024-byte cluster is allocated to the file.

Using RECOVER as a Last Resort

In the DOS file system, subdirectories are a special type of file. If disk errors occur that damage subdirectory entries, CHKDSK is unable to repair the errors. For these types of errors, the RECOVER command may be your only solution. Unfortunately, RECOVER may cause more problems than it solves.

RECOVER has two modes of operation. In the first, it recovers parts of a file that contains defective sectors. DOS itself is unable to read a file with a defective sector. If you use the following syntax, the readable sectors of the file are converted into a new file without the bad sectors.

RECOVER *drive:path*\filename.ext

Because any information that was in the bad sectors is lost, the file probably is of little use. If the file is a simple text file, it may be usable, but program files likely will not run (or if they do, may cause damage to other files). The positive part of the process is that the bad sectors will be marked as bad in the FAT and are not reused.

The second RECOVER mode works at the disk level to recover all the files on the disk. This mode, however, is very dangerous. All of the files and directories on the disk will be converted to files in the root directory. They will be named FILEnnnn.REC (starting with FILE0001.REC and incrementing for each file). As with CHKDSK, the limitations on the number of root directory entries applies. The following is a disk directory listing (using DIR A: /S) before the RECOVER command is issued:

```
Volume in drive A is DATA 01
Volume Serial Number is 3E23-15DA

Directory of A:\

NEWP    BAT        37 04-30-91  12:55p
OLDP    BAT        20 04-30-91  12:55p
DATA         <DIR>     05-06-91   9:47a
        3 file(s)         57 bytes

Directory of A:\DATA

.            <DIR>     05-06-91   9:47a
..           <DIR>     05-06-91   9:47a
SCREEN00 TXT    583 05-06-91   9:15a
SCREEN01 TXT    657 05-06-91   9:45a
SCREEN02 TXT    491 05-06-91   9:47a
        5 file(s)      1731 bytes

Total files listed:
        8 file(s)       1788 bytes
              356352 bytes free
```

Next, use the command RECOVER A:. DOS provides the following warning:

```
The entire drive will be reconstructed,
directory structures will be destroyed.
Are you sure (Y/N)?
```

If you press Y to continue, RECOVER prompts with the following:

```
Press any key to begin recovery of the
file(s) on drive A:
```

RECOVER then reports that 6 files have been recovered. Notice that this does not match the five files that were on the disk. The difference is that the subdirectory named DATA also is converted to a file. If you enter DIR A:, you will see the following message:

```
Volume in drive A has no label
Volume Serial Number is 3E23-15DA

Directory of A:\

FILE0001 REC    1024 05-06-91   9:53a
FILE0002 REC    1024 05-06-91   9:53a
FILE0003 REC    1024 05-06-91   9:53a
FILE0004 REC    1024 05-06-91   9:53a
FILE0005 REC    1024 05-06-91   9:53a
FILE0006 REC    1024 05-06-91   9:53a
         6 file(s)        6144 bytes

Total files listed:
         6 file(s)        6144 bytes
                     356352 bytes free
```

In the preceding message, the volume label has disappeared, the DATA subdirectory has disappeared, and six files with the same size, date, and creation time reside in the root directory. If the disk had contained larger files, they would have had different sizes, but the sizes would all be adjusted up to allocate full clusters. As you can see, recovering even a small number of files with RECOVER takes a long time. If you want to practice using this command, make sure to use a floppy disk with files you do not care about.

To correct the problems caused by using RECOVER, use the Norton Disk Doctor (NDD) program included with the Norton Utilities. This utility includes an option for recovering from the RECOVER command. If, however, you have such severe disk problems that RECOVER is your last resort, you have to examine each FILEnnnn.REC file to try and determine what it originally was, rename it, and go to the next file. The EDIT, TYPE, or DEBUG commands may help you examine the files.

Summary

Staying in control of your disks by learning to use the disk-level commands is important. These commands are used to prepare and directly access disks. Without understanding these commands fully, you can destroy entire disks full of valuable data with a single keystroke.

Chapter 4 helps you understand disk commands and gives you the knowledge you need to safely use them. With the information from this chapter, you can prepare your hard disk, create special-purpose boot disks, and recover from many types of disk errors. After completing this chapter and taking the precautions described, you should have greater confidence in your ability to handle difficult disk-management situations.

In Chapter 5 you will learn how to use tree-structured directories effectively and how to navigate your directories quickly and efficiently.

```
                    MS-DOS Shell
File  Options  View  Tree  Help
┌────┐   ┌────┐   ┌──────┐
│    │A  │    │B  │      │C
└────┘   └────┘   └──────┘
```

5

Navigating Directories

Chapter 4 shows you how to stay in control of your disks using disk-related commands. In this chapter, you learn how to use hierarchical (or tree-structured) directories to increase your productivity.

Topics covered in this chapter include learning to use directory structures, creating and removing directories, moving through directories and keeping track of your location, simplifying directory use with PATH and APPEND, and copying directory structures with the XCOPY command.

Commands for Managing Directories

Several DOS commands help you create, display, and navigate tree-structured directories. These include:

❏ **MD** (or **MKDIR**). Creates directories.

❏ **RD** (or **RMDIR**). Deletes directories.

❏ **CD** (or **CHDIR**). Moves between directories.

❏ **TREE**. Displays directory structure.

❏ **PROMPT**. Keeps track of your current location within the directory structure.

❏ **PATH** and **APPEND**. Simplifies searching for program and data files.

❏ **XCOPY**. Copies directory structures.

147

Learning about Directories

Hierarchical directories can help make using your PC much easier by helping you organize your programs and their associated data files. In addition to examining how directories function, this chapter shows you how to do the following:

❏ Create and remove directories.

❏ Move to a particular directory and quickly return to the original directory.

❏ Create a visual map of directory structures.

❏ Have DOS provide an important reminder of your current location.

❏ Run programs regardless of their location on the disk and help your programs find their required files.

❏ Duplicate directory structures by creating directories and copying files with a single command.

Understanding the Function of Directories

Directories help you organize different files on disk drives. You can, for example, place most of your DOS files in one directory, any word-processing files in another directory, database files in another, and so on. In fact, when you begin to use directories to organize the functions of the various files on your hard disk drive, a natural structure emerges.

Establishing Logical Structure

Different tasks and functions you perform with your computer can be organized into specific directories with the different DOS commands discussed in this chapter. Consider the following groups of functions:

DOS files
    DOS utility programs
    Batch files

Word processing
    Word processor program files
    Documents

Database
    Database manager program files
    Databases

Spreadsheet
    Spreadsheet program files
    Worksheets

If you organize your files in a logical manner, you find that it is much easier to use each type of program and manage the program's associated data files. In fact, you may want to expand the levels of your system's organization. If you use a spreadsheet program, for example, to maintain and calculate your budget, compute your taxes, and prepare sales estimates, you may want to expand the Spreadsheet structure to include the following:

Spreadsheet
    Spreadsheet program files
    Worksheets
        Budget
        Taxes
        Sales

You may want to subdivide several branches of your PC's directories into logical groups. If you do this, you establish a strong basis for setting up the directory structure of your hard disk drive.

Understanding Why Directories are Necessary

Creating directories to help you logically organize your files is one of the best reasons why you should be familiar with directories and directory commands. There are also other more practical reasons why you should understand DOS directories.

File Limitations in the Root Directory

If you want to place all of your files in the primary directory (also called the root directory—a reference to the "tree" structure of hierarchical directories), you probably cannot fit these files in the root directory. DOS places an absolute limit of between 112 and 512 files in the root directory, depending on the type and capacity of the disk. Even though this seems to be a considerable number of files, it is possible to have thousands of files stored on a hard disk drive.

Directories, commonly referred to as subdirectories, are special types of DOS files. Unlike the root directory, subdirectories do not have a predefined size. You can place as many files as you like within a subdirectory—it increases in size as much as necessary.

File Names Cannot be Duplicated

One limitation of DOS is that duplicate file names cannot be in the same directory. If you copy a file into a directory and it has the same name as an existing file, the new file replaces the existing file.

This limitation can be a problem because most application programs are distributed on floppy disks and they contain setup programs with the same file names. In many cases, the program developer provides a program that you use to copy the application program to your hard disk drive and to configure the program to match your system. The name of the program that sets up the application program is often something like SETUP.EXE. Each application program requires its own unique setup program. Imagine the chaos that would result if you tried to install several applications in the root directory?

Another common file name is READ.ME (or some variation). Unless each application has its own subdirectory, this file is overwritten by each new application's READ.ME file.

Understanding the Importance of the Root Directory

New PC users are often confused by the term *root directory* even if they understand the concept of structured tree directories. Every disk, whether it is a hard disk drive or a floppy disk, has a root directory that you do not create and cannot name. Some confused PC users may ask, "if you cannot name the root directory, why is it called the root directory?"

The root directory is the base that you use to build subdirectories. This directory is at the base, or root, of the directory structure. DOS does provide you with a name for the root directory. The backslash (\) refers to the root directory when it precedes any other part of a command argument except for the drive designator. The following command requests a directory listing of the root directory on the current drive:

```
DIR \
```

The next command requests a directory listing of the DOS directory:

```
DIR C:\DOS
```

This directory is actually a subdirectory that is located one level below the root directory on the C drive.

The root directory is one directory that is common to other directories because every subdirectory is built on its base. If you need to issue a command that refers to a directory in another branch of the directory tree, the root directory is always at the base of the pointer to the requested subdirectory.

Understanding the importance of the root directory and the value of subdirectories will help you in the next sections that examine the commands you can use to create, manipulate, and use tree-structured directories.

Windows/DOS Shell	

One of the major advantages of file management with a graphical user interface is that you can see a representation of the directory tree as you work. See Chapter 12 for more information about DOS Shell and examples of the way it presents the directory tree structure.

Creating Logical Directory Structures

As you practice the examples and exercises in the following sections, use a floppy disk drive instead of your hard disk drive. Although tree-structured directory systems are more commonly used on hard disks than on floppy disks, there is no restriction in DOS that prevents you from creating subdirectories on any type of disk. It is easier to try out the examples on floppy disks and then use what you learn to develop the best structure for your own situation. Regardless of the practice method you choose, the commands are identical whether you work with a hard disk or a floppy disk.

Developing Directory Structures

Before you create directories, consider the directory structure you want to use. As you saw earlier, organizing files by function is a good starting point. Other considerations apply as well. In the following sections you learn how to do the following:

- ❏ Decide on a logical directory structure based on function.
- ❏ Create directory names that make directories easier to use.
- ❏ Create a complete structured tree directory.

Deciding on the Directory Structure

A logical breakdown into separate functions is usually the best way to start developing your directories. The sample organization that was suggested earlier might help you organize your PC files.

The first thing you should to if you want to organize your directories is to make a list that outlines every function your system performs. This list can be similar to the list in the section on establishing logical structures. Break down and list each function as a logical group so that you can see that your programs are used for specialized functions in addition to more generalized use. The spreadsheet program, for example, lists the special functions as well as any general operations performed with the application:

> Spreadsheet
>> Spreadsheet program files
>> Worksheets
>>> Budget
>>> Taxes
>>> Sales

Be as complete as possible with your list—you can always combine groups of specialized functions if you find they do not warrant their own subdirectory.

After you map out individual functions, continue with the next step—determining the best naming scheme.

Windows
Because of the integrated nature of the Windows environment, Windows users may find it easier to group documents (whether word processing, spreadsheets, databases, or others) by task. Thus, a Windows user might have a subdirectory called PROJECTS, which contains a subdirectory for each project.

Naming Directories Effectively

Directory names follow many of the same rules as file names:

❑ Directory names can contain up to eight characters.

❑ Directory names can have an extension of up to three characters following a period.

❑ You can use the characters A through Z, 0 through 9, and the following:

  ^ $ ~ ! # % & - { } ( ).

❑ DOS does not accept special characters, such as , . \ < > | * ? +, although a single period is allowed if followed by one to three characters.

❑ You can use extended characters (ASCII 128 to 255) in a directory name.

❏ Directories may be nested several levels deep. A file's complete path name, however, cannot exceed 66 characters, including the drive designator and the colon (:) that follows it.

❏ Two subdirectories within a directory cannot have the same name.

Although these specific rules apply, you may want to apply some of your own rules as well. Use directory names, for example, that clearly indicate the directory's contents. This limitation helps you remember that each directory contains the files you need. Do not use extensions on directory names, however, because it is easy to confuse a directory name that has an extension with the name of a file. When you examine the PATH statement in a later section, you will learn that program directory names should be kept short by not placing program directories too many levels deep in the directory structure.

Using MD To Create the Directory Structure

The DOS Make Directory command, MD (or MKDIR), creates directories. MD has the following syntax:

`MD drive:directory name`

To create a directory called 123 as a subdirectory of the root directory on the A drive, type the following command:

`MD A:\123`

The MD command does not confirm that it has created a directory. If no errors occur, the DOS prompt simply returns. If you attempt to create a directory and you use a name that already exists, DOS responds with the message:

`Directory already exists`

MD is unable to create a subdirectory before its parent directory exists. For example, if you attempt to create a directory A:\123\DATA before the directory A:\123 exists, DOS responds with the message:

`Unable to create directory`

If the directory you want to create is a subdirectory immediately below the current directory, you can eliminate both the drive designator and the backslash. To create a directory called DOS as a subdirectory of the root directory on the A drive, first make sure the A drive is the current drive and the root directory is the current directory by typing the following commands:

`A:`
`CD \`

The CD command (for Change Directory) is covered later in this chapter. To create the DOS directory, simply type:

```
MD DOS
```

The MD command does not confirm that directories are created, so type **DIR** to see that the two directories are listed as in the following lines:

```
Volume in drive A is DIRECTORIES
Volume Serial Number is 1479-11E5
Directory of A:\
COMMAND   COM   47867   03-08-91      5:05a
123   <DIR>         05-07-91     10:42a
DOS   <DIR>         05-07-91     10:38a
3 file(s)   47867 bytes
        1093120 bytes free
```

Now that you know the 123 directory exists, you can issue the command:

```
MD 123\DATA
```

The backslash is used as a separator between directory names. In this example, the backslash between 123 and DATA means that the DATA directory is a subdirectory of the 123 directory. The command MD 123\DATA creates the DATA directory as a subdirectory of the 123 directory, which is a subdirectory of the current directory.

This command does not produce an error message because the parent directory (123) of the DATA directory already exists. Create three more subdirectories that are subordinate to the 123\DATA directory by issuing the following commands:

```
MD A:\123\DATA\BUDGET
MD 123\DATA\SALES
MD \123\DATA\TAXES
```

Note that each of the three variations of the MD command functioned properly. In each case enough information was supplied so the command could find the proper pathway to the parent directory and create the new directory.

Figure 5.1 shows the structure of the directories that you just created. As you can see, the 123 directory and the DOS directory are both at the same level—that is, both are subdirectories of the A (or root) directory. The DATA directory is the next level, and is a subdirectory of the 123 directory. Finally, the DATA directory has three subdirectories: BUDGET, SALES, and TAXES.

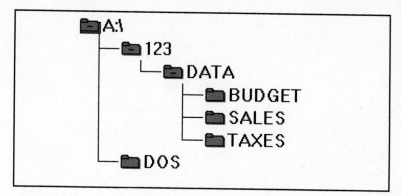

Figure 5.1:
The disk directory structure created with MD commands.

In this example, the 123 directory is the parent directory of the DATA directory, that in turn is the parent of BUDGET, SALES, and TAXES. The root directory is the parent of both the 123 and DOS directories. These relationships become important when you want to move between different directories.

Removing Directories from the Structure

If you no longer use a particular program or subdirectory of a project that you finished, or if you want to rename an existing directory, you should know how to remove directories.

There are several commands you can use when you remove directories. In the following sections you learn how to:

❏ Remove empty directories with the RD command.

❏ Handle directories that are not empty with the DIR, DEL, and ATTRIB commands.

Using RD to Remove Directories

DOS provides the RD (or RMDIR) command for removing directories. The syntax of the command is the following:

RD *drive:directory*

To remove the A:\DOS\BATCH directory, for example, use the command:

RD A:\DOS\BATCH

The RD command functions much like the MD command. Both the drive designator and the first backslash (indicating the root directory) may be optional, depending on the current drive and directory.

Windows/DOS Shell

It is more efficient to use a graphical system than the DOS command line to create or change your directory structure because you can see the effect of your actions. In addition, both DOS Shell and Windows provide tools for moving files between directories without having to first copy them and, as a separate step, delete the originals.

Removing Directories that are not Empty

You cannot use the RD command to remove a directory that contains files because removing the directory also deletes any files and any subdirectories contained in the directory.

Suppose the A:\DOS\BATCH directory contains files and you type the following command:

    RD A:\DOS\BATCH

Instead of removing the directory, DOS reports:

    Invalid path, not directory,
    or directory not empty

The error message indicates three possible errors. The Invalid path message means that the directory name you typed was incorrect. This could be due to a simple typing error or a misspelled path name. This message also displays if you do not specify the complete path name needed to find the desired directory from the current DOS location. Suppose, for example, that the current directory is the A:\123 directory shown in Figure 5.1. If you type the following command, you tell DOS to remove a subdirectory named DOS\BATCH that is subordinate to the A:\123 directory:

    RD DOS\BATCH

Clearly, as you can see in Figure 5.1, there is no directory named A:\123\DOS\BATCH.

The second error message is not directory. This message signifies that the RD command can only remove directories—not standard DOS files. (Recall that directories are a special type of DOS file that require directory commands instead of file commands.)

The `directory not empty` message tells you that the directory you tried to delete still contains either files or subdirectories. You have to empty the directory before you can remove it.

To determine if the A:\DOS\BATCH directory contains files or subdirectories or both, type the following:

```
DIR A:\DOS\BATCH
```

DOS responds with the following information:

```
Volume in drive A is DIRECTORIES
Volume Serial Number is 1479-11E5
Directory of A:\DOS\BATCH
.            <DIR>          05-07-91     12:56p
..           <DIR>          05-07-91     12:56p
DISK1    TXT      210       05-01-91      4:37p
DISK2    TXT      210       05-01-91      4:37p
4 file(s)         420 bytes
          1089024 bytes free
```

Although the A:\DOS\BATCH directory appears to contain two files and two subdirectories, the first two lines are actually special DOS references.

```
.            <DIR>          05-07-91     12:56p
..           <DIR>          05-07-91     12:56p
```

The single period (or dot) is a reference to the current directory—in this case the A:\DOS\BATCH directory. The double dots (. .) refer to the parent of the current directory—in this case A:\DOS. You often can use the single or double dots as a shorthand method for supplying arguments to commands. The DEL . command, for example, is equivalent to DEL *.*. If your current directory were the A:\DOS\BATCH directory, the command DIR .. is the same as DIR A:\DOS.

Now that you know the single dot (.) and double dot (..) entries are not subdirectories of A:\DOS\BATCH, you can delete the files in A:\DOS\BATCH and then try the RD command again. Type the command:

```
DEL A:\DOS\BATCH\*.*
```

This command can remove all of the files in a directory. After you press Enter, DOS prompts:

```
All files in directory will be deleted!
Are you sure (Y/N)?
```

Type **Y** if you want to proceed. Next, re-enter the command to remove the A:\DOS\BATCH directory:

```
RD A:\DOS\BATCH
```

Once again, DOS responds with the familiar message:

```
Invalid path, not directory,
or directory not empty
```

Clearly there is still a problem. Rechecking your command shows that the directory name is spelled correctly and the path is specified. Perhaps a file survived the DEL command. Check the directory listing again by typing:

```
DIR A:\DOS\BATCH
```

This time DOS responds with this message:

```
Volume in drive A is DIRECTORIES
Volume Serial Number is 1479-11E5
Directory of A:\DOS\BATCH
.           <DIR>           05-07-91    12:56p
..          <DIR>           05-07-91    12:56p
        2 file(s)         0 bytes
              1090048 bytes free
```

The only two listings are the single (.) and double (..) dot files that you now know are not files or subdirectories of A:\DOS\BATCH. Why, then, does the error message display when you try to delete this sample directory?

Programs occasionally create hidden files. Before copy protection schemes were widely abandoned, manufacturers used hidden files (and even hidden subdirectories) as a form of copy protection. If you try to remove an old, copy-protected program, you may find it has left hidden files that prevent you from easily removing no longer needed directories. Fortunately, DOS provides another tool that enables you to examine and change file attributes. The ATTRIB command can show you any hidden files that do not appear with DIR unless you use the /A:attributes argument. To use ATTRIB to check the A:\DOS\BATCH directory, type the following:

```
ATTRIB DOS\BATCH\*.*
```

In this case, DOS responds with this message:

```
H  A:\DOS\BATCH\DISK3.TXT
```

Windows/DOS Shell
Both Windows and DOS Shell present attribute information in an easy-to-read format that enables you to change attributes while you view them.

This tells you that a hidden file, DISK3.TXT, remains in A:\DOS\BATCH. The DEL command does not delete hidden files, so you must change DISK3.TXT's file attributes so it is not marked as a hidden file.

```
ATTRIB -H DOS\BATCH\DISK3.TXT
```

This line removes the hidden file attribute from DISK3.TXT. You can now delete the file using the command:

```
DEL DOS\BATCH\DISK3.TXT
```

Finally, remove the directory by typing this line:

```
RD DOS\BATCH
```

This time DOS gives you no error message. Just to be sure the directory is gone, type the following:

```
DIR DOS /S
```

This command requests a directory listing for A:\DOS and any of its subdirectories. DOS responds with these messages:

```
Volume in drive A is DIRECTORIES
Volume Serial Number is 1479-11E5
Directory of A:\DOS
  .          <DIR>          05-07-91     10:38a
  ..         <DIR>          05-07-91     10:38a
     2 file(s)         0 bytes
Total files listed:
     2 file(s)         0 bytes
          1091072 bytes free
```

There are no subdirectories shown for A:\DOS, so you finally were successful in removing A:\DOS\BATCH.

DOS Shell   ▼ ▲

The DOS Shell File List can be set to include hidden and system files.
When this feature is activated, these files can be manipulated in the
same way as regular files. To display hidden and system files, use the
File Display option under the Options menu.

Using FORMAT /Q To Remove Directory Structures

If you want to remove individual directories from a disk, you must use the RD
command. You cannot use the DEL command because directories are a special type of file. This means that removing a large number of files and
subdirectories from a disk can involve many steps. DOS 5 provides a shortcut
method for quickly removing all files and subdirectories in a single step. The
FORMAT /Q command performs a "quick format" of the disk. Although this
destroys any files on the disk, it is the fastest method of preparing a disk for
reuse. Chapter 4 covered the FORMAT command options in detail.

Moving around the Directory Structure

There is more to efficient directories than just logical directory structures—
you must also have an efficient way to move through the structure. The next
few sections show you how to use the CD command to navigate your directories. Later in the sections you look at some advanced techniques that make it
much easier to quickly move to any branch of the tree with a minimum of
keystrokes.

You learn how to use the CD (or CHDIR) command to perform the following
tasks:

❑ Determine the current directory.

❑ Change the current directory.

❑ Create batch files that remember the current directory and enable
   you to quickly return to the original directory after moving to another directory.

❑ Create a DOSKEY macro shortcut method for moving to a specific
   directory.

A Note on Directory Paths

Although directory paths are discussed in several places in the text, some basic concepts need to be reviewed:

❑ Each disk has a "root" directory that is referred to by an initial backslash (\).

❑ Unlike any other directories on a disk, the root directory does not have a name.

❑ All named directories are subdirectories subordinate by one or more levels relative to the root directory.

❑ A complete path name starts with the drive designator and shows the complete route from the root directory, through all subordinate directories, and ends with the file name.

❑ A single period or dot (.) can be used as shorthand for the current directory. Double periods (..) can be used as shorthand for the parent of the current directory.

DOS Shell

The DOS Shell provides a visual representation of all the directories on the disk. The current directory is highlighted and you can use the arrow keys to move through the tree. All the shortcuts for working with directory names in commands are still available. In addition, a number of other shortcuts are available (for example, moving to a directory by typing the first letter of the directory name). These features are discussed in detail in Chapter 12.

Determining the Current Directory with CD

In order to navigate effectively in a directory structure, you must first know your current location in the directory. Later in this chapter you learn how to use the PROMPT command to force DOS to constantly inform you of the current directory. If you decide not to modify your prompt, you can simply type **CD** and DOS responds by displaying the current directory. If you are still working with the sample disk created earlier, DOS might respond with this path:

```
A:\123\DATA\BUDGET
```

With no parameters, the CD command simply displays the current directory. This is handy, especially if you use someone else's PC and you don't want to make any changes to their system.

Changing the Current Directory with CD

To change the current directory instead of just displaying it, add a path to the CD command. You may have to use a path argument that includes the entire path from the root directory or you may be able to use a simplified path. The path statement you can use depends on the relationship of the new directory to the current directory before the command is issued.

To see how this path structure works, refer to the directory structure shown in Figure 5.1. Suppose that when you issue the CD command without any arguments, DOS responds with this message:

    A:\123\DATA

To change the current directory to A:\DOS, you must reference the complete path from the root directory to the A:\DOS directory. The A:\DOS directory is not subordinate to the A:\123\DATA directory. In addition, A:\DOS is not subordinate to the A:\123 directory, which is the parent of the current directory. The only common element shared by the current directory A:\123\DATA and the desired A:\DOS directory is the root directory on the A drive. For this reason, you must type the following command to make the change:

    CD \DOS

Notice that the drive designator is not used. When you change current directories on the current drive, you do not have to include the drive designator.

Suppose that instead of changing to the A:\DOS directory, you want to change the current directory from A:\123\DATA to A:\123\DATA\TAXES. In this case, the desired directory is subordinate to the current directory, so you need only type the following:

    CD TAXES

To confirm that the current directory has indeed changed, type **CD** and DOS responds:

    A:\123\DATA\TAXES

As an alternative to the command CD TAXES, you can type the command and include the entire path from the root to the TAXES directory:

    CD \123\DATA\TAXES

This, however, might lead you to make a common syntax mistake. While both CD TAXES and CD \123\DATA\TAXES are correct, the following shortcut is incorrect:

```
CD \TAXES
```

If you type this line and press Enter, DOS responds with this message:

```
Invalid directory
```

Remember that the initial backslash refers to the root directory. Thus, the command CD \TAXES tells DOS to change the current directory to A:\TAXES, not A:\123\DATA\TAXES.

Occasionally, you can use a shortcut when you want to change directories because the parent of the current directory can be entered as two periods (..). Assume you were successful in changing the current directory to A:\123\DATA\TAXES, but you found that you instead needed to make the A:\123\DATA\SALES directory current. DOS provides two ways to make this change. First, you can type:

```
CD \123\DATA\SALES
```

You also can type the following line:

```
CD ..\SALES
```

Either command changes the current directory. The second command line, however, is shorter, faster to type, and less prone to typing errors.

The CD command also enables you to change the current directory on another drive without making the other drive the default drive. If the current default drive is the C drive, you can change the current directory on the A drive by typing:

```
CD A:\DOS
```

You can simplify the use of many commands by changing the current directory on a noncurrent drive because the current directory on a drive is always used as the default directory for the file-related commands.

Using Batch Files To Track Directories

Although the sample disk directory structure, illustrated in figure 5.1, has deliberately been kept simple, you can see that changing the current directory often requires a large number of keystrokes. Even more complex is the task of changing the current directory, performing whatever function required the change, and then returning to the original directory. DOS does not provide a "return to original directory" command. In the next exercise, you learn how to create this command.

A Note on Customizing DOS

This example makes use of redirection, a concept that is covered in detail in Chapter 7. Batch files are covered in depth in chapter 13.

To create your own command, start by creating a file called THISDIR.TXT. This file is used as a template by the first batch file when it creates a batch file that saves the current directory. A copy of this file is on the enclosed disk as THISDIR.TXT. To create it yourself, type the following:

```
CD \DOS
COPY CON THISDIR.TXT
@ ECHO OFF
SET THISDIR=
```

Do not press Enter after the equal sign (=). Instead, make sure the cursor immediately follows the equal sign (=, with no spaces), and then press the F6 function key. This places the ^Z (Control Z) characters on the screen. After you do this, press Enter.

If you made no mistakes in the exercise, DOS responds with the familiar message:

```
1 file(s) copied
```

Next, you need the main batch file THISDIR.BAT, which does most of the work. Type the following lines:

```
COPY CON THISDIR.BAT
@ECHO OFF
REM Save the current directory in the CURDIR file in the DOS directory
CD > \DOS\CURDIR
REM Make a copy of THISDIR.TXT and calls it HERE.BAT
COPY \DOS\THISDIR.TXT \DOS\HERE.BAT
REM Append the current directory to the SET THISDIR= command in HERE.BAT
TYPE \DOS\CURDIR >> \DOS\HERE.BAT
REM Run HERE.BAT to set the THISDIR environment variable to the current
directory
CALL \DOS\HERE
REM Delete the temporary files
DEL \DOS\HERE.BAT
DEL \DOS\CURDIR
```

After you enter the final line, press the F6 function key and then the Enter key. DOS once again responds with the `1 file(s) copied` message.

The final batch file is used to create the file to return you to your original directory. Enter these commands:

```
COPY CON HOME.BAT
@ECHO OFF
CD %THISDIR%
SET THISDIR=
```

After typing the final line, press the F6 function key immediately after the equal sign (=), and then press Enter.

Again, DOS responds with the `1 file(s) copied` message to confirm your commands.

In order to use these batch files, type the following at the DOS prompt to save the current directory:

```
\DOS\THISDIR
```

You are then free to change to any other directory on the same disk. To return to the original directory, simply type:

```
\DOS\HOME
```

Later in this chapter you learn how to use the PATH command to simplify running program files that are not in the current directory. Once you do, if your PATH environment variable includes the \DOS directory, you simply type THISDIR to save the current directory, and HOME to return to the original directory.

Streamlining CD with Macros

DOS 5 has an advanced feature called *macros* that you use with the new DOSKEY command. Macros are covered in more detail in Chapter 13, but the following examples show you one way to use macros to streamline the process of changing directories.

Imagine that you often need to work with files in the A:\123\DATA\TAXES directory. Depending on your current drive and directory, you may have to enter either one or two commands to make the A:\123\DATA\TAXES directory current. You may or may not be able to use a short path name for the directory, depending on the directory that is current on drive A.

To make sure the commands you enter always have the same effect, it is safest to type two commands at the DOS prompt. The first command line ensures that the A drive is the current drive, and the second line uses a complete path name to specify the \123\DATA\TAXES directory. The two commands you would type in the sample directory are the following:

```
A:
CD \123\DATA\TAXES
```

To turn these commands into a DOSKEY macro, type the following command:

```
DOSKEY TAXES=A:  $T CD \123\DATA\TAXES
```

Then, when you type TAXES at the DOS command prompt, the two commands are executed and the A:\123\DATA\TAXES directory becomes the current directory.

DOSKEY macros disappear when you turn the power off or reboot the system. Chapter 13 shows you how to save your macros for future use.

The DOS Shell program offers an alternative to the CD command for changing the current directory. In many cases, however, typing a command at the command prompt is faster.

Using TREE To Map Your Directory Structure

Figure 5.1 displays the directory structure of the exercise disk in a clear, easily understood map. In this section, you learn how to use the TREE command to produce a similar map. With a map of a disk's directories, you will find that it is much easier to move around the disk and keep track of your files.

The following sections show you how to accomplish the following tasks:

- ❑ Use the TREE command to display all or part of the map of a disk's directory structure.
- ❑ Force TREE to use graph characters that you can print on any printer or import into a word processor for editing.
- ❑ Display the names of the files in the directories displayed by TREE.

Displaying the Directory Map with TREE

Several factors determine whether TREE displays all or part of a disk's directory map. If you specify neither a drive nor a directory, the map shows every directory that is subordinate to the current directory on the current drive. If you specify a drive, the TREE map shows every directory that is subordinate to the current directory on the specified drive. If you specify a directory but not a drive, TREE lists all the directories subordinate to the specified directory on the current drive. Finally, if you specify both a drive and a directory, the map show all directories subordinate to the specified directory on the specified drive.

If the exercise disk you created for this chapter is in drive A, for example, the A drive is the current drive, and the root directory is the current directory. If you type **TREE**, a map displays like the map in figure 5.2.

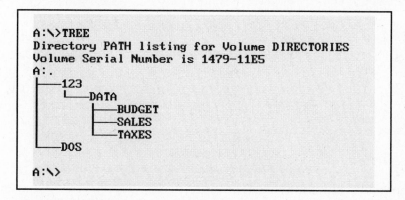

```
A:\>TREE
Directory PATH listing for Volume DIRECTORIES
Volume Serial Number is 1479-11E5
A:.
├───123
│   └───DATA
│           ├───BUDGET
│           ├───SALES
│           └───TAXES
└───DOS

A:\>
```

Figure 5.2:
The directory structure shown by the TREE command.

As you can see, the map displayed by TREE is similar to the map shown in figure 5.1. Obviously, this map is useful in navigating the disk directory structure. Sometimes, however, you may not need a complete map. It may, for example, be easier to keep track of your 123 data directories if the map only shows directories subordinate to the A:\123 directory. If you type **TREE 123**, a list appears, similar to figure 5.3.

```
A:\>TREE 123
Directory PATH listing for Volume DIRECTORIES
Volume Serial Number is 1479-11E5
A:123
└───DATA
        ├───BUDGET
        ├───SALES
        └───TAXES

A:\>
```

Figure 5.3:
A partial directory map produced by TREE.

The map is restricted and only shows the directory structure in the A:\123 branch of the tree.

Using ASCII Characters in the TREE Map

The horizontal and vertical lines TREE uses to display its map do not print properly on some printers. In addition, word processing programs often use the same codes to display accented characters instead of lines. If your printer does not support the graphics characters or if you try to import the directory map into a word processing program, you may see a display similar to this:

```
Directory PATH listing for Volume DIRECTORIES
Volume Serial Number is 1479-11E5
A:.
√ÄÄÄ123
|   ¿ÄÄÄDATA
|       √ÄÄÄBUDGET
|       √ÄÄÄSALES
|       ¿ÄÄÄTAXES
¿ÄÄÄDOS
```

The TREE command includes a switch that forces it to create the map with standard ASCII characters like the vertical bar (|), the plus sign (+), the slash (\), and the hyphen (-). If you type TREE /A, DOS displays the following lines:

```
Directory PATH listing for Volume DIRECTORIES
Volume Serial Number is 1479-11E5
A:.
+--123
|   \--DATA
|       +--BUDGET
|       +--SALES
|       \--TAXES
\--DOS
```

Even though this map is rougher than the normal TREE display, it is certainly better than the previous map that displayed accented characters.

A Note on Redirecting Tree Maps

If you wish to import the disk directory map into a word processing document, redirect the output of the TREE command to a file (redirection is covered in Chapter 7). Type the following command to place the map into the file, then import it as a text file:

```
TREE /A >DISK.MAP
```

Using TREE To Display Files in Subdirectories

Sometimes it is helpful to have a map of the location of your files on a disk. The TREE /F command does just this—it lists the files and the disk's structure map. Remember, however, that this form of the command shows all of the files in the specified directories. You may want to limit the map to a particular subset of the disk directory structure to keep the list from becoming too large.

To display the location of the files in the data directories under the A:\123 directory, for example, you can either specify the A:\123\DATA directory as an argument to the TREE command, or make the A:\123\DATA directory current via the CD command. Figure 5.4 shows how the TREE /F command displays the file locations on the directory map.

```
A:\123\DATA>TREE /F
Directory PATH listing for Volume DIRECTORIES
Volume Serial Number is 1479-11E5
A:.
    ├──BUDGET
    │      QTR1_BUD.WK1
    │      QTR2_BUD.WK1
    │      QTR3_BUD.WK1
    │      QTR4_BUD.WK1
    │
    ├──SALES
    │      QTR1_SAL.WK1
    │      QTR2_SAL.WK1
    │      QTR3_SAL.WK1
    │      QTR4_SAL.WK1
    │
    └──TAXES
           QTR1_TAX.WK1
           QTR2_TAX.WK1
           QTR3_TAX.WK1
           QTR4_TAX.WK1

A:\123\DATA>
```

Figure 5.4:
A directory map showing file locations.

Alternatives to TREE in DOS 5

Both the CHKDSK and the DIR commands include options that display a map of the files on a disk. These maps, however, are not as useful for navigating the disk directory structure. If you type CHKDSK A: /V, for example, the following list appears:

```
Volume DIRECTORIES created 05-07-1991 10:41a
Volume Serial Number is 1479-11E5
Directory A:\
```

```
A:\IO.SYS
A:\MSDOS.SYS
A:\COMMAND.COM
Directory A:\123
Directory A:\123\DATA
Directory A:\123\DATA\BUDGET
A:\123\DATA\BUDGET\QTR1_BUD.WK1
A:\123\DATA\BUDGET\QTR2_BUD.WK1
A:\123\DATA\BUDGET\QTR3_BUD.WK1
A:\123\DATA\BUDGET\QTR4_BUD.WK1
Directory A:\123\DATA\SALES
A:\123\DATA\SALES\QTR1_SAL.WK1
A:\123\DATA\SALES\QTR2_SAL.WK1
A:\123\DATA\SALES\QTR3_SAL.WK1
A:\123\DATA\SALES\QTR4_SAL.WK1
Directory A:\123\DATA\TAXES
A:\123\DATA\TAXES\QTR1_TAX.WK1
A:\123\DATA\TAXES\QTR2_TAX.WK1
A:\123\DATA\TAXES\QTR3_TAX.WK1
A:\123\DATA\TAXES\QTR4_TAX.WK1
Directory A:\DOS
    1213952 bytes total disk space
      71680 bytes in 2 hidden files
       3072 bytes in 6 directories
      75776 bytes in 13 user files
    1063424 bytes available on disk
        512 bytes in each allocation unit
       2371 total allocation units on disk
       2077 available allocation units on disk
     651264 total bytes memory
     505216 bytes free
```

Although all of the directories are listed, the display is clearly not usable as a map for navigating around in the directories.

The DIR command includes a new /S switch in DOS 5 that tells the DIR command to process subdirectories. If you type the command DIR A: /S, the following screen displays:

```
Volume in drive A is DIRECTORIES
Volume Serial Number is 1479-11E5
Directory of A:\
COMMAND   COM   47867   03-08-91   5:05a
```

```
FIG55B      DOC         0   05-08-91    2:32p
IO          SYS     33430   03-08-91    5:05a
MSDOS       SYS     37394   03-08-91    5:05a
        4 file(s)          118691 bytes

Directory of A:\123\DATA\BUDGET
QTR1_BUD    WK1      2072   04-16-91   12:02p
QTR2_BUD    WK1      1903   02-15-91    7:32a
QTR3_BUD    WK1      2467   01-19-91   11:36a
QTR4_BUD    WK1      1600   03-16-91   11:53a
        4 file(s)            8042 bytes

Directory of A:\123\DATA\SALES
QTR1_SAL    WK1      2207   04-19-91    2:02p
QTR2_SAL    WK1      1933   02-18-91    8:23a
QTR3_SAL    WK1      2533   01-17-91    9:43a
QTR4_SAL    WK1      1730   03-17-91   12:53a
        4 file(s)            8403 bytes

Directory of A:\123\DATA\TAXES
QTR1_TAX    WK1      2072   04-22-91   12:02p
QTR2_TAX    WK1      1899   02-23-91    7:32a
QTR3_TAX    WK1      2345   01-24-91   11:36a
QTR4_TAX    WK1      1576   03-17-91   11:53a
        4 file(s)            7892 bytes
Total files listed:
       16 file(s)     143028 bytes
                    1061888 bytes free
```

Even though this is more useful than what results when you use the CHKDSK /V command, it is clear that the TREE command is the best choice for producing a map of your disk's directory structure.

DOS Shell ▼ ▲

The DOS Shell permits you to view a list of all files on your disk that can be sorted several different ways. The Search command creates a list of files similar to the one from DIR/S.

The DIR/S/B command creates a list of files that match the search criteria without the directory information. This file can then be used in batch files to manipulate the listed file.

Using PROMPT To Display the Current Directory

Earlier you learned that issuing the CD command without any arguments makes DOS display the current directory. You can use the PROMPT command to cause the current directory to always display on the DOS command line.

PROMPT is a command that assigns a value to the environment variable of the same name: PROMPT. There are thirteen predefined parameters that can be used to set the value of the PROMPT variable. You also can include any other text at the prompt. One of the predefined parameters, $P (for PATH), tells DOS to include the current drive designator and the current directory in the DOS prompt. The predefined parameters you can use with the PROMPT command are illustrated in table 5.1.

Table 5.1
PROMPT Parameters

Code	Character	Description
$Q	=	Equal sign
$$	$	Dollar sign
$T		Current time
$D		Current date
$P		Current drive and path
$V		MS-DOS version number
$N		Current drive
$G	>	Greater-than sign
$L	<	Less-than sign
$B	|	Pipe
$H		Backspace (erases previous character)
$E		Escape code (ASCII code 27)
$_		Carriage return and linefeed

If no value has been set for PROMPT with the PROMPT or SET PROMPT= commands, DOS only displays the drive designator and a greater-than symbol as the DOS prompt:

A>

To change the DOS prompt so it shows the current drive and directory, type the following command:

```
PROMPT $P
```

Even though this command works, you may find it produces a slightly confusing DOS prompt because there is no separator between the current directory and any command you might type following the prompt. To modify the prompt for clarity, include the $G parameter:

```
PROMPT $P $G
```

This changes the displayed DOS prompt to show the current drive and directory, a space, and then the greater-than symbol.

A Note on the DOS Prompt and Setup

If the DOS 5 Setup program does not find a PROMPT command in the AUTOEXEC.BAT file, it automatically places the following line in the file:

```
PROMPT $P$G
```

NetWare

You can set the prompt in your NetWare Login Scripts with the DOS SET Login Script Command. The correct syntax is: DOS SET PROMPT = "PG". Note the quotation marks around the value. These marks will not show up when you check the PROMPT environment variable by typing **SET** at the DOS prompt. The marks are necessary to the NetWare DOS SET command when setting any environment variable.

Simplifying Directory Searches with PATH and APPEND

Tree-structured directories greatly assist in organizing your application programs and their associated data files. Unfortunately, this same organization adds a certain level of complexity as well. When you want to run a program or use a data file that is not in the current directory, for example, you must specify the complete path name to a file or DOS won't find the file. You can use the PATH and APPEND commands, however, to help DOS find files and solve this problem.

In the following sections you learn how to use the PATH and APPEND commands to run programs and access data files without having to consider their location in the disk directory structure.

Understanding the Difference between PATH and APPEND

DOS accepts three file extensions for executable programs: BAT, COM, and EXE. Unless a file uses one of these three extensions, DOS does not recognize it as a program file. The PATH command provides extended search capabilities for program files. In other words, PATH may help you start your word processor from another directory, but it cannot help the word processor find your documents.

Windows/DOS Shell	

Both Windows and DOS Shell provide an association feature that enables you to activate a program by selecting a document. If the document files are well-organized, this command solves the problem of linking documents and applications. This feature is discussed in detail in Chapter 12.

The APPEND command is similar to the PATH command except that it works with program files and, more importantly, data files. The APPEND command is similar to the PATH command except that it works with data files—not just program files. If you include an APPEND command with a PATH command, you can access many types of files.

NetWare

Do not attempt to change the path manually using PATH=... NetWare requires that you use its MAP utility to create any NetWare Search Drives that allow NetWare to set the DOS PATH. The correct syntax for setting the PATH to include the WINDOWS directory on the local hard drive might be: MAP INSERT S2:=C:\WINDOWS. (Map a search drive to C:\WINDOWS, add C:\WINDOWS to the path, and make this new drive the second drive in the MAP and PATH.) Typing **MAP** by itself at the DOS prompt, when logged into a NetWare server, supplies a list of all current drive mappings.

NetWare

The NetWare MAP utility performs almost exactly the same way as the DOS APPEND /X:ON routine. MAP finds both executable and data files on SEARCH DRIVES much like the APPEND command does for local DOS drives. APPEND may be used for local DOS drives, but MAP INSERT S{search drive number}:={server volume name}:{directory name} should be used when you need the functionality of APPEND on a NetWare Drive.

Using PATH and APPEND

Effective use of the PATH and APPEND commands requires that you learn several tasks. In the following sections you learn how to:

❏ Use the PATH and SET commands to set and display a program search path.

❏ Add directories to the program search path.

❏ Store the current program search path so you can set a different PATH and then return to the original PATH.

❏ Use the APPEND command to set a data file search path.

Setting Program Search Paths with PATH

The earlier example showed you how to use batch files to navigate through complex tree-structured directories. These exercises also introduced a problem with tree-structured directories: you have to specify the path name to the batch files whenever you want to use them, because you want to use the batch files regardless of your location in the directory tree. This is not too much of a burden when the batch files are located in the \DOS directory, but DOS provides an easier way.

DOS uses an environment variable called PATH to specify the directories that should be searched when the command processor looks for an external command. You'll recall from chapter 3 that the standard DOS command processor, COMMAND.COM, contains a table of commands—the internal DOS commands—that it can execute without calling outside programs. External DOS commands are provided by the program files that the Setup program normally places in C:\DOS. In fact, however, any program placed anywhere on your disks can be considered an external command.

The PATH environment variable can be set in several different ways. The internal DOS command SET can be used to set the value of any environment variable including PATH. The internal DOS command PATH is used specifically to set the PATH environment variable. PATH can be used in the following configurations: with or without an equal (=) sign, with no arguments to display PATH, or with a semicolon as its only argument to clear the PATH.

The most straightforward way to set the PATH environment variable is to use the PATH command with the desired program search directory as the argument. Type the next command to place the value A:\DOS in the PATH environment variable:

PATH A:\DOS

After you press Enter to execute this command, any programs in the A:\DOS directory can be run regardless of the current directory. The PATH command can also be issued with an equal sign:

PATH=A:\DOS

The equal sign is optional—the PATH command ignores it if it is included.

The PATH variable, like any other environment variable, can also be specified with the SET command. To perform the same function as the previous two PATH commands, type:

SET PATH=A:\DOS

All three methods produce identical results. You can display the current value of PATH just as easily. Simply type **PATH** with no arguments to display the PATH variable. DOS responds with this message:

PATH=A:\DOS

To display the values of all currently set environment variables, type **SET** with no arguments. DOS responds with several lines similar to the following:

```
COMSPEC=A:\DOS\COMMAND.COM
PROMPT=$P $G
PATH=A:\DOS
DIRCMD=/P /O:GNE /A:-D
```

Adding to Your Program Search Path

As you add new programs and new directory branches to your disk, you soon find that only referring to the \DOS directory in the program search path is inadequate. Suppose you change your current directory to the \123\DATA\BUDGET directory and then decide to work on your QTR4_BUD.WK1 worksheet. You can change your current directory to the

\123 directory or you can start 123.EXE by entering the command **\123\123**.

The PATH environment variable can hold quite a few entries. In fact, the PATH command, like any other DOS command, can accept up to 127 characters on the command line. You really can include up to 122 characters in the PATH environment variable because the word PATH and the necessary trailing space take 5 characters.

Each new directory you specify must be separated from any others by a semi-colon. To include both the A:\DOS and A:\123 directories in the program search path, for example, you must type the following command:

```
PATH A:\DOS;A:\123
```

A Note on Searching for Program Files

When searching for program files, DOS first looks in the current directory. If the search is unsuccessful, the directories specified by the PATH environment variable are searched in the order they are listed. This can result in unexpected results if program files with the same name are included in more than one directory on the program search path. If both A:\DOS and A:\123 contain programs called SETUP.EXE, for example, issuing the command SETUP runs A:\123\SETUP.EXE only if the current directory is A:\123. If any other directory is current, the same command executes A:\DOS\SETUP.EXE.

As you continue to add new directories to the PATH environment variable, you may reach a point when retyping the entire command line is too much work. Unfortunately, DOS does not provide a way to add to the existing definition of environment variables from the command line. There are two ways, however, to add additional directories to the PATH environment variable. The method you choose depends on the change you intend to make—whether it is permanent or temporary.

Windows/DOS Shell

Both Windows and DOS Shell use the PATH environmental variable when searching for commands. In DOS Shell, the path can be temporarily changed for the entire environment. In Windows, each DOS window maintains its own PATH environmental variable. Changes to the path affect only those DOS windows where they are executed.

A PATH command is usually one of the lines you include in your system's AUTOEXEC.BAT file. The same PATH command is executed every time you boot your system and the same directories are included in the program search path. To make a permanent change to the PATH, edit the line in the AUTOEXEC.BAT file.

A Note on Editing the AUTOEXEC.BAT File

To edit the PATH command contained in the AUTOEXEC. BAT file, use EDIT, the DOS full screen editor. To do so, type:

```
EDIT C:\AUTOEXEC.BAT
```

This loads the editor and the AUTOEXEC.BAT file. Move the cursor to the line containing the PATH command and make any necessary changes. To save your changes and exit the editor, press Alt, File, Exit, and Yes.

Temporary additions to the PATH environment variable are a little more difficult. You cannot simply enter a command telling PATH or SET to make the addition. You can create a small batch file, however, that enables you to add to the program search. A copy of this file is on the enclosed disk as EXTEND.BAT. To create this file, type the following:

```
COPY CON EXTEND.BAT
@ECHO OFF
REM First show the current PATH
ECHO Old path was %PATH%
REM Test to make sure a new directory was specified
IF "%1"=="" GOTO NONE
REM Test to make sure the new directory exists
IF NOT EXIST %1\NUL GOTO BAD
GOTO ADD
:NONE
ECHO You did not specify the name of a directory to add to the PATH
GOTO END
:BAD
ECHO Specified directory does not exist
GOTO END
:ADD
REM Add the new directory
PATH %PATH%;%1
:END
REM Now show the new path
ECHO New path is %PATH%.
```

After typing the final line, press the F6 function key to add a Control Z (^Z), then press Enter to complete the file.

After you press Enter, DOS responds with the following message:

```
1 file(s) copied
```

To use the batch file, simply type:

EXTEND new_directory

The batch file then displays the existing directory path.

The input line is then checked to make sure you typed a parameter. If you forgot to include a new directory to add to the existing path, the batch file informs you and then shows you that the path is unchanged.

The batch file then performs an indirect test to make sure the specified directory exists. It cannot directly test to see if a directory exists. The NUL device exists in every directory. If you test for the NUL device and specify the directory, however, the directory itself must exist or the test fails.

The new directory is added to the existing PATH variable if you type the command:

PATH %PATH%;%1

This command demonstrates that the PATH command and the PATH environment variable are not the same. In this line, %PATH% returns the current value of the PATH environment variable. The PATH command concatenates this value with the value of %1—the new_directory parameter you typed on the command line, and sets the PATH environment variable using the combined value.

Finally, the new value of the PATH environment variable is displayed.

Storing and Restoring the PATH

The EXTEND.BAT batch file can help you add new directories to the program search path for the current session. Sometimes, however, EXTEND.BAT is not the appropriate command for your work. If you add so many directories to the PATH environment variable, for example, that adding a new directory would exceed the 122-character limit, the EXTEND.BAT command does not work. In addition, if you need to use programs that appear late in the program search path, and other programs with the same names appear earlier, you cannot use EXTEND.BAT.

In both of these examples, it is better to do the following: store the current program search path, specify a new value for PATH, and then restore the original value after you use the program that needs the new PATH.

Recall from the EXTEND.BAT example that you can specify the current value of an environment variable in a batch file by adding a percent sign on both sides of the variable name. In the next line, %PATH% represents the value of the PATH environment variable:

```
PATH %PATH%;%1
```

In a batch file you can use the SET command to set an environment variable. To create a batch file that stores the existing program search path and sets a new path to the directory you specify, enter the following lines:

```
COPY CON NEWPATH.BAT
@ECHO OFF
SET OLDPATH=%PATH%
PATH %1
```

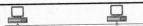 **NetWare**

Although storing and restoring the PATH may make sense for stand-alone DOS-based workstations. NetWare does not tolerate manual modifications to the PATH lightly. The NetWare MAP command is used in batch files to set and reset the NetWare MAP to point to different directories that also set the DOS PATH. This technique is useful in maximizing NetWare performance. When starting your word processor on a NetWare LAN, for example, you might have a batch file that contains the following:

MAP G:=SYS:USERS/FRED makes drive G point to your own personal directory if your name is FRED.

G: switches the default drive to G.

MAP INSERT S2:=SYS:WP50 changes the DOS path to point to include the WP50 directory as well as create a MAP DRIVE.

WP executes the wordprocessing software finding it on the search drive.

F: returns you to the default NetWare drive.

MAP DELETE G: removes the NetWare definition for drive G.

MAP DELETE S2: removes the search drive and path entry for WP50.

Although this may look confusing at first, this method works very well and allows for easier support of a NetWare installation.

This batch file is on the disk as NEWPATH.BAT. After typing the final line, press the F6 function key to add a Control Z (^z) character, then press Enter to complete the file. DOS then responds with this message:

```
1 file(s) copied
```

To use the new batch file, simply type the following and then press Enter:

```
NEWPATH new_program_search_path
```

A Note on the NEWPATH Batch File

Unlike EXTEND.BAT, NEWPATH.BAT does not check for errors. If you want to add error checking, use the tests shown in EXTEND.BAT as an example.

After you issue the `NEWPATH new_program_search_path` command, the old value of the PATH is stored in an environment variable called OLDPATH. The next batch file restores PATH to the value stored in OLDPATH and is on the enclosed disk as OLDPATH.BAT.

```
COPY CON OLDPATH.BAT
@ECHO OFF
PATH %OLDPATH%
SET OLDPATH=
```

After you type the last line, press the F6 function key immediately after the equal sign (=) to add a Control Z (^Z) on the last line, then press Enter.

DOS responds with the following message:

```
1 file(s) copied
```

OLDPATH.BAT does not use any arguments, so to restore PATH to its original value, type `OLDPATH` and then press Enter.

Using APPEND To Set the Data File Search Path

The APPEND command is, in effect, a PATH command for data files. You use the command in a similar way, but APPEND includes some switches that control its behavior.

APPEND is an external DOS command. As a result, it does not automatically set an environment variable. If you specify the /E switch when you first load

APPEND, however, an environment variable named APPEND is created and updated whenever you issue an APPEND command.

Additional APPEND options include:

- ❏ **/X:on**. Adds full data-file search capabilities while programs execute.
- ❏ **/X:off**. Removes full data-file search capabilities while programs execute.
- ❏ **/PATH:on**. Enables you to search for data files using the APPEND search path, even if a complete pathname was provided.
- ❏ **/PATH:off**. Restricts searching for data files using the APPEND search path, if a complete pathname was provided.

If either the /E or /X switches are used, they must be specified the first time the APPEND command is used during a session.

To specify a data file search path with the APPEND command and to create an environment variable called APPEND, enter these commands:

```
APPEND /E
APPEND A:\123\DATA\TAXES
```

To examine the environment variables, simply type SET and DOS responds by displaying the currently set variables:

```
COMSPEC=A:\DOS\COMMAND.COM
PROMPT=$P $G
PATH=A:\DOS
DIRCMD=/P /O:GNE /A:-D
APPEND=A:\123\DATA\TAXES
```

Copying Directories Using XCOPY

The XCOPY (or eXtended COPY) command offers several advantages over the standard COPY command. You can, for example, specify that XCOPY copies files based on whether their archive bit is set (meaning that the file has been modified), whether they were created or modified after a specified date, or whether you respond to a prompt. XCOPY also can be instructed to copy subdirectories—even if they are empty.

NetWare

Although XCOPY presents several new features and works well when copying from a local drive to a NetWare drive, files already on a NetWare drive usually have attribute settings that XCOPY does not transfer. To copy a file on a NetWare drive to a NetWare drive, use the NCOPY command, which offers many of the features of DOS XCOPY. NCOPY also copies NetWare file attributes, such as SHAREABLE or INDEX. If you use XCOPY by mistake, remember to use the NetWare FLAG command to set the proper file attributes.

Comparing XCOPY to the File Commands

Most file-related commands are covered in detail in Chapter 6. Even though XCOPY performs many file-related functions, its extended directory-related capabilities should be mentioned. Do not assume, however, that this means XCOPY is only intended for copying directories or directory structures. The XCOPY command is an improved, much more extended copy command.

Using XCOPY's Options

In this last section of chapter 5, you learn to use XCOPY to accomplish the following tasks:

❏ Copy modified files based on their archive bit or file date.

❏ Prompt before DOS copies files.

❏ Duplicate directory structures on the same or another disk.

Using Attributes To Control what XCOPY Copies

When files are created or modified, DOS uses one of the file's attributes (contained in the file's directory entry) to indicate that the file has not been backed up. This attribute, known as the archive attribute, can then be used to ensure that files are backed up (via the BACKUP command) or copied with the XCOPY command. Two XCOPY switches control whether XCOPY uses this attribute.

The first is the /A switch, which instructs XCOPY to only copy files that have their archive attribute set. To copy any worksheets that have been modified from A:\123\DATA\TAXES to B:\, for example, type the following:

```
XCOPY A:\123\DATA\TAXES B:\ /A
```

If you use the archive attribute because you want to ensure that files have been modified and need to be copied or backed up, you can use the /A switch, but it doesn't quite complete the job. XCOPY has another switch, /M, that copies the same files and then resets the archive attribute to indicate that the files have been backed up. To copy the same files as above, but to keep them from being included the next time you issue the same command, type the following command (instead of the previous command):

```
XCOPY A:\123\DATA\TAXES B:\ /M
```

Another XCOPY option, the /D:date switch, instructs XCOPY to copy files based on their file date. If you want to copy any of the tax worksheet files created or modified after July 4, 1991, for example, simply enter the following command:

```
XCOPY A:\123\DATA\TAXES B:\ /D:07/04/91
```

Using Prompts To Control what XCOPY Copies

Even if XCOPY had no other options except for its capability to prompt you before you copy a file, it would still be a useful command. Suppose you wanted to copy to another disk (B:, for example) the files BRIAN.WK1, PASS.WK1, TEST2.WK1, TEST4.WK1, and TEST5.WK1 from the following list.

BIORHYTM.WK1	TEST2.WK1
BRIAN.WK1	TEST3.WK1
BUDGET.WK1	TEST4.WK1
DATAMYTE.WK1	TEST5.WK1
GRAPH.WK1	TRIG.WK1
PASS.WK1	TRIGTEST.WK1
TEST.WK1	

If you use XCOPY with the /P switch you can enter a single command:

```
XCOPY *.WK1 B: /P
```

XCOPY then displays each matching file name followed by the (Y/N)? prompt. To copy a file, press **Y**; to bypass a file, press **N**. After you process the list, XCOPY informs you with the number of copied files.

Copying Directories with XCOPY

Another unique feature of XCOPY is the capability to copy subdirectories and directory structures, even if they are not empty. In fact, you can use XCOPY to copy the directory structure without copying any files.

Windows' File Manager has the capability to copy entire directories. The graphical interface makes it easy to duplicate a directory and its contents (files and subdirectories) to a new location on the same disk or to another disk. You can also move the directory rather than copying it.

The XCOPY /S switch is used to copy files and any non-empty subdirectories. Suppose, for example, you want to copy all of the files from the A:\123\DATA directory and any of its subdirectories to the B drive. Simply type the following command:

```
XCOPY A:\123\DATA B: /S
```

DOS then responds with the following information:

```
Reading source file(s)...
A:\123\DATA\BUDGET\QTR1_BUD.WK1
A:\123\DATA\BUDGET\QTR2_BUD.WK1
A:\123\DATA\BUDGET\QTR3_BUD.WK1
A:\123\DATA\BUDGET\QTR4_BUD.WK1
A:\123\DATA\SALES\QTR1_SAL.WK1
A:\123\DATA\SALES\QTR2_SAL.WK1
A:\123\DATA\SALES\QTR3_SAL.WK1
A:\123\DATA\SALES\QTR4_SAL.WK1
A:\123\DATA\TAXES\QTR1_TAX.WK1
A:\123\DATA\TAXES\QTR2_TAX.WK1
A:\123\DATA\TAXES\QTR3_TAX.WK1
A:\123\DATA\TAXES\QTR4_TAX.WK1
        12 File(s) copied
```

In addition to copying the twelve files, XCOPY creates three directories on the B drive. The three directories are B:\BUDGET, B:\SALES, and B:\TAXES. These three directories are the subdirectories of the specified source directory, A:\123\DATA. To create the same directories on the B drive as on the A drive, the command must be changed to this:

```
XCOPY A:\123\DATA B:\123\DATA /S
```

The specified target directory in this example does not already exist on the B drive, so DOS prompts with this message:

```
Does DATA specify a file name
or directory name on the target
(F = file, D = directory)?
```

Type **D** to tell XCOPY to create the target directory and proceed with the copy.

Suppose, however, that the A:\123\DATA\SALES directory was empty. In that case, only eight files would have been copied and two directories created. The /E switch instructs XCOPY to also copy empty directories.

XCOPY can also be used to duplicate a directory structure without copying any files. If you want to copy the complete directory structure that exists on the disk in the A drive, but none of the files, XCOPY can quickly accomplish the task. The key is to specify a source file that does not exist and then use the /S and /E switches.

Creating the same directory structure on the B drive as currently exists on the A drive with the MD command requires the following steps:

```
MD B:\123
MD B:\123\DATA
MD B:\123\DATA\BUDGET
MD B:\123\DATA\SALES
MD B:\123\DATA\TAXES
MD B:\DOS
```

For each directory you want to create, you have to enter a command. With XCOPY, however, you can create the entire directory structure with two commands.

To begin, use the DIR /S command and specify an unusual file name. You might try this line:

```
DIR A:\ZZZ.ZZZ /S
```

If DOS reports with the familiar `File not found`, ZZZ.ZZZ is not used as a filename on the A drive (if it was found, select another unlikely name to test).

After you determine a file name that is not used on the A drive, type the following command to duplicate the directory structure from the A drive on the B drive:

```
XCOPY A:\ZZZ.ZZZ B: /S /E
```

DOS responds with this message:

```
File not found--ZZZ.ZZZ
       0 File(s) copied
```

Although no files are copied, the complete directory structure is copied.

The previous examples illustrate that if you specify a partial directory path for either the source or the target, you can instruct XCOPY to create specific portions of the directory tree. XCOPY is a powerful command that can save you considerable work.

Summary

Creating tree-structured directories help you control and maintain your files. In order to effectively use directories, you must learn to create logical structures that are easy to understand and navigate, learn the commands used to extend program and data search paths, and learn those used to move through the directory tree.

Tree-structured directories can be very complex, especially when they include many different branches. If you use the commands covered in this chapter, you will be proficient in tracking your current directory location, moving to other directory branches, and returning to the original directory location.

This chapter showed you how to create batch files and macros to make navigating directories even easier. In addition, you read about creating maps of your directories and forcing DOS to show you where you are in a directory tree. The commands you used in this chapter will help you extend your program and data search paths, and copy entire directory structures with a single command.

6

Keeping in Control of Files

Chapter 5 examined the commands used to navigate tree-structured directories. It also showed you some tricks to make working with directories much easier. Chapter 6 covers commands that work at the file level to help you manage your programs and data.

File commands are used more often than most other types of DOS commands. If you want to control your files, you need to understand file attributes and know how to use them; know how to copy, erase, and rename files; and understand how to backup your files effectively. You also need to know how to examine files after you modify them. This chapter shows you how to maximize the performance of these tasks and get the most from your files.

File-Related Commands

The file-related commands covered in this chapter include the following:

- ❏ ATTRIB
- ❏ COPY
- ❏ VERIFY
- ❏ FC
- ❏ COMP
- ❏ Type
- ❏ DEL (ERASE)
- ❏ UNDELETE
- ❏ REN (RENAME)
- ❏ BACKUP
- ❏ RESTORE

Using File Commands

In the following sections you learn how to use file attributes to increase your work in DOS. You learn how to use file attributes to protect files and reduce the burden of file backups. You also learn how to use the new features of DOS 5 that enable you to set defaults for commands that can be dangerous to your files. Finally, several examples illustrate how the file commands can be used to examine files and enable you to free space on your hard disk drive.

Understanding File Directory Entries

The file listing you see when you use the DIR command only shows part of each file's directory entry. Each directory entry actually contains eight fields (although currently only seven are used). Depending on the switches you specify, the DIR command may display between two and five of those fields. Table 6.1 shows the fields in DOS file entries.

Table 6.1
Fields in DOS File Entries

Field	Size (bytes)
Filename	8
Extension	3
Attribute	1
Unused	10
Time	2
Date	2
FAT entry	2
File Size	4

The *Filename* entry contains the ASCII code for the characters that make up the name of a file. If the file name is shorter than eight characters, the field is filled with space characters to the right of the last character's position. When a file is erased, the first character in the filename field of the directory entry is changed to an ASCII 229 (å) character. If the first character in the filename entry is a period, the entry is for a subdirectory. If the second character is also a period, the current entry is used to show the starting cluster of the parent of the directory.

The *Extension* entry contains the ASCII code for the characters in the file's extension. This field can contain zero to three characters and, like the file name entry, the extension entry is always filled starting at the left. In addition, any unused positions on the right are filled with space characters.

The *Attribute* field entry is only a one-byte field, yet it has room for eight different pieces of information (only six pieces are actually stored in its field). The attribute field is often called the *attribute byte* and each of the six pieces of information is called a *file-attribute bit.* If the bit associated with a particular file attribute is set to one, that attribute is active. If the bit is set to zero, the attribute is turned off. Table 6.2 shows the file-attribute bits that constitute the file-attribute byte.

Table 6.2
Breakdown of the File-Attribute Byte

Bit#	Attribute	Description
0	Read-only	Enables a file to be read but not written to.
1	Hidden	Prevents a file from being displayed by the DIR command unless the /A:H switch is used. Also prevents files from being erased.
2	System	Prevents a file from being displayed by the DIR command unless the /A:S switch is used. Also prevents files from being erased.
3	Volume label	Identifies the directory entry as the volume label for the disk.
4	Subdirectory	Identifies the directory entry as a subdirectory.
5	Archive	Automatically set to one whenever a file is created or modified. It is used by programs such as BACKUP and XCOPY to control whether files will be processed.
6	Unused	
7	Unused	

The ten byte unused directory entry field (or unused 10 in Table 6.1) is reserved for future extensions to the DOS file system.

The *Time* field contains the time a file was created or modified. This entry is a 2-byte unsigned integer that is created using the following formula:

```
(Hour * 2048) + (minute * 32) + (second / 2)
```

Even though the directory listing only shows hours and minutes, when you create or modify a file, the time is actually stored to the nearest two seconds.

The *Date* field contains the date a file was created or modified. This entry is a 2-byte unsigned integer that is created using the following formula:

```
((Year - 1980) * 512) + (Month * 64) + (Day)
```

With this formula, 127 years of calendar dates can be stored in two bytes. All dates for DOS use 1980 as year zero. The original IBM PC was introduced in 1981, so 1980 was made the zero base year for the system calendar.

The *FAT* entry shows the offset from the beginning of the FAT table to the file's first allocated cluster. The FAT itself shows which of the other clusters are allocated to the file.

The *File Size* entry is a 4-byte unsigned integer that shows the size of the file in bytes.

ATTRIB Displays and Controls File Attributes

The ATTRIB command has been available since DOS 3 was introduced, although the 3 version could access only a file's read-only attribute. The DOS 3.1 ATTRIB command was enhanced to enable access to the archive bit. In DOS 3.3 the /S switch was added so ATTRIB could change either of these two bits for files in subdirectories. The DOS 5 ATTRIB command also can control the hidden and system attributes.

The following syntax is used to display or change file attributes:

```
ATTRIB ±R ±H ±S ±A drive:\path\filename  /S
```

Use the plus sign (+) to set the designated attribute on; use the minus sign (-) to turn it off. The letters R, H, S, and A correspond to the four attributes ATTRIB can control. If you supply no attribute arguments, ATTRIB displays attributes for any files that meet the specified filename (or all files if you do not specify a filename).

NetWare

The more advanced ATTRIB commands in DOS 5 work even better than previous versions on a NetWare drive, but lack support for the SHARE-ABLE and INDEX attributes found in the NetWare FLAG command. Either of these commands may be used to set the read-only and read-write attributes of any file, but FLAG must be used to set attributes not available with ATTRIB.

Displaying File Attributes

To display the file attributes for the files on a basic boot floppy disk, type the following command:

```
ATTRIB A:
```

DOS responds by displaying this information:

```
SHR  A:\IO.SYS
SHR  A:\MSDOS.SYS
  A  A:\COMMAND.COM
```

In this example, you can see that IO.SYS and MSDOS.SYS are both marked as System, Hidden, Read-only files. COMMAND.COM has its Archive attribute set.

Using ATTRIB To Protect Files

You need the three files listed in the previous section on a boot disk. For this reason, make sure COMMAND.COM cannot be accidently erased. One way to do this is to change the COMMAND.COM read-only attribute by setting it to On. Use the following command to accomplish this task:

```
ATTRIB +R A:\COMMAND.COM
```

When you use ATTRIB to set file attributes, DOS does not report that the command was successful. To verify that COMMAND.COM's attributes were actually changed, type this command:

```
ATTRIB A:\COMMAND.COM
```

DOS shows you that COMMAND.COM's read-only attribute was actually changed by displaying:

```
  A  R  A:\COMMAND.COM
```

If you want to change IO.SYS and MSDOS.SYS by removing their system attributes, simply type:

```
ATTRIB -S A:\*.SYS
```

With this command, however, DOS does respond with the following message:

```
Not resetting hidden file A:\IO.SYS
Not resetting hidden file A:\MSDOS.SYS
```

To understand what this message means, type the **ATTRIB A:** command again, and DOS displays:

```
SHR    A:\IO.SYS
SHR    A:\MSDOS.SYS
  A R A:\COMMAND.COM
```

You can see that none of the file attributes for either IO.SYS or MSDOS.SYS were affected. An earlier DOS message said Not resetting hidden file, so your next move should be to change the hidden attribute for both files. Enter the next command:

ATTRIB -H A:*.SYS

After you enter this command, DOS responds with this message:

```
Not resetting system file A:\IO.SYS
Not resetting system file A:\MSDOS.SYS
```

Even though you can use DOS to set the hidden and system attributes independently, you cannot set or reset only one of them if the other has been set. To reset both the hidden and system attributes for these files, type the following:

ATTRIB -S -H A:*.SYS

Then, to display the changed attributes, enter this line:

ATTRIB A:

DOS responds with the message:

```
 R A:\IO.SYS
 R A:\MSDOS.SYS
 A R A:\COMMAND.COM
```

If you set any of these three file attributes, it makes a file read-only and prevents it from being erased. Setting the hidden or system attribute can, however, lead to other complications. You may have problems locating your files because both of these attributes hide the file from a normal directory listing. In addition, if you change any files that programs use during operation to hidden or system files, the programs may not function properly.

Windows/DOS Shell

Both Windows and DOS Shell provide a visual display of this information. One of the advantages to the visual display is that, as you change attributes, the new attributes are displayed without having to re-execute the command.

If you follow the suggestions in Chapter 5 about placing program and data files in separate directories, you can use the read-only attribute to protect your program files from being accidentally erased. If you have Lotus 1-2-3 installed on your hard disk drive, for example, and the program files are in a directory named C:\123, you can protect the program files by typing the following command:

```
ATTRIB +R C:\123\*.*
```

Programs like 1-2-3 enable you to change defaults within the program and save the new default settings for future work sessions. You cannot save any new settings if the configuration file is a read-only file.

To configure 1-2-3 so you can update its default settings, change the file attributes for 1-2-3's configuration files so they are not read-only files. 1-2-3 uses the extension CNF for its configuration files. Type the following command to enable the default settings (if you use another program, substitute the program's file extension):

```
ATTRIB -R C:\123\*.CNF
```

A Note on the 1-2-3 Install Program

In 1-2-3, the files that contain the drivers for hardware setup use the extension SET. If you are going to use the INSTALL program to change items in the hardware setup, make sure you remove the read-only file attribute from the SET file.

Controlling Backups with File Attributes

The final file attribute that ATTRIB can access is the archive attribute. You can use this attribute to control which files are backed up or copied. In chapter 5 you learned that the XCOPY command can examine the archive attribute to determine if a file should be copied. Later in this chapter you learn that the BACKUP command has a similar feature.

Whether you use the BACKUP command or the XCOPY command to back up your files, you can save time and reduce the number of floppy disks you use if you make intelligent use of the archive file attribute. Backups are intended to protect you from loss in the event of disk error. If you can reinstall your programs from the original program disks, why back up your program files every time you decide to back up your data? Why not just back up data?

Program files have their archive bit set when they are installed. Immediately after you install a new program, you should use the ATTRIB command to reset the archive attribute. In the earlier example of 1-2-3, you would type the following command to reset the archive attribute for all of the files in your 1-2-3 program directory:

```
ATTRIB -A C:\123\*.*
```

Later, when you use the BACKUP or XCOPY commands, use the appropriate switches (discussed with each command) to ignore files that have not been modified. Incidentally, if you change either the program's hardware configuration or default settings, the archive attributes for the modified configuration files are set—this ensures that the files are backed up with the data files.

Ensuring Accurate File Copies

Copying files is one of the first procedures you learn when you start using a PC. Many users, however, never realize the large number of options DOS provides for making copies and ensuring that the copies are accurate. The following sections examine some of these options and show you how to use them.

NetWare

When files are copied with the DOS COPY command on a NetWare drive, the file attributes are set to Non-Shareable Read-Write. To maintain existing Shareable or Read-Only settings when copying files already on a NetWare drive, you should use the NetWare NCOPY command. For example, NCOPY STUFF.TXT \NEWSTUFF\STUFF.TXT copies STUFF.TXT from the current directory maintaining any Shareable and/or Read-Only attributes the file had in its current location, and setting these in the destination.

Controlling Copy Options

The basic form of the COPY command is simple—you follow the command with the source and destination parameters. Nevertheless, there are times when you need to control the copy process. The COPY command has three switches that you can use to provide this control.

One switch is the /V switch, which verifies that the destination file was written correctly. This switch does slow the copy process slightly, but it also assures you that the destination file is correct. The COMP and FC commands discussed later in this chapter provide another, possibly more reliable method of insuring the accuracy of the destination file.

The second switch, /A, instructs COPY to treat the copy as an ASCII copy. If you use the /A switch, the file that immediately precedes the /A switch and all remaining files on the command line (until a /B switch is encountered) are considered ASCII text files. When you perform an ASCII copy, the following rules apply:

❏ The source file is copied up to the first end-of-file character (Ctrl-Z). The copy of the source file does not include the first end-of-file character nor anything that follows it.

❏ An end-of-file character is added to the end of the destination file.

❏ The source file size listed in the directory is ignored.

❏ ASCII copies are the default when you combine files.

The /B switch instructs the COPY command to treat the copy as a binary copy. If you use /B, the file that immediately precedes the /B switch and all remaining files on the command line (until an /A switch is encountered) are considered binary files. When you perform a binary copy, the following rules apply:

❏ The entire source file is copied, including any Ctrl-Z characters.

❏ An extra end-of-file character is not added to the end of the destination file.

❏ The source file size listed in the directory is used.

❏ Binary copies are the default except when you combine files.

Combining ASCII Files with COPY

Combining files with the COPY command saves considerable work. Suppose you buy a new piece of software that requires a specific system configuration for proper operation (see chapter 4 for a discussion of this subject). The installation program for the new software often modifies or replaces your system's existing CONFIG.SYS and AUTOEXEC.BAT files. The new software purchased may do this without even advising you of the change.

After you lose your carefully constructed copies of the CONFIG.SYS and AUTOEXEC.BAT files, you must be more careful and ensure that you have copies of these files in different names or in a separate directory. If you install a new program that destroys CONFIG.SYS or AUTOEXEC.BAT, you can combine your saved copy with the one created by the newly installed program, edit the combined file, and create a new file that meets both your needs and those of the new program.

Imagine that your system's CONFIG.SYS file looks like this:

```
DEVICE=C:\DOS\SETVER.EXE
DEVICE=C:\DOS\HIMEM.SYS
DOS=HIGH,UMB
DEVICE=C:\DOS\EMM386.EXE RAM
FILES=60
BUFFERS=3
BREAK=ON
DEVICEHIGH=C:\DOS\SMARTDRV.SYS 2048 512
SHELL=C:\DOS\COMMAND.COM C:\DOS\ /E:512 /p
```

After you install a new program (DUMBPROG.EXE), you find that your other programs can no longer access extended memory and your hard disk drive is slow. When you examine CONFIG.SYS, you find it has changed and now includes the following:

```
FILES=30
BUFFERS=20
DEVICE=C:\DUMBPROG\DUMBPROG.SYS /XYZ 235 -P
DEVICE=C:\DUMBPROG\DUMBONE.SYS /BJU 851
DEVICE=C:\DUMBPROG\DUMBTWO.SYS /9331
DEVICE=C:\DOS\ANSI.SYS
```

As you suspected, the DUMBPROG installation program was produced by someone who assumed you were only going to run DUMBPROG on your system and therefore did not consider that you might possibly have important commands in the CONFIG.SYS file. In order to correct the problem, you must repair CONFIG.SYS.

The first step is to rename the new, defective CONFIG.SYS file by typing the following:

```
REN CONFIG.SYS CONFIG.DUM
```

Next, combine the original CONFIG.SYS file that you copied to a new file called CONFIG.GUD before you installed the DUMBPROG program. Combine CONFIG.GUD with CONFIG.DUM to create the revised CONFIG.SYS file:

```
COPY CONFIG.GUD+CONFIG.DUM CONFIG.SYS
```

DOS responds with this message:

```
1 file(s) copied
```

To see what the new CONFIG.SYS file contains, type the following command:

```
TYPE CONFIG.SYS
```

The new, combined file is displayed:

```
DEVICE=C:\DOS\SETVER.EXE
DEVICE=C:\DOS\HIMEM.SYS
DOS=HIGH,UMB
DEVICE=C:\DOS\EMM386.EXE RAM
FILES=60
BUFFERS=3
BREAK=ON
DEVICEHIGH=C:\DOS\SMARTDRV.SYS 2048 512
SHELL=C:\DOS\COMMAND.COM C:\DOS\ /E:512 /p
FILES=30
BUFFERS=20
DEVICE=C:\DUMBPROG\DUMBPROG.SYS /XYZ 235 -P
DEVICE=C:\DUMBPROG\DUMBONE.SYS /BJU 851
DEVICE=C:\DUMBPROG\DUMBTWO.SYS /9331
DEVICE=C:\DOS\ANSI.SYS
```

With the exception of an extra set of lines for controlling the number of open files and buffers, you probably can use this combined CONFIG.SYS file with only minor modifications. One change you can make is to remove the following lines:

```
FILES=30
BUFFERS=20
```

To do this, enter the command:

```
EDIT CONFIG.SYS
```

After CONFIG.SYS appears, move the cursor to the beginning of each of these two lines, add the word REM, then save the file and exit from EDIT. Press Alt, File, Exit, and Yes.

When you reboot your system, the commands included in the original CONFIG.SYS file and the necessary ones from the CONFIG.SYS file produced by DUMBPROG will execute.

In this example, you successfully combined a file with another file using the default ASCII mode. Other cases may require you to combine binary files. The following example demonstrates how you can use the /B switch to combine two binary files.

Windows

When working with text files, Windows provides several options to the user. The best approach for combining files is to use the Notepad utility.

Combining Binary Files with COPY

Program files, such as those with a COM or EXE extension, are not good candidates for combining. You could not, for example, combine your favorite word processor and your favorite spreadsheet program files to create a combination word processor and spreadsheet program. There are, however, other types of binary files that you can successfully combine.

Print files that contain graphics, for example, often contain characters that the COPY command recognizes as an end-of-file character. If you want to combine graphics files such as a letterhead and a letter that uses graphics fonts, you must use the binary mode instead of the ASCII mode. If you don't use the binary mode, each file is read only until an end-of-file character is encountered.

Suppose, for example, that your letterhead is contained in a graphics print file called LETRHEAD.GRA and the letter is in LETTER.GRA. To combine the two files and send the result to the printer, you would type the following command:

```
COPY LETRHEAD.GRA/B+LETTER.GRA PRN
```

The /B switch instructs COPY that both LETRHEAD.GRA and LETTER.GRA are binary files. If the body of the letter was an ASCII text file named LETTER.TXT, however, you would type the following command:

```
COPY LETRHEAD.GRA/B+LETTER.TXT/A PRN
```

Verifying the Accuracy of Copies

DOS provides several ways to verify that destination files are accurate copies of the source files. Even though errors are rare when you make copies, a single error may be all that is necessary to make the copy unusable or even dangerous. Imagine if you copied a program like FORMAT.COM and there was an error that caused the program to perform an unconditional format of your hard disk drive instead of a floppy disk in drive A. This is just one example of the importance of making accurate copies and monitoring the copy process.

Using the /V Switch

The COPY and XCOPY commands include a /V switch that reads the destination file to ensure that it was written correctly. To copy a file and verify the copy, use the following syntax:

```
COPY source destination /V
```

If you want to copy the AUTOEXEC.BAT file from the C drive to a disk in the A drive and verify the copy, type the following:

```
COPY C:\AUTOEXEC.BAT A:\ /V
```

Using VERIFY

DOS also provides the command VERIFY that you can use to turn on or off the verification of all disk writes. To check the current status of write verification, type:

```
VERIFY
```

DOS responds with one of the following messages:

```
VERIFY is off
VERIFY is on
```

To enable disk-write verification, type:

```
VERIFY ON
```

To disable disk-write verification, type:

```
VERIFY OFF
```

The VERIFY command provides only a minimal level of protection. When enabled, disk-write verification simply ensures that data was not written to a bad disk sector. VERIFY does not provide absolute assurance that the destination file is an accurate copy of the source file. VERIFY does, however, provide an extra measure of protection for commands, such as BACKUP, that produce files that cannot be verified by other means (such as COMP and FC).

Using COMP and FC

Two DOS commands, COMP and FC, are used to compare files. You can use either command to determine if files are identical, but the FC command includes a few more options than COMP.

The syntax for the COMP command is as follows:

    COMP *filename1 filename2* /D /A /L /N=number /C

The switches in the command line are the following:

- ❏ /D: Displays differences in decimal format instead of the default hexadecimal format.

- ❏ /A: Displays differences in ASCII characters instead of ASCII codes.

- ❏ /L: Displays line numbers for differences instead of showing the number of bytes from the beginning of the file.

- ❏ /N=number: Enables you to compare different sized files by comparing only the first specified number of lines in each file.

- ❏ /C: Disregards case of ASCII letters so that "DOS" and "dos", for example, would be considered a match.

The syntax of the FC command for comparing ASCII files is as follows:

    FC /A /C /L /LBn /N /T /W /nnnn *filename1 filename2*

The syntax of the FC command for comparing binary files is the following:

    FC /B *filename1 filename2*

The switches in the FC command line are the following:

- ❏ /A: Abbreviates the output of differences by displaying only the first and last lines for each set of differences.

- ❏ /B: Performs a byte-by-byte comparison instead of trying to resynchronize if it finds differences.

- ❏ /C: Disregards case of ASCII letters so that "DOS" and "dos", for example, would be considered a match.

- ❏ /L: Compares files as lines of ASCII text and tries to resynchronize if it finds differences.

- ❏ /LBn: Sets the number of lines in the compare buffer, thus setting the maximum allowable number of consecutive mismatched lines.

- ❏ /N: Displays the line numbers on an ASCII comparison.

- ❏ /T: Does not expand tabs to spaces.

- ❏ /W: Compresses tabs and spaces for comparison so that any number of consecutive spaces and tabs will match.

❑ /nnnn: Specifies the number of consecutive lines that must match after a mismatch before FC resynchronizes the files.

Both COMP and FC accept wild cards for the filename arguments.

Suppose you have two copies of a program file called PROG1.EXE and you want to find out if they are the same. To perform a binary comparison with the COMP command, enter the command:

```
COMP PROG1.EXE C:PROG1.EXE
```

DOS responds with the message:

```
Comparing PROG1.EXE and C:PROG1.EXE...
```

If differences exist, you see a message:

```
Compare error at OFFSET 3734
file1 = 31
file2 = 32
```

COMP can identify up to ten differences between two files. After the comparison is complete, you are prompted:

```
Compare more files (Y/N) ?
```

Answer **N** to end the comparison. In order to do the same binary comparison with the FC command, type:

```
FC /B PROG1.EXE C:PROG1.EXE
```

DOS responds with the message:

```
Comparing files PROG1.EXE and C:PROG1.EXE
00003734: 31 32
```

Notice that COMP and FC reported the same difference at the same byte offset. In both cases, PROG1.EXE on drive A is reported as having the hexadecimal value 31 at offset 3734, and the file on drive C has the hexadecimal value 32 at the same location. A difference exists between the two files, but the binary comparisons do not provide enough information for you to understand the discrepancy.

An ASCII comparison of the files may help. To perform an ASCII comparison with COMP, type:

```
COMP PROG1.EXE C:PROG1.EXE /A
```

This time DOS responds:

```
Comparing PROG1.EXE and C:PROG1.EXE...
Compare error at OFFSET 3734
file1 = 1
file2 = 2
```

Now you can see that the difference between the two files is that PROG1.EXE on the A drive has the decimal value 1 at offset 3734, and the file on the C drive has the decimal value 2 at the same location. This difference may be a little easier to understand when DOS presents ASCII characters instead of hexadecimal codes, but the information remains relatively cryptic. Try using FC to make an ASCII comparison between the two files. Type the following command:

FC /L PROG1.EXE C:PROG1.EXE

DOS responds with the information:

```
Comparing files PROG1.EXE and C:PROG1.EXE
***** PROG1.EXE
----------\x0d\x0a POS Version 5.11  \x0d\x0a--------------------\x0d\x0a
***** C:PROG1.EXE
----------\x0d\x0a POS Version 5.12  \x0d\x0a--------------------\x0d\x0a
*****
```

By using the /L switch, you instructed FC to display the lines that differ. Finally, you can see the difference between the source file and the copy in an understandable manner—the program copy on the A drive is listed as version 5.11 and the one on the C drive is listed as version 5.12.

Of course, this example was simplified—normally you would expect two versions of a program to differ in more than just an internal version number.

As you have seen, both COMP and FC find the smallest differences between files. If you want to make sure two copies are identical, you can use either command. COMP is usually faster than FC because FC has to build two internal tables for comparing lines of differences. COMP, on the other hand, simply tracks up to ten bytes worth of differences between the files. If the two files are different sizes, you must use FC unless you use the COMP /N=number of lines switch to limit the comparison to a specified number of lines at the beginning of the files.

Examining Files with TYPE

The TYPE command is used to display ASCII text files. If you want to see what AUTOEXEC.BAT contains, for example, but do not want to make any changes, you can enter:

```
TYPE AUTOEXEC.BAT
```

As you learn in Chapter 7, the output of the TYPE command is often piped to the MORE filter, as in the following command:

```
TYPE AUTOEXEC.BAT | MORE
```

You also can print a copy of the AUTOEXEC.BAT file by redirecting the output of TYPE (also discussed in Chapter 7):

```
TYPE AUTOEXEC.BAT > PRN
```

The TYPE command does not accept wild cards, so to examine several ASCII files you can either reissue the command for each file, or you can combine TYPE with the FOR statement.

If you want to print all of the batch files located in the C:\DOS\BATCH directory, for example, use the TYPE and FOR commands in either of the following command lines:

```
FOR %%X IN (*.BAT) DO TYPE %%X >PRN--this is the batch file syntax

FOR %X IN (*.BAT) DO TYPE %X >PRN--this is the command line syntax
```

If you use the TYPE command in this manner, all of the batch files are printed together. It is difficult to understand which lines belong to which batch file in this configuration. The following batch files illustrate a better way to type ASCII text files.

Create the first batch file, TYPE1.BAT, by entering the following commands:

```
COPY CON TYPE1.BAT
@ECHO OFF
IF "%1"=="" GOTO END
FOR %%X IN (%1) DO CALL TYPEFILE %%X
:END
```

After typing the last line, press the F6 function key (^Z will appear), and then press Enter. DOS responds with this message:

```
1 file(s) copied
```

Next, create the second batch file, TYPEFILE.BAT, by entering:

```
COPY CON TYPEFILE.BAT
ECHO %1 >PRN
TYPE %1 >PRN
ECHO ^L >PRN
```

A Note on the TYPEFILE.BAT Batch File

To enter the ^L in the last line, hold down the Alt key, use the keypad on the right side of the keyboard to type **012**, then release the Alt key. ^L is the formfeed, and will cause each file to be typed starting on a new sheet of paper.

After you type the last line, press the F6 function key (^Z will appear), and then press Enter. DOS responds with this message:

```
1 file(s) copied
```

To use these batch files, simply enter the following command:

```
TYPE1 filespec
```

You can enter a single file name for the filespec argument or use wild cards to print a series of files. Each file name is printed at the top of a new page followed by the lines in the file. If you do not include the filespec argument, nothing is printed. Files that contain control characters like the ^L (formfeed) in TYPEFILE.BAT make the printer eject the page when the control character is reached in the file.

Understanding DEL and UNDELETE

The DEL, or ERASE, command marks files as deleted by changing the first character in the file's directory entry to hexadecimal E5 (decimal 229 – å) and by marking the file's cluster chain in the FAT as free. These changes do not actually erase the file, but they prevent DOS from displaying the file in a directory listing, and they let DOS reuse both the directory entry and the freed clusters.

You often can recover a file with the new UNDELETE command in DOS 5. Recall from the earlier discussion of directory entries that one of the fields in each directory entry is the pointer to the first cluster that was allocated to the file. When a file is deleted, that first cluster is marked as free in the FAT, but the rest of the cluster chain remains linked. The FAT field in the directory entry for the deleted file still points to the beginning cluster even though that position in the FAT is marked as free. DOS can reuse the clusters; however, until the clusters are reused, the data from the deleted file remains on the disk.

NetWare

UNDELETE does not work for NetWare drives. The NetWare SALVAGE command may be used with limited or amazing results depending on the version of NetWare. NetWare 2.X allows for the SALVAGE of the last file or group of files deleted to be undeleted. NetWare 3.X contains a complete menu-driven utility that can salvage any deleted files whose original location has not been reused by the system even if the file was deleted several months ago.

Keep in mind that DOS reuses both the directory entry and the freed clusters that belonged to deleted files with no regard for how important those files were. If you accidently delete a file, you should undelete it immediately. The longer you wait to recover deleted files, the less your chance of success.

Using DEL Safely

The DEL command has two safeguards built in. If you enter the DEL command in any variation that indicates all files in a directory, such as DEL *.*, DEL ., or DEL .., DOS prompts you with the following confirmation:

```
All files in directory will be deleted!
Are you sure (Y/N)?
```

This gives you the chance to confirm that you want to delete all of the files in the specified directory. DOS does not warn you, however, if you use a wildcard filespec that is not global. If you enter the following, for example, any files with an EXE extension are deleted immediately—even if they were the only files in the directory:

```
DEL *.EXE
```

Before you use a partial wildcard filespec argument with the DEL command, always check the filespec with the DIR command. You should, for example, precede the previous command with the following command:

```
DIR *.EXE
```

Then, if any files are displayed that should not be deleted, you would know your partial wildcard filespec argument should be more restricted.

Another choice offered by DEL is the /P (for Prompt) switch. If you include this switch, each filename matching the specified filespec is displayed along with the following prompt:

```
Delete (Y/N)?
```

This extra level of verification can prevent you from accidently deleting files if you used an invalid partial wildcard filespec argument. With DOS 5, you can even make DEL use the /P switch as its default by creating a DOSKEY macro (see Chapter 13 for more information on creating DOSKEY macros and saving them in batch files for later use). Enter the following to create a DOSKEY macro for the DEL command:

```
DOSKEY DEL=DEL $1 /P
```

Windows/DOS Shell

An advantage to a graphical environment is that you have an opportunity to see the files that your command will affect. In addition, both applications can be set to prompt you for permission before deleting each file.

Recovering Deleted Files with UNDELETE

UNDELETE is a powerful new command included with DOS 5. The UNDELETE command recognizes that deleted files remain on the disk until they are overwritten by other files. The syntax for the UNDELETE command is the following:

```
UNDELETE filename /LIST or /ALL  /DT or /DOS
```

The arguments for the UNDELETE command are defined as follows:

- ❏ /LIST: Lists, but does not recover, the deleted files in the specified directory that are available to be recovered.

- ❏ /ALL: Undeletes all of the specified files without prompting by supplying the first character of the filename from the delete tracking file if possible. Otherwise, it uses the first available character from the following list:

    #%&-0123456789ABCDEFGHIJKLMNOPQRSTUVWXYZ

- ❏ /DT: Uses information contained in the delete tracking file to recover only deleted files.

- ❏ /DOS: Uses information contained in the MS-DOS directory listing to recover only deleted files.

The UNDELETE command uses information contained in a special file called the delete tracking file if the file is available. Otherwise, it uses information on deleted files contained in the directory listing. The delete tracking file is created by the MIRROR command, and is covered in detail in Chapter 8.

Windows

The Format command in the Windows' File Manager uses the standard DOS FORMAT command. Therefore, disks formatted with File Manager under DOS 5 will contain the necessary files to use the UNFORMAT and UNDELETE commands. The default in Windows (and in DOS Shell) is to prompt for confirmation before each file is deleted (as though the /P switch were used).

Suppose you were writing a book and during the course of your work you saved each chapter in a file on a floppy disk. When you enter the command, `DIR A:\`, DOS responds with the following message:

```
Volume in drive A is DOCUMENTS
Volume Serial Number is 3D0F-17FA
Directory of A:\

CHAP4    DOC   111441  05-06-91  11:32a
CHAP5    DOC    79369  05-09-91   3:58p
CHAP6    DOC    41939  05-14-91   4:43p
 3 file(s)  232749 bytes
 980480 bytes free
```

If you accidentally type `DEL *.DOC` and delete the chapters that you saved on the A drive, you can recover them with the UNDELETE command. In the meantime, however, if you type `DIR A:`, DOS responds with the following bad news:

```
Volume in drive A is DOCUMENTS
Volume Serial Number is 3D0F-17FA
Directory of A:\

File not found
```

To recover your lost files, use the UNDELETE command by entering the following command:

```
UNDELETE A: /ALL
```

DOS responds with the following message:

```
Directory: A:\
File Specifications: *.*

    Deletion-tracking file not found.

    MS-DOS directory contains   3 deleted files.
    Of those,   3 files may be recovered.

Using the MS-DOS directory.

    ?HAP6   DOC    41939   5-14-91    4:43p   ...A

File successfully undeleted.

    ?HAP4   DOC   111441   5-06-91   11:32a   ...A

File successfully undeleted.

    ?HAP5   DOC    79369   5-09-91    3:58p   ...A

File successfully undeleted.
```

Now, when you type `DIR A:\`, DOS tells you that the three files have returned:

```
Volume in drive A is DOCUMENTS
Volume Serial Number is 3D0F-17FA
Directory of A:\

#HAP4    DOC   111441   05-06-91   11:32a
#HAP5    DOC    79369   05-09-91    3:58p
#HAP6    DOC    41939   05-14-91    4:43p
    3 file(s)   232749 bytes
    980480 bytes free
```

The first character in the directory listing for each deleted file is changed to å, which is the special character that indicates deleted files. As a result, no record of what the first character of the file name should be is available. Notice that the first character of each file name has been changed to a pound sign (#). UNDELETE uses the previous list of characters to provide a new first character. If a delete tracking file existed, UNDELETE would have used the information in the delete tracking file to provide the original first character. In the next section, you learn how to use the REN command to change the first character of recovered files.

If you save new files on a disk before you try to recover accidently deleted files, fewer deleted files can be recovered. Suppose, for example, you saved another chapter on the disk before you realized that three chapters had been accidentally deleted. Instead of recovering three files, UNDELETE might be able to recover only two. If the new file was considerably larger, you may not be able to recover any of the files.

Understanding REN

The REN command (also typed as RENAME) changes the name of files. REN works within a single directory; that is, REN cannot be used to move files from one directory to another. REN renames files, but cannot rename subdirectories. Also, REN cannot change a file's name if another file already has the new name.

To rename a file, use the following syntax:

REN drive:\path**oldname newname**

Note that **newname** cannot have a drive or path specified. To change the name of A:\WORDPROC\DOCUMENT\CHAP1.DOC to A:\WORDPROC\DOCUMENT\CHAP1.TXT, use the following command:

REN A:\WORDPROC\DOCUMENT\CHAP1.DOC CHAP1.TXT

The REN command also accepts wild cards. You can, for example, change the pound sign (#) character in the following three files that UNDELETE named in the previous example:

```
#HAP4      DOC   111441   05-06-91   11:32a
#HAP5      DOC    79369   05-09-91    3:58p
#HAP6      DOC    41939   05-14-91    4:43p
```

You can change the first character to the letter C by entering the following command:

REN #*.* C*.*

REN does not inform you that the change has taken place, so type **DIR** to confirm the change and DOS responds with the following message:

```
Volume in drive A is DOCUMENTS
Volume Serial Number is 3D0F-17FA
Directory of A:\

CHAP4      DOC   111441   05-06-91   11:32a
CHAP5      DOC    79369   05-09-91    3:58p
CHAP6      DOC    41939   05-14-91    4:43p
        3 file(s)232749 bytes
        980480 bytes free
```

If you attempt to rename a file and the new name you specify matches an existing file, REN advises you with the following message:

```
Duplicate file name or file not found
```

If you specify a path and include the new name, you will see the following message:

```
Invalid parameter
```

Understanding BACKUP and RESTORE

The BACKUP and RESTORE commands enable you to protect your files quickly and efficiently from data loss by copying them to another disk or, if necessary, to disks. The BACKUP command offers an advantage over other methods of backing up your files, such as COPY and XCOPY, because it utilizes the entire space on the target disk. When the target disk becomes full, BACKUP prompts you to install a new disk and then continues.

NetWare

The DOS BACKUP and RESTORE commands do not attempt to back up the NetWare bindery database. Because this information is essential to restore a NetWare drive properly, use the NetWare LARCHIVE and LRESTORE commands that back up the NetWare drive to any local drive, including floppies. If you insist on using the DOS BACKUP and RESTORE commands, first run the BINDFIX program, found in the SYSTEM directory, on the NetWare drive. This routine first makes a backup of the current NetWare bindery information to an ordinary DOS file and then makes any necessary corrections or adjustments. This backup copy of the bindery can be backed up like any other DOS file using BACKUP, and can later be used to restore the bindery database after a DOS RESTORE command.

A consistent and efficient way to back up data files and other files is important. You may find that replacing data can be costly and time consuming, or even impossible. A backup of your data protects you from hardware failures, software problems, and the largest data destroyer, human error.

The files produced by BACKUP cannot be used directly. They are special format files that can be read only by the RESTORE command. In fact, if you request a directory listing for one of the backup disks, you will see a message similar to the following:

```
Volume in drive A is BACKUP  001
Volume Serial Number is 0676-15D8
Directory of A:\

BACKUP    001   85516   05-15-91   9:37a
CONTROL   001     379   05-15-91   9:37a
   2 file(s)   85895 bytes
   275456 bytes free
```

If you instruct BACKUP to keep a log of the backup copy, you can examine the log file to determine which files are contained in the backup files. The following listing, for example, shows the log file associated with the backup that created the preceding backup:

```
5-15-1991 9:36:43
001  \WIN30\WINWORD\DOCUMENT\CHAP6.DOC
001  \WIN30\WINWORD\DOCUMENT\BJUBIO.DOC
001  \WIN30\WINWORD\DOCUMENT\BYLAWOLD.DOC
001  \WIN30\WINWORD\DOCUMENT\CHAP12IN.DOC
001  \WIN30\WINWORD\DOCUMENT\CHAP4IN.DOC
```

Windows

You should only run the BACKUP and RESTORE commands from the DOS command line. Do not run these commands from within a DOS window.

Deciding which Files To Back Up

Even though backing up your files is the best way to avoid losing valuable data, most PC users tend to delay this task because it is inconvenient and time-consuming. If you also put off backing up data, remember two important facts. First, replacing lost data often takes a much longer time than performing a full backup on low-density floppy disks, the most time-consuming of any backup methods. Second, backups can be done quickly if you logically think about your files' contents and back up only a minimum number of files.

The BACKUP command has many options that you can use to limit the number of files included in a backup. You can limit, for example, the number of files to be backed up by specifying certain subdirectories and file specifications, and by specifying a date or time of files. Also, you can use the file-archive attribute as a limiter.

When you plan on backing up files, remember that most of the files on a typical hard disk drive are program files. The original program disks (or the backup copies you created when you installed the program) are perfectly good backups for these files. You do not, therefore, need to bother including program files in your backups.

Suppose the C:\WORDPROC directory, for example, contains the program files for a word processing program. The directory has two subdirectories, C:\WORDPROC\DOCUMENT, which contains document files, and C:\WORDPROC\LIBRARY, which contains templates installed by the installation program. The following lines show the total size of the files in these three directories:

```
C:\WORDPROC
 3,197,001 total bytes in 55 files

C:\WORDPROC\DOCUMENT
 172,411 total bytes in 9 files

C:\WORDPROC\LIBRARY

 163,551 total bytes in 14 files

Total of all files found
 3,532,963 total bytes in 78 files
```

In order to back up the entire group of 78 files in these three directories, you would need to use ten 360K disks, five 720K disks, three 1.2M disks, or three 1.44M disks. If you limit your backup to the nine files in C:\WORDPROC\DOCUMENT, however, a single disk of any capacity can hold the entire backup. The partial backup saves 5% as many bytes as a complete backup, yet backs up 100% of your data.

Perhaps some of your data files were unchanged since the previous backup. You probably have documents that you refer to occasionally without modifying them. If you limit your backup so that only documents modified since the last backup are included, you might be able to cut the number of bytes of backup even more than the preceding example by as much as half.

Using BACKUP Intelligently

After you determine which files should be backed up, you can make rapid, intelligent backups. The first step is to use ATTRIB to reset (or turn off) the archive attribute of your program files. This command is discussed earlier in this chapter, but a short review here may be helpful.

Use the following syntax to reset the archive attribute of your program files :

    ATTRIB -A drive:\path to program directory*.*

Use the same command format to reset the archive attribute for any samples, templates, fonts, or other files installed in separate directories as part of the program's installation. You only need to use the ATTRIB -A command prior to your first backup after installing a program. The archive attribute remains off unless a file is modified.

BACKUP resets the archive attribute when it backs up a file. If you specify the /M argument to the BACKUP command, files that had their archive attribute turned off by ATTRIB, BACKUP, or XCOPY, will not be included in the backup. If, for example, CHAP1.DOC is backed up June 1st and not modified before your June 7th backup, it will not be backed up on June 7th.

The BACKUP command uses the following syntax:

    BACKUP *source destination-drive:* /S /M /A /F :size /D:date /T:time /
    L:drive: path\logfile

In the preceding syntax, *source* denotes the files, drive, or directory you want to back up. The *destination-drive:* variable sets the drive for saving backup files. You can use the /S switch to back up subdirectories of the specified directory. By using the /M switch, you can back up only those files created or modified since the last backup. The /A switch appends backup files to an existing backup disk instead of overwriting any existing files.

When you use the /F:size variable in the preceding syntax, you can specify the capacity of the disks that have not been formatted. The /D:date variable backs up only files created or modified on or after the specified date, whereas the /T:time variable backs up only files created or modified at or after the specified time. Also, the /L:drive:path\logfile variable creates a log file to record the backup operation.

You must always specify the source of the files to be backed up, as well as the destination drive. All of the other arguments are optional, but can be important or necessary to back up specific files that need backups.

To back up any files in the C:\WORDPROC directory, for example, and its subdirectories that have been modified since the last backup, enter the following:

    BACKUP C:\WORDPROC A: /M /S

DOS responds with the following message:

```
Insert backup diskette 01 in drive A:

WARNING! Files in the target drive
A:\ root directory will be erased
Press any key to continue . . .

*** Backing up files to drive A: ***
Diskette Number: 01
```

Next, DOS tells you the name of each file as it is backed up. You would see, for example, a message similar to the following:

```
\WORDPROC\DOCUMENT\CHAP6.DOC
\WORDPROC\DOCUMENT\BJUBIO.DOC
\WORDPROC\DOCUMENT\BYLAWOLD.DOC
\WORDPROC\DOCUMENT\CHAP12IN.DOC
\WORDPROC\DOCUMENT\CHAP4IN.DOC
```

This message indicates that five files (out of 78) are backed up. If the /M switch had not been included in your BACKUP statement, all 78 files would have been backed up. This process saves you time and disks.

BACKUP resets each file's archive attribute as it is backed up. If you re-enter the same command, DOS responds with the following warning:

```
WARNING! No files were found to back up
```

The BACKUP command normally writes over any files in the root directory of the destination disk. If you want to add more backup files to the destination disk, instead of replacing the ones that are already there, use the /A switch. To add, for example, new or modified documents to the previous backup, type the following command:

BACKUP C:\WORDPROC A: /M /S /A

DOS responds with the following prompt:

```
Insert last backup diskette in drive A:
Press any key to continue . . .

*** Backing up files to drive A: ***
Diskette Number: 01
```

DOS then displays the names of the files being backed up. The new files are added to the existing BACKUP.xxx file.

If a destination disk has not been formatted, BACKUP automatically formats it using the default capacity of the disk drive. If you work with low-capacity disks in a high-capacity drive, use the /F:size argument to specify the capacity of the disk. If, for example, your A drive is a 1.44M high-capacity drive but you use 720K disks for your backups, use the following command:

```
BACKUP C:\WORDPROC A: /M /S /A /F:720
```

The /D:date and /T:time switches can be used to further restrict which files are backed up, although the /M switch combined with the ATTRIB command probably provides better control. If you use the /D:date or /T:time switches, make sure the date or time template you use includes every file that you need to back up.

The final BACKUP switch, /L:drive:path\logfile, records an ASCII text file that shows the date and time of the backup, the disk number, and the name of each backed up file. If the /L switch is used without the drive:path\logfile argument, a file called BACKUP.LOG is created in the root directory of the source disk. The BACKUP.LOG file looks like this:

```
5-15-1991 13:06:50
001  \WORDPROC\DOCUMENT\CHAP6.DOC
001  \WORDPROC\DOCUMENT\SCREEN00.DOC
001  \WORDPROC\DOCUMENT\SCREEN01.DOC
```

To print a copy of BACKUP.LOG to keep with your backup disks, type:

```
TYPE BACKUP.LOG > PRN
```

BACKUP does not copy the three DOS system files, IO.SYS, MSDOS.SYS, and COMMAND.COM. This prevents a later use of RESTORE from copying an older version of the DOS system files over a newer version.

Restoring Your Files

You must use RESTORE to access the backup files, because files created by BACKUP are a special format that you cannot simply copy and then use. Usually, BACKUP is used many times before RESTORE. In fact, you may never use RESTORE because backups are intended to protect you from losing data when problems occur.

RESTORE has the following syntax:

```
RESTORE drive1: drive2:path\filename /S /P /B:date /A:date /E:time /
L:time /M /N /D
```

The arguments for the RESTORE command line are as follows:

- ❑ *drive1:*   The drive containing the backup files.
- ❑ *drive2:*path\filename: The file(s) to restore.
- ❑ /S: Restores all subdirectories.
- ❑ /P: Prompts before restoring read-only files or files modified since the last backup.
- ❑ /B: Restores only files modified on or before the specified date.
- ❑ /A: Restores only files modified on or after the specified date.
- ❑ /E: Restores only files modified at or earlier than the specified time.
- ❑ /L: Restores only files modified at or later than the specified time.
- ❑ /M: Restores only files modified since the last backup.
- ❑ /N: Restores only files that no longer exist on the destination disk.
- ❑ /D: Displays but does not restore files on the backup disk that match specifications.

The DOS 5 version of RESTORE can restore backup files created by any previous version of BACKUP. If you back up your files before installing DOS 5, you can restore those files without any difficulty.

Before you use RESTORE to restore backup files, consider whether the backed up files will replace more recent versions of the same files. If you are not sure which copy of a file you want, copy the more recent one to another disk before overwriting the file with the backed up copy.

To check which files will be restored, use the /D switch as in the following command:

```
RESTORE A: C: /D
```

When you type the previous command and press Enter, DOS responds with the message:

```
Insert backup diskette 01 in drive A:
Press any key to continue . . .

*** Files were backed up 05-15-1991 ***

*** Listing files on drive A: ***
Diskette: 01
\WORDPROC\DOCUMENT\SCREEN00.TXT
\WORDPROC\DOCUMENT\MAXDOS5.ZIP
```

```
\WORDPROC\DOCUMENT\CHAP6.DOC
\WORDPROC\DOCUMENT\SCREEN01.DOC
\WORDPROC\DOCUMENT\CHAP6.DOC
\WORDPROC\DOCUMENT\SCREEN00.DOC
\WORDPROC\DOCUMENT\SCREEN01.DOC
```

To restore your files from the backup without automatically overwriting any files that have changed since they were backed up, use the /P switch. To restore files with a DOC extension, for example, that prompts you before it overwrites any newer versions, type:

RESTORE A: C:*.DOC /P

DOS responds with the following message:

```
Insert backup diskette 01 in drive A:
Press any key to continue . . .

*** Files were backed up 05-15-1991 ***

*** Restoring files from drive A: ***
Diskette: 01

WARNING! File CHAP6.DOC
was changed after it was backed up
Replace the file (Y/N)?
```

Answer **Y** to replace the file on drive C with the backed-up file, or **N** to skip this file. Next, RESTORE displays the names of files as they are restored:

```
\WORDPROC\DOCUMENT\SCREEN01.DOC
```

Once again, RESTORE finds a file that has changed since it was backed up:

```
WARNING! File CHAP6.DOC
was changed after it was backed up
Replace the file (Y/N)?
```

Notice that the file is again CHAP6.DOC. When the command BACKUP C:\WORDPROC A: /M /S /A was issued, the original backed up version of the file was not replaced, and the new copy was appended to the end of the BACKUP.001 file. Again, answer **Y** or **N** at the prompt. RESTORE then continues until all specified files have been processed.

RESTORE creates as many subdirectories as it needs to restore the files you specify. The following command, for example, can be used if you backed up your hard disk drive before you installed DOS 5 and changed the partition size.:

```
RESTORE A: C:\*.* /S /N
```

The directory tree will be rebuilt and any files that are not already on the C drive (the DOS 5 files are already on the drive) will be restored.

Summary

Chapter 6 covered a series of common DOS commands that are often taken for granted because they are used for basic operations. Knowing how to take advantage of the features of the file commands—both new to DOS 5 features and ones that already existed—will help you better control your files. By using the ATTRIB command to control file attributes, for example, you can make backing up your files a quick and simple task, thus ensuring that you are more likely to maintain timely backups. In chapter 6 you also learned of shortcuts to correcting problems caused by software installation programs.

In Chapter 7 you learn more about how filters, pipes, and redirection can be used to increase your productivity.

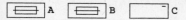
7

Using Filters, Pipes, and Redirection for Productivity

In Chapter 3 you learned about commands' standard input and standard output. In this chapter you will learn how to use three basic but powerful tools to modify the manner in which DOS commands receive their inputs and route their outputs. This chapter presents filters, pipes, and redirection. These three tools can save you time and allow you to accomplish everyday tasks more efficiently. Some of the tasks in this chapter can be accomplished only by using filters, pipes, or redirection.

You also will learn how to use these DOS capabilities to customize existing commands into new personalized commands of your own. As you work through the example in this chapter, you will learn how to use filters, pipes, and redirection as connectors, which can combine commands into new and creative tools.

Each of this chapter's examples use some of the following commands:

- ❏ COPY
- ❏ DIR /O
- ❏ DOSKEY
- ❏ EDIT

- ❏ FIND /I /V /C
- ❏ MORE
- ❏ SORT /+
- ❏ TYPE

As you practice using these commands, you will learn to use DOS to set up a simple database, store as a file the information you type at the console, sort

221

and search text files, combine several DOS commands so that they behave as one command, and run several programs in sequence by issuing only one command. You also will learn how to print error messages and other types of information in a file, make a printout of a directory list, and work with simple macros.

The following sections show you how to set up and use a simple text database of names, addresses, and phone numbers. You do not need any external application programs to create, edit, or produce reports from the database. You will learn how to perform data entry, data processing, and output tasks using only DOS.

Creating a Simple Database

To many computer users, the term "database" means an elaborate, dedicated file whose structure is complex and whose creation is difficult. While it is true that database applications software—such as Paradox and dBASE IV—are relatively complex products, a database *file* does not have to be complex. In its simplest form, a database is nothing more than a collection of related records. Each record contains items of information about an individual entry. A database can contain records pertaining to inventory part numbers, sales prices of retail items, family history, or just about any other type of information.

If your database needs are simple, you may not even need to use a database application program; DOS may provide all the database management capabilities you need. To learn more about this, try creating a simple database of names, addresses, and telephone numbers in DOS. The following pages show you how to set up the database, and how So that you can get more practice with DOS commands, you will see how to create a simple name, address, and phone number database that you can access from the DOS prompt.

The first task is to set up the database. Do not worry about creating an elaborate database; you can start small for now and add entries as you go. Think of the names, addresses, and phone numbers of at least five people you know. Limit the information about each person to 80 characters, which is the maximum number of characters that will fit in a single line on-screen. Better still, limit the information to 60 or 70 characters to leave room for the DOS command prompt.

The database is a text file called FRIENDS.DAT. You might select another name, but if you do, use your selection in place of FRIENDS.DAT when trying the sample commands presented in this chapter. In this file, each line represents a database record. Each record contains a name, address, and phone number, which are separated by at least two blank spaces. For subsequent commands to work properly with each line, you must pay attention to the spacing of the items in each line. For now, use the MS-DOS Editor to type in the information, if you have DOS 5. If you are using a previous version of the operating system, use EDLIN or skip to the end of this discussion, where you will learn how to use COPY redirection to load your information.

Windows ▼ ▲

The Windows environment includes many small applications designed to improve your productivity. Many of the tasks accomplished at the command line using a complex series of files, pipes, and redirection can be done using a single Windows tool. The database example included in this chapter is an excellent introduction to the concepts of file manipulation. But, compared to the Cardfile database utility that is bundled part of the Windows environment, creating a database as a text file is a primitive approach.

Using the DOS Editor To Create the Database

To get into the DOS 5 full-screen editor, type **EDIT** at the DOS command prompt. For the editor to work, you must have QBASIC.EXE in the current directory or in your system's search path. If the EDIT program does not work, copy QBASIC.EXE into your \DOS directory, or into another directory that is listed in your computer's search path. If you need help setting up the editor, see the discussions on paths and environment variables in Chapter 9.

A Note on EDIT and Your Monitor

EDIT is a full-screen graphic program. It can work with any monitor, but by default is set for use with a color monitor. Use the /B switch if you have a black-and-white screen. Use the /G switch if you are using a CGA monitor. If you have EGA, VGA, or any other type of monitor, do not use any switches.

The initial editing screen contains a message that refers you to the help manual. For now, press Esc to clear the message. Then type the names, addresses, and phone numbers that will make up your database. You can use the arrow keys to move around in your text.

There are two ways to get into the editor and specify the file you want to use. First, you can use the file name as a parameter when you issue the EDIT command. This is what the command will look like:

```
EDIT FRIENDS.DAT
```

When you are done working on the file, you can save it by issuing the SAVE command. Type Alt-F to open the File menu and then type **S** for Save. DOS saves the file under the name you used when you started the editor.

Second, you can get into the editor by typing **EDIT** with no parameters. When you open the editor in this manner, however, you must supply a file name when you want to save the file to disk. When you are ready to save your work, press Alt-F to open the File menu. If you have not previously saved the file, press **S** to select Save, and DOS prompts for the name of the file. Press **A** to select Save As when you want to store the data under a file name that DOS does not already have.

To exit from the editor, press Alt-F to display the File menu, and then press **X** (for Exit).

Using the DOS COPY Command To Create the Database

You also can enter information by using the DOS COPY command. If you do not have the DOS 5 editor or another text editor, such as EDLIN, you should use this method to create your database. The COPY command "copies" the information you type at the console directly into a file.

Before you begin entering the database information, use COPY to create the FRIENDS.DAT file, as follows:

```
COPY CON FRIENDS.DAT
```

Next, type each line of information from the keyboard. Correct any mistakes in the line before you press Enter at the end of the line. (Remember that when you are copying data from the console device, you cannot back up a line.) After you type the last line, press F6 or Ctrl-Z, and then press Enter. DOS saves the information in a new file named FRIENDS.DAT.

Viewing the Database

Next, use the DOS TYPE command to look at your file, as follows:

```
TYPE FRIENDS.DAT
```

This chapter's sample files contain the following information:

```
Timothy  Fredricks 4321 Wandering Lane, Friendswood TX    321-7123
Bill     Burton     823 South Hampton St. New York NY     782-4232
Sam      Clarion   92383 East Samton Lane, New Jersey     312-2133
Charles  Browning  432-A Any Lane, Bloomington, IN        432-2344
Doug     Downley   4231 Candlerock Way, Indianapolis, IN  234-4322
```

The TYPE command is useful for viewing short text files. You will see other examples of TYPE later in the chapter. If your file looks correct, you are ready to use the database to help you learn about filters.

DOS Shell

The DOS Shell environment offers a special tool for examining the contents of files quickly. The View File Contents command (under the File menu) can generate a text (ASCII) or hexadecimal display of a file's contents. The hexadecimal view is useful when you need to examine binary files. One of the features missing from the TYPE command (even when used with MORE) is the capability to move backward through a file. The View File Contents window gives you a great deal of flexibility through its use of scroll bars to move through the document.

Using DOS Filters

To some DOS users, filters are a mystery. Yet, everyone can relate to filters in the right context. Chances are you have had some experience with filters. Think, for example, of a coffee filter. You put ground coffee beans in the filter and then pour water through it. The filter traps the coffee but allows the water to pass through. When the water emerges from the filter, its color and flavor are changed. Computer filters work in much the same way. In DOS, filters are commands that take in data, change it in some way, and then output the result.

DOS filters can help you view, sort, and select parts of a file. MORE, SORT, and FIND are three DOS commands that filter data.

Filters are always used to manipulate information. Data does not just pour through these three commands; rather, the filters change or alter the data in some way. MORE divides continuous output into screen-size sections and waits for you to press a key before displaying more. FIND looks for strings in the output data and returns only a subset of the lines used as input. SORT arranges input in a different order before outputting it. Filters get their default inputs from the keyboard, but also can accept input from files and the output of other commands.

MORE

Earlier in this chapter, you used the TYPE command to view the contents of your FRIENDS.DAT file. When you issued the TYPE command, DOS simply displayed the file's entire contents on-screen. TYPE is very handy for viewing the contents of a small file, but does not work as well when you want to view a file that contains more than one screenful of information. When you use TYPE by itself to view the contents of a long file, the information scrolls up the screen very rapidly, and does not stop so that you can read it. You can press Ctrl-S or Pause to stop the scrolling, but it is sometimes difficult to stop the scroll before information scrolls past the top edge of the screen. You can avoid the scrolling problem by using the MORE filter.

The MORE filter receives an input—in this case, the contents of a data file—and displays it on the monitor in screen-size portions. You can use MORE with the TYPE command to pipe the output through the filter for the same results, as follows:

```
TYPE READ.ME | MORE
```

When you issue this command, DOS displays the contents of READ.ME one screenful at a time. To see the next screenful of information, you can press any key except Pause. Notice the use of the vertical bar (|), which is the DOS pipe symbol. Pipes are discussed later in this chapter.

In Chapter 8, you will use the MORE filter and redirection to look into a file, as follows:

```
MORE < READ.ME
```

This example shows the file being redirected through the filter. Redirection is explained in detail later in this chapter.

SORT

When you use the SORT filter, DOS arranges a file's contents in alphabetical order and displays the sorted data on-screen. SORT does not make any changes to the file; rather, the filter simply displays the file's contents in sorted order. The original file remains as you left it.

Suppose, for example, that you want to view the contents of the database in FRIENDS.DAT, with its entries placed in alphabetical order. To do this, issue SORT as follows:

```
SORT < FRIENDS.DAT
```

DOS alphabetizes the database's entries, and displays the results on-screen, as follows:

```
Bill     Burton    823 South Hampton St. New York NY    782-4232
Charles  Browning  432-A Any Lane, Bloomington, IN      432-2344
Doug     Downley   4231 Candlerock Way, Indianapolis, IN 234-4322
Sam      Clarion   92383 East Samton Lane, New Jersey   312-2133
Timothy  Fredricks 4321 Wandering Lane, Friendswood, TX  321-7123
```

Notice that the alphabetical order is based on the first character in each line. By default, SORT alphabetizes from the first character, even if the character is a space. When sorting a file, SORT does not distinguish between upper- and lowercase letters.

You can reverse the sort order by adding the /R switch to the SORT command.

In the preceding example, DOS sorted the database entries according to the letters in the first column of each line. You can tell SORT, however, to arrange a file's contents according to the letters in other columns. If you were careful to start each last name in the same column, you can sort the file by last name by using the /+ switch. The /+ switch causes SORT to arrange the data according the information in a specified column. In the sample FRIENDS.DAT, each last name begins in the tenth column. Use the following command to display the entries in alphabetical order by last name:

```
SORT /+10 < FRIENDS.DAT
```

This SORT command displays the following information:

```
Charles  Browning  432-A Any Lane, Bloomington, IN      432-2344
Bill     Burton    823 South Hampton St. New York NY    782-4232
Sam      Clarion   92383 East Samton Lane, New Jersey   312-2133
Doug     Downley   4231 Candlerock Way, Indianapolis, IN 234-4322
Timothy  Fredricks 4321 Wandering Lane, Friendswood, TX  321-7123
```

You can see that SORT has ordered the lines based on last names. Keep SORT's positional capability in mind when you create other DOS databases. By starting each item of all records at the same relative position, you can sort your database on any item.

The SORT command also is handy to use with files that have been exported from spreadsheet applications into ASCII format.

FIND

When you use the FIND filter, the action is more like panning for gold than making coffee. FIND separates the information you want from the rest of the information in the file. You use FIND to search every line of a file for occurrences of a specified string of characters. When DOS finds a match, it directs the entire string to the screen. If a line does not contain a match, FIND strains out that line.

FIND is a standard DOS command also works as a filter. If you do not specify a file, FIND can take input from the keyboard, a pipe, or a redirected file.

Suppose that you want to find any line in the FRIENDS.DAT file that contains the letters "NY." You can easily do this by issuing FIND as a standard command, as follows:

```
FIND "NY" FRIENDS.DAT
```

Notice that FIND uses two parameters. The first parameter indicates the string to be matched. When you specify the string, you must surround it with quotation marks ("") in the command line. This allows blank spaces to be included in the search string. The second parameter is the name of the file to be searched. FIND displays only those lines that contain a string matching the first parameter.

When you issue the preceding command, DOS searches FRIENDS.DAT for any line that contains the string NY, and displays that line on-screen, as follows:

```
Bill    Burton    823 South Hampton St. New York NY    782-4232
```

FIND Switches

FIND features many useful switches. You can use the /N switch to add line numbers to the output. The numbers refer to the line in the file where the match was found. In the case of the sample FRIENDS.DAT file, Bill Burton's line would be preceded by [2], and Charles Browning's line would be preceded by [4]. The number shows the line's position in the original file, not FIND's output.

Use the /I switch to tell FIND to ignore differences in case. Try this by using FIND as a filter and adding the /I switch:

```
FIND /I "ny" < FRIENDS.DAT
```

DOS displays all lines containing the string ny, NY, nY, or Ny:

```
Bill     Burton  823 South Hampton St. New York NY     782-4232
Charles  Browning 432-A Any Lane, Bloomington, IN      432-2344
```

You can see how FIND would be useful for reporting pricing information from a sales database or last names for a given first name in a name and address database. You simply specify the text you want to find.

You can use the /C switch to count the number of lines that contain the specified string. You also can use the /C switch along with the string " " (one blank space) to count the total number of lines in the file, because each line has at least one space.

By specifying the /V switch, you can use FIND to filter out lines that contain a specified string. Suppose that you want to search the FRIENDS.DAT file for a list of friends who do not live in New York. Enter the following form of the FIND command:

```
FIND /V "NY" < FRIENDS.DAT
```

The following results appear on-screen:

```
Timothy  Fredricks 4321 Wandering Lane, Friendswood, TX   321-7123
Sam      Clarion   92383 East Samton Lane, New Jersey     312-2133
Charles  Browning  432-A Any Lane, Bloomington, IN         432-2344
Doug     Downley   4231 Candlerock Way, Indianapolis, IN  234-4322
```

Limitations to FIND Searches

There are limits to searches you can do with FIND. The search string must be contained in one line; you cannot search for a string that is interrupted by a carriage return. This is not a problem in the sample database, however, because each listing resides on only one line. Further, you cannot use wild cards in either file names or extensions. If you could, you might specify more than one file to be searched at one time. To do searches over more than one file, you must use the FOR command, which is described in Chapter 13.

Some of the FIND switches conflict and cannot be used in combination with each other. For example, /C counts only the number of lines containing the specified string. Only a number and no other text is output. The /N switch attaches the line number to each line of text output. You cannot add a line number when the line is not there, so you cannot use /N and /C in the same FIND command. If you try it, DOS simply ignores the /N and returns the number requested by the /C switch.

Using DOS Pipes

Computer *pipes* work in much the same way as hoses or water pipes. Water is poured into one end of the pipe and comes out the other. The pipes are not only a connection between the faucet and the water main, but they keep the water from running all over the floor. Computer pipes take the output from one command and connect it to the input of another command. The DIR command, for example, produces a list of directory names. This list could be piped from DIR to another command, which sorts the list.

Pipes are helpful when you want to direct output from a command to a temporary file, and then use that file as input for another command. Use the vertical bar (|) in this situation to set up a pipeline.

Pipes connect two different commands that must otherwise be used separately. A pipe is most useful when you want to place more than one command on a command line or when you are creating personalized commands of your own from the ones DOS gives you. The vertical bar looks a little like a pipe. At least it looks more like a miniature pipe than does the ampersand symbol (&), so it is a good choice to represent the pipe.

Using Pipes with Filters

Later in this chapter, you will find an example in which DOS takes the output from DIR and stores it in a file. In another example, DOS sorts the contents of this file. Here are the two commands you will issue to perform those operations:

```
DIR > LISTFILE.TXT

SORT < LISTFILE.TXT
```

Because the DOS filters MORE, SORT, and FIND can be used with redirection or pipes, both of the preceding lines can be combined into one step. The following command, which makes use of a pipe (|), does both tasks:

```
DIR | SORT
```

DOS 5, however, also features a DIR switch, which can sort the output. If you have DOS 5, you can type this command:

```
DIR /O:n
```

The /O switch is available only with the latest version of DOS. It allows you to tell DIR the order in which you want the directory listing to appear. There are many possibilities. This example uses *n*, which stands for *name*. The directories from this example would be output in alphabetical order by name. You can substitute any of the following letters for *n*:

Parameter	Function
-n	reverse alphabetical order
e	alphabetic by extension
-e	reverse alphabetic by extension
d	date and time (earliest first)
-d	reverse date and time (latest first)
s	size (smallest first)
-s	reverse size (largest first)
g	directories before files
-g	directories after files

A Note on Pipes and TEMP

You must have a TEMP environment variable set before you can use pipes. If the preceding example did not work for you, type **SET** at the DOS prompt to find out if the TEMP variable is set in your system. If the example did work, your AUTOEXEC.BAT file probably contains a line that looks something like this:

```
SET TEMP=C:\WINDOWS\TEMP
```

Do not worry if your TEMP directory is not the same as the one shown here. The TEMP directory can be any directory you have in your path but do not use for any other purpose. Look in the section on environment variables in Chapter 9 if you need help setting up a TEMP variable.

Network software usually has a command to let you see who else is on the system. If that command name is WHO, the following example displays a sorted list of users:

```
WHO | SORT
```

The OS/2 LAN Server uses the command NETWHO to list the identities of other users on the system. Users on this type of network would type the example this way:

```
NETWHO | SORT
```

If you only want to know if Mary is logged on, use this command:

```
WHO | FIND /I "MARY"
```

The /I switch tells FIND to locate all matches regardless of case. This example would find MARY, Mary, or mary.

Any program that reads from the terminal can read from a pipe instead. Any program that writes to the terminal can write to a pipe instead. You can use as many pipes in a command as you wish. Suppose, for example, that you want to find all directory listings that contain the string "MY" and print them to the terminal one screenful at a time. Enter the following command:

```
DIR | FIND "MY" | MORE
```

The output from this command might look something like this:

```
DUMMY    DAT    5249 05-09-91  8:00p
MYINFO   DOC     421 05-09-91  8:05p
MYDATA   TXT    1240 05-09-91  8:25p
MYRA            425 05-09-91  8:26p
MOMMY    BAT     830 05-09-91  8:27p
```

As your FRIENDS.DAT database grows to more than one screenful of information, you can use pipes to help control the display of the database. When you want to view the database one screen at a time, you can use the following command:

```
TYPE FRIENDS.DAT | MORE
```

The results of this command will look just the way it would if you used TYPE without the MORE filter, because the file is not big enough to be broken into screen-size chunks. The output is still being filtered through MORE, but it all fits on one screen.

You can use the MORE command and pipes in combination with DIR, SORT, and TYPE. You may have other utilities or batch files on your computer that can be piped into MORE.

If your list of friends is very long, you may want to sort the results of a query. Use the following command to display a sorted list of friends who live in New York:

```
FIND /I "NY" FRIENDS.DAT | SORT
```

Here are the results of the FIND piped through SORT:

```
Bill    Burton   823 South Hampton St. New York NY    782-4232
Charles Browning 432-A Any Lane, Bloomington, IN       432-2344
```

Using Pipes To Combine Commands

By using pipes to tie commands together, you can execute several commands in sequence. Use the following command, for example, to create a directory named NEWSTUFF and then make it the current directory:

```
MD NEWSTUFF | CD NEWSTUFF
```

You also can use pipes to run programs in sequence. The next example changes directories, runs a word processing program, changes to another directory, and then runs a grammar-checking program:

```
CD \WP51 | FLWP | CD \G4 | G4
```

This is a handy tool for amusing children. You can use the following command, for example, to start several computer games in turn with just one command:

```
CD \GAMES | TETRIS | BEYOND | CHESS
```

This command starts the game TETRIS. When the player exits from TETRIS, TETRIS ends and BEYOND starts. When the player exits from BEYOND, that game ends and CHESS begins. Keep this in mind if you ever have to amuse a child in an office while you work. Perhaps it will eliminate some interruptions.

Windows ▼ ▲
If entertaining children in an educational fashion is an important goal, the Windows environment offers a number of advantages. Not only are the games more visually appealing, but the Windows interface makes applications more accessible. In the standard Windows environment, a child can begin to learn to use a program while creating refrigerator art using Paintbrush. A word of warning, however: The very ease of use in Windows makes it possible for a child to wreak havoc in document files unless you make sure to restrict the child to using only "safe" programs.

Using Redirection

Redirection is the most easily understood of DOS' special tools. An everyday example are gutters or drain pipes found on houses. Rain water runs down the roof and before it falls over the edge, it is redirected to a corner of the house by the gutter. If that gutter runs into a creek, the water is being redirected again. The creek will rise both because rain is falling directly into the creek and because additional water is being redirected into the creek.

DOS redirection works with both input and output. Input normally comes from one place. When dealing with computers, that is usually a keyboard. But data can be redirected from another location. Some programs get input from a file. You will learn how to redirect a file into a command. The normal output on a computer goes to the screen. But it could also be redirected to a file or to the printer.

You no doubt understand what is happening in redirection without really understanding exactly what DOS is actually doing. When a user tells a command where to send its output, the user is redirecting the output. This is because output is always directed to the same place unless the user tells the operating system to send the output elsewhere. On its own, DOS always writes the output of a command to the screen. You can send the output to a file instead by using the greater-than symbol (>). Here is a simple example:

```
DIR > LISTING
```

When you issue this command, the directory listing is not printed to the screen; it is stored in a file named LISTING.

There is also a default method of input. Most commands get the data they need from the keyboard. If you want a command to get information from a file, you must use the less-than sign (<) to direct the file's data into the command.

Similarly, you can use the < redirection symbol to redirect a file so that it is used as input for a filter. You can use the following command, for example, if you want to sort the contents of the file FILELIST.TXT:

```
SORT < FILELIST.TXT
```

DOS alphabetizes the file's contents and displays the sorted list on-screen. As shown earlier, you can add the > redirection symbol to route the sorted output into another file, as follows:

```
SORT < FILELIST.TXT > SORTEDLT.TXT
```

You also can redirect the output to the printer. Use the name of the port to which your printer is connected, as follows:

```
SORT < FILELIST.TXT > LPT1
```

A Note about Printer Port Designators

In versions of DOS predating DOS 5, the preceding command is written with a semicolon after the printer port designator LPT1, like this:

```
SORT < FILELIST.TXT > LPT1;
```

Some commands, such as PRINT, send output primarily to the printer, but also can display messages on-screen. If you redirect the PRINT command's output to a file, the file will contain only the messages that are generated by the command. The file is printed to the printer, not to the file. Try the following example:

```
PRINT C:\AUTOEXEC.BAT > TMPFILE.TXT
```

When you issue this command, DOS prints the contents of AUTOEXEC.BAT, but TMPFILE.TXT contains this message:

```
C:\AUTOEXEC.BAT is currently being printed
```

If DOS does not find AUTOEXEC.BAT, an error message is generated. This message is output to the screen, but not to the file. You cannot use > to redirect all error messages.

Windows/DOS Shell

Files created by redirecting output are created as actual disk files. As such, they are accessible to the entire Windows or DOS Shell environment. If you create a file in a DOS command window, you can switch to another window and manipulate the new file.

Redirecting Output to NULL

Many computer users place the PAUSE command in their AUTOEXEC.BAT file after the DATE and TIME commands. (PAUSE is commonly used in other types of batch files, as well, as shown in Chapter 13.) When PAUSE is used, the batch file stops executing until the user presses a key. The following message appears at the bottom of the screen:

```
Press any key to continue . . .
```

You can specify a different message by writing it next to the command. Here is an example of PAUSE with a customized remark:

```
PAUSE Press any key to begin installing program
```

The text `Press any key to begin installing program` appears at the bottom of the screen when the PAUSE command executes. There may be times, however, when you want to use the PAUSE but have no text appear on-screen. In this instance, you must use redirection to send output to a dummy device, called NULL. The following command eliminates all messages from PAUSE:

```
PAUSE > NULL
```

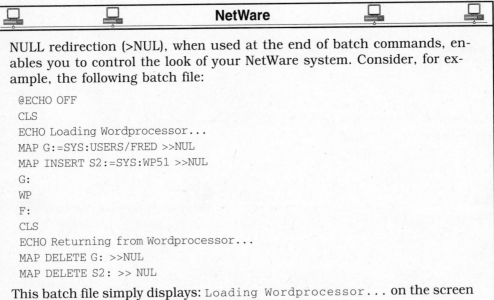

NetWare

NULL redirection (>NUL), when used at the end of batch commands, enables you to control the look of your NetWare system. Consider, for example, the following batch file:

```
@ECHO OFF
CLS
ECHO Loading Wordprocessor...
MAP G:=SYS:USERS/FRED >>NUL
MAP INSERT S2:=SYS:WP51 >>NUL
G:
WP
F:
CLS
ECHO Returning from Wordprocessor...
MAP DELETE G: >>NUL
MAP DELETE S2: >> NUL
```

This batch file simply displays: `Loading Wordprocessor...` on the screen while it sets up NetWare drive mappings. It also displays: `Returning from Wordprocessor...` while it deletes the drive mappings. Try this in one of your own batch files on the network and see how much nicer it looks. The astute reader may have noticed the >> instead of > in the batch file example. The >> stands for appended output and is a little faster than > when redirecting ouptut to NUL.

Combining Redirection and Pipes

Sometimes you may want to use both redirection and pipes in a single command line. The following command copies all directory listings containing the string "MY" to a file called MYPROGS.TXT:

```
DIR | FIND "LOG" > MYPROGS.TXT
```

As you may recall, you used the following command in the earlier section on filters:

```
FIND /I "NY" < FRIENDS.DAT
```

You can use the following command to direct the output to a file:

```
FIND /I "IN" < FRIENDS.DAT > INFRNDS.DAT
```

Chapter 8 will show you how to direct output to a file to keep a list of a directory's contents. Specify a file name to hold the list, which you can use to maintain directory integrity. You can refer to the list to see if any files have been deleted or added accidently. The following command creates the list, sorts it alphabetically, and stores it in a file named DIRNAME.LST:

```
DIR | SORT > DIRNAME.LST
```

You also can direct the output to the printer. You might want to do this if you are working with floppy disks. Because disk management is easier if you keep a paper printout with each disk, you can use the following command to print the disk's directory list:

```
DIR A: | SORT > PRN
```

NetWare

Use the NetWare CAPTURE command before redirecting output to a network printer. CAPTURE usually directs output from LPT1: and PRN: to the first network printer.

You also can use the TREE command to include all subdirectories in your list. The /F switch must be used to include file names. You can make a list of not just the directory, but also of subdirectories with TREE. The backslash (\) starts the listing from the root directory. There is no reason to sort when using TREE, so the command looks like this:

```
TREE \ /F > PRN
```

Pipes are used with one temporary file at a time. If your task involves two temporary files, you will need to use more than a one-line command. The following three commands let you compare two directory listings so that you can determine which files are in only one directory:

```
DIR C:\UTIL > UTIL1.TXT
DIR C:\OLDUTIL > UTIL2.TXT
FC UTIL1.TXT UTIL2.TXT
```

Using Filters, Pipes, and Redirection with DOSKEY

DOSKEY is a terminate-and-stay-resident (TSR) program that has several functions. You can use DOSKEY's command-history capabilities to recall or edit a previously issued command. You can find examples of this DOSKEY function in Chapter 3.

You also can use the program as a macro builder to build, edit, store, and execute macros. This section shows how DOSKEY macros use filters, pipes, and redirection. For a more detailed discussion of DOSKEY and macros, see Chapter 13.

A *macro* is a series of commands that is stored for later use. DOSKEY can be used to save one or more DOS commands in RAM. This saved list of commands is given a name, which you can type whenever you want to run the commands.

Running a macro is very much like using a batch file. A batch file is created by saving commands in a file. You create a macro, however, by placing commands in a macro definition. Batch files can be any length, but DOS macros are limited to 127 characters. A batch file can move you to another location or call other programs. Macros just execute the commands one at a time in order. You can press Ctrl-C to end the execution of a batch file, but you must press Ctrl-C once for *every* command in a macro. Because macros are stored in RAM, they run faster than batch files, which are stored on disk. When you turn off your computer, however, your DOS macros are lost.

To create a macro, you call DOSKEY and then type the name of the macro followed by the commands to be included in the macro. You cannot use the special pipe and redirection characters in the macro definition. Instead, you must use the following codes:

Code	Character
$L	<
$G	>
$GG	>>
$B	|

The following simple macro sorts FRIENDS.DAT and saves the sorted output in a file called SFRIENDS.DAT:

```
DOSKEY ORDERIT=SORT$LFRIENDS.DAT$GSRT-FNDS.DAT
```

Be sure to use two different file names. If you use FRIENDS.DAT for both files, DOS tries to put sorted input into the same place from which it is taking data out to be sorted. You are likely to lose all your data that way. Use two distinct files when sorting a file and storing the sorted data.

This is not just important with DOSKEY, but also with commands typed at the command line. Do NOT try something like this:

```
TYPE FRIENDS.DAT >> FRIENDS.DAT
```

If you keep appending a file onto itself, it will continue to grow until you run out of disk space. Until that happens, your machine is hung up. Now that you understand pipes and redirection, however, you are not likely to make such a mistake.

Nothing should happen when you type the command. Remember that a macro just stores the directions and carries them out when you type **ORDERIT**. The macro should give you the same results as if you had typed the following command:

```
SORT < FRIENDS.DAT > SFRIENDS.DAT
```

Here is another example that searches a directory for files that contain the letters "MY", and then and prints them to the screen one page at a time:

```
DOSKEY MYDIR=DIR$BFIND/I "my"$BMORE
```

Call the command by typing **MYDIR** at the DOS prompt. The macro directions appear on-screen as follows:

```
DIR|FIND/I "MY"|MORE
```

Generally it pays to be concise, but use spaces where you need them. In this case, if you do not place a space after the /I switch, you cause DOS to return an error message saying that /I is an invalid switch.

DOSKEY can record groups of commands that you use often. You can record all the macros once and save them in a batch file by issuing the following command:

```
DOSKEY /MACROS > DOMACROS.BAT
```

If you call DOMACROS.BAT from your AUTOEXEC.BAT, all macros will be loaded each time you log on.

Summary

When you know how to use pipes, filters, and redirection, you add a new dimension to your DOS-level work. Filters, pipes, and redirection are techniques that make DOS more productive. If you have not yet taken advantage of these DOS tools, perhaps you will work them into your everyday DOS activities. Here are the important concepts you should take from this chapter:

❏ Filters are programs that take an input, perform a transformation on the input, and write an output. MORE, SORT, and FIND are three commonly used filters.

❏ Pipes are used to move the output from one program to the input of another.

❏ Redirection is used in two instances. You can redirect input from a file instead of the keyboard. You also can redirect output to a file instead of the screen. Output also can be appended to an existing file.

❏ Special symbols must be used with using redirection with DOSKEY macros.

The next chapter teaches you techniques that will help you ensure your data's integrity. Nothing in computing is as disappointing as the loss of an important file, directory, or even an entire disk. Chapter 8 shows you how to guard against such losses.

8

Ensuring Data Integrity

The computer enables you to perform many tasks more quickly and efficiently than when working manually. Unfortunately, the computer also introduces risks that you do not face when working manually. You may, for example, copy new files over old files that you want to keep. You can accidentally wipe out entire directories or lose hours of work in only a few seconds.

For these reasons, you need to know more than simply how to use applications or basic DOS commands. Before you can use computers efficiently, you must learn how to maintain data integrity.

When you work toward preserving data *integrity*, you are working to ensure that your data is complete and correct. Complete, correct data can be the difference between confused fumbling and finishing on time. Do you know which files you need and where they are? To find a file, do you first have to weed through a hard disk full of forgotten garbage, old information, and unused applications? Do you always know where the latest version of each file is stored? Do you forget which file contains what information?

This chapter will encourage you to follow good work habits to ensure data integrity. You will learn how to sort directories to maintain order and make archive directory listings. The chapter also covers commands that let you undelete files and unformat accidently formatted disks, change the attributes of important files, as well as learn how and when to use the DOS commands to backup and restore your files.

241

The commands used by the tasks in this chapter include the following:

❑ ASSIGN	❑ SORT
❑ ATTRIB	❑ SUBST
❑ BACKUP	❑ UNDELETE
❑ COPY	❑ UNFORMAT
❑ MIRROR	❑ VERIFY
❑ RECOVER	❑ XCOPY
❑ RESTORE	

This chapter teaches you how to work efficiently with DOS. In the following sections, you will learn how to organize your work and avoid common pitfalls that plague many computer users.

Understanding Files and Data Integrity

A computer stores information in files. Many different types of files exist and can store programs, data, or a combination of information.

Characters in a filename can be any of the letters from A to Z, the numbers 0 to 9, or any of the following characters (separated by commas): ?, -, ^, $, ~, !, #, %, &, +, {, }, (,). You cannot use the comma, period, spaces, or any other special characters in file names.

Unfortunately, exceptions to these rules do exist that can frustrate the user. Occasionally, you may be able to save a file name containing a space when using applications that do not enforce the "no space" rule. If, for example, you are saving the file SALLY.OK in a word processor program, you may accidently put in a space and save it as SALLY. OK. Notice the extra space at the beginning of the extension. This is a common typing error. Some word processors catch it, whereas others save the file name just as you have typed it. Getting a space in a file name or extension is easier than getting it out. Because COMMAND.COM reads the space character as a parameter delimiter, your attempt to use a space in a file name parameter appears to be two parameters to COMMAND.COM.

A Note on Spaces in File Names

Some applications, such as PC Tools, use spaces as a form of copy protection. If you decide to remove the application from your hard drive, you must either use the uninstall program (if the application supplied one) or learn how to delete files containing spaces. Read Chapter 9 to learn how to create similar copy-protected files of your own.

If you save the file with the space in the file name, you may encounter problems when you list the files. When you type the DIR command from the DOS prompt, you may not see the space in the file name when you list the directory. All the file names look normal. If you look at the directory, it shows that the file SALLY.OK exists, but when you enter the command DIR SALLY.OK, you get the following message:

```
File not found
```

Although you cannot see what the file name really is, you can track it down and rename or delete it. This is done with a step-by-step narrowing of the files to be listed. You know it exists because you see it using the DIR command. You also can see it listed when you type DIR S*.*. You can track down the problem by adding one letter at a time. You soon will find that SALLY.* is listed in the file. Now you know the problem must be in the extension. If this is the only file listed, you can delete it or rename it at this point.

In this example, the space is in the first position of the extension. If you use the command DIR SALLY.O*, therefore, you do not see a listing of the file. This tells you that a problem with the first letter in the extension exists. Once you know where the extra space is located, put a ? wild card in that spot. The DIR SALLY.?OK command lists the file and you can rename it using the following command:

```
REN SALLY.?OK SALLY.OK
```

The REN command is used to rename the file to a similar name but without the space.

By using a step-by-step elimination, you have found that you can list this file individually. This process will work for any problems you might have with difficult to delete files.

Windows/DOS Shell

Windows and DOS Shell enable you to select files from a list by high-lighting them. This eliminates the need to accurately type the file name and lets you manipulate any file—even if you cannot type the file name.

Examining File Contents To Maintain Integrity

The TYPE command is the easiest command to use for looking inside a file. It is most useful if the file contains ordinary ASCII characters, as in the following example:

TYPE AUTOEXEC.BAT

```
@echo off
SET COMSPEC=C:\DOS\COMMAND.COM
PATH C:\;C:\DOS;C:\UTIL;C:\WP51;C:\WINDOWS
C:\WINDOWS\mouse.com /Y
PROMPT $P$G
SET TEMP=C:\WINDOWS\TEMP
```

A binary file created by a program contains more than just ASCII characters. The output probably will contain many unreadable characters. In general, you may want to avoid using TYPE on a binary file for no other reason than to omit the annoying beeps and unstoppable screen scrolls. The TYPE command, however, sometimes shows enough characters that you can use it to answer specific questions about the contents of a file.

Another disadvantage with the TYPE command is its limited usefulness for long files. Any output that is longer than what the screen can show scrolls off the screen. The scroll can be stopped, however, if you have a slow machine and you can type Ctrl-S or Pause very quickly. To cancel Ctrl-S, press any key.

Most PC users, however, enjoy using a fast machine and the MORE command instead of a slow machine and the TYPE command. As you saw in the last chapter, you can view a long file by redirecting it through the MORE command. The following is an example of the MORE command:

MORE < READ.ME

The first screen of information is displayed and the following prompt appears at the bottom of the screen:

```
-- More --
```

You can press any key to see the next screen of information.

You also can use the MORE and TYPE commands with pipes. See Chapter 7 for other examples using the MORE command.

DOS Shell

The DOS Shell provides the View File Contents command (under the File menu) to use in place of the TYPE command. Not only does it provide a text (ASCII) view, but it also can display information in a hexadecimal format that is useful for examining binary files. The View File Contents window gives you control over your positioning within a file through its use of scroll bars to move through the document.

Checking Times, Dates, and Sizes of Files

Many computer users work with data files on both hard disks and floppy disks. Perhaps you do most of your work on the hard drive, but copy certain files to floppies after modifying them. Many users also share data with other users. Some users may modify the files' contents. In many of these situations, more than one copy of the same file is available and those copies may or may not be the same. Files with the same names can be exact copies or older versions of the same file. How, then, can you compare these files?

The quick check is to use the DIR command to view the size and date of the file. Copying or renaming the file does not change the time or date. If they are the same for each file, they probably are the same file. If you need to be sure, use the COMP or FC command discussed in Chapter 6. COMP and FC are able to compare files for exactness.

DOS Shell

By using the Dual File View within DOS Shell, you can obtain a listing of two separate directories for comparison. The graphical representation of the directory tree makes it easy to move around and compare a number of files in different directories without having to remember their full filename, including the path.

Maintaining Integrity while Copying Files

The COPY command is used to make a duplicate of an existing file. The new file can have a new name or new location, or both. If you want to move a data file from the hard drive to a floppy, use the following command:

```
COPY MYSTUFF.DAT A:MYSTUFF.DAT
```

The new file can be given a new name by using it in the second parameter. The following is a similar command that copies the file and it renames YOURCOPY.DAT.

```
COPY MYSTUFF.DAT A:YOURCOPY.DAT
```

Wild cards can be used with the COPY command to copy many files at the same time. The following example command makes a second copy of every file with the DAT extension. The new copies have the same base name but a different extension.

```
COPY *.DAT *.BAK
```

DOS lists the file names as it copies the files. If not enough space is on the target media (such as a floppy disk) to store all the data, DOS stops copying and tells you how many files have been copied. The following message, for example, signifies that the target media (the drive receiving files) has run out of space on the fourth file:

```
JOHN.DAT
KATHY.DAT
ZACHARY.DAT
KALINA.DAT
Insufficient disk space
3 file(s) copied
```

Look for the Insufficient disk space message when you are copying files from your hard disk to a floppy so you can delete them from the hard disk. Do not assume that it is safe to delete the source files until you have verified that all were successfully copied to the floppy.

You also can use the COPY command to combine two text files into one new one, such as the following:

```
COPY JAN.DAT + FEB.DAT YEAR.DAT
```

In the preceding command, January and February data (JAN.DAT and FEB.DAT) are combined into a new file called YEAR.DAT. If you have DAT files for the whole year (and no other files in that location with the DAT extension), you can combine them all at once with the following command:

```
COPY *.DAT YEAR.ALL
```

Be sure that you do not form a target file name that matches a source wildcard file name. In the last example, had the target file been called YEAR.DAT, COPY would match the newly created target file in the directory with *.DAT and try to COPY its contents to itself. The contents of YEAR.DAT would be lost before the final copy was made. You can specify another directory for the target file when combining files with wildcard parameters. COPY will not find the target file in the current directory and mistake it for a source file.

Maintaining Integrity while Deleting Files

You can easily make a typing error and delete a different file than you intended. You should get into the habit of always using the /P switch to avoid this. The /P switch adds a prompt to ask for confirmation before DOS deletes a file. The command and request look similar to the following:

```
DEL JUNE01.DAT /P
```

```
JUNE01.DAT, Delete (Y/N)?
```

No default answer is available to this question. You must answer **Y** if you want the file(s) deleted, or **N** if you do not want the file(s) deleted.

Wild cards can cause trouble because it is easy to include more files than you realize. If you use wild cards with the DEL command, DOS asks for confirmation on each file. Another trick is to precede each DEL command with the same values using the DIR command. You may want to delete all your files that are called CHAPTER.*xxx*. You know you have CHAPTER-1.DAT, CHAPTER-2.DAT, CHAPTER-3.TXT, and CHAPTER-4.DOC. You can save time by deleting them all with the following command:

```
DEL CH*.*
```

Again, you should check the contents of the directory before deleting any files in them. In the preceding example, for instance, if you have a file called CHUCK.LOV that you want to keep, you should define the parameter further (CHA*.*, for example) so you do not delete the file. Make sure you include only those files you want to delete by first using the following command:

```
DIR CHA*.*
```

Mistakes can happen even to those who are careful. DOS 5 has a new command, UNDELETE, that enables you to undelete a deleted file. This command is explained in detail later in this chapter.

Recovering Data from Defective Disks

DOS provides the RECOVER command for recovering files and complete disks when CHKDSK cannot. Use the RECOVER command only when absolutely necessary. Do not casually experiment with RECOVER, as it can be very dangerous. It is designed to recover data from a damaged file one cluster at a time. It renames files and directories so you are left to wonder which file was which. Later in this chapter, you are shown that you should not use the command at all except under dire circumstances. If you maintain regular backups of your data, you should never have to use RECOVER.

You may have occasions, however, when the RECOVER command can be useful. You can use the RECOVER command to regain as much information as possible from damaged sectors of a disk. Information is read into a new file one sector at a time. Data stored in bad sectors, however, is lost. Files using those sectors have areas that cannot be restored. For this reason, partially recovered files may not be useful when crucial information is lost. You may be able to use most of a text file that RECOVER has processed, but it is unlikely that a recovered program or binary data file that is missing parts will be useful. Damaged sectors are marked as bad, so reusing the disk later is not a problem. You should be cautious, however, about reusing a disk that has failed because of bad sectors. The disk may deteriorate further and you will face data loss again.

The following is an example showing how difficult using the RECOVER command can be. You can try this type of example by using DISKCOPY to create an experimental disk from one containing a few files and directories. DO NOT experiment with using RECOVER on your hard disk or an original floppy! You may, for example, initially have the directory as shown in the following entries in a directory on your A: drive:

```
ONE       <DIR>    04-29-91  3:39a
HELV    PST    1261 12-11-91  9:47p
HELV-NBL PST    1261 12-11-90  9:47p
TIME    PST    1274 12-11-90  9:52p
TIME-ROM PST    1264 12-11-90 10:09p
          5 File(s)   345088 bytes free
```

If you type RECOVER A: at the DOS prompt to recover your A: drive, you are shown the following message:

```
Press any key to begin recovery of the
file(s) on drive A:
9 file(s) recovered
```

The following shows how the RECOVER command names the recovered files in a directory listsing:

```
FILE0001 REC   2048 04-29-91  3:38a
FILE0002 REC   2048 04-29-91  3:38a
FILE0003 REC   2048 04-29-91  3:38a
FILE0004 REC   2048 04-29-91  3:38a
FILE0005 REC   1024 04-29-91  3:38a
FILE0006 REC   2048 04-29-91  3:38a
FILE0007 REC   2048 04-29-91  3:38a
FILE0008 REC   2048 04-29-91  3:38a
FILE0009 REC   2048 04-29-91  3:38a
         9 File(s)   345088 bytes free
```

As you can see, the subdirectory ONE no longer appears. The directory listing shows no subdirectories. Actually, the entry for the subdirectory is shown as just another file in the root. Notice also that most files are 2048 bytes in size. You have to be a detective to identify these files. For text file identification, you can use the TYPE and FIND commands while searching for a clue among the FILEnnnn.REC files. If you can identify a file, rename it. Just remember that parts of the file may be missing. Binary program and data files may be impossible to identify, but you might find a recognized version number or record header at the beginning of a file.

If you cannot avoid using the RECOVER command, keep in mind these simple precautions. Try to recover files one at a time. This can be done if you know the file name. Also, files are recovered to the root directory, which is limited to 512 files or directories. If you restore files one directory at a time, you can go over this limit and RECOVER will stop.

RECOVER has other limitations, as well. It cannot be used on a drive formed by the ASSIGN, JOIN, or SUBST commands. Also, files cannot be recovered from a network drive, nor can you use wild cards (* or ?) to recover files. This means that you must specify either a file or a drive explicitly.

Understanding Directories and Data Integrity

As you know, a disk is used to store many files that are divided into directories. This division looks somewhat like an upside-down tree. When DOS is installed on a hard drive, the files are stored into a directory called DOS. Many other commercial packages also set up directories of their own when installed. WordPerfect, for example, might be found in a directory called \WP51, whereas Lotus 123 might be found in a directory called \123R3. This initial directory organization is done for you, but this section discusses directory strategies for you to follow when making your own directories and reorganizing the structure of existing ones.

Using Directory Commands

When your drive is formatted, it has one directory already on it, called the *root directory*. Because all the items on a disk are either files or directories, all the entries in your root also are either files or directories. Type the DIR command and look at the different entries. You should see something similar to the following:

```
Volume in drive C is HARD DISK 1
Volume Serial Number is 3B13-11D8
Directory of C:\

DOS         <DIR>        03-06-91  10:19a
COMMAND  COM     37557   04-07-89  12:00a
CONFIG   SYS       152   04-09-91   6:12p
WINDOWS     <DIR>        04-09-91   3:56p
AUTOEXEC BAT       234   05-23-91   5:23p
MOUSE       <DIR>        04-03-91   9:42a
70 Files(s) 833312 bytes free
```

The names of your subdirectories are followed by <DIR>. All other items are files. A root directory on a hard drive can contain up to 512 entries. Other directories may contain any number of files and subdirectories, but DOS slows down when searching listings of more than 150 entries.

You have three basic commands to manipulate directories. New directories are made one at a time and must hang off an already existing directory. Use the MKDIR, or MD, command to make a new directory. This new directory appears as an entry in the current directory (the one you are in) unless you specify another path.

The second basic command is the RMDIR, or RD, command that lets you delete a directory. The directory to be deleted must be empty before you delete it, so first delete its files and subdirectories. You cannot, however, remove the current directory while you are in it. You receive the following error message if you try to delete a directory that contains files, that does not exist, or that you are currently in:

```
Invalid path, not directory, or directory not empty
```

DOS looks for the directory to be removed in the current directory unless you specify a different path. Be especially careful about stating the path if you have more than one directory with the same name in two different locations in the directory tree.

The third basic command is the CHDIR, or CD, command that lets you change to a new current directory. Chapters 5 and 7 cover these three commands in more detail.

Handling Difficult To Remove Directories

DOS will not let you delete the current directory of any disk. If you want to delete the current directory, you must backup one level and then remove the directory. If, for example, the current directory is called TOOLS and you want to delete it, use the following commands:

```
CD ..
RD TOOLS
```

In the first command, the double period (dot dot) refers to the directory that is one level up from the current directory. A single period (dot) in a file listing or path parameter signifies the current directory. You will occasionally see DOS use these shorthand names when you use DIR while in a subdirectory.

If the directory TOOLS was not deleted and it appears not to have files in it, you may have hidden files stored there. The ATTRIB command can be used to unhide files, as with the following commands:

```
ATTRIB -h TOOLS\*.*
DIR TOOLS
```

If files now appear, you can delete them and remove the subdirectory.

Keeping Track of Directory Listings

Sometimes knowing what is supposed to be in each directory is helpful. Several large applications, for example, copy many files to a directory. After a few months of using the program, you may find that one of its features no longer works correctly. If this is the case, you want to be sure none of the original files needed to run the program have accidently been deleted. Short of reinstalling the whole program, how can you tell that all the files are still there? Perhaps you have copied many files from one place to another and have accidently specified the path incorrectly. How can you delete only the unwanted files and leave those that belong? You should keep directory listings of those subdirectories that contain many files. The following command sorts your directory listing and copies it to a file:

```
DIR | SORT > DIRNAME.LST
```

The output also can be directed to a printer if a hard copy list is more convenient, using the following command:

```
DIR | SORT > LPT1
```

You can use the TREE command to document directory listings. The TREE command shows not only the files in the directory, but all subdirectories as well. Use the following command to see a complete list of your directories and subdirectories:

```
TREE > DIRNAME.TRE
```

If you decide to use both of the preceding commands, be sure to use different file names. When using the > character, DOS writes over any existing file of that name. If you have a subdirectory of that name, you get an error message. Also, do not try to pipe the TREE command through SORT because the result will not make sense. If you sort the output of the tree structure, all the directories are ordered together. This is not at all useful.

Changing a Drive's Identity

You may find that temporarily renaming a directory is useful. If you have two sizes of floppy drives on your machine, you probably will discover a use for the ASSIGN command. It is not uncommon to buy a software package in the size of your B: drive, usually a 3 1/2-inch disk. Later, you may find that the program assumes the drive from which you are installing is the A: drive. Often, the install program works correctly, but a problem may arise when you change printer drivers many months later. Instead of buying a new program in a different size disk, or even copying the data to another disk size, you can reassign your disk drives. The following command assigns the logical drive A to the physical drive B:

```
ASSIGN A=B
```

After you assign the A drive to the B drive, you can put disks in the B drive when your programs expect them to be in the A drive. When you are finished using your program, you can reset all drives to their original drives by typing ASSIGN with no parameters.

Another method for temporarily changing the name of a drive is to use the SUBST command, instead of the ASSIGN command. The result of using the following command is exactly the same as the preceding ASSIGN example.

```
SUBST A: B:\
```

The second parameter, B:\, must be a directory, not just a drive. When renaming drives, use the \ character to specify the root directory. The affect is the same as renaming the drive. The SUBST command, however, can be used only with existing drives. You can create additional logical drives by adding the following line to CONFIG.SYS:

```
lastdrive= Z
```

Drives are set from A so this command ensures 26 drives will be created. If you use the command lastdrive=F, for example, 6 logical drives are created.

The SUBST command can be used to rename drives and directories. If you find yourself typing long directory names repeatedly, try shortening them by substituting a shorter name. You may have, for example, a file to be uploaded called NEWDOC that is stored in C:\COMM\PROCOMM\UPLOAD\PROJECT directory. This can be a long path to remember and to type correctly. You can shorten the path to something easy to remember with the following command:

```
SUBST Z: C:\COMM\PROCOMM\UPLOAD\
```

All references to the directory C:\COMM\PROCOMM\UPLOAD\ can now be made using z:. You also can access the file with z:\NEWDOC. This works only if you have the statement lastdrive=z in your CONFIG.SYS file.

Exercising Sound Hard Drive Management

The PC platform supports an increasing number of media. Until recently, each had its own errors and problems, causing users to lose data and valuable time. This situation, however, is changing with the arrival of disks and tapes that have error correction that virtually eliminates disk errors, even with constant use.

New technology has its limits, however. A user still can wipe out valuable data by misplacing, mislabeling, and mishandling disks and tapes.

Making Hard Drives Safer

Organization of the drive can be a key to safety. If you keep all your letters and memos in one directory, for example, you can back up the data easily and routinely. You also may wish to have your database files in one directory that can be easily backed up and restored if they are destroyed.

The hard drive is an electro-mechanical device that can and does experience problems. Bad spots develop, which results in a `BAD TRACK 0, DISK UNREADABLE` message. A variety of causes for this condition exist, some of which require reworking the drive and replacing all the platters. The mean time between failures (MTBF) often is listed with the documentation that comes with your computer. If not, the MTBF is available through the OEM. A typical MTBF is 40,000 hours, which is nearly 5 years. This is the average; you may experience a failure at any time, not precisely on the drive's 5th anniversary. Be prepared, however, for messages such as the following:

```
Not ready reading drive C. Abort, Retry, Fail?
```

This can be a warning that things are going bad with the drive or even the controller. If you have diagnostic programs, use them to detect problems before they happen. No action is as worthwhile as always backing up your disks frequently.

Protecting Floppy Disks

Floppy disks and their cousins, the 3 1/2-inch micro-floppies, are made of a thin polymer coated with a substance that can be altered by magnetic flux. The larger 5 1/4-inch floppies are indeed floppy because they bend easily. Dirt can enter through the large cutouts used by the tracking and read/write mechanisms.

The smaller 3 1/2-inch are enclosed, do not bend, and have a slide cover that protects the media. The recording matter inside is made of the same material as its larger relative and also is easily destroyed through carelessness.

Floppy disks are sensitive to heat. Do not leave them in your car in the summer. Watch out for spills, as well as static. Large motors, appliances, televisions, and stereo speakers all produce magnetic fields that can weaken or destroy the data on disks. Keep your disks away from these items. Remember that an office fire or flood can destroy your PC and its data. It is wise to keep a backup set off site in case your office set is damaged.

Keep floppies in their original containers or purchase commercially available diskette holders. These holders provide a better solution because they are tough plastic, not cardboard, and keep out dust, as well as deflect spilled coffee or other liquids.

Protecting Disk Media

DOS comes with several built-in diagnostic commands that indicate disk problems. DOS also has utilities that can recover data from damaged media.

The CHKDSK command, along with the /F parameter, for example, returns lost clusters. The command also is informative. It can show you are losing an increasing amount of your disk to bad sectors. Normally, you use the command to fix problems when clusters are lost because of file allocation table (FAT) problems. You can use the *.* parameter to decide whether your files are contiguous or badly fragmented, which suggests that you should pack your disk with commercially available disk unfragment programs. Chapter 4 shows you how to use CHKDSK.

Using UNDELETE To Recover Lost Data

DOS offers a command that attempts to undo a mistakenly issued DEL or ERASE command. You should use the UNDELETE command as soon as you discover that important data has been erased. UNDELETE, however, is not infallible. It does not work well if other files have been written to the disk after the data was deleted. Also, if you run a commercially available disk compactor, you have little chance of finding your deleted file.

By having the MIRROR utility resident in memory, you increase your chances of undeleting a file. Still, you should not rely upon this utility. Having several recent copies of data might be a better strategy. This is especially important if UNDELETE retrieves only a very truncated portion of the original file. In a case where you might have this happen, you should go back to your previous copy of the file.

The following is an example showing how undelete works. The directory contains the following files:

```
SPEEDU   WK   28982   05-04-89   1:23a
BK4309   WK    3145   04-26-90  11:20a
PHONET   WQ   12289   12-27-90  12:15a
IXP19    WQ    7092   02-03-91   1:40a
CHECK    WQ    1741   03-08-91   7:45a
5 file(s)   53249 bytes
   252928 bytes free
```

If you accidently type in DEL *.*, the preceding files are deleted. To undelete the files, type in UNDELETE A: and the following message is displayed:

```
Directory: A:\
File Specifications: *.*
Deletion-tracking file contain
5 deleted files.
Of those  5 files have all clusters available,
0 files have some clusters available,
0 files have no clusters available.
DOS directory contain  5 deleted files.
Of those,  5 files may be recovered.
Using the deletion-tracking file.
CHECK  WQ  174  3-08-91  7:45  Deleted  5-03-91 12:05p
All of the clusters for this file are available. Undelete (Y/N)?y
File successfully undeleted.
IXP19  WQ  709  2-03-91  1:40  Deleted  5-03-91 12:05p
All of the clusters for this file are available. Undelete (Y/N)?y
File successfully undeleted.
PHONET  WQ  12289  12-27-90  12:15  Deleted  5-03-91 12:05p
All of the clusters for this file are available. Undelete (Y/N)?y
File successfully undeleted.
BK4309  WK  314  4-26-90  11:20  Deleted  5-03-91  12:05p
All of the clusters for this file are available. Undelete (Y/N)?y
File successfully undeleted.
SPEEDU  WK  2898  5-04-89  1:23  Deleted  5-03-91 12:05p
All of the clusters for this file are available. Undelete (Y/N)?y
File successfully undeleted.
```

If you issue the DIR A: command, the directory looks like it did when you began:

```
CHECK     WQ   1741   03-08-91    7:45a
IXP19     WQ   7092   02-03-91    1:40a
PHONET    WQ  12289   12-27-90   12:15a
BK4309    WK   3145   04-26-90   11:20a
SPEEDU    WK  28982   05-04-89    1:23a
    5 file(s)   53249 bytes
   252928 bytes free
```

Using UNFORMAT To Reverse an Accidental FORMAT

You should write-protect disks that you do not wish to format; however, accidental formats do happen. Your chances of retrieving this data are increased by having MIRROR running in memory. Run it in test mode first using the /TEST switch to see what data can be retrieved. You can rebuild the partition using the /PARTN switch.

Immediately after recovering data, backup or copy the data to other media. The rebuilt disk or diskette is unreliable. You are merely trying to retrieve lost data. You still have the responsibility of making the computer environment safe by determining what happened. Determine if the problem is a data entry error or if something is wrong with the hardware.

Before reinstalling the data, you must create a new media. Use FDISK if the partition table has been destroyed. Reformat the disk and load your data and programs. Put MIRROR.COM in your AUTOEXEC.BAT to ensure unformat and undelete work optimally.

Both undo commands work best in an environment in which MIRROR has been running during DELETE or FORMAT. Mirror your hard drives in your AUTOEXEC.BAT file and run MIRROR as a TSR to protect vital data.

You can mirror all your hard drives, creating a most recent version MIRROR.FIL on all hard drives. If you are changing data often and the data is very crucial, you may opt to run the MIRROR command as a TSR for a single disk. It can be run in this manner for only one drive, so choose the one that is most likely to have something go wrong. The MIRROR command takes up about 6K of memory on an IBM XT. This is a small trade-off to ensure data integrity. Further, if you have the memory and saving the data is crucial, make MIRROR memory-resident. Mirror the A: drive, for example, if your word processing staff routinely stores documents to that drive.

You also need to change the batch file that calls the word processor so it loads in MIRROR. If you have WordPerfect in WP51 and call that from your root directory, a batch file to load up MIRROR and protect the A: drive during a word processing session can look similar to the following:

```
REM Make Mirror Memory resident to prevent damage or lost data
CD \WP51
MIRROR /TA
WP
REM Now Unload the Mirror program from memory
MIRROR /U
CD\
```

This batch file is used to help safeguard your daily activity without intervention from you.

The following is an example of the UNFORMAT command and the resulting DOS message. A floppy disk has been accidently formatted while MIRROR was running as a TSR on that drive.

```
UNFORMAT A:

Insert disk to rebuild in drive A:
and press ENTER when ready.
Restores the system area of your disk by using the image file created by
the MIRROR command.
WARNING !!       WARNING !!
```

The UNFORMAT command should be used only to recover from the inadvertent use of the FORMAT command or the RECOVER command. Any other use of the UNFORMAT command may cause you to lose data. Files modified since the MIRROR image file was created may be lost, as in the following example:

```
Searching disk for MIRROR image.
The last time the MIRROR or FORMAT command was used was at 12:11 on 05-03-91.
The MIRROR image file has been validated.
Are you sure you want to update the system area of your drive A (Y/N)? y
```

The system area of drive A has been rebuilt and you may need to restart the system. Using the DIR command, you can see that your files have been returned, as in the following:

```
CHECK    WQ1    174   03-08-91   7:45a
MIRROR   FIL   3891   05-03-91  11:37a
IXP19    WQ!    709   02-03-91   1:40a
MIRROR   BAK    614   05-01-91   6:26p
PHONET   WQ1   1228   12-27-91  12:15a
BK4309   WK1    314   04-26-91  11:20a
SPEEDUP  WK1  28982   05-04-88   1:23a
SECOND   TST     64   05-03-91  11:37a
NEW      TST     64   05-03-91  11:37a
OCONFIG  BAT     15   03-12-91   3:45p
    10 file(s)   98592 bytes
    252928 bytes free
```

Use the MIRROR command after creating partitions and formatting a hard drive. Stick a floppy into drive A: and make a MIRROR image of the partition table. After you do this, store the floppy in a safe place. You probably will never need it, but should something happen to your partition table, you will have it on a floppy.

Understanding the Threat of Computer Viruses

Admittedly, there is much hype surrounding the subject of sabotage known alternately as computer viruses, worms, Trojan horses, and so on. It seems as though with the approach of every Friday the 13th, another Friday the 13th virus is released. Perhaps the damage from this form of irresponsible behavior is overrated.

You should, however, take some precautions regardless of the threat. Have a virus checking program in your tool chest. Run it occasionally. Be suspect of certain conditions that arise, such as unexplainable lost data, error messages flashing across the screen that were never there before, and spurious hardware problems.

If you move a program or data from one computer to another, be sure both are not infected. If you bring things to work from your home computer, scan your files with the latest shareware or commercial diagnostic program.

Most bulletin boards now routinely scan all their software to check for viruses. You also should check the program yourself if you obtained it from a BBS. You should practice safe computing and not spread anything that will wipe out data or programs.

Another avenue of transmission is getting disks from friends. Have they checked out their computer? You should assume that they have not. Be on guard. Do not accept disks from friends without checking them out. Watch what you put on your machine.

If you find someone engaged in this activity, you should remind him of the consequences, both legal and in terms of real human effort.

Maintaining Data Integrity with General Computing Practices

Data integrity depends not just on using commands correctly and safely. You also can customize your environment to increase data integrity. The power of DOS can be used to prevent system errors. Users also should follow simple practices to decrease the number of human errors.

Customizing DOS To Increase Data Integrity

DOS comes with a series of external commands. If used incorrectly, these can negate the best thought-out archive routines. It is important to be aware of these commands and have a strategy that augments the operating environment's security. This is singularly true for computers remotely accessed, as is the case with most consultants and large multi-site companies. They have many computers to worry about, but lack day-to-day access.

If you are responsible for the care of other peoples' computers, customizing DOS should be something you do to prevent lost data.

Hiding RECOVER.COM

RECOVER.COM is a DOS command that most users should never use. Some users are tempted to try RECOVER because its name implies "getting lost data back." Perhaps RECOVER should have been named DESTROY. Given a simple drive name, the command will wreck havoc upon all the executable files and directories. The RECOVER command renames everything to FILE*nnnn*.REC, in which *nnnn* is some increasing number. You also lose your entire directory tree.

Because it is rare to use RECOVER.COM, you should consider moving it to some directory other than the root or DOS directory. Perhaps you have a directory full of seldom used utilities. Put RECOVER.COM there, or delete it entirely. Remember, you have a copy of it on your original DOS diskettes if you ever need it. If you do leave RECOVER on a disk, tell the PC's normal user(s) not to use the command.

Making FORMAT a Batch File and Renaming FORMAT.COM

The FORMAT command erases an entire disk, laying out tracks and sectors. This is necessary before using a new diskette. Hard drives sometimes will need to be formatted as well. When the disk is formatted, the contents of the disk are lost. The default form of FORMAT puts null values on all the data areas. Problems occur with the FORMAT command when it is used mistakenly, erasing media that contains important data.

Another problematic situation exists in environments that have many PCs with different capacity drives. The users are taught to format their diskettes, but are not taught about the different types of drives. When they use the disk in another machine, they find that the diskette cannot be read because it has been formatted at a different capacity.

With the following batch file, FORMAT.BAT, the computer prompts the user for the size of diskette. You also can write it to force the users to use a common size so disks can be interchanged among machines. The batch file's contents are the following:

```
@echo off
REM my format batch program to make all 3.5 drives 720k.
REM the old DOS program format.com is named myformat.com.
REM extra parameters after command there for command line variance
REM in case a new version of DOS allows for more than two parameters.
MYFORMAT %1 %2 %3 /F:720
REM all done
```

The user formats the floppy by entering:

FORMAT A:

or

FORMAT B:

Additional security measures can be added to MYFORMAT.BAT by prohibiting formatting on certain drives. To do this, you need to have several batch programs—one for each disk on your system. FORMAT.BAT can parse these and call the correct external batch format procedure. In this manner, formatting is allowed on drives A: or B:, but disallowed on C, as in the following example:

```
@echo off
if "%1" == "" call nodrive
if %1 == a: call MFORMATA.BAT
if %1 == b: call MFORMATB.BAT
if %1 == c: call MFORMATC.BAT
if %1 == d: call MFORMATD.BAT
```

MFORMATA.BAT and MFORMATB.BAT are batch files similar to the previous batch file. The contents of the batch file called to format a 1.2M floppy in the A: drive, for example, would be the following:

```
REM FORMAT A 5 1/4 FLOPPY IN A: TO 1.2
MYFORMAT A: /F:1.2
```

Each batch program calls the renamed FORMAT.COM (MYFORMAT.COM) and executes a format upon a drive. MFORMATC.BAT can be programmed to abort if the user tries to format the hard drive. You might allow formatting of the hard drives by asking for a password first. This restricts who can format the hard drives, as well as making the non-restricted user pause and think before clearing the media of data. The idea is to protect the hard drives from an accidental erasure. DOS 4 and 5 have several safety features that prompt the user before formatting the disk. With these versions, formatting does not proceed unless the volume name is typed in correctly. The user has to answer the prompt with y for the disk be formatted.

Removing Drive Reassignments

Another safety feature you may wish to add is to reassign both the SUBST and ASSIGN commands to their defaults. ASSIGN makes the computer think that one disk drive is actually another. By typing `ASSIGN B=C`, for example, you make all references to the drive B look on the C drive. `ASSIGN A=B`, on the other hand, makes all calls to A look on the B drive. You can reset the drives to have their original identifier by typing in ASSIGN without any parameters. DOS refuses to format a SUBST or ASSIGN drive.

Avoiding Data Loss to APPEND.COM

You might use APPEND.COM in batch files that execute obsolete application programs that cannot traverse subdirectories. You also can use APPEND.COM when an old program requires the increased data search path and cannot find the data on its own. Remember to reset the APPEND condition when you no longer need it by including the following line:

```
APPEND ;
```

This command, however, does have side effects. Although useful and necessary in a few cases, the APPEND command is not something you want to have turned on all the time. It can interfere with DOS commands and the way they work so you should use extreme caution when using it. Also, when you use this command, data can be written to an incorrect subdirectory, which may hamper the user in locating his files.

Using DOS To Avoid Mistakes

Many ways of using DOS features to protect your data are available to you. This section suggests several commands and options that can be used to prevent data loss due to user error.

Using DIR Before DEL

Protect yourself when using wild cards by using the DIR command before you execute a command. You may wish, for example, to delete all the files with a BAK extension. Before you do this, type the following command:

```
DIR *.BAK
```

Look at the screen to see if the directory contains anything you want to keep. Once you have verified this is the group of files you wish to delete, press F1 and F3 to repeat the previous command and change DIR to DEL, as in the following command:

```
DEL *.BAK
```

Using the /P Option with DEL and RESTORE

Make it a habit to use the /P switch when deleting or restoring files. This can be time consuming when deleting many files, but it safeguards your data if you are doing a wildcard delete. The /P switch simply slows things down a bit. When you use /P with the DEL or ERASE commands, the computer prompts you file-by-file with the following:

```
Delete (Y/N)
```

This gives you a second chance to stop deleting files you want to keep.

Also, you may have noticed a particular set of parameters more dangerous than others. Using the ?? wildcard characters, for example, might have caused you problems in the past. If you know you have problems with parameters such as this one, you should force yourself to think twice and use the /P option when you are deleting files.

Using /P and /D Options with RESTORE.EXE

Make sure you do not overwrite your CONFIG.SYS or AUTOEXEC.BAT files. Protect the boot programs IO.SYS and MSDOS.SYS by using /P with RESTORE.EXE. With DOS 5, the BACKUP command no longer saves the IO.SYS and the MSDOS.SYS files. This makes it safer to do a restore without parameters, but the problem still exists in prior versions of DOS.

You always should remember to avoid restoring the two boot records. They reside on specific locations on your boot drive. If you restore them, they change position and are moved to a non-bootable position in your root directory. The machine does not boot if this happens. To preview what is restored, use the /D parameter. To prevent restoring system files, type the following:

```
RESTORE A: C:/D
```

You see a list of files scroll by. If you execute the RESTORE command with date or time selection parameters, you see a subset of the backup files. Possible restore switches are /B, /A, /E, /L, /M, and /N. The /N switch, for example, restores only those files that no longer exist on the target disk. To preview what the RESTORE command does, type `RESTORE A: C:/N/D |MORE`. This filters the command through the MORE command so you get only one screen at a time. This does not, however, restore anything to the target; that is, it just shows you what would be restored. The screen displays what can be restored, giving you a choice of restore parameters.

Using ATTRIB To Protect Files

The following shows you how the ATTRIB command can be used to protect files. By typing ATTRIB *.*, you can see which attributes have been set, similar to the following message:

```
A:\CHECKS.WQ1
A:\MIRROR.FIL
A:\IXP191.WQ!
A:\MIRROR.BAK
A:\PHONETM.WQ1
A:\BK43090.WK1
A:\PCTRACKR.DEL
A:\SPEEDUP.WK1
A:\SECOND.TST
A:\NEW.TST
A:\OCONFIG.BAK
```

You should practice this with a floppy that has no critical files on it. Set the read-only attribute with ATTRIB +R *.W??. If you try to delete one of the files with DEL PHONETM.WQ1, the following message appears:

```
Access denied
```

You also can hide a file by typing ATTRIB +H PHONERM.WQ1. The DIR *.WQ1 command no longer shows the file.

You should consider making your CONFIG.SYS and AUTOEXEC.BAT files read-only with the ATTRIB command. You do not want to lose this work. A great deal of valuable time can be spent setting up these files correctly. Also, loading high-memory device drivers and installing DOS commands, such as FASTOPEN, require some experimentation to get correct. With each machine, configuration is different, and loading these commands and device drivers can be tricky.

Occasionally, a commercial software distributor includes its own CONFIG.SYS in the release diskettes. They do this to force your computer to have the correct number of buffers and files. Sometimes an INSTALL program intentionally overwrites your CONFIG.SYS file. This happens with some smaller software vendors. Most of the large commercial software packages display a message that warns you when the program is going to modify these files.

Usually, they make backups of each file. Some make this modification optional, telling you what the changes should be and asking you to put them in yourself after the program installation is finished.

As a safe practice, write down the configurations suggested and put them in yourself. If you keep these protected by having the file attributes set to read-only, you must unprotect them before you edit. Remember to use ATTRIB to change the protection back to read-only.

This small amount of work can prevent very large headaches. The following is a suggested procedure to unprotect, change, and re-protect your system files:

```
ATTRIB +R CONFIG.SYS
ATTRIB +R AUTOEXEC.BAT
ATTRIB CONFIG.SYS
ATTRIB AUTOEXEC.BAT
```

The last two lines in the preceding syntax are used to verify that the file has been modified to read-only. ATTRIB shows you a screen reports similar to the following:

```
R      C:\CONFIG
R      C:\AUTOEXEC
```

Minimizing Data Integrity Problems

Several methods are available for you to avoid losing and storing incorrect data. In golf, having consistency, such as in your swing, pays off. This is true in most activities, especially organizing your computer disks. You should always be consistent when doing routine tasks.

When working with a pile of disks, tapes, or forms, set up a system to organize them. When one disk is finished, move it to the finished pile. Stack the finished ones upside down with each succeeding piece on the one before it so you have a reverse-order stack. When you are done with the entire task, you simply turn the stack over and they are in the correct order, with number one on top and the final disk on the bottom.

Often, keeping a checklist helps organize time-consuming tasks. This is beneficial especially when you assign work to another person. They simply work through the list, checking a box as each step is completed.

If you encounter a problem, document it. Write the message on your checklist if you are using one. Print it on the label of the disk or tape, but use a marker that does not damage the media. You also might put a small memo or Post-it note on the floppy.

Using Caution with New Procedures

Problems can arise when changing to a new procedure. A new backup routine, for example, is released by a major software house. You immediately purchase a copy and start using it that day.

What could be so wrong with doing that? Nothing, if you label all your disks with a comment stating which backup method you used. You should consider going through all your old backup disks and marking those as well, indicating which backup method was used.

Using Copies To Protect Original Software

Make a copy of new software distribution disks before you load it onto your machine. Always load from the copy, not the original. The original should be kept either with the manuals or in a plastic diskette container. It is convenient to have all your original software in one place. Commercially available cases can hold between 50 and 100 floppies. One or two of these should be all you need for your original software. Be sure to store new releases, drivers necessary for your screen and hard drives, network software, and application software.

Label the copies you have made of your software and store them in a safe place. These are the copies you are working with and perhaps occasionally reloading. Write-protect the original when you make copies. It is easy to switch file specifications or fail to swap disks when prompted. A mistake can overwrite the floppy that you wish to copy . The DISKCOPY command is very dangerous for this reason. Put a write-protect tab on the original before you use DISKCOPY. Otherwise, you might accidently copy from the blank to the program disk, virtually destroying an expensive piece of software.

Use the CHKDSK command before and after the copy to see if all hidden files have been copied. Copy protection is no longer in vogue, but it still exists. One way you can determine if something is copy-protected is to use the CHKDSK command. This command reports the contents of the disk. If anything is on it that looks unusual, such as bad sectors, many hidden files, or anything else other than data files, you may have to use a commercial backup program. These programs are designed to defeat copy protection and can be used to make a legitimate copy of software you have purchased. See the license agreement that came with the software if you are unsure.

If you are stuck with software that is copy-protected or uses the *key-disk* method of operation, exercise extreme caution. The key-disk method is a copy protection scheme that requires the original disk to be in drive A:. This disk must be verified as the original before the program will run. Keep the write tab on the key disk if the verification process allows it. Some copy protection schemes write data to the key disk for verification, so using a write-protect tab will not work. If the program halts and tells you to remove the tab, you will have to leave the tab off.

If the key-disk is destroyed, you must ship it back to the vendor and wait for another copy. You should protect it because you will not be able to use the program until you receive another copy.

Avoiding Illegal Software

Remember that boot-leg software is one way computer viruses are spread. Avoid using bootleg software and protect your data. Also, protect yourself from expensive litigation by owning all the software you use. The piracy laws are getting tougher, whereas the price of software continues to drop. You have to decide whether it is worth the $200 savings having a boot-leg copy of your word processor. How much does it cost when the manufacturer takes you to court? Remember, a single anonymous phone call can put you into litigation.

Locking Your Computer

If your computer contains sensitive personal or payroll records, keep your computer locked. Locking your computer keeps prying hands away from confidential information.

A determined snoop, however, still can find a way around a locked computer. On some machines, the lock makes it impossible to open the machine, but many of the newer machines can be opened even if they are locked. If your machine can be opened, the hard drive can be removed and plugged into another computer. The information can then be viewed, printed, and copied, and the disk returned to your machine. If privacy is very important, use a software lock to password protect your applications and data. These are available from computer stores and through shareware distributors. They protect the data by requiring a password before allowing access to a drive, a program, or a data file.

Using ATTRIB To Hide Data

The ATTRIB + h DIRNAME command hides a directory. If you have a directory named PAYROLL, hide it. The title alone invites a curious mind. A hidden directory is not displayed by the TREE command, further ensuring no one accidently discovers where you have hidden your data.

Backing Up Important Data

If you have never lost any data, you probably are tempted to skip this section. Readers who have lost data on a floppy probably have learned to back up floppies. Readers who have had a hard drive crash, probably make regular backups from the hard drive. In this instance, it is unfortunate that experience often is the best teacher.

Backing up provides you with easy insurance against many hardware and software failures. In this section, you will learn many backup procedures to be used in several different situations.

Making a Complete Backup

You may have several instances when the hard disk needs to be completely backed up. Other times, it may be more efficient for you to back up only your data files. Sometimes, you may want to make a backup of data from a directory and include all its subdirectories. If you have many data files, you may find it more efficient to back up only those that have changed since the last backup. At other times, you may find it wiser to use an alternative to the BACKUP command.

Despite the backup schedule you choose to follow regularly, you may find times when the entire hard drive should be backed up, such as in the following cases:

❏ You have decided to change the partition size of your hard drive. This always is a potential danger. It is easy to understand how making a partition smaller might cause a loss of data, but the same loss can occur when you make a partition size larger. Back up your entire hard drive whenever using the FDISK command to do anything other than to display partition data.

❏ You are moving your computer. Hard disks are sensitive items and always should be treated gently. Many errors occur after bangs and bumps that jar the drive. This risk is magnified when the computer is packed into a box, loaded in a vehicle, and moved to a new location. If your computer is moved any great distance, back up all your data first. This especially is important if it is spending anytime in an airplane cargo hold or on a truck.

❏ Your hard drive is running out of space and you are going to devote a couple hours to housekeeping functions. Before you delete large amounts of data, move many files around, or do any major reorganization, make a backup of your disk.

❏ You do not want to spend a large amount of time reorganizing your hard drive. Your hard drive organization is something to be proud of. Once every program is in the state you want it, you should back up your drive. You can always reinstall all those difficult to load programs from the original disks, but a backup at this point may save you from a delay later.

❏ You have decided it is time for your child to become computer literate. Although watching your child sitting at your chair typing away is something special, remember that your data can be wiped out with some childish experimentation with ERASE or DELETE. Children, however, are not the only people who are guilty of making silly mistakes. When you cannot afford to lose data and a novice user begins sharing your machine, back up the entire hard drive.

❏ You have decided to begin learning about all the mysteries of DOS, as well as clean up unneeded files. This probably is a combination that has zapped all users at some time or another. If you are going to learn how DOS really works by deleting every file in the root that you cannot identify, first take some precautions. Make an emergency boot disk and backup your hard drive.

The easiest way to back up a hard drive is to have a second hard drive installed. You simply copy the data on the primary drive onto your extra hard drive. You also can use the BACKUP command and use the second hard drive to store the backup files. Unfortunately, having a second hard drive can be expensive.

If you get a tape drive configured for your system, you can use it to make convenient backups. Generally, these tape drives come with software and you should follow the manufacturers' recommendations. Even if you invest in a tape drive, you should learn about DOS BACKUP and RESTORE because you can use them when you want to make a partial disk backup.

For backing up to floppies, invest in the largest size disk your machine reads. The more data a disk holds, the fewer disks you need.

Windows

Although you may never experience problems performing backups from within Windows, you should always exit the Windows environment completely before using the BACKUP and RESTORE commands.

Preparing To Back up Files

Disk errors occur infrequently, but the worst time for them to occur is during a backup. Before beginning any backup, you should use the VERIFY command. When VERIFY is on, every time a disk writes it is followed by a confirmation procedure. This extra step verifies that the data just written can be read without error. Turn it on by typing VERIFY ON. When finished, you can return to normal operations by typing VERIFY OFF. Typing the command without parameters tells you whether it is currently on or off.

To use the BACKUP command, you must specify what drive you are backing up and where you want the new files to be sent. To back up a hard drive with subdirectories, you must use the /S switch to include those subdirectories in the backup. To backup the C drive onto floppies in A, use the following set of commands:

```
VERIFY ON
BACKUP C:\*.* A: /S
VERIFY OFF
```

With DOS 5, you no longer need to format disks before beginning a backup. If DOS detects an unformatted disk, it formats it automatically. A switch is available that can be used to force a format size to be different than the default. If you have a high-density A drive but want to back up to low-density disks, for example, you can use the following command sequence:

```
VERIFY ON
BACKUP C:\*.* A: /F:360 /S
VERIFY OFF
```

You should get in the habit of always using the /F switch. Using it acts as a reminder to match the disk type to the way it is formatted.

You should backup only to floppies that contain no errors. If you format a stack of them before a backup, you can pick out those with errors. If you format them while doing the backup with the /F switch, pay attention to the format message. You will be told if any sectors are bad and given a chance to continue using the disk or to format another. If you are going to be using new pre-formatted disks, look at them with CHKDSK first to make sure they are good disks.

Taking Care of Backup Disks

Be very careful to take each floppy disk out after it is used and replace it with another. If you accidently press Enter before you change disks, DOS does not realize that the disk is the same. A warning that all information on the disk is lost is displayed, but you need to pay attention to the messages. If you forget to switch the disks, DOS writes data over the previous volume.

Though it is not necessary to use formatted disks, you should have several of them around. DOS still does not estimate how many floppies are needed before doing a backup. If you run out or need to abort the process for any other reason, use Ctrl-C.

Making Partial Backups

Once you have made a backup of your entire hard drive, you can backup only a group of selected files quite simply. All you need to do is specify the correct files. Because your data changes much more often than your programs, it makes sense to back up data files more often. Partial backups save time and use fewer disks. The following is an example for backing up word processor data files:

```
VERIFY ON
BACKUP C:\WP51\DOCS\*.* A:
VERIFY OFF
```

You also can backup only a partial directory. The following is an example showing you how to backup only those files concerned with an XYZ extension:

```
VERIFY ON
BACKUP C:\WP51\DOCS\*.XYZ A:
VERIFY OFF
```

DOS prompts you for the correct disk sequence. DOS' warning that the root directory files are to be erased is normal. As DOS backs up the files, it lists the files on-screen. The BACKUP command and screen output look similar to the following example:

```
VERIFY ON
BACKUP C:\WP51\DOCS\*.XYZ A:

Insert Backup diskette 01 in drive A:

WARNING: Files in the target drive
A:\ root directory will be erased
Press any key to continue

*** Backing up files to drive A: ***
Diskette Number: 01
\WP51\DOCS\CHAP1.XYZ
\WP51\DOCS\CHAP2.XYZ
```

```
\WP51\DOCS\CHAP3.XYZ
\WP51\DOCS\CHAP4.XYZ
\WP51\DOCS\CHAP5.XYZ
\WP51\DOCS\CHAP6.XYZ
\WP51\DOCS\APPEND.XYZ
\WP51\DOCS\INTRO.XYZ

Insert Backup diskette 01 in drive A:

WARNING: Files in the target drive
A:\ root directory is erased
Press any key to continue...
```

If you do not have enough room for all the files on one disk, you will see a prompt to insert another disk.

Making Incremental Backups

You may want to make an incremental backup if you have many data files, but use only a few of them very often. Perhaps you have 23 data files in your database program, but you rarely change more than four of them. You can save a great deal of time if you backup only those four files each night.

You may have times when you do not want to back up all of a group of files from a directory. In the preceding example, six chapters are in a group of files. If you write a seventh chapter, you should include it in the same group of backups. You do not need to backup the first six again as they have not changed. Use the following command if you want to backup the new chapter in addition to any files modified since the last backup.

```
VERIFY ON
BACKUP C:\WP51\DOCS\*.* A: /M
```

The BACKUP command deletes any old copies of a file as the newer version is backed up. If you do not want the older version to be deleted, use the /A switch.

Keeping Track of Backups

It is not enough just to make a backup at regular intervals. You also must know where to locate your backups and how to use the RESTORE command. You must be able to restore files in the same order in which they were backed up.

Labeling Backup Disks

Be sure to label each disk used for a backup. Files should be restored in the correct order. A good convention is to put the date and a short description on every disk. Also, write the number of the disk over the number of total disks. As the disks are backing up, you might make labels like the following :

    C:*.* July 15, 1991   1 of

After the backup is complete, go back and add the total number of used disks. If 15 disks are used, the final label will read similar to the following:

    C:*.* July 15, 1991   1 of 15

Find a supply of stickers that can be removed easily. Some adhesive-backed labels self-destruct when you try to remove them. Others come off cleanly. Mail order supply catalogs are full of good alternatives. A small investment in good labels is worth the money. Anyone with access to a mainframe or mini-computer has seen the wobbly tape syndrome, in which so many labels are on top of each other, the tape itself is out of balance. Sometimes these extra labels shear off, jamming up mechanisms.

If you maintain a large archive from different machines, try color coding. Labels come in many different colors. Use colors consistently to help identify where a disk came from.

Logging Backup Disks

Log files are especially useful when doing incremental backups. Each backup used with the /L option creates a log containing the date and time of the backup. Also, a list of the files included in it appears with the number of the disk that they are on. If you do not specify a location with the backup, then it is stored in the root directory of the source log. If a log already exists, the new log is appended to the end of the existing file.

To illustrate the way logs work, use the following files of a small directory that are backed up with the following command:

```
BACKUP C:\DATA B: /S /L
```

A file called BACKUP.LOG is created and stored in the root directory of C. The following displays the contents of this file:

```
5-17-1991  7:35:52
001  \MACRO.WK1
001  \GRADES.AM
001  \UPFILE.TXT
001  \TEMP\TEST1.TXT
001  \TEMP\TEST2.TXT
```

Only five files are included in this backup. The files of the subdirectory TEMP are included because the /S switch is used. BACKUP.LOG lists all the complete file names of all the files that are backed up, as well which disk they are on. In this case, they all fit on the first disk.

This file takes up very little space considering how convenient it can be. It can be used to locate where a file is stored, as well as reminding you of its backup date. It especially is useful when restoring files of a backup set.

Restoring From Backup Disks

To access the backed up files, you must use the RESTORE command. Assume that you have accidently deleted all the files with the XYZ extension. You can replace them from the floppy with the following command:

```
RESTORE A: C:\WP51\DOCS\*.XYZ /P
```

The /P switch prompts you for permission to restore files that have been changed since the last backup. Accuracy depends on your system clock. You should always use the /P switch when you use the RESTORE command.

The RESTORE command is easy to use. Specify the directory you are restoring from and where you want the files to go. You must remember, however, to restore files to the same directory from where they were backed up. If you do not remember what directories they were in, try viewing the files without restoring them by using the /D switch, as in the following command:

```
RESTORE A: C:\WP51\DOCS\*.XYZ /D
```

As with the backup command, use the /S options for subdirectories. The following command can be used after you crash your hard drive to restore all backed up files. Use the /S switch when restoring subdirectories.

```
RESTORE A: C:\WP51\DOCS\*.* /P /S
```

Backing Up System Files

A different procedure must be used with system files. BACKUP cannot backup the IO.SYS, MSDOS.SYS, and COMMAND.COM system files. Be sure to use the SYS command to copy these files onto a floppy. The following is an example command that moves them onto a floppy in the A drive:

```
SYS C:\ A:
```

Using Alternative Backup Commands

You should not use BACKUP with directories that have been redirected with the ASSIGN, JOIN, or SUBST commands. The RESTORE command cannot restore those files. This means that on a network you can backup only those directories to which you have direct access.

Sometimes XCOPY is a better choice for making a backup than the BACKUP command. If you want to save only a few files, you may find the XCOPY command easier to use because you do not need the RESTORE command to get the files again. This can be useful especially when moving files from one machine to another. It also can be useful when you want to restore the files to a different directory structure than the one from which they came.

Just as in backup and restore, the /S option is used when files in subdirectories are to be copied. The following is a command that copies the XYZ extension files:

```
XCOPY C:\WP51\DOCS\*.XYZ A:
```

The files from C:\WP51\DOCS\ are copied to the destination floppy A:. If you do not include the destination, the files are copied onto the current directory. The destination might be an existing directory. It also might end in \. Otherwise, DOS asks you if the files should be copied onto a file or a directory. The screen looks similar to the following:

```
XCOPY C:\WP51\DOCS\*.XYZ A:\DOCS

Does destination specify a file name
or directory name on the target
(F - file, D - directory)?
```

You should type an F if you wish the files to be copied to the file DOCS. Type a D if you wish DOS to make the directory \DOCS on A: and to copy the files there.

The XCOPY command cannot be used to copy system files or hidden files. If hidden files are to be backed up, you must first use the ATTRIB command to change the attributes, or use another method. XCOPY also should not be used if the files to be backed up do not fit onto one disk. DOS copies what it can and then warns you that all files did not fit. Unlike BACKUP, however, XCOPY does not prompt you for a second disk.

Windows	

The Windows environment simplifies this process by allowing you to drag a copy of a directory and all of its files and subdirectories onto floppy driver icons. This creates a copy of the directory and its contents on the floppy disk in much the same way as using XCOPY.

Following a Backup Schedule

Regardless of the utility you choose to use when backing up files, you should select a backup schedule and follow it. Make complete backups on the occasions described earlier in this section and backup data files regularly. The schedule is prescribed according to the amount of data you feel you can afford to lose. If you are not currently working on anything crucial, then a weekly backup may be what you need. If, however, losing a week of work would cause you many problems, then you should consider backing up modified files each day.

It also is a good idea to use several different sets of disks for backups and to rotate them. If, for example, you decide to backup certain data files each day, keep five sets of backup disks. Label them Monday through Friday and use the appropriate set on each day of the week. If you make backing up a habit and simplify the record keeping, you are much more apt to do it.

Backing Up a Single Document

If you are doing edits on a lengthy document, make a backup before you begin. This should be a habit for you. No matter what happens during the session, you always have a safe copy tucked out of harm's way. Go back to the previous version should you encounter disaster. All you lose is a few hours work, rather than months.

Backing Up Work from Applications

Many programs now enable you to back up certain files automatically. Sometimes a switch is available that lets you make a backup each time you save a file. This can be a good security measure because if you lose the file or make changes you later regret, a backup of an older version exists.

Be careful about thoughtlessly setting this option, however. Sometimes it can cause you trouble. If you save your work on floppies or have little free space, you will find that the automatic backup files fill up your media quickly. Sooner of later you probably will get caught being unable to save your current file because several unwanted backup files are taking up needed space. If you decide to have an automatic backup made, remember to delete unneeded backups periodically.

Another option that is becoming more common is to have the software save the file you are working on automatically and intermittently. If this option exists for you, it is probably variable and preset for 60-minute intervals or so. If you do not want to lose even an hour of work, then you should reset the time to every 15 minutes. The automatic save is so fast that you are hardly ever inconvenienced when it occurs.

Summary

This chapter discussed many ways that DOS can be used to ensure data integrity. Data integrity is a large and important topic. Using complete and correct data is important when doing any job on a computer. This chapter looked at many of the topics covered in other chapters, but with an eye toward doing each job as safely as possible.

UNDELETE and UNFORMAT are commands that are new to DOS 5. This chapter shows you how they can be used to save as much lost data as possible. Special attention is paid to the examples using UNDELETE, UNFORMAT, and MIRROR. Although ATTRIB is not new, many of the switches are.

An entire section devoted to tips for making DOS a safer environment, especially for the novice user, is provided in this chapter. These tasks will be particularly useful to those users who are responsible for many computers.

Backing up is perhaps the most important section in this chapter. Good tools are available to make daily and weekly backups less of a chore. Not only are tasks shown to demonstrate the procedure, but advice is given so you can decide how often and with what method you should back up your files.

9

Building on Your DOS Repertoire

So far, Part Two has shown you most of the commands that you need to know to be effective at the DOS prompt. This chapter covers the final topics that you will need to know before moving to Part Three. You will see techniques that are useful to intermediate users. This chapter covers environment variables, ANSI.SYS, MODE, graphics, and secrets. Although some of the commands in this chapter are not often found in other DOS books, they can be very useful.

The exercises in this chapter make use of the following commands:

❏ COMMAND   ❏ PROMPT

❏ COMSPEC   ❏ SET

❏ DATE   ❏ TIME

❏ PATH

This chapter also will teach you how to work with environment variables, invoke a second command processor, add date and time stamps to printouts of your files, and customize your system's path and prompt.

Changing Environment Variables

As you learned in Chapter 3, *environment variables* are modifiable pieces of information that are available to every program running on your machine. The PATH and PROMPT, for example, are variables. DOS stores these variables by name in an area of memory called the *environment.* You can look at this area of memory by issuing the SET command. Type **SET** at the DOS prompt now. You might see something like this:

```
COMSPEC=C:\DOS\COMMAND.COM
TEMP=C:\WINDOWS\TEMP
PATH=C:\;C:\DOS;C:\UTIL;C:\BATCH;C:\WINDOWS;C:\MOUSE;D:\
PROMPT=$P :-$G
```

The variable's name is on the left, and the variable's value appears to the right of the equal sign. You can use SET to modify each of the values. Later in this chapter, you will learn how to change specific values. The following variable, for example, sets the value of the DOS prompt:

```
SET PROMPT=$T$G
```

 **NetWare**

DOS variables are very handy on a NetWare system. Consider the example in which one batch file is expected to start a spreadsheet application for several workstations, each of which uses a different video display. You can have a monochrome workstation, a CGA color workstation, and a VGA color workstation. By loading a customized environment variable (SET SCREEN=MONO, SET SCREEN=CGA, and SET SCREEN= VGA respectively) in each workstation's AUTOEXEC.BAT file, you cause each workstation to contain a variable called SCREEN, which defines its display type. You can now use a single batch file that recognizes these different variables. This batch file can contain the following lines:

```
IF "%SCREEN%"="MONO" 123 MONO.SET
IF "%SCREEN%"="CGA" 123 CGA.SET
IF "%SCREEN%"="VGA" 123 VGA.SET

...
```

Note that environment variables can be set to contain many other things, such as CPU type, extended or expanded memory availability, keyboard type, math coprocessor support, the location of the workstation, and other information.

NetWare

Many NetWare installations make extensive use of the DOS environment variables and NetWare itself puts a heavy toll on the available environment space. For this reason, include SHELL= C:\COMMAND.COM / E:4096 /P in your CONFIG.SYS file. This sets aside 4K for environment space rather than the meager amount DOS supplies by default. You should make sure that the directory points to the location of COMMAND.COM. SHELL=A:\COMMAND.COM is correct for floppy-based and most diskless workstations. The /E:XXXX parameter should be set in steps of 256 bytes. 4K should be more than enough for most situations.

Environment variables are useful to programs because a program can inspect a variable's contents to determine operational mode, initialization information, or file information. The dBASE IV program, for instance, decides where to write its temporary work files by consulting the environment for the value of the variable DBTEMP.

You cannot use variables as command parameters at the DOS prompt, but you can use them as parameters in batch files. You utilize environment variables in batch files by enclosing the name of the variable in percent signs. For example, the string %PATH% is replaced by the path specified by the variable. Read the section on paths for examples.

Understanding COMSPEC

The COMSPEC variable tells DOS where to find the file COMMAND.COM, which contains all the operating system's internal commands. As you know, COMMAND.COM is a command processor that reads, translates, and executes standard commands. The command processor is invoked when you turn on your computer. After you type a command's name and press Enter, DOS searches COMMAND.COM for the command.

NetWare

COMSPEC is usually set on a NetWare drive by default to point to the directory containing DOS. NetWare can figure out the version of DOS in use and the default login script automatically sets NetWare drive Y to point to this directory. Your DOS 5 files should be placed in the directory \PUBLIC\IBM_PC\MSDOS\V5.00 even if your computer is not an IBM brand. COMSPEC=Y:COMMAND.COM should be placed in your LOGIN SCRIPT so NetWare can find COMMAND.COM.

You should not change the COMSPEC variable unless you move COMMAND.COM to a new location. After an application has run, DOS attempts to reload the transient portion of COMMAND.COM, and searches for COMMAND.COM at the location indicated by the COMSPEC variable. If COMMAND.COM is not at that location, your system will stop.

Modifying Variables Using a Second Command Processor

At some point you may want to invoke a second command processor. This enables you to execute DOS commands from within a program and then return to the program. Many programs already permit you to do this with ease. Various applications have different names for this function; some programs call it something like "SYSTEM," while others call it "EXIT TO DOS" or "DOS COMMANDS."

You also can use the COMMAND command to invoke a new command processor yourself. This is not a basic command and should be used only for customization or security. Any changes you make—such as changing directories or deleting files—remain in effect when you return to the primary processor. Environmental changes, however, are lost. The second command processor receives a *copy* of the environment and does not have access to the master environment. When the secondary command processor exits, so does the copy of the environment, along with any additions or modifications. Here is an example that starts a secondary command processor with 1024 bytes of environment space:

```
COMMAND /E:1024
```

The new processor must also be named COMMAND.COM. You must specify its location, if it is not located in the root directory. In this example, the location is specified as C:\DOS:

```
COMMAND C:\DOS
```

When you specify a location for COMMAND.COM, DOS changes the value of COMSPEC to match.

Add the /P switch to make the new COMMAND.COM the primary processor. Do not use the /P switch, however, without first considering the consequences. When the /P switch is issued, you cannot exit from the newly invoked processor and return to the original command processor. Without the /P switch, the second command processor is temporary, and you can exit from it by typing **EXIT** at the DOS prompt. You use the /P switch to make a secondary command processor with an increased environment size permanent.

Use the /E switch with a numeric value to increase the number of bytes reserved for the environment space. This should not be necessary, however, unless you are using SET to define several new variables. The value must be between 160 and 32768. DOS rounds off the value to the next 16-byte-multiple value. By default, DOS supplies 256 bytes to the environment. Variables use one byte for character of name and value. Remember that every byte of memory you give to the environment is a byte that is unavailable to programs. Most users operate with the default 256-byte value. If you get an Out of environment space message while assigning variables or running batch files, you will have to increase the environment's size. The following command accesses a new permanent command processor with an increased environment:

```
COMMAND C:\DOS /E:512 /P
```

If you have a batch file that requires more environment space or modifies variables to values you do not want to keep, you can use the /C switch with the command name. The /C switch, followed by a command such as a batch file name, causes the secondary command processor to exit automatically after the command terminates. To run the batch file TEMPVARI.BAT in a secondary command environment with increased variable capacity, issue this command:

```
COMMAND /C TEMPVARI /E:2048
```

When TEMPVARI is finished, DOS returns control to the primary command processor; all variables in the primary environment are unchanged.

Creating Your Own Variables

You can create new environment variables on the command line and in batch files by using the SET command. Remember that variables are meaningful only to programs that reference them. The following command, for example, creates a variable called DRIVERS and specifies the string "INSTALLED" as the variable's value:

```
SET DRIVERS=INSTALLED
```

You might use this kind of variable in a batch file. The file might set the DRIVERS to be "installed" at the beginning of a procedure and then change the value to " " (nothing) at the end of the procedure. Lines within the batch file can check the value of DRIVERS and use the value in branching decisions. You also can create variables that have multiple values, like the PATH variable.

Expanding the Environment

The size of the DOS environment is limited. If you or your programs create variables, you may run out of environment space. When you try to expand the environment beyond its limit, DOS displays an `Out of environment space` message. You can use the SHELL command, however, to increase this space. Add the following command to your CONFIG.SYS file and reboot the system:

```
SHELL=C:\DOS\COMMAND.COM /E:1024 /P
```

If your COMMAND.COM resides in any directory other than the root directory, be sure to use the correct path in this command. The amount of environment space will automatically increase the next time you reboot. For most users, 1024 bytes is plenty of space. If you still run out of space, you can increase the environment space even more.

Using the DOS Date and Time Functions

DOS keeps track of the date and time when each file was created. If you use RENAME or COPY on a file, DOS does not change the file's date or time stamp. DOS does change the file's date and time stamp, however, whenever you modify the file and resave it. You can see the date and time for each file by using DIR. This information can help you determine which version of two files is newer. By comparing dates, you can avoid copying an old version of a file over a newer version when copying or restoring files.

Most newer computers have a system clock that stores the date and time. This information is stored in CMOS (battery-backed memory) and you usually can view it by executing your system's setup command or key sequence. You also should be able to use your system's setup command to change the date and time settings. If your computer enables you to do this, then it probably has a battery that supplies power to the clock function when the machine is turned off. Batteries seem to last an amazingly long time, but eventually will need to be replaced. If your computer begins to lose the correct time or if other CMOS settings become lost, have your battery checked or replaced.

If you do not have a system clock, you should add the DATE and TIME commands to your AUTOEXEC.BAT file. If you do not have an AUTOEXEC.BAT, DOS asks for the date and time even if your computer does have a clock. To set the date at the DOS prompt, use the DATE command. DOS displays the following prompt:

```
Current date is Thu 05-16-1991
Enter new date (mm-dd-yy):
```

Change the date by following the pattern in parentheses. If the date is July 4, 1991, type **07-04-91**. The TIME command works almost the same way. Type **TIME** and you will see the following prompt:

```
Current time is 9:25:33.51a
Enter new time:
```

Again, follow the pattern. You do not have to change the seconds and you can specify the time in a 12- or 24-hour format. To set the clock to 3:30 p.m., you can type either **15:30** or **3:30p**. If you choose to use a 12-hour format, always remember to put an "a" or a "p" after the time, to represent a.m. or p.m.

Adding the Date or Time to Printed Files

At some time, most users wish they could tell what time or date a file was printed. When you are working with many similar printouts, you can easily get them mixed up. If you find yourself in this situation, you may want to tell DOS to add the date or time to your draft-quality printouts.

The following command adds the date to the end of a text file:

```
DATE < CR.DAT | FIND "C" >> yourfile.doc
```

In this syntax, DATE calls the DOS DATE command. Of course, you substitute a real file name in place of *yourfile.doc*. CR.DAT is a file containing only a carriage return. The carriage return is directed into the DATE command so that the computer does not lock up while waiting for you to type in a different date. Try the DATE command again if you do not remember why the carriage return is needed. You need to create this file before using the preceding command. Use the DOS COPY command to create the file and place a carriage return in the file, as follows:

```
COPY CON CR.DAT
```

Next, press Enter (to place the carriage return in the file), and then press F6 (to close the file). Press Enter to execute the COPY command. Issue the command **DIR CR.DAT** to make sure that the new CR.DAT file is in your directory. If you use TYPE to view the file's contents, you will see a carriage return but no text.

Now type **DATE < CR.DAT** to see what happens. The result should be the same as if you had typed the carriage return yourself.

DATE < CR.DAT is piped into FIND, which extracts only the line containing the date. This prevents the line Enter new date (mm- dd-yy) from also being appended to your file. Be sure to use an uppercase **C** to enable FIND to locate the line containing Current in the output of DATE. FIND is case-sensitive unless you use the /I switch with it.

DOS then appends the date to the end of the file. Now you need only to print the file.

The following batch file uses the preceding command and prints the file:

```
DATE_PRN.BAT
COPY %1 TMPPRN
DATE < CR.DAT | FIND "C" >> TMPPRN
PRINT TMPPRN
DEL TMPPRN
```

This batch file copies your data file and appends the date onto the copy, then prints and deletes the copy. The advantage to using this batch file is that it does not change the original file. The command can be used many times without repeatedly appending new dates to the end of the file. No matter how many times the file is printed, only one date appears each time.

The batch file does not create CR.DAT; you still must create CR.DAT yourself before running the batch file. Make sure that CR.DAT is stored in the same directory as this batch file. You can call the batch file by typing the following command:

DATE_PRN.BAT *yourfile.doc*

You can use the same process to attach the time to the end of a file. Just substitute the TIME command for the DATE command. Further, you can add both the date and the time with one additional line.

Controlling TEMP

Like all variables, TEMP cannot be accessed directly from the prompt. You cannot, for example, use the command CD TEMP. Environment variables are used only by programs. When you need to use a variable, you can call it from a batch file. When used in a batch file, the variable's name should be surrounded by percent signs, such as %TEMP%. DOS looks up and inserts the correct value.

When you pipe to filters like MORE, DOS creates temporary files on the default disk. If you are logged to a copy-protected or nearly full floppy, DOS may not be able to complete the pipe operation. DOS 5 provides a solution to these problems. If you have trouble using pipes, set the TEMP variable to a hard disk directory such as C:\. DOS uses the location specified by TEMP to create the temporary file(s). As the command sequence finishes, it deletes the temporary files. Assign a drive and directory in AUTOEXEC.BAT by including a command like this one:

```
TEMP=C:\WINDOWS\TEMP
```

Many programs—such as Windows, compilers, and databases—use temporary files and will add the variable assignment to your AUTOEXEC.BAT for you when you install the package. If you do not have such an application, you should create a directory for the storage of temporary files. Then insert a TEMP= line in AUTOEXEC.BAT to tell DOS where the directory is.

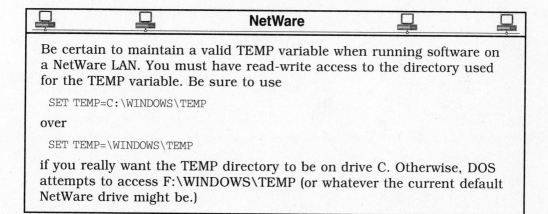

NetWare

Be certain to maintain a valid TEMP variable when running software on a NetWare LAN. You must have read-write access to the directory used for the TEMP variable. Be sure to use

```
SET TEMP=C:\WINDOWS\TEMP
```

over

```
SET TEMP=\WINDOWS\TEMP
```

if you really want the TEMP directory to be on drive C. Otherwise, DOS attempts to access F:\WINDOWS\TEMP (or whatever the current default NetWare drive might be.)

Using Paths for Productivity

The PATH command specifies a list of directories, which DOS searches for executable files that are not in the current directory. Executable files are those that have a COM, EXE, or BAT extension. Put the PATH command in a line near the top of AUTOEXEC.BAT, if the file contains other commands that are located in places other than the current directory. If you set the PATH variable first, you do not have to write the entire path for any other commands that are invoked in AUTOEXEC.BAT.

Chapter 5 features several examples of paths. A path consists of many different values, which are separated by semicolons. Consider the following path statement:

```
PATH=C:\;C:\DOS;C:\UTIL;C:\BATCH;C:\WINDOWS;C:\MOUSE;D:\
```

You can view your PATH statement's contents along with other variables simply by typing **SET** at the DOS prompt. To see the path alone, type **PATH** at the command prompt. Every time you type something at the DOS command prompt and then press Enter, DOS verifies whether your entry was a valid command. The operating system first looks at the internal commands and then checks the current directory. Finally, DOS searches all the directories listed in the path. If you have two executable files with the same name, DOS executes the one in the directory that is listed first in the path.

DOS always executes internal commands first. These are commands like DIR and COPY, which are stored in COMMAND.COM. After internal commands, COM files, EXE files, and finally BAT files are executed, in that order. If, for example, you have the files DOIT.BAT, DOIT.COM, and DOIT.EXE in one directory, DOIT.COM will always be the one to run if you type **DOIT**. You can get DOIT.BAT or DOIT.EXE to run by including the appropriate extension when you type their names at the DOS prompt.

Perhaps you have a program in your path called WP.EXE and a batch file called WP.BAT. If you want to use the batch file to run the program, you must have WP.BAT positioned before WP.EXE in the PATH statement. Because the current directory is searched first, you also must not be in the same directory as a program called WP.EXE. Generally, you should not use the name of the program as the name of the batch file.

You can force DOS to search for nonexecutable files. You can use APPEND to make another directory seem as though it were appended on the current directory. You can review APPEND in Chapter 5.

Arranging the Path for Efficiency

Performance deteriorates when DOS must search more than 150 files or locations when looking for a file. When you have a large disk with a complex nested directory and a long path, your operating system may have to search more than the optimal number of files each time it looks for a command to execute. You can take several steps to limit the number of files through which DOS must search.

Remember, you always find something in the last place you look. The same is true for DOS. Once DOS finds a program, it stops searching. You can limit the amount of time DOS must spend searching for executable files by placing frequently used files in directories that are close to root level. You also can change the order of the directories as they are listed in your path, to move the most frequently accessed ones closer to the front of the PATH statement.

Sometimes a directory may contain only one executable file. Even if you want to use the program from anywhere in the directory tree, it seems like a waste of space to include it in the path. Consider making a short batch file to change directories and then run that file. You can even give the batch file a shortened name to save yourself typing. Here is a sample batch file:

```
CD\COMM\KERMIT
KERMIT
```

If this file were called DIAL.BAT, you would run it by typing **DIAL**. The first line makes current the directory in which the program is located. If the application uses other files, DOS will find them. Remember that DOS searches the current directory for all files, not just the executable ones. The last line is the command to start the program.

Keep all your BAT files in a \BATCH or \UTIL directory and put that directory's name in your system's search path. The batch file will be found and run regardless of the directory you are in. This will keep the path short.

The PATH variable must contain fewer than 127 characters. If your applications are nested, you probably will not be able to list them all directly. You also might try to keep your directory names short and remove any excess spaces from your PATH statement. If you still do not have room to list all the directories needed, try using the SUBST command. Give a directory a different name and include the new name in the path. Make sure that you have assigned a high-enough drive letter by using LASTDRIVE in CONFIG.SYS. The highest-acceptable drive indicator is the letter Z. Here is an example of SUBST:

```
SUBST Z: C:\WRITING\PAPERS\FUNNY\QUOTES
```

This enables you to take C:\WRITING\PAPERS\FUNNY\QUOTES out of the path and replace it with Z:.

Using a Batch File To Add a Directory to the Path

Unless you use the DOS editor or another commercially available text editor, you cannot add a directory to the PATH statement without retyping the entire statement. First, you must issue the PATH command at the DOS prompt to see the current path. Then you must use SET PATH= and type in the entire path, including the existing directories and the ones to be added. Here is a batch file that will save you the trouble:

```
ADDPATH.BAT
SET PATH=%PATH%;%1;%2;%3;%4
REM This adds up to four directories to the path
echo
%1,%2,%3,%4 have been added to the path statement.
REM  Now display it.
PATH
```

When you need to add directories to an existing path, type ADDPATH and then up to four directory names. Of course the names must fit within the 127-character limit of the entire path. Because the new directories are attached to the end of the path, any that do not fit in that space will not be added. The existing path does not change. If you do not specify four new directories, the path will have extra semicolons on the end. DOS simply ignores the extra semicolons, but they will count toward the 127-character path limit.

Using Different Paths for Different Applications

If you are working on several projects, you may want to have several path settings available. Sometimes you will want to add or change startup commands for a special project that lasts only days or weeks. At the end of that time you will want to return your system back its present state. If you find yourself constantly changing and modifying startup files, you should consider having several startup files handy and picking the one you need.

It is possible to put all options in one file and "comment out" the lines you do not currently need. To comment out a line, simply place the string "REM" at the beginning of the line. You can use REM in either the AUTOEXEC.BAT or CONFIG.SYS file to tell DOS to ignore a line. You can comment out your current settings and add lines to make changes for a special project. When the special project is complete, simply delete the changes and remove the REMs from the original lines.

It also is possible to keep an optimized path for each project. Put each path in a different file, by using BAT as the extension. Other variables, such as TEMP, can be changed in the same file. You might have two paths, for example, called P_WRITE.BAT and P_DRAW.BAT. P_WRITE.BAT might look like this:

```
REM P_WRITE.BAT
PATH C:\;C:\DOS;C:\UTIL;C:\WP51;\C:G4;C:\FASTBACK
```

P_DRAW.BAT might look like this:

```
REM P-DRAW.BAT
PATH C:\;C:\DOS;C:\UTIL;C:\WINDOWS
```

You should probably also have a path listed in your AUTOEXEC.BAT with the directories needed for all tasks. When you begin to work on a project that requires a specialized path, simply call the batch file that contains it. To set up the environment for writing, use this command:

```
P_WRITE
```

It is even possible to turn the path on and off. First direct your existing path to a file, as follows:

```
PATH > PATH_ON.BAT
```

Now you can turn the path off by using **PATH=;**. To verify that there is no path, use the SET command to see the status of all the environment commands. Type **PATH_ON** to reset your path.

Customizing the Prompt

One of the easiest ways to customize your computer's display is by changing the appearance of your prompt. You can use the PROMPT command interactively to experiment with different styles of prompts. When you decide what kind of prompt you want, set it permanently with a line in AUTOEXEC.BAT. If you use different shells, you can customize a prompt for each shell, to remind you which shell is current.

Adding Text Strings to a Prompt

You can use any text string you like as a prompt. For example, you can demand some respect from your computer by customizing your prompt to look like this:

```
Yes Karen?>
```

To get this affect, simply issue the PROMPT command as follows:

```
PROMPT Yes Karen?
```

Of course, you should insert your own name in the prompt. Try this simple command sometime when things aren't going well and the computer seems to be developing an "attitude." It may not be informative or useful, but it can't be any less satisfying than honking in traffic.

You can probably think of other satisfying things to make your computer say. Express yourself and be as silly as you want. Make your prompt into a happy face, like this:

```
PROMPT :-)
```

Every command line will smile at you. If you don't think so, try it and tilt your head far to the left. Do you wear glasses? Try this combination:

```
PROMPT 8-)
```

Adding Special Prompt Parameters

Another simple—but more useful—way to change the prompt is to specify one or more of DOS' PROMPT parameters. Each parameter is a dollar sign ($) followed by a letter or symbol; you can choose from many options. DOS is not case-sensitive in its treatment of these parameters, so you can type them in either upper- or lowercase. Try changing your prompt now. Use the following command, for example, to change the prompt to be a dollar sign:

    PROMPT $$

To make the prompt an equal sign (=), use the following command:

    PROMPT $Q

You are not limited to using only one of the prompt parameters. You can use any of them in combination. Other parameters display the date, time, or current directory path. One of the most frequently used prompts is the PG combination. $P tells the current drive and path and $G is the greater-than sign. Many believe this is the best default PROMPT to use on any machine. The greater-than sign is used for clarity and helps to separate the prompt from the data you type.

The $P helps avoid directory and subdirectory confusion by letting you know where you are after a command has been executed. The disadvantage to using the $P parameter, however, is that DOS will always seek out the drive name after each command. This can slow the system down if you often work from floppy disks.

The following list shows all the single-character PROMPT parameters:

Parameter	Displays
$Q	= (equal sign)
$$	$ (dollar sign)
$T	Current time
$D	Current date
$P	Current drive and path
$V	MS-DOS version number
$N	Current drive
$G	> (greater-than sign)
$L	< (less-than sign)
$B		(vertical bar)

Parameter	Displays
$_	(Blank space) Carriage return and linefeed
$H	Backspace (erases previous character)
$E	Escape code (ASCII code 27)

The following example uses several of the parameters at the same time:

```
\PROMPT /----\$_$b $n$g $b$_\----/$_
```

The command generates a prompt that looks like this:

```
/----\
| C> |
\----/
```

If you make your customized prompt too long, there may not be enough space on the command line for some commands. This can be a problem even if you use only the $P parameter, if you work in directories that are many layers deep. Use the escape and an underscore when you want your next command to appear on the line under the prompt. Unfortunately, this also can be a problem with some utilities, which assume that the prompt is only one line long.

The date and time parameters (DT) may give you more information than you want. Perhaps you only want to know the day and the month rather than the whole date. Do you really need to know the exact second of the time? For example, the PROMPT $T command displays the following prompt:

```
14:26:42.25
```

The first two numbers are the hour on a 24 hour clock. The next two numbers are the minutes. The last four characters give you the number of seconds. All these characters, however, do not have to appear in the prompt. You can eliminate the last few characters from the prompt by adding a $H for each character you do not want to see. Type the following command to show only the hour and minutes:

```
PROMPT $T$H$H$H$H$H$H
```

The $H actually backspaces over a character; if you have a slow display, you will probably notice a flicker. The prompt should now look like this:

```
14:26
```

If this command did not work, you probably got a message saying you were out of environment space. See the previous section on the environment to learn how to increase the amount of space available for variables.

The vertical bar (|) and the greater- and less-than symbols (< and >) cannot be typed directly as text in the PROMPT command. Instead, you must enter the correct parameter to make these characters appear in your prompt. Otherwise, DOS would not know if you wanted them to be printed in the prompt of if you were trying to use redirection or pipes.

You can combine text and the parameters to create complete messages like the following one:

```
PROMPT date is $D:
```

If you are executing a COMMAND shell, you may want to customize the prompt to remind users that they are in a shell, and that they must type **EXIT** to return. Use the following command to do this:

```
PROMPT Please enter a DOS command or type EXIT $P$G
```

If you use the PROMPT command with no parameters, your prompt changes to a default showing only the drive and the greater-than symbol. To show how the prompt was most recently set, type **SET** at the command prompt. You will see all the environment settings, including PROMPT.

Summary

A good understanding of primary and secondary command processors and enviroments is important for learning more advanced batch file techniques. At the DOS prompt, you can likely assign PATH and PROMPT values that DOS uses. Although these variables are usually assigned in AUTOEXEC.BAT, you can modify them at any time. You have seen some techniques for expanding the environment by issuing the COMMAND command. By redirecting TIME and DATE outputs, you can add a date or time stamp to printer output.

The next chapter presents memory configuration considerations. If your PC's memory configuration is not properly optimized, you may be wasting computing power. Todays PCs are more complex than the original PCs and are capable of using far more memory. DOS 5 recognizes the additional memory of todays PCs and offers commands and directives to allocate memory resources.

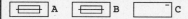
Part Three

Configuring DOS for Optimal Memory Usage

Controlling Devices

The DOS Shell

Tapping the Power of Macros and Batch Files

Programming with QBASIC

295

10

Configuring DOS for Optimal Memory Usage

A major concern of most users is how to get the most from their systems. The CPU type and amount of available RAM impose limits on a system's efficiency. Short of revamping hardware, the proper management of these resources is the most important determination of system performance. This is particularly important with memory, because poor management may prevent programs from running on the system. This chapter focuses on the aspects of DOS that control the operating system's performance and memory usage.

A computer system is defined by the type of CPU it uses, because the CPU imposes absolute limits on what the system can do. If you change the CPU type, you change the type of system you work with. Memory, however, is a more flexible resource, and you can improve the performance of an existing system by adding more memory. As the operating system and programs become more sophisticated, additional RAM can be put to even better use.

Earlier chapters discussed the way in which the operating system manages storage memory—floppies and hard disks. *Storage memory*, or *secondary memory*, controls how much information can be stored on your system. *System memory*, or *primary memory*, is used as the CPU's work space. When you copy a file from one disk to another, it is briefly stored in the work space. Calculations and data manipulations performed by programs use the same work space, and the operating system itself must be contained within this area. In fact, part of the system memory is used by the operating system for managing other portions of memory.

297

In addition to improved tools for managing secondary memory, DOS 5 provides better management of system memory. Before moving on to a discussion of memory management, it is important to understand the definitions and terminology used when discussing memory. If this is new information for you, the following section provides a solid foundation in memory-management concepts. If you are familar with memory management, you should review the information in order to understand the current terminology used by Microsoft.

Understanding Memory

If you work in the DOS environment, you are familiar with the term "640K barrier," which means that DOS was originally designed to recognize 640 kilobytes as the entire memory area. Developers thought that this memory amount would always be more than sufficient for any type of application. This 640K memory area is referred to as *conventional memory.*

In early versions of DOS, the conventional memory was the total available memory; any application had to share this space with the operating system and other data. As systems evolved, other types of memory were added which helped to alleviate the problem. Any program (including the operating system), however, must have links to this memory area. Thus, the 640K barrier remains, although changes in computer design have helped to ease the memory crunch.

In addition to the 640K designated for use by applications and the operating system, an additional block of memory is generally set aside for storing information needed by the operating system for management of the computer system. This memory region extends from 640K to 1M and is called the *Upper Memory Area (UMA).*

Memory is managed by its *memory address*, not by its physical location. When the CPU needs to communicate with a portion of memory, it sends out a message using the memory address to identify the location it seeks. It is the reponsibility of the operating system and the hardware to make sure that the informations gets to the correct physical location.

Originally, the memory in the UMA consisted of information contained in the system *ROM (read-only memory)* and RAM *(random-access memory)* on special hardware devices, such as video cards. Only some of the addresses were used and many of them had no physical memory attached at all. These holes in memory presented no problem because the system avoided these addresses; there was no record of any information stored there.

It became commonplace to install additional RAM that could be addressed using this memory range (640K to 1M). This was done because RAM has a faster access speed than ROM and system performance was improved by copying information from the ROM chips. In some cases, information from the device RAM is copied into this system RAM to shorten the access cycle.

This process is referred to as using *shadow RAM*. In most modern systems, the upper portion of the UMA often contains copies of the system BIOS and the lower portion of this region contains information used to manage the display. In general, the higher the resolution of the display, the more system memory must be devoted to the screen drivers. This is separate from any memory which may be part of the video card itself.

As mentioned previously, not all of the memory in the UMA is used by the system. Now, however, most systems have 384K of RAM in the UMA; the gaps reference actual RAM and can be used by the operating system or applications. DOS 5 enables you to load device drivers and programs into these unused portions. These segments of memory in the UMA are referred to as *Upper Memory Blocks (UMBs)* and require the use of a UMA manager. DOS 5 includes UMA-management capabilities, as part of EMM386.EXE, for use on systems that have a 386 or 486 processor.

There is no standard method for implementing the 384K of the UMA on various system boards or even whether it is addressable as RAM by the operating system. On some systems, the UMA is still a combination of ROM, device RAM and empty addresses. On others, it can be used only as shadow RAM or activating the UMA removes memory from the extended memory pool.

A Note on Counting Memory

Although the dictionary defines the meaning of *kilo* as one thousand, kilo means slightly more in computer jargon. In keeping with the binary nature of computer systems, kilo means 2 raised to the 10th power, or 1,024. Thus, the term *kilobytes* means 1,024 bytes rather than 1,000 bytes.

Thus, the 640K limit is 640 * 1024 bytes, or 655,360. This is the figure reported by the MEM command as the available conventional memory on a system with a full 640K of memory.

By extension, rather than referring to 1 million (a thousand thousand), the prefix *megabyte* refers to 1,024K or 1,024 * 1,024 bytes. Thus, a megabyte is actually 1,048,576 bytes.

Another way to take advantage of memory gaps is to use them to reference non-contiguous memory on an expansion board. This approach is referred to as *expanded memory (EMS)*, and it uses the available memory locations in the UMA to refer to memory which is on a separate add-in card. This memory does not become part of the standard system memory pool; it is managed instead by an additional driver.

The advantage of expanded memory is that the driver can quickly substitute different blocks of memory into the addresses and can provide access to all memory on the expansion board. These blocks of memory are *pages* and the locations in the UMA used for swapping form the *page frame*. Each address in the page frame can be swapped to different sections of memory on the card, so more expanded memory can be accessed than there is free memory in the UMA.

Although expanded memory was the first approach to breaking the 640K barrier (and Lotus, Intel, and Microsoft endorse it with the creation of the LIM standards), expanded memory is not a good choice for most DOS users because it must be managed by a third-party driver and is not under the direct control of DOS. There are exceptions to this, such as 286 systems using high-speed serial communications. In these systems, the switching of the CPU between real and protect modes causes problems on 286 systems with non-intelligent com: ports.

In order to access memory above 1M, new features were added to the CPU design that are only available on 286 and newer processors. The first 64K above 1M is set aside for memory management and can be directly accessed by DOS 5. This area is referred to as the *High Memory Area (HMA)* and contains part of the operating system. This area is only available on systems with memory installed above 1M.

Extended memory (XMS) is a continuation of the standard memory pool and exists above the HMA. This memory can be used by programs designed to take advantage of these specialized processor commands and is either under the direct management of the operating system or directly addressed by applications. In the latter case, the memory is controlled by an interrupt from the application and is not available to the operating system. The HIMEM.SYS command is the portion of the operating system used to control the HMA and extended memory. In addition, the DOS expanded-memory manager, EMM386.EXE, can be used to emulate expanded memory for those programs that require it.

Figure 10.1 summarizes the divisions of the system memory pool and the components of the operating system used to control each division. Notice that the expanded memory takes up portions of the UMA but is not under the direct control of DOS.

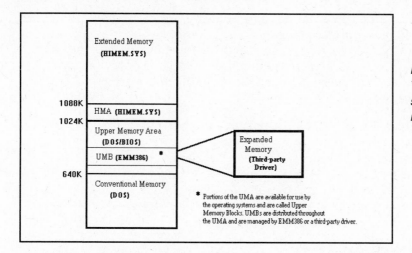

Figure 10.1:
The operating system's view of memory.

In order to make the most of your memory, you should know exactly what type of memory is available on your system and which programs can use each area. Many users find that the improved memory management of DOS 5 makes an investment in extended memory more attractive. The type of CPU that you have in your system, however, limits the type of memory management DOS 5 is able to provide.

CPU Limitations on Memory Management

The good news is that DOS now provides a full range of memory-management tools for utilizing system memory. The bad news, however, is that there are restrictions on whether or not you can use these tools, depending on the type of CPU you use.

The original IBM-compatible personal computers used an 8088 or 8086 processor chip. These chips were capable only of utilizing memory below the 1M limit because of a limitation on the size of memory address that they could recognize. The original developers of DOS decided to divide this 1M between the work space available to programs (640K) and the upper memory area (384K). Although expanded memory may result in more than 1M of usable memory, the memory is mapped into the UMA (below 1M) and the 8088/8086 processors can still address it.

Extended memory requires that the processor be able to handle larger addresses than the 8088/8086. To use extended memory, you must use a 80286, 80386 or 80486 system. Although all of these processors are able to address significantly more memory than 1M, systems typically are enhanced with 3M of extended memory for a total system memory size of 4M.

The commands contained in the 80386 and 80486 processors enable them to control extended memory in more powerful ways. Some benefits include the capability to use extended memory as though it were expanded memory and the capability to move sections of programs from storage memory (generally the hard disk) to the system work space. This capability is referred to as being able to use *virtual memory*.

Table 10.1 summarizes the types of memory management available for various CPU types.

Table 10.1
Memory Types Available by CPU type

Memory	8086/8088	80286	80386/80486
Conventional	Yes	Yes	Yes
UMA	Yes	Yes	Yes
HMA	No	Yes	Yes
Extended	No	Yes	Yes
Expanded	Yes	Yes	Yes
Expanded Emulation	No	No*	Yes
Virtual Memory	No	No	Yes

*Emulators available from third-party developers.

As Table 10.1 shows, the 80386 and 80486 processors offer the greatest amount of flexibility in availability of memory-management types.

Windows ▼ ▲

The types of memory management provided also relate to the Windows modes that are available on each system. The controlling factor in running 386-enhanced mode is that virtual memory must be available. Real mode uses features available in any of the Intel chips. Standard mode uses the features of the 80286.

Checking Available Memory

The first step in getting the most from your DOS installation is to determine what resources are available to you. The DOS MEM command reports the amount of installed memory detected by the operating system. To use this command, type **MEM** at the command prompt. The resulting screen will resemble the following:

```
 655360 bytes available to MS-DOS
 569184 largest executable program size
3145728 bytes total contiguous extended memory
      0 bytes available contiguous extended memory
1854464 bytes available XMS memory
    64K High Memory Area available
```

The preceding list indicates that the system has a full 640K of conventional memory and 3M of extended memory installed as part of the system work space. *Contiguous extended memory* refers to memory that bypasses the operating system and is managed directly by application programs. *XMS memory* refers to the extended memory available to the operating system. Because there is extended memory installed, the HMA exists but is not being used in this example. If the system had expanded memory installed, you would see two additional lines: the total amount and currently available amount of expanded memory.

Information about the contents of the UMA is obtained by using the /C parameter on the MEM command, which gives you a map of the programs in both conventional memory and the UMA. The following appears on the screen:

```
Conventional Memory :
Name            Size in Decimal        Size in Hex
-------------------------------------------------------
MSDOS           12304    ( 12.0K)         3010
SETVER            400    (  0.4K)          190
HIMEM            1184    (  1.2K)          4A0
EMM386           8400    (  8.2K)         20D0
SMARTDRV        18592    ( 18.2K)         48A0
MOUSE           14320    ( 14.0K)         37F0
ANSI             4192    (  4.1K)         1060
COMMAND          2624    (  2.6K)          A40
WORD           385408    (376.4K)        5E180
COMMAND          2784    (  2.7K)          AE0
COMMAND          2800    (  2.7K)          AF0
FREE               64    (  0.1K)           40
FREE           201904    (197.2K)        314B0
Total  FREE:   201968    (197.2K)
Upper Memory :
Name            Size in Decimal        Size in Hex
-------------------------------------------------------- SYSTEM
172064   (168.0K)        2A020
FREE             16320    ( 15.9K)         3FC0
```

```
FREE                73696    ( 72.0K)            11FE0
Total  FREE:        90016    ( 87.9K)
Total bytes available to programs (Conventional+ Upper):    291984
(285.1K)
Largest executable program size:        201728   (197.0K)
Largest available upper memory block:    73696   ( 72.0K)
    3145728 bytes total contiguous extended memory
          0 bytes available contiguous extended memory
    1854464 bytes available XMS memory
          MS-DOS resident in High Memory Area
```

The previous list indicates that there is 197K of conventional memory available (notice that, in addition to the various DOS modules, 376.4K is being used by Microsoft Word) and that 72K of the UMA is available. The 168K in the UMA is unavailable to the operating system. The final line indicates that portions of DOS are loaded into the HMA.

The MEM command also has two other parameters that can be used to get a more detailed description of memory usage. The parameters are:

/P: The *program flag* results in a display listing the location of each program segment loaded into memory. The information is organized by location in memory.

/D: The *debug flag* provides the same information as the program flag, but also includes information about device drivers and other internal system features.

A Note on Memory Notation

All information within the computer is stored in *binary* format (using only 0 and 1) with a series of *bits*. Each bit can be either on (1) or off (0) and, in the standard U.S. system (ASCII), it takes eight bits (or one *byte*) to store a single character.

Locations in memory can be thought of as numbered slots, starting at slot 0, at the beginning of memory, and continuing through the extended memory. The number of each slot corresponds to the *memory address*. These memory addresses must also be represented in a binary format. Although 8 bits is sufficient to define any character from the keyboard, it can describe memory addresses only up to 256 bytes. Obviously, more bits are required to enable the addressing of all the locations in memory. For example, the memory address for the 1M mark requires 20 bits.

To simplify the process of writing memory addresses, most programs (and DOS utilities) use *hexadecimal notation*. In hexadecimal notation (or

A Note on Memory Notation—continued

hex), a single character is used to represent four bits. In order to do this, hexadecimal notation uses 16 characters to represent numbers. In addition to 0 through 9, the system uses A through F. With this convention, the 1M mark is presented with five Fs rather than twenty 1s. Thus, the 20-bit address of the 1M mark can be notated with five hexadecimal characters. In writing, hexadecimal numbers are indicated with a lower-case h at the end (FFFFFh).

Prior to the 80386, memory addresses were processed 16 bits at a time with Intel chips. This meant that a memory address above 640K (FFFF) had to be broken into two parts—an offset and a segment address. These were represented as two four-digit hexadecimal numbers separated with a colon (:). To find the actual address, the first number was shifted one place to the left (FFFF became FFFF0) and the two numbers were added. With hexadecimal notation, the 1M mark is usually represented as FFFF:000F. Because the actual address is created by adding the the segment and the offset, however, a single memory address can be notated in more than one way (for example, the 1M mark can also be referenced as F0F0:F0FF).

On the 8088/8086 system, each segmented memory address corresponded directly with a physical memory address. With the advent of the 80286, however, memory addressing has become more complicated. The segment portion of the address is used as an index to a memory location rather than to a physical address. Thus, the segment portion of the address does not directly correspond to a physical location, rather to a reference in a table. The entry in the table determines the physical memory location.

In order to distinguish between segmented memory addresses and physical memory locations, it is the convention to write the physical memory address as a single hexadecimal number and to use the segmented format to refer to internal representations of addresses that may not directly correspond to physical memory. Not only is it easier to write the entire physical address as a single hexadecimal number, but each address is referenced with a unique notation. It is this newer system that the DOS utilities such as MEM use when reporting memory contents. In this notation, the 640K mark is 9FFFF and the 1M mark is FFFFF. The start of the HMA is at 100000 (notice the additional digit).

The following shows the listing produced by MEM /D:

```
00F360      MEM       0000A0       Environment
00F410      MEM       0176F0       Program
026B10      MSDOS     0794D0       -- Free --
09FFF0      SYSTEM    028010       System Program
0C8010      MSDOS     003FC0       -- Free --
0CBFE0      SYSTEM    002020       System Program
```

This list shows the information located on either side of the 640K mark. Notice that the MEM command uses a five-digit reporting system for hex addresses in which 09FFF0 represents a location just below the 640K mark (0FFFFF). The address of the next free block corresponds roughly to the 800K mark.

The MEM command is the best tool for viewing memory usage. It enables you to examine how much memory is available and how it is being used. Each of the memory regions is managed by a different memory manager and additional information about memory usage is available through those drivers. Before you can begin to understand how to efficiently use the memory in your system, it is important to understand how it is managed.

Memory Managers

All memory requires that a portion of the operating system be dedicated to managing the transfer of information into and out of the memory registers. Conventional memory is controlled by routines internal to the DOS environment. An external memory manager is required to access other types of memory (UMA, HMA, extended, or expanded). These memory managers form links between conventional memory and the other memory regions, so they must always be installed in a portion of conventional memory.

Device drivers must be installed before you attempt to use the memory they manage. With conventional memory, the installation is done automatically as part of the DOS boot procedure. Other memory managers should be loaded as part of the CONFIG.SYS file if they are going to be used by the operating system. You can use the DEVICE= command to load these managers; they should be loaded at the start of the CONFIG.SYS file to avoid problems when you attempt to access the memory.

HIMEM.SYS—Extended Memory and the HMA

If your system has extended memory, load HIMEM.SYS as the first line in the CONFIG.SYS file. This extends the range of memory in the system work space to include all contiguous memory. It also makes the HMA available for use by DOS or other applications and device drivers.

Because extended memory is linear and needs no swapping of pages or links with the UMA (unlike expanded memory), the extended-memory management provided by HIMEM.SYS generally gives the best performance when it uses the default values. If you experience trouble installing HIMEM.SYS on your system, check the command reference for the /MACHINE:, /A20CONTROL:, and /CPUCLOCK: settings, which can be used to resolve some hardware conflicts.

There are two settings that affect extended-memory management. The first is /SHADOWRAM:, which prevents the system from duplicating information from the ROM chips into RAM and frees up the memory for use by the system work space. On systems that have less than 2M of memory, HIMEM automatically attempts to disable shadowing. This setting works only on systems that permit the operating system to control the shadowing process—if your system does not permit the operating system to take control, the parameter is ignored. On systems that have more than 2M of memory, you can include this parameter to see whether there is any effect on the amount of available extended memory. Boot your system with the /SHADOWRAM:OFF flag on the DEVICE=HIMEM.SYS line in CONFIG.SYS and type **MEM** to check the available memory.

The second parameter that can change the way HIMEM manages extended memory is /NUMHANDLES=. This setting allows you to specify how many segments of extended memory will be available for use by the operating system. For most installations, the default setting of 32 is sufficient. If your applications report that there is no available extended memory when some should exist, try increasing this number. Each additional handle requires six bytes of memory. Doubling the number of handles requires an additional 192 bytes, or .2K, of conventional memory.

Some older programs are incapable of recognizing extended memory as managed by HIMEM.SYS. These applications expect to be able to access memory by using the Interrupt 15h Interface. If you have applications that require extended memory when they use this scheme, the /INT15= parameter enables you to reserve a portion of extended memory for control by the 15h interrupt. You specify the amount of memory that HIMEM should leave for the older scheme to manage. Because HIMEM generally provides better memory management, you should specify the minimum amount necessary to allow the programs to function.

As part of extended-memory management, HIMEM is responsible for handling access to the HMA. Remember that the HMA is the first 64K above the 1M mark and is only available on systems with extended memory. The HMA is unique in that it is assigned as a single memory block, which means that control of the HMA is an all-or-nothing affair—the first device or application specified in your CONFIG.SYS or AUTOEXEC.BAT file that requests the HMA is granted exclusive control of its use.

For most installations, you use the HMA to hold a portion of the operating system. The only exception is if you have devices or programs that require the use of the HMA, such as a Weitek coprocessor. Most applications (including DOS) never release control of the HMA, so, when permission is granted, the HMA is dedicated to that application.

The /HMAMIN setting enables you to specify a minimum size for HMA requests. This excludes programs that request small amounts of HMA resources in favor of programs that use the memory area more effectively. The only time you need this setting is when a device that uses the HMA must be loaded in the CONFIG.SYS file, and it makes a request for HMA resources that you don't want to authorize. If possible, you should reorder the lines in the CONFIG.SYS and AUTOEXEC.BAT files so that those applications that should be granted HMA resources appear first. Alternatively, check the settings available for the offending application to see if you can disable its request for HMA resources. If both of these approaches fail, experiment with gradually increasing settings to exclude the specific program.

Once you establish the extended memory as part of the available system memory, you should load in any device drivers or applications that will use that memory. This includes disk-caching programs, such as SMARTDrive, and any utility programs that remain resident in extended memory.

Expanded-Memory Managers

Because each manufacturer is free to implement physical memory in a different way on its memory expansion board, each manufacturer develops its unique expanded-memory driver. The drivers must conform to the rules for accessing expanded memory, as outlined by the Lotus-Intel-Microsoft specification, but they were always a third-party product (not part of the distributed DOS). DOS performs all of the memory access through these third-party drivers.

If you have expanded memory installed in your computer, you should first check the board's manual to see whether the memory can be reconfigured as extended memory. If so, you will get better performance and greater flexibility with the board configured as extended memory. If you have applications that require expanded memory, you can use EMM386 to emulate expanded memory when you need it (this is discussed in the next section). If you want to use physical expanded memory, you must load the driver supplied by the manufacturer. If you experience difficulties associated with the management of your expanded memory, check with the manufacturer to see if an updated driver is available.

EMM386.EXE—the UMA and Expanded-Memory Emulation

Prior to the release of 386 machines, the UMA was considered off-limits to applications and its only approved uses were to hold information about video devices and shadow ROM. The LIM expanded-memory specification enabled manufacturers to reference unused addresses and map in expanded memory, but the management was still controlled by third-party drivers, rather than by DOS. Third-party developers created UMA managers for 8088 and 80286 computers that enable the loading of information into the unused portions of the UMA, but these managers are not a part of DOS and the ways they handle addresses in the UMA can vary.

Because 386 machines implement a number of special memory-management commands (and these features are critical for good performance), Microsoft created a driver, EMM386, to manage the UMA for all 386 machines. EMM386 can also provide access to the free-memory blocks in the UMA for use by DOS and can be used for either device drivers or small applications.

Windows

The services provided by EMM386 are used by Windows when it is in standard mode. In 386-enhanced mode, Windows uses an internal memory manager for the expanded-memory emulation it provides. The Upper Memory Area management provide by EMM386 benefits Windows users because it frees up more conventional memory for running large applications.

In DOS 5, the driver is changed from a SYStem file to an EXEcutable program. Although EMM386 must still be loaded with a DEVICE= statement in the CONFIG.SYS file, its settings can be modified while the system is running. This allows you to load the UMA manager and still disable it when appropriate.

A Note on the Weitek Coprocessor

DOS 5 also provides support for the Weitek math coprocessor with EMM386. The Weitek coprocessor requires access to the HMA and only programs that are designed to recognize the Weitek can use this support.

The UMA management provided by EMM386 serves two primary purposes. Each of these functions is independent and must be activated during the installation process if it is to be used during the DOS session. The first function is to provide DOS access to the UMA for loading device drivers or small programs; the second is to use UMA blocks and extended memory to emulate expanded memory. Because this second feature requires that an extended-memory manager be present, EMM386 should always be loaded after the extended-memory manager (HIMEM.SYS).

The primary purpose of EMM386 is to manage the UMA. Because of the variety of functions of the UMA, there are a number of settings that affect the way in which EMM386 operates. The first of these settings determines the combination of functions EMM386 serves. The choices are the following:

- ❏ **No Parameter**.. Enables expanded-memory emulation, but does not grant access to the UMA.
- ❏ **RAM**. Enables expanded-memory emulation and grants access to the UMA.
- ❏ **NOEMS**. Does not provide expanded-memory emulation but grants access to the UMA.

If you elect to use EMM386 for expanded-memory emulation (you do not specify NOEMS), there are a number of additional settings that control how the UMA is specified for use. These settings fall into three major groups: the first controls how the expanded-memory emulation is coordinated with other system resources, the second setting determines which sections of the UMA are under the control of EMM386, and the third setting controls how EMM386 uses those areas for expanded-memory emulation. Some of these settings are described in the next section; for a complete listing of settings, see the Command Reference. In addition to these parameters, which must be specified when EMM386 is installed, you also have the option of turning EMM386 support off without rebooting the system.

Before changing any of these parameters, be sure to create a bootable disk containing a copy of your CONFIG.SYS file, your AUTOEXEC.BAT file, and any device drivers that are needed to start your system. It is important to maintain these backup files because it is possible to grant EMM386 control over portions of the UMA required by your system (and your computer either will not boot correctly or boot at all).

Managing EMM386 and System Resources

If expanded-memory emulation is selected, EMM386 tries to take control of all available extended memory for use as emulated expanded memory. This feature can be disabled by including the OFF parameter on the

DEVICE=EMM386 line in your CONFIG.SYS file. To use expanded-memory emulation, you must reactivate EMM386 at the command line using the ON parameter. Another option is to install EMM386 in AUTO mode, which activates expanded-memory emulation only when expanded memory is requested by an application. The only disadvantage of this approach is that expanded memory may not be available if other applications have previously requested extended memory.

In addition to totally disabling the expanded-memory emulation, you can restrict EMM386's use of the extended memory region. This is done by specifying either how much expanded memory should be emulated, or how much extended memory should be left after EMM386 assumes control.

To specify an amount of expanded memory to be emulated, simply include a size parameter as part of the EMM386 command. This parameter determines the amount of memory granted to EMM386 and defaults to 256K. The value must be expressed in 16K segments (the number specified must be divisible by 16).

Extended memory is excluded with the L= parameter, which allows you to specify the amount of extended memory to be reserved. This memory remains under the control of HIMEM.SYS and is not available for expanded-memory emulation.

Two other settings can be used to affect the system performance. If you are in a multitasking environment, adjusting the A= parameter may improve performance. (Windows disables EMM386 and is not affected by this parameter.) If your system uses direct memory access for data transfer (excluding floppy disk access), you can adjust the amount of memory available for DMA by using the D= parameter.

Excluding UMA Memory Segments from EMM386 Control

EMM386 automatically scans the UMA for available memory. In most systems, this process identifies any memory which is not dedicated to other uses and turns control of that address over to EMM386. Occasionally, however, this automatic detection process does not work. The following parameters control which segments of memory are controlled by EMM386:

❑ **/X=.** Excludes a portion of the UMA from the control of EMM386. Use this setting only if you have problems with EMM386 conflicting with a portion of the operating system contained in the UMA.

❑ **/I=.** Enables you to force control of a section of memory to EMM386. This setting is ignored if the memory has been explicitly excluded from EMM386 control by the use of the x setting.

Managing the Expanded-Memory Emulation

There are three different ways to specify the starting address for the page frames created by EMM386 when it is emulating expanded memory. The settings all serve the same function and enable you to select from the same group of addresses. The valid addresses are in the ranges C000h through E000h and 8000h through 9000h and are in increments of 400h. The three methods are:

- ❏ **M**. Enables you to use a numeric code for the address.
- ❏ **FRAME=**. Enables you to specify the address in hexadecimal.
- ❏ **/P**. Enables you to specify the address in hexadecimal.

You can also specify the starting address for a specific page by using the /p*n*= parameter. You can use this parameter for any of the pages (0 through 255), but the first four pages (0 through 3) must be contiguous for compatibility with the LIM 3.2 standard. In general, you use one of the parameters above to specify the starting address and then use the following parameter to move specific pages:

- ❏ **/pn=**: Enables you to specify the address (in hexadecimal) for page *n*.

You can also specify the area to be used out of conventional memory for EMS "banking." The b= setting controls where the 16K pages are placed and can be in the range 1000h through 4000h. You rarely need to change this configuration setting and should do so only if you experience conflicts.

Finally, you can specify the number of memory handles available to EMM386 with the h= setting. You only need to change this setting only if your applications report that there are no expanded-memory handles available.

Summary

The management of the conventional memory area is controlled directly by DOS and requires no special settings in the CONFIG.SYS file. Other types of memory require memory managers and the order in which they are installed is critical.

If your system has extended memory, you should install HIMEM.SYS as the first DOS device in your CONFIG.SYS file (following any drivers required to boot the system). If you have more than 2M of memory, you should try the /SHADOWRAM:OFF parameter to see if this procedure increases the amount of memory available in your system. (On systems with less than 2M of memory, this is the default). Install any device that requires extended memory immediately following the installation of HIMEM.SYS. Remember that because the HMA is controlled by HIMEM.SYS (and is managed on a first-come, first-served basis), the first application that you load that uses the HMA gains control unless it is excluded by the /HMAMIN switch.

If you use an expanded-memory board that can't be reconfigured to extended memory, you should next load its driver. If you use an expanded-memory board on a 386 or 486 computer, you are prevented from using EMM386 to gain access to the UMA.

The EMM386 driver must be installed in your CONFIG.SYS file in order to gain access to the UMA or to expanded-memory emulation. If you do not need expanded-memory emulation, use the NOEMS switch to gain access to the maximum memory in the UMA. On DMA systems, you should use the D= switch to reserve buffer space for data transfer.

If you need expanded-memory emulation, use the RAM switch to enable both EMS emulation and AUTO switch to enable expanded-memory emulation only when needed by an application. You may want to control the amount of memory used for emulation by using the L= switch to reserve extended memory. If you experience conflicts in the UMA when using EMM386, use the parameter settings to specify the portions of memory used for expanded-memory emulation.

Creating the DOS Environment

Previous versions of DOS required that all components of the operating system be located within conventional memory. Numerous third-party developers have profited by creatively circumventing this requirement. DOS 5 enables you to distribute portions of the operating system into other memory locations. If you have extended memory and are using HIMEM.SYS, a portion of DOS itself can be loaded into the HMA. If you have a 386 or 486 machine with extended memory and EMM386 is installed, the UMA can be used to hold device drivers and utility programs.

Specifying the Location of DOS in CONFIG.SYS

After installing the memory managers and any applications that will reside in memory, you should specify the location and memory management to be used by DOS. Whether DOS is located in the HMA (and whether it uses the UMA) is determined by including the DOS specifier in the CONFIG.SYS file. On 386 and 486 systems, the DOS specifier allows you to free up the maximum amount of conventional memory for use.

Windows

The ability to increase the amount of free conventional memory is one of the greatest benefits to Windows users in DOS 5. The more conventional memory available, the better Windows performs. The amount of conventional memory available is crucial for Windows users who wish to run large DOS programs. The amount of memory free in a DOS window is directly proportional to the amount of available conventional memory when you enter Windows.

Because 8088/8086 systems do not have extended memory and the UMA is not under the control of the operating system, there are no options about how DOS is loaded—it will be in conventional memory. On 286 systems with extended memory, you can locate a portion of DOS into the HMA, but because the UMA is not under the control of EMM386, it is unavailable. On 386 and 486 systems, HIMEM.SYS must be installed to move DOS from conventional memory to the HMA. Both HIMEM.SYS and EMM386.EXE must be installed to load device drivers or applications into the UMA.

If you use a 286, 386, or 486 system, if you have extended memory, and if the HMA is not needed for another application or device (such as the Weitek math coprocessor), you can load DOS into the HMA using the DOS=HIGH instruction. (You must specify HIGH or DOS loads into conventional memory.)

If you want to load information into the UMA, you must specify the UMB parameter on the DOS specification, which can be specified with or without the HIGH parameter. If you do not specify UMB, the UMA is not available for loading devices or utilities (but is still available for use by EMM386 for use in emulating expanded memory). Although both a LOW setting (loads DOS into conventional memory) and a NOUMB setting (doesn't permit DOS into the UMA) exist, these are the defaults and need not be specified. The three meaningful settings for the DOS specification are:

❏ **DOS=HIGH**. Loads DOS into the HMA, but does not permit loading device drivers or applications into the UMA.

❏ **DOS=HIGH,UMB**. Loads DOS into the HMA and permits use of the UMA for device drivers or applications.

❏ **DOS=UMB**. Loads DOS into conventional memory and permits use of the UMA for device drivers or applications.

After you configure your memory managers, load applications into expanded or extended memory, and configure DOS for the most effective use of your memory, you are ready to load any device drivers or applications that will be part of the operating system environment.

Device Drivers

Device drivers are portions of the operating system that are written for specific hardware components and are added individually as needed. They contain the necessary programming code to allow the device to communicate with the operating system. They are loaded as part of the CONFIG.SYS file and remain in memory while the computer is active.

Prior to DOS 5, device drivers had to be located in the conventional memory area. With this access now provided to the UMA on 386 and 486 machines, some of the device drivers can be loaded in the upper memory area, which frees conventional memory for other uses.

Device drivers are made part of the operating system with the DEVICE= command in the CONFIG.SYS file. This command places the driver into memory and forms the necessary links with the operating system. In DOS 5, there are two commands that can be used to load a device driver: DEVICE=, which loads a driver into conventional memory, and DEVICEHIGH=, which loads a driver into the UMA. With DEVICEHIGH=, if there is no room available in the UMA, the driver is loaded into conventional memory, as if you had specified DEVICE=. Both DEVICE= and DEVICEHIGH= enable you to specify parameters for the device driver following the device driver name.

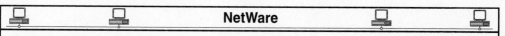

NetWare

The current NET5.COM file, supplied with the distribution disks, does not yet come in XMSNET5 (extended-memory compatible) and EMSNET5 (LIM expanded-memory compatible) flavors. This puts a strain on workstation memory if you use XMSNETx or EMSNETx before upgrading to DOS 5. You can make up for this memory loss by setting DOS=HIGH in the CONFIG.SYS file.

The memory managers, HIMEM.SYS and EMM386.EXE, are device drivers that control the way in which the operating system interacts with the memory installed in the system. Because these drivers deal with memory in very complex ways, they must be loaded into conventional memory with the DEVICE= command to function properly.

The device drivers included in DOS 5 that do not directly manage memory are not as sensitive as HIMEM.SYS and EMM386.EXE. The drivers listed in Table 10.2 can be loaded into the UMA with the DEVICEHIGH= command. SETVER.EXE is not a device driver, but it must be part of the environment to emulate previous versions of DOS. The sizes given are approximate and based on the example setting in the DOS Command Reference.

Table 10.2
Standard DOS Device Drivers

Driver Name	Device Managed	Size in Hex	(Decimal)
ANSI.SYS	Keyboard	1060h	(4.1K)
DISPLAY.SYS	Display	2060h	(8.1K)
PRINTER.SYS	Printer	2D60h	(11.3K)
EGA.SYS	EGA Displays	CD0h	(3.2K)
DRIVER.SYS	Logical Drives	E0h	(0.2K)
SMARTDRV.SYS	Disk-Caching	4570h	(17.4K)
RAMDRIVE.SYS	RAM Drives	104A0h	(65.2K)
SETVER.EXE*	Emulates DOS versions.	190h	(.4K)

* The size of SETVER changes as entries are added or removed. This is the value for the default list.

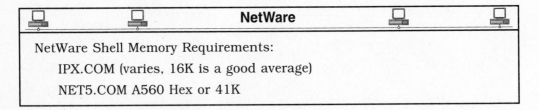

NetWare

NetWare Shell Memory Requirements:

IPX.COM (varies, 16K is a good average)

NET5.COM A560 Hex or 41K

Not all files with the SYS extension are device drivers. Specifically, COUNTRY.SYS and KEYBOARD.SYS contain information used by DOS in communicating with devices, but they are not actual device drivers. If you attempt to load one of these files with a DEVICE= or DEVICEHIGH= command, your system will freeze up and you must restart it with a different CONFIG.SYS file (booting from a floppy disk).

In addition to the drivers included as part of the DOS 5 environment, many device drivers are written by third-party developers to support their specific hardware products. These include such common add-ons as a mouse, a digitizing tablet, and a large screen. Each of these add-ons requires a driver, which is loaded as part of CONFIG.SYS. Depending on how well-written they are, these drivers may or may not function when loaded into the UMA with DEVICEHIGH=. Most third-party manufacturers make an effort to keep their products as compatible as possible with the operating system. If you experience problems with a driver, contact the manufacturer to see if there is an update.

Utility Programs

Many users make use of utility programs to add features to the DOS environment. If the utility programs you use are memory-resident (active whenever the DOS system is active), and if they do not require COMMAND.COM or special shortcut keys, they can be loaded as part of the DOS environment with either the CONFIG.SYS or AUTOEXEC.BAT file.

These utilities may be part of the DOS environment or they may be developed by third-party publishers. As with all third-party products, some utility programs may not function when they move out of conventional memory. If you experience problems with utility programs that are loaded into upper memory, check with the publisher to see if an updated version is available.

The utilities that are part of the DOS environment are often referred to as external DOS commands. The major difference between these types of programs and the other external DOS commands is that utility features remain in memory as part of the DOS environment, whereas commands are executed once (in conventional memory) and then forgotten by the system. The commonly used DOS features loaded as utility programs are summarized in Table 10.3.

Table 10.3
External DOS Utilities

File Name	Size	Purpose
FASTOPEN	5.5K	Speeds hard-disk access.
MIRROR	6.5K	Provides capacity to undelete files.
NLSFUNC	2.7K	Enables access to foreign-language features.
SHARE	6.0K	Provides file-locking for older DOS applications.
GRAPHICS	5.8K	Provides graphics support for BASIC and QBASIC programs.
DOSKEY	4.0K	Provides a command-line macro facility.
PRINT	5.6K	Enables printing via the DOS environment.

Note: The following two files require differing amounts of memory, depending on the function in use:

MODE		Enables device configuration (see Chapter 11).
KEYB		Changes keyboard mappings.
DOSSHELL	N/A	Provides a Graphic User Interface to the DOS environment.

Note: Installing DOSSHELL makes it your permanent shell. You can not exit to DOS.

As with device drivers, DOS 5 provides greater control over the locations of utility programs in memory. The INSTALL= command makes a program part of the DOS environment and loads it into conventional memory. The LOADHIGH= (LH=) command also makes the program part of the DOS environment, but loads it into the UMA, rather than into conventional memory. Like DEVICEHIGH=, if no memory is available in the UMA, the utility is loaded into conventional memory. Unlike other memory loaders, however, LOADHIGH= must be located in the AUTOEXEC.BAT file, rather than in the CONFIG.SYS file. You can specify parameters for the utility, following the utility name on either the INSTALL= or LOADHIGH= command.

Using the UMA Effectively (80386 and 80486 Systems)

The first step to load device drivers is to make a backup system disk for your current system. Next, check that the following three lines appear in your CONFIG.SYS file. The lines must be in the order given, but there may be additional lines inserted between any of the three lines.

```
DEVICE=HIMEM.SYS /SHADOWRAM:OFF
DEVICE=EMM386.EXE NOEMS
DOS=HIGH, UMB
```

Use the /SHADOWRAM qualifier only if it provides additional extended memory and system performance does not suffer. If you use the HMA for another purpose, you may omit the HIGH parameter on the DOS= command line. If you need expanded-memory emulation, replace the NOEMS parameter on the EMM386= line with RAM.

These commands are necessary to make the UMA available for loading device drivers or applications. Once you have established the memory management for the UMA, you should check how much memory is used by each device driver and how much memory is actually available in the UMA.

To determine how much memory is required, add the necessary lines to your CONFIG.SYS to load all of your device drivers into conventional memory with the DEVICE= statement, and load all of your utilities with the INSTALL= statement. This is necessary to gather the information necessary to relocate drivers and utilities into the UMA.

When you have added all of the drivers and applications to the environment, use the MEM /C | MORE command to view the memory usage. The reason for the pipe through MORE (| MORE) is that the output requires more than one screen and the MORE command allows you to view the output one screen at a time.

The first screen of output lists each device driver and the amount of memory it uses. Create a list of the drivers including their memory usage in both decimal notation and in hexadecimal (the last column). The last section of the output provides information about which Upper Memory Blocks (UMB) are available. You should list each UMB rather than the total amount. Each driver and utility must be contiguous within the UMA. In other words, each single driver or utility must fit entirely into a single UMB. More than one driver can share a UMB, but they can't be split between two blocks.

Using the information that you gathered, you can now develop an ideal model for moving as many drivers and utilities from conventional memory to the UMA. Unfortunately, you cannot specify where a particular device will be loaded and all drivers will load before any utilities. This means that you must use trial and error to try to force the combinations you want. Also, unless all of your device drivers and utilities are well-behaved, your first plan may not work because you may find that one of your drivers or utilities does not work in the UMA.

When you have your list of which devices and/or utilities go into each UMB, you are ready to load them. Load the driver that is to be located at the lowest address in memory first with DEVICEHIGH=. Always specify the SIZE= parameter to make sure that enough memory is reserved for the driver to function. Check that the segment you just loaded is working correctly by booting the system and utilizing the features controlled by that driver or utility. Only after you are sure that the previous load was successful should you move on to the next item.

After you are confident that the driver or utility is working properly, you can try the item to be located at the next memory address. Move one driver or utility to the UMA at a time and check after each move to make sure everything is functioning properly. Always specify the parameter size on device drivers. Use the MEM /C command to find out where each segment is being loaded and experiment with the order of the LOADHIGH= and DEVICEHIGH= statements to make the best use of memory. Although this approach may take a little longer, it ensures that each driver and utility is functioning properly.

DOS Shell

The DOS Shell is an extension of the DOS environment, rather than a new layer of the operating system. The DOS Shell's performance is automatically optimized when you optimize DOS' performance. Windows, on the other hand has different performance characteristics, and configuring the DOS environment for maximum performance does not produce the best performance in Windows.

Summary

To create the DOS environment, the first step is to determine where DOS itself will be located and whether or not you have access to the UMA. If there is access, you should load DOS into the HMA with the DOS=HIGH statement. If you use EMM386 or another upper-memory manager, you should specify DOS=UMB to allow links between the operating system and the UMA. On 386 machines, you should combine the two to free the maximum amount of conventional memory. (The statement would be DOS=HIGH, UMB.) Be sure to install both HIMEM.SYS and EMM386.EXE with the proper parameters prior to issuing the DOS command.

If you are able to use the UMA, you must now determine what drivers or utilities will be loaded into that area. Follow these steps:

1. Use a DEVICE= statement in your CONFIG.SYS file to load all of the device drivers into conventional memory.

2. Use an INSTALL= statement to load any utilities that become part of the DOS environment.

3. Use MEM /C | MORE to develop a list of memory used by each driver and utility. Be sure to note the amount of memory in hexadecimal format for each device driver.

4. Record the size and location of each UMB as reported by MEM /C.

5. Develop a plan for the location of each driver or utility in the UMA. Try to fill all of the available UMA space (more UMA use means more conventional memory). It is better to load five small drivers that fill the space than one large utility that leaves memory gaps. Remember that each driver or utility must fit entirely within its UMB.

6. Use the appropriate UMA command (DEVICEHIGH= for device drivers and LOADHIGH= for utilities) to move the first segment to the UMA. Always specify the size of the memory usage for devices on the DEVICEHIGH= command.

7. Check that the moved driver or utility functions correctly before you try to load another one. After each move, check that all features function smoothly.

8. Experiment with the order of the DEVICEHIGH= and LOADHIGH= statements to get the maximum use of the UMA.

These steps create a DOS environment that provides maximum free conventional memory, a primary consideration in configuring DOS. The other area of concern is the rate of data transfer.

Data Transfer

In addition to using memory to hold the operating system and applications, the same shared work space is also used to hold the data being used by the program. Each application manages its own data when it is loaded into the system work space, but the operating system moves that information from secondary storage (the hard disk or floppy) to the work space.

Unless you perform complex calculations, lag times of data transfer are much more noticeable than delays resulting from processor speed. Freeing memory enables you to run larger and more sophisticated programs and proper management of the operating system's data transfer improves data transfer speed.

The most critical factor in data transfer is the structure of the secondary storage. There is slower response time for file access if there are several group subdirectories or if the file system is fragmented. To gain the maximum performance, you should follow the recommendations in Chapter 4 on managing your hard disk.

Configuration Settings

Although each application manages its own data resources, the operating system is responsible for providing the necessary resources for the management of the data in work space memory. The availability of these resources is controlled by a series of statements in the CONFIG.SYS file, and each statement affects a different aspect of data transfer. The resources are discussed in the following sections.

Windows
If you use Windows extensively, you may wish to configure the DOS environment for maximum Windows performance rather than for performance at the command line. Because of the way Windows handles memory and data transfer, you do not need as many buffers, but you do need additional file handles. For more information about configuring Windows with DOS 5, see Appendix A.

NetWare
Do not set BUFFERS= to a high number just because the NetWare server has a 1.3GB hard disk. You actually hinder performance rather than help it.

Buffers

A buffer is an area of memory set aside for holding information that is being transferred from secondary storage to the work space. Information that has been recently accessed, but is no longer in the work space, may still be in the buffer. The operating system always checks the buffer first to see if the information is available there. If it is, it can be quickly loaded into the work space without having to access the secondary storage. Because memory access is significantly faster than storage access, system performance is greatly improved. An additional use for buffers is to improve disk access when there are a large number of subdirectories, because the time required to search a complex disk structure has a major impact on system performance.

Buffers can be particularly helpful in programs, such as word processors, in which you may be going back and forth between two sections of text. Rather than having to read and write the sections from disk, DOS is able to use the buffers to hold the information. The advantage of using the BUFFERS=S= setting is lost if you use a disk-caching program (discussed in the next section), because caches perform the same functions more effectively.

Despite the fact that the BUFFERS=S= setting is related to storage size rather than work space, the default value for the BUFFERS=S= setting is based on the amount of RAM available in the system. In general, it is a good idea to increase the number of buffers based on the size of the storage device. The maximum number of buffers that can be defined before you see a performance loss has increased to approximately 50 in DOS 5. Table 10.4 summarizes the recommended number of buffers, based on the size of the storage device (hard disk).

Table 10.4
Recommended Buffers

Hard Disk Size	Number of Buffers
(40M	20
>=40M, but <80M	30
>=80M, but <120M	40
>=1200M	50

One restriction on the number of buffers you specify is that each buffer requires memory to store the information. Because each buffer holds one entire sector (.5K) plus some overhead for management, a single buffer requires approximately 525 bytes of storage. Assuming you have a standard size hard disk (40M), and you specify the recommended number of buffers (30), you are devoting almost 16K to buffer space.

If DOS is loaded into conventional memory, the size of programs that can be loaded is affected. If DOS is loaded HIGH, the buffer space is created with DOS in the HMA and does not reduce the amount of conventional memory available for applications. If you load DOS into the HMA, specify the recommended number of buffers. If you load DOS into conventional memory, and are experiencing memory shortages, reduce the number of buffers available.

The best way to determine the number of buffers to use is through experimentation. If you have too few buffers specified, DOS always has to go to the storage device for its information. If you have too many buffers specified, DOS wastes time searching the buffers prior to going to the disk for new information. If possible, use a disk-caching program instead of increasing the number of buffers.

NetWare

You must also set FILE HANDLES = XX in a SHELL.CFG file to control the number of open files available to your workstation on the NetWare server (place this file wherever you start the NetWare IPX.COM program). The CONFIG.SYS FILES=XX command is good only for local drives.

Files

The FILES= setting is used to limit the number of file handles that are available. This setting determines the number of files that can be opened by DOS at one time. As with the other configuration settings, this primarily affects the performance of applications, rather than the operating system. The file controlled by this setting is very different from the number of files that you may be viewing, as each application may open a number of support files.

Using a word processor as an example, when two files are opened in individual windows, the application also has several files open. These additional files might include files containing the actual program code, a dictionary file or two, a style sheet file, and a glossary of macros. For systems that are primarily dedicated to word processing, the typical setting for FILES= is 20.

Spreadsheets and databases require additional open files to function, as do Graphic User Interfaces (GUIs) such as Microsoft Windows. If you use a spreadsheet, database or GUI, you should increase the file limit to 30. Although the effect on memory is minor, you should not increase the FILES= setting beyond 40, unless requested by a specific program.

File Control Blocks

The use of a *File Control Block (FCB)* is a file-access method that has been retained from DOS 1. Newer versions of the operating system (including DOS 5) use file handles to control the access. The number of file handles, rather than FCBs, is controlled by the FILES= setting. If a file is opened using a file handle, it does not use a FCB. You should change the FCBS== setting from the default only if requested to do so by a program's installation procedure.

Stacks

The STACKS= setting controls how much memory is set aside for handling hardware interrupts. This memory is used by the application to manage its interactions with the processor system. The setting enables you to specify both the number of stacks and their individual sizes. The total amount of memory required is determined by multiplying these two values. On non-IBM machines, the default installation is STACKS==9,128. This allocates nine stacks of 128 bytes each, for a total memory requirement of 1,152 bytes (or just over 1K). You should not change this setting unless it is recommended by your hardware manufacturer, unless you are using Windows (see Appendix A for a discussion of the STACKS= setting and Windows).

Disk-Caching

There are three primary approaches to improving disk-access speeds with disk-caching, and all three are established with settings in the CONFIG.SYS file. Each of them offers specific performance benefits and they can be used in various combinations. The following section discusses the three methods.

Secondary Buffers

The first approach is to use the BUFFERS=S= setting to create a secondary buffer for data. With this scheme, when the operating system goes to the disk for information, it gets the current segment and also the segment that follows. Access then improves with applications in which information moves sequentially, because the data you request next is already waiting in memory. Examples of programs that benefit from a secondary buffer include word processors and graphics applications.

Secondary buffers are specified in the BUFFERS= setting as a second value. The command BUFFERS=S=30,8 creates 30 standard buffers and eight secondary buffers. If you use secondary buffers, it is recommended that you set the number available to the maximum (8). This is an effective approach if you are not using a disk-caching program such as SMARTDrive.

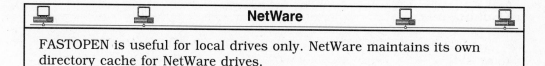

FASTOPEN is useful for local drives only. NetWare maintains its own directory cache for NetWare drives.

FASTOPEN

The second method of improving disk access is to track the location of frequently used files through the use of the FASTOPEN utility and the creation of a file-name cache. FASTOPEN is installed in memory and keeps track of the files that you access. If you request a file that has been used recently, FASTOPEN speeds access by enabling the operating system to go directly to the necessary file, rather than to search the hard disk.

Although the primary programs that benefit from FASTOPEN are database applications, other types of applications can also derive advantages from the utility. Applications such as AutoCAD, for example, use a variety of support files that must be constantly swapped. FASTOPEN tracks their locations and decreases the time required for the applications to switch functions.

FASTOPEN requires two memory locations to function. The primary location of the utility is responsible for monitoring file usage and maintaining the name cache. The utility can either be located in conventional memory or installed in the UMA by using the LOADHIGH= command. In order to make room in the conventional memory area, the name cache can be moved to expanded memory (or emulated-expanded memory) with the /X parameter. Each tracked file requires 48 bytes in the name cache and you can track approximately 200 files in 10K of memory. You can specify up to 24 drive designators as well as the number of files to be tracked for each.

For example, the command LOADHIGH=FASTOPEN C:50 D:10 /X loads the actual utility program into the UMA (assuming space is available), creates the name cache in expanded memory (or emulated-expanded memory if no physical expanded memory is available), and tracks 50 files on the C drive and 10 files on the D drive.

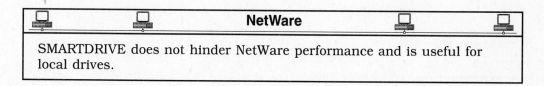

SMARTDRIVE does not hinder NetWare performance and is useful for local drives.

SMARTDrive

The third method of improving data access is to use SMARTDrive to provide more intelligent disk-caching. These services are an extension of those provided by the BUFFERS= command, but SMARTDrive is much more efficient in the ways it handles data transfer. Instead of defining individual segments in which information can be stored, you provide SMARTDrive with a portion of memory that stores information from the disk. This segment of memory is divided into regions based on the track size of your hard disk.

Windows	

SMARTDrive is intended for use with Windows. You may find that there are other cache programs that give better performance with DOS applications. Because each user has different needs and priorities, no single solution works for all situations. When you establish your cache configuration, the best way to determine the selection that works best is by experimentation.

Like the standard DOS buffers, SMARTDrive buffers both input (reading) and output (writing) requests from applications. Unlike the BUFFERS=S= command, however, information is only written to disk when it is modified. SMARTDrive stores recently used information, so that the data may already be in memory when a program requests a file to read. SMARTDrive always loads the sectors following the information just read (the same way DOS does when you specify a secondary buffer). SMARTDrive, like FASTOPEN, keeps track of which sectors are most frequently used. It uses this information to determine which parts of the cache should be emptied and which are likely to be requested.

Like FASTOPEN, SMARTDrive uses two distinct regions of memory—one for the program and one for the actual cache. The utility itself can be loaded into either conventional memory (with DEVICE=) or the UMA (with DEVICEHIGH=). The cache can be located in extended memory (the default) or expanded memory (using the /a parameter).

You must also specify the size of the cache to be used. This requires balancing the benefits available from the caching system against the demands of your programs. If you can't dedicate at least 512K of either expanded or extended memory to the cache, it is better to use secondary buffers with the BUFFERS= command. A cache larger than 2M does not produce noticeable improvement and should be avoided.

If you have memory (either extended or expanded) that is not being used by your applications, dedicating it to the SMARTDrive cache may improve performance. Begin with a cache size of 1024K and experiment to see if increasing it improves performance. (Cache sizes must be divisible by 16.)

In addition to specifying the location and starting size of the cache, you can also include a minimum size. Some programs, such as Microsoft Windows, are able to dynamically adjust SMARTDrive based on disk activity and memory requirements. The minimum value specified should be at least 256K because smaller caches don't provide sufficient benefit to justify the loss of memory.

Using a RAM Disk

Buffering methods are most useful if you frequently recall the same information frequently. If you move through a file or group of files and don't reuse the information, however, a cache system may not be effective. The problem is that each time new information is read in, old information is dropped from the cache. If you read a significant amount of information and then try to access information you used before, it may no longer be in the cache and the system has to perform a disk access. Unlike cache schemes that improve general system performance, RAM disks are used to improve the performance of a specific application.

Occasionally, you need to continuously access a file or group of files. This file may be an applications temporary file, a particularly large document file, a database or a series of spreadsheet files. With a RAM disk, you can load all of the information into memory at one time, allowing you to access information more quickly. Unlike a caching scheme, a RAM disk enables you to determine which files will be stored in the work space memory.

One disadvantage of this approach is that the memory devoted to the RAM disk is no longer available for use by applications. Because most modern applications require all available conventional memory, use a RAM disk only in extended or expanded memory. A second disadvantage is that the contents of the RAM disk are not protected in case of a power loss (or a forgetful user turning off the system). Any file on a RAM disk that is modified must be copied back onto a storage device.

To determine whether the creation of a RAM disk will improve the performance of a specific application, monitor the amount of disk activity that occurs while you are using the program. Most systems have a light that indicates when the hard disk is being accessed. If this light is usually on when you run a particular application, the creation of a RAM disk may improve your system's performance.

You specify the creation of a RAM disk by including a DEVICE= (or DEVICEHIGH=) reference to the RAMDRIVE.SYS driver. There are two parameters that you must specify when you create a RAM disk. The first parameter is the type of memory—expanded memory or extended memory (use /A for expanded memory and /E for extended memory). The second parameter is the size of the RAM disk.

The first step in creating a RAM disk for an application to identify which files the application needs. In general, it is a good idea to initially load your document files onto the RAM disk. If that does not provide sufficient improvement, try loading just the application files. Only if that fails should you load both the application and document files. To determine how large a disk you will need, copy all the files you are placing onto the RAM disk into a subdirectory and use the DIR command to get a directory size.

In addition to these files, create a subdirectory called TEMP on the RAM disk and set the environmental variables TEMP and TMP to point to it. The amount of space required for this subdirectory varies depending on the programs you are using. Consult your application's documentation for a more specific answer.

When the RAM disk is established from the CONFIG.SYS file, you must copy the appropriate files onto the RAM disk. This is best done with the AUTOEXEC.BAT file (see chapter 13). In addition, you should create a subdirectory and use the SET command to point to it with the TEMP and TMP variables.

Summary

The data-transfer rate of your system is one the most telling considerations in determining how fast the system operates. The first step in improving data-transfer rates is to make sure that your hard disk is well-tuned: use an efficient directory structure and regularly defragment your files, as discussed in Chapter 4.

The way in which you allocate system resources determines how the system handles data transfer. These settings are established in the CONFIG.SYS file and have a major effect on system performance. In most cases, the default values for these resources are not the optimal values. The recommended configuration settings for a system running spreadsheet applications and Windows from a 40 to 80M hard disk are:

```
BUFFERS=S=30
FILES=30
```

Be aware that some programs have different requirements and may require you to make additional modifications. The FCBS= and STACKS= settings can be left at their default values unless you experience difficulties with your system.

If you use a system without expanded or extended memory, you should add a secondary buffer using the BUFFERS=S= command. A typical setting would be BUFFERS=S=30,8. If you use the same group of files regularly, but not as a group, you should also install FASTOPEN (preferably in the UMA).

On a system with expanded or extended memory, you should install SMARTDrive. Experiment with its settings to determine the configuration that provides optimal performance.

A RAM disk may be useful if you have a program that is slowed down because of the amount of disk activity it must perform. If possible, you should create the RAM disk in either extended or expanded memory. A RAM disk in conventional memory reduces the number of programs that you can run.

Recommended Configurations

Each system has unique characteristics that may require special consideration when configuring its memory resources. Table 10.5 presents some general guidelines for the creation of CONFIG.SYS files. Be sure to read the section on getting the most out of expanded memory if you have a 286, 386, or 486 processor and expanded memory. If you have a 286 system and a UMA manager that works with DOS 5, follow the recommendations for a 386/486 system. These recommendations assume that your applications do not need expanded memory. To activate expanded-memory emulation, change the NOEMS parameter to the RAM parameter on the EMM386 installation.

Table 10.5
Recommended System Configurations

Processor	Memory Available	CONFIG.SYS
ANY	Conventional Only	DOS=LOW BUFFERS=S=20,8 FILES=20 INSTALL=FASTOPEN.EXE
ANY	Conventional Expanded	DOS=LOW (expanded-memory manager) BUFFERS=S=20 FILES=20 DEVICE=SMARTDRV.EXE /A DEVICE=RAMDRIVE.EXE /A

Table 10.5—continued

Processor	Memory Available	CONFIG.SYS
286/386/486	Conventional Extended	DEVICE=HIMEM.SYS /SHADOWRAM:OFF DOS=HIGH DEVICE=EMM386.EXE NOEMS BUFFERS=S=20 FILES=20 DEVICE=SMARTDRV.EXE
386/486	Conventional UMA	DEVICE=HIMEM.SYS /SHADOWRAM:OFF DEVICE=EMM386.EXE NOEMS DOS=UMB BUFFERS=S=20, 8 FILES=20 INSTALL=FASTOPEN.EXE
386/486	Conventional UMA Extended	DEVICE=HIMEM.SYS /SHADOWRAM:OFF DEVICE=EMM386.EXE NOEMS DOS=HIGH, UMB BUFFERS=S=20, 8 FILES=20 DEVICEHIGH=SMARTDRV.SYS

If the UMA is available, you should change as many DEVICE= statements to DEVICEHIGH= as possible (except for HIMEM.SYS and EMM386.EXE). In addition, experiment with replacing INSTALL= statements in the CONFIG.SYS file with LOADHIGH= statements placed in your AUTOEXEC.BAT file.

Bear in mind that these are simply guidelines and that the best method for determining the systems configuration is intelligent experimentation.

Getting the Most from Expanded Memory

If possible, you should reconfigure your expanded memory as extended memory. If not, and if you are not using a 80386 system, you should load SMARTDrive into the expanded memory region. If you create a 1M cache and still have available expanded memory, create a RAM disk in the remaining space. Use this area to hold any temporary files created by the system (SET TEMP= and TMP= to point to a directory on the RAM disk). Also, experiment with relocating frequently used applications onto the RAM Disk. Unless you notice a significant improvement in system responsiveness, you should not place data files on the RAM disk.

If you are on a 80386 or 80486 system, you should determine whether any of your programs requires expanded memory. In many cases, the improved performance that can be obtained by disabling the expanded memory manager, and using HIMEM.SYS and EMM386.EXE to manage the UMA, will be worth the loss of the expanded memory. Another option is to create two sets of configuration files—one using the physical expanded memory and one permitting EMM386 to manage the UMA. A technique for automating this process is discussed in Chapter 13.

Getting the Most from Extended Memory

Extended memory is currently the best option for improving your system performance. If you need expanded memory for your applications, use EMM386 to emulate only as much expanded memory as is required by your applications. Use SMARTDrive and locate its cache in the extended memory region (unless you have expanded memory that is not being used). Many applications can utilize extended memory for their processing, so be sure to leave sufficient memory free for any program that requires it. In general, if you are using currently released programs, your performance will be better if you allow the programs to manage extended memory rather than configuring it as a RAM disk.

A Final Word about Configuring DOS

This chapter discussed managing your system's memory resources. The most important rule in memory management is to be selfish in how you allocate your resources. Install the absolute minimum regarding programs that require conventional memory. This is particularly important for device drivers and utility programs that remain a permanent part of your DOS environment. Even using the UMA does not free you from having to limit these resources. The memory available in the UMA is very limited and any drivers or utilities that do not fit will be installed in your conventional memory. The next chapter discusses using device drivers efficiently.

11

Controlling Devices

DOS, like every operating system, provides an interface between the user and the computer system. The DOS interface provides users with a layer of control that they can use to customize and add new functions to their computer systems. This control extends not only to the CPU, but also to the devices connected to the system. Common devices include the display, printers, disk drives, the keyboard, and the computer's I/O ports (parallel and serial ports).

In this chapter you learn how to use DOS commands and device drivers to customize your DOS environment and add new devices. Even if you already use all of the devices available to your system, the commands and device drivers discussed in this chapter help you optimize each device and make those devices work together more efficiently.

In the section on displays, you learn how to use DOS's device drivers to control output to the display, and how to use the MODE command to set some of the visual characteristics of your computer's display. Both techniques provide a level of customization not present in the standard DOS installation. The section on printers shows you how to use the PRINTER.SYS device driver to swap code pages, the GRAPHICS command to control printing of graphics, and the PRINT command to print in the background.

If you have added a new floppy disk drive to your system or need to gain better control of your disk drives, the section on disk drives has the answers you need. In it you learn how to use the DRIVER.SYS device driver to set the logical format for a floppy disk drive, the ASSIGN command to redirect drive I/O, the JOIN command to link drives together, and the SUBST command to make directories appear as separate drives.

When your disks are configured the way you want, move on to the section on keyboards, where you learn to switch character sets, define a new console, and control keyboard sensitivity. The chapter finishes with a discussion of the MODE command, and how you can use it to control parallel and serial ports.

Before you can gain more control over your system's devices, you must understand, at least to some degree, the way DOS interacts with devices. The next section examines device drivers and other methods you use with DOS to control devices.

Windows ▼ ▲

If you create multiple DOS sessions within each window, each session has a copy of the DOS environment. Any changes to devices or environmental variables made within a DOS window affect that window only. The changes are not made part of the global Windows environment.

Working with Device Drivers and Commands

Some of the common devices attached to a typical PC include input devices such as the keyboard, mouse, and parallel and serial ports; output devices such as the display and printer; and storage devices such as disk drives. The level of control you exert over a device depends on the way you use the device, the features you want to add to it, and other factors. Nevertheless, there are two primary ways you control devices: through device drivers or with DOS commands.

Controlling Devices with Device Drivers

You learned in previous chapters that device drivers are mini-programs that DOS uses to communicate with the devices in your computer system. To better understand how you control these devices, it is important that you take another look at device drivers.

A *device driver* is a small program or section of program code that serves as an interface between a device and the DOS kernel, which in turn controls the interface between the device driver and an application. Device drivers usually are installed via a DEVICE= or DEVICEHIGH= setting in the CONFIG.SYS file. These types of drivers usually have a SYS file extension.

Many device drivers provided by third-party vendors are provided in a second form, which has a COM file extension. This type of driver is loaded by simply typing the name of the driver and providing any necessary command line switches. Functionally, the two types of drivers are identical. If you are not familiar with how device drivers are installed, review the previous chapters that discuss the CONFIG.SYS file and system basics. Each section in this chapter also has examples that show you how to install device drivers.

Device drivers, whether installed via CONFIG.SYS or at the command line, are not the only means for controlling devices. DOS also includes commands, both internal and external, that provide for device control.

Controlling Devices with DOS Commands

Although DOS often does not directly interact with add-on peripherals without some form of device driver, it does include commands for controlling standard devices. Some DOS commands can be used to control more than one device. The MODE command, for example, provides control of the keyboard, display, and I/O ports.

Most DOS commands that provide some form of device control are external commands with COM extensions. Whether the command is internal or external, you type the name of the command, followed by the appropriate switches. The command, which is actually a mini-program, either runs a single time and sets the device, or installs as a TSR that is ready when you need to use it. The method you use varies according to the function of the device.

Now that you are familiar with the methods you can use to control the devices in your system, you are ready to learn how to control your computer's display.

Controlling the Display

Most DOS users do not realize that they can control output to the display from the DOS command line. Much of the time, control of the display is implemented in the user's applications, and need not be controlled from the command line. There are times, however, when you may need to modify the display yourself, rather than have an application do it.

In this section you learn to use the ANSI.SYS, DISPLAY.SYS, and EGA.SYS device drivers to control output to the display. You also learn to use the MODE command to switch between 40- and 80-column display, color or monochrome, and set the number of screen lines. ANSI.SYS is discussed first because it must be installed for a few of the other commands to work.

```
┌──────────────────────────────────────────────────────────────┐
│ ▬                     DOS Shell                         ▼ │ ▲ │
├──────────────────────────────────────────────────────────────┤
│  DOS Shell uses a series of special files to control the         │
│  graphics display within the DOS Shell. If you change the type   │
│  of graphics adapter being used, you must change these files     │
│  as well. The affected file extensions are GRB and VID. The      │
│  currently installed drivers are named DOSSHELL.GRB and          │
│  DOSSHELL.VID. The actual driver files are on the DOS            │
│  Installation diskettes and are of the format type.GR_ and       │
│  type.VI_; type is the type of video adapter (VGA, MONO, etc.).   │
└──────────────────────────────────────────────────────────────┘
```

Installing ANSI.SYS

ANSI.SYS is a device driver supplied with DOS that acts as an intermediary between the keyboard and the CPU, and also acts as an intermediary between the display and the CPU. When ANSI.SYS has been installed, you can change the way DOS interprets your keyboard's scan codes (the codes generated when you press a key), control display color, and use special characters to control the display's appearance.

Before you can use the capabilities that ANSI.SYS provides, you must install it. As with other device drivers, ANSI.SYS installs via a DEVICE= statement in the CONFIG.SYS file. To install ANSI.SYS, add the following line to the CONFIG.SYS file:

```
DEVICE=C:\DOS\ANSI.SYS
```

The previous example assumes that your system's DOS files are stored in a directory on drive C named \DOS. With DOS 5, if you prefer to load ANSI.SYS into reserved memory and decrease memory usage below 640K, type the following line:

```
DEVICEHIGH=C:\DOS\ANSI.SYS
```

Whether device drivers such as ANSI.SYS can be loaded into reserved I/O address space depends on your system configuration. If you experience problems after loading a device high, move it back below 640K. Remember that after altering CONFIG.SYS, you must reboot the system for the changes to take effect.

Using ANSI.SYS

If ANSI.SYS has not been loaded in CONFIG.SYS, DOS uses the basic I/O routines that are built into the DOS kernel. In most cases, these are adequate. If ANSI.SYS has been loaded, however, all keyboard input is directed through ANSI.SYS, as is all output to the screen.

Normally, characters that you type on the command line are unaffected by ANSI.SYS. In order for ANSI.SYS to interpret your keystrokes as directives to it, rather than just standard keyboard input, you must use a special character to alert ANSI.SYS that you are issuing it a command. For this reason, each ANSI.SYS command must be preceded by an escape character.

Unfortunately, there is no way to issue an escape character directly from the keyboard. As a result, you cannot simply issue a command directly to ANSI.SYS by typing it. There are, however, two ways around this problem.

Using Escape Characters in Files

You can use a text editor, including the DOS EDLIN editor and the MS-DOS Editor (EDIT.COM), to create files that contain escape code sequences. Then, the file can be directed through ANSI.SYS if you use the TYPE command.

The Escape Character in EDLIN

To issue an escape character in EDLIN, press Ctrl-V, followed by a left bracket ([). When you enter the escape code in EDLIN, the line looks like this:

```
1:*^V[
```

After you save the file and then load it back into EDLIN, you no longer see the v. Instead, you see only the caret (^) and bracket ([), as in the following line:

```
1:*^[
```

The Escape Character in the MS-DOS Editor

You can also enter an escape character with the MS-DOS Editor, which is a much better text editor than EDLIN.

To enter an escape character in the MS-DOS Editor, press Ctrl-P, then the Esc key, followed by the left bracket ([). The Editor enters the escape character as a left arrow.

Other Ways To Insert an Escape Character

You may also be able to use other word processors, such as Microsoft Word, to create text files that contain escape characters. In Word, press and hold the Alt key and type **27** on the numeric keypad. This enters an ASCII 27, which is the escape character. Again, the printable character that represents the escape character is a left arrow. Check your word processor's documentation to determine how to enter ASCII codes into a document, then enter ASCII 27 followed by a left bracket.

Directing Files through ANSI.SYS with TYPE

After you create a file that contains commands for ANSI.SYS, you can use the DOS TYPE command to direct them to the ANSI.SYS driver. To understand how this process works, create a simple text file that directs ANSI.SYS to move to row 12, column 35 on the display and print a message in blinking characters. The control characters are explained later in the chapter. For now, simply type the characters as shown in the following example.

1. Type **EDIT HELLO** and press Enter.
2. Type the following, using Ctrl-P,Esc wherever you see the left arrow symbol: ①[12;35H①[5mHELLO WORLD!①[0m
3. Press Alt,F,S to save the file.
4. Press Alt,F,X to exit the MS-DOS Editor.
5. Type **CLS** to clear the display.
6. Type **TYPE HELLO** and press Enter.

When you use the TYPE command to output the contents of the HELLO file to the display, it is directed through ANSI.SYS. ANSI.SYS detects the escape characters and manipulates the display accordingly.

Character-attribute codes and cursor-movement commands for ANSI.SYS are discussed in more detail later in the chapter. Before you learn about them, examine the second method you can use to send characters to ANSI.SYS—the DOS PROMPT command.

Entering Escape Characters with PROMPT

As you learned in previous chapters, the DOS PROMPT command can be used to set the DOS command line prompt. You can use PROMPT to make the date, time, current drive, or other information appear as the system's command prompt.

You can also use the DOS PROMPT command to direct escape characters to ANSI.SYS. When you issue a PROMPT directive, it is directed through ANSI.SYS, as is all other keyboard input. PROMPT can be used in a batch file or directly from the command line. Therefore, the PROMPT command is the only way you can send escape codes directly to ANSI.SYS without placing the commands in a file.

To use the PROMPT command, type **PROMPT**, followed by one or more special PROMPT character strings. Each character is preceded by the $ character. Table 11.1 lists the character strings that can be included with the PROMPT command.

The character strings for the PROMPT command were covered in a previous chapter. The last item in Table 11.1, the $e code, is used to direct commands to ANSI.SYS. Use the HELLO message in the previous exercise, but this time, use the PROMPT command to send it to ANSI.SYS.

Table 11.1
PROMPT Command Parameters

Symbol	Effect
$q	= (equal sign)
$$	$ (dollar sign)
$t	Current time
$d	Current date
$p	Current drive and directory
$v	MS-DOS version number
$n	Current drive
$g	> (greater-than symbol)
$l	< (less-than symbol)
$b	I (vertical bar, or pipe)
$_	Carriage return/linefeed
$h	Backspace
$e	ASCII code 27, the escape character

Saying HELLO WORLD! with PROMPT

Although it is unlikely you will want to use the HELLO WORLD! message in the previous example as a system prompt, the following exercise shows you that you can achieve the same effect from the command line. This process is much simpler because you are typing a single command and not using a text editor. Type the following line and press Enter:

```
PROMPT $e[12;35H$e[5mHELLO WORLD!$e[0m
```

When you press Enter, the command prompt jumps to the middle of the
screen and displays the familiar `HELLO WORLD!` prompt. The prompt remains in
one location until you reset the prompt because you assigned the string as
the prompt, rather than sending it to ANSI.SYS a single time with the TYPE
command. To reset the prompt, type the following and press Enter:

```
PROMPT =
```

If you prefer a different prompt, enter it instead of the previous sample line.

Moving the Cursor with ANSI.SYS

One of the main uses for ANSI.SYS is to move the cursor to a specific row
and column on the display. The HELLO WORLD! example uses cursor-movement directives to position the cursor at row 12, column 35. As you have
seen, cursor movement via ANSI.SYS can be accomplished using the PROMPT
command or a text file that is printed to the display.

Each of the cursor-movement instructions, which are listed in Table 11.2, are
preceded by the escape character and left bracket. The left bracket is in addition to any left bracket required as part of the escape character. EDLIN, for
example, requires that you type Ctrl-V and a left bracket to enter an escape
character. If the escape character is then followed by a cursor-movement
command, type another bracket for the movement command:

```
1:*^V[[12;35H
```

Note that each of the cursor-movement commands is followed by a single
character, which in the previous example is `H`. The final character is case-
sensitive (DOS differentiates between upper- and lowercase letters), so you
must type it as shown in Table 11.2.

Table 11.2
ANSI.SYS Cursor Movement Commands

Command	Function
Esc[_row;col_**H**	Moves the cursor to the specified row and column. If no row and column numbers are specified, the cursor moves to the home position at row 0, column 0.
Esc[_row;col_**f**	Functions the same as **Esc[**_row;col_**H**.
Esc[_lines_**A**	Moves the cursor up the number of lines specified by _lines_.
Esc[_lines_**B**	Moves the cursor down the number of lines specified by _lines_.

Table 11.2—continued

Command	Function
Esc[_columns_**C**	Moves the cursor to the right the number of columns specified by _columns_. If the value for _columns_ is omitted, the cursor moves one column to the right. If the cursor is at the right edge of the display, it will not wrap to the next line.
Esc[_columns_**D**	Moves the cursor to the left the number of columns specified by _columns_. If the value for _columns_ is omitted, the cursor moves one column to the left. If the cursor is at the left edge of the display, it does not wrap to the previous line.
Esc[s	Saves the current cursor position.
Esc[u	Restores the cursor to the position previously saved with **Esc[s**.
Esc[2J	Clears the display and returns the cursor to row 0, column 0. This is functionally identical to the CLS command.
Esc[K	Erases all characters from the current position to the end of the line.

Now, put some of those cursor-movement commands to use. Create a PROMPT setting that displays the current drive and directory, stores the current position, places the date and time on the top line, then returns to the previously saved position. You can enter the following line directly at the command prompt, or place it in the AUTOEXEC.BAT file to incorporate it into your startup sequence:

```
PROMPT $p$g$e[s$e[0;53;H$d $t$e[K$e[u
```

The previous PROMPT command places the date and time starting at column 53, which makes the last character of the time appear near the right edge of the display on an 80-column display. If you use a different number of columns, alter the column number in the prompt accordingly.

Changing Screen-Character Attributes

In addition to moving the cursor using ANSI.SYS, you can control the visual characteristics of text on the display, including attributes such as bold, underscore, blinking, reverse video, and hidden text, and also change the foreground and background color of text. Changing the color or other visual characteristics of text simply requires issuing the correct ANSI.SYS display control code:

Esc[*n;n;n*...**m**   Sets character attributes such as display mode and color of foreground and background. The valid entries for *n* are listed in Table 11.3.

Table 11.3
Graphics Mode Functions for ANSI.SYS

Text attributes:

Value	Effect
0	All attributes off (default)
1	Bold
4	Underscore (MDA displays only)
5	Blinking
7	Reverse video
8	Hidden

Foreground Color:		*Background Color:*	
Value	Effect	Value	Effect
30	Black	40	Black
31	Red	41	Red
32	Green	42	Green
33	Yellow	43	Yellow
34	Blue	44	Blue
35	Magenta	45	Magenta
36	Cyan	46	Cyan
37	White	47	White

Use the ANSI.SYS text attribute command to change the date and time prompt in the previous example. The following line shows the date in bold and the time as yellow on black:

```
PROMPT $p$g$e[s$e[0;53;H$e[1m$d  $e[1;33;40m$t$e[K$e[0m$e[u
```

The prompt string is now fairly long. Use the MS-DOS EDIT command to add the prompt line to the AUTOEXEC.BAT file to incorporate the custom prompt automatically. Load AUTOEXEC.BAT into the DOS Editor, add the line, and resave the file.

Setting Display Mode with ANSI.SYS

Another way you can control the display with the ANSI.SYS driver is to change the display mode. If you use a standard color VGA system, it defaults to 80-column by 25-line color text mode. You can, however, change the display's mode if you use the following ANSI.SYS command:

Esc[=nh Sets display mode. Valid entries for n are listed in Table 11.4.

Table 11.4
Display Mode Command Values

Value	Effect
0	40 x 25 monochrome text
1	40 x 25 color text
2	80 x 25 monochrome text
3	80 x 25 color text
4	320 x 200 4-color graphics
5	320 x 200 monochrome graphics
6	640 x 200 monochrome graphics
7	Enable line wrap
13	320 x 200 color graphics
14	640 x 200 16-color graphics
15	640 x 350 monochrome graphics
16	640 x 350 16-color graphics
17	640 x 480 monochrome graphics
18	640 x 480 16-color graphics
19	320 x 200 256-color graphics

In addition to affecting the system's display, ANSI.SYS can be used to redefine the keyboard's scan codes. What scan codes are and how to define them with ANSI.SYS are covered later in this chapter in the section on keyboards.

The next section examines the DOS device driver DISPLAY.SYS, which provides support for code page switching on the display. Before you can understand how to use DISPLAY.SYS, you first must understand code pages.

Working with Code Pages

As you learned in previous chapters, computers use ASCII codes to represent characters, numbers, and symbols. When the computer prints an uppercase "A" for example, it prints ASCII 65. These ASCII characters are set up in a code page that defines the character set. Think of the code page as simply a table of numbers from 0 to 255, each of which represents a character, whether the character is a letter, number, or symbol.

Character sets for different countries are not the same, so DOS uses a different code page for each selected country (some countries naturally use the same code page as another). There are five code pages that DOS supports, as shown in Table 11.5:

Table 11.5
Code Pages Supported by DOS 5.0

Code Page	Country
437	United States
850	Multilingual
860	Portuguese
863	Canadian-French
865	Nordic

Each code page contains characters for the associated language. Therefore, a given ASCII value may not result in the same character with two different code pages. Multiple code pages provide you with a much higher number of characters than does a single code page. To access the additional characters, simply tell DOS to switch code pages.

The following sections show you how to implement code-page switching for the display and printer.

Using DISPLAY.SYS

The DOS device driver DISPLAY.SYS provides support for code-page switching on the system's display. Once DISPLAY.SYS is installed and configured properly, you can switch code pages and access new sets of characters. With DISPLAY.SYS installed, you can switch to different code pages without rebooting the system.

DISPLAY.SYS can be used with LCD, EGA, and VGA display adapters. Although there are command line switches for DISPLAY.SYS that specify MDA and CGA display adapters, the code pages for these two display modes are fixed, and code-page switching is not implemented for MDA and CGA displays.

As with all other device drivers, the DISPLAY.SYS driver is installed via a DE-VICE= statement in the CONFIG.SYS file. The following line lists the general form of the DISPLAY.SYS command line:

```
DEVICE=C:\DOS\DISPLAY.SYS CON: = (type,codepage,added codepage,
subfonts)
```

The first parameter, which in the above example is `c:\DOS`, specifies the location of the DISPLAY.SYS file. If DISPLAY.SYS is located in a drive and directory other than C:\DOS, change the entry accordingly.

The `CON:` parameter defines the system console—the combination of keyboard and display. Although a colon (:) is included after CON, it is optional and can be omitted.

The `type` parameter specifies the video adapter type. As mentioned previously, there are entries for the Monochrome Display Adapter (MDA) and Color Graphics Adapter (CGA) displays, but they have no effect. The following are valid entries for the type parameter:

Parameter	Display Type
MONO	Monochrome Display Adapter (MDA)
CGA	Color Graphics Adapter (CGA)
EGA	Enhanced Graphics Adapter (EGA) and Video Graphics Array (VGA)
LCD	Convertible LCD

The `codepage` parameter specifies the code page to be used and can be any code page number listed in Table 11.5 (437, 850, 860, 863, or 865).

The `added codepage` parameter specifies the maximum number of additional code pages the display adapter will use. These additional code pages are accessed via the MODE command. Valid entries range from 1 to 6, depending on the type of display adapter used. EGA and VGA displays can use a maximum of six code pages, and LCD adapters can use a maximum of one code page.

The last parameter, subfonts, specifies the number of subfonts the display adapter supports for each code page. The number varies according to the type of display. On a CGA display the correct value is 0, and DISPLAY.SYS defaults to 0 if CGA is specified for the *type* parameter and no value is supplied for subfonts. The correct entry for LCD displays is 1, and DISPLAY.SYS defaults to 1 if *type* is set to LCD and no value is specified for *subfonts*. Finally, the entry for EGA and VGA systems can be 1 or 2. DISPLAY.SYS defaults to 2 if *type* is set to EGA and no value is specified for *subfonts*.

The following example installs DISPLAY.SYS for an EGA display using two code pages, Multilingual and Norwegian, with a maximum of two added code pages:

```
DEVICE=C:\DOS\DISPLAY.SYS CON: = (EGA,850,865,2)
```

In the previous example, the Norwegian code page 865 is the existing code page, and the Multilingual code page 850 is the specified code page.

Remember that if you do not plan to use code-page switching for the display, there is no need to install DISPLAY.SYS.

Changing Display Modes with the MODE Command

By default, your computer system probably uses an 80-column, 25-line display. There may be times, however, when you want to switch to a display mode that offers more lines. If you try to list a particularly large directory with the DIR command, for example, and the entire list does not fit on the display, even with the /W switch, increasing the number of lines might make the entire directory fit on the display.

The DOS MODE command, which is covered in many of the sections in this chapter, provides a means for changing the display mode from the DOS command line. MODE selects a display adapter and mode or reconfigures the active display.

Windows   ▼ ▲

You cannot use the MODE command within Windows to change the display characteristics for the Windows environment. Changes made are unique to the DOS window.

Using MODE on a CGA Display

There are different forms for the MODE command, depending on the type of display adapter in use. The following is the first of the three possible command syntaxes:

```
MODE display,shift,t
```

The form of the MODE command shown above is for the CGA display adapter. The `display` variable defines the type of display mode to be used, and can be set to one of the modes listed in Table 11.6.

Table 11.6
Display Mode Settings for the MODE Command

Setting	Meaning
40 or 80	Specifies the number of columns.
bw40 or bw80	Specifies monochrome display and number of columns.
co40 or co80	Specifies color display and number of columns.
mono	Specifies monochrome display with 80 columns.

The *display* variable is optional, and if it is not specified, the current display mode is used.

The `shift` parameter can be set to R for *right*, or L for *left*. If included, this parameter shifts the display to the right or left, as specified. If the *display* parameter is set to 40, or is omitted and the display is currently in 40-column mode, the display is shifted one character. If the *display* parameter is set to 80, or is omitted and the display is currently in 80-column mode, the display is shifted two characters.

The `t` parameter causes a test pattern consisting of characters to be generated on the display, which can be used to adjust the position of the display via prompts generated by MODE. Most systems never use this parameter because this form of the MODE command applies only to CGA displays.

Setting Display Mode and Screen Lines—All Displays

A more common use for the MODE command is to change the display mode and number of screen lines. By default, most systems use 80-column by 25-line displays. The display type and number of screen lines, however, can be changed with a single MODE command:

```
MODE display,n
```

In the previous example, *display* can be any of the settings listed in Table 11.6 with the exception of mono. It is not possible to change the number of lines on a MDA or CGA display. The number of lines can be 25, 43, or 50, depending on the type of display. Some displays support all three, but others do not. Note that ANSI.SYS must be loaded in the CONFIG.SYS file before you can specify the number of screen lines.

To set the display for 80-column color and 50 lines, type the following MODE command:

```
MODE CO80,50
```

To switch back to a default 80-column by 25-line display, include the *display* parameter but omit the *n* parameter:

```
MODE CO80
```

This form of the MODE command is useful for changing the display characteristics of the console display, but it can also be used to change the display mode of an auxiliary console that has been defined with the CTTY command. The CTTY command is discussed later in this chapter in the section on keyboards.

Setting the Console with MODE

The last form of the MODE command controls the console display. The primary difference from the previous form of the MODE command is that CON is specified, followed by the number of columns and screen lines:

```
MODE CON COLS=c LINES=l
```

The *c* parameter can be set to either 40 or 80. Valid entries for *l* are 25, 43, or 50, depending on the type of display. As before, not all displays support all settings. VGA displays, however, do support all three. To set the console on a VGA system to 80 columns by 50 lines, use the following MODE command:

```
MODE CON COLS=80 LINES=50
```

The MODE command can also be used to switch code pages for the display.

Using EGA.SYS

DOS 5.0's DOS Shell acts as a user interface between the operating system (DOS) and the user. As you have read in previous chapters, the DOS Shell includes a Task Switcher that enables you to switch between applications without first exiting them.

To use the Task Switcher on a system with an EGA display adapter, you must use the device driver EGA.SYS. EGA.SYS saves and restores an application's display when the Task Switcher is used to switch to and from the application. To install EGA.SYS, use the following entry in the CONFIG.SYS file:

```
DEVICE=C:\DOS\EGA.SYS
```

There are no optional parameters for the EGA.SYS device driver. Its location in the CONFIG.SYS file, however, is important. To conserve memory on an EGA system that uses a mouse, install EGA.SYS before the mouse driver is installed. Either place the EGA.SYS line in CONFIG.SYS before the line that loads the mouse driver, or load the mouse driver from the command line (if the mouse includes a COM-type driver that can be installed via AUTOEXEC.BAT or the DOS command line).

Controlling the Printer

The printer is a peripheral that most users do not think much about. Applications generally take control of the printer to control printer setup, print graphics, and perform other tasks. Many of those tasks, however, can be controlled from the DOS command line. Two DOS commands and an included device driver enable you to print graphics screens, print in the background, and control other aspects of your printer.

The first of these three DOS utilities is PRINTER.SYS. This command provides you with a way to switch code pages on some printers.

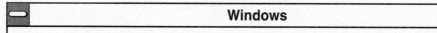

Windows

The Configure Printer dialog box used by Windows controls the same features as the DOS commands that modify printer characteristics. If you want to change the printer characteristics within Windows, use the Configure Printer option.

Installing and Using PRINTER.SYS

Before you can implement code-page switching for your printer, you must install the PRINTER.SYS driver. As with other device drivers, use the DEVICE= command in CONFIG.SYS to install the driver. In addition to specifying the driver itself, you must also specify the printer port to be affected, the printer model, and the code page that you want to use. The following example shows the required parameters:

DEVICE=C:\DOS\PRINTER.SYS LPTx: = (type, *codepage, added codepage)*

The printer port can be PRN, LPT1, LPT2, and LPT3. The **type** parameter in the previous example defines the printer type to be affected. DOS directly supports only three types of printers. Therefore, there are three possible valid entries for *type* as shown below:

Type	Printer Model
4201	IBM 4201 Proprinter family and 4202 Proprinter XL
4208	IBM 4207 or 4208 Proprinter X24 or XL24
5202	IBM 5202 Quietwriter III

The **codepage** parameter can be any of the valid code page numbers listed in Table 11.5. The final parameter, added codepage, specifies the number of code pages, in addition to *codepage*, that the printer will support. The discussion of the MODE command later in this chapter explains how to access additional code pages. The following sample entry specifies the Proprinter XL24 printer, Multilingual code page, and two additional code pages:

```
DEVICE=C:\DOS\PRINTER.SYS LPT1 = (4208, 850, 2)
```

You can specify settings for multiple printer ports with the same command. The following example uses the same settings as in the previous example, but sets up LPT2 for a different configuration:

```
DEVICE=C:\DOS\PRINTER.SYS LPT1 = (4208, 850, 2) LPT2 = (4201, 863, 2)
```

You can also specify more than one code page for a single port. If you have a Quietwriter III printer with a cartridge that contains two code pages, for example, specify the device as follows:

DEVICE=C:\DOS\PRINTER.SYS LPT1 = (5202,(437,850),0)

Note that the multiple pages must be enclosed in additional parentheses, and that 0 is specified as the number of additional code pages.

Windows	

In Windows, the task of background printing is handled by Print Manager and requires no additional steps. If you install the PRINT utility within a DOS window, you have two print spoolers—PRINT and Print Manager.

DOS Shell

The PRINT utility must be installed prior to entering DOS Shell to print files with the DOS Shell menu commands. It does not need to be installed to print from applications.

Text versus Graphics Display Mode

There are two general types of display modes available on your system—text and graphics. If the display is showing a screen of text and you press the Print Screen (PrtSc or Print Scrn) key, the text on the display is directed to the printer. If the display contains a graphic image, however, the image will not print properly. To print graphic images on the printer with the Print Screen key, you must use the DOS conversion command called GRAPHICS.

The GRAPHICS command enables you to print graphics displays on a printer. GRAPHICS, which is a memory-resident program, performs as a filter for the Print Screen key—if the GRAPHICS command has been installed and the user presses Print Screen, the output is directed through the GRAPHICS program where it is converted as necessary to print properly on the printer. If the display shows only text, GRAPHICS has no effect on the data that flows to the printer. In addition, if the attached printer does not support graphic modes, GRAPHICS has no effect.

Printing Graphics Screens with GRAPHICS

The GRAPHICS command supports the CGA, EGA, and VGA graphics modes. It must be in memory to process a print request, so you must execute the command prior to printing. There are a number of optional parameters that can be included with the GRAPHICS command. The general form of the command follows:

```
GRAPHICS printer d:path\filename /R /B /LCD /PB:STD/PB:LCD
```

Using Printer Options with GRAPHICS

The `printer` parameter specifies the type of printer connected to the system, and changing the `printer` parameter affects the way GRAPHICS converts the data before it goes to the printer. Table 11.6 lists the printer types supported by the DOS 5 GRAPHICS command.

Table 11.6
Printer Types Supported by GRAPHICS

Parameter	Printer Type
color1	IBM Color Printer with black ribbon.
color4	IBM Color Printer with RGB (red, green, blue, and black) ribbon.
color8	IBM Color Printer with CMY (cyan, magenta, yellow, and black) ribbon.
hpdefault	All Hewlett-Packard PCL printers.
deskjet	Hewlett-Packard Deskjet Printer.
graphics	IBM Personal Graphics Printer, IBM Proprinter, or IBM Quietwriter Printer.
graphicswide	IBM Personal Graphics Printer with 11-inch carriage.
laserjet	Hewlett-Packard LaserJet.
laserjetii	Hewlett-Packard LaserJet II.
paintjet	Hewlett-Packard PaintJet.
quietjet	Hewlett-Packard QuietJet.
quietjetplus	Hewlett-Packard QuietJet Plus.
ruggedwriter	Hewlett-Packard RuggedWriter.
ruggedwriterwide	Hewlett-Packard RuggedWriter Wide.
thermal	IBM PC-convertible Thermal.
thinkjet	Hewlett-Packard ThinkJet.

The following line invokes GRAPHICS for the Hewlett-Packard DeskJet printer:

```
GRAPHICS deskjet
```

If no printer is specified, GRAPHICS defaults to the graphics option. If the printer you use is not compatible with one of those listed in Table 11.6, you can create a *printer profile* for your printer.

Creating and Using Printer Profiles

Your DOS directory contains a file called GRAPHICS.PRO, which contains definitions for the standard printers that DOS 5 supports. When you invoke GRAPHICS without specifying a printer profile, it looks for the file GRAPHICS.PRO in the current directory, then in the directory containing the GRAPHICS.COM program.

You can incorporate special capabilities of your printer by creating a new printer profile. To create a profile, make a backup copy of GRAPHICS.PRO, then modify GRAPHICS.PRO as necessary. You can create a new printer profile with a different filename instead, and specify the filename on the GRAPHICS command line, as shown in the following line:

```
GRAPHICS myprinter C:\DOS\MYPRINT
```

Unfortunately, the GRAPHICS.PRO file is not documented in the *MS-DOS User's Guide and Reference*. If you are familiar with the printer control sequences and capabilities of your printer, however, you should be able to successfully modify GRAPHICS.PRO, or create and specify a different printer profile.

If you use the GRAPHICS command to load a profile, and you then attempt to load another profile (by issuing another GRAPHICS command), the second profile must be smaller than the one originally loaded. If the second profile is larger, you must restart the system and load the desired profile.

The /R, /B, and /LCD GRAPHICS Switches

There are three switches that control the way graphics print on the printer— /R, /B, and /LCD. The /R switch causes the image to be reversed, with white characters on a black background. This is identical to what displays on the screen, but is opposite of the default for printed images, which is black on white. Note that the printer does not actually print white characters—the paper is white (usually), and when the image is printed, only the background is printed. The paper then "shows through" where the foreground would normally be printed.

The /B switch is used with a color printer to enable and disable printing the background. If the display background is blue, for example, and you invoke the GRAPHICS command with the /B switch, the printer prints a blue background. If the /B switch is omitted, the background is not printed. The paper color then serves as the background color.

The /LCD switch prints an image in the LCD (Liquid Crystal Display) aspect ratio instead of the standard CGA aspect ratio. Optionally, the PB:LCD switch can be used instead of the /LCD switch. The PB:STD and PB:LCD switches are discussed next.

The PB:STD and PB:LCD GRAPHICS Switches

The final two switches that can be used with the GRAPHICS command are PB:STD and PB:LCD. The PB in these switches stands for *Print Box*, which define whether GRAPHICS uses a standard-size print box, or the smaller LCD-size print box, when it prints graphics.

If you lack a screen-capture utility and need to capture graphics images and print them, use the GRAPHICS command to set up your printer to print the image. Although you will not be able to save the image to a file for editing or later printing, GRAPHICS enables you to successfully print the image.

Using PRINT To Print in the Background

The last of the DOS commands that enhances printing is the PRINT command. Like GRAPHICS, the PRINT command operates as a memory-resident program. PRINT is capable of processing print jobs in the background while you continue to work on the system. In other words, PRINT frees your system almost immediately when you issue a print request, rather than tying up the system until the print job has finished (or all of the job has been sent to the printer's buffer).

To understand how PRINT functions, you must first understand multitasking and what the terms background and foreground mean. The system's CPU processes *tasks*. Printing a document is a task, servicing a spreadsheet program is a task, and accepting and interpreting keyboard input is a task. When a computer *multitasks*, it performs more than one task at a time.

A system that is multitasking, however, does not actually perform the tasks at exactly the same time. Instead, it services one task for a very short period of time (typically less than a second), then services another task, and another, until it returns to the original task. This task-switching happens so quickly that it appears the computer is servicing many tasks at once, when it really services them one after the other.

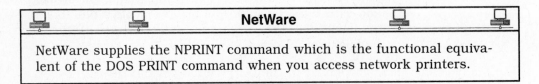

NetWare

NetWare supplies the NPRINT command which is the functional equivalent of the DOS PRINT command when you access network printers.

A task can be run in the *background*, which means it receives a lower amount of CPU time than the primary task, which runs in the *foreground*. PRINT runs in the background, so print jobs processed through the PRINT command generally receive a smaller percentage of CPU time and a lower priority than whatever foreground process you use.

Installing PRINT

The first time you invoke the PRINT command, you can specify a number of parameters that control its function. After the initial load, you cannot reset the parameters unless you restart the system to reset the PRINT options. You can, however, issue the PRINT command as many times as necessary to schedule and control print jobs.

The general form of the PRINT command is the following:

```
PRINT /D:device /B:bufsiz /U:busytick /M:maxtick /S:timeslice /
Q:maxfiles /T d1:path\file1 (...additional files) /C /P
```

As you can see, the /U and /M parameters relate to something called *ticks*. A tick refers to a CPU clock tick, which is 1/18.2 seconds. A certain number of ticks simply refers to a specific amount of time. The /S parameter, *timeslice*, also refers to an amount of time. Each of the parameters is explained in Table 11.7, which describes each of the parameters for the PRINT command.

Table 11.7
PRINT Command Switches

Switch	Effect
/D:device	Specifies the device to be affected. Valid entries for the parallel ports are PRN, LPT1, LPT2, and LPT3. Valid entries for the serial ports are COM1, COM2, COM3, and COM4. Note that PRN and LPT1 reference the same port. If device is specified, it must be the first switch. If device is not specified, PRINT prompts for a device name.
/B:bufsiz	Sets the size of the internal print buffer, in bytes. The default value is 512 bytes, and the maximum value is 16384 bytes (16K). Increasing the buffer size generally makes printing faster, but reduces the amount of memory available to other programs.
/U:busytick	Specifies the number of clock ticks PRINT waits for a printer to become available (not in use by another application, printer on-line, etc.). Valid entries are 1 through 255, with a default of 1.
/M:maxtick	Specifies the maximum number of clock ticks the printer can use to print a single character. If the time is exceeded, an error message is generated. Valid entries are 1 through 255, with a default of 2.

Table 11.7—continued

Switch	Effect
/S:timeslice	Specifies the number of clock ticks allocated for background printing. Valid entries are 1 through 255, with a default of 8. Increasing the value for timeslice gives more time to background printing, at the expense of other applications. Decreasing the timeslice value makes foreground tasks run more smoothly, at the expense of printing speed.
/Q:maxfiles	Sets the maximum number of files that can be placed in the print queue. Valid entries are 4 through 32, with a default of 10.
/T	Removes all print requests from the queue (clears the queue).
d1:path\file1	Specifies the name of the file to be printed. This entry can contain a drive or directory in addition to a file name. You can include multiple file names based on the value of /Q:maxfiles.
/C	Cancels background printing of the specified file.
/P	Places a file in the queue for printing and places PRINT in print mode.

To load the PRINT utility with all of its default settings, simply issue the prompt command by itself, and DOS generates a message that PRINT has been installed:

```
C:\>PRINT
Name of list device [PRN]: LPT1
Resident part of PRINT installed
PRINT queue is empty
C:\>
```

Working with PRINT Switches

As mentioned previously, only the file name and the /T, /C, and /P parameters can be specified more than once with the PRINT command. All other switches relating to clock ticks, devices, maximum numbers of files, and buffer size can only be set the first time PRINT is invoked. To change these parameters, you must restart the system (reboot) and invoke the PRINT command with the appropriate settings.

The following example places the file MYFILE in the queue to be printed:

```
PRINT /P MYFILE
```

If the /P is omitted when a file name is included on the PRINT command line, the file is placed in the queue. If the /P parameter is included on the command line before a list of files, each of the files following the /P is placed in the queue until a /C parameter is encountered. Then, the file name before the /C parameter is cancelled. In the following example, all of the files except FILE4 are placed in the queue. FILE4 is assumed to already be in the queue, and is cancelled:

```
PRINT /P FILE1 FILE2 FILE3 FILE4 /C
```

If the /P parameter is included after a file name or group of file names, it places in the queue the file appearing before it on the command line, as well as any files appearing after it (until a /C parameter is encountered). In the following example, FILE1 is cancelled, FILE2 and FILE3 are placed in the queue, and FILE4 is cancelled:

```
PRINT /C FILE1 FILE2 /P FILE3 FILE4 /C
```

To put it simply, both the /C and /P switches apply to file names listed on either side of the switch.

If the /T parameter is used to terminate printing, all print requests are cleared from the queue, including the job that is currently printing. To terminate all printing and clear the queue, use the following command:

PRINT /T

The following are additional characteristics of the PRINT command:

- ❏ Files are printed in the order they are entered into the queue, in first-in and first-out order.
- ❏ PRINT cannot be used on a network server.
- ❏ If PRINT is installed but not active (no files in the queue) you can use the printer for other tasks. If PRINT is active, you cannot use the printer for other printing tasks without first terminating all scheduled print jobs.
- ❏ If the device specified with PRINT does not exist, it may cause the computer to perform erratically. If you make a mistake and enter a non-existent device, reboot the system and enter a correct device name.
- ❏ Files scheduled in the queue must remain in the disk location specified when the file was placed in the queue. If PRINT has been directed to print a file on drive B, for example, the diskette in drive

B must contain the appropriate file, and the diskette may not be removed before the file has been printed.

❏ Tabs are converted to spaces in increments of eight (such as a tab to positions 8, 16, 24, etc.).

Now that you are familiar with the commands and device drivers available in DOS 5 that control the system's printer, you are ready to move on to the commands and drivers that control the system's disk drives.

Controlling Disks

Previous chapters explained DOS 5's commands for manipulating files and directories. Most users familiar with DOS are comfortable moving around in the file system, copying and deleting files, and working with directories. There are also DOS commands and drivers that affect disk drives at the device level, which many users are not familiar with.

These DOS commands and device drivers enable you to connect an external floppy drive to the system, provide a means to reassign drive IDs, join two drives together so that they are recognized as a single drive, and cause a directory to be recognized as a separate drive. This section of the chapter examines those commands and drivers. The first topic, DRIVER.SYS, adds quite a bit of flexibility to your control of floppy disk drives.

Using DRIVER.SYS

DRIVER.SYS is a device driver included with MS-DOS that controls floppy drives. For most systems, DRIVER.SYS is optional. Systems that use an external floppy drive, however, almost always require DRIVER.SYS in order for the drive to function properly. DRIVER.SYS is also useful for assigning a new drive ID to an existing drive, and changing the drive's logical type.

On systems that have a single floppy disk drive, DOS automatically assigns logical drive IDs A and B to the single floppy drive. This capability enables you to access the floppy as either A or B, which makes it possible to perform an XCOPY with a single drive. Normally, it is not possible to perform a cyclical (same disk) XCOPY—you cannot, for example, XCOPY from A to A. It is possible to perform an XCOPY from A to B on a single-floppy system, however, because DOS automatically assigns both logical IDs A and B to the drive, even though both are the same physical drive.

What happens when there are two physical drives in the system recognized as A and B, and one is a 1.2M, 5 1/4-inch disk drive and the other is a 1.44M, 3 1/2-inch drive? If you are copying from one drive to the other, XCOPY will work. If, however, you need to copy from a disk of the same size as the destination disk (the copy), XCOPY will not work. DOS does not duplicate another drive ID for either floppy drive as it does when there is only a single drive because logical drive ID B has been assigned to the physical drive B.

Fortunately, DRIVER.SYS offers a way around this problem. If you use DRIVER.SYS you can assign a new logical drive ID to the necessary floppy drive, then XCOPY using the single drive, just as you would with a system that has only one drive. The first step is to install DRIVER.SYS.

Installing DRIVER.SYS

Like other device drivers, DRIVER.SYS installs in the system's CONFIG.SYS file via a DEVICE= statement. DRIVER.SYS must potentially control a wide range of floppy formats. As a result, there are a number of possible switches that can be included in the command line. The line that follows is the general syntax for DRIVER.SYS:

```
DEVICE=d:path\DRIVER.SYS /D:ddd /F:f /T:ttt /S:ss /H:hh /C /N
```

The *d:path*\ parameter specifies the location of the DRIVER.SYS file. Normally, it is located in the directory containing the rest of the DOS files, which is often C:\DOS.

The */D:ddd* parameter specifies the drive number. The /D: is required, and the *ddd* specifies the drive number. Drive numbers begin at 0 and increment by one. Drive A uses drive number 0. If the system has two floppy drives, drive B is drive 1. If you are adding an external floppy drive, specify the next available drive number. If you want to assign a new logical drive ID to an existing drive, specify the existing drive's ID number. An example of this is discussed later in the chapter. The *ddd* parameter may be set from 0 to 127, but numbers greater than 3 are generally not supported on most systems. Drive numbers 0 through 3 provide for a total of four physical floppy drives.

The */F:f* parameter specifies the type of drive, or *form factor*, to be used. The */F:f* parameter provides the simplest method for specifying a drive type. Valid entries for *f* are the following:

Setting	Form Factor
0	160K/180K or 320K/360K
1	1.2M
2	720K
7	1.44M
9	2.88M

To install DRIVER.SYS for the first external floppy drive on a system that contains two internal floppy drives, and define it as a 1.44M drive, use the following command:

```
DEVICE=C:\DOS\DRIVER.SYS /D:2 /F:7
```

No other switches are needed to specify the number of tracks or sectors the drive requires.

There are occasions, however, when you need to specify the number of tracks and sectors for the drive. The /T:ttt parameter in the previous syntax line specifies the number of tracks. Valid entries range from 1 to 999. The default is 80, unless form factor 0 has been specified with the /F switch. If the /F switch is used, the default is 40 tracks.

The /S:sss parameter specifies the number of sectors per track. Valid entries are 9, 15, 18, and 36 sectors. If a form factor is specified with the /F switch, the number of sectors defaults to an appropriate number, as follows:

Form Factor	Sectors per Track
/F:0	/S:9
/F:1	/S:15
/F:2	/S:9
/F:7	/S:18
/F:9	/S:36

In general, it is not necessary to specify the number of tracks or sectors, because the /F switch can be used to default tracks and sectors to appropriate values. The /F switch can be omitted, however, and the track and sector switches used in its place. The following defines drive 2 as a 1.44M drive:

```
DEVICE=C:\DOS\DRIVER.SYS /D:2 /T:80 /S:18 /H:2 /C
```

Note that there are two additional parameters included in the previous example—/H:h and /C. The /H:h parameter specifies the number of heads for the drive. Valid entries for h are 1 through 99. The default is 2. It is unlikely that floppy drives will ever have more than two heads, and the higher possible values for the h parameter are holdovers from earlier versions of DRIVER.SYS that were capable of controlling non-standard hard drives. Future devices, however, may support more than two heads for devices serviced by DRIVER.SYS.

The /C parameter in the previous example specifies *change-line support*, which determines whether the drive can detect when the drive door is closed.

The switches you use depend on the type of drive and the effect you want to achieve. The following section examines the use of DRIVER.SYS to assign multiple logical drive IDs to the same physical floppy drive.

Making a Single Floppy Drive Look Like Two

One of the most useful implementations of DRIVER.SYS is to assign more than one logical-drive ID to a single floppy disk drive. A previous section discussed one example—when a system contains two floppy drives: a 1.2M, 5 1/4-inch floppy disk drive and a 1.44M, 3 1/2-inch drive. You cannot perform an XCOPY using only the 3 1/2-inch floppy disk drive, because XCOPY cannot perform a cyclical copy (a copy where the source and destination drives are the same).

You can, however, assign a new logical-drive ID to the drive, and then use XCOPY to copy between the original drive ID and the new drive ID. It does not matter that the two logical-drive IDs reference the same physical drive. All that matters is that the logical-drive IDs be different.

When DRIVER.SYS is installed, the newly installed floppy disk drive receives the next available drive ID. If the system has two floppy disk drives (A and B), and two logical hard drives (C and D), for example, the new floppy ID assigned to the copy of DRIVER.SYS will be E. Even if the drive already has a logical-drive ID assigned to it, such as A, it will also take on the new ID. This is what makes it possible to perform an XCOPY with a single drive.

The following command installs DRIVER.SYS for an existing drive 0 (drive A) as a 1.2M drive with change-line support enabled (tracks, sectors, and heads are defaulted):

```
DEVICE=C:\DOS\DRIVER.SYS /D:0 /F:1 /C
```

If there are two physical floppy drives and two hard drives in the system, the drive installed by the previous DEVICE= statement receives the drive ID E. To perform a cyclical XCOPY using the drive, use the following command:

```
XCOPY A: E:
```

Assignment of Drive IDs

DOS uses a consistent method for assigning drive IDs, so you always know which ID a device receives. Drive ID A is reserved for the first floppy disk drive, and B is reserved for the second floppy disk drive. Hard disk drives always start at ID C, and each hard disk, whether physical or logical, receives the next available drive ID. If a hard drive is partitioned into four logical drives, for example, it is recognized as C, D, E, and F.

In the previous example, drives added by DRIVER.SYS or RAMDRIVE.SYS are recognized starting with drive G. The order in which the DRIVER.SYS and RAMDRIVE.SYS entries appear in CONFIG.SYS determines their drive assignments. Using the example of two physical floppy drives and four logical hard drives (C through F), the following lines in CONFIG.SYS receive drive assignments as noted:

```
DEVICE=C:\DOS\DRIVER.SYS /D:0 /F:1 /C    ;drive G
DEVICE=C:\DOS\DRIVER.SYS /D:2 /F:7 /C    ;drive H
DEVICE=C:\DOS\RAMDRIVE.SYS 1024 512 128  ;drive I
DEVICE=C:\DOS\DRIVER.SYS /D:3 /F:7 /C    ;drive J
```

Note that the first DRIVER.SYS entry references drive 0. Therefore, the first floppy drive is recognized as both drive A and drive G.

DRIVER.SYS is the only device driver for physical disk drives provided by DOS. In addition to DRIVER.SYS, DOS includes three commands that provide a great deal of control over drives and directories. The first of the three commands is ASSIGN.

Using ASSIGN To Reassign Drives

The ASSIGN command redirects disk commands from one logical drive ID to another. When you redirect a drive with the ASSIGN command, all drive I/O goes to the redirected drive, instead of to the actual drive.

The syntax for ASSIGN is the following:

ASSIGN *d1=d2* ...

d1 represents the existing drive assignment, and *d2* represents the redirected drive. More than one assignment can be made on the same command line. The following command swaps drives A and C:

ASSIGN A=C C=A

All I/O operations destined for the hard drive at C are redirected to floppy drive A. All I/O directed at floppy drive A is redirected to drive C.

There are very few uses for the ASSIGN command. One use, however, is to "trick" a program that expects to have a program disk in drive A look for the data on the hard drive instead. In this case, only drive A needs to be reassigned:

```
ASSIGN A=C
```

When the application attempts to look for the required data on drive A, it is redirected to drive C. The application is not aware that the drive has been reassigned.

In general, you should not use the ASSIGN command unless you have a valid, specific reason to do so. Never use the ASSIGN command with other commands that modify the logical structure of a disk, such as ERASE, BACKUP, FDISK, FORMAT, and so on. Also, do not use ASSIGN in conjunction with the JOIN or SUBST commands, which are explained next. It is too easy to change the logical structure of your disk, and then to accidentally destroy information because you have forgotten that they are redirected.

Using the JOIN Command

The ASSIGN command is just one way to trick DOS into thinking a drive is something that it really is not. The JOIN command adds a disk drive to the directory structure of another disk. This is functionally equivalent to mounting a file system under UNIX.

The directory structure of a diskette in drive B can be joined to drive C, for example, under a directory called \FLOPPYB (the directory name can be anything—\FLOPPYB is just an example). You can activate and access the floppy by making drive C active, then use the CD command to change to the joined directory:

```
C:\>C:
C:\>CD \FLOPPYB
```

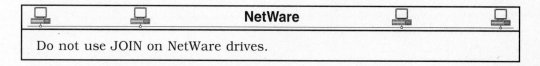

NetWare

Do not use JOIN on NetWare drives.

If you list a directory or perform any other disk operation on \FLOPPYB, the diskette in drive B will be affected.

The format for the JOIN command is the following:

    JOIN *d1: d2:\directory*

The *d1:* parameter is the drive to be joined. The *d2:* parameter specifies the drive to which *d1* is being joined, and *directory* specifies the name of the directory under which *d1* is joined. To mount drive B under the directory \FLOPPYB, use the following command:

    JOIN B: C:\FLOPPYB

There are certain requirements for the JOIN command to work. First, the directory under which the drive is mounted must be located under the root directory (a subdirectory). A drive cannot be joined to a root directory. The directory need not be directly under the root directory. The following example is a valid use of JOIN:

    JOIN D: C:\PROJECT\DRIVED

Note that you can join hard disk drives as well as floppy disk drives. Also, the directory under which D is joined is not directly under the root of drive C.

Another restriction to the use of JOIN is that the directory to which the drive is joined must not exist, or, if it does, it must be empty. If the directory does not exist, the JOIN command creates it. A directory that is joined cannot be used for any other purpose until the joined drive has been detached (discussed shortly).

When a drive is joined, it cannot be referenced by its original logical drive ID. In the previous example, in which drive D is joined to drive C, you cannot access drive D until the drive is detached. An attempt to change to drive D, for example, results in the following error message:

    Invalid drive specification

You cannot join a drive to the current directory. The directory must exist as a subdirectory under the current directory or as a directory or subdirectory under another drive or directory.

There are a number of commands that do not function with a joined drive. They include the following:

BACKUP	DISCOPY	LABEL	RESTORE
CHKDSK	FDISK	MIRROR	SYS
DISKCOMP	FORMAT	RECOVER	

In addition, do not use the ASSIGN or SUBST commands when JOIN is in effect.

Listing and Detaching Joined Drives

When used by itself without any switches, the JOIN command displays a list of all currently joined drives. To detach a drive, use the following command:

```
JOIN d1: /D
```

If, for example, you wish to detach drive B, type the following:

```
JOIN B: /D
```

Remember that JOIN creates the destination directory if it does not exist. If you do not wish to keep the new directory after the drive has been detached, you must use the RMDIR command to remove the directory.

SUBST—the Opposite of JOIN

The JOIN command takes a drive and grafts it onto the directory structure of another disk; the SUBST command does just the opposite. It takes a directory from a drive and makes it appear as a separate drive. The following is the format for the SUBST command:

```
SUBST d1: d2:path
```

The *d1:* parameter specifies the drive ID to be associated with the directory, and *d2:path* specifies the directory to be associated with the drive ID. The specified drive ID does not have to exist, nor does it have to be the next available drive ID. It must, however, have a logical-drive ID less than that of the value of LASTDRIVE, which is an environment variable that specifies the last available drive ID.

By default, LASTDRIVE is set to the last logical drive assigned in the system. If the system has two logical hard disk drives, LASTDRIVE assumes the value D. If new drive IDs are assigned via RAMDRIVE.SYS or DRIVER.SYS, DOS updates the value of LASTDRIVE accordingly. The *MS-DOS User's Guide and Reference* incorrectly states that LASTDRIVE defaults to the drive that is after the last drive in use by the system. Instead, The default is the last drive being used, not the one after it.

You can, however, set LASTDRIVE yourself and make drive IDs available that otherwise would be unavailable. Add the following statement to the CONFIG.SYS file, for example, so you can use all drive IDs from A through Z:

```
LASTDRIVE=Z
```

NetWare

If you set LASTDRIVE=Z on a NetWare workstation, you make more work for yourself in correcting old LOGIN scripts that contain references to *1:, *2:..., rather than specific drive letters F:, G:... The NetWare MAP command works like SUBST, and can be used to assign a drive letter to a SUBDIRECTORY. More recent versions of NETWARE supporting the MAP ROOT command allow full emulation of the SUBST command.

After you enter this command, you can use SUBST to assign any drive ID. Each drive made available by the LASTDRIVE setting, however, takes memory. Set LASTDRIVE only as high as necessary. If there are two hard drives in the system, for example, and you want to SUBST two directories to two new drives, set **LASTDRIVE=F**.

Assume, for example, that you want to make the directory \TEMP in drive C appear as a separate drive, and that there are two hard drives in the system (using two logical IDs). Set **LASTDRIVE=E** in CONFIG.SYS, then use the following command to associate \TEMP with the last available drive ID:

```
SUBST E: C:\TEMP
```

Note that if you use SUBST to create an alias for a directory, and you specify a drive ID that is already in use (such as for a physical drive), the pre-existing drive will not be accessible until the aliased directory is detached. The aliased drive simply takes its place, as far as DOS is concerned.

The same general rules apply to the SUBST command as to the JOIN and ASSIGN commands. Do not use the ASSIGN or JOIN commands in conjunction with SUBST. Also, do not use commands that change the structure of a disk if you use SUBST. Such commands are listed in the section on using JOIN.

Viewing and Detaching Drives with SUBST

To view drives that have been aliased with the SUBST command, simply use the command without any parameters. DOS responds by listing every drive that has been aliased by SUBST:

```
C:\>SUBST
    E: => C:\QEMM
    F: => C:\DESQVIEW
C:\>
```

To detach a directory from an aliased drive ID, use the following form of the SUBST command:

    SUBST *d1:* /D

To detach the directory that has been aliased to drive E with the SUBST command, type the following:

    SUBST E: /D

You can use SUBST at any time. Nevertheless, you should consider using SUBST only at system startup to avoid problems. Do not use SUBST to substitute a directory that is in use by an application. Do not shell out of a program, for example, then use SUBST to substitute its directory.

Windows/DOS Shell

Both Windows and DOS Shell create a secondary command environment to execute DOS commands that are not part of their standard menus. Any changes made within these secondary environments are not maintained in other windows. Therefore, you should not use the ASSIGN, JOIN or SUBST commands from within a window. You can use these commands before you enter the GUI environment (DOS Shell or Windows). Changes made with DRIVER.SYS are installed during the boot process and are in place when you start Windows or DOS Shell.

Controlling the Keyboard

There are three DOS commands that provide control over the system's keyboard. They enable you to switch character sets (code pages), change the device recognized as the console, and set keyboard response rate. The second command, CTTY, is discussed next.

Changing Consoles with CTTY

A *console* is a device through which standard input and output are directed. The system's keyboard and display are the default console. DOS recognizes the console by the device name CON.

Although CON is the default console, you can change to a different console device using the DOS command CTTY. If, for example, you have a terminal connected via one of the computer's COM ports and you want to use it as the system console for input and output to the system, you can use the CTTY command to tell DOS to redirect input and output to and from the COM port. Also, some devices such as bar-code readers and Point-of-Sale systems may need to be set up as the system console.

The format for the CTTY command is as follows:

```
CTTY device
```

The *device* parameter specifies the device through which standard I/O is directed. Valid entries for *device* include:

PRN   CON COM3

LPT1 AUX COM4

LPT2 COM1

LPT3 COM2

To set the serial port COM1 as the system console, use the following command:

```
CTTY COM1
```

Note that the necessary parameters for baud rate, data bits, stop bits, and other communication parameters must first be set for COM1 with the MODE command. The MODE command and configuring I/O ports are discussed in the next section of this chapter.

Once COM1 has been defined as the system console, DOS accepts standard input from COM1, and directs standard output to COM1. If a terminal is connected to COM1, you can enter DOS commands on the terminal instead of the system's keyboard. Output that is normally directed to the system's display appears on the terminal's display. To reset the system to make CON the console, issue the following command from the terminal:

```
CTTY CON
```

You can then begin to enter commands from the system console.

Setting Keyboard Sensitivity with MODE

Even though you cannot change the response of most keyboards (the amount of pressure required to activate a key), you can change how DOS handles a key that is pressed. You can use the MODE command to set the repeat rate for a key that is pressed and held down, and you also can set the amount of time that elapses before DOS begins to repeat characters when the key is held down.

The form of the MODE command to control keyboard sensitivity is the following:

```
MODE CON RATE=rate DELAY=delay
```

The `rate` parameter specifies the number of repetitions per second for the character. Valid entries for *rate* are 1 through 32, and the default is 20 for IBM AT-compatible keyboards, and 21 for IBM PS/2-compatible keyboards. The `delay` parameter specifies the time delay before DOS begins to repeat the character. The delay parameter is expressed in 1/4-second increments, and valid entries are 1 through 4, a delay from .25 to 1 second. The default is 2, which provides a 1/2 second delay.

To set the repeat rate to 20 and the delay to a full second, type the following command:

```
MODE CON RATE=20 DELAY=4
```

You must provide an entry for both rate and delay.

Controlling I/O Ports

This final section of the chapter examines the method you use to set up the system's I/O ports, including the parallel and serial ports. In addition to setting an I/O port's communication settings, you can use the MODE command to redirect a parallel port to a serial port.

Setting Parallel Port Settings with MODE

The MODE command enables you to specify the number of columns, line spacing, and retry values for a parallel port. The format of the command is as follows:

```
MODE LPTx c,l,r
```

The `LPTx` parameter specifies the port to be affected, and can be any of the system's parallel ports, including LPT1, LPT2, and LPT3.

The `c` parameter specifies the number of columns (characters) per line. There are two possible settings: 80 and 132. The default is 80.

The `l` parameter specifies the spacing between lines, and can be either 6 or 8. The default is 6.

The `r` parameter, which specifies retry values, requires a bit more explanation. When the system attempts to access a parallel port and the port is not available after a specified period of time because the attached device is off-line or already in use, the system *times-out*, meaning that it stops trying to send information through the port and generates an error condition. The *r* parameter determines how the MODE command handles a time-out condition (the device is not available after the MODE command is issued).

The possible values for *r* are listed in the command reference for MODE in Section IV. In general, the default value n (or none) is acceptable for most users. This default causes the MODE command to take no retry action. The *r* parameter can be omitted if the default is to be used.

To set LPT2 for 132 columns and a line spacing of 8, use the following command:

```
MODE LPT2 132,8
```

You need not enter values for both columns and lines if you wish to use the current value for one of the settings. To set the port back to a line spacing of 6 and maintain 132 columns after you issue the previous command, use the following MODE command:

```
MODE LPT2 ,6
```

The comma in this case acts as a place-holder for the parameters.

In most cases, the column and line-spacing parameters are controlled from a user's application instead of the command line. The application is capable of setting line spacing, number of columns, and many other printer parameters.

The *retry* value, which follows the line-spacing parameter is useful when you have difficulty printing. If the system continues to time-out for some reason, use the MODE command to instruct the system to continue trying to re-send the information to the printer. Use a value of *p* for the *retry* parameter, which causes the system to continue to try to send the information to the printer without timing out:

```
MODE LPT2 ,,p
```

Do not use retry values for a printer or other parallel device located on a network. Refer to the Command Reference for more information on retry parameter values.

Setting Serial Ports with MODE

Just as MODE sets values for parallel port operation, it also can be used to set the system's serial port parameters. The MODE command requires more parameters when you want to control serial ports because there are more communication settings involved with serial ports than there are with parallel ports. The format for the command is the following:

```
MODE COMn,b,p,d,s,r
```

The n parameter specifies the port to be affected. Valid entries are 1 though 4. The b parameter specifies the port's baud rate, and can be any of the following:

Setting	Baud Rate
11	110 baud
15	150 baud
30	300 baud
60	600 baud
12	1200 baud
24	2400 baud
48	4800 baud
96	9600 baud
19	19200 baud

The *p* parameter controls the port's use of the parity bit for parity checking. It can be set to n (none), e (even), o (odd), m (mark), or s (space). The default is e (even).

The d parameter specifies the number of data bits the port will use. Valid entries are in the range of 5 through 8, with a default of 7.

The s parameter controls the number of stop bits, which is actually a timing value used to synchronize communication. The s parameter can be set to 1, 1.5, or 2. For a baud rate of 110, the default is 2. For all other baud rates, the default is 1.

The r parameter specifies the retry action, just as the same parameter controls retry for parallel ports. As with parallel ports, the default is n, for none, and retry values should not be used with devices connected across a network.

To set up COM2 for 2400 baud, no parity checking, 8 data bits, and 1 stop bit, use the following command:

```
MODE COM2 2400,N,8,1
```

Note that most applications that use a communications port will set the parameters correctly. You may have applications, however, that require the port to have been set previously with MODE.

For more information on retry values for serial ports, refer to the Command Reference.

Redirecting Ports with MODE

In addition to setting communications parameters for the serial and parallel ports, MODE can also be used to redirect a parallel port to a COM port. This is useful if you have an application that expects the printer to be connected to an LPT port, and does not recognize printers connected to COM ports.

Parallel ports transfer data one full byte at a time, whereas serial ports transfer data one bit at a time. Fortunately, the conversion from byte-transmission to bit-transmission occurs automatically in hardware, so you do not have to worry about compatibility problems.

To redirect LPT1 to COM1, for example, use the following MODE commands. The first specifies communication parameters for the serial port, and the second redirects the parallel port to the serial port:

```
MODE COM1 9600,N,8,1,B
MODE LPT1:=COM1:
```

To specify any other combination of ports, simply replace the ports as necessary. Any parallel port can be redirected to any serial port.

You must set the communication parameters for the serial port with MODE before redirecting the parallel port to it, and a retry value must be included if the device is a printer. The previous example set the retry parameter for COM1 to B, which causes it to return a busy signal if the port is busy.

Using MODE To Display Device Status

The final use for the MODE command is to display the status of devices connected to your computer system. You can choose to display the status of a single device, or display the status of all connected devices. To list the status of all devices, simply issue the MODE command with no other parameters. DOS responds with a complete status listing.

```
C:\>MODE
Status for device LPT1:
-----------------------
LPT1: not rerouted
Retry=NONE
```

```
Code page operation not supported on this device
Status for device LPT2:
---------------------
LPT2: not rerouted
Status for device LPT3:
---------------------
LPT3: not rerouted
Status for device CON:
---------------------
Columns=80
Lines=25
Code page operation not supported on this device
Status for device COM1:
---------------------
Retry=NONE
Status for device COM2:
---------------------
Retry=NONE
C:\>
```

To list the status of a specific device, specify the name of the device and use the /status switch:

   MODE *device* /status

Use the following command, for example, to list the status of the console:

   MODE CON /STATUS

DOS responds by listing only the status of the console.

Summary

Applications often control your computer system's devices. You can control those devices, however, at the DOS command line. You can set a special system prompt, switch character sets for the keyboard and display, and switch between display adapter modes with a single command.

If you use the PRINTER.SYS device driver with the PRINT and GRAPHICS commands, you can control the way the system's printer functions. Most useful is PRINT, which enables you to print in the background while you continue to work.

You can use the CTTY and MODE commands, respectively, to change the system console and set keyboard sensitivity.

The MODE command enables you to configure the system's parallel and serial ports. Most applications set up these ports correctly, but some require that they be configured from the command line. Also useful is the capability to redirect a parallel port to a serial port with the MODE command.

Perhaps most useful of all of these device-control commands and drivers are the ones associated with disk drives. DRIVER.SYS offers an excellent means for adding new drives to the system and fooling DOS into thinking it has more drives than it really does. ASSIGN provides you with a way to fool DOS into recognizing drives by a different logical drive ID.

Even though the JOIN and SUBST commands are functionally opposite, they both provide you with powerful tools for organizing disks and directories from the command line. The JOIN command enables you to join one drive to another drive as a directory. The SUBST command does just the opposite—it makes a directory look like a separate drive.

The commands examined in this chapter provide a set of tools you can use to customize your DOS environment, speed your work by placing printing tasks in the background, and gain a finer degree of control over the devices in your system.

12

The DOS Shell

Previous chapters discussed performing tasks with the *Command Line Interface (CLI)*, which is the technical term for the process of entering commands at the DOS prompt. This chapter introduces the DOS Shell and shows you how to perform many of the same tasks in this new environment. In addition, you will discover the ways in which the DOS Shell can be used to manage programs and documents and improve your efficiency on the computer. The DOS Shell provides a new user interface which is designed to complement the DOS environment rather than to replace it.

A standard CLI, including the traditional DOS prompt, relies on your memory for recalling specific commands. Each command must be entered in its entirety, generally without any additional prompting from the system. This is fine when the number of commands are few, but it becomes more difficult to remember unfamiliar tasks when the operating system is more complex.

These problems, combined with a desire to make computers accessible to more users, led to the concept of a menu-based environment. In a menu-based system, the options are displayed on-screen, you select a menu containing the category of command to execute, and a list of individual menu options is displayed that correspond to the actual command. The system then prompts you to provide the necessary information for each portion of the process. There is usually an activation key to bring up the menus and most systems permit you to avoid the menu system entirely. Lotus 1-2-3 and WordPerfect are examples of menu-based environments.

Although menu-based systems offer a number of advantages, they still do not provide a unified approach to commands. Developers are free to use their own individual terms and shortcut keys to refer the same action. In addition, you are still required to understand the command *syntax*. Syntax refers to the structure of the command—the order in which the various parts must be entered. Finally, the system is still verbal (language-based) and you must remember the meaning of each of the commands. In this context, verbal refers to the type of learning style being used. A learning style is an educational model that divides the process of obtaining knowledge into three primary methods: *verbal* (you learn language—command definitions), *visual* (you learn by watching), and *kinesthetic* (you learn by doing).

The *Graphical User Interface (GUI)* was introduced to improve menu-based systems. A GUI is also menu-based, but it is based on actions rather than words. A central component to the GUI environment is the mouse (or another pointing device), so that you perform tasks by physical actions rather than through words. A well-developed GUI gives you both options—a kinesthetic memory of the actions or the verbal alternative of command definitions.

An underlying concept of the GUI environment is the imposition of a standard system of commands. A GUI provides a common structure shared between programs—common tasks are performed the same way in all programs that conform to the GUI. Finally, a graphical environment utilizes the metaphor of a window. Unlike other environments in which commands are entered at a single specific location (the prompt), portions of the screen in graphical environments perform specific tasks with actions. Because most graphical environments allow you access to more than one task, the screen area is divided into smaller working areas called *windows*. Gaining familiarity with these features is an important aspect of learning to use a graphical environment and is the topic of the second major section, "The Basics of the DOS Shell Window."

Versions of DOS prior to DOS 4 offered only a CLI, but DOS 5 adds a a reasonable alternative with the DOS Shell. Although DOS 4 offers a primitive shell system, the DOS 5 Shell becomes a complete user environment and adds many of the features of a complete GUI as part of the standard DOS package. To be precise, the DOS 5 Shell is a *Graphical Shell* rather than a Graphical User Interface. Unlike a full user interface, a shell only manages the operating-system tasks (it does not impose a standard interface onto application programs).

The Functions of the DOS Shell

A user interface totally controls the way in which you interact with the computer system. A shell, however, only affects the actions that are part of the operating system. These actions include file- and directory-management tasks, program-management tasks, and necessary system-resource management tasks. The DOS Shell does not control the system configuration features—they are still managed through the CONFIG.SYS and AUTOEXEC.BAT files.

File and directory management is accomplished with a graphical interface similar to the File Manager in Microsoft Windows 3.0. In addition to the standard file features found in the DOS CLI (Copy, Rename, and Delete), you are also provided with the capability to move files in a single step and to search for files based on specific criteria. All of this is presented in a graphical format that displays the relationship between files and directories. A new feature, unavailable in the Windows File Manager, gives you the capability to list all of the files on the disk and to sort them based on a variety of keys. Directory management includes the standard options of creating and deleting directories, with the added capability of renaming existing directories.

Program management includes many of the features of Windows Program Manager and combines them with the traditional menuing environment of the DOS CLI. As in Windows, documents can associate with the corresponding applications (when you open the document, the proper application is also started). *Open* is the term used by most GUIs to refer to the process of starting an application. You can either open the application directly or open it via an associated document.

The DOS Shell also enables the creation of program groups, which are clusters of programs presented as a group. Moving beyond the restrictions in Windows, program groups may contain subgroups and you can nest as many levels as you wish. This feature was the primary tool available in the DOS 4 Shell and it made an effective menu-based system. The DOS 5 Shell retains the capability to add help information to each menu item.

The major disadvantage of the DOS 5 Shell is that, unlike the Windows Program Manager, you can only display a single group at a time. If you want to move to a new group, you must move through a tree structure similar to the file/directory structure used by DOS.

In addition to providing a visual system for manipulating the DOS environment, the DOS Shell also provides features for managing system resources. You can enable a task-swapping environment which permits you to move between multiple programs. On the surface, this feature is similar to the multitasking features of Windows, but with DOS Shell only one application can be active at a time. The others are quickly available, but they are inactive. The DOS Shell is intended for standard DOS applications which, unlike Windows applications, are designed to have full control of the environment.

The Interface Spectrum—from DOS 4 through Windows

One of the first implementations of a DOS shell was the DOS 4 version of DOS Shell. Unlike other implementations, the DOS 4 version was restricted to the creation of lists of menu items that could be nested to provide a front-end to the DOS environment. Although it functioned in a graphics mode and offered file- and directory-management tools, these features were not well-integrated. As with a standard menu-based system, you were provided with a list of options; some of the options were commands and others led to a different level within the menu system.

The advantage to the DOS 4 Shell was that its menu system could be customized. Users could create their own menu items and menu lists, and system administrators could create environments in which users were guided through their options. It had few features, however, that recommended it to the more sophisticated DOS user. In fact, most of its features had been previously available through the use of a sophisticated batch-file system that presented the illusion of a menu system.

The MS-DOS Executive (shown in fig. 12.1) was part of the early implementation of Windows. The MS-DOS Executive provided many of the features available in the current DOS Shell, but it required the addition of the Windows interface to the DOS environment. While there were advantages to this combination, the demands on system resources made it an inefficient system for all but the most powerful systems.

Figure 12.1:
The MS-DOS Executive.

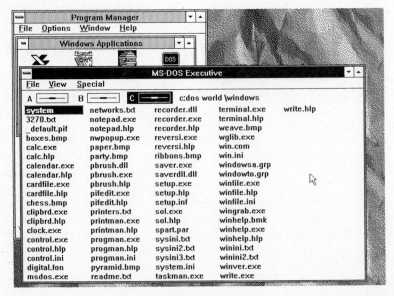

The current version of Windows includes all the functions of the DOS Shell as well as a number of other features. The components of the Windows environment that correspond to the DOS Shell are the Program Manager and the File Manager. The features of these two programs can be integrated to provide the functionality of the current DOS Shell. The analogous approach is to run the two applications so that they share the screen, as shown in figure 12.2.

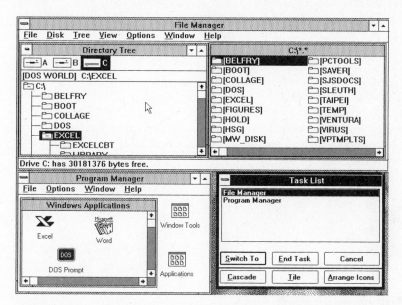

Figure 12.2:
Windows' File Manager and Program Manager.

Windows is designed for high-powered systems; it places a heavy load on system resources and has significant features that are available only on a 386 or 486 system. Windows is a full GUI that provides a standard environment for Windows programs designed specifically to take advantage of its capabilities. Even though Windows requires DOS as an operating system, it hides DOS from you. DOS applications are still permitted in the environment, but are "guests" rather than "members."

Windows applications are *multitasking applications*; not only can more than one application be available at once, but the ones in the background (not currently being accessed by the keyboard or mouse) can share the processor and continue to work. In 386-enhanced mode (available only on 386 or 486 systems with extended memory), Windows extends this capability to DOS applications. In standard mode, Windows offers task-swapping for DOS applications in the same way as the DOS Shell.

For many people, the major disadvantage of Windows is its system requirements. Unlike the DOS Shell, Windows offers only limited functionality on 286 systems and requires a graphic monitor to function at all. Although all the features of the DOS Shell are available within Windows on a 286, the addition of Windows uses system resources that could be dedicated to programs. The only reason to use Windows in its standard mode rather than the DOS Shell is if there are Windows-specific applications (such as Pagemaker, Word for Windows, or Excel) that you want to access.

The DOS Shell offers numerous advantages over the standard DOS prompt. The first is that several file- and directory-management features are only available when using the DOS Shell. These include the capabilities to copy a group of files that do not share common characteristics, to rename directories, and to obtain lists of all the files, regardless of their locations within the directory structure. Added to this is an integrated help system to guide you through unfamiliar tasks. The DOS Shell also provides the capability to associate documents with applications and to switch between multiple applications without having to return to the DOS prompt. Finally, the Shell enables you to create program groups and menu levels that are fully integrated into the management environment.

Unlike Windows, the DOS Shell runs on any IBM-compatible systems (on systems that use an EGA display, you must install EGA.SYS as a device driver. In fact, the DOS Shell offers a text-display option that doesn't require a graphics display (see fig. 12.3) and the DOS Shell takes advantage of high-performance systems. A good example of this is the graphical version of the interface available on any system with a graphics display (see fig. 12.4).

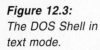

Figure 12.3:
The DOS Shell in text mode.

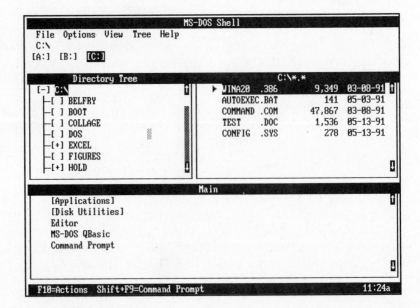

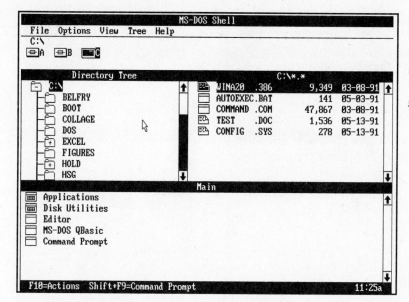

Figure 12.4:
The DOS Shell in graphics mode.

As with most interfaces, the underlying CLI is still available. If, at any time, you want access to the standard DOS prompt, it is always available via a menu selection. The most difficult aspect of transferring from a CLI to a GUI or a graphical shell is the transition from learning words to learning actions. Although many people have been exposed to mice or other pointing devices as part of a word-processing or desktop-publishing package, they still make people uncomfortable. The benefits of using the DOS Shell outweigh the difficulties of becoming comfortable with the mouse. And, fortunately, just like riding a bicycle, knowledge of how to use a GUI remains even after a period of disuse.

The Basics of the DOS Shell Window

To activate the DOS Shell, simply type **DOSSHELL** at the command prompt. If you have a graphics display, select the Display command under the Options menu. You can now select the best display option from the list. Use the Preview option to determine which selection you prefer prior to selecting the OK button.

The windows available in the DOS Shell environment are much more restricted than they would be in a full GUI. This is advantageous because there is less to learn and maintain. Figure 12.5 shows the standard portions of the DOS Shell window. Each of these sections serves a distinct function. If your view of the DOS Shell differs from the one shown, don't worry—there are five different screen views that can be presented. Each of them share a common structure, but have some differences. To obtain the view shown in figure 12.5, select Program/File List from the View menu.

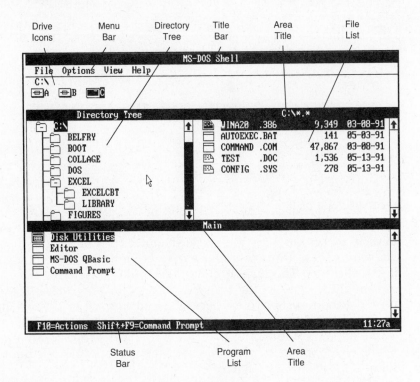

Figure 12.5:
The standard DOS Shell.

❑ **Title Bar**. Indicates that you are in the DOS Shell.

❑ **Area Title**. Indicates the various shell tasks that are available. These include the Directory Tree, the File List (the title shows the current directory), the Program List (the title shows the current group), and the Task List. The active area is indicated by a change in the area title region (not visible in the figure, the Directory Tree is active).

❑ **Drive Icons**. Indicate which drives (including network drives) are under the control of the operating system. Floppy drives, hard drives, and networked drives are indicated with different icons.

❑ **Status Bar**. Provides information about what options are available from your current location.

❑ **Menu Bar**. Available DOS Shell options. Moving between the various areas may change the individual menu items which are accessible.

In addition to these general window areas, each window contains indicators that control the functioning of that area. These options include:

❏ **Scroll Bar**. Located at the right side of each window, enables you to move the display to show additional information. The elevator or scroll box (the small box on the scroll bar) moves the window over the list of information. When it is at the top (as in the Directory Tree area in fig. 12.5), you see the top of the list. Moving it downward reveals more of the list. If there is no scroll box (as in the Program List in fig. 12.5), then all of the information on the list is being displayed.

❏ **Selection Indicator**. The highlighting that shows which items from the list are currently selected. The root directory (C:\) is selected in the Directory Tree area in figure 12.5.

In addition to the various windows components, you probably have an indicator showing the location of your mouse. The easiest way to find the mouse indicator is to watch the screen while moving your mouse. The indicator should move as you move the mouse. If you are unfamiliar with the mouse, "up" is defined as the direction toward the mouse cord (its tail). If you orient the mouse with the cord away from you, moving the mouse to the right causes the indicator to move to the right. Learning to use a mouse requires practice, so don't be discouraged if you feel clumsy or uncoordinated.

The other major component of a window environment is a *dialog box*, which is the mechanism used by the graphical environment to communicate with you. The existence of a dialog box is indicated by a series of dots (or, more properly, an ellipse). A typical dialog box is shown in figure 12.6. This particular dialog box appears when you change the selection of files to be displayed.

A dialog box can have a variety of components. each of which communicates in a specific way. The standard dialog box components are:

❏ **Button**. Like the OK, Cancel and Help options in figure 12.6, these choices move you away from the dialog box. The OK option closes the dialog box and performs the action based on the information provided. If required information is missing, an error is displayed or the action is not performed. The Cancel button closes the dialog box, but does not perform the action. The Help button provides more information about the effects of completing the various options on the dialog box.

❏ **Text Area**. Like the name option in figure 12.6, a text box enables you to enter new text information. If the text is highlighted, typing new information replaces the existing text. The left- and right-arrow keys are used to move across the text. When the text is highlighted, pressing the right-arrow key takes you to the end of the phrase and allows you add additional information (for example, adding a subdirectory to the directory name).

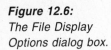

Figure 12.6:
The File Display Options dialog box.

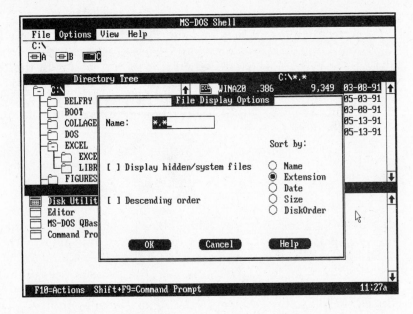

❏ **Check Box**. Like the Display hidden/system files or the Descending order options in figure 12.6, these are questions that can be answered with a Yes or No response. A check in the box (as in the Descending order option) indicates that the answer is Yes (things should be in descending order). A blank (as in the Display hidden/system files) indicates that the answer is No (do not display hidden or system files).

❏ **List Boxes**. Like the Sort by: group, option boxes are used to select a single item from a group. In this case, the information can be sorted by Name, Extension, Date, Size, or DiskOrder, but not a combination of these.

❏ **Selection List**. Not shown in figure 12.6, this is a small window within the dialog box that contains options for the user to select. An example of this type of component can be seen in the Change Scheme dialog box (the Colors... selection under the Options menu).

Using (and Avoiding) the Mouse

Like most graphical environments, the DOS Shell enables you to perform a task in several different ways. The primary difference is in how much you use the mouse. Most people are introduced to a graphical system by a mouse advocate who uses the mouse to perform every action, whether or not it is the most efficient method. As you become more experienced with using the environment (and with the mouse), you will discover which tasks are best suited to the mouse or the keyboard. The best way to discover what works for you is by experimenting with both.

Every menu and menu item can be accessed from the keyboard by a key sequence. Pressing the Alt (or F10) key activates keyboard selection. At this point, you can press the left- and right-arrow keys to move to the desired menu, and then use the down-arrow (or Enter) key to cause the menu to display. Or you can display the File menu (with the down-arrow or Enter keys) and then use the left- and right-arrow keys to move to another menu. You can also press the proper letter to activate the menu you need. The menu activation letters are indicated by a different format than the rest of the menu name.

When the menu you want is displayed, you can select an item with the up- and down-arrow keys, and then press Enter to activate the command. Alternatively, you can use the activation letter for the menu item.

With the mouse, you can point to the menu name (move the mouse indicator so that it is over a portion of the name), drop down the menu (click the active button), and then click on the item you want. Releasing the mouse button activates the menu item. Or you can point to the menu name, hold the mouse button down and move to the menu item. Releasing the button selects the item.

Each of these methods accomplishes the same result—a menu item is selected and activated. In addition, you can combine these methods and use the mouse to drop down the menu, and then use the activation letter to select the desired item. Pressing Esc or clicking on a different area of the screen closes a menu without making a selection.

Within dialog boxes, you can use the Tab key to move from one section to another, and you can use the space bar to select an item. Within List Boxes, you need to use the arrow keys to move between choices. Pressing Enter activates the default option button (the default is fine if it is one of the options or if it is indicated by the cursor location). Moving to an option button and pressing Enter selects that option. You can also use the arrow keys to move through the box or the mouse.

The selection bar within the screen areas can be moved using the up- and down-arrow keys. In the File List area, there is a difference between a file that is selected and one that is under the selection bar. How this difference is indicated depends on the type of monitor you use. The Tab key moves you between screen areas. Whenever you can use the Tab key to move forward, Shift+Tab moves you in the opposite direction.

You can scroll through lists by using the up- and down-arrow keys or the mouse. The PgUp and PgDown commands can be used to move the window a full screen at a time. Each scroll bar has an up-arrow at the top and a down-arrow at the bottom to move the scroll box. Pointing to an arrow and holding down the mouse button causes the scroll box to move in that direction. Another approach is to point to the scroll box and drag it (by moving the mouse while keeping the button down) to a new location.

The DOS Shell Menus

Although most actions can be accomplished by using just the mouse, most people will regularly use the menus. Figure 12.7 displays the various menus and their menu items. Many menu items also have a shortcut key that enables you to execute that command without even accessing the menu. These shortcut keys are indicated on the menu map on the right side of each menu section.

The DOS Shell uses a series of conventions to indicate the status of the menu items. As mentioned previously, commands that require additional user input with a dialog box are indicated with an ellipse (three dots following the menu item name). Items that are not available are dimmed or removed from the menu. Generally, this occurs when the proper type of object for the command is not currently selected. Some menu items serve as toggled commands. These commands have two settings—ON and OFF. When the setting is set to ON, it is indicated by a small diamond to the left of the menu name.

Whenever you begin to learn a new program, the most important command is the one that returns you to a familiar environment. In the case of the DOS Shell, it is the Exit command, located on the File menu. The shortcut key for this command is Alt+F4. The Exit command takes you to whatever directory is selected in the Directory Tree.

The Help Command

As you learn, it is very important to know how to access the Help feature. The most obvious way to activate the Help system is by selecting the Help menu on the far right of the menu bar. Two entry-level sections, Using Help and Shell Basics, are provided to guide new users through the common DOS Shell activities. When you are comfortable with the basics, there are separate sections that detail Commands and Procedures, as well as a summary of the keyboard commands. Rounding out the Help system is a comprehensive index to all commands, procedures, and general topics.

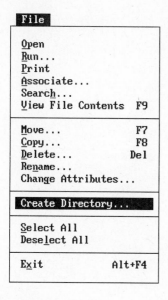

```
┌─────────────────────────────────┐
│ File                            │
├─────────────────────────────────┤
│ Open                            │
│ Run...                          │
│ Print                           │
│ Associate...                    │
│ Search...                       │
│ View File Contents    F9        │
├─────────────────────────────────┤
│ Move...               F7        │
│ Copy...               F8        │
│ Delete...             Del       │
│ Rename...                       │
│ Change Attributes...            │
├─────────────────────────────────┤
│ Create Directory...             │
├─────────────────────────────────┤
│ Select All                      │
│ Deselect All                    │
├─────────────────────────────────┤
│ Exit                  Alt+F4    │
└─────────────────────────────────┘
```

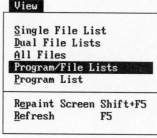

```
┌─────────────────────────────────┐
│ View                            │
├─────────────────────────────────┤
│ Single File List                │
│ Dual File Lists                 │
│ All Files                       │
│ Program/File Lists              │
│ Program List                    │
├─────────────────────────────────┤
│ Repaint Screen  Shift+F5        │
│ Refresh              F5         │
└─────────────────────────────────┘
```

```
┌─────────────────────────────────┐
│ Tree                            │
├─────────────────────────────────┤
│ Expand One Level  +             │
│ Expand Branch     *             │
│ Expand All        Ctrl+*        │
│ Collapse Branch   -             │
└─────────────────────────────────┘
```

Figure 12.7:
The DOS Shell menu map. The File menu items change when you move from the Directory List or File List to the Program List or Task List. Both versions of the File menu are shown in figure 12.7. The Tree menu does not display when you view the Program List only or when the All Files view is selected.

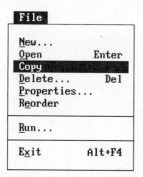

```
┌─────────────────────────────┐
│ File                        │
├─────────────────────────────┤
│ New...                      │
│ Open            Enter       │
│ Copy                        │
│ Delete...       Del         │
│ Properties...               │
│ Reorder                     │
├─────────────────────────────┤
│ Run...                      │
├─────────────────────────────┤
│ Exit            Alt+F4      │
└─────────────────────────────┘
```

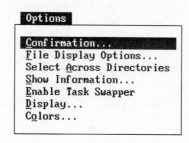

```
┌──────────────────────────────────┐
│ Options                          │
├──────────────────────────────────┤
│ Confirmation...                  │
│ File Display Options...          │
│ Select Across Directories        │
│ Show Information...               │
│ Enable Task Swapper              │
│ Display...                       │
│ Colors...                        │
└──────────────────────────────────┘
```

```
┌──────────────────┐
│ Help             │
├──────────────────┤
│ Index            │
│ Keyboard         │
│ Shell Basics     │
│ Commands         │
│ Procedures       │
│ Using Help       │
├──────────────────┤
│ About Shell      │
└──────────────────┘
```

In addition to accessing the information through the Help menu, help can also be obtained by pressing the F1 key at any point. For standard portions of the DOS Shell, this activates the Help utility. In the Program List, the help you receive is part of the construction of program groups and is dependent on how well the custom user environment was constructed.

File and Directory Management

The DOS Shell enables you to access most of the file and directory management commands of DOS via the File List. This section of the DOS Shell is most similar to the Windows' File Manager and provides a simplified environment for doing tasks previously accomplished at the command prompt. In addition, several new features are also available.

These new features combine menu commands and the Directory Tree and File List areas. Because of the graphical nature of the file display, it is possible to select groups of files for manipulation even if they share no similar characteristics. Before discussing the various tasks that are performed in the File List, it is important to understand the various ways in which the DOS Shell can present file and directory information.

Displaying the Contents of Directories

The View menu is used to change the display of information within the DOS Shell window. To change the display, simply select one of the five options from the top portion of the menu. Of the five different views available, four of them enable you to access the File commands. Three of these options present information about both the files and the directories, and all three of these views use the same basic structure for the File List. The fourth option, View All Files, uses a slightly different format and is discussed later in this section. The fifth view, Program List, does not give any control over the file structure and is discussed in the section "Working with Program Groups." The default view is the Program/File List (shown in fig. 12.8).

Figure 12.8:
The Program/File List view.

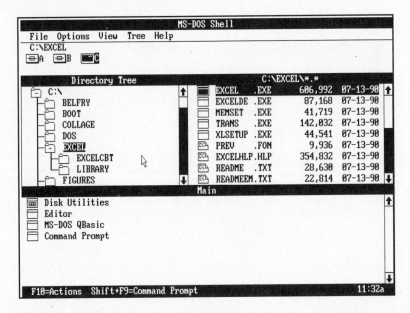

The Program/File List view is the most flexible because it gives you access both to the file and directory management tools as well as to the program groups. If you need to do extensive file manipulation with a directory (for example, to back up your current projects from a document directory), the Single File List view (shown in fig. 12.9) is a practical option.

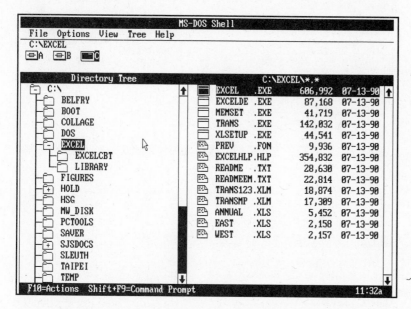

The Single File List view hides the Program List, but enables you to list significantly more files. You still have access to both the Directory Tree (for moving between directories) and the Drive Icons. This allows you to move files from the current directory to another location. The final directory-oriented display, Dual File List views (shown in fig. 12.10), is useful when you need to work with files in two directories.

The Dual File List view also removes the Program List from the screen. Rather than filling the entire display with a single file view, it enables you to work with two separate directory structures, which is useful for comparing the contents of directories and for changing the organization of information within a file structure. Notice that the Drive Icons are also duplicated, which enables you to compare information between drives.

Changing the Viewed Directory

All of these views give you access to the Directory Tree(s) and the displayed files. The Directory Tree is used to determine which directory is displayed in the File List and it functions like an outline of your directory structure (you can use the Tree menu to expand or collapse levels). In graphics mode, a directory is represented with a file folder; in text mode, the symbol is a pair of square brackets. Each directory is displayed with a line tracing its path back up to the root (\).

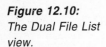
Figure 12.10:
The Dual File List view.

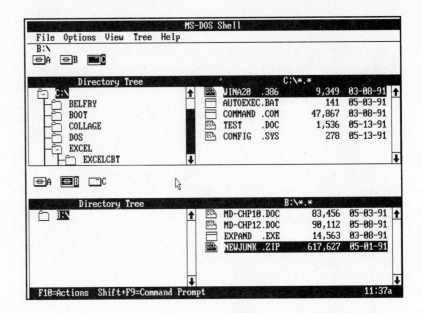

A directory that can be expanded (it contains subdirectories which are not being displayed) is indicated with a plus sign (+) in the middle of the directory representation (either with the folder icon or between square brackets). If you use the mouse, you can click on a directory to expand or collapse its subdirectories. If you use the keyboard, however, you must first move the selection bar to the desired directory, and then use the plus key (+) to expand the directory or the minus key (-) to collapse it. Of course, you can also use the menu commands if the appropriate directory is selected.

In addition to expanding a single level, you can expand all of the subdirectories' levels under a selected directory by using the Expand Branch command from the menu or by pressing the asterisk key (*). If you want to expand the entire Directory Tree, either select the Expand All command from the menu or use the Ctrl+* combination.

As you move through the Directory Tree, the File List updates to display the contents of the currently selected directory. If you use the mouse, simply point to the directory you want displayed. With the keyboard, you can use the arrow keys to move through the tree.

When you enter the first letter of a directory name on the current level, you move to that directory. If more than one directory share the same starting letter, pressing the letter key again moves you to the next directory with that starting letter. You move down the Directory Tree list as though it were all one level. In other words, if you select a letter that has a corresponding name as a subdirectory, you jump into that subdirectory.

Organizing the Displayed Files

The File Display Options command under the Options menu produces the dialog box shown in figure 12.11. This dialog box allows you to select which files are displayed (based on their file names) and the organization within the File List. In addition, you can specify whether or not Hidden/System files are included in the display.

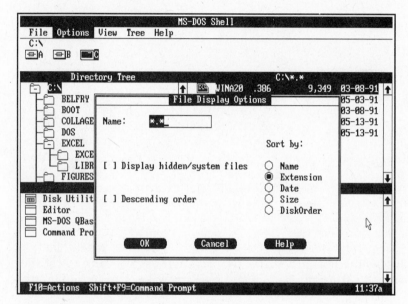

Figure 12.11:
The File Display Options dialog box.

The Name text box enables you to enter a template for the file names that are displayed (using the wild card symbols discussed in Chapter 3). All files within the current directory that match the template are displayed in the File list. The order of the display is controlled by the Descending order check box. If blank, the list is sorted in ascending order. If checked, the list is displayed in descending order.

The file information used to organize the File List display is controlled by the Sort by: group. The first four options in the Sort by: group—Name, Extension, Size, and Date—are self-explanatory. When combined with the selection options available through the name template, they give you a great deal of flexibility in the way in which you can display the File List. The DiskOrder sort option is most useful in the All Files view, in which it gives you an indication of the disk structure.

Updating the Display

The Refresh command (F5) is used to update the directory and file listings. This is particularly useful when you work with a network drive that can be modified by another user or when you change the disk in a floppy disk drive. Any time you create or delete a file or directory via a program (rather than the DOS Shell commands), you must use the Refresh command to update the listings. The Repaint command is used when the graphics adapter in your system has trouble updating the display. This command causes the screen image to re-create and should restore any missing or garbled portions (this frequently occurs following the use of a Terminate and Stay Resident program).

Selecting Files

Selecting an individual file is much like selecting a directory in the Directory Tree. With the mouse, you simply point and click. With the keyboard, you use the arrow keys to move to the file you want or use the first letter of the file name. You will always have at least one file highlighted, but not necessarily selected. If you have a file selected and decide you don't want to complete an action, you can simply select the next file and continue with your new action. If you want to clear all selections and highlight the first file in the File List, use the Deselect All command under the File menu. The Deselect All command has a shortcut key combination of Ctrl+\ (backslash).

If you want to select a group of files that are located together in the File List, click on the first name, hold down the shift key, and then click on the last name to be included in the list. If you use the keyboard, move to the first file name and hold down the shift key as you use the arrow keys to move through the list.

If you use a mouse and want to select a group of files scattered throughout the File List, you can hold down the Ctrl key while clicking on the file names. If you use the keyboard, move to the first file name and press Shift+F8. This activates the Add option (indicated in the status bar) and enables you to add another file to the selection. To select the file to add, use the arrow keys to move to the file and press the space bar. To add another file, simply move to the file and press the space bar. Press Shift+F8 again to end the process of adding files.

If you want to remove a file from a group selection, you can hold down the shift key and click on the file to be removed or press Shift+F8, move to the appropriate file name and press the space bar. Note that if the Add feature is already selected, you do not need to press Shift+F8.

If you want to select all of the files in the display, use the command Select All from the File menu or press Ctrl+/. If you select a group of files and decide you want to start over with a new selection, use the Deselect All command.

The Select Across Directories command under the Options menu is one of the toggle switches that is set by selecting it. If it is not active (no symbol appears to the left of the name), moving within the Directory Tree cancels any selection. You are restricted to selecting files within the active directory only. If you activate Select Across Directories (a diamond appears to the left of the name), your selection remains active as you change the active directory. Although this is most apparent with the Dual File List views (in which two different directories can be displayed), it works with any File List view.

You must use one of the methods discussed previously for selecting files that are not located in a continuous group (either hold down the Ctrl key while clicking, or activate the add feature with Shift+F8 and use the space bar to select the next file to be include in the group). There is no indicator to remind you that files are selected in another directory, so you are responsible for remembering the files you select. If you are unsure if files are selected in another directory, use the Deselect All command (Ctrl+\) to make sure nothing is currently selected.

Common File Actions

Most of the file tasks that can be performed within the DOS Shell have an equivalent that is performed at the DOS command line. This section details the various operations that can be performed on files. Unless otherwise indicated, all of the commands can be done on a single file or a group of files.

Each action has at least two ways in which it can be accomplished—with the keyboard and with the mouse. Where appropriate, other alternatives (including shortcut keys) are also indicated.

The DOS Shell gives you the option of being warned when a particular action will destroy an existing file. In the dialog box, selecting OK allows the file to be destroyed and selecting Cancel stops the action. It is important to remember that OK is the default option and will be selected if you press Enter.

The warnings are controlled by the Confirmation dialog box under the Options menu (shown in fig. 12.12). There are two types of actions that can cause a file to be destroyed—deleting the file and replacing one file with another (renaming or moving). In addition, you can elect to have any file manipulation with the mouse require an explicit confirmation. The warning takes the form of a confirmation dialog box and appears for each file in a group.

❏ **Delete**. Highlight the file(s) and select Delete from the File menu.

Highlight the file(s) and press Del.

Figure 12.12:
The Confirmation
dialog box.

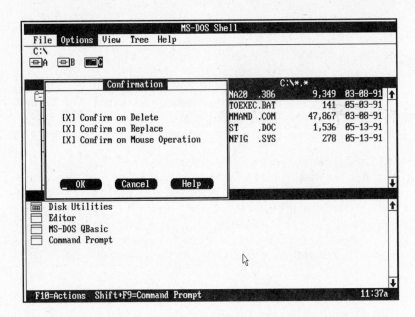

❏ **Copy**. Highlight the file(s) and select Copy from the File menu. You are prompted for the new file name(s).

Highlight the file(s) and press F8. You are prompted for the new file name(s).

If you are copying a file from one directory to another, you can hold down the Ctrl key and drag the file(s) from the File List to the directory on the Directory Tree.

❏ **Move**. Highlight the file(s) and select Move from the File menu. You are prompted for the new location.

Highlight the file(s) and press F7. You are prompted for the new location.

Drag the file(s) from the File List to the new location on the Directory Tree.

❏ **Rename**. Highlight the file and select the Rename command from the File menu.

❏ **Print**. Highlight the file and select the Print command from the File menu. To use the Print command, the Print utility must be installed before entering the DOS Shell. If you forget to install PRINT.COM, you have to exit the DOS Shell, install PRINT.COM, and then re-enter the DOS Shell to enable printing.

In addition to the internal DOS commands, available as part of the DOS Shell, the external DOS commands can be added as part of a Program Group and accessed via the Program List. In fact, the default group contains several disk utilities, including Disk Copy, Quick Format, Format, and Undelete.

Common Directory Actions

One of the areas in which the DOS Shell offers significantly more power than the standard DOS prompt is in directory actions. In addition to creating new subdirectories and deleting empty directories, you can also rename existing directories. Directory commands must be executed from the keyboard or via the command menus.

❑ **Create**. To create a directory, select the directory to be the parent for the new subdirectory, and then select the Create Directory command from the File menu.

❑ **Delete**. As part of the DOS environment, the DOS Shell requires that a directory be empty before it can be deleted. To delete the contents of a directory, move to the File List, use the Select All command, and then select Delete. Or move to the File List, press Ctrl+/, and then press the Del key.

❑ **Rename**. To rename a directory, highlight the directory name and select the Rename command from the File menu.

Tools for Finding a File

In addition to the visual display of the directory structure, the DOS Shell has a number of other features that help you locate specific files. The first of these is the All Files view, as shown in figure 12.13. This command (under the View menu) replaces the standard list displays with a single list containing all the files on the list. The Directory Tree is replaced with information about the currently selected file.

If you know the name of the file you seek, sort the All Files view by name, and then move to the appropriate location in the list. Clicking on a file name displays information about the file and the directory in which it resides (see fig. 12.14). In the first section of the file information, you are provided with the name of the file and its attributes. The second section contains the size of the file. If more than one file is selected, the number of files and the total size of the group is reported. The next section identifies the directory where the file is stored, the size of the directory, and the number of files it contains. The final section contains summary information for the entire disk.

Figure 12.13:
The All Files view.

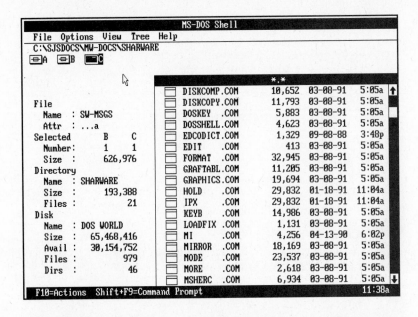

Figure 12.14:
The File/Directory Information dialog box.

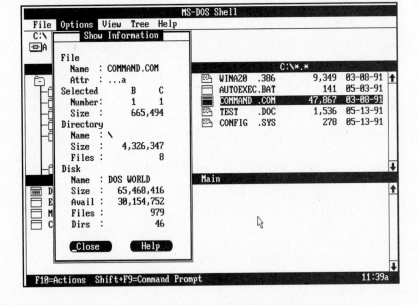

With group selections, the file and directory information sections continue to display information about the first file selected. The same information can be obtained in the Single File List views and Dual File List views by highlighting a file (or group of files), and then selecting Show Information from the Options menu.

You can change the attributes associated with a file by using the Change Attributes command under the File menu. This command displays the dialog box, shown in figure 12.15, and enables you to specify the Read, Archive, Hidden, and System attributes for a file. (For more information about these attributes, see the ATTRIB command in the Command Reference.)

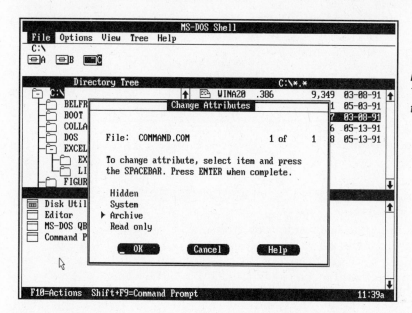

Figure 12.15:
The Change Attributes dialog box.

The All File view can also be used as a tool for system maintenance. If you display the files sorted by extension, you can group together all files of a specific type. You can delete backup and temporary files that have been automatically created by programs and are no longer needed. Rather than having to search throughout the hard disk, you can list them as a contiguous group, select them, and then delete them in one session.

You can also use the DiskOrder display option to get a rough idea of your disk structure. In general, your EXE, SYS and COM files should be located at the start of your disk because they do not change. By grouping these files into a block, you minimize the speed at which your disk will fragment because more frequently changed files are also grouped at the end of your disk with any available free space.

If you know part of the name of a file, but not its location, you can use the Search command from the File menu to help you find it. This command displays the dialog box, shown in figure 12.16, and enables you to specify wild cards when searching for the file. Thus, to list all files that start with the letters MD and have the DOC extension, enter **MD*.DOC** as the search text.

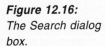

Figure 12.16:
The Search dialog box.

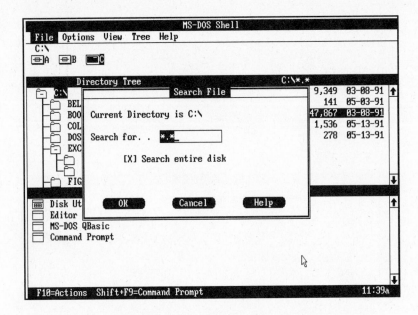

The Search command is an even more powerful tool if you use file-naming conventions. For example, if all invoices are identified by the starting letters IN and their file names are composed of the year, month, and day (in two-digit formats), you can use the command **IN9105??.*** to list all the invoices for May, 1991. DOS searches down the Directory Tree, starting at the root and displays a single list of all files that match the string, no matter where they were on the disk. When you press Esc, you return to the regular shell.

You will occasionally find a file that seems to have the right name, but not be sure it is the one you need. The View File Contents command (F9), under the File menu, displays the contents of the file in ASCII or Hexadecimal format. This is only useful for identifying the text within files (unless you have programming skills), but it is often faster than opening an application and loading the file, especially if it is not the correct file and you have to try again.

The View File Contents command displays a new window of information (see fig. 12.17). The Display menu is very simple and offers you the choice of an ASCII view (a standard text format) or a Hex(adecimal) view. The View menu contains two options: Repaint (retains its standard function) and Restore View (returns you to the standard DOS Shell display). You can also use the Esc key to restore you to the selected List display.

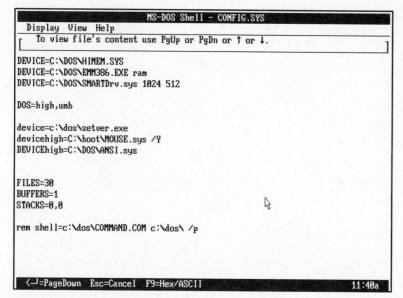

Figure 12.17:
The File Contents window.

Starting an Application

Not only does the DOS Shell provide a complete environment for managing files and directories, but it also offers a variety of ways to manage application files. Although the Program Groups and Task List are the primary ways to work with applications, you can still access your programs without having to add them to Program Groups or to work with the Task List. Any application that you normally start from a command prompt can be activated by using one of several methods. The only restriction is that the DOS Shell itself uses some memory resources so you may not be able to run all your memory-intensive applications.

Using the Run Command

If the program is installed so that it can be started from any directory on the disk (its directory is on your PATH), you can start it in the same way by using the Run command under the file menu. You simply select the Run command and enter the name of the application. If you want to open a document with the application, you can include its name as part of the command line, as you would at the command prompt (for example, WORD MY-FILE)

In addition to starting applications that are on your PATH, the Run command allows you to enter the name of any executable file on your disk, as you would at the command prompt. If you want to use the Run command for a program that is not on your path, you must specify the full path to the file (for example, \WORD\WORD.EXE).

Using the File List

You also use the File List to gain access to your programs. To start a program from the File List, you must first find the program's application file. For most programs, this is the file with the application name and a EXE extension. When you highlight the name of the application file, you can either use the Open command under the File menu or double-click on the file name to start the program. (A double-click is created by pushing the mouse button twice rapidly.)

Opening an Application from a Document

One of the most useful features of the DOS Shell is its capability to associate documents with applications, enabling you to select a document from the File List and have the DOS Shell open the appropriate application. This means that you don't need to start the application and then load the document—it's all done in one step. You can create associations for any application that accepts a document file name as part of the command line. The only restriction is that each type of document extension may only be associated with a single application (all of your TXT files, for example, must be associated with the same program). A single application can have more than one type of document associated with it.

The association is a link between the file extension of the document and the application file. To create an association, you can start either with the application or a document with the proper extension. You can use the Associate command (under the File menu) to create the link, and you can select several files to associate at one time. If they are applications, you are prompted for each one; if they are documents, you are prompted for each unique extension.

To define an association starting with an application, first select the application that will be used and choose the Associate command. You are presented with a dialog box that prompts you to enter the file extensions that are to be associated with the selected application. Most extensions have three characters and should not include the period that separates the file name from the extension. If you wish to associate more than one extension with a single application, enter the extensions in the same dialog box and separate their names with a single space.

To define an association starting with a document, select the document and choose the Associate command. You are prompted with a dialog box that lists the extension of the selected document file and asks you to enter the name of the application. Unless the application's directory is on your PATH, you should enter the full name of the application's file, including the directory names.

When the association is created, you can either select a document and use the Open command, or you can double-click on the document name in the File List. This opens the application and loads the document as if you had entered the application and document name at the command prompt.

Creating a Program Environment

Although it is possible to access programs through the File List or the Run command, the DOS Shell is designed to provide a user environment with the Program List. The Program List contains groups and individual program items that can be selected with the mouse or the keyboard. The Program List is in the lower portion of the screen in the Program/File List view and is the entire screen in the Program List view (as shown in fig. 12.18). You must select one of these two views from the View menu in order to use the Program List capabilities of DOS Shell.

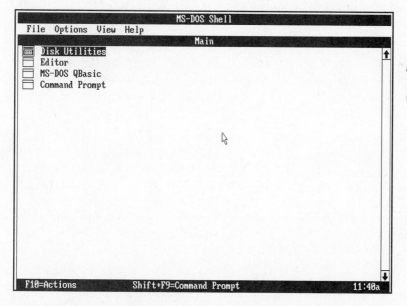

Figure 12.18:
The Program List
view.

The Program List portion of the DOS Shell provides the same basic functions as the Program Manager does in Windows. These features are new to standard DOS and allow the creation of a custom user environment in which access to programs is structured for maximum convenience. These programs are added as individual program items that can be consolidated into program groups. Program groups can be nested (you can have a program group within another group) in the same way that directories and subdirectories can. You can think of the Program List as a tree structure, similar to the Directory Tree, with the individual program items as the files and the program groups as the directories.

The Initial Program List

When you move into the Program List area, several menu changes occur. The File menu loses all of the file- and directory-management commands (Print, Associate, View File Contents, Search, Move, Rename, Change Attributes and Create Directory). This occurs because you are no longer working with the files and directories shown in the File List, rather with the program groups. Several new commands are added, including New, Properties, and Reorder. In addition, the Copy and Delete commands affect program groups or items rather than individual files or directories.

Several features from the Options lists are also unavailable, though the menu does not change its structure. Because the Directory Tree is no longer active, the Tree menu is no longer displayed. Finally, the Refresh command is also removed because the Program List can be changed only through direct modification.

The standard DOS Shell has two defined groups. The first, Main, exists for any user environment and is the upper level of the program tree. In the standard environment, there are three program items at the main level—QBasic, the Editor, and the Command Prompt. Each of these items activates another component of the DOS Environment.

The Command Prompt program item enables you to access the familiar CLI environment of the standard prompt. You can perform any tasks from the standard DOS environment. To return to the DOS Shell, simply enter **EXIT** and then press an additional key. Although it is possible to start an application with this method, it is preferable to use the File List or the Run command. The Editor command takes you into the new DOS full-screen editor (discussed in Chapter 13) and the QBasic command takes you into the QBasic environment, which is discussed in Chapter 14.

The Disk Utilities option on the default Program List is a program group. On a text display, this is indicated with square brackets around the name. On a graphics display, icons are displayed to the left of the name with a different icons representing program items and program groups.

Any item within the Program List can be activated by using the techniques for selecting a file from the File List. You can either double-click on the appropriate name or select the name followed by the Open command from the File menu. In addition, you can also use the Enter key as a shortcut for the Open command. In most cases, the Open command is more awkward and you will want to use either the mouse or the Enter key. If you move down a level in the group structure, the name of the parent group is always displayed as the first item of the list. Selecting this item moves you back up through the program tree. You can also press Esc to move to the parent group.

With the Program List, the programs you use regularly to perform your duties are available as part of your custom environment and you also still have access to any program via the Run command. The command works the same in any area of the DOS Shell and allows you to start an application that is located anywhere on your system by specifying the full name and location of the application file.

Working with Program Groups

As mentioned previously, the structure of the Program List resembles the traditional directory structure of DOS. Using this example, the program groups serve the same function as the directories and subdirectories of DOS. DOS directories contain files of various sorts and subdirectories, just as program groups contain program items (accessing a single application), or further levels of program groups.

The Main program group is similar to the root directory in that it is always at the top of the tree. Many users find it simplest to put their commonly used programs in the Main group and use other program groups to hold less frequently used programs. In fact, programs that you seldom use may not be included as program items at all, but instead may be accessed via the Run command. The fact that you can have program items as part of the first level is one of two major differences between the Task List and the Program Manager in Windows. The other major difference is that you can have more than one level of program groups.

Another approach is to group programs by their functions. In this model, you might have a Word Processing group, a Spreadsheet group, and a Graphics group. Each of them might contain several different applications that serve similar functions. A variation on this approach is to create groups that are task-oriented. In this model, you might have a Memo group, a Budget group, and a Presentation group. Because each program group is defined individually, you can have the same application represented as different program items in different groups.

A more sophisticated environment might use several levels to organize the applications. In this model, the Presentation group could have the most often used applications at the group level and less commonly used applications in program groups within Presentations. These groups can include a Graphics group and a File Conversion group.

In addition to serving as an organizational tool, program groups can also be used to provide a measure of security in managing program access. This is particularly useful for system administrators who want to use the DOS Shell as a front-end system to provide user access to a networked system. The only additional work that must be done to use the DOS Shell in this fashion is to develop a batch file that assigns network mappings and starts the DOS Shell. This procedure is discussed in Chapter 13.

Not only does the DOS Shell enable the system administrator to establish basic password protection for both groups and items, but it also enables the development of a customized help system. Each group or item can display a user-defined help message when the F1 key is pressed. The features Title, Password, and Help are part of the group properties. Group properties can be established when a new program group is created, or at any time by using the Properties command under the File menu.

Creating or Modifying a Program Group

To create a new program group, you must be in the group that will be the parent group. If you create a group of the main level, you should be at the top of the program tree. The name of the current group is displayed as the title of the Program List.

When you select New from the File menu, you are presented with the choice of creating a new program group or program item. To create a group, select Program Group and press Enter (or select OK). The dialog box shown in figure 12.19 appears with the title Add Group. This is the same dialog box that appears if you select an existing group and use the Properties command. If you are modifying an existing group, the dialog box title will be Program Group Properties.

As indicated in the dialog box, the only required field is the Title field. The information from this field is displayed as the program group name in the Program List. The information inserted as the Help Text is displayed when the user presses the F1 key. Because pressing the Enter key activates the default option button (OK) and closes the dialog box, you can't use the Enter key in your help message. To start a new line, enter ^m, which generates a single paragraph mark. You can specify up to 255 characters.

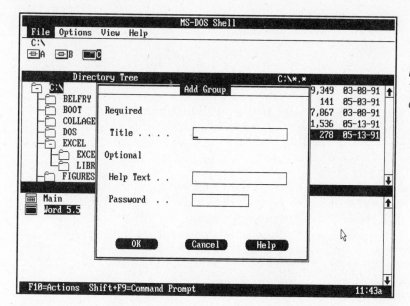

Figure 12.19:
The Program Group dialog box.

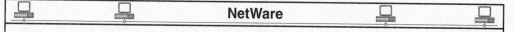

NetWare

The DOSSHELL is a nice network menu system. Make sure to create a separate group for NetWare applications so you don't attempt to execute them when you're not logged in. It is difficult to configure the shared version of DOSSHELL in the \PUBLIC\IBM_PC\MSDOS\V5.00 subdirectory, but it is worth it in the long run. Try using DOSSHELL from a local drive first until you feel confident with DOSSHELL.

You can also enter a *group password*, which prevents any user from viewing the contents of the group. This is a more global level of security than an *item password*, which prevents the unauthorized user from starting that particular application but still displays the contents of the group. If you install passwords in your Program List, you will want to make the DOSSHELL.INI file a read-only file. The passwords are encrypted and cannot be read for the INI file, but they can be deleted entirely, which removes the password protection.

Changing the Contents of a Program Group

It is most convenient if the items which are frequently used are at the top of the group list, saving the trouble of having to read through the entire group searching for the proper item. If it is a commonly used item, positioning it at the bottom of the group is also effective because then it is simple to find and select.

The Reorder command under the File menu is used to rearrange the items within a program group. To use it, select the item to be moved, and then activate the Reorder command. You are asked to select the new position for the item and to press Enter to reorganize the list. The item is inserted before the item you select as the new location. It is easiest to arrange a program group by working downward—move the item that will be first and then the item that follows. This forces the unused items to the bottom of the list.

The Copy command can be used to duplicate program items between groups. Program items are copied when you want to duplicate the link to a program with different parameters or when two programs use a similar configuration. In many cases, it is a good idea to create a default program item with the standard configuration for your system, which can be copied when you want to create a new item. To use the Copy command, select the item to be duplicated and then activate the Copy command. You are then prompted for the group where the item should be inserted.

The Delete command is used to remove a program item or a program group. As with directories, a program group can't be deleted if it still contains items. You must delete all of the items within the group by using Select All and then Delete (Ctrl+/, Del). After all of the items are removed, you can remove the group itself. If a group or item has a password, you are prompted for the password prior to completing the delete operation.

Creating a Program Item

Because the DOS Shell is a part of the DOS environment, rather than another complete layer of operating system (as is Microsoft Windows), it is a simple matter to add standard DOS applications to the program groups, particularly if you use the Program List only as a menu system. If you use the Task List and the task-swapping features available within DOS Shell, the situation becomes somewhat more complex. The settings associated with task-swapping are discussed in the next section.

If you use Windows products regularly, you must create your user environment as part of the Windows environment, rather than within DOS Shell. The DOS Shell is intended as a graphical shell for managing DOS programs; it is not designed to manage the Windows environment as a task. Furthermore, the Program Information Files (PIFs) that allow DOS programs to function in the Windows environment are significantly more sophisticated than the task-swapping descriptions created for programs in the DOS Shell environment. Windows offers better control over how programs share resources. Although it is possible to activate the DOS Shell from within Windows, it should not be used for program management under Windows.

Selecting the New command from the File menu gives you the choice of creating a new program item or program group. You must be in the group that item is to become part of prior to executing the command. Selecting the Program Item option displays the dialog box shown in figure 12.20 with the title Add Program Item. As with program groups, the properties of an item can be changed after its creation by using the Properties command under the File menu. If you are modifying a program item, the title will read Program Item Properties.

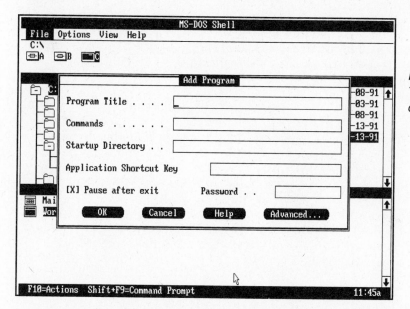

Figure 12.20:
The Program Item dialog box.

The required fields are the Program Title field (displays as the name of the program item) and the Commands field. The Commands field contains the command(s) to be executed when the program item is selected. This field can also include codes to request that you supply additional parameters to complete the command line. These are entered in a format similar to the one used for batch files.

A series of commands can be entered, separated with a semicolon (;). Any command that is valid at the command prompt can be used, including DOS commands that utilize redirection and pipes. If a parameter is to be supplied, it is indicated with a percent sign (%) and a number. You can't skip a number, but numbers do not need to be assigned sequentially left to right (for example, you could use WORD %3 %1 %2). You are prompted for the parameters in a sequence based on the parameter numbers, not their order in the command. You can use up to nine parameters; repeating the parameter code causes the parameter value to be repeated in the command. The final step in assigning a program item is to provide the necessary information for the prompt dialog boxes, used to obtain the parameter information.

Before selecting OK and entering the prompt information, all other program item information should be completed. The Startup Directory can be used to cause the DOS Shell to change to the specified directory before it executes the command in the Commands field. Some programs require that they be started from a particular directory to function properly. On the other hand, programs that specify a starting directory internal to the program are not affected by this setting.

As mentioned previously, you can assign a password to an individual program item. The same caution applies to a program item password as to a group password—you can remove the password by editing the DOSSHELL.INI file, unless it is made a read-only file.

The Pause After Exit option causes the program to pause and wait for you to press a key before returning to the DOS Shell when you exit the program. This is useful if the application displays a final message that the user needs to see.

The application shortcut keys and most of the Advanced options are used with task swapping and are discussed in the next section. These are relevant only if you use the task-swapping environment and need not be complete if you use the DOS Shell as a simple menu system. The exception is the Help field, which is accessed with the Advanced button. This field works like the Help field for a Program Group and contains the information that is displayed when the F1 key is pressed.

When all of the appropriate fields are complete, pressing OK results in a dialog box, like the one in figure 12.21, for each parameter specified on the Commands line that you must supply. If no parameters are required, you are immediately returned to the standard DOS Shell window.

Although all of the information in this dialog box is optional, you should complete as much information as possible, so users know what is expected. The Window Title is the information to be displayed as the title for the dialog box. Completing this field is important—it provides a professional look to your environment. The Program Information is the text displayed at the top of the dialog box to guide the user in completing the required information. The Prompt Message appears to the left of the text field where the parameter is to be entered. You are limited to 18 characters for this prompt. Finally, you can specify Default Parameters to be used when the user selects OK without entering any text. An example of a parameter configuration (see fig. 12.22) and the resulting dialog box (see fig. 12.23) are presented to demonstrate the relationship between the fields and the resulting dialog box.

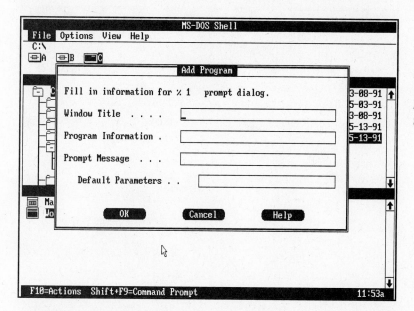

Figure 12.21:
The Parameter Prompt Configuration dialog box.

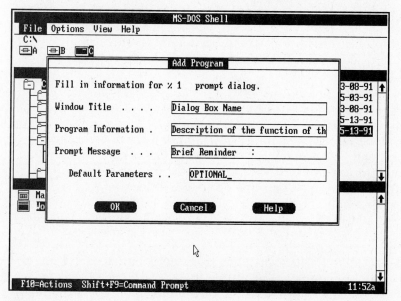

Figure 12.22:
The Parameter Configuration dialog box.

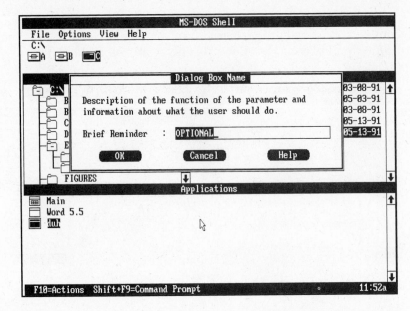

Figure 12.23:
The resulting dialog box for parameter %1.

Remember that these final steps are necessary only when you use replaceable parameters that must have values supplied by the user. If you use the DOS Shell as a simple menu system, you need only complete the Program Title and the Commands fields, which create the program item and tell DOS what command to execute. Startup Directory and Pause after Exit are optional, although some programs require that they be completed to function smoothly. The Password is never required by the DOS Shell and is available as a tool for system administrators. All the other settings are part of the task-swapping environment and are discussed in the next section.

Task Swapping

A major benefit of using the DOS Shell over the standard DOS environment is the capability to run more than one application at a time. This feature is referred to as task swapping and is activated by the Enable Task Swapping command on the Options menu. When this options is selected, the Program List area is reduced to a half-screen width and shares the lower portion of the screen with the Task List in the Program/File List view (as shown in fig. 12.24).

Task swapping, as provided by the DOS Shell, is intended as a way to enable you to use more than one application at a time. It is not intended as a complete environment for sharing information between applications. There are facilities for selecting which program is active, but neither the Task List nor the DOS Shell provide any facilities for moving information between programs. To accomplish that type of integration, you need to look to a more comprehensive windowing environment (Microsoft Windows or QuarterDeck's DesqView).

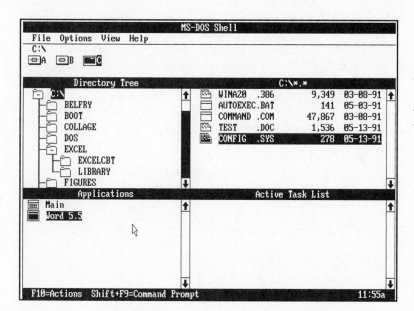

Figure 12.24:
The Program/File
List view with Task
Swapper

NetWare

DO NOT Attempt to use the Task Swapping feature of DOSSHELL when logged into a NetWare system. Microsoft recommends strongly against this.

Using the Task List

The Task List is used to manage the currently available programs. Because the swapping provided by the DOS Shell is between individual DOS applications, all applications are run as full-screen windows. When you move between applications, or when you move between an application and the DOS Shell, the entire screen is redrawn with new information.

If you are in the DOS Shell, you can select any application from the Task List by double-clicking (or selecting the application name and activating the Open command). If you are in an application, you can return to the DOS Shell window by pressing Ctrl+Esc. If you wish to add an application to the Task List, you can either select it from the Program List or execute it via the Run command.

If you are in an application and want to move to another application in the Task List, it is best to use the Alt+Tab key combination. If you keep pressing the Alt key and use the Tab key to move through the active programs, the name of the window you are activating is displayed as a banner across the top of the page. When you are at the proper application, release the Alt key and the window's contents are redrawn. You can also use the Alt+Esc key combination to cycle through the Task List, but the screen is redrawn for each application. The delay while the screen is redrawn is significant, so, unless the next application in sequence is the one you want, the Alt+Esc combination is much slower than Alt+Tab.

The Task List is only displayed in the Program/File List and All Program views. If you select one of the other views while the Enable Task Swapping option is selecting, the Task List (and Program List) are hidden, but the commands to move between active applications are still available (Alt+Tab, Alt+Esc, and Ctrl+Esc).

When the Enable Task Swapping command is selected, and there is at least one active program, you are required to exit each program individually before you can disable task swapping or exit the DOS Shell. Although the Exit command is apparently available (it is not dimmed), you must close each program individually (using whatever keystrokes it requires) before it allows you to exit the DOS Shell. The Enable Task Swapping command is dimmed as soon as a single application is added to the Task List. The other commands under the Options menu are available if a File List is displayed, but they do not affect the Task List.

The Advanced Program Item Options

Several of the commands in the Program Item properties dialog box are relevant when task swapping is activated. The Shortcut key command enables you to specify a key combination to jump directly to that application if it is active on the Task List. This is particularly useful for quickly moving within a standard group of programs that are usually active.

The settings in the Advanced dialog box (shown in fig. 12.25) are used to control the way programs behave as tasks. These settings are accessed via the Advanced button in the Program Item Properties dialog box. There is a limit to the number of programs that can be active at one time and an error message displays if you attempt to start additional programs. Your only option is to then close some of your other applications.

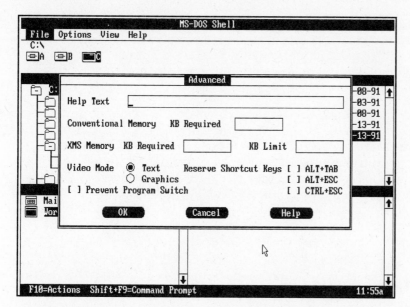

Figure 12.25:
*The Program Item
Advanced dialog
box.*

Many of these settings are changed only if you experience problems. For example, the only times you should use the Graphics setting for the Video Mode are if you are using a CGA monitor, if the DOS Shell has trouble redrawing the screen when you swap in or out of a particular application, or if the DOS Shell is running in a window as part of Microsoft Windows (see Appendix A).

The Reserve Shortcut Keys are useful if you have an application that uses one or more of these key combinations to activate a command within the application. Checking one of the boxes tells the DOS Shell environment to ignore that key combination and enables the program to use it as a shortcut. If you have an application that uses all three of the Reserved Shortcut Keys, you may want to leave one available for the DOS Shell. Otherwise, you must exit the program to return to the DOS Shell or swap to a different application.

If you have an application that is particularly sensitive to the swapping environment, but that can be activated from within the DOS Shell with no problem, you may want to set the Prevent Program Switch option. This option, which requires you to exit the program to return to the DOS Shell or to swap to another application, is useful if you have an application that causes problems in the environment when you swap away from it (system crashes or memory conflicts, for example).

The main group of settings in the Advanced dialog box refers to memory management. The most important of the three is the KB Limit setting, located at the far right of the XMS Memory line. This setting is used to determine whether a program is granted access to extended memory. If left blank, a program is not permitted any extended memory. If set to -1, a program may use all available extended memory. If a program seizes control of all the installed extended memory and refuses to relinquish it to other programs, you can specify a limit on the maximum amount it can request by entering a value in kilobytes.

The other two memory settings, Conventional Memory KB Required and XMS Memory KB Required, are used to specify the amount of memory that must be present before a program can start. Specify these settings only if you have trouble with a program trying to start (and then crashing), or if you receive a message from the application advising you of insufficient memory. If you specify these settings, make them as low as possible so that the program is more likely to be able to start. If insufficient memory (of either kind) is present, a message displays indicating that the program can't start. These settings are independent; you can specify one or the other or both.

When a Program Crashes

If a program crashes when task swapping is enabled, you should return to the DOS Shell. It is a good idea to exit all of your active programs (saving any open documents) and exit the DOS Shell. Restart the DOS Shell, and then add the applications you need to reactivate to the task list. This process of completely exiting and restarting your applications ensures that the environment is clean when you reopen your applications.

If an application crashes and does not return you to the DOS Shell window, you can use one of the key combinations to return to the DOS Shell window. If you can't swap away from the crashed application, you must reboot your system and you lose any unsaved data.

If you can swap away from the crashed application's window, you should close each application and then exit DOS Shell. Select each active task (except for the one that crashed) and exit the application (again, first save any open documents). When all the other applications are closed, select the crashed application and choose the Delete command from the File menu. This removes the application from the Task List, but it should only be used as a last resort. Finally, exit the DOS Shell. You can now restart the DOS Shell and reactivate your applications.

If you can return to the DOS Shell but other applications won't activate, select the crashed application and delete it from the Task List. You should now be able to cycle through the other applications and close each one (remembering to save your documents). Again, exit and restart the DOS Shell to ensure that you have a clean environment.

Customizing the DOS Shell

There are many features of the DOS Shell that the average user can change and have recorded from session to session. For example, you can change the types of display, program items, program groups, or views. Like many modern programs, the DOS Shell uses the INI extension for the file that contains its customization settings (DOSSHELL.INI). Although this file can be edited directly, most of the settings that the average user manipulates can be controlled from within the program.

When you change a setting in the DOS Shell, the values are stored immediately. Unless you keep a backup copy of the DOSSHELL.INI file, you can't undo any of the changes that you make. One change that's fun to make is to alter your shell environment by changing the colors of the various components.

Changing the Color Scheme

The colors used for each of the windows components is part of a collection of colors referred to as a *color scheme*. The standard DOS Shell contains a collection of present color schemes that can be selected via the Colors command on the Options menu. Using the dialog box shown in figure 12.26, you select the color scheme you want to use. (You can use the preview option to see which colors will be used for the various components.)

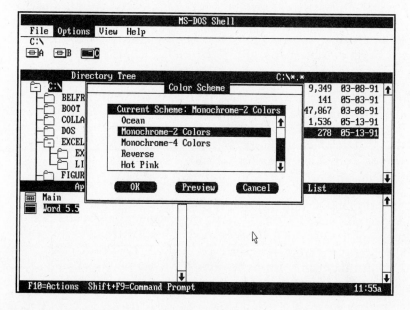

Figure 12.26:
The Colors dialog box.

Although it is tempting to select a color scheme based on its appeal, it is more important that it be comfortable for your eyes. Make sure that you can easily identify all of the critical portions of your display. Of course, no decision is final and you can also change the color scheme if it begins to bother you (or if you get bored with it). It is also possible to define your own color schemes, as discussed in the "Creating Color Schemes" section).

The DOSSHELL.INI File

The initialization file used by DOSSHELL is a standard ASCII file that can be edited in any word processor that reads and writes "Text Only" or "ASCII" files. If you don't have a favorite word processor, you can use the Edit command to activate the DOS Editor. Most of the file records settings that can be established with the DOS Shell menus. There are, however, a few settings that are accessible only by directly editing the file. In addition, if you add a substantial amount of new information, it is easier to edit the file directly.

The settings in the initialization file are divided into two sections—[savestate] and [programstarter]. Each setting must be in the proper group for it to be recognized. The section names must be enclosed in square brackets and should not contain spaces. The initialization files are not case-sensitive and you may use upper-, lower-, or mixed-case letters.

Any time you directly edit the initialization file, it is a good idea to create a backup copy before you begin. This is easily done: select the DOSSHELL.INI file in the DOS directory, choose the Copy command, and then create a duplicate file called DOSSHELL.OLD. If you then experience problems trying to use your edited DOSSHELL.INI file, you can copy the backup from DOSSHELL.OLD and replace DOSSHELL.INI. This restores your original settings.

Table 12.1 lists the settings that are controlled by menu items on the DOS Shell menus. Each of these settings is automatically updated when you change the corresponding settings on the appropriate menu. Many of these settings only appear in the initialization file if their value has been changed from the default. The default value is indicated with an asterisk. Except where noted, all settings are part of the [savestate] section.

Although it is possible to change these settings directly, it is easier and safer to use the DOS Shell menus and let the system record the changes. In addition, the mouseinfo setting is established if you use a non-Microsoft mouse or an older version of the mouse driver. The settings in table 12.2 control the general DOS Shell environment but are not available via menu commands. It is therefore necessary to directly edit these settings if you wish to change them.

Table 12.1
DOSSHELL.INI Menu Settings

Setting	Values	Menu item (MENU:item)
screenmode	graphics text*	OPTIONS:display
resolution	low# medium# high# veryhigh#	OPTIONS:display NOTE: # is replaced with a digit.
filemanagermode	shared* singletree twotree systemtree	VIEW NOTE: Shared is Program/File systemtree is All Files.
task list	enabled disabled*	OPTIONS: Enable Task Swapper.
switching		This duplicates task list.
filemanager	enabled* disabled	This setting is in the [programstarter] section and controls whether the File List is displayed. It is used in combination with filemanagermode.
sortkey	name* extension date size diskorder	OPTIONS:file display options (Sort by:)
sortorder	ascending* descending	OPTIONS:file display options (Sort Order:)
displayhiddenfiles	enabled disabled*	OPTIONS:file display options
replaceconfirm	enabled* disabled	OPTIONS:confirmation (on replace)
deleteconfirm	enabled* disabled	OPTIONS:confirmation (on delete)
mouseconfirm	enabled* disabled	OPTIONS:confirmation (on mouse action)
crossdirselection disabled*	enabled directories	OPTIONS: select across

Table 12.1—continued

Setting	Values	Menu item (MENU:item)
currentcolor		This setting is in the [programstarter] section and stores the name of the current color scheme.

Table 12.2
DOSSHELL.INI Environment Settings

Setting	Values	Purpose
beep	enabled disabled	Controls whether the system beeps on errors.
swapmouse	enabled disabled	Controls which mouse button is used for selection. Enabled makes the right button the active one.
command		This setting is in the [programstarter] section and stores the name of the current command processor.

In addition to these settings, there are *expressions* in the initialization file that are used to establish the options available in the DOS Shell environment. Unlike other settings that are single lines of information, these expressions contain multiple levels of data. Expressions include the program groups and program items, the associations, and the color schemes. All three of these expressions are stored in the [programstarter] section of the INI file.

Each of the three expressions is defined by a single entry; items within the group are indicated by curly brackets ({ }). The group name must end with an equal sign (=) pointing to a group within curly brackets. The curly brackets determine how the settings are grouped. The organization used by the INI file is recommended, but not required. If you were to write a section as a single line the format would be:

```
associations={association={program=word.exe extension=DOC}
association={program=editor.com extension=BAS}}
```

Alternatively, you might decide to organize things so that the major entries stand out. An example might be:

```
associations = {
  association={program=word.exe extension=DOC}
  association={program=editor.com extension=BAS}
  }
```

Regardless of which method of organization you use, it is crucial that the curly brackets match. Each time a group of settings is created with a left bracket, it must be closed with a right bracket. The three expressions can appear in any order. They are presented here in order of increasing complexity.

Associations

The *associations* expression contains a group of settings for each extension having an association within the DOS Shell. The association group has two settings within it: program and extension. The format for this expression is:

```
associations =
{
  association =
  {
    program =
    extension =
  }
  association =
  {
    program=
    extension=
  }
}
```

Notice that the expression name is *associations* (plural) and the individual groups of settings are referred as an *association* (singular). You may have as many groups within the expression as you wish. Each association must have both of the individual settings (program and extension). *Program* indicates the full path and name of the application. *Extension* refers to the three characters that identify the file type to be linked to the program. It does not matter how you create associations within the DOS Shell—each extension is given an individual setting subgroup, meaning that a program can be listed in more than one association.

Color Schemes

The individual setting *currentcolor* (at the beginning of the [programstarter] section) holds the name of the active color scheme that must be defined in the *color* expression. The color expression is also part of the [programstarter] section and is broken into *selection* entries that identify a color scheme. The order of the selection entries determines the order they are displayed in the Colors dialog box.

Each selection must have a *title* of one or more words and definitions for the foreground and background windows. The foreground and background sections contain the same list of features and are used to control the active (*foreground*) and inactive (*background*) areas on the screen. The general format for the colors section is:

```
color =
{
  selection =
  {
    title =
    foreground =
    {
      SETTINGS (See table 12.3
    }
    background =
    {
      SETTINGS (See table 12.3
    }
  }
  selection =
  {
    title =
    foreground =
    {
      SETTINGS (See table 12.3.)
    }
    background =
    {
      SETTINGS (See table 12.3.)
    }
  }
}
```

Each color scheme, or *selection*, must include the setting for both the foreground and background for each component listed in table 12.3. As shown in the previous example, the individual settings are grouped by foreground and background within the selection. Each component is assigned a color from the standard sixteen color set. The first set of eight colors include: black, blue, green, red, cyan, magenta, brown and white. Each of these may be modified by the prefix *bright* to obtain the second set of eight (brightblack, brightblue, and so forth) with the exception of brown. There is not a brightbrown. The sixteenth color is brightyellow.

Table 12.3
The Window Components for Color Schemes

Setting	Description
base	The text within each area.
border	The lines dividing the areas. The background setting is not used.
elevator	The background setting controls the color of the box on the scroll bars. The foreground setting is not used.
scroll bar	The foreground setting controls the color of the arrow. The background setting controls the background color of the entire scroll bar region.
drivebox	The drive icon (foreground) and icon bar (background).
driveicon	The drive letter indicator.
highlight	The active area title bar and the item currently under the cursor.
titlebar	The title bar for inactive areas
selection	The currently selected item(s).
menu	The menu bar and pull-down menus.
disabled	An unavailable item on a menu.
accelerator	The accelerator key used to activate the menu or menu item. The background setting is used only in text mode.
dialog	The information on a dialog box.
button	The buttons on a dialog box. The button border is the same color as the button text.
cursor	The location of the cursor. The cursor setting is used only in text mode.
shadow	The shadow which appears behind dialog boxes. The shadow setting is used only in text mode.
alert	Not used.
menubar	Not used.

Unless noted, the foreground setting has the color of the letters displayed against the background color. The settings can be listed in any order and are duplicated for the foreground and background. If you are not going to use a color scheme, you may want to remove it from the initialize file to minimize the amount of unnecessary text.

Program Groups

The final expression is the *group* entry. This entry lists all of the information used to create the Program List. If you are building a complex menu system, or including lengthy help information, it is best to edit this file directly. Like the other expressions, items within the group are defined by a collection of settings. Unlike other expressions, the group expression can be nested (a group expression can contain another group expression).

The group expressions translate to the program groups and program items on the Program List. The first level of the group expression corresponds to the MAIN entry on the Program List (the root or top level). Within this first level, you can add individual programs (using a *program expression*) or additional levels of groups. A group expression must have a title setting and a program expression must contain a command setting and a title setting. The default structure for the DOS Shell Program List (used if the DOSSHELL.INI file is missing or contains no group expression) is:

```
group =
{
  program =
  {
    command = COMMAND
    title =  Command Prompt
  }
}
```

This example defines the MAIN group and adds one program item—the Command Prompt. The DOSSHELL.INI file, installed as part of the DOS 5 environment, adds two programs in the MAIN group (on the first level) and creates a subgroup (Disk Utilities) containing six additional programs. The basic structure is:

```
group = {
  program = {
    command = EDIT %1
    title = Editor
  }
  program = {
```

```
      command = QBASIC %1
      title = MS-DOS QBasic
   }
group = {
title = Disk Utilities
program = {
   command = diskcopy %1
   title = Disk Copy
   }
program = {
   command = backup %1
   title = Backup Fixed Disk
   }
program = {
   command = restore %1
   title = Restore Fixed Disk
   }
program = {
   command = format %1 /q
   title = Quick Format
   }
program = {
   command = format %1
   title = Format
   }
program = {
   command = undelete %1
   title = Undelete
   }
}
```

As with the colors expression, the order of the items within the expression determines the order they are displayed in the program list (in the example, the program items are moved before the group item). To create additional groups, you enter another group expression. Remember, it is the curly brackets (not the indentation) that determine the structure of the list.

In addition to the command and title settings, a group expression can contain the help and password settings. The *help* setting contains the text that is accessed with the F1 key. You can enter the **^m** combination to insert a new line into the text. Because the passwords must be encrypted by the internal scheme used by the DOS Shell, you can't use the password setting to install a new password. You can, however, delete a password by directly editing this setting.

The program expression can contain settings for each of the options on the Program Item Properties dialog box. The settings that can be included are summarized in table 12.4.

If parameters are included in the command setting for a program expression, a *dialog expression* must be used to define the dialog box that prompts for the value to be used for the parameter. The dialog expression can have several entries, but must include the *parameter* setting. This setting forms the link between the symbol used on the command line and the dialog box. The value used must be a parameter setting contained on the command line (parameter = %1).

The other settings are optional and correspond to fields on the Parameter Configuration dialog box. The settings are:

title   The title to be displayed at the top of the dialog box.

info   The text to be displayed within the dialog box.

prompt   The prompt used within the dialog box (appears next to the field where the user will enter text).

default   The value to be used if no information is entered into the dialog box.

Table 12.4
Program Item Properties in DOSSHELL.INI

Setting	Meaning (Values)
Standard Settings:	
directory	Startup Directory
password	See previous discussion about limitations
pause	Pause after exit (enabled/disabled)
shortcut	Application Shortcut Key (as displayed)
shortcutcode	Application Shortcut Key (numeric code)
Advanced Items:	
help	Help information (use ^m for newline)
prevent	Prevent Program Switch
kbrequired	Conventional Memory KB Required
xmsrequired	Extended Memory KB Required

Table 12.4—continued

Setting	Meaning (Values)
xmslimit	Extended Memory KB Limit
alttab	Alt+Tab (enabled/disabled)
altesc	Alt+Esc (enabled/disabled)
ctrlesc	Ctrl+Esc (enabled/disabled)
screenmode	Video Mode (text/graphics)

Taken together, these settings and expressions can be used to create all of the entries in the Program List. The two main expressions, group and program, correspond to the Program Groups and Program Items which are displayed on the Program List. The third expression, dialog, is used when parameters are specified on a command setting. The remaining settings correspond to the fields on the Program Group Properties and Program Item Properties dialog boxes.

Summary

The DOS 5 Shell adds many features to the standard DOS environment. Although it is not a comprehensive Graphical User Interface (GUI), the DOS Shell serves as a complete Graphical Shell and allows the user to perform any required file-, directory-, or program-management tasks.

The DOS Shell provides the user with the option of using the mouse in a fully graphical environment, but also accommodates users who are more comfortable with the keyboard. In addition, there is a comprehensive Help facility available by at the touch of a button (F1).

Unlike Windows, the DOS Shell can run on any DOS platform. In some areas, such as file management, the features provided with the DOS Shell exceed those available within Windows 3. Although the File List is limited to display the contents of only one (Program/File List view or Single File List view) or two (Dual File List view) directories at a time, it enables you to view the entire Directory Tree as well as the contents of the selected directory. In addition, the All Files view permits you to work with all of the files on your system in a listing. The DOS Shell provides a graphical method for performing all of the common file- and directory-management tasks as well as the ability to rename directories, move files, and search for particular files.

Access to programs is provided in several ways, including a Run command that functions like a command prompt, double-clicking on a program name, and opening a document associated with an application. The Program List provides a simple, comprehensive menu system with nested groups and the option of adding on-line help. Moving beyond the limits of the standard DOS environment, the DOS Shell offers task-swapping in which multiple applications can be available for immediate access. Unlike Windows, however, only the current application is actually processing. The others are available but in a suspended state. This is managed through the use of the Task List.

All of these features are presented is in an easy to use, well-integrated environment that can be fully customized. Many of the tasks that formerly required the use of utilities or batch files can now be accomplished as part of the DOS Shell or through a graphical menu system. You are now granted many of the advantages of the Windows environment without having to sacrifice DOS applications. Best of all, these benefits are part of the standard DOS environment.

A   B   C

13

Tapping the Power of Macros and Batch Files

Most DOS users find it impractical to try to remember all the DOS commands, because there are so many of them and so many parameters for each one. Ask a DOS expert what the parameters are for the PRINT command, and he probably will not be able to give you an answer. Experts do, however, understand such parameters and know how to look them up.

Experienced users often make DOS remember things for them, or make DOS carry out complex commands or strings of commands automatically. They do this by using *batch files*.

This chapter shows you what a batch file is and how it works. You start by stringing simple commands together to create a batch file, and then move to advanced techniques using variable parameters, conditional branching, and error checking. Batch files are so easy to create that even if you have no programming experience, you can still take advantage of these useful and powerful tools.

Following the sections on batch files is a detailed discussion of *macros*. You learn how macros differ from batch files, what their advantages and disadvantages are, and even how to integrate macros and batch files to make them work together.

427

Batch File Commands

While you can use virtually any DOS command in a batch file, DOS features eight commands that are specifically meant for use in batch files. These batch-specific commands can be used at the DOS command line, but they generally make more sense and are more useful from within a batch file.

These eight batch-specific commands perform such tasks as executing other batch files, performing conditional testing and program branching, manipulating batch file variables, and generating output on the display. This chapter discusses the following batch-specific commands:

❑ **CALL**. Executes a batch file from within another batch file. The secondary batch file is called a *nested batch file*.

❑ **ECHO**. Generates output, which usually appears on the system's display. The ECHO command is your primary means of passing information to the batch file's user.

❑ **FOR**. A very powerful command that allows successive operations (a *loop*) to be performed on a set of items. The set can consist of file names, commands, and other items.

❑ **GOTO**. The GOTO statement is used in a batch file to cause execution to jump (go to) from one location in the batch file to another.

❑ **IF**. The IF statement is used to test for error conditions, compare two strings, or verify the existence of a file or directory. An IF NOT variation is used to check for the opposite conditions.

❑ **PAUSE**. The PAUSE command does what its name implies. It pauses the batch file's operation to allow for the display of messages and to allow the user to abort the batch file before a critical operation takes place.

❑ **REM**. The simplest of the batch-specific commands, REM simply adds nonexecuting comments to a batch file.

❑ **SHIFT**. The SHIFT command causes batch file variables to be replaced with one another, like shifting the order of information in a stack.

Before you start using these commands, you need an understanding of what batch files and macros are.

Understanding Batch Files and Macros

When you work with DOS commands, you type a command and press Enter, and the command executes. The command may be an internal or external

DOS command, program, or other executable file. But what if you have a sequence of commands that you must execute often? Or one or more complex commands that are difficult to remember (such as the parameters for the PRINT command)? Batch files and macros provide solutions to these problems.

A batch file is nothing more than an ASCII text file containing a list of DOS commands or program file names. The batch file may contain a single command or hundreds. When you type the name of the batch file and press Enter, DOS executes the commands in the batch file one after the other until they have all been executed. When you execute a batch file, you are telling DOS to execute a *batch* of programs or commands. In essence, batch files give you a way to make DOS press its own keys.

Macros are very similar to batch files. The main exception is that macros are stored in memory, while batch files are stored on disk. Although macros have fewer commands and capabilities, they can perform many of the same functions that batch files do.

Finding Uses for Batch Files and Macros

Experienced DOS users are most often the ones who use batch files and macros. They understand batch file and macro concepts and know that batch files in particular can be used to perform complex tasks very easily. Beginning and intermediate users, however, also can benefit from the use of batch files and macros. These two shortcuts can free you from trying to remember cryptic and complex commands, making DOS much easier to use.

Any repetitive task that you execute on a regular basis is a good candidate for a batch file or macro. The mapping of network drive IDs is a good example of a task that should be automated through a batch file. Because the ability to access applications and data on the network often depends on consistent drive mapping (always having a particular program located on a specific logical drive), you should automate the task with a batch file to ensure that everything is set up correctly and consistently from session to session. You could create, for example, a batch file called GONET that loads your network software and shell, maps network drive IDs, and then logs on to the network.

As already mentioned, batch files are especially helpful because they free you from having to remember command parameters. An example is the FORMAT command. If you want to format a 720K, 3 1/2-inch floppy disk in a 1.44M drive, you must issue the FORMAT command with the correct switch. If not, DOS attempts (and fails) to format the disk as a 1.44M disk. To avoid this problem, you can create a batch file or macro called FORMLOW that automatically executes the FORMAT command with the necessary switches. When you have the batch file or macro in place, you never again need to remember the necessary commands or switches.

You probably perform certain tasks each time you start your system. You can automate these tasks through your computer's AUTOEXEC.BAT file.

Examining AUTOEXEC.BAT

As previous chapters discussed, DOS checks for the existence of two files whenever you boot the computer. The first file, CONFIG.SYS, controls system configuration. After DOS executes the statements in CONFIG.SYS, it looks for a file called AUTOEXEC.BAT in the root directory of the boot drive. The commands in AUTOEXEC.BAT (if it exists) are executed automatically by DOS.

AUTOEXEC.BAT is a standard DOS batch file. Like other batch files, it can include commands and program file names, perform conditional branching, set environment variables, and perform any of the tasks that can be carried out by any other batch file. The only thing unique about AUTOEXEC.BAT is its file name—AUTOmatic EXECuting BATch file. Because of its name, this file's contents are executed automatically during system start-up.

Tasks that you perform each time you boot the system should be incorporated into your AUTOEXEC.BAT file. By automating these tasks, you save time and effort, and eliminate the possibility of manual errors. The following is just one example of a possible AUTOEXEC.BAT file. It sets the prompt, path, and an environment variable called TEMP, loads a mouse driver, and issues two commands to set up a workstation's network software:

```
PROMPT $P$G
PATH=C:;C:\DOS;D:\WINDOWS;C:\UTIL
SET TEMP=D:\WINDOWS\TEMP
C:\MOUSE\MOUSE /2
IPX
NET5
```

Your AUTOEXEC.BAT file may be simpler than the one above, or it may be more complex. Whatever the case, use AUTOEXEC.BAT to save time and effort, and eliminate errors.

Before you can customize the AUTOEXEC.BAT file or create other batch files, you must be able to use a text editor. Therefore, the next section describes the MS-DOS Editor.

Using the MS-DOS Editor

Batch files are ASCII files, meaning they contain only ASCII characters, such as letters, numbers, and certain punctuation marks. They are text-only files that do not contain control codes or special characters.

You can use any text editor to create a batch file as long as the editor can save the file in ASCII format. The DOS EDLIN program, for example, can be used to create batch files. Unfortunately, EDLIN is an awkward program to use. DOS offers a much better alternative—the MS-DOS Editor.

This section offers a brief examination of the editor and some of its features. It is not meant to be a complete overview, but it does explain the editor's commands that relate to batch file creation. For a more detailed look at the MS-DOS Editor, refer to the *MS-DOS User's Guide and Reference.*

Running the MS-DOS Editor

The MS-DOS Editor is easy to start. The editor's executable file—EDIT.COM— is located in the directory containing the rest of the DOS files (usually C:\DOS). If the DOS directory is on the system path or if C:\DOS is the current directory, simply type the following command and press Enter to start the editor:

```
EDIT
```

When the editor starts, you see the screen shown in figure 13.1.

Note that the directory containing QBASIC.EXE must also be on the path for the MS-DOS Editor to run. If it is not, or the file QBASIC.EXE no longer exists, you cannot run the editor.

The Editor's Menus

The MS-DOS Editor uses a standard, *SAA-compliant* menu. SAA is an acronym for System Application Architecture, which is a standard developed by IBM for standardization of application interfaces. Many applications for the DOS, Windows, and OS/2 environments use a common program menu structure defined by the SAA standard. They are characterized by drop-down menus that typically include menus called File, Edit, and Help, to name but a few. The SAA standard also specifies the location of the menus—the File menu, for example, is always the left-most option in an SAA-compliant menu.

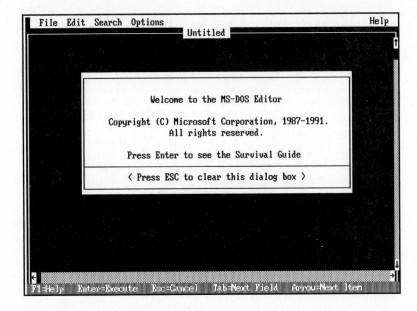

Figure 13.1:
The MS-DOS Editor's start-up screen.

To access the editor's menus, press Alt to activate the editor's menu bar. The menu bar contains five menu options—File, Edit, Search, Options, and Help. When you press Alt, the first letter of each option is highlighted. To select a menu option, simply press the highlighted letter of the appropriate command. A menu drops down that displays the commands available from the current menu. To select an option from the drop-down menu, press the highlighted letter of the desired command or use the keyboard cursor keys to highlight the command, then press Enter.

Optionally, you can use a mouse to access the editor's menus. Place the mouse pointer on the desired menu and press the select button (left button). When the corresponding menu drops down, use the mouse pointer to select the command from the menu.

The File Menu

The editor's File menu contains commands for opening and saving files, printing, and exiting from the editor. The File menu contains the following commands:

❏ **New**. Enables you to edit a new file

❏ **Open**. Opens an existing file

❏ **Save**. Saves the file, using the current file name

❏ **Save As**. Saves the file, using a new name

❏ **Print**. Prints the file

❏ **Exit**. Exits from the editor

Many of the editor's commands use *dialog boxes* to interact with the user. A dialog box is a rectangular menu containing information or data fields. The File Open dialog box, shown in figure 13.2, is a typical dialog box. It appears when you select the Open command from the editor's File menu.

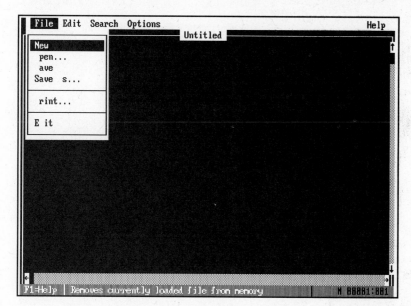

Figure 13.2:
The MS-DOS Editor's File Open dialog box.

Using the MS-DOS Editor's Dialog Boxes

Take this chance to practice using the editor's dialog boxes. The following steps use the File Open dialog box to open your system's AUTOEXEC.BAT file:

1. Type **EDIT** to run the MS-DOS Editor.
2. Press Esc to clear the start-up dialog box.
3. Press Alt, F, O to open the File Open dialog box.
4. Type **C:\AUTOEXEC.BAT** and press Enter.

Your system's AUTOEXEC.BAT file loads into the editor and displays on-screen. Instead of using the editor's menu to load the file, you also can specify the name of the file when you invoke the editor, as follows:

```
EDIT C:\AUTOEXEC.BAT
```

Take the opportunity now to save a backup of your AUTOEXEC.BAT file. If your AUTOEXEC.BAT file becomes corrupted for some reason, you will still have a duplicate on the hard disk that can be copied to AUTOEXEC.BAT.

1. Select Alt, F, A to open the Save As dialog box.
2. Type **AUTOEXEC.MAX** and press Enter.

Now that your AUTOEXEC.BAT file is safely backed up, the next section will familiarize you with the Editor's Edit commands.

Using the Edit Menu

The Edit menu provides commands that let you copy, move, and delete text within a file. This menu is particularly useful for duplicating text without re-typing it. The Edit menu contains the following commands:

❏ **Cut**. Removes selected text from the file and places it in a temporary storage buffer.

❏ **Copy**. Copies selected text to the buffer. You then can paste the text from the buffer into another part of the file.

❏ **Paste**. Inserts text from the buffer that has previously been cut or copied.

❏ **Clear**. Like the Cut option, Clear removes selected text from the file, but does not save it in the buffer.

To get a little practice using the Edit menu, move the first line of your AUTOEXEC.BAT file to the bottom of the file. Take the following steps:

1. Place the cursor at the beginning of the first line.
2. Press Shift-End.
3. Select Alt, E, T to cut the highlighted text to the buffer.
4. Place the cursor at the bottom of the file.
5. Select Alt, E, P to paste the text onto the last line.

You probably use the File and Edit menus the most when creating and editing batch files. For information on using the rest of the Editor's menus, see the *MS-DOS User's Guide and Reference*.

Now that you are familiar with the basic features of the MS-DOS Editor, you are ready to begin creating batch files.

Creating Batch Files

A batch file is a simple thing to create. You just decide what function the batch file should perform, determine the correct commands that must be issued to perform the task, then place the commands (one after the other) in a text file. The text file becomes the batch file.

Suppose that you want to create a simple batch file that performs a directory listing of the root directory of drive C, the \DOS directory on drive C, and any files in the root directory of drive D that do not have file extensions (such as subdirectories). Enter the following commands in the editor and save the file as LIST.BAT:

```
DIR C:\
DIR C:\DOS
DIR D:\*.
```

Select AIT, F, A and enter **LIST.BAT** as the file name. When you have saved the file, exit from the editor.

Running a Batch File

DOS recognizes three types of files as being executable files; that is, files that you can run as programs simply by typing their name at the DOS prompt. The first two, COM and EXE files, you are probably already familiar with from previous chapters. DOS knows how to read COM and EXE files and execute them appropriately. DOS also recognizes files with a BAT extension as batch files. When you type the name of a batch file at the DOS command line and press Enter, the command interpreter (COMMAND.COM) reads the lines in the batch file and executes them one at a time.

To test the LIST.BAT batch file created in the previous section, type the following and press Enter:

```
LIST
```

The batch file executes, and each line of it appears on-screen as it is executed. The batch file performs a directory listing of C:\, then C:\DOS, and finally, all files in the root directory of drive D that have no file extension. The directory listings scroll up the screen without stopping.

Stopping a Batch File

The LIST.BAT batch file is a good example of a batch file that runs out of control. It displays directory listings without giving you time to view them.

There are commands you can place in a batch file to make it pause at appropriate times; these commands are discussed a little later in the chapter.

To terminate a batch file while it is executing, press Ctrl-C. DOS displays the following prompt:

```
Terminate batch job (Y/N)?
```

Press **Y** to terminate the batch program without performing any additional tasks. Press **N** to allow the batch program to continue working. If you press any other key, DOS displays the prompt again.

Now that you know how to create, start, and stop batch files, you can go on to learn how to add greater power to your batch files by using batch subcommands.

Using Batch Subcommands

As you have learned in previous chapters, DOS includes internal and external commands, device drivers, and commands specific to CONFIG.SYS. DOS also includes a handful of commands that are reserved exclusively for use in batch files. These batch file commands are often called *batch subcommands*. This section shows you what some of these subcommands are and how to implement them in your batch files. The first of these subcommands, ECHO, enables you to place messages in a batch file; the batch file displays the messages on-screen as it executes.

Using ECHO to Display Messages

By adding features that make a batch file interactive with the user, you make the batch file considerably more powerful. One of the necessities for making a program interactive is to provide some means of communicating instructions and messages to the user. DOS provides the ECHO command for displaying messages from an executing batch file.

You can use ECHO to turn off the echoing (display) of commands to the prompt line. Normally, commands in a batch file display as the lines are executed. In the LIST.BAT file, for example, each of the three DIR commands displays as it executes, although the commands may flash by too quickly to be read.

By turning off ECHO, you prevent those commands from appearing on-screen. If the commands in a batch file do not generate any output, turning ECHO off at the beginning of the batch file causes the batch file to execute "silently." Its commands execute, but nothing happens on-screen while it works.

To turn off command echoing, add the following command to the batch file where you want echoing to stop:

```
ECHO OFF
```

As commands execute, they no longer show up on-screen. The first ECHO OFF statement, however, *does* display (echoing does not stop until *after* the ECHO OFF statement has been executed). To prevent this statement from displaying, place an @ symbol in front of the command, like this:

```
@ECHO OFF
```

To turn echoing of commands back on when the batch file has performed its task, issue the ECHO command again, but this time to turn ECHO on:

```
ECHO ON
```

Because echoing is not enabled until *after* the ECHO ON statement, there is no need to place the @ symbol in front the ECHO ON statement—ECHO is off when it is executed, so the ECHO ON does not display.

As mentioned already, you also can use ECHO to display messages from within the batch file as it executes. To display a message, simply use the ECHO command followed by the message. The following is a fragment from a batch file that uses the ECHO command:

```
@ECHO OFF
ECHO Welcome to Maximizing DOS 5.0
ECHO     and
ECHO Tapping the Power of Batch Files and Macros
ECHO ON
```

When this batch file executes, it displays the following output:

```
Welcome to Maximizing DOS 5.0
    and
Tapping the Power of Batch Files and Macros
```

If you omit the first line (@ECHO OFF), the commands display, followed by the result of the command. This results in a double line, as follows:

```
C:\>ECHO Welcome to Maximizing DOS 5.0
Welcome to Maximizing DOS 5.0
C:\>ECHO  and
        and
C:\>ECHO Tapping the Power of Batch Files and Macros
Tapping the Power of Batch Files and Macros
```

Remember that to make the messages display properly, you must turn ECHO off.

ECHOing Blank Lines

ECHO also can be used to skip a line in a batch file. This is useful if you want to put some space between one message and the next, or between a message and a command that will display on the screen.

You cannot, however, simply use the ECHO command without a message. ECHO, when used by itself, displays the status of command echoing. If ECHO has previously been turned off, for example, issuing the ECHO command by itself results in the following:

```
ECHO
ECHO is off
```

You can use a single character, such as a period, as the echoed message, which comes very close to having a blank line. If you want a truly blank line, however, you must use DOS' invisible character—ASCII 255.

To create a blank line using ECHO, type the ECHO command followed by a space, then press Alt-255 (use the numeric keypad). The cursor jumps one character to the right as the ASCII 255 character is inserted in the line. You are not be able to see it, however, because ASCII 255 has no graphic representation. The following example outputs two blank lines by echoing ASCII 255 to the display in two different ECHO commands:

```
ECHO <Alt,255>
ECHO <Alt,255>
```

When DOS executes the ECHO statement, it prints an ASCII 255 to the display and drops down to the next line, ready to execute the next statement. Because the ASCII 255 is invisible, you get the effect of a blank line.

Remember that to enter the ASCII 255 character, you must press and hold the Alt key, then press 255 on the numeric keypad. When you release the Alt key, the character is inserted in the line.

Making Noise with ECHO

At times it is useful to signal a user when some type of action needs to be taken while a batch file is executing. If you need to get the user's attention, you can have DOS sound the compter's bell. You may want to use the bell when the user is supposed to replace diskettes during a copy or backup, when the batch file pauses, or after a particularly long command sequence during which the user may have stepped away from the system.

To use the bell in a batch file, issue the ECHO command with a Ctrl-G. Each Ctrl-G sounds the bell once. To sound the bell three times, use the following command:

```
ECHO ^G^G^G
```

Note that for the Ctrl-G to function properly, you must enter it by holding down Ctrl while you press G. If you type a caret (^) followed by a G, DOS simply echos the characters ^G to the screen; it does not sound the bell.

You also can use the ECHO command to send directives to ANSI.SYS. These ECHO commands can be used to position the cursor on-screen, change screen color, and perform the same types of screen manipulation functions discussed in Chapter 11. Echoing to ANSI.SYS through a batch file is discussed in detail later in this chapter.

Using PAUSE To Pause a Batch File

Recall earlier in the chapter that you can suspend or terminate a batch file by pressing Ctrl-C. In some cases, Ctrl-S also suspends a batch file's execution, and pressing the space bar restarts it. Both of these methods, however, are haphazard. Neither provides a sure way of pausing the batch file at a specific point, and both require that the user stop the batch file, instead of the batch file stopping itself.

The PAUSE command can pause an executing batch file. PAUSE, however, serves a dual purpose—it also displays a message. When used by itself, PAUSE displays a standard message:

```
Press any key to continue . . .
```

DOS then waits for the user to press a key. When a key has been pressed, the batch file continues executing. Therefore, PAUSE offers a means of pausing the batch file's execution at a specific line.

You can use PAUSE to display an optional message if ECHO is on. To display your own message with PAUSE, simply include the message after the command, as follows:

```
PAUSE When you are ready to continue, please press a key.
```

When the PAUSE statement executes, the new message is displayed first, followed by the standard `Press any key to continue . . .` message. ECHO must be on for the optional message to display, which means that the PAUSE command will be printed on-screen, also. Because the standard message is always displayed, you may want to leave ECHO off and use the standard PAUSE message along with an echoed statement, as follows:

```
ECHO When you are ready to go on,
PAUSE
```

When DOS executes the two statements, the output looks like this:

```
When you are ready to go on,
Press any key to continue . . .
```

You can elimininate the PAUSE message altogether. That way, your ECHO message can specify what action to take, and the PAUSE command simply pauses and waits for a key to be pressed. To use PAUSE without displaying its message, redirect the output of the PAUSE command to the DOS NUL device, as follows:

```
ECHO Press Ctrl-C to exit, or any other key to continue.
PAUSE>NUL
```

DOS responds to these two commands by displaying the ECHO message, but does not display the Press any key to continue . . . message:

```
Press Ctrl-C to exit, or any other key to continue.
```

Redirecting output to the NUL device is like dropping it into a bottomless pit. As long as you do not need the output, NUL is a good way to dispose of it cleanly.

Now that you are familiar with a few batch file subcommands, combine them with the FORMAT command to create a batch file for formatting a floppy disk.

Using a Batch File To Format a 720K Diskette

The following batch file, called FORM720.BAT, uses the FORMAT, ECHO, and PAUSE commands to format a 3 1/2-inch floppy disk in drive B in 720K format:

```
@ECHO OFF
ECHO Insert a diskette in drive B:.
ECHO When you are ready to format the diskette,
PAUSE
ECHO !!! About to FORMAT the diskette in drive B: !!!
ECHO Press Ctrl-C to abort, or
PAUSE
FORMAT B: /F:720
```

You can see from the previous batch file that PAUSE is not only useful, but also very necessary for many batch files. The PAUSE command adds a layer of security to the FORMAT command in this case, pausing the batch file before FORMAT is executed and giving the user the option of aborting before FORMAT is invoked. If PAUSE were not used in this batch file, the disk in drive B would be formatted immediately without any chance of aborting the FORMAT before any data on the disk is potentially lost.

Using REM To Add Comments to a Batch File

A good programmer sprinkles comments liberally throughout a program. These comments, which do not function as part of the final program, serve two primary purposes: they explain the function of the code to other programmers, but more important, they explain the code to the *programmer writing the code*. After all, programs are often extremely complex, and it is very easy to forget what a section of code does, and even easier to forget how it works, even if you wrote the code. By placing comments in the program, the programmer can skim over his "notes" right in the code and see at a glance what each particular section of code does.

The same can be true for batch files—particularly very complex ones. It makes sense, then, to add comments in batch files just as you would in a C or Pascal program. The batch command REM is used for just that purpose.

REM is one of the easiest commands to use. You simply type **REM**, followed by a comment. When DOS finds an REM statement in a batch file it is executing, it ignores the entire line. Now you can add some remarks to the FORM720.BAT file, and change the ECHO and PAUSE commands to redirect the PAUSE output to NUL:

```
@ECHO OFF
REM  *** Have the user insert disk and press a key: ***
REM  **************************************************
ECHO Insert a diskette in drive B:.
ECHO When you are ready to format the diskette,
ECHO Press the Enter key.
PAUSE>NUL
REM  **************************************************
REM
REM  *** Have the user verify the FORMAT, or abort: ***
REM  **************************************************
ECHO !!! About to FORMAT the diskette in drive B: !!!
ECHO Press Ctrl-C to abort, or any other key to continue.
PAUSE>NUL
FORMAT B: /F:720
REM  **************************************************
```

Although the remarks in the new FORM720.BAT file add quite a few lines, they make it much easier to follow the logic and flow of the batch file. The file now also contains REM statements without a comment, to provide a space between lines for readability. If you want to add blank lines without comments, you can do so simply by inserting a blank line with the Enter key. DOS ignores blank lines when it processes batch files.

There is one thing to be aware of when using REM. If you have not previously issued the ECHO OFF statement in the batch file, the REM line is displayed on-screen, much like an ECHO command. If ECHO has been turned off, however, the remarks do not appear on-screen.

Passing Information to Batch Files through Replaceable Parameters

Many times, batch files can function on their own, without any additional input or direction from the user. At other times, however, the user needs to pass information to the batch file. The batch file then can use that information when it processes its commands.

Take the FORM720.BAT file, for example. It only formats a 3 1/2-inch, 720K diskette in drive B. Adding the ability to format either drive A or B in any of the available formats would make the batch file much more useful. To make the batch file work properly, you enable the user to specify the drive to format and the disk capacity in bytes. DOS lets you use *replaceable parameters* in batch files for just such purposes.

Using Replaceable Parameters in Batch Files

DOS allows a batch file to use up to ten parameters that can be replaced in the batch file when it is executed. These parameters are included on the command line when the batch file is invoked, and are passed to the batch file based on their location on the command line.

Assume that you have created a batch file called PREPDISK.BAT, which you use to format disks in drives A and B, making available all of the possible formats. You pass the drive ID and capacity to the batch file by including them on the command line:

```
PREPDISK B: 720
```

But what represents the parameters in the file, and why are they called *replaceable* parameters? Examine the following PREPDISK.BAT file to find out:

```
@ECHO OFF
REM  *** Display the drive and format entered by user: ***
REM  ****************************************************
ECHO <Alt,255>
ECHO You have asked %0 to format a diskette in drive %1
ECHO with a capacity of %2 bytes.
ECHO <Alt,255>
ECHO When you are ready to format the diskette,
ECHO press the Enter key.
PAUSE>NUL
ECHO <Alt,255>
REM  ****************************************************
REM
REM  *** Have the user verify the FORMAT, or abort: ***
REM  ****************************************************
ECHO !!! About to FORMAT the diskette in drive %1 !!!
ECHO Press Ctrl-C to abort, or any other key to format
ECHO the diskette in drive %1.
PAUSE>NUL
FORMAT %1 /F:%2
REM  ****************************************************
```

Note the *%n* variables (where *n* represents a number) in many of the batch file's program lines. These are replaceable parameters. Their order, or the value of *n*, corresponds to the location of the parameter typed on the command line. The following illustrates the position of available parameters by showing a sample use of the PREPDISK batch file with two parameters:

```
PREPDISK   B:    720
%0         %1    %2
```

As you can see, %0 is the first entry on the line (the PREPDISK command), %1 is the first command parameter, and %2 is the second command parameter. If the batch file supported more than two parameters (not including %0), you could place each parameter on the command line and have DOS replace them in the batch file at the appropriate time. Therefore, valid parameters are %0 through %9.

To see how the batch file works, simply plug in the appropriate parameters wherever you see a corresponding %n value. For example, type the following to see how PREPDISK.BAT works:

```
PREPDISK B: 1440
```

PREPDISK.BAT responds with:

```
C:\DOS>PREPDISK B: 1440
You have asked PREPDISK to format a diskette in drive B:
with a capacity of 1440 bytes.
When you are ready to format the diskette,
press the Enter key.
!!! About to FORMAT the diskette in drive B: !!!
Press Ctrl-C to abort, or any other key to format
the diskette in drive B:.
Insert new diskette for drive B:
and press ENTER when ready...
C:\DOS>
```

Now that you are familiar with parameters, you can create a more useful batch to move files from one drive/directory to another. The batch file works by first copying the specified files, then deleting the originals.

Creating a MOVE Command for DOS

The following is the listing for the MOVE.BAT file:

```
@ECHO OFF
REM  *** This batch file moves a file from one directory
REM  *** to another by copying it, then deleting
REM  *** the original. Multiple files can be moved.
ECHO <Alt,255>
ECHO %0 is preparing to move the file(s) %1 to the
ECHO %2 directory.
ECHO <Alt,255>
ECHO The original file, %1, will be erased.
ECHO Press Ctrl-C to abort the move, or
PAUSE
ECHO Moving %1 to %2
COPY %1 %2
ERASE %1
```

You can see that the batch file simply takes the first parameter (%1) and copies it to the directory represented by %2. It then erases the file represented by %1. All that is happening is DOS is filling in the blanks whenever it finds the %n variable.

As is, however, this MOVE.BAT file is a dangerous command. It does not verify that the source file exists, nor does it verify that the destination directory exists. If the COPY fails, the ERASE command still takes place; instead of moving the file, routine simply erases it.

To make MOVE.BAT foolproof, you must add some error checking to it. Error checking is covered in detail later in this chapter, where you learn how to make MOVE.BAT foolproof. First, examine some other ways you can use replaceable parameters in batch files.

Using More than Ten Parameters—the SHIFT Command

Generally, batch files use two to three parameters at most. Rarely is a batch file so complex that it uses all nine possible variables (disregarding the batch file name, which is stored in %0). DOS does, however, provide for the possibility of more than nine parameters with the SHIFT command.

SHIFT works by shifting the values of the batch file parameters one space to the left. In other words, SHIFT throws out the value of %0 and places the value of %1 in %0. It places the value of %2 in %1, and so on. If there are ten or more parameters specified on the command line, the tenth parameter is stored in %9 after the SHIFT command is executed. The values are just "bumped" down the line one space every time the SHIFT command is executed.

To see how the SHIFT command works, try creating and running the following SHIFTIT.BAT batch file:

```
@ECHO OFF
ECHO %%0  %%1  %%2  %%3
ECHO Current variable values are:  %0 %1 %2 %3
SHIFT
ECHO   SHIFTed variables are now:  %0 %1 %2 %2
```

Next, type the SHIFTIT command and pass it three command-line parameters. DOS responds as follows:

```
C:\DOS>SHIFTIT one two three
  %0  %1  %2  %3
Current variable values are: SHFITIT one two three
SHIFTed variables are now: one two three three
```

You can see from this example that the SHIFT command simply moves the value of each parameter to the left. Also, notice that the last value, %3, retains its original value because there is nothing to its right to SHIFT into its place.

Also notice that the second line includes %%0, %%1, and so on. To display a variable name, such as %1, without having it expanded to display the value, use a double percent sign (%%) in front of the character, rather than a single percent sign.

The SHIFT command is particularly useful in batch files that use looping operations to perform a repetitive task on a number of possible values. The batch file can be passed a large string of parameters, and the SHIFT command can SHIFT them into position as needed. Examples of loop structures are discussed later in this chapter.

Using Environment Variables as Named Parameters

You learned in earlier chapters that DOS uses environment variables for a number of tasks. Environment variables store the PATH string, the locations of temporary directories, memory management variables for programs, and many other pieces of information that DOS and applications can use when they execute.

You can pass environment variables to a batch file just as you would a replaceable command-line parameter. To do so, simply enclose the environment variable name by two % symbols. For example, assume that you have the following AUTOEXEC.BAT file:

```
PROMPT=$P$G
IPX
NET5
WORDDIR=F:\APPS\WORD
DOCSDIR=\MYDOCS
```

Further, assume that somewhere in your network start-up routine you map the network directory containing the program WORD to logical drive ID F:. The following batch file—called WORD.BAT—uses the value of WORDDIR automatically to locate the WORD program's executable file, and the DOCSDIR as the directory in which to place document files (the start-up directory for WORD):

```
@ECHO OFF
ECHO Changing to the %DOCSDIR% directory and running
ECHO WORD from the %WORDDIR% directory . . .
REM
REM   Next line makes drive C active:
C:
REM   Next line changes to the DOCSDIR directory:
CD %DOCSDIR%
REM   Next line executes WORD from the WORDDIR directory:
ECHO ON
%WORDDIR%\WORD.EXE
```

The batch file generates the following output:

```
C:\DOS>WORD
Changing to the C:\MYDOCS directory and running
WORD from the F:\APPS\WORD directory . . .
C:\MYDOCS>F:\APPS\WORD\WORD.EXE
```

You can use environment variables to insert drive IDs, passwords, directories, and other items of information into a batch file. The capability to integrate environment variables into batch files is particularly useful on a networked system. Each user's AUTOEXEC.BAT file can set a group of common environment variables according to the user's needs, then a single batch file can be invoked by all users regardless of the value of the environment settings. The batch file acts as a template, and the environment variables fill in that template.

Performing Conditional Branching and Error Checking

Most programs are not executed linearly. In other words, execution does not start at the first line of the program and continue through to the last line. Program flow jumps around within the program as the user interacts with it by selecting commands and options, and as error conditions are generated.

This "jumping around" in the program is called *conditional branching* because the program *branches* to a new section of the program, based on a given set of *conditions* or as conditions change while the program is running. Those conditions might include the occurrence of errors, or *error conditions*. If a particular error occurs, for example, the program branches to a specific section of code to handle the error. The process of detecting error conditions is called *error checking*.

Batch files can implement conditional branching and error checking. They do this using the CALL, GOTO, IF, IF NOT, and FOR commands. The following sections describe these commands in detail.

Using GOTO To Jump Around

The GOTO command, or a command very similar to it, is present in nearly every programming language. GOTO simply causes program execution to jump to ("go to") a specific section of program code. The use of GOTO statements is frowned on in many programming languages, because in those languages the use of GOTO represents poor program logic and program flow. These languages include much more powerful and useful commands for directing program flow.

In batch files, however, GOTO is perfectly acceptable. In fact, GOTO represents the only way you can branch from one place to another in a batch file (which is, obviously, why it is acceptable).

Some programming languages, such as BASIC, use program line numbers to determine where to jump to when the GOTO command is issued. The command GOTO 100 in a BASIC program, for example, instructs the program to jump immediately to program line 100 and begin executing the code at that location. Other languages use labels to label sections of the program. The GOTO command is then used to jump to a labeled section. The batch file GOTO command also uses labels.

Labeling Batch File Sections

Complex batch files are broken into sections, each of which performs a certain function. The sections are labeled, providing the GOTO command a means by which it can jump from one section to another. To label a section of a batch program, include the label name preceded by a colon on the line above the section:

```
:START
REM  This section of the program is labeled START.
ECHO Starting the task...
:MIDDLE
REM  This section performs another group of tasks.
ECHO Working on another task....
:FINISH
REM  This section finishes execution
ECHO Cleaning up for exit...
:END
REM  This section does nothing. It provides a label to jump
REM  to in case of an error. Because it is at the end of
REM  the batch file, jumping to :END will end the batch
REM  file without executing any more commands.
```

GOTO is most often used with the IF and IF NOT statements to jump to a specific label when a particular condition occurs. Before looking at the IF

command, however, you should note that the following program contains a
simple but handy use for GOTO—making multiple duplicates of a disk:

```
@ECHO OFF
:START
ECHO Place diskette in drive %1 and press return.
PAUSE>NUL
MKDIR %1\MYAPP
COPY C:\MYAPP\*.* %1\MYAPP
ECHO Files have been copied.
GOTO :START
```

This example creates a loop that keeps the batch file executing until the user
presses Ctrl-C. If DOS finds a labeled line before it has been told to GOTO a
given label, it ignores the label and executes the statement after it. When it
processes a GOTO command, DOS starts at the beginning of the batch file
and begins searching for a label that matches the one specified with the
GOTO command. When it finds the appropriate label, it resumes executing
the batch file on the line directly following the label.

Label names can be longer than eight characters, but only the first eight are
recognized. DOS recognizes the label :THIS_IS_A_LABEL, for example, as
THIS_IS_. Therefore, DOS would consider the labels THIS_IS_A_LABEL and
THIS_IS_A_NEUTRON_DETECTOR to be the same. Whichever label appears
first in the batch file is the one that would be executed following either of the
next two commands:

```
GOTO THIS_IS_A_LABEL
GOTO THIS_IS_A_NEUTRON_DETECTOR
```

This means that the last label may never be executed unless the batch file
branches to a line of code above it, and continues linearly through the file
until it comes to the duplicated label. It will never specifically branch to the
duplicated label using a GOTO statement.

Now that you understand how labels and the GOTO command work, examine
a more common use for GOTO—error checking.

Error Checking in Batch Files

Simple batch files can often operate without performing any type of error
checking. The statements in the file are executed one after the other regardless of the outcome of each line. It is important in many cases, however, for
the batch file to perform some form of checking to make sure the batch file is
not improperly destroying data or doing something else unexpected. The

MOVE.BAT file listed previously in the chapter is a prime example of a batch file that should include error checking.

You perform error checking in batch files primarily by checking for the existence or nonexistence of variables, directories, files, and other bits of information. Depending on whether the checked data exists, you branch to an appropriate place in the batch file using the GOTO command. *Branching* means you jump to a specific location in the batch file and execute the statements at the new location. In the case of a terminal failure (an error preventing the batch file from continuing), you jump to the end of the batch file to terminate it without executing any more statements (as in the :END section in a previous batch file).

The primary error-checking tool in batch files is the IF subcommand. The IF statement can be used directly from the command line, but it is more useful inside a batch file. There are three forms for the IF statement, each of which is shown in the following example:

```
IF ERRORLEVEL number command
    IF ERRORLEVEL 1 GOTO FAIL
IF string1==string2 command
    IF %1=="Hello" ECHO Hello to you, too!
IF EXIST filename command
    IF EXIST *.BAK ERASE *.BAK
```

These three listed forms verify whether the specified condition is true. If it is, the command following the IF statement is executed. In addition, a NOT modifier can be used with any IF statement, as follows:

```
IF NOT ERRORLEVEL number command
IF NOT string1==string2 command
IF NOT EXIST filename command
```

Instead of checking the condition to see if it is true, using IF NOT checks to see if the condition is *NOT* true. If the conditions is not true, the command following the IF NOT statement is executed.

Using IF ERRORLEVEL

A few DOS commands and many programs generate exit codes when they terminate. The exit code is a numeric value that represents a particular condition, which often represents a specific error. Usually, an exit code of 0 means that the command or program terminated normally without errors. Any other value usually indicates that an error occurred.

The XCOPY command is one DOS command that generates exit codes when it exits. XCOPY uses the following exit codes:

Code	Meaning
0	Files were copied without error.
1	No files were found.
2	User pressed Ctrl-C to terminate.
4	Initialization error. Not enough memory or disk space, invalid drive, or invalid command syntax.
5	Disk write error.

The following sample batch file tests the exit code from an XCOPY command and echoes an appropriate message:

```
XCOPY A: B: /S
IF NOT ERRORLEVEL 0 GOTO OOPS.
ECHO XCOPY functioned without any errors.
GOTO :END
REM  The previous two lines execute only if ERRORLEVEL=0
:OOPS
IF ERRORLEVEL 1 ECHO No files found on drive %1.
IF ERRORLEVEL 2 ECHO You pressed Control+C to cancel XCOPY.
IF ERRORLEVEL 4 ECHO An initialization error occurred.
IF ERRORLEVEL 5 ECHO Could not write to drive %2.
:END
```

Most DOS commands do not return exit codes. The following is a list of the few DOS commands that *do* return an exit code:

BACKUP	GRAFTABL	RESTORE
DISKCOMP	KEYB	SETVER
DISKCOPY	REPLACE	XCOPY
FORMAT		

You will see how exit codes can be incorporated in the PREPDISK.BAT file a little later in this chapter. First, examine a few other uses for the IF command.

Using IF string1==string2

Another use for the IF command is to check two variables or strings to see if they match each other (or if they do *not* match). This might include, for example, checking the value of a variable to see if it matches a certain drive letter. The following lines, for example, could be added to the PREPDISK.BAT file discussed earlier in the chapter:

```
IF %1=="C:" GOTO NOFORMAT
FORMAT %1 /F:%2
GOTO END
:NOFORMAT
ECHO You cannot format drive C:!!!!!!
ECHO Exiting without formatting...
:END
```

Typing the following command on the PREPDISK.BAT command line results in the batch file generating the error message shown in the ECHO statement listed previously:

```
PREPDISK C: 720
```

The %1 parameter, which in this case assumes the value C:, is compared with "C:" to see if they match. If they do match, the IF statement causes the error message to be echoed, and the next line directs batch execution to the :END label.

This form of the IF statement is most often used to evaluate batch file parameters to determine a course of action. It can be used , for example, to determine which type of diskette is to be formatted, and use that determination to branch to the appropriate section in the batch file.

But what if the user forgets to enter a parameter? The batch file will still attempt to perform its function, even with the necessary parameter missing. It is a good practice, then, to make sure that the user has not omitted a parameter. To do that, first compare the parameter to a null string, as follows:

```
IF "%2"=="" GOTO NOFORMAT
... <other batch file commands>
:NOFORMAT
ECHO You did not specify a disk format to use for
ECHO drive %1. You must specify the disk type, such
ECHO as PREPDISK B: 720.
```

The value of %2 is compared with " ", which represents a null string (nothing is inside the quotation marks). If the user forgets to provide the %2 parameter, DOS assumes a null value. Notice that in the first line of the preceding partial batch file, %2 is in quotation marks. If the quotation marks are omitted and the parameter is not entered on the command line (%2 is null), the IF statement evaluates as follows:

```
IF =="" GOTO NOFORMAT
```

This generates a syntax error because a value for *string1* must be provided, even if it is null (" "). Adding the quotation marks around the %2 parameter would make the IF statement evaluate as follows (assuming that no %2 parameter was specified):

```
IF ""=="" GOTO NOFORMAT
```

In this case, the statement evaluates true because the two NULs equal each other.

Finishing the PREPDISK.BAT File

You now know enough batch commands to put together a decent PREPDISK.BAT file that performs error checking, prevents the user from formatting the hard drive, and is relatively foolproof. The following is a commented listing for PREPDISK.BAT:

```
@ECHO OFF
REM *************************************************************
REM  Make sure the user has entered a drive ID. If a drive ID
REM  has been entered, jump to the CHK_lowA label to verify that
REM  the drive ID is valid.
IF NOT "%1"=="" GOTO CHK_lowA
ECHO You must specify a drive ID for PREPDISK.
GOTO :END
REM *************************************************************
REM  Check to make sure the user has asked to format either
REM   drive A: or B: (must check for a: and A:, as well as
REM   b: and B:, since IF is case sensitive.
REM
REM  ****  Check for a:
:CHK_lowA
IF NOT %1==a: GOTO CHK_upA
REM  If %1 is a:, check the %2 parameter for correct form factor
REM   by jumping to the CHK_FMAT label.
GOTO CHK_FMAT
REM
REM  ****  Check for A:
:CHK_upA
IF NOT %1==A: GOTO CHK_lowB
GOTO CHK_FMAT
REM
REM  ****  Check for b:
:CHK_lowB
IF NOT %1==b: GOTO CHK_upB
```

```
GOTO CHK_FMAT
REM
REM  ****  Check for B:
:CHK_upB
IF NOT %1==B: GOTO WRONG_ID
REM  The previous IF was the last chance. %1 has been checked
REM  to see if it is equal to a:, A:, b:, and B:.
REM  If %1 was not B:, execution transfers to the WRONG_ID label.
REM  *************************************************************
:CHK_FMAT
REM
REM  First, check to make sure a form factor parameter was entered.
IF NOT "%2"=="" GOTO FORM_OK
ECHO You must enter a form factor for PREPDISK, such as:
ECHO      PREPDISK B: 1.44    or   PREPDISK B: 1440
GOTO END
REM  *************************************************************
:FORM_OK
REM
REM  Next, check the byte value entered as %2 to verify the
REM  form factor for the format command. If the value is correct,
REM  jump to the GOFORMAT label to format the diskette. Note that
REM  only the 360K, 720K, 1.2Mb, 1.44Mb, and 2.88Mb form factors
REM  are supported by this batch file. Also, note that not all of
REM  the possible values for the form factor parameter are supported
REM  (such as the 720kb or 1.44mb values).
REM
IF %2==360 GOTO GOFORMAT
IF %2==720 GOTO GOFORMAT
IF %2==1200 GOTO GOFORMAT
IF %2==1.2 GOTO GOFORMAT
IF %2==1440 GOTO GOFORMAT
IF %2==1.44 GOTO GOFORMAT
IF %2==2880 GOTO GOFORMAT
IF %2==2.88 GOTO GOFORMAT
REM  *************************************************************
REM  The next label is accessed if the %2 form factor parameter
REM  does not match one of the accepted values.
REM
:DROPOUT
ECHO You have entered a form factor of %2, which is either not
ECHO recognized or not supported. Please verify the value, then
ECHO enter it in the form nnnn or n.nn (1440 or 1.44).
GOTO :END
REM  *************************************************************
REM  If %1 and %2 were valid parameters, attempt to format the disk.
REM
```

```
:GOFORMAT
ECHO You have asked %0 to format a diskette in drive %1
ECHO with a capacity of %2 bytes.
ECHO
ECHO When you are ready to format the diskette, press Enter.
PAUSE>NUL
ECHO
REM **************************************************************
REM
REM  Have the user verify the FORMAT, or abort: ***
REM
ECHO !!! About to FORMAT the diskette in drive %1 !!!
ECHO Press Ctrl-C to abort, or any key to continue...
PAUSE>NUL
FORMAT %1 /F:%2
REM **************************************************************
REM  Check the exit code from the FORMAT command.
:CHK_EXIT
IF ERRORLEVEL=3 ECHO Control+C was used to abort the FORMAT.
IF ERRORLEVEL=4 ECHO A fatal error occurred during the FORMAT.
IF ERRORLEVEL=5 ECHO You pressed N when prompted to proceed with FORMAT
GOTO END
REM **************************************************************
REM  Display error message: wrong drive ID was specified!
:WRONG_ID
ECHO You have attempted to format a drive other than A: or B:, or
ECHO you did not enter a drive on the PREPDISK command line.
ECHO PREPDISK will not format a hard disk!!!
ECHO Please re-enter the PREPDISK command line with the correct
ECHO drive ID.
GOTO END
REM **************************************************************
REM  Give the batch file a clean ending.
:END
ECHO Exiting from PREPDISK
```

PREPDISK.BAT is relatively long, considering the fact that it only formats a disk and does nothing more. It does, however, do quite a bit of error checking. PREPDISK.BAT is still not complete; a little later in this chapter you will learn to use the FOR command to eliminate many of the IF statements from the file.

PREPDISK.BAT illustrates two uses for the IF command: error checking and evaluating variables. The final use for the IF command is to check for the existence of a file. There is no command that directly checks for the existence of a directory, but you can check for a specific file in the directory in question, as you learn in the next section.

Using IF To Check for Files and Directories

The final form of the IF command checks for the existence of a specified file. Indirectly, you can use this form of IF to check for the existence of a directory. The formats for checking for the existence of a file with the IF command are the following:

```
IF EXIST filename command
```

or

```
IF NOT EXIST filename command
```

MOVE.BAT, which was discussed earlier in this chapter, is an example of a batch file that should use file checking. MOVE.BAT copies a specified file (or files) to a different disk or directory, then erases the original file (or files). It should first verify that the source file exists, then verify that the destination directory exists before attempting the operation. If either condition evaluates false, MOVE.BAT should abort the file operation.

The following sample line for MOVE.BAT checks for the existence of the source file (or files):

```
IF EXIST %1 ECHO Source files found.
```

Entering the following command line would cause the previous line to check for the existence of the file SOURCE.TMP in C:\FILEDIR:

MOVE C:\FILEDIR\SOURCE.TMP D:\NEWPLACE\SOURCE.TMP

Further, the IF command does check for the existence of multiple files. Entering *.* as the file name, for example, would cause IF to evaluate the condition as true if there were any files in the source directory:

MOVE C:\FILEDIR*.* D:\NEWPLACE

You cannot directly check for the existence of a directory. You can, however, check for its existence indirectly by checking for the existence of a file called NUL. The NUL device is present in all directories, so checking for its existence validates the existence of the directory by association—if the file exists, then the specified directory must also exist.

To check for the existence of a directory, use a command similar to the following:

IF EXIST D:\NEWPLACE\NUL ECHO The destination directory exists.

Now, put those two techniques to work in the MOVE.BAT file.

Cleaning Up MOVE.BAT To Add File Checking

The following is the listing for the MOVE.BAT file. It includes an IF statement to check for the existence of the source file(s), and another IF statement to check for the existence of the destination directory.

```
@ECHO OFF
REM *** This batch file moves a file from one directory
REM *** to another by copying it, then erasing
REM *** the original. Multiple files can be moved.
REM
REM ************************************************************
:CHECK_NUL
REM Check to make sure source and destination parameters have
REM been entered.
IF "%1"=="" GOTO NO_PARM1
IF "%2"=="" GOTO NO_PARM2
REM ************************************************************
:CHECK_EX
IF NOT EXIST %1 GOTO NO_FILE
IF NOT EXIST %2\NUL GOTO NO_DIR
REM If MOVE.BAT gets this far, both the file(s) and directory
REM exist, and the move will be started.
ECHO
ECHO Moving %1 to %2
COPY %1 %2 /V
ECHO Press Control+C to prevent the source file(s) from being
ECHO deleted. Press any other key to delete the source file(s).
ECHO NOTE!!! Press Ctrl-C if you have received an error
ECHO message from the COPY command.
PAUSE>NUL
ERASE %1
ECHO File move operation completed successfully.
GOTO END
REM ************************************************************
:NO_PARM1
REM Execute this section if no source file(s) was specified.
ECHO You must specify the source file(s) to be moved.
GOTO END
REM ************************************************************
:NO_PARM2
REM Execute this section if no destination directory is specified.
ECHO You must specify a destination directory for the file(s).
GOTO END
REM ************************************************************
:NO_FILE
```

```
REM  This section is executed if the source file(s) does not exist.
ECHO The file(s) %1 does not exist.  Aborting file move operation.
GOTO END
REM  ***********************************************************
:NO_DIR
REM  This section is executed if the destination directory does
REM  not exist.
ECHO The destination directory %2 does not exist. Aborting
ECHO file move operation.
GOTO END
REM
REM  The previous GOTO is not necessary, but it is good practice
REM  to include a jump to END, just in case you later add another
REM  section after this one (before the :END label is reached).
REM  ***********************************************************
:END
```

Now that error checking has been added to MOVE.BAT, it is a safe batch file to use. Note that it also performs a verify operation after the copy to ensure that the file(s) copied correctly. It pauses after the copy to let the user abort the pending file deletion. If the /V (verify) switch results in an error message, the user can abort the file deletion.

There are two other commands that can be used in batch files to perform branching operations. The next section covers the first of them, CALL, which allows you to run a batch file within another batch file.

Using CALL To Nest Batch Programs

A batch file usually contains a number of commands. DOS is quite able to execute command after command, as long as the commands are internal or external DOS commands, or standard programs with COM or EXE file extensions. DOS has a bit of a problem, however, when it tries to run a batch file from within another batch file.

When DOS finds a batch file nested in another batch file, it runs the nested batch file and then terminates. In other words, DOS never returns to the originating batch file to complete its execution. Consider the following example, called NEST.BAT:

```
VER
ECHO Hello World!
PREPDISK B: 1.44
MOVE C:\DOCS\*.DOC D:\BACKUP
ECHO All done!
```

When you run NEST.BAT, it executes the VER command, then the first ECHO command, and then runs PREPDISK. After it completes PREPDISK, however, DOS drops back to the command line. It does not execute either the MOVE batch file or the final ECHO command.

There is a way, however, to make DOS execute the nested batch files and return to the original batch file to complete its execution. The command DOS provides for that purpose is CALL.

The CALL command is simple and straightforward. You simply issue CALL, followed by the name of the batch file to execute and any necessary parameters for the called batch file. The following shows the previous batch file, NEST.BAT, which has been altered to use the CALL command:

```
VER
ECHO Hello World!
CALL PREPDISK B: 1.44
CALL MOVE C:\DOCS\*.DOC D:\BACKUP
ECHO All done!
```

Now when NEST.BAT is executed, all its commands execute. Remember that using CALL is just like issuing a command from the DOS command line. If the desired batch file is not in the current directory or on the path, you must specify its location. The following example assumes that MOVE.BAT and PREPDISK.BAT files reside in the directory C:\BATCH:

```
VER
ECHO Hello World!
CALL C:\BATCH\PREPDISK B: 1.44
CALL C:\BATCH\MOVE C:\DOCS\*.DOC D:\BACKUP
ECHO All done!
```

That is all there is to using the CALL command! The last of the commands that DOS provides for conditional execution is the FOR command. FOR is discussed in the next section.

Conditional Looping with FOR

The FOR command, one of the least seldom-used DOS batch commands, is one of the most powerful. Like the other batch commands, FOR can be used from the command line or from within a batch file. FOR is not meant to be used for conditional branching, although it does perform conditional testing. Instead, FOR is used to perform a command on a group of files.

A good example of such an operation is this: suppose that you copy a group of files from a floppy disk to a directory on your hard drive, only to find out you copied them to the wrong directory. Assume that there were 50 files on the floppy. If they all have the same file extension, and the destination directory did not contain any files with that extension before the copy, you can use a single ERASE command with a wild-card file specification and erase them all. It is unlikely, however, that you will be that lucky.

The FOR command is the perfect tool for the job of erasing those unwanted files. All you have to do is read the floppy disk to find out which files to erase, then erase the matching files from the hard disk's directory. Before learning how to do that, examine the format for the FOR command as it is used directly from the command line:

    FOR %*variable* IN (*set*) DO *command parameters...*

To use the FOR command in a batch file, the only requirement is to add another % symbol in front of the variable:

    FOR %%*variable* IN (*set*) DO *command parameters...*

The *variable* is not the same as a standard replaceable variable in a batch file. It represents a single-character variable letter that is replaced within the FOR command, not within a batch file. For that reason, you cannot use the %0 through %9 batch file replaceable parameters as the loop variable in the FOR command. As you do learn a little later, however, you can use replaceable parameters for other uses in the FOR command.

The following command checks the disk in drive B and erases matching files from the C:\DOCS directory on the hard drive:

    FOR %F IN (B:*.*) DO ERASE C:\DOCS\%F

The %F represents a parameter that is replaced in the C:\DOCS\???? path string. Through each iteration of the FOR loop, the files on drive B are replaced in the ERASE C:\DOCS\%F command, one-by-one. The (*set*) in this case is all the files on drive B (B:*.*).

For example, if the first file on drive B is THISFILE.TXT, the first iteration of the FOR command would look like this (replacing the %F parameter):

    FOR %F IN (B:*.*) DO ERASE C:\DOCS\THISFILE.TXT

Note that the examples given above use a single % sign in front of the loop variable. This indicates that the command must be typed from the DOS command line. To include the preceding examples in a batch file, add a second % in front of the variable character. Also, the variable character can be any alphabetical character, as long as both variable names on the command line match each other.

Using FOR with Replaceable Batch Parameters

Although you cannot use the replaceable batch parameters %0 through %9 as the loop *variable* in a FOR command, you can incorporate replaceable batch parameters in other locations in a FOR command. For example, create a batch file that uses the FOR command to erase selected files from a selected disk. The file and disk specifications are included on the batch file command line.

The following is the listing for a batch file called ZAP.BAT. Note that because the command is used in a batch file, it uses %% in front of the variable name:

```
FOR %%F IN (%1\%2) DO ERASE %%F
```

Assume that you want to use ZAP.BAT to erase all files with a DOC extension on drive B. You can perform that task with a simple wild-card ERASE command, but use the ZAP.BAT file instead to illustrate how batch parameters can be replaced in a FOR command:

```
ZAP B: *.DOC
```

The ZAP.BAT file substitutes **B:** for %1 in the FOR command's set, and ***.DOC** for %2. Assume that the first DOC file on drive B: is MYFILE.DOC. The first iteration of the FOR loop results in the following command:

```
FOR %F IN (B:\*.DOC) DO ERASE B:\MYFILE.DOC
```

As it is, ZAP.BAT is not a very useful batch file. You can achieve the same effect simply by typing the following:

```
ERASE B:*.DOC
```

Nevertheless, ZAP.BAT illustrates that you can use replaceable batch parameters within a FOR command, as long as you do not use it for the loop variable. You do learn shortly how to make the ZAP.BAT file much more useful.

Using Multiple Sets in a FOR Command

What makes the FOR command so powerful is its flexibility. Part of that flexibility comes from the fact that you can use multiple sets in a single FOR command. Use that technique to expand ZAP.BAT's usefulness. The following is a sample ZAP.BAT file that erases three types of files with a single command:

```
FOR %%F IN (%1\*.%2 %1\*.%3 %1\*.%4) DO ERASE %%F
```

To erase all files on drive B with TMP, BAK, and OLD file extensions, type the following command:

```
ZAP B: TMP BAK OLD
```

ZAP.BAT now works this way: it runs through the FOR loop using the first value in the set, which is %1*.%2. When it has processed all files matching that form (which evaluates to B:*.TMP) it runs through the loop again using the second value for (set), which is %1*.%3. Because %3 has the value BAK, the second pass erases all of the BAK files on drive B (because it evaluates to B:*.BAK). When the second pass is completed, the third pass executes, which uses the set value %1*.%4. This third pass erases all of the files on drive B with a file extension of OLD.

Now ZAP.BAT has a capability that the standard ERASE command does not have; that is, it can be used to erase multiple file types with a single command.

Using Multiple Commands with FOR

Another reason the FOR command is so flexible is that you can use it to perform multiple commands on the same set. Consider the MOVE.BAT file: it uses two commands, COPY and ERASE, to move files from one place to another. The FOR command can do it with a single line:

```
FOR %%F IN (COPY ERASE) DO %%F %1
```

Assume that this line is contained in a batch file named MOVE2.BAT. To copy all the BAK files in C:\DOCS to C:\BACKUP, then erase all of the BAK files from C:\DOCS, issue the following commands:

```
CD \BACKUP
MOVE2 C:\BAK\*.DOC
```

With the MOVE2.BAT file, you must first change to the destination directory, then issue the MOVE2 command. The passes for the FOR command would translate into the following:

```
FOR %%F IN (COPY ERASE) DO COPY C:\DOCS\*.BAK
FOR %%F IN (COPY ERASE) DO ERASE C:\DOCS\*.BAK
```

You must first change to the destination directory because of the way the COPY command is executed—it does not specify a destination directory. This is because the ERASE command, which is executed using the same template, cannot use a destination directory specification.

Now that you have seen that multiple sets can be incorporated in a single FOR statement, make a change to the PREPDISK.BAT file to make it smaller.

Shortening the PREPDISK.BAT File with FOR

Change PREPDISK.BAT to eliminate the :CHK_lowA, :CHK_upA, :CHK_lowB, and :CHK_upB sections, and replace them with a single FOR command. Also, eliminate the multiple IF statements that check the form factor in the :FORM_OK section. The new listing for PREPDISK.BAT is as follows:

```
@ECHO OFF
REM ***********************************************************
REM  Make sure the user has entered a drive ID. If a drive ID
REM  has been entered, jump to the CHK_DRIV label to verify that
REM  the drive ID is valid.
IF NOT "%1"=="" GOTO CHK_DRIV
ECHO You must specify a drive ID for PREPDISK.
GOTO :END
REM ***********************************************************
:CHK_DRIV
REM  Check to make sure the user has asked to format either
REM  drive A: or B: (must check for a: and A:, as well as
REM  b: and B:, since IF is case sensitive.
REM
FOR %%I IN (a: A: b: B:) DO IF %1==%%I GOTO CHK_FMAT
REM ***********************************************************
REM  If the batch file does not branch to CHK_FMAT before it
REM  reaches this point, the drive ID was entered incorrectly.
REM  So, branch to the WRONG_ID label...
GOTO WRONG_ID
REM ***********************************************************
:CHK_FMAT
REM
REM  First, check to make sure a form factor parameter was entered.
IF NOT "%2"=="" GOTO FORM_OK
ECHO You must enter a form factor for PREPDISK, such as:
ECHO      PREPDISK B: 1.44   or   PREPDISK B: 1440
GOTO END
REM ***********************************************************
:FORM_OK
REM
REM  Next, check the byte value entered as %2 to verify the
REM  form factor for the format command. If the value is correct,
REM  jump to the GOFORMAT label to format the diskette. Note that
REM  only the 360K, 720K, 1.2Mb, 1.44Mb, and 2.88Mb form factors
REM  are supported by this batch file. Also, note that not all of
REM  the possible values for the form factor parameter are supported
REM  (such as the 720kb or 1.44mb values).
REM
```

```
FOR %%F IN (360 720 1200 1.2 1440 1.44 2880 2.88) DO IF %2==%%F GOTO
GOFORMAT
REM ************************************************************
:DROPOUT
REM  This section is executed if the %2 form factor parameter
REM  does not match one of the accepted values.
REM
ECHO You have entered a form factor of %2, which is either not
ECHO recognized or not supported. Please verify the value, then
ECHO enter it in the form nnnn or n.nn (1440 or 1.44).
GOTO :END
REM ************************************************************
:GOFORMAT
REM  If %1 and %2 were valid parameters, attempt to format the disk.
REM
ECHO You have asked %0 to format a diskette in drive %1
ECHO with a capacity of %2.
ECHO
ECHO When you are ready to format the diskette, press Enter.
PAUSE>NUL
ECHO
REM ************************************************************
REM
REM  Have the user verify the FORMAT, or abort: ***
REM
ECHO !!! About to FORMAT the diskette in drive %1 !!!
ECHO Press Ctrl-C to abort, or any key to continue...
PAUSE>NUL
FORMAT %1 /F:%2
REM ************************************************************
:CHK_EXIT
REM  Check the exit code from the FORMAT command.
IF ERRORLEVEL=3 ECHO Ctrl-C was used to abort the FORMAT.
IF ERRORLEVEL=4 ECHO A fatal error occurred during the FORMAT.
IF ERRORLEVEL=5 ECHO You pressed N when prompted to proceed with FORMAT.
GOTO END
REM ************************************************************
:WRONG_ID
REM  Display error message: wrong drive ID was specified!
ECHO You have attempted to format a drive other than A: or B:.
ECHO PREPDISK will not format a hard disk!!!
ECHO Please re-enter the PREPDISK command line with the correct
ECHO drive ID.
GOTO END
```

```
REM  *********************************************************
:END
REM  Give the batch file a clean ending.
ECHO Exiting from PREPDISK
```

You can see that adding a few FOR commands has reduced the size of the PREPDISK.BAT file considerably. To streamline it even further, you can eliminate the REM statements and cut down the size of some of PREPDISK's messages.

Using ANSI.SYS Directives in Batch Files

You learned in Chapter 11 that the ANSI.SYS driver can be used to set screen colors and text attributes, and position the cursor. If ANSI.SYS has been installed, you also can use ANSI.SYS directives in your batch files. Communicating with ANSI.SYS from a batch file is as easy as using the ECHO command.

As you probably recall from Chapter 11, sending a directive to ANSI.SYS requires that you issue an escape, followed by a left bracket ([). The method you use to enter the escape sequence depends on the text editor you use. With the MS-DOS Editor, you press Ctrl-P followed by the Esc key. Then, press the [key. With EDLIN, press Ctrl-V followed by a double left bracket ([[). Enter the desired control directive following the escape sequence.

Use ANSI.SYS directives to dress up the MOVE.BAT file:

```
@ECHO OFF
REM  *** This batch file moves a file from one directory
REM  *** to another by copying it, then erasing
REM  *** the original. Multiple files can be moved.
REM
REM  *********************************************************
:CHECK_NUL
REM  Check to make sure source and destination parameters have
REM  been entered.
IF "%1"=="" GOTO NO_PARM1
IF "%2"=="" GOTO NO_PARM2
REM  *********************************************************
:CHECK_EX
IF NOT EXIST %1 GOTO NO_FILE
IF NOT EXIST %2\NUL GOTO NO_DIR
REM  If MOVE.BAT gets this far, both the file(s) and directory
REM  exist, and the move will be started.
```

```
ECHO
ECHO Moving [32m%1[0m to [33;1m%2[0m
COPY %1 %2 /V
ECHO Press [31mCtrl-C[0m to prevent the source file(s) from being
ECHO deleted. Press any other key to delete the source file(s).
ECHO [31;1mNOTE!!! Press Ctrl-C if you have received an error
ECHO message from the COPY command.[0m
PAUSE>NUL
ERASE %1
ECHO [32mFile move operation completed successfully.[0m
GOTO END
REM  *********************************************************
:NO_PARM1
REM  Execute this section if no source file(s) was specified.
ECHO You must specify the source file(s) to be moved.
GOTO END
REM  *********************************************************
:NO_PARM2
REM  Execute this section if no destination directory is specified.
ECHO You must specify a destination directory for the file(s).
GOTO END
REM  *********************************************************
:NO_FILE
REM  This section is executed if the source file(s) does not exist.
ECHO The file(s) %1 does not exist.  Aborting file move operation.
GOTO END
REM  *********************************************************
:NO_DIR
REM  This section is executed if the destination directory does
REM  not exist.
ECHO The destination directory %2 does not exist. Aborting
ECHO file move operation.
GOTO END
REM
REM  The previous GOTO is not necessary, but it is good practice
REM  to include a jump to END, just in case you later add another
REM  section after this one (before the :END label is reached).
REM  *********************************************************
:END
```

You can see that as long as ANSI.SYS is installed, it is a simple matter to send directives to it to control the display. Just ECHO the directive, and it will be filtered through ANSI.SYS.

Using Macros

In the first part of this chapter, you learned to construct batch files to perform complex and repetitive tasks. With a little patience and a small investment of time, you can put together a batch file that performs any task you could perform from the keyboard, but does it much more quickly.

Batch files, however, are not the only method DOS offers for enhancing your productivity. DOS also lets you create *macros*. A macro is a string of commands that you can define by name. You execute the macro by typing its name on the command line. DOS then executes the commands that are defined in the macro. This is virtually identical to a batch file. There are two primary differences, however, between macros and batch files. First, batch files are stored on disk, while macros are stored in memory. Second, batch files can be any length, while macros are limited to no more that 128 characters.

Considering the Advantages and Disadvantages of Macros

Macros have some advantages over batch files. Because they are stored in memory instead of on disk, macros execute more quickly than batch files can. Macros are relatively easy to create, while batch files usually take a little more development time.

Macros also have disadvantages when compared to batch files. Because they are stored in memory, they are not permanent; that is, when the system is shut off or rebooted, the macros are lost. A macro can be defined from a batch file, however, which makes it a simple thing to redefine a macro after resetting the system.

Another disadvantage to using macros is that the macros—and DOSKEY, the DOS program used to create them—both take up memory. If your system is lacking available memory, defining macros can make the lack of available RAM even worse. By default, DOSKEY sets aside 512 bytes for macros, and uses another 3K of RAM for itself. Unless you direct DOSKEY to create a larger storage area for macros, the loss of 3.5K of RAM is a small price to pay for the flexibility that DOSKEY and macros provide. If you work with the DOS command line to any degree, DOSKEY is indispensable.

Installing DOSKEY

DOSKEY is a memory-resident program that, in addition to storing macro definitions in memory, also provides a command-line editor. DOSKEY maintains a history of the commands you enter on the command line. Using the cursor and function keys, you can select commands that you have entered previously, making it unnecessary to retype them.

To load DOSKEY, type:

```
DOSKEY
```

and press Enter. This installs DOSKEY with the default command buffer size of 512 bytes. If, after using DOSKEY for awhile, you decide you need more memory for commands or would like to allocate less memory to DOSKEY, start the program as follows:

```
DOSKEY /BUFSIZE=nnn
```

The *nnn* parameter specifies the size, in bytes, of the buffer. To load DOSKEY with a buffer of 300 bytes, type:

```
DOSKEY /BUFSIZE=300
```

Entering Commands with DOSKEY

When DOSKEY has been installed, you enter commands at the command line just as you do without DOSKEY. One of the main differences, however, is that you can enter more than one command on a line. Without DOSKEY, you can enter only one command on the command line. To enter multiple commands with DOSKEY, separate each command by a carriage return symbol (not an actual carriage return). To enter a carriage return symbol, press Ctrl-T. For example, to copy files to a new directory and then erase the original files (much like the MOVE.BAT file), type the following:

```
COPY C:\DOCS\*.BAK D:\NEWDIR <Ctrl-T> ERASE C:\DOCS\*.BAK
```

A carriage return symbol (¶) appears on the command line when you press Ctrl-T:

```
COPY C:\DOCS\*.BAK D:\NEWDIR ¶ ERASE C:\DOCS\*.BAK
```

You can string as many commands together as you like, provided the total number of characters does not exceed 128.

Editing Commands with DOSKEY

DOSKEY's command history is one of its most useful features. DOSKEY keeps track of commands you have entered. Instead of retyping a command, you can use the cursor keys and function keys to select a previously entered command. To select the last command, for example, press the up-arrow key. As you keep pressing the up-arrow key, DOSKEY cycles through the commands that you have entered. When you find the one you want and it is displayed on the command line, press Enter to execute it.

The following keys control the command list in DOSKEY:

Key	Function
Up arrow	Displays the previous command in the command history list
Down arrow	Displays the next command in the command history list
F7	Displays the entire command history list
F8	Cycles through the commands that begin with the letter you specify before pressing F8
F9	Prompts for the number of a command in the command history list (the list is displayed with F7)
PgUp	Displays the oldest command (at the top of the list)
PgDn	Displays the most recent command (at the bottom of the list)
Esc	Clears the command from the command line

One of the most useful DOSKEY control keys is F8. If you type the first letter of a command, then press F8, DOSKEY finds the first command in the list that begins with the selected letter (or letters). Successive F8 keys cycle through other commands with the same first letter.

Once you have selected a command from the command history list, you can edit it. To edit a command, use the left- and right-arrow keys to position the cursor at the point where you want to begin editing. By default, DOSKEY will be in replace mode, and anything you type replaces the character underneath it. To insert characters in the command line, press Ins. This places DOSKEY in insert mode, and any characters you type will be inserted in the command line. Pressing Ins again toggles DOSKEY back to replace mode.

Most of the other cursor control keys can be used with DOSKEY. Table 13.1 lists the cursor control keys you can use with DOSKEY.

Now that you have a working knowledge of DOSKEY you can put it to use defining macros.

Table 13.1

DOSKEY Cursor Control Keys

Key	Function
Home	Moves the cursor to the beginning of the command line
End	Moves the cursor to the end of the command line
Left arrow	Moves the cursor one character to the left
Right arrow	Moves the cursor one character to the right
Ctrl-left arrow	Moves the cursor one word to the left
Ctrl-right arrow	Moves the cursor one word to the right
Backspace	Moves the cursor one character to the left. (If DOSKEY is in insert mode, the character to the left is deleted.)
Del	Deletes the character under the cursor and shifts remaining characters to the left
Ctrl-End	Deletes all characters from the current cursor position to the end of the line
Ctrl-Home	Deletes all characters from the current cursor position to the beginning of the line
Ins	Toggles between insert and replace modes
Esc	Clears the command line

Creating, Running, and Stopping Macros

Creating a macro using DOSKEY is fairly simple. Once DOSKEY has been installed, you issue the DOSKEY command again, followed by the name to assign to the macro and the commands to be executed. The following command would create a macro that performs a directory of three types of files with a single command:

```
DOSKEY DIR3=DIR *.DOC $T DIR *.TXT $T DIR *.BAT
```

Note that instead of the Ctrl-T (ASCII 20) character, you use a $T to separate one command from another in a macro. If you use the Ctrl-T instead, DOS interprets the command immediately. In the previous example, using Ctrl-T instead of $T causes DOS to execute the three commands immediately, one after the other, instead of simply defining the macro in memory. Whenever you want to include more than one command in a macro, you must separate the commands with $T.

To run the macro, just type its name on the command line and press Enter:

```
DIR3
```

DOS responds by running the commands in the macro definition.

You usually test a macro after you create it. If the macro works properly, you can go on to define other macros. If the macro does not work, however, you can easily edit it by using DOSKEY. Simply press the up-arrow key until the macro definition is displayed, then edit the command line using the DOSKEY editing keys. When the macro is fixed, press Enter to redefine it. DOSKEY replaces the original definition with the new definition.

When you run a batch file, pressing Ctrl-C terminates execution of the batch file. You also use Ctrl-C to terminate a macro. There is a difference, however, between terminating batch files and terminating macros. When you press Ctrl-C while a macro is executing, only the active command terminates. You must press Ctrl-C for every command in the macro. In the DIR3 macro defined above, you must press Ctrl-C three times to terminate the macro.

Using Replaceable Parameters in Macros

You learned earlier in the chapter that the %1 through %9 parameters can be used in a batch file as replaceable parameters. You can enter parameters on the command line when you invoke the batch file, and the parameters are passed to the batch file and inserted where appropriate. Macros also can use replaceable parameters. Instead of the % character as the parameter identifier, a $ character is used. Valid parameters are $1 through $9.

The following macro illustrates the use of replaceable parameters in a macro. Like the MOVE.BAT file, the MOVEIT macro moves a file or files from one directory to another by first copying, then erasing the original files:

```
DOSKEY MOVEIT=COPY $1 $2 /V $T ERASE $1
```

To move all of the BAK files from the current directory to the directory C:\TEMP, issue the following macro command:

```
MOVEIT *.BAK C:\TEMP
```

DOS replaces the command-line parameters in the macro following the same rules as for batch files:

```
COPY *.BAK C:\TEMP ¶ ERASE *.BAK
```

Note that DOS also interprets the $T as a carriage return.

Saving Macros

You cannot save a macro in a file. Macros must be defined from the command line using DOSKEY. You can, however, redirect a DOSKEY macro definition command to a batch file, or directly create a batch file that contains the commands necessary to define a macro. The batch file can then be run to define the macro. To save the MOVEIT macro in a batch file called MV.BAT, for example, use the following command:

```
ECHO DOSKEY MOVEIT=COPY $1 $2 /V $T ERASE $1 > MV.BAT
```

The DOS output redirection symbol (>) is used to redirect the ECHO command to a file called MV.BAT. Now that the macro definition is saved in a batch file, you can define the macro whenever you need it simply by running MV.BAT. If you want to save all of the macros in memory to a batch file, use the following command:

```
DOSKEY /MACROS > MACROS.BAT
```

This saves all macros in memory to a file called MACROS.BAT. You can then redefine all of the macros by running MACROS.BAT. If you simply want to view all of the defined macros, but do not want to redirect them to a file, use the following command:

```
DOSKEY /MACROS
```

Because you can use a batch file to define a macro, you may want to create a single macro file that contains all of your macro definitions. You can then CALL the macro definition batch file from your AUTOEXEC.BAT file to define the macros at system start-up. Whenever you want to add a macro to the file, simply define it and append it to the existing macro definition file.

For example, assume that you keep a macro definition file called MACROS.BAT that contains all your most commonly used macros. You want to add the MOVEIT macro to MACROS.BAT. To append it to the MACROS.BAT file, type the following at the command line:

```
ECHO DOSKEY MOVEIT=COPY $1 $2 /V $T ERASE $1 >> MACROS.BAT
```

This command uses the DOS output append symbol (>>) to redirect and append the macro definition to the MACROS.BAT file. If MOVEIT already exists in MACROS.BAT, it will be duplicated at the end of the file. When MACROS.BAT is executed, the first MOVEIT macro is defined, but is then replaced by the last MOVEIT command in the file. Therefore, whenever there is a duplicate definition in the file, the last one replaces any preceding macros with the same name.

It is too easy, however, to use the wrong redirection symbol and wipe out everything in MACROS.BAT—if you use the > symbol (output redirect) instead of >> (output append), the macro definition is redirected to the file rather than appended. If the MACROS.BAT file already exists, it is replaced by a new file of the same name. Any other macros in the original file are lost. To eliminate the possibility of using the wrong redirection symbol, create a macro called DEFINE to create a macro and append it to MACROS.BAT:

```
DOSKEY DEFINE=ECHO DOSKEY $* $G$G MACROS.BAT
```

To define a new macro called DIRW and append it to MACROS.BAT, just type the following command:

```
DEFINE DIRW=DIR /W
```

To understand how the DEFINE macro works, you must examine the rest of the replaceable parameters supported by DOSKEY.

Using Redirection and Replaceable Parameters

In addition to the $1 through $9 parameters supported by DOSKEY, you can use the parameters listed in Table 13.2 when defining a macro.

Table 13.2
Additional DOSKEY Parameters

Parameter	Function
$*	Saves all the text following a macro command name (all parameters included on the macro command line) as a single replaceable parameter.
$L (or $l)	The same as the input redirection symbol, <. Redirects input from a file to the macro command line.
$G (or $g)	The same as the output redirection symbol, >. Redirects output from the macro command line to a file.
GG (or gg)	The same as the output append symbol, >>. Appends output to a specified file.

Take a second look at the DEFINE macro to see how it works:

```
DOSKEY DEFINE=ECHO DOSKEY $* $G$G MACROS,BAT
```

When you type **DEFINE** followed by a command definition, that command definition is stored in the parameter **$***. DEFINE uses ECHO to output the

DOSKEY command, followed by whatever you typed as a parameter on the DEFINE macro command line. The result is the appended to the MACROS.BAT file using the output append parameter GG. Consider the DIRW definition listed earlier in this section:

```
DEFINE DIRW=DIR /W
```

The DEFINE command translates that into the following:

```
ECHO DOSKEY DIRW=DIR /W >> MACROS.BAT
```

All DEFINE really does is take your macro definition input and *safely* redirects it to MACROS.BAT. Naturally, you do want to include the DEFINE macro definition in the MACROS.BAT file or in your AUTOEXEC.BAT file. Then, the DEFINE command will be available whenever you need it. You can edit MACROS.BAT directly to add a DEFINE macro to it, or if DEFINE is already defined in memory, simply type the following to append it to MACROS.BAT:

```
DEFINE DEFINE=ECHO DOSKEY $* $G$G MACROS.BAT
```

Removing a Macro from Memory

When you redefine a macro that already exists, the new definition takes the place of the old one. If you want to remove the definition altogether, rather than replace it with something else, redefine the macro but leave the definition blank. For example, to remove the DIRW macro from memory, type the following:

```
DOSKEY DIRW=
```

The macro is removed from memory.

Saving Time and Trouble—Suggestions for Macros and Batch Files

What you can do with macros and batch files is limited only by your imagination and ability to understand and use DOS commands. This last section of the chapter lists some ideas for batch files and macros you may want to create.

❏ **Automate Network Access**. Install network shell software and drivers, map network drives to common and standard logical drive IDs, turn on print capturing (if required), start network message handler, and log onto the network.

❏ **Start Applications**. Change to directory (which can be specified using a replaceable command-line parameter), set environment variables necessary for the application to run, perform any other required setup, then execute an application.

❏ **Incremental Backup**. Check file attributes and backup any file that has changed since the last backup was performed.

❏ **Full System Backup**. Perform a full system backup to disk, tape, or floppy.

❏ **Manipulate Path**. Save the PATH to a variable called OLDPATH, set a new PATH for an application, start the application, and when the application terminates, restore the OLDPATH.

These are just a few of the many tasks you can perform using batch files and macros. Whenever you find yourself performing a repetitive task, it is time to create a macro or batch file.

Summary

Although many complex tasks require you to develop a program by using traditional programming techniques and languages, you also can use batch files and macros to perform even the most difficult and complicated command-line processes. Further, you can easily learn to create batch files because there are only a few batch-specific commands.

Remember that batch files are ASCII files containing DOS commands. A batch file is essentially a task list. Each task on the list is executed in the order it appears in the file. You can, however, perform conditional testing, branching, and error checking. For that reason, batch files are not always executed top to bottom—complex batch files loop and jump around within the structure of the file.

The commands specific to batch files are

CALL	IF
ECHO	PAUSE
FOR	REM
GOTO	SHIFT

The FOR command, in particular, is a very powerful command. You can use FOR to perform the same task on a set of files, variables, or commands.

Macros are not as powerful as batch files, but they are faster because they are stored in memory instead of on disk. Macros can consist of multiple commands, as long as the total command string does not exceed 128 characters.

You use DOSKEY, DOS' command-line editor, to create a macro. With DOSKEY installed, you can scroll through a list of commands that you have previously entered, edit those commands, list them, direct them to a file, and define them as macros that can be invoked by name. DOSKEY uses only 3.5K of memory by default, and its benefits more than outweigh the small amount of memory it uses.

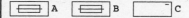
14

Programming with QBASIC

QBASIC is a programming language that is supplied with DOS 5. It replaces the venerable GW-BASIC, supplied with several previous DOS versions. It is similar in appearance and function to Microsoft's QuickBASIC products, but lacks QuickBASIC's compile and library options. This is because QBASIC, like GW-BASIC, is an interpreted language, and QuickBASIC is a compiled language. Let's look at the differences between the two.

Interpreted versus Compiled

An *interpreted language* environment, such as QBASIC, operates in the following manner:

1. QBASIC is first loaded into memory, in the same way software packages such as word processors are.

2. The programmer is then presented with QBASIC's Editor. The editor functions like a specialized word processor, accepting valid QBASIC terms and statements that are typed in (see figure 14.1).

3. The collection of QBASIC terms and statements are what form a QBASIC program. A program can be designed to accomplish a task that ranges from the very simplistic to the extremely complex.

4. Once the program is written, it is ready to be executed. In QBASIC, execution requires the interpreter to read and process each line that performs the appropriate action. This (hopefully) produces the programmer's desired result.

477

```
File   Edit   View   Search   Run   Debug   Options           Help

File                 Edit                      View

New                  Cut          Shift+Del    SUBs...                  F2
Open...              Copy         Ctrl+Ins     Split
Save                 Paste        Shift+Ins    Output Screen            F4
Save As...           Clear              Del

Print...             New SUB...
Exit                 New FUNCTION...


Search               Run                       Debug

Find...              Start        Shift+F5     Step                     F8
Repeat Last Find  F3 Restart                   Procedure Step          F10
Change...            Continue           F5
                                               Trace On

Options                           Help         Toggle Breakpoint        F9
                                               Clear All Breakpoints
Display...           Index                      Set Next Statement
Help Path...         Contents
Syntax Checking      Topic: Contents      F1
                     Using Help      Shift+F1

                     About...
```

Figure 14.1:
QBASIC Menus

In order to run the program, QBASIC's interpreter must be present; without the interpreter, the program is nothing more than a collection of words, just like a letter.

A *compiled language* (like QuickBASIC) operates in much the same manner as the interpreted language (until step 4). At this point, a compiler takes the place of the interpreter and pre-processes the program before it is executed. This step creates a *stand-alone executable program* that can be executed without the presence of the QuickBASIC language. This approach has some definite advantages with respect to execution speed and the distribution of finished programs. It does, however, present the programmer with a more complicated programming environment.

A View of QBASIC

QBASIC is a very powerful language, and, in the tradition of the BASIC language, is still very easy to use. Some of its features include the following:

❑ QBASIC contains more than 220 built-in statements and functions, and it maintains a readable *English-like* syntax.

❑ On-line help is provided, including program examples for many of the statements and functions.

❏ The built-in editor is easy to use, operating in the same manner as the DOS Editor.

❏ Automatic syntax checking is provided (each line of code you enter is checked for proper format and content).

❏ Built-in debugging features enable you to incrementally execute programs and view changes in variables as they happen.

❏ The speed of execution is more than adequate for most applications.

❏ QBASIC is fully upward-compatible with Microsoft QuickBasic and Microsoft Basic Professional Development Systems for even more power and flexibility.

These features place substantial programming power in the hands of the user, in an easy-to-use package.

The Scope of this Chapter

Entire books can be filled with the detailed explanation of languages such as QBASIC. The approach of this chapter is to limit the scope to certain classes of statements and their uses. In doing so, several sample programs are included, which illustrate the statements and some of their applications.

It is hoped that what you read and see here will encourage you to experiment with the language and look beyond these examples to use QBASIC to solve some of your simple programming problems.

Variables

Simply stated, *variables* are the names given to the locations in memory where values are stored. For example, to store the dollar amount of a customer's credit limit, you might name a variable *CreditLimit*. In this variable, you can store a numeric value representing the customer's credit limit. Because QBASIC allows such descriptive names for variables, the programmer (as well as anyone else who reads the program) has an excellent idea of what is stored there.

QBASIC places the following restrictions on naming variables:

❏ A variable name can contain as many as 40 characters. It cannot, however, be the same name as a QBASIC reserved keyword.

❏ The first character must be a letter (either upper- or lowercase) from A through Z.

❏ The rest of the variable name may contain numbers, letters (of either case), or periods.

❏ The final character of a variable name may be used to denote the type of value the variable contains. Five characters ($, %, !, &, and #) have special meanings for this purpose.

As indicated in the last section, QBASIC variables have a certain type. These types are either *string* variables or *numeric* variables.

String Variables

String variables contain text information. They can be any combination of letters, numbers, punctuation marks, etc. Some examples of a string would be:

> *"QBASIC is a very powerful language."*

> *"The temperature reached 87 degrees today!"*

The length of the string may be from 0 through 32,767 characters.

Declaring a String Variable

You may create a string variable by placing the type declaration character **$** at the end of its name:

> *Month$="January"*

This statement creates the string variable *Month$*, and assigns the value *January* to it. When placing a value into a string variable, the desired value must always be contained within double-quote marks. Remember the $ is actually part of the variable's name, and must be included.

Another method of declaring a string variable involves using the **DEF**type *[letter] (-[letter])* command. This allows you to set a default type for variables not defined by other means. Using the **STR** option in place of *type* would signify string. For example, the command *DEFSTR M* declares all untyped variables starting with the letter M to be string variables. Therefore, the following statement is a valid declaration of the string variable *Month:*

> *Month="January"*

A second form of this command allows you to declare for a range of letters:

    DEFSTR A-F

Numeric Variables

Numeric variables, as the name implies, contain numbers. QBASIC further separates numeric variables into four specific types, limiting the range of values each can contain. Table 14.1 lists the variable names and respective ranges of values.

Table 14.1
Numeric Variable Types

Variable Name	Minimum Value	Maximum Value
Integer	-32,768	32,767
Long Integer	-2,147,483,648	2,147,483,647
Single Precision		
Positive	3.402823E+38	2.802597E-45
Negative	-2.802597E-45	-3.402823E+38
Double-Precision		
Positive	1.79769313486231D+308	4.940656458412465D-324
Negative	-4.940656458412465D-324	-1.79769313486231D+308

Declaring Numeric Variables

As with string variables, numeric variables can be declared using a type declaration character at the end of its name:

```
Counter%=1              ' Integer Variable
LoopCount&=40000        ' Long Integer Variable
InvAmount!=567.89       ' Single-Precision Variable
AtomicWeight#=5.63433432  ' Double-precision Variable
```

Each of these statements creates the named variable and assigns the value of it to the right of the = sign. Remember that the type declaration characters (%, &, !, #) are part of the variable name and must be included.

There are also forms of the **DEF***type [letter] (-[letter])* command for defining numeric variables. Examples of each are:

```
DEFINT C  ' Integer Variables
DEFLNG L  ' Long Integer Variables
DEFSNG I  ' Single-Precision Variables
DEFDBL A  ' Double-Precision Variables
```

These statements define untyped variables, beginning with the letter C as integer variables, the letter L as long integer variables, the letter I as single-precision variables, and the letter A as double-precision variables.

Arrays

Arrays are a special type of variable that give the programmer a great deal of flexibility and power. An *array* is a variable of a single type (either string or numeric) and name. Thousands of values can be stored in a single array, with each one differentiated by a subscript. The *subscript* is the address of the value within an array.

It may help to look at an array as a sort of apartment building. The building itself has a single name (just like an array). Within this single building hundreds of tenants can live, each with his/her own apartment (just as there can be hundreds of values within an array). Apartments within a building are usually numbered, giving each one a unique address (again, just like the elements of an array). To send a piece of mail to any one of these tenants, you must address it to the building and then the specific apartment. An address to the Jones' apartment might look like this:

Mr. & Mrs. Bob Jones

Greene Townhouse Apt. 3

123 Main Street

Anytown, AnyState, AnyZip

The second line of the address references the apartment building and a specific apartment number. This information is required to get to the desired tenants: the Jones'.

An array operates in the same manner. To get to the desired value, you must reference the array name and its subscript (its address within the array).

Declaring an Array

An array is declared by dimensioning it. In the dimension statement, you name the array, set its type, and determine the maximum number of elements it may contain. For example, the following statement dimensions an array:

```
DIM Month$(12)
```

This creates a string array, named *Month$*, with room for 12 string values. (You need to use the statement Option Base 1 to prevent QBASIC from counting 0, giving you 13 array variables.)

Each individual value is then referenced like this:

```
Month$(1)                   ' the 1st value in the array
Month$(2)                   ' the 2nd value in the array
  .
  .
  .
Month$(12)                  ' the 12th value in the array
```

To store information into the array, treat it like any other variable:

```
Month$(1)="January"         'stores "January" in 1st array element
Month$(2)="February"        'stores "February" in 2nd array element
  .
  .
  .
Month$(12)="December"       'stores "December" in 12th array element
```

In the example, the array is set up so that the subscript number directly corresponds with the actual month. This is a very common and useful method of declaring arrays. It provides a logical link between the array subscript, in this case, 1 through 12, and the array values (January through December).

Loops and Conditional Statements

This section addresses two QBASIC properties that encompass most of a program's logic: loops and conditional statements.

All of the statements in this section (except for the *SELECT CASE* conditional statement) deal with evaluating an expression, which produces a true or false answer. Usually this involves comparing two variables in one of the following forms:

```
variable1 = variable2      'Is variable1 equal to variable2?
variable1 > variable2      'Is variable1 greater than variable2?
variable1 < variable2      'Is variable1 less than variable2?
variable1 <> variable2     'Is variable1 not equal to variable2?
variable1 >= variable2     'Is variable1 greater than or equal to variable2?
variable1 <= variable2     'Is variable1 less than or equal to variable2?
```

For example, the expression x%=1 will be true when x% does equal the number 1. At all other times, it will evaluate as false.

Loops

Loops can be defined as a block of two statements (such as FOR and NEXT), between which other QBASIC statements are inserted. These statements are performed until certain conditions, set by the loop, are fulfilled. Two examples of loops are the *FOR..NEXT* loop and the *DO..LOOP* statement.

FOR..NEXT Loops

The syntax of a *FOR..NEXT* loop looks like this:

```
FOR counter = startval TO endval [STEP incrval]
    [statements..]
NEXT [counter]
```

❑ *FOR* is the QBASIC statement that marks the beginning of the loop. It is here that all parameters for the execution of the loop are initialized and evaluated at each pass. The loop stops when the *FOR* statement evaluates *counter* to be greater than *endval*. At this point, the program continues at the statement immediately following the *NEXT* statement.

❑ *counter* is a numeric variable (most likely an integer type) that keeps track of the loop's iterations.

❑ *startval* is the beginning value for *counter*.

❑ *endval* represents the desired ending value (or when you want the loop to stop) for *counter*.

❑ *[STEP incrval]* is an optional clause that contains the number by which *counter* is incremented each time one cycle of the loop is executed. If the *STEP* clause is omitted, the default *incrval* value is 1.

❑ *NEXT* is a QBASIC statement that marks the end of the loop. It is here that *counter* is incremented by the *incrval*. Once this is done, control is then passed back to the *FOR* statement.

To illustrate this, let's consider the following simple *FOR..NEXT* loop:

```
FOR x% = 1 TO 10
    PRINT "Hello"
NEXT x%
```

This loop prints the word *Hello* 10 times. Using the previous nomenclature, *counter* would be *x%*, *startval* would be 1, *endval* would be 10, and *incrval* would have defaulted to 1.

As you will see in the examples for this chapter, *FOR..NEXT* loops are excellent vehicles for executing processes (such as printing) a specified number of times.

DO..LOOP Statement

The basic idea behind the *DO..LOOP* statement is identical to the *FOR..NEXT* loop. A *statement*, or group of statements, is performed until certain conditions are met. The *DO..LOOP* is more flexible in the fact that its execution does not have to rely on a counter reaching a set value. It can be a more logical condition, such as *"stop when someone presses the escape key."*

There are two possible forms of the *DO..LOOP* statement:

```
DO
    [statements]
LOOP {WHILE [UNTIL] expression}
```

and

```
DO {WHILE [UNTIL] expression}
    [statements]
LOOP
```

Both forms must include a valid *expression* and the use of either the *WHILE* or *UNTIL* clause.

An *expression* must be able to be evaluated as a true or false answer (as previously explained).

The *WHILE* clause executes the loop as long as the *expression* evaluates **true**.

The *UNTIL* clause executes the loop as long as the *expression* evaluates **false** (or until it evaluates **true**).

Choosing between the Two Forms

In the first form (DO..LOOP{WHILE [UNTIL] expression}) the *expression* is evaluated at the end of the block. This means the statements within the block will always be executed at least once, even if the *expression* is already fulfilled. The second form evaluates the *expression* at the beginning of the block. This means the statements within the block will only be executed if the *expression* is not fulfilled. Selecting the form to use will depend on the specific operation of the statements contained within the *DO..LOOP* statement.

For example, imagine you want to input an *account number* which must be validated before you can continue. By choosing the first form, and placing the input statements within the block, you can input a valid account before exiting with a single set of input statements. The following example illustrates this:

```
AcctNumb$ =""
DO
   [statements to input the account number]
LOOP UNTIL AcctNumb$ = "123456"
```

This simple DO..LOOP statement executes until you input an *AcctNumb$* equal to *123456*.

On the other hand, if you want to perform a group of processes that are contingent upon a customer's account balance, choose the second form. This way, you don't enter the block unless the balance is within your set limits.

```
DO WHILE AcctBal! >= 5000
   [statements]
LOOP
```

This loop executes as long as the variable AcctBal! is greater than or equal to *5000*.

Conditional Statements

QBASIC's conditional statements enable programs to make decisions and perform the appropriate actions, based on those decisions. Two basic forms exist for this process: the *IF* statement and the *SELECT CASE* statement.

IF Statement

The *IF* statement evaluates an expression or expressions and uses the outcome to branch to the appropriate set of statements.

Two possible forms of the *IF* statement exist. The first from is on a single line, as in the following:

IF *expression* THEN [*statement(s)*] [ELSE [*statement(s)*]]

The second method uses block form, as in the following:

```
IF expression THEN
[statements]
[ELSE
   [statements]]
END IF
```

In the single-line form, the physical end of the line concludes the *IF* statement. In the block form, the keyword *END IF* signifies the end. In either case, the *ELSE* clause is optional. Omitting it implies that if the statement is false (not true), nothing needs to be done.

The *IF* statement starts by evaluating the *expression*. If it is found to be **true**, the statements immediately following *THEN* are performed until the *ELSE* clause is encountered or until the end of the statement is reached. If the expression evaluates **false**, and the *ELSE* clause exists, the statements immediately following *ELSE* are executed until the end of the *IF* statement. This is illustrated in the following example:

```
IF AvailCredit! >= OrderAmt! THEN
   PRINT "Credit Is Ok"
ELSE
   PRINT "Order Cannot Be Processed"
END IF
```

In this example, if the numeric variable *AvailCredit!* is greater than or equal to the numeric variable *OrderAmt!*, the program prints the message *Credit Is Ok*. Otherwise, the message *Order Cannot Be Processed* is displayed.

A Note on the IF Statement

The IF statement also has an optional *ELSEIF* clause. Although this option is quite valuable, it creates a more complex *IF* statement. In cases where it could have been used, this book has opted for the more readable *SELECT CASE* statement.

SELECT CASE Statement

The SELECT CASE statement offers you a structured method of evaluating a variable against several possible values. The statement's basic syntax and structure is as follows:

```
SELECT CASE variable
   CASE [IS] value(s) [TO value] [,]
   [statements]
   [CASE [IS] value(s) [TO value] [,]
   [statements]]
   [CASE ELSE
   [statements]]
END SELECT
```

The *SELECT CASE* block begins by stating the *variable* to be evaluated. This can be any valid string or numeric variable.

Individual *CASE* statements are then listed. One should exist for each value (of *variable*) that requires processing.

An optional *CASE ELSE* clause, followed by the appropriate statements, can also be listed. This statement following the *CASE ELSE* clause is processed every time all of the *CASE value* statements fail.

The optional *IS* clause enables you to use comparison characters (<,>,>=,<=,<>) other than the implied = (equal) sign.

The optional *TO* clause enables you to specify a *value* range. For example, the *SELECT CASE* statement that follows would process the values under the second *CASE* if *LowValue%* were between 4 and 7:

```
SELECT CASE LowValue%
   CASE 1 TO 3
   [statements]
   CASE 4 TO 7
   [statements]
   CASE 8 TO 10
   [statements]
         .
END SELECT
```

The final option is using the comma (,) as a separator. This enables you to have compound value criteria for the same *CASE* statement. The comma is an implied *OR* statement, meaning the following *SELECT CASE* statement would process the statements under the first CASE if *LowValue%* were between 4 and 7 or less than 38:

```
SELECT CASE LowValue%
   CASE 4 TO 7, IS < 38
   [statements]
      .
      .
      .
END SELECT
```

Displaying Information on the Screen

One of the keys to a well-written program is the display of timely messages and prompts, as well as easy-to-read output. There are several commands in the QBASIC language that facilitate this. Three of these commands, *LOCATE*, *PRINT* and *PRINT USING*, are discussed in the following sections.

LOCATE Statement

The *LOCATE* statement enables you to position the cursor at a certain row and column on the screen. The next statement producing output is displayed at that location.

The syntax for the *LOCATE* statement is as follows:

```
LOCATE [row], [column], [visible], [[start], [stop]]
```

❏ *row* is the number of the row on which the cursor will be displayed. The range is usually from 1 to 25, but can vary depending on the display adapter.

❏ *column* is the number of the column in which the cursor is displayed. The range is either from 1 to 80 or from 1 to 40, depending on the current QBASIC SCREEN setting.

❏ *visible* is either 1 or 0. The number 1 displays the cursor and 0 hides it. The default is 1.

❏ *start*, *stop* are used to change the size of the cursor.

In the following example, the LOCATE statement positions the cursor at row 10, column 10. The subsequent PRINT statement then displays the message *Hello World* at that position.

```
LOCATE 10,10
PRINT "Hello World"
```

The LOCATE statement can be used to position the cursor for input statements as well.

PRINT Statement

The *PRINT* statement displays data on the screen or printer. The syntax for the *PRINT* statement is as follows:

```
PRINT data [,] [;]
```

❏ *data* is any string or numeric variable. It can also be literal string or number (for example, "Hello World" or 12.34)

❏ ; (semicolon) and , (comma) are used to display more than one piece of data on the same line. The semicolon (;) displays data items without spaces between them. Use the comma (,) to separate data places 14 spaces between each item.

In the following example, the output from the statements is *My Name is Jeff*:

```
Name$ = "Jeff"
PRINT "My Name Is ";Name$
```

PRINT USING Statement

The *PRINT USING* statement adds to the flexibility of the *PRINT* statement by enabling the data to be formatted to a certain size and appearance.

The syntax of the *PRINT USING* statement is as follows:

```
PRINT USING formatstring ; data
```

❏ *formatstring* contains the formatting characters for the subsequent *data*. This can be contained in a string variable or a literal string ("$$#,###.##"). Several characters exist for formatting both numeric and string data$mdconsult QBASIC's on-line help for a complete list.

❏ *data* is the actual data to be output.

The *PRINT USING* statement can contain only one *formatstring*, but it can contain several pieces of *data*.

In the following example, the output from these statements would be:

Total Credit Limit: $45,000. Available: $18,000

```
CreditLimit! = 45000
AvailCredit! = 18000
PRINT USING "Total Credit Limit: $###,###. Available:$###,###";
        CreditLimit!;AvailCredit!
```

Accepting Input from the Keyboard

QBASIC has several methods by which the programmer can request input from the user. The examples in this chapter rely primarily on two methods: the *LINE INPUT* statement and the *INKEY$* statement.

LINE INPUT Statement

LINE INPUT accepts data entered from the keyboard and places it into a string variable. All characters are accepted, even commas and quotation marks. The maximum number of characters that can be accepted via *LINE INPUT* is 255.

The syntax for the *LINE INPUT* statement is as follows:

```
LINE INPUT ["prompt";] [;]variable$
```

The optional *prompt* clause displays a descriptive message on the same line that *variable$* is prompted for.

The following example displays the message *Enter Your First Name* on the screen and waits for input. Once the user has responded and pressed Enter, his input is placed in the string variable *FirstName$*.

```
LINE INPUT "Enter Your First Name: ";FirstName$
```

INKEY$ Function

Unlike the *LINE INPUT* function, which waits for the user to respond, *INKEY$* reads a character from the keyboard and immediately returns the result to the program. This makes it a very useful tool for reading function-key and arrow-key responses.

The syntax for the *INKEY$* function is as follows:

```
variable$ = INKEY$
  -and-
IF INKEY$<>""THEN...
```

The second form simply assigns the *INKEY$* value to a string variable. This method is desirable because the value of *INKEY$* at the time the statement is issued can be processed by referencing *variable$*.

In the following example, a small loop repeats indefinitely until you press a key. The keystroke is then placed in *r$* and the loop is exited.

```
DO
   r$ = INKEY$
LOOP UNTIL r$<>""
```

Basic Sequential File Input and Output

Several of the examples in this chapter involve input (reading) and output (writing) to *sequential files*. Sequential files are simple files that contain ASCII text with (in this case) each record on a separate line. To access these files for input and output, the QBASIC *OPEN* statement is used. To read the data from the files, use the *LINE INPUT* # statement. And finally, to write new data to a file, the QBASIC *PRINT* # statement is used.

OPEN Statement

The QBASIC *OPEN* statement, in this context, is used to open a sequential file for input or output. Opening a file for input enables you to read its contents without changing them. Opening a file for output immediately creates a new, empty file with the name you selected and readies it to be written to.

The syntax to open a sequential file for input is as follows:

```
OPEN fname FOR INPUT AS # filenumber
```

❑ *fname* is either the file's actual name enclosed in double quotes ("AUTOEXEC.BAT") or a string variable containing the file's name (*FileName$* if the string variable *FileName$* contains a valid file name).

❑ *filenumber* is the number associated with the file. It must be in the range from 1 through 255. Each file must have a *filenumber* unique to all others open at that time.

In the following example, the file AUTOEXEC.BAT is opened for input as file number 1:

```
FileName$="AUTOEXEC.BAT"
OPEN FileName$ FOR INPUT AS #1
```

Opening a file for output is done in the same manner, except the word *OUTPUT* is substituted for *INPUT*. Be careful: opening a file for OUTPUT immediately creates a new empty file with name you supply. This overwrites any existing file with the same name.

LINE INPUT # Statement

The *LINE INPUT* # statement reads data from a sequential file and places it into a string variable. Any delimiters, such as commas or semicolons, are ignored.

The syntax for the *LINE INPUT* # statement is as follows:

```
LINE INPUT # filenumber, invari$
```

❑ *filenumber* is the number associated with the file being read from. When the file was opened for INPUT, you specified a *filenumber*; this should be that same number.

❑ *invari$* is the string variable that contains the input information.

The following example reads a record from the previously opened *AUTOEXEC.BAT* file and places that information into *info$*.

```
OPEN "AUTOEXEC.BAT" FOR INPUT AS #1
LINE INPUT #1, info$
CLOSE 1
```

PRINT # Statement

The *PRINT* # statement writes ASCII text data to a sequential file. The data written will not be formatted or delimited in any manner.

The syntax for the *PRINT* # statement is as follows:

```
PRINT # filenumber, outvari$[;,]
```

❑ *filenumber* is the number associated with the file being written to. When the file was opened for OUTPUT, you specified a *filenumber*; this should be that same number.

❑ *outvari$* is the string containing the data to be written. You can specify multiple strings for output on the same *PRINT* # statement line. Separating them with a semicolon (;) places the subsequent strings immediately after the preceding ones. Separating them with a comma (,) places the subsequent strings in the next print position (14 characters apart).

The following example writes the data *January Sales Figures Follow* into the previously opened *TEST.TXT* file:

```
info$="January Sales Figures Follow"
OPEN "TEST.TXT" FOR OUTPUT AS #1
PRINT #1, info$
CLOSE 1
```

Miscellaneous Functions and Statements

QBASIC contains numerous functions and statements for performing specialized tasks. The examples presented in this chapter utilize several of them. As
a means of general introduction, each one is listed and explained briefly. The
explanation is confined to a specific implementation of the function or statement. For a broader definition, refer to QBASIC's on-line help.

ASC(*stringvari*) Function

ASC returns the ASCII or IBM extended value for the first character in
stringvari. The number returned can be from 0 through 255. The *ASC* function is a useful means for determining when arrow keys and PgUp, PgDn, or
other keys are pressed. (See the sample program FILEMODI.BAS as well as
several others).

CHR$(*numbvari*) Function

CHR$ performs the opposite operation of the *ASC* function. *numebvari* must
be in the range from 0 through 255. The *CHR$* function presents a useful
means for including characters that can't be typed, such as Tab and Enter, in
your programs. (See the Boxer procedure)

CLS statement

The CLS statement clears the screen.

COLOR [textcolor], [background] Statement (in text screen mode)

The COLOR statement is the means by which the color of the text and background on a color monitor can be changed. *textcolor* and *background* are inte-
gers in the range from 0 through 15. Each number represents a different
color. You can, for instance, change the display to black characters on a
white background by issuing the following color statement: COLOR 0,7. (See
the sample program COLORCHG.BAS for an illustration of this).

CONST *variname* = expression Statement

The *CONST* statement enables you to assign a descriptive name (such as
TRUE) to an expression (such as **-1**), producing a more readable program. An

added benefit of this statement is that once a constant is initialized, it cannot be inadvertently changed elsewhere in the program. (Several of the sample programs set TRUE and FALSE up as constants).

DATE$ Function

Used as a function, *DATE$* returns the current system date. (See the sample program CALENDAR.BAS)

ERR Function

The *ERR* function returns the number corresponding to the last QBASIC error which occurred. This information, combined with the *ON ERROR GOTO* statement, enables you to set up error-handling routines. (Several of the sample programs contain this function).

FILES [*filespec*] Statement

The *FILES* statement displays the list of files that match *filespec* (C:*.BAT, for example). If *filespec* is not found or is invalid, *ERR* is set to the appropriate error number. Otherwise, the matching file(s) is displayed on the screen. (The sample program FILEINPT.BAS uses the *FILES* statement to test for the existence of a file).

INSTR(*[startpos,]stringexpr1, stringexpr2*) Function

The *INSTR* function performs a search on the string *stringexpr1* for the first occurrence of the string *stringexpr2* starting at the position, *startpos*. If the search is successful, the numeric position where *stringexpr2* starts in *stringexpr1* is returned. Otherwise, 0 is returned. In the following example, *xpos%* would equal **7**. (See the sample program DIRSIZE.BAS)

```
xpos% = INSTR(1,"BYTES AVAILABLE","AVAILABLE")
```

LEFT$(*stringvar,numbchar*) Function

The *LEFT$* function starts at the leftmost character of the string variable, *stringvar*, and extracts the first *numbchar* characters. For example, the following statements set *part$* equal to *ABCD*. (See the sample program FINDNEWS.BAS)

```
alphab$ = "ABCDEFGHIJKL"
part$ = LEFT$(alphab$,4)
```

LEN(*stringvar*) Function

LEN returns the number of characters contained in the string *stringvar*. This information, combined with the *LOCATE* statement presents an easy method of centering output on the screen. For example, the following statements centers the words *AUTOEXEC.BAT* on the first line of an 80-column screen. (See the sample program FILEVIEW.BAS as well as several others).

```
FileName$="AUTOEXEC.BAT"
LOCATE 1, (80-LEN(FileName$))/2
PRINT FileName$
```

LTRIM$(*stringvar*) Function

The *LTRIM$* function returns a copy of the string, *stringvar* with all leading spaces removed. (See the sample program CALENDAR.BAS)

MID$(*stringvar,startpos,[numbchar]*) Function

MID$ extracts a portion of the string, *stringvar*, beginning at the character position, *startpos*, and continuing for *numbchar*. For example, the following statements set *part$* equal to *CDEF*. (Several of the sample programs contain the *MID$* function)

```
alphab$ = "ABCDEFGHIJKL"
part$ = MID$(alphab$,3,4)
```

NAME *oldfile* AS *newfile* Statement

The NAME statement takes the file, *oldspec* and moves it to the file *newfile*. For example, the following statement moves the file *AUTOEXEC.BAT* from the root directory into the \DOS directory, and changes its name to *AUTOEXEC.OLD*. (See the sample program MOVE.BAS)

```
NAME "\AUTOEXEC.BAT" AS "\DOS\AUTOEXEC.OLD"
```

RTRIM$(*stringvar*) Function

The *RTRIM$* function returns a copy of the string, *stringvar* with all trailing spaces removed. (See the sample program FINDOLDS.BAS)

RIGHT$(*stringvar,numbchar*) Function

The *RIGHT$* function starts at the rightmost character of the string variable, *stringvar*, and extracts the last *numbchar* characters. For example, the following statements set *part$* equal to *IJKL*. (See the sample program FINDNEWS.BAS)

```
alphab$ = "ABCDEFGHIJKL"
part$ = RIGHT$(alphab$,4)
```

SHELL [*commstring*] Statement

The *SHELL* statement enables your program to execute a DOS command contained in the string *commstring*. This useful command enables you to insert options normally reserved for DOS execution into your programs. For example, the following statement formats a diskette from within a QBASIC program. (See the sample program DIRSIZE.BAS).

```
SHELL "FORMAT A:"
```

SLEEP [*numb*] Statement

The *SLEEP* statement suspends execution of a program for the number of seconds specified by the argument, *numb*, or until a key is pressed. (See the sample program POSTIT.BAS)

STR$[*numbvar*] Function

The *STR$* function converts a numeric variable, *numbvar*, into a string. (See the sample program CALENDAR.BAS).

VAL[*stringvar*] Function

The *VAL* function converts the string, *stringvar*, into a number. (See the sample program COLORCHG.BAS).

User-Defined Sub Procedures and Functions

Simply stated, sub procedures and functions are blocks of code that exist outside the main program and are called to perform specific tasks. They can be passed parameters by the calling program, and, in the case of a function, can also return a value. Processes that must be performed repeatedly throughout a program are excellent candidates for transformation into a sub procedure or function. The sample programs contained in this chapter contain both a sample sub procedure (Boxer), and a sample function (Selector).

Sub procedures and functions are declared within a QBASIC program through the use of the *DECLARE* statement. The *DECLARE* statement sets the basic parameters for calling the procedure:

```
DECLARE FUNCTION functioname [parameters]
DECLARE SUB subname [parameters]
```

❏ *functioname* and *subname* are the names of the procedures to be called. They can be up to 40 characters in length.

❏ *parameters* is the list of variables to be passed to the procedure. You must specify the types of the variables in the parameter list.

The DECLARE statements should exist at the beginning of the main module, before any executable statements.

The sub procedures and functions must then be created in forms shown in the following two sections.

Function

```
FUNCTION functioname [parameters] [SHARED] [STATIC]
   [statements]
   functioname = expression
END FUNCTION
```

❏ *functioname* is the name of the function.

❏ *parameters* is the list of variables to be passed to the function. You must specify the types of the variables in the parameter list.

❏ *SHARED* signifies that there are variables contained in the main module which the function needs to use, but was not explicitly passed.

❏ *STATIC* signifies that the values of any variables local to the function are to be preserved between calls to the function.

❏ The statement *functioname = expression* is the means by which a value is returned to the calling program.

Sub Procedure

```
SUB subname [parameters] [SHARED] [STATIC]
   [statements]
END SUB
```

❏ *subname* is the name of the sub procedure.

❏ *parameters* is the list of variables to be passed to the sub procedure. You must specify the types of the variables in the parameter list.

❏ *SHARED* signifies that there are variables contained in the main module that the sub procedure needs to use but was not explicitly passed.

❏ *STATIC* signifies that the values of any variables local to the sub procedure are to be preserved between calls to the sub procedure.

The following two statements illustrate actual calls to the sub procedure Boxer and function selector from the sample programs:

Call to the function *selector* with a predefined array *choice$*, screen coordinates (11 and 35) and default choice (1).

```
selectr% = selector%(choice$, 11, 35, 1)
```

The number corresponding to the choice made (in selector) is returned and stored in the variable selectr%.

Call to the sub procedure *Boxer* screen coordinates of the box (8 ,8 ,14 and 72) and a predefined box pattern, *boxstring$*.

```
Boxer 8, 8, 14, 72, boxstring$
```

For more detailed information on sub procedures and functions, refer to the actual code in the sample programs, and QBASIC's on-line help.

Sample Programs

CALCULTR.BAS

This program performs basic mathematic operations on a maximum of ten numbers.

Considerations:

The operations are performed from left to right.

The first argument should be a number (for the square root function, 3@ should be entered instead of @3).

This program does not recognize ( ) groupings.

Shows:

Procedure for parsing terms out of an input line.

Mathematical properties of QBASIC.

```
' CALCULTR.BAS
'
'    Calculator program which reads and parses an input line
'
'        Useage:
'                The operations are performed from left to right
'
'                The first argument should be a number (so for the
'                square root function, 3@ should be entered instead of @3)
'
'                This small program will not recognize () groupings
'
'                A maximum of ten number can be entered
'
CLS
' Set Up Variables
InNumb$ = "    "
' nmb = Number    oper$ = operation to perform
DIM nmb(10), oper$(10)
' Print Messages
LOCATE 23, 1: PRINT "+ = Add, - = Subtraction, * = Multiply, / = Divide,
      ^ = Power, @ = Square Root"
LOCATE 10, 10: PRINT "Enter Formula To Calculate: "
LINE INPUT InNumb$                ' Accept Input
' mult=*, additon=+, subtraction=-, division=/, ^=power, @=SQR Root
operator$ = "*+-/^@"
    z% = 1
    DO WHILE LEN(InNumb$) > 0
       ' parse out numbers
       innumber$ = ""
       DO
         innumber$ = innumber$ + MID$(InNumb$, 1, 1)
         InNumb$ = MID$(InNumb$, 2)
```

```
      LOOP UNTIL INSTR(1, operator$, MID$(InNumb$, 1, 1)) <> 0 OR
   LEN(InNumb$) = 0
     oper$(z%) = MID$(InNumb$, 1, 1)
     nmb(z%) = VAL(innumber$)
      z% = z% + 1
     InNumb$ = MID$(InNumb$, 2)
   LOOP 'while len(InNumb$)
   SELECT CASE oper$(1)
      CASE IS = "*"                              ' Multiplication
        ans = nmb(1) * nmb(2)
      CASE IS = "/"                              ' Division
        ans = nmb(1) / nmb(2)
      CASE IS = "+"                              ' Addition
        ans = nmb(1) + nmb(2)
      CASE IS = "-"                              ' Subtraction
        ans = nmb(1) - nmb(2)
      CASE IS = "@"                              ' Square Root
        ans = SQR(nmb(1))
      CASE IS = "^"                              ' Exponent
        ans = nmb(1)
        FOR x% = 1 TO nmb(2) - 1
          ans = ans * nmb(1)
        NEXT
   END SELECT
FOR opercntr% = 3 TO z%
   SELECT CASE oper$(opercntr% - 1)
      CASE IS = "*"
        ans = ans * nmb(opercntr%)
      CASE IS = "/"
        ans = ans / nmb(opercntr%)
      CASE IS = "+"
        ans = ans + nmb(opercntr%)
      CASE IS = "-"
        ans = ans - nmb(opercntr%)
      CASE IS = "@"
        ans = SQR(ans)
      CASE IS = "^"
        ans2 = ans
        FOR x% = 1 TO nmb(opercntr%) - 1
          ans2 = ans2 * ans
        NEXT
        ans = ans2
   END SELECT
NEXT
LOCATE 15, 10: PRINT "You Answer Is: "; ans
```

CALENDAR.BAS

Reads the default file: CALENDAR.TXT in the current directory and sees if there are any messages dated for today. It then displays these messages on the screen.

Considerations:

Recognizes dates in the following format:

"5/8", "May 8", or "05/08/91"

CALENDAR.TXT should appear as follows:

```
5/8 Call Bob Jones About Meeting
5/8 Review Expense Figures By 9:00am
etc..
```

Shows:

Sequential file input.

Use of DATE$ function.

```
' CALENDAR.BAS
'       Reads the default file: CALENDAR.TXT in the current directory
'       and sees if there are any messages dated for today.
'       It then displays these messages on the screen.
'
'
'           Recognizes dates in the following format:
'
'               "5/8", "May 8",  or "05/08/91"
'
'       CALENDAR.TXT should appear as follows:
'
'               5/8  Call Bob Jones About Meeting
'               5/8  Review Expense Figures By 9:00am
'                       etc...
'
'       CALENDAR.TXT must be in the current directory
'
'
'
ErrorCode% = 0
ON ERROR GOTO ErrRoutine
CONST true = -1
CONST false = 0
CLS
```

```
' load up month's name array
DIM Months$(12)
Months$(1) = "January": Months$(2) = "February": Months$(3) = "March"
Months$(4) = "April": Months$(5) = "May": Months$(6) = "June"
Months$(7) = "July": Months$(8) = "August": Months$(9) = "September"
Months$(10) = "October": Months$(11) = "November": Months$(12) = "December"
OPEN "calendar.txt" FOR INPUT AS #1     ' open file in CURRENT directory
IF ErrorCode% <> 0 THEN END
' evaluate today's date
InDate$ = DATE$
monthval% = VAL(LEFT$(InDate$, 2))
dayval% = VAL(MID$(InDate$, 4, 2))
yearval% = VAL(RIGHT$(InDate$, 4))
month$ = LTRIM$(STR$(monthval%)) + "/"
day$ = LTRIM$(STR$(dayval%))
MonthName$ = Months$(monthval%)
day$ = LTRIM$(STR$(dayval%))
' create search strings
search1$ = InDate$
search2$ = MonthName$ + " " + day$
search3$ = month$ + day$
' Read each record in file
FoundOne = false
x% = 1
DO                                      ' Read lines
   LINE INPUT #1, message$
   IF INSTR(1, message$, search1$) <> 0 OR INSTR(1, message$, search2$)
      <> 0 OR INSTR(1, message$, search3$) <> 0 THEN
     IF x% >= 22 THEN
        SOUND 320, 4
      LOCATE 23, 1: PRINT "Press Any Key To Continue"
       DO: z$ = INKEY$: LOOP UNTIL z$ <> ""
        x% = 1
        CLS
     END IF
    LOCATE x%, 1: PRINT message$: x% = x% + 1
    FoundOne = true
   END IF
LOOP UNTIL (EOF(1))
IF FoundOne THEN
   SOUND 320, 4
ELSE
   LOCATE 23, 1: PRINT "No Messages For "; InDate$
END IF
END
```

```
ErrRoutine:
      ErrorCode% = ERR
      SELECT CASE ErrorCode%
       CASE IS = 58
            LOCATE 22, 1: PRINT "File Already Exists, Press Any Key
    To Continue"
       CASE IS = 53
            LOCATE 22, 1: PRINT "File Not Found, Press Any Key To
    Continue"
       CASE IS = 64
            LOCATE 22, 1: PRINT "Incorrect File Name Entered, Press
    Any Key To Continue"
       CASE IS = 71
            LOCATE 22, 1: PRINT "Disk Not Ready Error, Press Any Key
    To Continue"
       CASE IS = 75
            LOCATE 22, 1: PRINT "Path/File Access Error, Press Any
    Key To Continue"
       CASE IS = 76
            LOCATE 22, 1: PRINT "Path Not Found Error, Press Any Key
    To Continue"
       END SELECT
  DO
    z$ = INKEY$
  LOOP WHILE z$ = ""
  RESUME NEXT
```

COLORCHG.BAS

This utility creates a batch file that changes the DOS color attributes.

Shows:

Use of INKEY$ Function.

Use of COLOR statement.

Sequential file output.

Use of SHELL statement.

2 Dimensional Arrays.

```
'   COLORCHG.BAS
'      Routine To Create A Batch File Which Will Change The DOS
'      color attributes
'
'
```

```
'
DECLARE FUNCTION selector% (choice$, StartRow%, StartCol%, Default%)
DECLARE SUB Boxer (tlrow%, tlcol%, brrow%, brcol%, boxstring$)
' Boxer may be called with several types of box configurations
' Box         Top Left    Top Right   Top         Bottom      Left
     Right       Bott Left   Bott Right
' pattern     Corner      Corner      Line        Line        Side
       Side        Corner      Corner
boxstring$ = CHR$(201) + CHR$(187) + CHR$(205) + CHR$(205) + CHR$(186) +
     CHR$(186) + CHR$(200) + CHR$(188)
DIM TextColor(9, 3) AS STRING            'Create Text Colors Array
DIM BackGround(9, 3) AS STRING           'Create Back Ground Colors
     Array
CLS
' Load Up Colors With Default Values
'               Text Color
' Color Name                Dos Value           QBASIC Value
TextColor(1, 1) = "Black": TextColor(1, 2) = "30": TextColor(1, 3) = "0"
TextColor(2, 1) = "Red":   TextColor(2, 2) = "31": TextColor(2, 3) = "4"
TextColor(3, 1) = "Green": TextColor(3, 2) = "32": TextColor(3, 3) = "2"
TextColor(4, 1) = "Yellow":TextColor(4, 2) = "33": TextColor(4, 3) = "14"
TextColor(5, 1) = "Blue":  TextColor(5, 2) = "34": TextColor(5, 3) = "1"
TextColor(6, 1) = "Magenta": TextColor(6, 2) = "35": TextColor(6, 3) = "5"
TextColor(7, 1) = "Cyan":  TextColor(7, 2) = "36": TextColor(7, 3) = "3"
TextColor(8, 1) = "White": TextColor(8, 2) = "37": TextColor(8, 3) = "7"
'TextColor(9, 1) = "Black On White": TextColor(9, 1) = "7"
'               Back Ground Colors
' Color Name                Dos Value
BackGround(1, 1) = "Black": BackGround(1, 2) = "40": BackGround(1, 3) = "0"
BackGround(2, 1) = "Red":   BackGround(2, 2) = "41": BackGround(2, 3) = "4"
BackGround(3, 1) = "Green": BackGround(3, 2) = "42": BackGround(3, 3) = "2"
BackGround(4, 1) = "Yellow":BackGround(4, 2) = "43": BackGround(4, 3) = "14"
BackGround(5, 1) = "Blue":  BackGround(5, 2) = "44": BackGround(5, 3) = "1"
BackGround(6, 1) = "Magenta":BackGround(6, 2) = "45": BackGround(6, 3) = "5"
BackGround(7, 1) = "Cyan":  BackGround(7, 2) = "46": BackGround(7, 3) = "3"
BackGround(8, 1) = "White": BackGround(8, 2) = "48": BackGround(8, 3) = "7"
'BackGround(9, 1) = "Black On White": BackGround(9, 1) = "7"
' Set Up Default Values
CurrText% = 8: CurrBack% = 1: CurrTCol% = 20: CurrBCol% = 50: sel% = 8
CurrCol$ = "TEXT": offset% = 5
' Display Screen
COLOR 0, 8: CLS : COLOR 7, 0
Boxer 1, 1, 20, 80, boxstring$
LOCATE 2, 31: PRINT "DOS Color Changer"
LOCATE offset% - 1, CurrTCol% - 2: COLOR 0, 7: PRINT "Text Color"
```

```
COLOR 7, 0: LOCATE offset% - 1, CurrBCol% - 2: PRINT "Back Ground"
Boxer 21, 1, 24, 80, boxstring$
LOCATE 22, 3: PRINT "o  Use Your Arrow Keys To Change Colors   o  Press
     <<TAB>> To Switch Columns"
LOCATE 23, 3: PRINT "o  Press <ESC> When You Are Finished"
' Print Colors On The Screen
FOR x% = 1 TO 8
   ' Black Will Display Black On White
   IF TextColor(x%, 1) = "Black" OR BackGround(x%, 1) = "Black" THEN
      bck% = 15
   ELSE
      bck% = 8
   END IF
   LOCATE x% + offset%, CurrTCol%: COLOR VAL(TextColor(x%, 3)), bck%
   PRINT TextColor(x%, 1)
   LOCATE x% + offset%, CurrBCol%: COLOR VAL(BackGround(x%, 3)), bck%
   PRINT BackGround(x%, 1)
NEXT
LOCATE CurrText% + offset%, CurrTCol% - 1: PRINT CHR$(26)
LOCATE CurrBack% + offset%, CurrBCol% - 1: PRINT CHR$(26)
' Main Program Loop
DO
   IF CurrCol$ = "TEXT" AND r$ <> CHR$(9) THEN
      LOCATE CurrText% + offset%, CurrTCol% - 1: PRINT " "
      CurrText% = sel%
      LOCATE CurrText% + offset%, CurrTCol% - 1: PRINT CHR$(26)
   END IF
   IF CurrCol$ = "BACK" AND r$ <> CHR$(9) THEN
      LOCATE CurrBack% + offset%, CurrBCol% - 1: PRINT " "
      CurrBack% = sel%
      LOCATE CurrBack% + offset%, CurrBCol% - 1: PRINT CHR$(26)
   END IF
   ' Displays A Line With Current Color Selections
   LOCATE 16, CurrTCol% + 6
   COLOR VAL(TextColor(CurrText%, 3)), VAL(BackGround(CurrBack%, 3))
   PRINT "Current Color Selection"
   COLOR 7, 0
   DO                                 ' Wait For A Key Press
     r$ = INKEY$
   LOOP UNTIL r$ <> ""
   IF LEN(r$) > 1 THEN
     IF CurrCol$ = "TEXT" THEN sel% = CurrText% ELSE sel% = CurrBack%
     rscancode% = ASC(MID$(r$, 2, 1))
     IF rscancode% = 72 THEN                    ' Up Arrow Pressed
        IF sel% = 1 THEN sel% = 8 ELSE sel% = sel% - 1
```

```
          END IF
       IF rscancode% = 80 THEN                    ' Down Arrow Pressed
          IF sel% = 8 THEN sel% = 1 ELSE sel% = sel% + 1
       END IF
    ELSE
       IF r$ = CHR$(9) THEN                        ' Tab Pressed
          IF CurrCol$ = "TEXT" THEN
             CurrCol$ = "BACK"
             LOCATE offset% - 1, CurrTCol% - 2: COLOR 7, 0: PRINT "Text
    Color"
             COLOR 0, 7: LOCATE offset% - 1, CurrBCol% - 2: PRINT "Back
    Ground"
          ELSE
             CurrCol$ = "TEXT"
             LOCATE offset% - 1, CurrTCol% - 2: COLOR 0, 7: PRINT "Text
    Color"
             COLOR 7, 0: LOCATE offset% - 1, CurrBCol% - 2: PRINT "Back
    Ground"
          END IF
       END IF
    END IF
LOOP UNTIL r$ = CHR$(27)
COLOR 7, 0
LOCATE 22, 2: PRINT SPACE$(77): LOCATE 23, 2: PRINT SPACE$(77)
'  A Batch File Named COLOR.BAT Will Be Created In The Root Directory Of
'  The Drive You Are Currently Logged Into.  This File Will Contain The
'  Necessary To Change The DOS Screen To The Color Scheme Selected Here.
DIM SHARED choice$(2)
choice$(1) = "Yes"
choice$(2) = "No"
LOCATE 22, 10: PRINT "Create \COLOR.BAT With Selections Made?"
selectr% = selector%(choice$, 22, 52, 1)
IF choice$(selectr%) = "Yes" THEN
   OPEN "\color.bat" FOR OUTPUT AS 1
   PRINT #1, "ECHO OFF"
   PRINT #1, "echo " + CHR$(27) + "[" + TextColor(CurrText%, 2) + ";" +
       BackGround(CurrBack%, 2) + "m"
   CLOSE #1
END IF
LOCATE 22, 2: PRINT SPACE$(77): LOCATE 22, 10
PRINT "Run \COLOR.BAT Before Exiting?"
selectr% = selector%(choice$, 22, 45, 1)
IF choice$(selectr%) = "Yes" THEN
   cmd$ = "\color.bat"
   SHELL cmd$
```

```
END IF
END
SUB Boxer (tlrow%, tlcol%, brrow%, brcol%, boxstring$) STATIC
 ' Figure Out Size Of Box
 SizeOfBox% = brcol% - tlcol% + 1
 ' Parse Out Box Characters
 tlc$ = MID$(boxstring$, 1, 1)
 trc$ = MID$(boxstring$, 2, 1)
 tln$ = MID$(boxstring$, 3, 1)
 bln$ = MID$(boxstring$, 4, 1)
 lsd$ = MID$(boxstring$, 5, 1)
 rsd$ = MID$(boxstring$, 6, 1)
 blc$ = MID$(boxstring$, 7, 1)
 brc$ = MID$(boxstring$, 8, 1)
 'Begin Box Creation
 LOCATE tlrow%, tlcol%
 PRINT tlc$; STRING$(SizeOfBox% - 2, tln$); trc$;
 FOR x% = tlrow% + 1 TO brrow% - 1
      LOCATE x%, tlcol%
      PRINT lsd$; SPACE$(SizeOfBox% - 2); rsd$;
 NEXT
 LOCATE brrow%, tlcol%
 PRINT blc$; STRING$(SizeOfBox% - 2, bln$); brc$;
END SUB
FUNCTION selector% (choice$, StartRow%, StartCol%, Default%) STATIC
selected% = Default%
DO
  IF selected% = 1 THEN COLOR 0, 7
  LOCATE StartRow%, StartCol%: PRINT choice$(1)
  COLOR 7, 0
  IF selected% = 2 THEN COLOR 0, 7
  LOCATE StartRow%, StartCol% + LEN(choice$(1)) + 2: PRINT choice$(2)
  COLOR 7, 0
  DO
    r$ = INKEY$
  LOOP UNTIL r$ <> ""
  IF LEN(r$) > 1 THEN
    rscancode% = ASC(MID$(r$, 2, 1))
    IF rscancode% = 77 THEN                  ' Right Arrow Pressed
      IF selected% = 1 THEN selected% = 2 ELSE selected% = 1
    END IF
    IF rscancode% = 75 THEN                  ' Left Arrow Pressed
      IF selected% = 2 THEN selected% = 1 ELSE selected% = 2
    END IF
  END IF
```

```
LOOP UNTIL r$ = CHR$(13)
selector% = selected%
END FUNCTION
```

DIRSIZE.BAS

Computes the size of file specifications input. Takes advantage of DOS 5 displaying the size during a directory.

Shows:

Sequential file input.

Use of SHELL statement.

Use of the INSTR function.

Arrays.

Use of PRINT USING statement.

```
' DIRSIZE.BAS
'      Computes The Size Of File Specifications Input
'
'       Takes advantage of DOS 5.0 displaying the size during a directory
'          command
'
'
'
CLS : LOCATE 1, 28: PRINT "File Size Totaler"
DIM DirName$(10)
DIM DirSize!(10)
x% = 0
LOCATE 9, 1: PRINT "Directory": LOCATE 9, 50: PRINT "Size"
DO
  x% = x% + 1
  DirName$(x%) = "": LOCATE 6, 1: PRINT SPACE$(79)
  LOCATE 5, 1: PRINT "Enter Up To 10 Directory Names, Or File
       Specifications (BLANKS To EXIT)"
  LOCATE 6, 1: INPUT DirName$(x%)
  LOCATE x% + 10, 1: PRINT MID$(DirName$(x%), 1, 40)
LOOP UNTIL DirName$(x%) = "" OR x% >= 10
x% = 1
total! = 0
DO
  cmd$ = "DIR " + DirName$(x%) + " /w > dirsze.dir"
  LOCATE 23, 1
  SHELL cmd$
```

```
      LOCATE 23, 1: PRINT "Calculating" + SPACE$(65)
      OPEN "dirsze.dir" FOR INPUT AS #1
      DO
        number$ = ""
        LINE INPUT #1, dir$
        IF INSTR(1, dir$, "file(s)") <> 0 THEN
           start% = INSTR(1, dir$, "file(s)") + 8
           DO WHILE MID$(dir$, start%, 1) = " "
              start% = start% + 1
           LOOP
           DO WHILE MID$(dir$, start%, 1) <> " "
             number$ = number$ + MID$(dir$, start%, 1)
             start% = start% + 1
           LOOP
           EXIT DO
        END IF
      LOOP WHILE NOT EOF(1)
      IF DirName$(x%) <> "" THEN
         total! = total! + VAL(number$)
         DirSize!(x%) = VAL(number$)
         LOCATE x% + 10, 42: PRINT USING "############"; DirSize!(x%)
      END IF
      CLOSE #1
      IF x% = 10 THEN EXIT DO
      x% = x% + 1
    LOOP UNTIL DirName$(x%) = ""
    LOCATE 23, 1: PRINT SPACE$(79)
    LOCATE 22, 36: PRINT "Total: "
    LOCATE 22, 42: PRINT USING "############"; total!
    KILL "dirsze.dir"                ' delete the temporary file
```

FILEINPT.BAS

Inputs a valid filename routine.

Shows:

Use of FILES statement.

Use of error routine ON ERROR GOTO.

```
' FILEINPT.BAS
'    Small file name enter routine
'
'      Uses The FILES command to check for existance of file
'
```

```
'
ON ERROR GOTO ErrRoutine
DO
  CLS
  LOCATE 10, 1: PRINT "Enter A Filename (or BLANKS TO Exit)"
  filename$ = ""
  LOCATE 11, 1: LINE INPUT filename$
  ErrorCode% = 0
  IF filename$ <> "" THEN
    FILES filename$
    LOCATE 12, 1: PRINT SPACE$(240)                ' clear out 3 lines
    IF ErrorCode% = 0 THEN
      LOCATE 12, 1: PRINT "File Found!  Press Any Key To Continue"
        DO
          r$ = INKEY$
        LOOP UNTIL r$ <> ""
      END IF
  END IF
  LOOP UNTIL filename$ = ""
END
ErrRoutine:
      ErrorCode% = ERR
     LOCATE 12, 1: PRINT SPACE$(77)
      SELECT CASE ERR
      CASE IS = 53
          LOCATE 22, 1: PRINT "File Not Found, Press Any Key To
Continue"
      CASE IS = 64
          LOCATE 22, 1: PRINT "Incorrect File Name Entered, Press
Any Key To Continue"
      CASE IS = 71
          LOCATE 22, 1: PRINT "Disk Not Ready Error, Press Any Key
To Continue"
      CASE IS = 75
          LOCATE 22, 1: PRINT "Path/File Access Error, Press Any
Key To Continue"
      CASE IS = 76
          LOCATE 22, 1: PRINT "Path Not Found Error, Press Any Key
To Continue"
      END SELECT
DO
  z$ = INKEY$
LOOP WHILE z$ = ""
RESUME NEXT
```

FILEMODI.BAS

This utility is used to comment/uncomment out lines in the AUTOEXEC.BAT
and CONFIG.SYS files.

Considerations:

This program does not make a backup of existing AUTOEXEC.BAT and
CONFIG.SYS files before it writes.

Shows:

Sequential file input.

Function use.

Procedure use.

Sequential file output.

Use of SELECT CASE.

Use of arrays.

```
'  FILEMODI.BAS
'      Routine to comment/uncomment out lines in AUTOEXEC.BAT and
'      CONFIG.SYS
'

CONST TRUE = -1
CONST FALSE = 0
' Declare functions and subroutines
'            SELECTOR% is called to choose between two possible options
'            BOXER is called to draw a box on the screen
'

DECLARE FUNCTION selector% (choice$, StartRow%, StartCol%, Default%)
DECLARE SUB Boxer (tlrow%, tlcol%, brrow%, brcol%, boxstring$)
ON ERROR GOTO ErrRoutine
' Boxer may be called with several types of box configurations
' Box        Top Left    Top Right    Top        Bottom      Left
'      Right       Bott Left   Bott Right
' pattern    Corner      Corner    Line       Line        Side
'      Side        Corner      Corner
boxstring$ = CHR$(201) + CHR$(187) + CHR$(205) + CHR$(205) + CHR$(186) +
      CHR$(186) + CHR$(200) + CHR$(188)
' Select file to edit
CLS
drive$ = " "
Boxer 8, 8, 14, 72, boxstring$                'Draw Box On The Screen
LOCATE 13, 10: PRINT "Enter A Single Letter (No colons or Slashes)"
```

```
DO
  LOCATE 9, 10: INPUT "Enter Your BOOT Drive (i.e. A,B,C,D, etc): ",
      drive$
LOOP UNTIL drive$ <> " "
DIM SHARED choice$(2)
choice$(1) = "AUTOEXEC.BAT"
choice$(2) = "CONFIG.SYS"
' calling pattern selected% = selector(choice$, StartRow%,
      StartCol%,default%)
LOCATE 13, 10: PRINT "Use Arrow Keys To Select File, Then Press RETURN"
LOCATE 11, 10: PRINT "Select File To Modify:"
selectr% = selector%(choice$, 11, 35, 1)
CLS
Boxer 1, 1, 20, 80, boxstring$
DIM SHARED alines$(301)
lincnt% = 1
filename$ = drive$ + ":\" + choice$(selectr%)    'Create File Name String
ErrorCode% = 0
OPEN filename$ FOR INPUT AS #1
IF ErrorCode% <> 0 THEN END
Boxer 21, 1, 23, 80, boxstring$
LOCATE 22, 4: PRINT " o Press Escape To Exit    o Press Enter To Toggle
      REM on/off "
LOCATE 2, (80 - LEN(choice$(selectr%))) / 2: PRINT choice$(selectr%)
    DO                                      ' Read lines into an
      array
      LINE INPUT #1, alines$(lincnt%)
       lincnt% = lincnt% + 1
   LOOP UNTIL (EOF(1)) OR lincnt% >= 300
   IF EOF(1) THEN
     alines$(lincnt%) = "<---- End Of File ---->"
     saveable = TRUE
   ELSE
     alines$(lincnt%) = "<---- File Too Large ---->"
     saveable = FALSE
   END IF
   CLOSE #1
' Set up variables for displaying lines
FirstRec% = 1                      'First Displayed Record
SelRec% = 1                        'Selected Record
TotalRec% = lincnt%                'Total Records
toplne% = 3                        'Beginning Line
bottlne% = 19
MaxRecs% = bottlne% - toplne% + 1  'Maximum Displayable Records
IF TotalRec% <= MaxRecs% THEN
```

```
        LastRec% = TotalRec%                'Last Record displayed
ELSE
        LastRec% = MaxRecs%
END IF
currrw% = toplne%                      'Current Relative Row Position
done = FALSE                           'Variable DONE controls execution of
                                       'main program loop

' Main Program Loop
DO
    xline% = toplne%
    FOR i% = FirstRec% TO LastRec%
        LOCATE xline%, 4
        PRINT MID$(alines$(i%) + SPACE$(ABS(76 - LEN(alines$(i%))))), 1,
            76): LastRec% = i%
        xline% = xline% + 1
    NEXT
    COLOR 0, 7
    LOCATE currrw%, 4
    PRINT MID$(alines$(SelRec%) + SPACE$(ABS(76 -
        LEN(alines$(SelRec%))))), 1, 76)
    COLOR 7, 0
     DO
      keypr$ = INKEY$
     LOOP WHILE keypr$ = ""
     IF LEN(keypr$) > 1 THEN
        keypr = ASC(MID$(keypr$, 2, 1))
     ELSE
        keypr = ASC(keypr$)
     END IF
     SELECT CASE keypr
        CASE IS = 27                        ' Escape pressed
            CLOSE #1
            done = TRUE
            IF saveable THEN
                Boxer 21, 1, 23, 80, boxstring$
                choice$(1) = "Yes"
                choice$(2) = "No"
                LOCATE 22, 2: PRINT "Do You Want To Save Your Changes? "
                selectr% = selector%(choice$, 22, 37, 1)     ' Call Selection
                                                             ' Procedure

                IF choice$(selectr%) = "Yes" THEN
                    OPEN filename$ FOR OUTPUT AS #1
                    FOR x% = 1 TO TotalRec% - 1
                        PRINT #1, alines$(x%)
                    NEXT
```

```
            CLOSE #1
          END IF
        END IF
   CASE IS = 71                          ' Home  Pressed
      SelRec% = 1: FirstRec% = 1: currrw% = toplne%
      IF TotalRec% <= MaxRecs% THEN
         LastRec% = TotalRec%
      ELSE
         LastRec% = MaxRecs%
      END IF
   CASE IS = 79                          ' End Pressed
      SelRec% = TotalRec%: LastRec% = TotalRec%
      IF TotalRec% > MaxRecs% THEN
         currrw% = bottlne%
      ELSE
         currrw% = TotalRec% + toplne% - 1
      END IF
      IF TotalRec% > MaxRecs% THEN
         FirstRec% = TotalRec% - MaxRecs% + 1
      ELSE
         FirstRec% = 1
      END IF
   CASE IS = 73                          ' PageUp Pressed
      IF FirstRec% - MaxRecs% <= 0 THEN
         SelRec% = 1
         FirstRec% = 1
      ELSE
         SelRec% = FirstRec% - MaxRecs%
         FirstRec% = FirstRec% - MaxRecs%
      END IF
      IF FirstRec% + MaxRecs% >= TotalRec% THEN
         LastRec% = TotalRec%
      ELSE
         LastRec% = FirstRec% + MaxRecs% - 1
      END IF
      currrw% = toplne%
   CASE IS = 81                          ' PageDown Pressed
      IF LastRec% + MaxRecs% > TotalRec% THEN
         LastRec% = TotalRec%
         IF TotalRec% > MaxRecs% THEN
            FirstRec% = LastRec% - MaxRecs% + 1
         ELSE
            FirstRec% = 1
         END IF
      ELSE
```

```
            LastRec% = LastRec% + MaxRecs%
            FirstRec% = LastRec% - MaxRecs% + 1
         END IF
       IF TotalRec% > MaxRecs% THEN
          currrw% = bottlne%
       ELSE
          currrw% = TotalRec% + toplne% - 1
       END IF
       SelRec% = LastRec%
    CASE IS = 80                              'Down Arrow Pressed
       IF SelRec% <> TotalRec% THEN
          IF SelRec% = LastRec% THEN
             FirstRec% = FirstRec% + 1
             SelRec% = SelRec% + 1
             LastRec% = LastRec% + 1
             currrw% = bottlne%
          ELSE
             SelRec% = SelRec% + 1
             IF SelRec% <> bottlne% THEN
                currrw% = currrw% + 1
             ELSE
                currrw% = bottlne%
             END IF
          END IF
       ELSE
          SOUND 320, 3.2
       END IF
    CASE IS = 72                              'Up Arrow Pressed
       IF SelRec% <> 1 THEN
          IF SelRec% = FirstRec% THEN
             FirstRec% = FirstRec% - 1
             SelRec% = SelRec% - 1
             LastRec% = LastRec% - 1
          ELSE
             SelRec% = SelRec% - 1
          END IF
       ELSE
          SOUND 320, 3.2
       END IF
          IF currrw% <> toplne% THEN
             currrw% = currrw% - 1
          ELSE
             currrw% = toplne%
          END IF
    CASE IS = 13                                  'Enter pressed
```

```
         IF alines$(SelRec%) <> "<---- End Of File ---->" AND
      alines$(SelRec%) <> "<---- File Too Large ---->" THEN
            zline$ = UCASE$(alines$(SelRec%))
          IF LEFT$(zline$, 3) = "REM" THEN
            alines$(SelRec%) = MID$(alines$(SelRec%), 4)
             DO                       ' Get rid of leading spaces
                spacr$ = LEFT$(alines$(SelRec%), 1)
                IF spacr$ = " " THEN
                   alines$(SelRec%) = MID$(alines$(SelRec%), 2)
                END IF
              LOOP UNTIL spacr$ <> " "
            ELSE
             alines$(SelRec%) = "REM " + alines$(SelRec%)
            END IF
         ELSE
            SOUND 300, 3.2
         END IF
      CASE ELSE
         SOUND 300, 3.2
    END SELECT
LOOP UNTIL done
END
ErrRoutine:
      ErrorCode% = ERR
     SELECT CASE ErrorCode%
     CASE IS = 58
          LOCATE 22, 1: PRINT "File Already Exists, Press Any Key
    To Continue"
     CASE IS = 53
          LOCATE 22, 1: PRINT "File Not Found, Press Any Key To
    Continue"
     CASE IS = 64
          LOCATE 22, 1: PRINT "Incorrect File Name Entered, Press
    Any Key To Continue"
     CASE IS = 71
          LOCATE 22, 1: PRINT "Disk Not Ready Error, Press Any Key
    To Continue"
     CASE IS = 75
          LOCATE 22, 1: PRINT "Path/File Access Error, Press Any
    Key To Continue"
     CASE IS = 76
          LOCATE 22, 1: PRINT "Path Not Found Error, Press Any Key
    To Continue"
     END SELECT
DO
```

```
  z$ = INKEY$
LOOP WHILE z$ = ""
RESUME NEXT
SUB Boxer (tlrow%, tlcol%, brrow%, brcol%, boxstring$) STATIC
 ' Figure Out Size Of Box
 SizeOfBox% = brcol% - tlcol% + 1
 ' Parse Out Box Characters
 tlc$ = MID$(boxstring$, 1, 1)
 trc$ = MID$(boxstring$, 2, 1)
 tln$ = MID$(boxstring$, 3, 1)
 bln$ = MID$(boxstring$, 4, 1)
 lsd$ = MID$(boxstring$, 5, 1)
 rsd$ = MID$(boxstring$, 6, 1)
 blc$ = MID$(boxstring$, 7, 1)
 brc$ = MID$(boxstring$, 8, 1)
 'Begin Box Creation
 LOCATE tlrow%, tlcol%
 PRINT tlc$; STRING$(SizeOfBox% - 2, tln$); trc$;
 FOR x% = tlrow% + 1 TO brrow% - 1
      LOCATE x%, tlcol%
      PRINT lsd$; SPACE$(SizeOfBox% - 2); rsd$;
 NEXT
 LOCATE brrow%, tlcol%
 PRINT blc$; STRING$(SizeOfBox% - 2, bln$); brc$;
END SUB
FUNCTION selector% (choice$, StartRow%, StartCol%, Default%) STATIC
selected% = Default%
DO
  IF selected% = 1 THEN COLOR 0, 7
  LOCATE StartRow%, StartCol%: PRINT choice$(1)
  COLOR 7, 0
  IF selected% = 2 THEN COLOR 0, 7
  LOCATE StartRow%, StartCol% + LEN(choice$(1)) + 2: PRINT choice$(2)
  COLOR 7, 0
  DO
    r$ = INKEY$
  LOOP UNTIL r$ <> ""
  IF LEN(r$) > 1 THEN
    rscancode% = ASC(MID$(r$, 2, 1))
    IF rscancode% = 77 THEN                    ' Right Arrow Pressed
      IF selected% = 1 THEN selected% = 2 ELSE selected% = 1
    END IF
    IF rscancode% = 75 THEN                    ' Left Arrow Pressed
      IF selected% = 2 THEN selected% = 1 ELSE selected% = 2
    END IF
```

```
    END IF
LOOP UNTIL r$ = CHR$(13)
selector% = selected%
END FUNCTION
```

FILEVIEW.BAS

This utility is used to view a text file.

Considerations:

File size is limited to 500 lines in length.

No check is made to ensure that a text file is being viewed.

Shows:

Sequential file input.

Procedure use.

Use of SELECT CASE.

Use of arrays.

```
' FILEVIEW.BAS
'      Utility to view text file
'
'        file size is limited to 300 lines in length
'
'
CONST TRUE = -1
CONST FALSE = 0
' Declare functions and subroutines
'            SELECTOR% is called to choose between two possible options
'             BOXER is called to draw a box on the screen
'
DECLARE FUNCTION selector% (choice$, StartRow%, StartCol%, Default%)
DECLARE SUB Boxer (tlrow%, tlcol%, brrow%, brcol%, boxstring$)
ON ERROR GOTO ErrRoutine          'Error Routine Setup
' Boxer may be called with several types of box configurations
' Box        Top Left    Top Right    Top        Bottom     Left
'      Right        Bott Left   Bott Right
' pattern    Corner       Corner      Line       Line       Side
'      Side        Corner       Corner
boxstring$ = CHR$(201) + CHR$(187) + CHR$(205) + CHR$(205) + CHR$(186) +
      CHR$(186) + CHR$(200) + CHR$(188)
Boxer 9, 1, 13, 80, boxstring$
```

```
' Select file to edit
filename$ = ""
CLS
DO
  Boxer 9, 1, 13, 80, boxstring$
  ErrorCode% = 0
  LOCATE 10, 2: PRINT "Enter File Name To View (or BLANKS TO Exit): "
  LOCATE 11, 2: LINE INPUT filename$
  COLOR 0, 0: VIEW PRINT 23 TO 24          ' Set color scheme to black on
                                           ' black.  Also set small view
                                           ' port.

    FILES filename$                        ' Search for file
    CLS : VIEW PRINT: COLOR 7, 0           ' Clear view port and reset
                                           ' color scheme.
LOOP UNTIL filename$ = "" OR ErrorCode% = 0
IF filename$ = "" THEN END
Boxer 1, 1, 20, 80, boxstring$
Boxer 21, 1, 23, 80, boxstring$
LOCATE 22, 4: PRINT " o Press Escape To Exit "
DIM SHARED alines$(301)                       'Create Array
lincnt% = 1
OPEN filename$ FOR INPUT AS #1                 'Open File For Seq. Input
LOCATE 2, (80 - LEN(filename$)) / 2: PRINT filename$
  DO                                      ' Read lines into an array
    LINE INPUT #1, alines$(lincnt%)
      lincnt% = lincnt% + 1
  LOOP UNTIL (EOF(1)) OR lincnt% >= 301
  IF EOF(1) THEN
    alines$(lincnt%) = "<---- End Of File ---->"
  ELSE
    alines$(lincnt%) = "<---- File Too Large ---->"
  END IF
  CLOSE #1
' Set up variables for displaying lines
FirstRec% = 1                        'First Displayed Record
SelRec% = 1                          'Selected Record
TotalRec% = lincnt%                  'Total Records
toplne% = 3                          'Beginning Line
bottlne% = 19
MaxRecs% = bottlne% - toplne% + 1    'Maximum Displayable Records
IF TotalRec% <= MaxRecs% THEN
  LastRec% = TotalRec%               'Last Record displayed
ELSE
  LastRec% = MaxRecs%
END IF
```

```
currrw% = toplne%                       'Current Relative Row Position
done = FALSE                            'Variable DONE controls execution of
                                        'main program loop
' Main Program Loop
DO
  xline% = toplne%
  FOR i% = FirstRec% TO LastRec%                'Display lines
     LOCATE xline%, 4
      PRINT MID$(alines$(i%) + SPACE$(ABS(76 - LEN(alines$(i%))))), 1,
      76): LastRec% = i%
      xline% = xline% + 1
  NEXT
  COLOR 0, 7                                    ' Highlight Current Line With
  LOCATE currrw%, 4                             ' Color Statement
  PRINT MID$(alines$(SelRec%) + SPACE$(ABS(76 -
     LEN(alines$(SelRec%)))), 1, 76)
  COLOR 7, 0
  DO                                            ' Wait For User To Press
    A Key
    keypr$ = INKEY$
  LOOP WHILE keypr$ = ""                  .
  IF LEN(keypr$) > 1 THEN                        ' See What Type Of Key Is
    Pressed
    keypr = ASC(MID$(keypr$, 2, 1))              ' Arrows or Paging Keys
    Pressed
  ELSE
    keypr = ASC(keypr$)                          ' Normal Key Pressed
  END IF
  SELECT CASE keypr
     CASE IS = 27                                ' Escape pressed
          CLOSE #1
          done = TRUE
     CASE IS = 71                                ' Home  Pressed
        SelRec% = 1: FirstRec% = 1: currrw% = toplne%
        IF TotalRec% <= MaxRecs% THEN
           LastRec% = TotalRec%
        ELSE
           LastRec% = MaxRecs%
        END IF
     CASE IS = 79                                ' End Pressed
        SelRec% = TotalRec%: LastRec% = TotalRec%
        IF TotalRec% > MaxRecs% THEN
           currrw% = bottlne%
        ELSE
           currrw% = TotalRec% + toplne% - 1
```

```
          END IF
      IF TotalRec% > MaxRecs% THEN
        FirstRec% = TotalRec% - MaxRecs% + 1
      ELSE
        FirstRec% = 1
      END IF
    CASE IS = 73                          ' PageUp Pressed
      IF FirstRec% - MaxRecs% <= 0 THEN
        SelRec% = 1
        FirstRec% = 1
      ELSE
        SelRec% = FirstRec% - MaxRecs%
        FirstRec% = FirstRec% - MaxRecs%
      END IF
      IF FirstRec% + MaxRecs% >= TotalRec% THEN
        LastRec% = TotalRec%
      ELSE
        LastRec% = FirstRec% + MaxRecs% - 1
      END IF
      currrw% = toplne%
    CASE IS = 81                          ' PageDown Pressed
      IF LastRec% + MaxRecs% > TotalRec% THEN
        LastRec% = TotalRec%
        IF TotalRec% > MaxRecs% THEN
          FirstRec% = LastRec% - MaxRecs% + 1
        ELSE
          FirstRec% = 1
        END IF
      ELSE
        LastRec% = LastRec% + MaxRecs%
        FirstRec% = LastRec% - MaxRecs% + 1
      END IF
      IF TotalRec% > MaxRecs% THEN
        currrw% = bottlne%
      ELSE
        currrw% = TotalRec% + toplne% - 1
      END IF
      SelRec% = LastRec%
    CASE IS = 80                          'Down Arrow Pressed
      IF SelRec% <> TotalRec% THEN
        IF SelRec% = LastRec% THEN
          FirstRec% = FirstRec% + 1
          SelRec% = SelRec% + 1
          LastRec% = LastRec% + 1
          currrw% = bottlne%
```

```
                ELSE
                  SelRec% = SelRec% + 1
                  IF SelRec% <> bottlne% THEN
                    currrw% = currrw% + 1
                  ELSE
                    currrw% = bottlne%
                  END IF
                END IF
              ELSE
                SOUND 320, 3.2
              END IF
            CASE IS = 72                          'Up Arrow Pressed
              IF SelRec% <> 1 THEN
                IF SelRec% = FirstRec% THEN
                  FirstRec% = FirstRec% - 1
                  SelRec% = SelRec% - 1
                  LastRec% = LastRec% - 1
                ELSE
                  SelRec% = SelRec% - 1
                END IF
              ELSE
                SOUND 320, 3.2
              END IF
                IF currrw% <> toplne% THEN
                  currrw% = currrw% - 1
                ELSE
                  currrw% = toplne%
                END IF
        CASE ELSE
            SOUND 300, 3.2
    END SELECT
LOOP UNTIL done
END
ErrRoutine:
    CLS : COLOR 7, 0: VIEW PRINT     ' Reset View Port and color scheme
    ErrorCode% = ERR
    SELECT CASE ErrorCode%
    CASE IS = 58
        LOCATE 22, 1: PRINT "File Already Exists, Press Any Key
To Continue"
    CASE IS = 53
        LOCATE 22, 1: PRINT "File Not Found, Press Any Key To
Continue"
    CASE IS = 64
```

```
        LOCATE 22, 1: PRINT "Incorrect File Name Entered, Press
Any Key To Continue"
   CASE IS = 71
        LOCATE 22, 1: PRINT "Disk Not Ready Error, Press Any Key
To Continue"
   CASE IS = 75
        LOCATE 22, 1: PRINT "Path/File Access Error, Press Any
Key To Continue"
   CASE IS = 76
        LOCATE 22, 1: PRINT "Path Not Found Error, Press Any Key
To Continue"
   END SELECT
DO
 z$ = INKEY$
LOOP WHILE z$ = ""
RESUME NEXT
SUB Boxer (tlrow%, tlcol%, brrow%, brcol%, boxstring$) STATIC
 ' Figure Out Size Of Box
 SizeOfBox% = brcol% - tlcol% + 1
 ' Parse Out Box Characters
 tlc$ = MID$(boxstring$, 1, 1)
 trc$ = MID$(boxstring$, 2, 1)
 tln$ = MID$(boxstring$, 3, 1)
 bln$ = MID$(boxstring$, 4, 1)
 lsd$ = MID$(boxstring$, 5, 1)
 rsd$ = MID$(boxstring$, 6, 1)
 blc$ = MID$(boxstring$, 7, 1)
 brc$ = MID$(boxstring$, 8, 1)
 'Begin Box Creation
 LOCATE tlrow%, tlcol%
 PRINT tlc$; STRING$(SizeOfBox% - 2, tln$); trc$;
 FOR x% = tlrow% + 1 TO brrow% - 1
     LOCATE x%, tlcol%
     PRINT lsd$; SPACE$(SizeOfBox% - 2); rsd$;
 NEXT
 LOCATE brrow%, tlcol%
 PRINT blc$; STRING$(SizeOfBox% - 2, bln$); brc$;
END SUB
FUNCTION selector% (choice$, StartRow%, StartCol%, Default%) STATIC
selected% = Default%
DO
  IF selected% = 1 THEN COLOR 0, 7
  LOCATE StartRow%, StartCol%: PRINT choice$(1)
  COLOR 7, 0
  IF selected% = 2 THEN COLOR 0, 7
```

```
      LOCATE StartRow%, StartCol% + LEN(choice$(1)) + 2: PRINT choice$(2)
      COLOR 7, 0
      DO
        r$ = INKEY$
      LOOP UNTIL r$ <> ""
      IF LEN(r$) > 1 THEN
        rscancode% = ASC(MID$(r$, 2, 1))
         IF rscancode% = 77 THEN                  ' Right Arrow Pressed
           IF selected% = 1 THEN selected% = 2 ELSE selected% = 1
         END IF
         IF rscancode% = 75 THEN                  ' Left Arrow Pressed
           IF selected% = 2 THEN selected% = 1 ELSE selected% = 2
         END IF
      END IF
   LOOP UNTIL r$ = CHR$(13)
   selector% = selected%
   END FUNCTION
```

FINDNEWS.BAS and FINDOLDS.BAS

FINDNEWS.BAS

Finds the newest file in the directory selected.

FINDOLDS.BAS

Finds the oldest file in the directory selected.

Shows:

> Parsing of date and time fields.
> Date and Time comparison.
> IF statement.

```
' FINDNEWS.BAS
'
'      Finds The Newest File In The Directory Selected
'
'
'
'
'
CLS : LOCATE 1, 28: PRINT "Find The Newest File"
LOCATE 5, 1: PRINT "Enter Directory Name To Search"
```

```
LOCATE 6, 1: INPUT DirName$
cmd$ = "DIR " + DirName$ + " > findlast.txt"
SHELL cmd$
FileLast$ = "": DateLast$ = "": TimeLast$ = ""
OPEN "findlast.txt" FOR INPUT AS #1
DO
  LINE INPUT #1, InLine$
  InLine$ = RTRIM$(InLine$)
  FileName$ = LEFT$(InLine$, 12)
  DateTime$ = RIGHT$(InLine$, 16)
  DateIn$ = LEFT$(DateTime$, 8)
  TimeIn$ = RIGHT$(DateTime$, 6)
  IF VAL(LEFT$(DateIn$, 2)) <> 0 AND VAL(LEFT$(TimeIn$, 2)) <> 0 AND
      FileName$ <> "FINDLAST TXT" AND INSTR(1, FileName$, ".") = 0 THEN
    DateComp$ = RIGHT$(DateIn$, 2) + LEFT$(DateIn$, 2) + MID$(DateIn$,
      4, 2)
    IF RIGHT$(TimeIn$, 1) = "p" THEN xtra% = 12 ELSE xtra% = 0
    TimeComp$ = STR$(VAL(MID$(TimeIn$, 1, 2)) + xtra%) + MID$(TimeIn$,
      4, 2)
    DateCompL$ = RIGHT$(DateLast$, 2) + LEFT$(DateLast$, 2) +
      MID$(DateLast$, 4, 2)
    IF RIGHT$(TimeLast$, 1) = "p" THEN xtra% = 12 ELSE xtra% = 0
    TimeCompL$ = STR$(VAL(MID$(TimeLast$, 1, 2)) + xtra%) +
      MID$(TimeLast$, 4, 2)
    IF DateComp$ > DateCompL$ OR (DateComp$ = DateCompL$ AND TimeComp$
      >= TimeCompL$) THEN
      FileLast$ = FileName$
      DateLast$ = DateIn$
      TimeLast$ = TimeIn$
    END IF
  END IF
LOOP UNTIL EOF(1)
LOCATE 10, 1: PRINT "The Newest File In This Directory Is: "; FileLast$;
      " "; DateLast$; " "; TimeLast$

' FINDOLDS.BAS
'
'     Finds The Oldest File In The Directory Selected
'
'
'
'

CLS : LOCATE 1, 28: PRINT "Find The Oldest File"
LOCATE 5, 1: PRINT "Enter Directory Name To Search"
```

```
LOCATE 6, 1: INPUT DirName$
cmd$ = "DIR " + DirName$ + " > findlast.txt"
SHELL cmd$
FileLast$ = "": DateLast$ = "99/99/99": TimeLast$ = "99:99a"
OPEN "findlast.txt" FOR INPUT AS #1
DO
  LINE INPUT #1, InLine$
  InLine$ = RTRIM$(InLine$)
  FileName$ = LEFT$(InLine$, 12)
  DateTime$ = RIGHT$(InLine$, 16)
  DateIn$ = LEFT$(DateTime$, 8)
  TimeIn$ = RIGHT$(DateTime$, 6)
  IF VAL(LEFT$(DateIn$, 2)) <> 0 AND VAL(LEFT$(TimeIn$, 2)) <> 0 AND
      FileName$ <> "FINDLAST TXT" AND INSTR(1, FileName$, ".") = 0 THEN
    DateComp$ = RIGHT$(DateIn$, 2) + LEFT$(DateIn$, 2) + MID$(DateIn$,
        4, 2)
    IF RIGHT$(TimeIn$, 1) = "p" THEN xtra% = 12 ELSE xtra% = 0
    TimeComp$ = STR$(VAL(MID$(TimeIn$, 1, 2)) + xtra%) + MID$(TimeIn$,
        4, 2)
    DateCompL$ = RIGHT$(DateLast$, 2) + LEFT$(DateLast$, 2) +
        MID$(DateLast$, 4, 2)
    IF RIGHT$(TimeLast$, 1) = "p" THEN xtra% = 12 ELSE xtra% = 0
    TimeCompL$ = STR$(VAL(MID$(TimeLast$, 1, 2)) + xtra%) +
        MID$(TimeLast$, 4, 2)
    IF DateComp$ < DateCompL$ OR (DateComp$ = DateCompL$ AND TimeComp$
        <= TimeCompL$) THEN
      FileLast$ = FileName$
      DateLast$ = DateIn$
      TimeLast$ = TimeIn$
    END IF
  END IF
LOOP UNTIL EOF(1)
LOCATE 10, 1: PRINT "The Oldest File In This Directory Is: "; FileLast$;
      " "; DateLast$; " "; TimeLast$
```

MOVE.BAS

This utility is used to rename (move) a file.

Shows:

Error routine.

Use of NAME statement.

```
' MOVE.BAS
'    Small routine to rename a file
'
'    Uses The FILES command to check for existance of file
'
ON ERROR GOTO ErrRoutine
DO
  ErrorCode% = 0
  CLS
  LOCATE 1, 32: PRINT "File Move Utility"
  LOCATE 10, 1: PRINT "Enter Existing File Name (or BLANKS TO Exit): "
  LOCATE 12, 1: PRINT "Enter New File Name: "
  oldfilename$ = ""
  LOCATE 11, 1: LINE INPUT oldfilename$
  IF oldfilename$ <> "" THEN
      COLOR 0, 0: VIEW PRINT 23 TO 24          ' Set color scheme to
        black on
                                               ' black.  Also set small
      view
                                               ' port.
      FILES oldfilename$                       ' Search for file
      CLS : VIEW PRINT: COLOR 7, 0             ' Clear view port and
        reset
                                               ' color scheme.
  END IF
  IF ErrorCode% = 0 AND oldfilename$ <> "" THEN
     LOCATE 13, 1: LINE INPUT newfilename$
     NAME oldfilename$ AS newfilename$
     IF ErrorCode% = 0 THEN
        LOCATE 22, 1: PRINT "File Moved, Press Any Key To Continue"
          DO
            z$ = INKEY$
          LOOP WHILE z$ = ""
     END IF
  END IF
LOOP UNTIL oldfilename$ = ""
END
ErrRoutine:
      CLS : COLOR 7, 0: VIEW PRINT     ' Reset View Port and color scheme
      ErrorCode% = ERR
      SELECT CASE ErrorCode%
       CASE IS = 58
            LOCATE 22, 1: PRINT "File Already Exists, Press Any Key
      To Continue"
       CASE IS = 53
```

```
        LOCATE 22, 1: PRINT "File Not Found, Press Any Key To
Continue"
    CASE IS = 64
        LOCATE 22, 1: PRINT "Incorrect File Name Entered, Press
Any Key To Continue"
    CASE IS = 71
        LOCATE 22, 1: PRINT "Disk Not Ready Error, Press Any Key
To Continue"
    CASE IS = 75
        LOCATE 22, 1: PRINT "Path/File Access Error, Press Any
Key To Continue"
    CASE IS = 76
        LOCATE 22, 1: PRINT "Path Not Found Error, Press Any Key
To Continue"
    END SELECT
DO
  z$ = INKEY$
LOOP WHILE z$ = ""
RESUME NEXT
```

POSTIT.BAS

This utility is used to place a message on the screen. You input the message (up to 256 characters). The message is then parsed into 40 character lines and displayed in a moving box on the screen until any key is pressed.

Show:

WordWrap parsing of a line into predetermined lengths.

Use of SLEEP statement.

```
' POSTIT.BAS
'       Program to place a message on the screen.
'       User inputs the message (up to 256 characters).
'       The message is then parsed into 40 character lines and displayed
'       in a moving box on the screen until a key (any key) is pressed.
'
DECLARE SUB Boxer (tlrow%, tlcol%, brrow%, brcol%, boxstring$)
' Boxer may be called with several types of box configurations
' Box          Top Left    Top Right     Top        Bottom      Left
'     Right        Bott Left   Bott Right
' pattern      Corner      Corner        Line       Line        Side
'     Side         Corner      Corner
boxstring$ = CHR$(201) + CHR$(187) + CHR$(205) + CHR$(205) + CHR$(186) +
    CHR$(186) + CHR$(200) + CHR$(188)
```

```
CLS
LOCATE 1, 33: PRINT "Message Display"
LOCATE 10, 1: PRINT "Enter Your Message:": LOCATE 11, 1: LINE INPUT mess$
' now let's see how many lines there are
MaxLines% = 7
TotLines% = 1
TempMess$ = mess$
MaxLineLen% = 40
DIM MessLine$(MaxLines%)
DO WHILE LEN(TempMess$) > MaxLineLen%
   x% = MaxLineLen% + 1
   DO WHILE MID$(TempMess$, x%, 1) <> CHR$(32)
      x% = x% - 1
   LOOP
   MessLine$(TotLines%) = RTRIM$(MID$(TempMess$, 1, x%))
   TempMess$ = MID$(TempMess$, x% + 1)
   TotLines% = TotLines% + 1
LOOP
IF TempMess$ <> "" THEN MessLine$(TotLines%) = RTRIM$(TempMess$)
CLS
StartRow% = 1: StartCol% = 1
DO
   Boxer StartRow%, StartCol%, StartRow% + TotLines% + 1, StartCol% +
      41, boxstring$
    FOR t% = 1 TO TotLines%
      LOCATE StartRow% + t%, StartCol% + 1: PRINT MessLine$(t%)
   NEXT
   SLEEP 10                    ' put machine to sleep for 10 seconds, or
      until
                              ' a key is pressed
   ' now draw a box with empty sides, this will blank out the old box
   Boxer StartRow%, StartCol%, StartRow% + TotLines% + 1, StartCol% +
      41, SPACE$(8)
   IF StartCol% + 10 + 41 > 80 THEN              ' compute new box
      position
      StartCol% = 1
    IF StartRow% + TotLines% + TotLines% + 2 > 23 THEN
        StartRow% = 1
    ELSE
      StartRow% = StartRow% + TotLines% + 2
    END IF
   ELSE
     StartCol% = StartCol% + 10
   END IF
LOOP UNTIL INKEY$ <> ""
```

```
SUB Boxer (tlrow%, tlcol%, brrow%, brcol%, boxstring$) STATIC
' Figure Out Size Of Box
SizeOfBox% = brcol% - tlcol% + 1
' Parse Out Box Characters
tlc$ = MID$(boxstring$, 1, 1)
trc$ = MID$(boxstring$, 2, 1)
tln$ = MID$(boxstring$, 3, 1)
bln$ = MID$(boxstring$, 4, 1)
lsd$ = MID$(boxstring$, 5, 1)
rsd$ = MID$(boxstring$, 6, 1)
blc$ = MID$(boxstring$, 7, 1)
brc$ = MID$(boxstring$, 8, 1)
'Begin Box Creation
LOCATE tlrow%, tlcol%
PRINT tlc$; STRING$(SizeOfBox% - 2, tln$); trc$;
FOR x% = tlrow% + 1 TO brrow% - 1
      LOCATE x%, tlcol%
     PRINT lsd$; SPACE$(SizeOfBox% - 2); rsd$;
NEXT
LOCATE brrow%, tlcol%
PRINT blc$; STRING$(SizeOfBox% - 2, bln$); brc$;
END SUB
```

Part Four

Command Reference

DOS 5 and Windows 3

NetWare Considerations

LAN Manager Considerations

Menu Map of the DOS 5 Editor

Command Reference

ANSI.SYS   Driver

Purpose

Enables you to modify screen output and keyboard input through ANSI escape sequences.

When To Use

The ANSI.SYS driver provides control over the format and location of character output on the screen and can be used to reinterpret input from the keyboard.

Common Syntax and Examples

    DEVICE=d:path\ANSI.SYS /X /K

or

    DEVICEHIGH=d:path\ANSI.SYS /X /K

The $d:$ parameter is the disk drive for the device driver.

The $path\$ parameter is the path for the device driver. If no path is specified, the root directory is assumed.

To install ANSI.SYS in conventional memory from the \DOS directory, type the command:

    DEVICE=\DOS\ANSI.SYS

535

After ANSI.SYS is installed, you can use it to change a variety of characteristics of the display and keyboard. For a discussion of how to use ANSI.SYS, see Chapter 11.

In the following discussion, $e represents the escape command. You can not simply type the dollar sign followed by the letter e, but must instead use an editor capable of creating the escape character. The [character is the left bracket key. All ANSI commands begin with these two characters.

You can use ANSI.SYS, for example, to change the colors of text and the background color. The syntax for assigning colors and screen attributes, without the spaces, is as follows:

$e [*foreground-color* ; *background-color* m

This is just a pattern. The actual commands do not contain spaces. The valid foreground are background combinations are listed as follows:

Color	Foreground	Background
Black	30	40
Red	31	41
Green	32	42
Yellow	33	43
Blue	34	44
Magenta	35	45
Cyan	36	46
White	37	47

Text on the display can be in normal format or have any of five attributes—bold, blinking, underlined, reverse video, or hidden. Hidden text is created by displaying it in the same color as the background. The syntax for changing text attributes is as follows:

$e [*Parameter* m

The format attributes include:

Format	Parameter
Attributes Off	0
Bold	1
Underlined	4
Blinking	5
Reverse Video	7
Hidden	8

In addition to making changes to the display, the ANSI commands can be used to set the display type. The format used is as follows:

$e [*Type* m

Type is one of the following values:

Display Characteristics	Type
40x25 Monochrome (text)	0
40x25 Color (text)	1
80x25 Monochrome (text)	2
80x25 Color (text)	3
320x200 4-color (graphics)	4
320x200 Monochrome (graphics)	5
640x200 Monochrome (graphics)	6
320x200 Color (graphics)	13
640x200 Color (16-color graphics)	14
640x350 Monochrome (2-color graphics)	15
640x350 Color (16-color graphics)	16
640x480 Monochrome (2-color graphics)	17
640x480 Color (16-color graphics)	18
320x200 Color (256-color graphics)	19

Additional ANSI.SYS commands include the following:

Example	Action
$e[*x;y*H	Moves the cursor to position *x, y* on the display.
$e[*x;y*f	Moves the cursor to position *x, y* on the display.
$e[*x*A	Moves the cursor up *x* rows and displays the prompt.
$e[*x*B	Moves the cursor down *x* rows and displays the prompt.
$e[*x*C	Moves the cursor forward *x* columns.
$e[*x*D	Moves the cursor backward *x* columns.
$e[s	Saves the current cursor position.
$e[u	Restores the cursor to the last saved position.
$e[=7h	Enables word wrap.
$e[=7l	Disables word wrap.
$e[K	Clears to the end of the line.
$e[2J	Erases screen and moves cursor to home position.
$e[0m	Screen display changes to normal (white on black).

To change the character that a key displays, you can use the character the key is currently displaying and the character that you want the key to display. Characters used directly must be put in quotation marks. To map the e key to an X, for example, type:

```
Esc["e";"X"p
```

After you execute the command, an X appears every time you type a lower-case e. The p in the command line must be lowercase and is always used when mapping a key. To eliminate every lowercase e, you have to use a second command that maps the uppercase:

```
ESC["E";"X"p
```

You often may want to reassign a key to a character that does not display. To do this, you need the ASCII character codes. To reassign the caret key (^) as an up arrow (↑), you would use:

```
ESC["^";24p
```

If you want the key to have its original assignment, you must map it to the original character. To do this, you must know the character code because you can no longer generate the original character at the keyboard.

Switches

/X   Enables independent mapping of the extended keys on the 101-key keyboard (i.e., the two Insert keys can have different assignments).

/K   Maps duplicate keys on the 101-key keyboard to the corresponding keys on the conventional keyboard (i.e., the Insert key in the group of six keys becomes the same as the Insert key on the numeric keypad.

Notes

❏ ANSI sequences are case-sensitive. You must use the appropriate upper-or lower-case character.

❏ You must specify the /K switch if you use the SWITCHES=/K setting in the CONFIG.SYS file.

APPEND   Network, External

Purpose

Enables application programs to find requested data files by looking for them in the appended directory list. Although primarily designed to find data files, APPEND will also allow execution of programs when used with the /X:ON switch.

When To Use

Use APPEND when you need to access data files but do not want to specify the path necessary to access those files.

Common Syntax and Examples

To establish the data file search path the first time, use the following command:

APPEND *d1:path1\;d2:path2\;...* /X:ON or /X:OFF /PATH:ON
or /PATH:OFF /E

The *d1:,d2:,...* parameters are drive names.

The *path1\,path2\,...* parameters are path names to the directories to be searched. You may list as many paths as you want on the command line.

To delete appended paths, type the command:

APPEND;

To view the search path, simply type:

APPEND

To search, for example, several directories and disks for a document, type the command line as follows:

APPEND c:doc;c:doc2;d:doc;d:doc2

Switches

/X	Redirects programs that use the MS-DOS function calls SEARCH FIRST, FIND FIRST, and EXEC.
/X:ON	Same as /X (turns APPEND on).
/X:OFF	Turns off APPEND but keeps path.
/E	Places the disk drive paths in the environment.
/PATH:ON	Processes files that have drives or paths included in the name.
/PATH:OFF	Does not process files with drives or paths in the name.

Notes

❏ APPEND normally finds data files that are accessed by applications using: Open file, Open handle, and Get file size DOS calls. If you find that a particular application does not find data files in an appended directory, try APPEND with the /X switch.

❏ To set more than one appended directory, use the semicolon (;) to seperate multiple paths, but do not use separate command lines.

OKAY:	APPEND C:\DOCS;D:\BUSINESS;C:\STUFF
NOT OKAY:	APPEND C:\DOCS
	APPEND D:\BUSINESS
	APPEND C:\STUFF

❏ See PATH.

ASSIGN   Network, External

Purpose

Redirects requests for read and write operations from one disk drive to another disk drive.

When To Use

Use when you want to rerout the activity from one drive to another drive, especially with older programs that can only read and write file on drives A and B.

Common Syntax and Examples

    ASSIGN d1:=d2:

or

    ASSIGN /STATUS

The d1 parameter is the letter of the disk drive the program or DOS normally uses.

The d2 parameter is the letter of the disk drive you want the program or DOS to use in place of the usual drive.

To clear the assignment, use the following command:

    ASSIGN

Switch

/STATUS or /STA or /S   Lists current assignments.

Notes

❏ You do not have to include the colon as part of the drive identification.

❏ The ASSIGN command is intended for use with floppy disk drives and network drives only. Do not use the ASSIGN command to change the designation of your hard disk drive.

❏ Never use the ASSIGN command on a drive that is currently being used.

❏ Some commands (e.g., BACKUP, JOIN, LABEL, RESTORE, and SUBST) require drive information and should not be used on a drive that has been changed with the ASSIGN command.

❏ Some commands (DISKCOPY and FORMAT) ignore drive reassignments.

ATTRIB   Network, External

Purpose

Set, resets, or displays file attributes including: Read-Only, System, Hidden, and Archive.

When To Use

Use the +R parameter to mark a file as read-only to curtail accidental erasure.

Use the +H or +S parameters to hide files from being displayed with the normal DIR command.

Use the +A parameter to control the setting of the Archive bit for better control of backups.

Use the -R, -H, -S, & -A parameters to undo any of these settings.

Common Syntax and Examples

```
ATTRIB +R or -R +A or -A +S or -S +H or -H d:path\filename /S
```

The `d:` parameter specifies the drive where the files are located.

The `path\` parameter is the path to the files to be displayed or changed.

The `filename` parameter is the name of the file to be displayed or changed. Wild cards are permitted.

Switches

/S   Sets or clears the attributes of the specified files in the specified directory and all subdirectories to that directory.

+R   Turns on the read-only attribute.

-R   Turns off the read-only attribute.

+A   Turns on the archive attribute.

-A   Turns off the archive attribute.

+S   Turns on the system file attribute.

-S   Turns off the system file attribute.

+H   Turns on the hidden attribute.

-H   Turns off the hidden attribute.

Notes

❏ Although ATTRIB +R can be used to set a file to READ-ONLY on Novell Netware LANS, the NOVELL FLAG *filename* SRO command should be used for files that need to be set as Shareable-Read-Only.

❏ Most NETBIOS based LANS require a files attribute to be set to Read-Only before the file may be shared. You may use the ATTRIB +R filename command to set the Read-Only attribute as required.

❏ DOS Commands using the Archive Bit—DOS XCOPY, BACKUP and RESTORE—can make use of the archive bit. For this reason, use the +A or -A settings for better control of these commands.

❏ ATTRIB will not work for directory names; therefore it may not be used to hide an entire directory, but only the directory's contents.

BACKUP   Network, External

Purpose

Usually used to make backup copies of the contents of a non-removable fixed disk to removable diskettes, although you can use BACKUP to backup files from any disk drive to a second disk drive or even the same disk drive.

When To Use

If you have important data on disk that cannot be replaced easily, use BACKUP. It is also a good idea to make at least one backup copy of an entire hard disk including all programs, configurations, and data files. One of the most devastating computer failures is a hard drive failure for which there is no backup. After such a failure, all applications must be completely re-installed and re-configured, and of course important data must be duplicated if at all possible.

One other reason to make a backup copy of important data and programs is to protect your work in case of fire or theft. For this reason, make a copy from a removable hard disk drive. Regular backups can also serve as good protection against "informed" users, viruses, and catastrophy.

Common Syntax and Examples

```
BACKUP d1:path\filename d2:/S/M/A/D:date/T:time/F:size/
    L:d:path\logflnam
```

d1: is the name of the disk or floppy disk drive to be backed up.

path is the initial directory path for backup.

filename is the name of the file(s) to back up. Wild cards are allowed.

Switches

/S   Creates backups of all subdirectory contents.

/M   Creates backups of files that have been modified since the last backup, and resets the archive attribute of the original file.

/A   Backs up files and add them to existing backup disk without erasing the existing files. (This switch is ignored for backups created with DOS version 3.2 or earlier.)

/F:size   Uses the FORMAT command to create backup disks in the *size* specified. If no size is specified, the disk is formatted to the default size for the drive being used. The following values are permissible for *size*:

160	160K, single-sided, double-density, 5 1\4-inch disk.
180	180K, single-sided, double-density, 5 1\4-inch disk.
320	320K, double-sided, double-density, 5 1\4-inch disk.
360	360K, double-sided, double-density, 5 1\4-inch disk.
720	720K, double-sided, double-density, 3 1\2 inch disk.
1200	1200K, double-sided, quaduple-density, 5 1\4-inch disk.
1440	1440K, double-sided, quaduple-density, 3 1\2-inch disk.
2880	2880K, double-sided, 3 1\2-inch disk.

The *size* parameter can be specified with no kilobyte notation (i.e, 720), with the single K notation (i.e., 720K), or with the Kb notation (i.e., 720Kb). For sizes about 1 megabyte, the *size* parameter can be expressed in megabytes with no megabyte notations (i.e., 1.2), with the single M notation (1.2M), or with the Mb notation (1.2Mb).

/D:*date* Specifies the oldest date to be included in the backups. Only files modified on or later than this date are included. See the COUNTRY command for the date formats.

/T:*time* Specifies the oldest time to be included in the backups. Only files modified on or later than this time on the specified day are included. See the COUNTRY command for the time formats.

/L:*d:path\logflnam* Creates a new log history file and adds an entry recording the results of the backup operation. The default is the root directory of the source drive and the filename BACKUP.LOG.

Notes

❏ Even though there are many theories about how often and when to perform backups, you should perform backups as often as you are willing to repeat a period of work. A user who performs a backup once every three months is asking for trouble. In the event of a hard disk failure, this person would have to duplicate up to three months of work. If you perform backups of important data daily, however, you would only have to duplicate a day's worth of work to catch up after a hard disk drive failure.

❏ BACKUP may be used to backup programs and data files on NOVELL NetWare LANS, but BACKUP will not backup important BINDERY information.

❏ You must have at least *read* access to any directories and files you intend to backup.

❏ Unlike most previous versions of BACKUP, the DOS 5.0 version will not backup the hidden DOS system files or COMMAND.COM. For this reason, keep the DOS 5.0 distrubution disks in a safe place so you can run your system after a hard drive failure.

❏ Files may only be restored to the directory from which they were backed up. To see a list of the files backed up and the directories they came from, look at the BACKUP.LOG file. BACKUP.LOG is created in the root of the current drive unless a specific path is named with the /L:*pathname* switch.

❑ Because backups should be performed often, rewriting the labels on disks each time you backup disks may be troublesome. A simpler method is to label backup disks A1, A2, A3... for as many disks as it takes for one complete backup. Label a second set of disks B1, B2, B3... and a third set as C1, C2, C3.... The date, time, and contents of the backup can be written down on a piece of paper kept with the backup diskettes.

❑ BACKUP automatically erases existing files on a backup disk unless you use the append switch /A.

BREAK   Internal

Purpose

Used to control the frequency of Ctrl-C checking during the processing of commands.

When To Use

Normally, DOS checks for a Ctrl-C interrupt only when it begins reading from the keyboard or writing to an output device (screen or printer). Use BREAK ON when you want the computer to check for a Ctrl-C interrupt command more frequently (including at the start of disk reads and disk writes). This enables you to interrupt disk activity.

Common Syntax and Examples

    BREAK ON or OFF

To activate more frequent Ctrl-C checking, use the following command:

    BREAK ON

To limit Ctrl-C checking to when the processor is reading from the keyboard or beginning output, type the command:

    BREAK OFF

To check the status of Ctrl-C checking, simply type:

    BREAK

Switches

None.

Notes

❑ Setting BREAK ON may slow down processing.

❑ Although ^C or ^Break may be used safely during most file read operations, unexpected results or even file damage may result from breaking out of a file write.

❑ You can use the BREAK command in CONFIG.SYS files.

BUFFERS=	Config

Purpose

Used to set the number of primary and secondary buffers used by the system for file transfer and data retention.

When To Use

Set the value of BUFFERS= based on the size of your hard disk drive and the requirements of your applications. Use the value that is greater. Use secondary buffers if you are not using a disk cache such as SMARTDrive.

Common Syntax and Examples

```
BUFFERS= primary, secondary
```

The *primary* parameter is the number of primary buffers that should be created. These buffers are used to hold data that has been recently read from the disk.

The *secondary* parameter is the number of secondary buffers that should be created. These buffers are used to hold "read-ahead" data.

Switches

None.

Notes

❑ The original value for BUFFERS= is based on the amount of memory installed in your system. In all cases, you should increase this number. The recommended setting for hard disk drives between 40M and 80M is BUFFERS=30.

❑ See Chapter 10 for a discussion of optimizing data transfer and improving system performance.

CALL   Batch, Internal

Purpose

Used to activate a program.

When To Use

The CALL command is used in a batch file to activate an existing batch file. The calling batch file (the one containing the CALL command) is suspended and the called batch file (the one referenced on the CALL command) is activated. CALL can also be used to activate any command that will run from the command line.

Common Syntax and Examples

```
CALL program prog-params
```

The *program* parameter must be the name of an executable file (BAT, EXE, or COM). The name may include path information.

The `prog-params` are parameters that will be passed directly to the called program.

To call the directory command, type the following:

```
CALL DIR
```

To specify the root directory to the DIR command, type:

```
CALL DIR \
```

Switches

None.

Notes

❑ You cannot use pipes or redirections on the CALL command line.

❑ You can use the CALL command to create an endlessly looping program. To do this, simply use CALL to activate the original program (i.e., use a CALL statement with the name of the batch file as the program).

❑ The difference between calling a program (with CALL) and activating it directly (by specifying the application name) is that the original program is not stopped when you use the CALL command.

❑ See Chapter 13 for more information about batch files and the batch file commands.

CHCP   Network, Internal

Purpose

Displays and changes the active code page. You can use CHCP to change the active code page for every device you use with your system.

When To Use

Use CHCP when you want to customize your system for international use.

Common Syntax and Examples

    CHCP nnn

The *nnn* parameter prepares system code pages defined in the CONFIG.SYS file by the COUNTRY command. The following code pages are supported:

Code Page	Country or Language
437	United States
850	Latin I
852	Latin II
860	Portuguese
863	Canadian-French
865	Nordic

To change the current code page to Nordic, type the following:

    CHCP 865

To display the current code page, simply type CHCP and DOS displays the message:

    Active code page: nnn

The *nnn* parameter is one of the valid code pages listed previously.

Switches

None.

Notes

❏ You must specify the location of the COUNTRY.SYS file with the COUNTRY command.

❏ NLSFUNC must be loaded prior to setting the code page with CHCP.

CHDIR (CD)   Network, Internal

Purpose

Changes the current default directory or displays the name of the default diretory.

When To Use

Use CHDIR when you want to change the current default directory to a different directory.

Common Syntax and Examples

CHDIR d:path

or

CD d:path

The d: variable is the valid disk drive name.

The path parameter is the valid directory path.

To show the current directory path on the current drive, type:

CHDIR

or

CD

To change to the directory \DOS on the current drive, type:

CD \DOS

or

CHDIR \DOS

Switches

None.

Notes

❏ If you do not indicate a disk drive, the current disk drive is used.

❏ When you give a path name, DOS moves from the current directory to the last directory specified in the path.

❏ If you want to start the move with the disk's root directory, use the backslash (\) character as the path's first character. Otherwise, DOS assumes that the path starts with the current directory.

❏ If you give an invalid path, DOS displays an error message and remains in the current directory.

CHKDSK   External

Purpose

Displays information on disk space usage, file fragmentation, cluster size, available RAM, and repairs several basic disk errors.

When To Use

Use CHKDSK when file fragmentation is suspected, whenever the system has accidentally been rebooted or powered down in the middle of an application program, to check available disk space and available RAM, or to view the current cluster size.

Common Syntax and Examples

```
CHKDSK d:path\filename /F/V
```

The d: parameter specifies the drive that contains the files to be checked for fragmentation.

The path\ parameter is the path to the files that you want to check for fragmentation.

The filename parameter is the name of the file to be checked for fragmentation. Wild cards are permitted.

Switches

/F   Fixes the file allocation table and other problems.

/V   Shows CHKDSK's progress and displays more detailed information about any errors the program finds (This switch is known as the verbose switch).

Notes

❏ Unless the /F switch is specified, CHKDSK will not correct any disk errors that it encounters.

❏ CHKDSK does not work on network drives.

CLEANUP (MS-DOS 5) Installation, External

Purpose

Used to delete the previous version of DOS saved by the DOS 5 installation procedure.

When To Use

Use the CLEANUP command if you know that all of your applications work with DOS 5 and if you no longer need your previous version of DOS.

Common Syntax and Examples

```
CLEANUP /B
```

The CLEANUP command does not require any parameters.

To remove the files that contain the previous version of DOS, type:

```
CLEANUP
```

Switch

/B   Specifies a monochrome (black and white) monitor.

Notes

❑ After you run CLEANUP, you cannot use UNINSTALL to move back to the previous version of DOS.

❑ This is the same command as DELOLDOS.

CLS Network, Internal

Purpose

Erases the screen.

When To Use

Use CLS when you want to erase the screen contents and return to a blank screen.

Common Syntax and Examples

```
CLS
```

Switches

None.

Notes

❏ All information on the screen is cleared, and the cursor is placed at the home position (upper left corner).

❏ This command affects only the active video display.

❏ If you use the ANSI control codes to set foreground and background colors, the color settings remain in effect.

❏ If you do not set the foreground or background colors, the screen reverts to light characters on a dark background.

❏ CLS affects only the screen, not memory.

COMMAND   External

Purpose

Loads or reloads the DOS Command interpreter.

When To Use

Use COMMAND when you want to load an additional copy of the command proecessor with different parameters. COMMAND.COM is automatically loaded when you turn on your computer unless another command processor is specified with the COMSPEC= command in CONFIG.SYS. COMMAND is also used to shell out of many DOS applications.

Common Syntax and Examples

```
COMMAND d:path /E:size /P /C string /MSG
```

`d:path` specifies the location of the command processor.

Switches

/E:size	Sets the size of the environment, which is a decimal number from 160 to 32,768 bytes, rounded up to the nearest multiple of 16.
/P	Keeps the copy permanently in memory.
/C string	Passes the string of commands (string) to the new copy of COMMAND.COM.
/MSG	Routes all system messages to memory for storage.

Notes

❑ Although you may set a larger environment size by typing COM-MAND /E:*size* at the DOS prompt, this causes two copies of COMMAND.COM to be loaded into memory. The preferred method is to add SHELL=*d:path*\COMMAND.COM /E:*size* /P, which will set the environment size of the original copy of COMMAND.COM in memory.

❑ COMMAND /C *filename* used to be the only method to have one batch file call another as a subroutine. More recent versions of DOS make this unnecessary with the use of the CALL command for batch files.

❑ See the SHELL command.

COMP   Network, External

Purpose

Compares the contents of two files or sets of files.

When To Use

Use COMP when you want to compare the contents of different files.

Common Syntax and Examples

```
COMP d1:path1\filename1 d2:path2\filename2 /D /A /L /N=lines /C
```

d1:path1 is the drive and path containing the first set of files to be compared.

filename1 is the file name for the first set of files. Wild cards are allowed.

d2:path2 is the drive and path for the second set of files to be compared.

filename2 is the file name for the second set of files. Wild cards are allowed.

Switches

/D	Uses decimal format to list file differences.
/A	Lists file differences as characters.
/C	Ignores case during comparison.
/L	Lists the line numbers that have file discrepancies.
/N=*lines*	Compares only the indicated number of lines.

Notes

❏ If you do not provide filenames, the COMP command will prompt you for the files to compare.

❏ *d1* and *d2* and *path1*\ and *path2*\ may be the same.

❏ *filename1* and *filename2* may also be the same.

❏ If you do not give a drive name for a set, the current disk drive is used. (This rule applies to *d1*: and *d2*:, as well as the drive that holds the command.)

❏ If you do not give a path for a file set, the current directory for the drive is used.

❏ If you do not enter a file name for a file set, all files for that set (primary or secondary) are compared (the same as entering *.*). Only the files in the secondary set with names matching file names in the primary set are compared.

❏ If you do not enter a drive name, path name, or file name, COMP prompts you for the primary and secondary file sets to compare. Otherwise, the correct diskettes must be in the correct drive if you are comparing files on diskettes. COMP does not wait for you to insert diskettes if you give both the primary and secondary file names.

❏ Only normal disk files are checked. Hidden or system files and directories are not checked.

❏ Files with matching names but different lengths are not checked. A message is printed indicating these files are different.

❏ After ten mismatches (unequal comparisons) between the contents of two compared files, COMP automatically ends the comparison between the two files and aborts.

❏ If you have a program that once functioned properly but is now acting strangely, check a good backup copy of the file against the copy you are using. If COMP finds differences, copy the good program to the disk you are using.

❏ Do not compare current files that you use with copies that have been archived by the BACKUP program. If your only backup copy of a program is in a backed-up file, use RESTORE to place the file in a directory, and then use COMP to compare the files.

❏ If you need to find the last revision of a file, look at its date and time in the directory to identify the most recent revision of a file. If you want to compare diskettes that have been copied with DISKCOPY, use DISKCOMP instead of COMP.

COPY   Network, Internal

Purpose

Copies one or more files from one device to another or to the same device.

When To Use

Use COPY when you move files from one subdirectory to another, from a diskette to a hard disk drive, to create text files, to make a duplicate of a file in the same directory with a different name, to copy a text or post-script file to a printer and any other situation that you need to copy from one device to another.

Common Syntax and Examples

To copy a file, use the COPY command in the following format:

```
COPY /A/B d1:path1\filename1 /A/B d2:path2\filename2/A/B/V
```

or

```
COPY /A/B d1:path1\filename1 /A/B + d2:path2\filename2 /A/B
    d3:path3\filename3 /A/B/V
```

d1:, d2: are valid disk drive names.

path1\, path2 are valid path names.

filename1 filename2 are valid file names. Wild cards are allowed.

d2:path2\filename2 is the destination for the copy.

Use the following syntax to join several files into one file:

```
COPY /A/B d1:path1\filename1 /A/B + d2:path2\filename2
```

Switches

/V   Verifies the copy has been recorded correctly.

/A   Indicates an ASCII file. For the source file, the COPY command copies all information in the file up to, but not including, the end-of-file marker (Ctrl-Z). Anything after the end-of-file marker is ignored. For the destination file, an end-of-file marker (Ctrl-Z) is added to the end of the ASCII text file.

/B   Indicates a binary file. For the source file, the entire file is copied as if it were a program file. Any end-of file markers are treated as normal characters and the EOF characters are copied. For the destination file, no end-of-file marker is added.

Notes

❏ Additional files in the form *d:path\filename* may be added up to a total of 255 files.

❏ Note that COPY defaults to copying files in binary format, but that it appends files in ASCII as the default. Make sure you use the /A or /B parameters correctly when you want to append two binary files.

❏ DOS copies files without checking to see that they were written to the destination correctly. To have DOS check the integrity of the copy, you may use the /V switch whenever you copy crucial files. Note that the copy process takes longer if the system must copy and then verify.

❏ The most that can be copied with a single command is one entire directory. To copy an entire directory tree (to copy an entire 1.2M Floppy to a 1.44M floppy) including all subdirectories, use the XCOPY command.

❏ See XCOPY, DISKCOPY.

COUNTRY= Config

Purpose

Used to establish the character set and conventions specific to a supported language.

When To Use

Use the COUNTRY= command when you use a character set or language conventions other than the default US set.

Common Syntax and Examples

```
COUNTRY=code, page, d:path\filename
```

The *code* parameter specifies which country code you want to use. The available codes are the following:

Country	Code	Default, Alternate
Belgium	032	850, 437
Brazil	055	850, 437
Canadian-French	002	863, 850
Czechoslovakia (Czech)	042	852, 850

Country	Code	Default, Alternate
Czechoslovakia (Slovak)	042	852, 850
Denmark	045	850, 865
Finland	358	850, 437
France	033	850, 437
Germany	049	850, 437
Hungary	036	852, 850
International English	061	437, 850
Italy	039	850, 437
Latin America	003	850, 437
Netherlands	031	850, 437
Norway	047	850, 865
Poland	048	852, 850
Portugal	351	850, 860
Spain	034	850, 437
Sweden	046	850, 437
Switzerland (French)	041	850, 437
Switzerland (German)	041	850, 437
United Kingdom	044	437, 850
United States	001	437, 850
Yugoslavia	038	852, 850

The *page* parameter specifies which of the two code pages should be used for the country. The default code page is listed first in the table.

The *d:* parameter is the disk drive for the country information file.

The *path* parameter is the path for the country information file.

The *filename* parameter is the filename for the country information file.

To specify the Canadian-French country formats using the default code page (863) from the COUNTRY.SYS file in the root directory, place the following line in the CONFIG.SYS file:

```
COUNTRY=002
```

To specify the Canadian-French country formats using the default code page (863) from the COUNTRY.SYS file in the \DOS directory, place the following line in the CONFIG.SYS file:

```
COUNTRY=002,,\DOS
```

Notice that you must include both commas to specify a different location for the file without specifying an alternate code page.

To specify the alternate code page for the Canadian-French country formats from the COUNTRY.SYS file in the \DOS directory, place the following line in the CONFIG.SYS file:

```
COUNTRY=002,850,\DOS
```

Switches

None.

Note

❑ Unless an alternate location is specified, the program assumes that the required file is in the root directory of the boot drive.

CTTY   Network, Internal

Purpose

Redirects the keyboard and screen input and output to another device or back to the default keyboard and screen.

When To Use

Use CTTY when you have a terminal attached to a serial port and you want to use it instead of the standard keyboard and screen. CTTY may also be used to direct keyboard and screen input and output through a modem.

Common Syntax and Examples

```
CTTY device
```

Switches

None.

Notes

❑ Set serial port configuration with the MODE command before you try to redirect keyboard and screen I/O with the command CTTY.

❑ Use CTTY with programs that directly access screen memory.

❑ Certain applications that directly access screen RAM are not compatible with CTTY.

DATE   Network, Internal

Purpose

Views or changes the system date.

When To Use

Use DATE when you need to know what day it is or need to set the date due to loss of battery or regular power.

DOS uses the current date and the current time to mark your files as you create or change them.

Common Syntax and Examples

DATE *mm-dd-yy* for North America

DATE *dd-mm-yy* for Europe

DATE *yy-mm-dd* for the Far East

The format for this command depends on the COUNTRY code set in the CONFIG.SYS file.

The date must be entered with numerals only—letters are not permitted. Valid values are the following:

mm	1-12
dd	1-31
yy	80-99 or 1980-2099

You can use hyphens(-), slashes(/), or periods(.) to separate the day, month, and year entries.

Switches

None.

Note

❏ See SELECT, TIME, COUNTRY, and DEVICE.

DEBUG   External

Purpose

Starts the DEBUG program that tests and removes errors from executable program files.

When To Use

Use DEBUG if you create programs in assembly language and want to test and remove errors from the program.

Common Syntax and Examples

DEBUG *d:path\filename testfile-parameters*

d:path\filename is the disk drive and path to the executable program file you want to test.

testfile-parameters is the command line information that must be passed to the program.

To start the program MYPROG.EXE, for example, with the DEBUG statement, type the following:

DEBUG MYPROG.EXE

Switches

None.

Note

❑ You can also start DEBUG without a filename. This format starts DEBUG and enables you to use the DEBUG commands to load a file. You can make changes to the file and then save it. The following commands are available:

Command	Description
?	Displays a list of DEBUG commands.
a	Assembles Intel 8086/8087/8088 mnemonics.
c	Compares two areas of memory.
d	Displays the contents of an area of memory.
e	Enters data into memory beginning at a given address.
g	Runs the program that is in memory.
h	Performs hexadecimal arithmetic.
i	Displays one byte of input from a given port.
l	Loads the contents of a file into memory.
m	Makes a copy of a block of memory.
n	Gives the name of the file for an l or w command or specifies file parameters.
o	Sends one byte of data to an output port.

Command	Description
p	Processes a loop, repeated instruction, interrupt or subroutine.
q	Quits the Debug session.
r	Registers display.
s	Searches memory for a pattern of bytes.
t	Single steps to the next instruction and displays registers, flags, and the next instruction.
u	Disassembles an instruction and displays the source assembler statement.
w	Writes the current file to disk.
xa	Allocates expanded memory.
xd	Deallocates expanded memory.
xm	Maps expanded memory pages.
xs	Shows status of expanded memory.

DEL (ERASE)   Network, Internal

Purpose

Removes the specified file or files from the specified directory.

When To Use

Use DEL when you no longer want certain files and you want to use the occupied space for new files.

Common Syntax and Examples

```
DEL d:path\filename /P
```

or

```
ERASE d:path\filename /P
```

The *d:* parameter specifies the drive that contains the files.

The *path* parameter is the path to the files to be deleted.

The *filename* parameter is the name of the file to be deleted. Wild cards are permitted.

The following example deletes a file named "writing:"

```
DEL writing
```

If you have two files named writing.old and writing.new, you can delete them with the following command:

```
DEL writing.*
```

Switch

/P   Causes DEL or ERASE to prompt you before a deletion occurs.

Notes

❑ If the /P switch is used, each file is displayed and you are prompted to confirm the deletion. You can either confirm the deletion with a **Y** or cancel the delete with an **N**.

❑ The DEL command enables you to use the * and ? wildcards to delete more than one file at a time. This is convenient, but this method of deleting files can be dangerous, so use wildcards cautiously.

❑ If you type DEL *.*, this tells DOS you want to delete all the files in the working directory. DOS then displays the prompt Are you sure?. If you type **Y** (for Yes) in response, DOS deletes all files in the working directory.

❑ To delete every file in another directory, type the DEL command followed by the directory name.

❑ If you delete a file, you can use the RECOVER command or the new UNDELETE command to attempt to recover it. If you have written other files, it may not be possible to recover the file.

DELOLDOS (MS-DOS 5)   Installation, External

Purpose

Used to delete the previous version of DOS saved by the DOS 5 installation procedure.

When To Use

Use the DELOLDOS command after you have determined that all of your applications work with DOS 5 and that you will no longer need your previous version of DOS.

Common Syntax and Examples

```
DELOLDOS /B
```

The DELOLDOS command does not require any parameters.

To remove the files containing the previous version of DOS, type:

DELOLDOS

Switch

/B   Specifies a monochrome (black and white) monitor.

Notes

❏ After you run DELOLDOS, you cannot use UNINSTALL to move back to the previous version of DOS.

❏ This command performs the same function as CLEANUP.

DEVICE=   Config

Purpose

Used to install device drivers into conventional memory.

When To Use

Use DEVICE= when you want a device driver to be located in conventional memory.

Common Syntax and Examples

DEVICE=*driver* *driver-params*

The *driver* parameter specifies the device driver to be loaded. If the driver is not located in the root directory, the name must include a path specification.

The *driver-params* parameter specifies any parameters that are to be used in configuring the device driver that you want to install.

To load the RAMDRIVE device driver, enter the following line in the CONFIG.SYS file:

DEVICE=RAMDRIVE.SYS

To specify that the RAM disk should be created in expanded memory (using the RAMDRIVE parameter /A), enter the following line in the CONFIG.SYS file:

DEVICE=RAMDRIVE.SYS /A

To use the RAMDRIVE.SYS driver located in the \DOS directory (on the boot drive), enter the following line in the CONFIG.SYS file:

DEVICE=\DOS\RAMDRIVE.SYS

Switches

None.

Notes

❏ See the DEVICEHIGH= command for information about loading device drivers into the Upper Memory Area.

❏ Do not attempt to load COUNTRY.SYS or KEYBOARD.SYS with the DEVICE command. They are not device drivers.

❏ If you use a third-party video driver, it must be loaded before DISPLAY.SYS.

❏ See Chapter 10 for a discussion of memory management and improving system performance.

DEVICEHIGH= (MS-DOS 5)   Config

Purpose

Used to load a device driver into the Upper Memory Area (UMA).

When To Use

Use this command to free conventional memory by moving device drivers into available Upper Memory Blocks (UMBs).

Common Syntax and Examples

```
DEVICEHIGH=driver driver-params
```

or

```
DEVICEHIGH SIZE=hexsize driver driver-params
```

The *driver* parameter specifies the device driver to be loaded. If the driver is not located in the root directory, the name must include a path specification.

The *driver-params* parameter specifies any parameters that are to be used in configuring the device driver that you want to install.

To load the RAMDrive device driver in the Upper Memory Area, enter the following line in the CONFIG.SYS file:

```
DEVICEHIGH=RAMDRIVE.SYS
```

To specify that the RAM disk be created in expanded memory (using the RAMDRIVE parameter /A), but the actual driver located in the Upper Memory Area, enter the following line in the CONFIG.SYS file:

```
DEVICEHIGH=RAMDRIVE.SYS /A
```

To use the RAMDRIVE.SYS driver located in the \DOS directory (on the boot drive) and load it into the Upper Memory Area, enter the following line in the CONFIG.SYS file:

```
DEVICEHIGH=\DOS\RAMDRIVE.SYS
```

Switch

SIZE=   Used to reserve a specific amount of memory in the Upper Memory Area for a device driver. The *hexsize* parameter specifies the minimum memory (in hexadecimal notation) required to load the driver in the Upper Memory Area.

Notes

❏ An Upper Memory Manager and an extended memory manager must be installed to use this command (EMM386.EXE and HIMEM.SYS).

❏ Communication between DOS and the Upper Memory Area must be enabled with the DOS=UMB setting in the CONFIG.SYS file.

❏ If there are no UMBs available, the device driver is loaded into conventional memory.

❏ Some device drivers will not work in the Upper Memory Area. These include EMM386.EXE and HIMEM.SYS, which must be installed in conventional memory. If you experience a problem after you load a utility into the Upper Memory Area, try loading it into conventional memory.

❏ To make sure that there is sufficient memory allocated for a driver when it is loaded into the Upper Memory Area, first load the driver into conventional memory using DEVICE= and use the MEM /C command to determine its size in hexadecimal. Then use the SIZE= switch to specify the amount of memory that should be reserved for the driver.

❏ Do not attempt to load COUNTRY.SYS or KEYBOARD.SYS with the DEVICEHIGH= command. They are not device drivers.

❏ If you use a third-party video driver, it must be loaded before DISPLAY.SYS.

❏ See DEVICE= for information about loading device drivers into conventional memory.

❏ See Chapter 10 for a discussion of memory management and improving system performance.

DIR   Network, Internal

Purpose

Views a list of files and subdirectories in a directory.

When To Use

Use DIR when you want to see the filenames and information about files in the current directory or other directories.

Common Syntax and Examples

```
DIR d:path\filename /P/W /A:attribute /O:order /S /B /L
```

The `d:` parameter specifies the drive where the files are located.

The `path\` parameter is the path to the files to be displayed.

The `filename` parameter is the name of the file to be displayed. Wild cards are permitted.

To display all of the files in the current directory of the current drive, type:

```
DIR
```

To display all of the files with a WKS extension in the current directory, type:

```
DIR *.WKS
```

Switches

/P	Displays the directory listing one page at a time. With the /P option, the directory pauses after the screen is filled. To continue the display of the directory, press a key.
/W	Selects a wide display of the directory. With the /W option, only filenames and their extensions are displayed. This usually enables the contents of the directory to fit on one page.
/A:attribute	Displays the files or directories with the appropriate attributes specified on the command line. Values for attribute include:

H   Hidden files

S   System files

D   Directories

A   Files with the archive bit on

R   Read only

The colon between the switch and the attribute is optional. A minus sign preceding any of the listed attributes prevents those types of files from being displayed.

/O:order   Controls the way the DIR command lists directory names and file names on the display. The following values can be used to determine the *order* that the DIR command uses for its lists:

N   Alphabetical by file name

E   Alphabetical by file extension

D   Sorts by the date and time

S   By file size—smaller files first

G   Directories listed before file names

The colon between the switch and the attribute is optional. A minus sign before any of the previous attributes requests the inverse of the attribute. The -N attribute, for example, indicates that DIR list the names of files and directories in the reverse alphabetical order.

/S   Displays the files in the specified directory and any subdirectories in the directory listing.

/B   Produces output containing only the file and directory names. This format is particularly useful when creating batch files.

/L   Displays all information in lowercase.

Notes

❏ Default DIR options such as sort order may be set in the environment variable: to have the DIR command always sort in name order, add SET DIRCMD=/O:N/ to AUTOEXEC.BAT. Any valid combination of DIR switches may be set in this manner. SET DIRCMD=*switches* may also be issued from a batch file or the DOS prompt to change the default DIR switches.

❏ If the COUNTRY command in the CONFIG.SYS file is set to a country other than North America, the directory date and time formats may differ.

DISKCOMP   External

Purpose

Compares the contents of two diskettes.

When To Use

Use DISKCOMP after you create a copy of a disk with the DISKCOPY command, in order to verify that the copy contains no errors.

Common Syntax and Examples

```
DISKCOMP d1: d2: /1 /8
```

d1 is the original disk for the comparison.

d2 is the comparison disk for the comparison.

To compare the disk in drive A with the one in drive B, use the command:

```
DISKCOMP A: B:
```

Switches

/1   Compares only one side of each disk.

/8   Compares only sectors 1 through 8.

Note

❑ The DISKCOMP command sets exit codes as follows:

Exit Code	Description
0	Both disks compared exactly.
1	Disks did not compare exactly.
2	User terminated DISKCOMP with Ctrl-C.
3	Unrecoverable (hard) read or write error.
4	Initialization error due to insufficient memory, invalid drive parameters, or bad command syntax.

You can use these codes in a batch file with the IF ERRORLEVEL command.

DISKCOPY   External

Purpose

Copies the contents of one diskette to another diskette.

When To Use

Use DISKCOPY if you want to make an exact replica of a disk, including placement of files and hidden files on the disk.

Common Syntax and Examples

        DISKCOPY *d1*: *d2*: /1 /V

d1 is the source disk for the copy.

d2 is the target disk for the copy.

To copy the enter contents of disk A onto a disk in drive B, use the command:

        COPY A: B:

Switches

    /1   Copies only 1 side of a disk.
    /V   Verifies the copy process.

Notes

❏ It is not possible to use DISKCOPY to copy between two different size disks. You may not copy, for example, from a 1.2M floppy to a 1.44M floppy using DISKCOPY. To copy files between dissimilar size disks, please see XCOPY.

❏ DISKCOPY will copy the system files and create a bootable disk from a bootable original.

❏ DISKCOPY erases all of the information on the target disk.

❏ Disks that have had a lot of file activity may be fragmented because space on the disk is no longer allocated sequentially. A fragmented disk performs slowly due to delays in finding, reading, or writing a file.

DISPLAY.SYS   Driver

Purpose

Enables support for code page switching for the display.

When To Use

Use the DISPLAY.SYS driver when you want to customize your display for international use by specifying an alternate code page.

Common Syntax and Examples

```
DEVICE=d:path\DISPLAY.SYS CON:=(type,page,extras,subfonts)
```

or

```
DEVICEHIGH=d:path\DISPLAY.SYS CON:=(type,page,extra,subfonts)
```

The *type* parameter specifies the type of video adapter in use. If it is omitted, the driver is configured to match your hardware. The parentheses must be entered. If you specify CGA or MONO, you cannot use code page switching. Other permissible values are EGA and LCD.

The *page* parameter specifies the code page to be supported. Possible values for the code pages and their respective country or language follow:

Code Page	Country or Language
437	United States
850	Multilingual (Latin I)
852	Multilingual (Latin II)
860	Portuguese
863	Canadian-French
865	Nordic

The *extra* parameter specifies the number of additional code pages that can be supported. For EGA adapters, the maximum is 6. For LCD adpaters, the maximum is 1.

The *subfont* parameter specifies the number of subfonts that can be supported for each page.

The *d:* parameter is the disk drive for the device driver.

The *path* parameter is the path for the device driver. If no path is specified, the root directory is assumed.

To install the DISPLAY.SYS driver in conventional memory and have it test for hardware type, use the command:

```
DEVICE=DISPLAY.SYS CON=()
```

To install the DISPLAY.SYS driver from the DOS directory and specify an EGA adapter and the Canadian-French code page, type the command:

```
DEVICE=\DOS\DISPLAY.SYS CON=(EGA,863)
```

Switches

None.

Notes

❏ If you install a third-party display driver and DISPLAY.SYS, be sure to install the third-party driver before you install DISPLAY.SYS.

❏ PRINTER.SYS is used to enable code page switching for parallel ports.

DOS= (MS-DOS 5)   Config

Purpose

Used to determine whether DOS is loaded into the High Memory Area (HMA) and whether device drivers and utilities can be accessed in the Upper Memory Area (UMA).

When To Use

The DOS= command is required to free conventional memory by moving portions of the DOS environment into the HMA and UMA. If you want to load DOS into the HMA, use the HIGH setting. If you want to load device drivers and utilities into the UMA, use the UMB setting. If you want to use both, use the HIGH and UMB settings together.

Common Syntax and Examples

```
DOS=HIGH or UMB or HIGH, UMB
```

HIGH and UMB are parameters that activate specific features of the DOS environment. The HIGH setting loads DOS into the High Memory Area. The UMB setting enables DOS to communicate with the Upper Memory Area.

To load DOS into the High Memory Area, use the command:

```
DOS=HIGH
```

If you load device drivers or utilities into the Upper Memory Area, you must use the following command:

```
DOS=UMB
```

If DOS is to be loaded into the High Memory Area and you are loading device drivers or utilities into the Upper Memory Area, type:

```
DOS=HIGH, UMB
```

Switches

None.

Notes

❏ By default, DOS is loaded into conventional memory and is not capable of communicating with device drivers or utilities contained in the Upper Memory Area.

❏ When you specify two parameters, they can be in either order (i.e., DOS=HIGH, UMB is the same as DOS=UMB, HIGH).

❏ To use the DOS=HIGH statement, an extended memory manager must be installed (HIMEM.SYS).

❏ To use the DOS=UMB statement, both an Upper Memory Area manager and an extended memory manager must be installed (EMM386.EXE and HIMEM.SYS).

❏ You can explicitly specify that DOS should be loaded into conventional memory with DOS=LOW. You can load DOS into conventional memory and activate communication with the Upper Memory Area by using either DOS=UMB or DOS=LOW, UMB.

❏ You can explicitly prevent communication between DOS and the Upper Memory Area by using DOS=NOUMB. To load DOS into the High Memory Area without activating communication with the Upper Memory Area, you can use either DOS=HIGH or DOS=HIGH, NOUMB.

❏ The default is equivalent to explicitly stating DOS=LOW, NOUMB.

❏ See Chapter 10 for a discussion of memory management and improving system performance.

DOSKEY (MS-DOS 5)   Network, External

Purpose

Installs the command line editor, which may be used to display a history of previously entered commands as well as set up aliases or macros.

When To Use

Use DOSKEY to create aliases for existing commands or keyboard macros as well as to quickly re-use previously entered DOS commands.

Common Syntax and Examples

DOSKEY /REINSTALL /BUFSIZE=*size* /MACROS /HISTORY /INSERT or
/OVERSTRIKE *macroname=text*

macroname=text creates a macro that performs a DOS command or set of commands.

macroname is the name to assign to the macro.

text is the set of DOS commands.

To start the DOSKEY program, type:

DOSKEY

After DOSKEY starts, use the following keys to edit command lines and create macros:

Key	Description
Up-arrow	Recalls the DOS command you used before the one currently displayed on the command line.
Down-arrow	Recalls the DOS command you used after the one displayed on the command line.
Page Up	Recalls the oldest (first) DOS command you used in the current session or in the buffer. (See /BUFSIZE=SIZE switch.)
Page Down	Recalls the most most recent (last) DOS command you used.
Left-arrow	Moves the cursor back one character on the current command line.
Right-arrow	Moves the cursor forward one character on the current command line.
Ctrl-Left-arrow	Moves the cursor back one word on the current command line.
Ctrl-Right-arrow	Moves the cursor forward one word on the current command line.
Home	Moves the cursor to the beginning of the command line.
End	Moves the cursor to the end of the command line.
Esc	Clears the command line from the screen.
F1	Copies one character from the command line buffer to the command line. The command line buffer is a memory buffer containing the last command you used.

Key	Description
F2	Searches forward in the command line buffer for the key. DOS copies the text from the command line buffer up to but not including key.
F3	Copies the rest of the command line buffer to the command line beginning with the position in the command line buffer corresponding to the cursor position on the command line.
F4	Deletes characters from the command line buffer. Characters are deleted from the beginning of the buffer up to, but not including, the key you specify.
F5	Copies the command line to the buffer and clears the command line.
F6	Puts an end-of-file (Ctrl-Z) character at the end of the command line.
F7	Displays the contents of the memory buffer (contains all commands of the current session), and a command number beginning with 1 for the oldest (first) command.
ALT+F7	Deletes all commands stored in the memory buffer.
string F8	Searches memory for a command to recall. The string is the first character or characters of the command you want DOSKEY to locate. Type the string and then press F8.
F9	Asks you to enter a command number and then displays the command associated with that number. Use F7 to display all commands and their numbers.
ALT+F10	Deletes all macro defintions.

The following chart lists the keys in alphabetical order by task:

Task	Key
Clear the command	Esc
Copy 1 character from buffer	F1
Copy remainder of buffer	F3
Delete character to next key	F4
Delete all commands stored	Alt-F7
Delete all macro definitions	Alt-F10

Task	Key
Display all commands stored	F7
Display command by number	F9
Move cursor back 1 character	Left-arrow
Move cursor back 1 word	Ctrl-Left-arrow
Move cursor forward 1 character	Right-arrow
Move cursor forward 1 word	Ctrl-Right-arrow
Move cursor to end of line	End
Move cursor to start of line	Home
Put EOF (Ctrl-Z) at end of line	F6
Recall newest command	Page Down
Recall next command	Down-arrow
Recall oldest command	Page Up
Recall previous command	Up-arrow
Save command to buffer	F5
Search buffer for next key pressed	F2
Search memory for command	F8

Switches

/REINSTALL	Installs a new copy of the DOSKEY program. The buffer is also cleared.
/BUFSIZE=size	Specifies the size of the buffer DOSKEY uses to store commands and macros. The minimum size is 256 bytes. The default is 512 bytes.
/MACROS or /M	Displays current DOSKEY macros. You can capture or print the macro definitions by using the (>) redirection symbol to redirect the list to a file or printer.
/HISTORY or /H	Displays all the commands stored in the memory buffer. You can capture or print this list by using the (>) redirection symbol to redirect the list to a file or printer.
/INSERT or /OVERSTRIKE	Specifies whether to start DOSKEY with insert on or off. If you use insert, DOSKEY is started with insert on. Otherwise, DOSKEY is started with insert off or overstrike on. The default is overstrike on.

Notes

❏ DOSKEY is a terminate and stay resident program that occupies 3K of memory. You can load DOSKEY with the LOADHIGH command to load the routine into extended memory.

❏ Use the following special characters to create a macro:

Character	Function
$G or $g	Redirects output. Use this character when you use the (>) redirection symbol in a command.
GG or gg	Appends output. Use this character when you use the (>>) append symbol in a command.
$L or $l	Redirects input. Use this character when you use the (<) redirection symbol.
$B or $b	Uses output of one command as input to another command. Use this character when you use the pipe (I) symbol.
$T or $t	Separates one command from another command.
$$	Uses the dollar sign character ($) in a command.
$1 to $9	Parameters passed to the macro on the command line. Similar to the way %1 is used with batch files.
$*	Remainder of command line after macro name to be substituted. Similar to $1 to $9 parameters except everything after macro name is included in one chunk to be substituted for $*.

❏ To create a macro that displays a directory listing in wide format and in alphabetical order, type the following command:

```
DOSKEY WDIR=DIR $1 /W /O:N
```

To issue the macro for the A drive, type the command:

```
WDIR A:
```

DOSSHELL (MS-DOS 5)   Network, External

Purpose

Starts the DOS Shell, which gives access to DOS commands through a mouse compatible graphics user interface. The Shell may also be loaded in a text mode and used from the keyboard without a mouse.

When To Use

Use DOSSHELL when you want to take advantage of the new DOS task switcher, which allows multiple DOS programs to be switched in and out of memory. The graphics user interface of the DOSSHELL also makes file and directory management easier. You may also want to use the DOSSHELL simply to take advantage of the built in Program Manager that acts as a menu system for your application programs.

Common Syntax and Examples

```
DOSSHELL /T:resN
```

or

```
DOSSHELL /G:resN
```

To start the DOS Shell program in monochrome low resolution text mode with 25 lines, use:

DOSSHELL /T:LOW25 /B

To start the DOS shell in high resolution graphics mode, use the command:

DOSSHELL /G:HIGH

Switches

/G   Uses graphics mode when starting DOS Shell.

/T   Uses text mode when starting DOS Shell.

res uses l,m,or h to specify low, medium, or high resolution.

n is the number for your hardware within the resolution category.

/B   Uses the monochrome (black and white) color scheme.

Note

❑ After you start the shell program, you can use the DISPLAY command on the Options menu to change the screen resolution.

DRIVER.SYS   Driver

Purpose

Creates logical drives.

When To Use

Use the DRIVER.SYS driver to define the logical drive characteristics associated with a physical drive.

Common Syntax and Examples

```
DEVICE=d:path\DRIVER.SYS /D:drive /C /F:type /H:number /S:sectors
    /T:tracks
```

or

```
DEVICEHIGH=d:path\DRIVER.SYS /D:drive /C /F:type /H:number /
    S:sectors /T:tracks
```

The /D: parameter identifies the drive number (*drive*). The drives are numbered sequentially with A being number 0. The second floppy drive is always B and number 1. The first hard disk drive is C and is number 2.

The /F: parameter uses the following codes to specify the *type* of drive:

Code	Drive Type
0	160K/180K or 320/360K
1	1.2M
2	720K (3 1/2-inch disk)
5	Hard Disk
6	Tape
7	1.44M (3 1/2-inch disk)
8	Read/Write Optical Disk
9	2.88M (3 1/2-inch disk)

The d: parameter is the disk drive for the device driver.

The path\ parameter is the path for the device driver. If no path is specified, the root directory is assumed.

To install the B drive with a 1.2M format, use the command:

```
DEVICE=DRIVER.SYS /D:1 /F:1
```

To indicate that the B drive recognizes when the door is open, type:

```
DEVICE=DRIVER.SYS=/D:1 /F:1 /C
```

Switches

/C	Indicates whether the drive reports when the drive door is open or closed. If /C is not specified, DOS cannot tell whether the floppy disk has been changed (i.e., the door has been opened).
/H:*number*	Specifies the number of drive heads. The default value is set by the /F: parameter.
/S:*sectors*	Specifies the number of sectors. The default value is set by the /F: parameter.
/T:*tracks*	Specifies the number of tracks.

Notes

❏ See the DRIVPARM setting for information about reconfiguring a drive that is already installed.

❏ If you assign more than one set of characteristics to a drive number, only the last set is retained.

DRIVPARM=   Config

Purpose

Used to modify the format DOS uses when communicating with an existing logical device.

When To Use

Use the DRIVPARM= setting whenever you install an external disk drive or want to configure a drive to a format other than its default. The DRIVPARM= setting can be used to change the format created using DRIVER.SYS.

Common Syntax and Examples

```
DRIVPARM=/D:drive /C /F:type /H:number /I /N /S:sectors /T:tracks
```

The /D: parameter identifies the drive number (*drive*). The drives are numbered sequentially with A being number 0. The second floppy drive is always B and number 1. The first hard disk is C and is number 2.

The /F: parameter specifies the type of drive (*type*) using the following codes:

0	160K/180K or 320/360K
1	1.2M
2	720K (3 1/2-inch disk)
5	Hard Disk
6	Tape
7	1.44M (3 1/2-inch disk)
8	Read/Write Optical Disk
9	2.88M (3 1/2-inch disk)

To reconfigure the B: drive to a 1.2M format, use the command:

```
DRIVPARM=/D:1 /F:1
```

To indicate that the B: drive recognizes when the door is open, type the following:

```
DRIVPARM=/D:1 /F:1 /C
```

Switches

/C	Indicates whether the drive reports when the drive door is open or closed. If /C is not specified, DOS cannot tell whether the floppy disk has been changed (i.e., the door has been opened).
/H:*number*	Number of drive heads. The default value is set by the /F: parameter.
/S:*sectors*	Number of sectors. The default value is set by the /F: parameter.
/T:*tracks*	Number of tracks.
/I	Used if the ROM BIOS does not support 3 1/2-inch drives.
/N	Used to specify a non-removable block device.

Notes

❏ Use the DRIVER.SYS device driver to define the relationship between logical and physical drives.

❏ Use ASSIGN, SUBST, or JOIN to create relationships between logical drives and between logical drives and directories.

ECHO   Batch, Internal

Purpose

Used to control whether command lines are displayed on the screen and also used to display a command to the screen.

When To Use

Use the ECHO OFF command to stop command lines from displaying on the screen. When command lines are not being displayed, you can use the ECHO command with a text string to display comments or prompts (the text string) on the screen. Use the ECHO ON command to reactivate the display of command lines. The ECHO command by itself reports whether command lines are being displayed.

Common Syntax and Examples

```
ECHO ON or OFF
```

To stop the display of command prompts, type:

```
ECHO OFF
```

To start the display of command prompts, type:

```
ECHO ON
```

To check whether command prompts are being displayed, simply type:

```
ECHO
```

Switches

None.

Notes

❏ ECHO is automatically turned back on when you exit a batch file.

❏ Use ECHO to display a single blank line.

❏ The at symbol (@) can be used before a command line in a batch file to suppress the display of the command line. A common use for this feature is when you first want to disable the display of command lines with the ECHO OFF command. Normally, the command ECHO OFF displays on the screen. The command @ECHO OFF produces no output on the screen.

❏ You cannot use the ECHO command to display the DOS redirection symbols (|, <, or >).

- ❏ The ECHO command is often used with the IF statement to produce prompts in batch files.
- ❏ See Chapter 13 for more information about batch files and the batch file commands.

EDIT (MS-DOS 5)   Network, External

Purpose

Starts the new DOS 5.0 full screen editor for creating, editing, and printing ASCII text files.

When To Use

Use EDIT whenever you need to edit or create a file consisting of more than a few lines. Replaces the DOS EDLIN command, which is a line oriented editor.

Common Syntax and Examples

        EDIT *d:path\filename* /B /G /H /NOHI

The *d:* parameter specifies the drive where the file is located.

The *path* parameter is the path to the file to be edited.

The *filename* parameter is the name of the file to be edited. Wild cards are not permitted.

Switches

/B	Uses the DOS Editor in black and white.
/G	Uses the color graphics adapter (CGA) monitor.
/H	Displays the highest possible number of lines for your monitor.
/NOHI	This switch is used so you do not use highlighting. This is useful for 8-color monitors rather than 16 color monitors.

Notes

- ❏ The files QBASIC.EXE and EDIT.COM must be in the current directory or search path for the DOS Editor to function correctly.
- ❏ EDIT supports the use of a Microsoft compatible mouse. Make sure the mouse drivers are loaded before starting EDIT to access the mouse.

❑ The commands are completely different from EDLIN, so use the built in help system. Pressing the F1 key will bring up help at any time.

❑ Wild cards are not allowed in file names.

EDLIN   External

Purpose

Used to activate the EDLIN line editor and load a file or portion of a file into the editing buffer.

When To Use

Use EDLIN when you want to edit a file in a simple line editor, when you have a file that is too large and you want to break it into smaller files, or when you want to change quickly the contents of a file without using a full-screen editor or word processor.

Common Syntax and Examples

```
EDLIN d:path\filename /B
```

The *filename* parameter is the name of the ASCII file (text file) that is to be loaded into the editing buffer. It may contain path information.

The *d:* parameter indicates the disk drive letter.

The *path* parameter is the path to the directory containing the file to be edited.

To load the CONFIG.SYS file into EDLIN, use the command:

```
EDLIN \CONFIG.SYS
```

Switch

/B   Normally, EDLIN reads a file until it encounters an end-of-file marker (Ctrl-Z). With the /B switch, EDLIN reads until the entire file has been read (as indicated by the file size), even if it encounters a Ctrl-Z character.

Notes

❑ The DOS function keys are available within EDLIN. See Chapter 3 for a discussion of these keys.

❑ If the entire file is loaded into memory, EDLIN displays the message:
End of input file.

❏ The following is a summary of the EDLIN commands. See the EDLIN commands section for a description of each command.

line	Displays the line indicated by line.
?	Displays the list of EDLIN commands.
a	Loads a portion of the file into memory when the entire file will not fit into available memory.
c	Copies a block of consecutive lines.
d	Deletes a block of consecutive lines.
e	Ends the EDLIN session and saves the file.
i	Inserts one or more lines after the current line.
l	Displays one or more lines.
m	Moves one or more lines.
p	Displays a file one page at a time. The number of lines per page depends on the screen mode you are using.
q	Quits EDLIN without saving the file.
r	Searches and replaces one string for another.
s	Searches for a string of one or more characters.
t	Merges the contents of a file with the current file in memory.
w	Writes a portion of the file in memory to disk.

❏ The maximum line length is 253 characters.

❏ Press F6 (which inserts a ^Z end of file marker) at the end of the last line of a batch file created with EDLIN to stop the BATCH FILE MISSING error on network systems.

❏ The asterisk (*) is used both as an EDLIN prompt and to indicate which line number is the current line.

❏ Wildcards are not allowed.

❏ Any line can be made current and edited by typing the line number. EDLIN displays the line and then prompts for any changes by displaying the line number followed by an asterisk. Pressing Enter retains the information on the line.

❏ If sufficient memory is unavailable for creating an editing buffer that holds the entire file, portions of the file are swapped between the file and memory. In low memory conditions (only a portion of the file is loaded), the W (Write) and A (Append) commands are used to manipulate which portion of the file is in memory. Information recorded with a W (Write) command is permanent and remains even if the editing session is terminated with a Q (Quit) command.

❏ EDIT is generally a better choice for most file editing because it offers a number of significant features in addition to being a full-screen editor.

❏ EDLIN requires over 200K less disk space than EDIT and QBASIC and is recommended when storage space is limited.

EDLIN: A   External

Purpose

Used to load additional lines into memory from an external file.

When To Use

The A command (Append) loads portions of a file when the entire file that you want to edit cannot be loaded into memory at one time.

Common Syntax and Examples

*numb***A**

The **A** command by itself loads from the specified file until the file editing buffer is 75% full.

If a *numb* parameter is specified, EDLIN loads that many additional lines from the file into the editing buffer.

Switches

None.

Notes

❏ This command causes the line numbers to change. To see the new numbers, use either the L or P command.

❏ A is not available if the entire file is loaded into memory.

EDLIN: C   External

Purpose

Used to duplicate lines within the EDLIN editor.

When To Use

The C command (Copy) copies a line or group of lines to a new location within the editing buffer. The command can also be used to duplicate the line or group of lines more than once at the new location.

Common Syntax and Examples

start, end, **target***, repeat* **C**

The **target** parameter specifies the location for the copied lines.

The *start* parameter specifies the starting line for the information to be copied.

The *end* parameter is used when specifying a range of lines to copy.

The *repeat* command is used to specify that more than one copy of the line(s) are to be inserted before the target line.

To copy the current line so that it is before line ten, type:

`,,10C`

To copy lines 1 through 5 so that they are before line ten, type:

`1,5,10C`

To copy line 1 three times and insert the copies before line two, use:

`1,,2,3C`

Switches

None.

Notes

❑ This command causes the line numbers to change. To see the new numbers, use either the L or P command.

❑ The line(s) being copied cannot contain the target line.

EDLIN: D   External

Purpose

Used to delete a line or group of lines from the editing buffer.

When To Use

The D command (Delete) is used to remove a series of lines from the editing buffer.

Common Syntax and Examples

start, end **D**

The *start* parameter indicates the line to be deleted. If no starting value is given, the current line is deleted. If both a *start* and *end* line are specified, the entire range (including the specified lines) is deleted.

The *end* parameter is used to indicate a range of lines to be deleted.

To delete the current line, use:

D

To delete lines 1 through 5, use:

1,5D

Switches

None.

Notes

❑ This command causes the line numbers to change. To see the new numbers, use either the L or P command.

❑ If you specify a line number for the start parameter that does not exist, no lines are deleted.

❑ If you specify a line number greater than the last line number in the editing buffer for the end parameter, all of the lines from start to the end of the editing buffer are deleted.

EDLIN: E   External

Purpose

Used to create a backup of the original file, save the current contents of the editing buffer under the file name and exit EDLIN.

When To Use

The E command (End) is used to terminate a session when you want to save the results.

Common Syntax and Examples

E

The E command uses no parameters.

To create a backup copy of the original file and save the contents of the editing buffer under the original filename, and then end the editing session, use the command:

    E

Switches

None.

Note

❏ You cannot save your work with the E (End) command if EDLIN cannot create a backup copy of the original file (i.e., a BAK version of the file exists and is marked read-only).

EDLIN: I   External

Purpose

Used to activate the insert mode of EDLIN.

When To Use

The I command (Insert) is used to insert new lines before the current line. This is the only way to add new lines to the contents of the editing buffer.

Common Syntax and Examples

    numb I

The *numb* parameter indicates the line that receives the inserted information. If *numb* is not specified, information is inserted before the current line. If a number greater than the number of lines in the file is specified, the information is inserted at the end of the editing buffer.

To insert a line before line 14, simply type:

    14I

Switches

None.

Notes

❏ EDLIN indicates that insert mode is active by displaying the line number followed by an asterisk (*).

❏ This command causes the line numbers to change. To see the new numbers, use either the L or P command.

❑ You can use either Ctrl-C or Ctrl-Z to terminate insert mode.

EDLIN: L   External

Purpose

Used to view a line or group of lines in the editing buffer.

When To Use

The default L command (List) is used to view a full screen of information
with the current line centered.

Common Syntax and Examples

        start, end L

The *start* parameter is used to specify the starting line to be listed. If no
end parameter value is supplied, an entire screen of information is displayed.

The *end* parameter is used with the *start* parameter to specify a range of
lines. If the lines to be displayed require more than a single screen, EDLIN
pauses after each full screen of information.

If no parameter values are supplied, the current line is centered on the
display starting before the current line and continuing after it. On a standard display with 23 lines, the display starts 11 lines before the current
line and continues with 11 more lines.

To display the lines surrounding the current line, type:

        L

The current line is not changed.

To display lines 12 through 19, type:

        12, 19L

The current line becomes line 12.

Switches

None.

Note

❑ If you specify *start* only, this command displays the same lines as
the P command.

EDLIN: M   External

Purpose

Used to relocate a line or group of lines within the editing buffer.

When To Use

The M command (Move) is used to move a line or group of lines to a new location.

Common Syntax and Examples

>   start, end, **target M**

or

>   start, **+count, target M**

The **target** parameter specifies the new location for the line(s).

The *start* parameter specifies the starting line for the information to be moved.

The *end* parameter is used when specifying a range of lines to move.

The *+count* parameter can be used to specify the number of lines to move rather than the ending line. You must include the plus sign (+) before the number.

To move the current line so that it is before line ten, type:

>   ,,10M

To move lines 1 through 5 so that they are before line ten, type:

>   1,5,10M

To move line 1 and the next 4 lines so that they are before line ten, type:

>   1,+4,10M

Switches

None.

Note

❏ This command causes the line numbers to change. To see the new numbers, use either the L or P command.

EDLIN: P   External

Purpose

Displays the contents of the editing buffer one screen at a time.

When To Use

Using the default, the P command (Page) is used to view the full screen of information following the current line.

Common Syntax and Examples

    start, end P

The *start* parameter is used to specify the starting line to be listed. If no *end* parameter value is supplied, an entire screen of information is displayed.

The *end* parameter is used with the start parameter to specify a range of lines. If the lines to be displayed require more than a single screen, EDLIN pauses after each full screen of information.

If no parameter values are supplied, the current line is used as the starting line and an entire screen of information is displayed.

To display the lines following the current line, type:

    P

The current line is the last line displayed.

Switches

None.

Note

❑ If you specify only the start parameter, this command displays the same lines as the L (List) command.

EDLIN: Q   External

Purpose

Used to abandon any changes to the file being edited.

When To Use

Use the Q command (Quit) when you do not want to save the changes you have made to the edited file.

Common Syntax and Examples

Q

The Q command is entered with no parameters.

To abandon the editing buffer, type:

Q

You will be prompted with the message:

```
Abort Edit (Y/N)?
```

Type **Y** to abandon the file. Entering **N** returns you to the editing buffer.

Switches

None.

Note

❑ Changes made with the W (Write) command in low memory situations are retained. If the entire file fits into memory, the W (Write) command has no effect.

EDLIN: R   External

Purpose

Used to find and replace occurrences of a text string.

When To Use

The R command (Replace) is used when you want to change some or all of the occurrences of a specific text string.

Common Syntax and Examples

```
start, end ? R old(Ctrl-Z)new
```

The *old* parameter specifies the string that you want to find. The text string begins immediately following the R command. If there is a space after the R, the string starts with a space (i.e., R a searches for a space followed by a lowercase a). If *old* is omitted, the text string from the previous R command is used. If there is no previous replace, then the value from the previous S command is used. If there is no previous search or replace, then the search ends.

The Ctrl-Z character is required before the *new* parameter value if a value for the *new* parameter is specified.

The *new* parameter contains the string that is inserted in place of the text string in the *old* parameter. If the Ctrl-Z character is omitted and the R command has been used previously, the previous value for the *new* parameter is used. If no previous R command has been used, or the Ctrl-Z character is included, all occurrences (See Note) of the text string in the *old* parameter are deleted.

The *start* parameter indicates the line where the search should begin. If omitted, the search begins on the line following the current line.

The *end* parameter indicates the last line to be searched. If omitted, the search ends at the end-of-file marker.

The ? parameter is used to enable you to approve each change. Without the ? being specified, the R command changes all occurrences (See Note) and then displays the changed lines. With the ? parameter specified, EDLIN stops at each occurrence and prompts with O.K.?. If you enter **Y** (or **y**) or simply press the Enter key, the change is made. If you enter **N** (or **n**), no change is made. In either case, you move to the next occurrence of the text string.

Switches

None.

Note

❑ Only the first occurrence of the old text string is replaced in each line.

EDLIN: S   External

Purpose

Locates occurrences of a text string.

When To Use

The S command (Search) is used when you want to move between occurrences of a specific text string.

Common Syntax and Examples

> start, end, ? **S**string

The string parameter is the text string that you want to find. The text string begins immediately following the **s** command. If there is a space after the **s**, then the string starts with a space (i.e., **s** **a** searches for a space followed by a lowercase a). If string is omitted, the text string from the previous **s** command is used. If there is no previous search, then the old value from the previous R command is used. If there is no previous replace, then the search ends.

The start parameter indicates the line where the search should begin. If omitted, the search begins on the line following the current line.

The end parameter indicates the last line to be searched. If omitted, the search ends at the end-of-file.

The ? automatically continues Search. Normally, Search stops at the first occurrence of the text string. You can then repeat the **s** command with no parameters to move to the next occurrence. With the ?, you are prompted whether to stop. The actual prompt is: O.K.?. If you enter anything other than **Y** (or **y**), the search continues. Entering **N**, or simply pressing the Enter key, ends the search.

Switches

None.

Note

❑ This command does not change the line numbers.

EDLIN: T   External

Purpose

Used to incorporate the contents of a file into the material being edited.

When To Use

The T command (Transfer) is used when you want to include the entire contents of a second file in the material contained in the editing buffer. With this command, the contents of one file can be added to another at a point within the file.

Common Syntax and Examples

> target **T** *filename*

The *filename* parameter specifies the file to be inserted before the specified line. You can include path information in this parameter. The T command does not search the PATH for a match to the file.

The *target* parameter specifies the line before the line that receives the inserted information.

To include the file TEMP.TXT from the \HOLD directory and insert it before the current line, type:

```
T \HOLD\TEXT.TXT
```

To insert the material from the TEMP.TXT file before line ten, type:

```
10 T \HOLD\TEXT.TXT
```

Switches

None.

Note

❑ If you wish to add the contents of one file at the end of another file, use the COPY command.

EDLIN: W   External

Purpose

Used to write a portion of a file out to disk when the editing buffer cannot contain the entire file.

When To Use

The W command (Write) is used to store changes from the editing buffer when the entire file does not fit into memory. Use this command to free memory so that you can load additional lines from the original file in low memory situations.

Common Syntax and Examples

numb W

The *numb* parameter specifies the number of lines (from the beginning of the editing buffer) that should be written to the file. If omitted, W writes lines until the editing buffer is 75% empty.

To write the first twenty lines from the editing buffer to the file, type:

```
20W
```

Switches

None.

Note

❏ This editing command is not available if the entire file is loaded into memory.

EGA.SYS (MS-DOS 5)   Driver

Purpose

Used to manage task swapping under the DOS Shell on systems with EGA displays.

When To Use

Use the EGA.SYS driver if you use DOS Shell on a system with an EGA display.

Common Syntax and Examples

    DEVICE=d:path\EGA.SYS

or

    DEVICEHIGH=d:path\EGA.SYS

The EGA.SYS driver requires no parameters and is only used with the DOS Shell.

The d: parameter is the disk drive for the device driver.

The path\ parameter is the path for the device driver. If no path is specified, the root directory is assumed.

Switches

None.

Note

❏ For more information about the DOS Shell, see Chapter 12.

EMM386 (MS-DOS 5)   **Internal**

Purpose

Controls whether EMM386 is actively managing the Upper Memory Area or providing Weitek coprocessor support.

When To Use

Use the EMM386 to disable or enable expanded memory emulation or, if expanded memory emulation is active, to disable or enable Weitek coprocessor support. If device drivers or utilities are loaded into the Upper Memory Area, EMM386 cannot be disabled.

Common Syntax and Examples

```
EMM386 ON or OFF or AUTO
```

or

```
EMM386 W=ON or W=OFF
```

or

```
EMM386 ON or OFF or AUTO W=ON or W=OFF
```

The ON parameter specifies that EMM386 should be active (emulating expanded memory, managing the Upper Memory Area, or both).

The AUTO parameter specifies that expanded memory should only be emulated if a program requests it. If installed, management of the Upper Memory Area is active.

The OFF parameter specifies that EMM386 should not be active.

The W=ON parameter activates the Weitek coprocessor support.

The W=OFF parameter suspends the Weitek coprocessor support.

To activate the features installed by the EMM386.EXE driver, type:

```
EMM386 ON
```

To disable the features installed by the EMM386.EXE driver, type:

```
EMM386 OFF
```

To turn on support for the Weitek coprocessor, type:

```
EMM386 W=ON
```

To make expanded memory emulation available only when requested by programs and to enable Weitek coprocessor support, type:

```
EMM386 AUTO W=ON
```

Switches

None.

Notes

❑ The EMM386 command is available only if the EMM386.EXE driver has been installed. If you attempt to use the EMM386 command before installing the device driver, or if you do not have an 80386 or higher processor, DOS displays the following message:

```
EMM386 driver not installed
```

❑ EMM386 can be deactivated only if it is not providing Upper Memory Area management.

❑ To use Weitek coprocessor support, you must have a Weitek coprocessor, EMM386 must be installed and active (EMM386 ON or EMM386 AUTO), and the High Memory Area must be available (DOS must be loaded into conventional memory).

❑ If you attempt to use the w option with no Wietek processor installed in your system, DOS displays the following message:

```
Weitek Coprocessor not installed
```

❑ See the EMM386.EXE driver section and Chapter 10 for more information about the memory management capabilities of EMM386.

EMM386.SYS (MS-DOS 5)   Driver

Purpose

To emualate expanded memory using extended memory, to manage the Upper Memory Area, or both.

When To Use

The EMM386.EXE driver should be installed on any 386 or 486 machine that does not have another installed Upper Memory Area (UMA) manager. A UMA must be present to emualate expanded memory in extended memory.

Common Syntax and Examples

To activate expanded memory emulation only:

DEVICE=d:path**\EMM386.EXE** ON or OFF or AUTO memory W=ON or W=OFF
Mcode or FRAME=address or /Paddress Ppage=start X=beginexclude-
endexclude I=begininclude-endinclude B=location L=free
A=fastregs H=handles D=dma

or

DEVICE=d:path**\EMM386.EXE** ON or OFF or AUTO memory W=ON or W=OFF
Mcode or FRAME=address or /Paddress Ppage=start X=beginexclude-
endexclude I=begininclude-endinclude B=location L=free
A=fastregs H=handles D=dma **RAM**

or

DEVICE=d:path**\EMM386.EXE** ON or OFF or AUTO memory W=ON or W=OFF
X=beginexclude-endexclude I=begininclude-endinclude A=fastregs
D=dma **NOEMS**

The RAM setting indicates that EMM386 is providing both expanded
memory emulation and Upper Memory Management. The NOEMS setting
indicates that EMM386 is providing Upper Memory Management only. If
neither setting is present, EMM386 is providing expanded memory emulation only.

To have EMM386.EXE emulate expanded memory, but not manage the
Upper Memory Area, type:

DEVICE=EMM386.EXE

To have EMM386.EXE provide only expanded memory emulation if a program requests it, type:

DEVICE=EMM386.EXE AUTO

To have EMM386.EXE provide both expanded memory emulation and Upper Memory Area management, type:

DEVICE=EMM386.EXE RAM

To have EMM386.EXE use 128K and provide expanded memory emulation
using all except 1M of extended memory and to manage the Upper Memory
Area, type:

DEVICE=EMM386.EXE 128 L=1024 RAM

To have EMM386.EXE provide only expanded memory emulation and to set the page-segment frame at C400H and exclude the range D000h through E000h, type:

```
DEVICE=EMM386.EXE m2 X=D000-E000
```

or

```
DEVICE=EMM386.EXE FRAME=C400
```

or

```
DEVICE=EMM386.EXE /PC400
```

To have EMM386.EXE serve as an Upper Memory Manager only, type:

```
DEVICE=EMM386.EXE NOEMS
```

To have EMM386.EXE serve as an Upper Memory Manager and provide Weitek coprocessor support, type:

```
DEVICE=EMM386.EXE W=ON NOEMS
```

Switches

ON, OFF, AUTO	Determines whether EMM386 is actively providing memory management services.
memory	Specifies the amount of expanded memory (in Kilobytes) that is to be emulated by the EMM386.EXE driver.
W=ON or W=OFF	Controls whether support is provided for the Weitek coprocessor.
X=*beginexclude-endexclude*	Enables you to explicitly exclude an area of memory in the Upper Memory Area from use for page frames. The *beginexclude* and *endexclude* values must be in hexadecimal and can be in the range A000h through FFFFh. There can be more than one exclude range (repeat the entire x= command) and if the region is explicitly defined to be both excluded (x=) and included (i=), it will be excluded.
I=*begininclude-endinclude*	Enables you to explicitly include an area of memory in the Upper Memory Area for use for page frames. The *begininclude* and *endinclude* values

must be in hexadecimal and can be in the range
A000h through FFFFh. There can be more than one
include range (repeat the entire i = command) and if
the region is explicitly defined to be both excluded
(x =) and included (i =), it will be excluded.

M*code*   Defines the page-frame segment base using a *code*
from the following list:

Value	Base Address (Hexadecimal)
1	C000h
2	C400h
3	C800h
4	CC00h
5	D000h
6	D400h
7	D800h
8	DC00h
9	E000h
10	8000h
11	8400h
12	8800h
13	8C00h
14	9000h

This parameter cannot be used with either the FRAME=
or / P parameter.

FRAME=*address*   Defines the page-frame segment base using a specific
memory address. The valid addresses are listed under
the M parameter. This parameter cannot be used with
either the M or / P parameter.

/P*address*   Defines the page-frame segment base using a specific
memory address. The valid addresses are listed under
the M parameter. This parameter cannot be used with
either the FRAME= or M parameter.

P*page*=*start*   Defines the page-frame address for a specific page
(*page*). The page must be in the range 0 through 255.
The valid addresses are those listed under the M parameter as well as 9400h, 9800h, 9C00h, E400h,
E800h, and EC00h.

L=*free*

Specifies the amount of extended memory that is to remain free when EMM386.EXE is emulating expanded memory. The *free* variable should be in kilobytes. The default is 0.

B=*location*

Specifies the lowest valid address for the banking (or swapping) of expanded memory pages. The *location* variable can be any hexadecimal between 1000h and 4000h. The default is 4000h.

H=*number*

Specifies how many handles EMM386.EXE can use at one time. Permissible values are in the range 2 through 255 and the default is 64.

A=*fastregs*

The *fastregs* variable specifies the number of fast alternate register sets that are created for multitasking environments. Each register requires about 200 bytes of additional memory within the EMM386.EXE driver. Permissible values are in the range 0 through 254 and the default is 7.

D=*dma*

The *dma* variable specifies the amount of memory (in kilobytes) that should be allocated for direct memory access (dma) buffering. This amount excludes any data transfer to and from floppy disks. Possible values are in the range 16 through 256 and the default is 16.

Notes

❏ EMM386.EXE can be installed only on 386 and 486 systems.

❏ EMM386.EXE must be installed in conventional memory (not the Upper Memory Area).

❏ In general, EMM386.EXE is automatically configured for your system. You must decide, however, whether you want EMM386.EXE to provide expanded memory emulation only, expanded memory emulation and Upper Memory Area Management (add the RAM parameter) or to manage the Upper Memory Area and not provide expanded memory emulation (add the NOEMS parameter).

Other decisions include whether you want to enable Weitek coprocessor support (add W=ON) and if you want to restrict expanded memory emulation to when programs that request expanded memory (add the AUTO switch).

❏ Be careful to avoid confusing the OFF and ON settings with the W=ON and W=OFF settings. The first settings (OFF and ON) control whether EMM386.EXE provides services. The second (W=ON and W=OFF) control whether support is provided for the Weitek coprocessor. Both of these settings can be changed with the EMM386 command.

❏ Weitek support is only available if the High Memory Area is free (that is, if DOS is loaded into conventional memory).

EXE2BIN   Network, External

Purpose

Converts an EXE file to a COM-compatible BINary file.

When To Use

Programmers use EXEZBIN to convert small EXE programs to COM files.

Common Syntax and Examples

```
EXE2BIN d1:path1\in-file d2:path2\out-file
```

The *d1:path1* parameter is the disk and path to the input file.

The *in-file* is the file to be converted from an EXE format to a binary format.

The *d2:path2* parameter is the disk and path to the output file.

The *out-file* is the output file.

To convert the file CIRCUS.EXE to CIRCUS.BIN, for example, use the following command:

```
EXE2BIN CIRCUS.EXE
```

To convert the file CIRCUS.EXE and store the binary version in the file CLOWN.BIN, you would type:

```
EXE2BIN CIRCUS.EXE CLOWN.BIN
```

Switches

None.

Notes

❏ The default file name extension for the input file is EXE.

❏ If you do not give an output drive, path or file name, EXE2BIN writes the file to the current drive and path, and uses the input file name with an EXE extension as the output file name.

❑ The input file is converted to BIN format and is saved to the output file.

❑ The input file must be a valid EXE file, it cannot be packed, it cannot contain a STACK segment, and the resident code and data portion of the file combined must be less than 64K.

❑ Two conversion types are available. If the CSP:IP is specified as 0000:100H in the EXE file, the file runs as a COM file with the instruction pointer set at 100H by the ORG assembler statement. You use COM as the extension on the output file parameter.

❑ If no CSP:IP is given in the EXE file, a normal binary conversion is performed. If you need to perform segment fixes, EXE2BIN prompts you for the fixup value, which is the absolute segment where the program will be loaded. This, in effect, binds the program to a specified memory address. The command interpreter COMMAND.COM cannot load the program.

EXIT   Network, Internal

Purpose

EXIT leaves the current invocation of the command interpreter (if one exists).

When To Use

Use EXIT when you are creating a program, or when a batch program invokes additional instances of the command interpreter.

Common Syntax and Examples

```
EXIT
```

Switches

None.

Notes

❑ While running some programs, you can run a DOS command interpreter with the COMMAND command and then use EXIT to return to your program.

❑ If you started the COMMAND.COM program with the permanent /p switch, the EXIT command is disregarded.

❑ You cannot use EXIT if the /P parameter was used when the command processor was installed.

EXPAND (MS-DOS 5)   Network, External

Purpose

Expands a file to install it from the compressed installation disks.

When To Use

Use EXPAND when you want to decompress command files from the installation disks you received with DOS, if you accidentally delete a command, or when you want to upgrade to a new version of only some commands.

Common Syntax and Examples

    EXPAND *d1*:*path1****filename1** *d2*:*path2****filename2** *d3*:*path*

or

    EXPAND *d1*:*path1****filename1** *d3*:*path3****filename**3

The *d1*:*path1* parameter is the disk and path to the file or files you want to expand.

The *filename1* parameter specifies the file to be expanded.

The *d2*:*path2****filename2** parameter specifies additional files to be expanded.

The *d3*:*path3*\ parameter is the location where the expanded files are to be placed.

The *filename3* parameter can be used to specify the new name of the expanded file if you are expanding a single file.

To expand DOSSHELL.EX_ from the DOS 5.0 installation disk in drive A and rename it C:\DOS\DOSSHELL.EXE, for example, use the following command:

    EXPAND A:DOSSHELL.EX_ C:\DOS\DOSSHELL.EXE

Switches

None.

Note

❑ The EXPAND command is intended for recovering programs from the DOS 5 distribution diskettes. It will only work with Microsoft's compressed files.

FASTOPEN   External

Purpose

Starts the FASTOPEN program to keep directory information in memory so that DOS can quickly find frequently needed files.

When To Use

Use FASTOPEN when you have a few files you access frequently and if you want to improve the performance of your system.

Common Syntax and Examples

```
FASTOPEN d1:=n1 d2:=n2 ... /X
```

The $d1$ and $d2$ parameters specify drives that should be tracked for file usage.

The $n1$ and $n2$ parameters specify how many files should be tracked on the respective drive.

You can start FASTOPEN (from the root directory) in your CONFIG.SYS file with the following command:

```
INSTALL=FASTOPEN d:=n d:=n ... /X
```

d: is the disk drive where the FASTOPEN command should track opening files.

n is the number of files with which FASTOPEN can work. This must be a number between 10 and 999. The default value is 48.

To track 200 files on drive C using the copy of FASTOPEN in the C:\DOS directory, use the following command in your CONFIG.SYS file:

```
INSTALL=C:\DOS\FASTOPEN.EXE C:=200
```

Switch

/X   Specifies that the directory cache be created in expanded memory.

Notes

❏ FASTOPEN reduces access time by remembering the name and location of frequently accessed files in a cache area.

❏ FASTOPEN is compatible only with fixed disks. FASTOPEN will not work on a network or floppy disks.

❑ Do not attempt to load FASTOPEN from the DOS Shell as this will usually lock up your system.

❑ Although the program is not a big memory user, FASTOPEN requires 48 bytes per file.

FC   Network, External

Purpose

Displays differences between two files.

When To Use

Use FC to find the differences between two binary or text files.

Common Syntax and Examples

```
FC /A /C /L /LBn /N /T /W /nnn /d1:path1\filename1
   d2:path2\filename2
```

or

```
FC /B /d1:path1\filename1 d2:path2\filename2
```

*d1:path1**filename1** is the disk, path, and file name of the first file to compare.

*d2:path2**filename2** is the disk, path, and file name of the second file to compare.

To compare LETTER.DOC with MAILING.TXT, for example, use the following command:

```
FC /A LETTER.DOC MAILING.TXT
```

Switches

/A	Abbreviates the comparison output of ASCII. It compares by displaying only the first and last lines of each set of differences.
/C	Disregards the case of letters.
/L	Uses ASCII mode by synchronizing after finding a mismatch.
/LBn	Sets the number of lines for the internal buffer. The default is 100 lines. If more than this number of lines are different, the file comparison is ended.
/N	Displays the line numbers during the comparison.

/T   Does not expand tabs to spaces. FC treats tabs as spaces, with a tab being eight spaces. Use this switch to have tabs differ from spaces.

/W   Compresses tabs and spaces to single spaces during a comparison.

/nnn   Sets the number of lines that must match before FC states that a synchronization has occured.

/B   Compares in binary mode byte by byte and does not attempt to synchronize the files. Lists all differences. FC uses binary comparisons as the default for BIN, COM, EXE, LIB, OBJ, and SYS files.

Note

❑ Wild cards are allowed. Each first file name is compared to the corresponding second file name. If only one file is specified for either first or second file name, that file is compared to all the files that you specify by the wild card in the first or second file name.

FCBS=   Config

Purpose

Sets the number of file control blocks that can be in use at one time.

When To Use

Change this value from the default only when requested by a program.

Common Syntax and Examples

```
FCBS=blocks
```

The *blocks* parameter specifies the number of file control blocks that are to be allocated.

To increase the number of file control blocks to eight, include the following line in the CONFIG.SYS file:

```
FCBS=8
```

Switches

None.

Notes

❑ The default value for FCBS= is 4.

❑ The use of file control blocks has been replaced in most applications with the use of file handles, which are controlled by the FILES= setting. Change this setting only if a program requires it.

❑ See Chapter 10 for a discussion of optimizing data transfer and improving system performance.

FDISK   Network, External

Purpose

Configures a hard disk.

When To Use

Use FDISK when you are installing a new hard disk or you want to create, change, delete, display, or select partitions.

Common Syntax and Examples

```
FDISK
```

Switches

None.

Notes

❑ To change the size of a partition, you must delete that partition and create a new one of the size you want.

❑ The maximum partition size is 2G (2,000,000,000,000 bytes) or 2000M.

❑ If you delete a partition, you erase all the data stored in that partition.

❑ FDISK does not work on drives set up with the ASSIGN, SUBST, or JOIN commands.

FILES=   Config

Purpose

Sets the number of file handles that can be open at one time.

When To Use

Set the number of file handles to the maximum required by any of your programs.

Common Syntax and Examples

```
FILES=handles
```

The `handles` parameter determines the maximum number of file handles that can be allocated at one time.

To increase the number of file handles to 30, enter the following line in the CONFIG.SYS file:

```
FILES=30
```

Switches

None.

Notes

❑ The default value for FILES= is 8.

❑ This value must be increased to 30 to use Windows.

❑ See Chapter 10 for a discussion of optimizing data transfer and improving system performance.

FIND   Network, External

Purpose

Searches for a text string in one or more files.

When To Use

When you are looking for one or more occurances of a string. You can use this information to indicate which files you need to work with further.

Common Syntax and Examples

```
FIND /V /C /N /I "string" d:path\filename ...
```

The `"string"` parameter indicates the characters to search for. The string parameter must be enclosed in quotation marks.

The `d:path\filename` parameter is the disk and path to the file or set of files to search. Wild cards are not permitted. To use multiple files, use the FOR command with the FIND command.

To display all lines in SCHEDULE.TXT, that contain the string "lunch," for example, use the following command:

```
FIND "lunch" SCHEDULE.TXT
```

Switches

/V Displays all lines containing the string (**v**erbose option).

/C Displays a count of the lines containing the specified string.

/N Includes the line number on each line.

/I Ignores the case of letters when performing the search.

Notes

❏ If the string you are searching for contains quotation marks, use double quotation marks for each quotation mark within the string. "Hi," she said, for example, would be """Hi,"" she said".

❏ If you omit the file name, FIND can act as a filter, displaying only those lines that contain the specified string.

❏ If you use /V and /C in the same command, FIND displays those lines in the file not containing the specified string. If you use both /C and /N, the /N switch is ignored because only a count is displayed.

❏ FIND will not recognize carriage returns.

FOR   Batch, Internal

Purpose

Repeats a command for a series of values in a list.

When To Use

Use FOR at the command line or in a batch file to perform a task a specific number of times.

Common Syntax and Examples

```
FOR %variable IN (list) DO command
```

The *variable* parameter is used as a temporary variable to hold a value from the list. You can use any individual letter for this parameter. Its scope is limited to the individual FOR command and different FOR commands may use different *variable* parameters.

The *list* parameter is replaced by a list of values that are substituted one by one, in the order listed for the variable parameter. The items in the list are separated with a space. Wild cards can be used within the list.

The *command* parameter is any valid DOS command. It may include parameters, pipes, and redirections and generally includes a reference to the variable parameter.

To display the contents of the files TEMP1.TXT and TEMP2.TXT, for example, you would type the following:

```
FOR %f IN (temp1.txt temp2.txt) DO type %f
```

A more sophisticated version of the same command follows:

```
FOR %f IN (temp1 temp2) DO type %f.txt
```

To display the contents of all the files in the \HOLD directory with the TXT extension, use the command:

```
FOR %f IN (\hold\*.txt) DO type %f
```

To display the information a screen at a time from the command prompt, use the command:

```
FOR %f IN (\hold\*.txt) DO type %f
```

To include the same command in a batch file, type:

```
FOR %%f IN (\hold\*.txt) DO type %%f | more
```

Switches

None.

Notes

- ❏ If FOR is used in a batch file, you must use %% before the variable name (rather than a single %).
- ❏ See Chapter 13 for more information about batch files and the batch file commands.
- ❏ You can use piping and redirection with the FOR command.
- ❏ Take note of the new DIR/B command as it supplies file names in the correct format for use with the FOR command.

FORMAT   External

Purpose

Prepares a disk for use by DOS.

When To Use

When you want to prepare a new disk or diskette for use, or start over with an old disk or diskette.

Common Syntax and Examples

FORMAT *d*: /V:*label* /Q /U /F:*size* /B|/S

FORMAT *d*: /V:*label* /Q /U /T:*tracks* /N:*sectors* /B|/S

FORMAT *d*: /V:*label* /Q /U /1 /4 /B|/S

FORMAT *d*: /V:*label* /Q /U /1 /4 /8 /B|/S

d: is the disk drive letter of the disk you want to format. If you do not include any switches, FORMAT uses the drive type to determine how to format the disk.

To format the hard disk in drive C, for example, use the following syntax:

FORMAT C:

To format a floppy disk in drive A: as a single-sided disk, for example, use the following command:

FORMAT A: /1

Switches

/V:*label* Sets the volume label, up to 11 characters. If you do not give DOS a label to use for the disk, you will be prompted for one after the format is complete. You cannot use the /V switch with the /8 switch.

/Q Deletes the file allocation table (FAT) and the root directory of a disk that was formatted previously. Does not scan for bad tracks and sectors. Use this switch only to format a previously formatted disk you know is in good condition.

/U Specifies an unconditional format. This switch will prevent you from using the UNFORMAT command later.

/F:*size* Formats the disk to the size you specify. If size is not specified, the disk is formatted to the default size for the drive being used. The following sizes are valid:

Size	Format
160	160K, single-sided, double-density, 5 1/4-inch disk
180	180K, single-sided, double-density, 5 1/4-inch disk
320	320K, double-sided, double-density, 5 1/4-inch disk
360	360K, double-sided, double-density, 5 1/4-inch disk
720	720K, double-sided, double-density, 3 1/2-inch disk
1200	1200K, double-sided, quadruple-density, 5 1/4-inch disk
1440	1440K, double-sided, quadruple-density, 3 1/2-inch disk
2880	2880K, double-sided, 3 1/2-inch disk

The *size* value may be listed with no kilobye notation (i.e., 720), with the single K notation (i.e., 720K) or with the Kb notation (720Kb). For sizes over 1M (1000K), the *size* may be expressed in megabytes with no notation (1.2), with the single M notation (1.2M) or with the Mb notation (1.2Mb).

/B Reserves space for hidden system files (IO.SYS and MSDOD.SYS). In versions of DOS prior to Version 5.0, you are required to reserve this space prior to using the SYS command to copy system files.

/S Copies the DOS system files. If the files are not found, you are prompted to insert a system disk.

/T:*tracks* Specifies the number of tracks on the disk. When you combine T:tracks with the /N switch, it establishes the format of the disk. When possible, you should specify the size with /F switch instead. You cannot combine /F and /T switches.

/N:*sectors* Specifies the number of sectors per tracks on the disk and when combined with the /T switch, establishes the format of the disk. When possible, you should specify the size with /F switch instead. You cannot combine /F and /N switches.

/1 Formats only a single side of a floppy disk.

/4 Formats a 5 1/4-inch, 360K, double-sided, double-density diskette on a 1.2M drive. Some 360K diskette drives cannot read diskettes formatted with this switch. This switch may be used with the /1 switch to format a 5 1/4-inch, 180K single-sided diskette.

/8 Formats a 5 1/4-inch disk with 8 sectors per track. This switch is used for DOS versions prior to version 2.0.

Notes

❏ When the FORMAT command finishes, DOS displays the amount of disk space, how much is defective, how much is used by the operating system, and the available space.

❏ New to version 5.0 is the capability to do safe formatting. If you do not use the /U (unconditional format) option, FORMAT clears only the FAT (file allocation table) and the root directory. You can use the UNFORMAT command to restore them if you do not make further changes to the disk.

❏ Use the /Q switch to perform a quick format.

❏ Use the /U switch with a new disk.

❏ Do not use FORMAT on drives formed by using the ASSIGN, JOIN, or SUBST commands. FORMAT does not work over a network.

❏ The following codes may be checked by the errorlevel condition in a batch file with the IF command:

0   Successful format.

3   You pressed Ctrl-C to end FORMAT.

4   Fatal error other than 3 or 5.

5   User pressed N in response to `Proceed with format (Y/N)?` prompt.

❏ See the UNFORMAT command.

GOTO   Batch, Internal

Purpose

Transfers processing to a labelled point in a batch file.

When To Use

The GOTO command is used primarily with the IF statement to control the flow of a batch file.

Common Syntax and Examples

```
GOTO label
```

The *label* must be specified elsewhere within the program. Do not use the colon as part of the label name on the GOTO command.

Switches

None.

Notes

❏ The label being referenced is created by using a colon at the start of the text string. The label must appear by itself on the line. The colon should not be included on the GOTO command. Thus, the command GOTO NAME will jump to a line containing :NAME. Only the first eight letters of the label are recognized. You may use spaces in the label name.

❏ See Chapter 13 for more information about batch files and the batch file commands.

GRAFTABL   Network, External

Purpose

Allows the display of extended characters of a code page in graphics mode.

When To Use

Use GRAFTABL when you configure your system for foreign language support.

Common Syntax and Examples

```
GRAFTABL page
```

```
GRAFTABL /STATUS
```

The *page* parameter specifies a code page defined with the COUNTRY= setting. If it is omitted, GRAFTABL reports the current code page.

To specify the Canadian-French code page, for example, use the following:

```
GRAFTABL 863
```

To display the current code page, use the following command:

```
GRAFTABL /STATUS
```

Switch

/STATUS   Displays the current code page used by GRAFTABL.

Notes

❑ GRAFTABL affects only the extended graphics characters. Use the MODE or CHCP commands to change the full code page.

❑ The following codes may be checked by the errorlevel condition in a batch file with the IF command.

    0   Successfully loaded new code page.

    1   Successfully replaced previous code page.

    2   File error occurred.

    3   Incorrect parameter given.

    4   A DOS version other than 5.0 is in use.

❑ See the CHCP and MODE commands.

GRAPHICS

Network, External

Purpose

Starts a graphics program to allow printing of CGA, EGA, or VGA graphics.

When To Use

Use the GRAPHICS command when you want to set up a printer and send screen graphics to a printer.

Common Syntax and Examples

```
GRAPHICS type d:path\filename /R /B /LCD /PRINTBOX:STD or /
    PRINTBOX:LCD
```

The *type* parameter sets the type of printer. You can use any of the following values:

Parameter	Description
color1	IBM PC color printer with black ribbon
color4	IBM PC color printer with red, green, blue, and black ribbon
color8	IBM PC color printer with cyan, magenta, yellow, and black
hpdefault	Hewlett-Packard PCL printer
deskjet	Hewlett-Packard DeskJet printer
graphics	IBM Personal Graphics printer, IBM proprinter, or IBM Quietwriter printer
graphicswide	IBM graphics printer with an 11-inch wide carriage
laserjet	Hewlett-Packard LaserJet printer
laserjetii	Hewlett-Packard LaserJet II printer
paintjet	Hewlett-Packard PaintJet printer
quietjet	Hewlett-Packard QuietJet printer
quietjetplus	Hewlett-Packard QuietJet Plus printer
ruggedwriter	Hewlett-Packard RuggedWriter printer
ruggedwriterwide	Hewlett-Packard RuggedWriterwide printer
thermal	IBM PC-convertible Thermal printer
thinkjet	Hewlett-Packard ThinkJet printer

The `d:path\filename` parameter specifies the drive and path to the file containing the printer profile information. If you do not specify this information, DOS looks for GRAPHICS.PRO both in the current directory and in the directory containing GRAPHICS.COM.

To prepare your system for printing graphics characters from the screen, type the following command:

GRAPHICS

If you press Shift-PrtScrn, DOS scans the screen and sends the information to your printer.

Switches

`/R`	Prints the image as it appears on a standard video screen—white characters on a black screen. The default is black characters on a white screen.
`/B`	Prints the background color. Valid only for color4 and color8 printers.
`/LCD`	Prints the image using LCD size. Same as `/PRINTBOX:LCD`.
`/PRINTBOX:STD` or `/PRINTBOX:LCS` `/PB:STD` or `/PB:LCD`	Selects the print-box size.

Notes

❏ You press Shift-PrtScrn to print the contents of the screen. The screen is printed with four shades of gray if the computer is in 320x200 mode and the printer is color1 or graphics. If the computer is in 640x200 mode, the screen is printed in landscape orientation (sideways).

❏ You cannot use Shift-PrtScrn to print to a PostScript printer.

❏ The GRAPHICS command uses conventional memory.

❏ If you attempt to load a new graphics profile after one is previously loaded, you must use a smaller one than the first. Otherwise, you need to reboot your system using the new graphics profile. DOS gives you the following error prompt when this occurs:

```
Unable to reload with profile supplied
```

❏ See the PRINT command.

HELP (MS-DOS 5)   Network, External

Purpose

Displays information about the given command.

When To Use

Use this command when you want on-screen syntax information.

Common Syntax and Examples

```
HELP command
```

or

```
command /?
```

The *command* parameter is the command name about which you want help.

To get help on the CHKDSK command, for example, use one of the following commands:

```
HELP CHKDSK
```

or

```
CHKDSK /?
```

Switches

None.

Note

❏ The /? switch is available for every command in DOS.

HIMEM.SYS (MS-DOS 5)   Driver

Purpose

Manages extended memory.

When To Use

The HIMEM.SYS driver should be installed whenever a system has extended memory that is not being managed by a third-party extended memory manager.

Common Syntax and Examples

```
DEVICE=d:path\HIMEM.SYS /HMAMIN=min /NUMHANDLES=numxms /
   INT15=oldmem /MACHINE:type /A20CONTROL:ON or OFF /SHADOWRAM:ON
   or OFF /CPUCLOCK:ON or OFF
```

The *d:* parameter is the disk drive for the device driver.

The *path* parameter is the path for the device driver. If no path is specified, the root directory is assumed.

Switches

/HMAMIN=*min*	Specifies the minimum amount a program must request to gain access to the High Memory Area. Permissible values range from 0 through 63; the default is 0.
/NUMHANDLES=*numxms*	Specifies the number of extended-memory-block handles that can be allocated at one time. Permissible values range from 1 through 128; the default is 32.
/INT15=*oldmem*	Specifies the amount of memory that should not be controlled by the HIMEM.SYS driver.
/MACHINE:*type*	The default is the IBM PC/AT format. If you experience problems with the A20 handler (reported by HIMEM.SYS) or with loading DOS in the High Memory Area, you may have to specify the hardware type using a value from either the abbreviation or number column from the following list:

Hardware	Model	Abbreviation	Number
Acer	1100	acer1100	6
AT&T	6300 Plus	att6300plus	5
CSS Labs	css	12	
HP	Vectra	fasthp	14
HP	Vectra(A and A+)	hpvectra	4
IBM	PC/AT	at	1
IBM	PC/AT	at1	11
IBM	*PC/AT	at2	12
IBM	*PC/AT	at3	13
IBM	PS/2	ps2	2
Philips	philips		13

Hardware	Model	Abbreviation	Number
Phoenix	Cascade BIOS	pt1cascade	3
Toshiba	1600 and 1200XE	toshiba	7
Tulip	SX	tulip	9
Wyse	12.5 MHz 286	wyse	8
Zenith	ZBIOS	zenith	10

* Denotes Alternative Delay

`/A20CONTROL:` Determines whether HIMEM.SYS takes control of the A20 line even if it is active during the boot process. ON (take control) is the default setting.

`/SHADOWRAM:` Determines whether the shadowing of ROM information in RAM locations should be disabled. This is not supported on all hardware platforms. The default is OFF (no shadowing) on machines with 2M or less. The default is ON for machines with more than 2M.

`/CPUCLOCK:` Controls whether HIMEM.SYS tries to affect the clock speed of the CPU. Problems with HIMEM.SYS modifying the CPU speed may be corrected by specifying **CPUCLOCK:ON**. The default is OFF.

Notes

❑ With the default settings, the first program that requests access to the High Memory Area is granted access.

❑ See Chapter 10 for information about how HIMEM.SYS manages the High Memory Area and extended memory.

IF   Batch, Internal

Purpose

Evaluates a condition and selectively activates a command, based on the results of the evaluation (whether it is true or false).

When To Use

The IF command evaluates a given condition; DOS executes the given command when the condition is true. If the condition is false, the given command is not executed. IF is used extensively in batch files.

Common Syntax and Examples

```
IF NOT condition commmand
```

The NOT setting is optional and reverses the logic of the IF statement so that the given command is executed if the condition is false.

The *condition* parameter can be created by using the keyword ERRORLEVEL, using the keyword EXIST and specifying a file name or file names, or by creating a comparison using the == operator.

The *command* parameter can be any valid DOS command.

To determine whether the file TEMP.DOC exists in the \HOLD directory and, if it does, display "Found It" on the screen, use the following command:

```
IF EXIST \HOLD\TEMP.DOC ECHO Found It
```

To determine whether any files exist in the \HOLD directory and, if one does, display "Found it" on the screen, use the following command:

```
IF EXIST \HOLD\*.* ECHO Found It
```

To determine whether the \HOLD directory exists and, if it does, display "Found it" on the screen, type the following command:

```
IF EXIST \HOLD\NUL ECHO Found It
```

To perform an action if a file does not exist, use the NOT qualifier before the condition. To display "Not There" on the screen if the \HOLD directory does not exist, use the following command:

```
IF NOT EXIST \HOLD\NUL ECHO Not There
```

To jump to the label FOUND IT if the \HOLD directory exists, use the command:

```
IF EXIST \HOLD\NUL GOTO FOUND IT
```

In this case, you must have a line in your program that has :FOUND IT at the beginning of the line.

If you want to perform one action if the condition is true (that is, \HOLD exists) and another condition if it is false, you must use three labels and a structure similar to the following:

```
IF EXIST \HOLD GOTO FOUND
GOTO NOT FOUND
:FOUND
```

```
    Action to perform if condition is true.
  GOTO ENDIF
  :NOT FOUND
    Action to perform if condition is false.
  :ENDIF
```

Use the ERRORLEVEL switch to determine whether the previously executed command was successful. ERRORLEVEL will be equal to 1 if the command completed successfully.

You also can use strings and replaceable parameters in a condition. To check if the user entered the string A: as the first parameter to the batch file (and jump to the label DRIVE A if the parameter is A:), you could use:

```
IF %1==A: GOTO DRIVE A
```

or

```
IF "%1"=="A:" GOTO DRIVE A
```

These command lines test for an exact match. If the user entered a:, the condition would be false. To determine whether the user entered either A: or a: you must use two IF statements as in:

```
IF %1==A: GOTO DRIVE A
IF %1==a: GOTO DRIVE A
```

You can determine whether a parameter exists by using the following syntax:

```
IF NOT "%1"=="" GOTO IS PARAM
```

In this case, the quotation marks are required.

Switches

None.

Notes

❑ You can perform only a single action on an IF statement. To perform more than one action, you must use a labeled section and the GOTO statement.

❑ You can use the NOT qualifier with any type of condition (EXIST, ERRORLEVEL, or ==).

❑ Using a single equal sign (=) results in a syntax error.

❑ See Chapter 13 for more information about batch files and the batch file commands.

INSTALL= Config

Purpose

Loads a utility application into conventional memory.

When To Use

Use INSTALL= when you want the utilities to always be available in your DOS work session.

Common Syntax and Examples

```
INSTALL=utility utility-params
```

The *utility* parameter specifies the utility (application) to be loaded. If the application is not located in the root directory, the name must include a path specification.

The *utility-params* parameter specifies any parameters that are to be used in configuring the utility.

To load the FASTOPEN utility and have it track files on drive C, enter the following line in the CONFIG.SYS file:

```
INSTALL=FASTOPEN.EXE C:
```

To specify that FASTOPEN create its cache file in expanded memory (using the FASTOPEN parameter /x), enter the following line in the CONFIG.SYS file:

```
INSTALL=FASTOPEN.EXE C: /X
```

To use the copy of FASTOPEN.EXE located in the \DOS directory (on your boot drive), enter the following line in the CONFIG.SYS file:

```
INSTALL=\DOS\FASTOPEN.EXE C:
```

Switches

None.

Notes

❑ See the LOADHIGH= command for information about loading utilities into the Upper Memory Area.

❑ Installing utility applications is more memory efficient than starting them from the AUTOEXEC.BAT file unless you are using the LOADHIGH= command.

❑ See Chapter 10 for a discussion of memory management and improving system performance.

JOIN   External

Purpose

Connects or disconnects files and directories on one drive to or from another.

When To Use

Use when you want to access the files and subdirectories on two disk drives as if they were one drive.

Common Syntax and Examples

        JOIN *d1*: *d2*:*path*

    or

        JOIN *d1*: /D

The *d1* parameter specifies the drive to be connected to drive or directory specified by *d2*:*path*.

To add the information on drive A to the DOS directory on drive C, use the following command:

        JOIN A: C:\DOS

To cancel the connection, use the following command:

        JOIN A: /D

To see a list of the joined drives, use the following command:

        JOIN

The *d1*: parameter is the disk drive you want to join to a different drive.

The *d2*: parameter is the disk drive you want to join to d1.

The *path* parameter is the directory to join to d1:.

Switch

    /D   Cancels the specified JOIN command.

Notes

- ❏ After joining a drive to a subdirectory on another drive, the original drive letter will be invalid.
- ❏ The directory must be empty before you specify the path on the JOIN command.

❏ You cannot use the following commands with drives set up by JOIN command:

ASSIGN	FORMAT
BACKUP	LABEL
CHKDSK	MIRROR
DISKCOMP	RECOVER
DISKCOPY	RESTORE
FDISK	SYS

KEYB   Network, External

Purpose

Changes the keyboard layout and characters to one of five foreign languages.

When To Use

Use KEYB to configure a keyboard for a language other than U.S. English.

Common Syntax and Examples

    KEYB code,page,d:path\filename /E /ID:country

The *code* parameter sets the keyboard code.

The *page* parameter sets the code page.

The *d:path\filename* parameter is the DOS disk drive and path to the location of the keyboard definition file. KEYBOARD.SYS is the name of the default file.

To list the current codes, type the following command:

    KEYB

To use the Danish keyboard (Denmark), for example, type the following:

    KEYB dk

To install the Danish keyboard (Denmark) every time you use your system, enter the following as part of your CONFIG.SYS file:

    INSTALL=KEYB dk

Switches

/E   Required if using an 8086 (PC AT) computer with an enhanced keyboard.

/ID:*country*   Denotes the keyboard in use. Use for countries that have more than one keyboard layout. Valid entries include: France, Italy, and the United Kingdom. The *country* value must be a numeric value from the code page table.

Notes

❏ The following values are valid for the *code*, *page*, and *country* for those languages supported by DOS:

Language	Code	Page	Country
Belgium	be	850,437	
Brazil	br	850,437	
Canadian-French	cf	850,863	
Czechoslovakia(Czech)	cz	852,850	
Czechoslovakia(Slovak)	sl	852,850	
Denmark	dk	850,865	
Finland	su	850,437	
France	fr	850,437	120,189
Germany	gr	850,437	
Hungary	hu	852,850	
Italy	it	850,437	141,142
Latin America	la	850,437	
Netherlands	nl	850,437	
Norway	no	850,865	
Poland	pl	852,850	
Portugal	po	850,860	
Spain	sp	850,437	
Sweden	sv	850,437	
Switzerland(French)	sf	850,437	
Switzerland(German)	sg	850,437	
United Kingdom	uk	850,437	166,168
United States	us	850,437	
Yugoslavia	yu	852,850	

❏ You must have the (code) *page* that you specify installed on your system in order to use it.

❏ The following codes are reported by the KEYB command. These may be used in an IF structure as part of an ERRORLEVEL condition.

0 Successful.

1 Invalid keyboard code, code page, or syntax.

2 Missing or bad keyboard definition file.

4 Error in communicating with the CONSOLE (CON) device.

5 The code page you requested is not prepared.

❏ Press Ctrl-Alt-F1 to switch to the default keyboard definition. A mode called "typewriter mode" is available by pressing Ctrl-Alt-F7. Press Ctrl-Alt-F2 to use the alternate definition you set up with the KEYB command.

LABEL   External

Purpose

Creates, changes, or deletes a volume label for a disk.

When To Use

Use the LABEL command to keep track of which disk you are using.

Common Syntax and Examples

        LABEL *d:label*

The *d:* parameter is the drive letter of the disk you want to label.

The *label* parameter is the new volume label (up to 11 characters).

To display the disk label for the current drive, use the following command:

        LABEL

To change the disk label for the disk in drive A, use the following command:

        LABEL A:

If you do not specify a label, DOS displays a message in the following form:

    Volume in drive A is xxxxxxxxxxx
    Volume Serial Number is xxxx-xxxx
    Volume label (11 characters, ENTER for none)?

You can specify the label as follows:

```
LABEL A: WORKDISK
```

Switches

None.

Notes

❏ When you format a disk for DOS, you have the option of giving it a label with FORMAT/V. You use the LABEL command to change or delete a volume label, or to add one if you did not specify one.

❏ You can use the DIR or VOL commands to see if the disk is already labeled.

❏ LABEL does not work on drives involved with the ASSIGN, JOIN, or SUBST commands.

LASTDRIVE= Config

Purpose

Sets the drive letter for the last logical drive that is directly accessed by your system.

When To Use

Use this command to extend the number of logical drives recognized by your system. This is useful if you want to create logical drives during a DOS work session.

Common Syntax and Examples

```
LASTDRIVE=drive-id
```

The *drive-id* is the drive letter of the last drive that is available on your system.

To set the last available drive to F, enter the following line in the CONFIG.SYS file:

```
LASTDRIVE=F
```

Switches

None.

Notes

❏ The default for LASTDRIVE= is one more than the last physical drive in your system (so that, if you have a single hard disk named C:, LASTDRIVE= is set to D:).

❏ To use commands that create logical drives, you must increase the number of available drive letters. Examples of the commands that require an available drive letter are ASSIGN and SUBST.

❏ This setting does not control the drive mappings created by network software.

❏ Each logical drive requires a segment of memory and should be left at the default unless a program requires it be changed.

LOADFIX (MS-DOS 5)   External

Purpose

Forces a program to load above the 64K mark.

When To Use

Use the LOADFIX application loader when you receive the message `Packed file corrupt` after you try to execute an application in conventional memory.

Common Syntax and Examples

```
LOADFIX d:path\application
```

The `application` parameter is the name of the program that produces the `Packed file corrupt` message.

The `d:` parameter is the disk drive for the application.

The `path\` parameter is the path for the application. If no path is specified, the path is searched for the application.

Switches

None.

Notes

❏ If the application that generates the message is one that you often use, place the complete command (including both LOADFIX and the application name) in a batch file and start the application using the batch file.

❑ The error message results from moving device drivers into the Upper Memory Area, which frees memory below the 64K mark. Some applications are not capable of using that memory region.

LOADHIGH= (LH=) (MS-DOS 5)   Batch, Internal

Purpose

Loads utilities into the Upper Memory Area (UMA).

When To Use

Use this command to free conventional memory by moving utilities (either DOS commands or terminate-and-stay-resident applications) into available Upper Memory Blocks (UMBs).

Common Syntax and Examples

```
LOADHIGH=utility utility-params
```

or

```
LH=utility utility-params
```

The *utility* parameter specifies the utility (application) to be loaded. If the application is not located in the root directory, the name must include a path specification.

The *utility-params* parameter specifies any parameters that are to be used in configuring the utility.

To load the FASTOPEN utility into the Upper Memory Area and have it track files on drive C, enter one of the following lines in the AUTOEXEC.BAT file:

```
LOADHIGH=FASTOPEN.EXE C:
```

or

```
LH=FASTOPEN.EXE C:
```

To specify that FASTOPEN should create its cache file in expanded memory (using the FASTOPEN parameter /x) and use the Upper Memory Area to manage the cache, enter the following line in the AUTOEXEC.BAT file:

```
LOADHIGH=FASTOPEN.EXE C: /x
```

or

```
LH=FASTOPEN.EXE C: /x
```

To use the copy of FASTOPEN.EXE located in the \DOS directory (on your boot drive), enter the following line in the CONFIG.SYS file:

```
LOADHIGH=\DOS\FASTOPEN.EXE C:
```

or

```
LH=\DOS\FASTOPEN.EXE C:
```

Switches

None.

Notes

❏ The LOADHIGH= command will not work in the CONFIG.SYS file. It can be installed only via the AUTOEXEC.BAT file or at the command line.

❏ An Upper Memory Manager and an extended memory manager must be installed to use this command (EMM386.EXE and HIMEM.SYS).

❏ Communication between DOS and the Upper Memory Area must be enabled with the DOS=UMB setting in the CONFIG.SYS file.

❏ If there are no UMBs available, the utility is loaded into conventional memory.

❏ Some utilities will not work in the Upper Memory Area. If you experience a problem after loading a utility into the Upper Memory Area, check with the manufacturer for a new version or load the utility into conventional memory.

❏ See Chapter 10 for a discussion of memory management and improving system performance.

MEM
Internal

Purpose

Determines memory usage.

When To Use

Use the MEM command when you want to obtain information about your system's memory, especially when you relocate device drivers and utilities into the Upper Memory Area and when you attempt to free sufficient memory to run a program that reports insufficient memory available.

Common Syntax and Examples

MEM /CLASSIFY or /PROGRAM or /DEBUG

To get general information about memory usage, type:

MEM

To get the information required to determine whether device drivers or utilities can be used in the Upper Memory Area, use:

MEM /CLASSIFY

or

MEM /C

Switches

You can use the initial letter rather than the full name for any of the following switches.

/CLASSIFY   Lists the contents of conventional memory and the Upper Memory Area by program. You can use /C instead of /CLASSIFY.

/PROGRAM   Lists the contents of memory by memory address and size specifying owner (such as SYSTEM). You can use /P instead of /PROGRAM.

/DEBUG   Lists the contents of memory by memory address and size specifying the name of the installed application segment (such as device driver names). You can use /D instead of /DEBUG.

Notes

❏ The MEM command actually reports the status of six types of memory. They are conventional memory, the Upper Memory Area, LIM 4.0-compliant expanded memory (Total and Free EMS memory), the High Memory Area, XMS-compliant extended memory (Available XMS memory), and extended memory managed by Interrupt 15h (Available contiguous extended memory). The Total contiguous extended memory is all memory available above 1M (whether handled by an XMS manager or Interrupt 15h). MEM reports whether DOS is loaded into the High Memory Area.

❏ See Chapter 10 for a discussion of memory management and improving system performance.

MIRROR (MS-DOS 5)   Network, External

Purpose

Records information about the contents of one or more disks. MIRROR often is used in conjunction with the UNFORMAT or UNDELETE commands to recover contents of previously formatted disks or where information was deleted.

When To Use

Use MIRROR when you want to protect information on a floppy disk or hard disk drive from accidental formatting or deletion.

Common Syntax and Examples

        MIRROR *d*: /L /T*drive-entries*

    or

    MIRROR /U

    or

    MIRROR /PARTN

The *d*: parameter specifies the driver for which file history information should be maintained.

To unload the deletion-tracking program, type the following:

        MIRROR /U

To save the system's hard disk partition table, type the following:

        MIRROR /PARTN

Switches

/1	Retains only the most recent information about the disk rather than completely redoing the information file each time.
/T*drive*:	Terminate-and-stay-resident deletion-tracking program for use in recovering deleted files with the UNDELETE command.
-*entries*	List of disk sizes and default entries and file sizes.

Disk Size	Entries	File Size
360K	25	5K
720K	50	9K
1.2MB	75	14K
1.44MB	75	14K
20MB	101	18K
32MB	202	36K
>32MB	303	55K

/U   Disables the deletion-tracking program.

/PARTN   Saves the information on the disk partition.

Notes

❏ To remove the memory-resident deletion-tracking program, remove any memory-resident programs loaded after it was loaded and then enter MIRROR /U to disable.

❏ For maximum effectiveness, the MIRROR command should be added to the AUTOEXEC.BAT file so that the system information will be updated at each startup.

MKDIR/ (MD)   Network, Internal

Purpose

Creates a directory or subdirectory.

When To Use

Use this command when you want to create a new directory or subdirectory to store a program or data.

Common Syntax and Examples

MKDIR *d:path1*

or

MD *d:path2 name*

The *d:* parameter specifies the drive where the new subdirectory is to be created.

The *path1* parameter specifies the full name of the new subdirectory.

The *path2* parameter specifies the location where the subdirectory is to be created. The default is the current directory.

The *name* parameter specifies the name of the new subdirectory.

If you need a directory to store word processing data on the current drive, for example, you can create the directory by typing:

MKDIR WPDATA

or

MD WPDATA

If you need a subdirectory for your data on a drive that is not the current drive, simply type:

MD C:\WPDATA\LEGAL

Switches

None.

Notes

❑ You cannot create a subdirectory with the same name as a file in the parent directory.

❑ Although DOS will accept extensions on directory names, it is generally not a good idea to use them as it makes it too easy to confuse them with files.

MODE   Network, External

Purpose

The MODE command can perform several tasks including displaying the status of devices, changing system settings, and reconfiguring and redirecting ports and devices.

When To Use

The MODE command should be used to establish the communication settings for communication ports, the configuration of the display and keyboard, and for redirecting output between two ports. Each of the major functions of the MODE command has a different syntax and is discussed separately.

Displaying Device Status

MODE displays the status of a specific device or of all devices attached to the system.

Common Syntax and Examples

```
MODE device /STATUS
```

device refers to the device that you want to check with the STATUS switch.

To obtain the status of all devices that are recognized by the mode command, enter:

```
MODE
```

To display the status of the console, type the following:

```
MODE con
```

Switch

/STATUS or /STA is for requesting the status of redirected parallel printers.

Note

❏ The output produced when listing all devices requires more than one screen and should be redirected through the MORE command.

Configuring Serial Ports

MODE is used to configure serial ports for communication with modems or printers.

Common Syntax and Examples

MODE *comm*: baud=b parity=p data=d stop=s retry=r

or

MODE *comm*: b, p, d, s, r

comm sets the asynchronous communications (COM) port to configure, options are COM1, COM2, COM3, or COM4.

baud= sets the baud rate where b is the transmission rate in bits per second. You may use either the value or the actual baud rate for b. Use one of the following options:

Value	Baud Rate
11	110
15	150
30	300
60	600
12	1200
24	2400
48	4800
96	9600
19	19200

parity= sets the parity bit to check for errors. The options for p are n(none), e(even), o(odd), m(mark),and s(space) with a default of e.

data= sets the number of data bits in a character. Options for d are 5, 6, 7, or 8 with a default of 7.

stop= sets the number of stop bits at the end of a character. Options for s are 1, 1.5, or 2 with a normal default of 1.

retry= sets the retry action if a time-out occurs. Options for r include the following:

e	Returns an error from a status check of a busy port.
b	Returns a busy message from a status check of a busy port. Same as the p variable in earlier versions.
p	Continues retrying until port accepts output.
r	Returns a ready message from a status check of a busy port.
n	Takes no retry action. This is the default.

You can configure the COM1 port to 2400 baud with no parity checking and eight data bits/one stop bit with infinite retry with any of the following lines:

```
MODE COM1 baud=2400 parity=n data=8 stop=1 retry=p
```

or

```
MODE COM1: 2400, n, 8, 1, p
```

or

```
MODE COM1: 24, n, 8, 1, p
```

Switches

None.

Notes

❑ You may not mix the two methods of specifying parameters. You must use the parameter names (e.g., baud=) either for all values or for none of them.

❑ Your computer may not support all of these values, so check your system's manuals for the values it will support. Also check the manuals for the devices attached to your system.

Configuring Printers

MODE is used to configure communication ports for use with printers and other output devices.

Common Syntax and Examples

```
MODE lptn: cols=c lines=l retry=r
```

lptn sets the parallel port to send information. Options are LPT1, LPT2 or LPT3.

cols= sets the number of characters per line. Options for *c* are 80 or 132 with 80 as the default.

lines= sets the number of lines per inch. Options for *l* are 6 or 8. 6 is the default.

retry= sets what should happen if there is a time-out or when there is an error when you attempt to print. Options for *r* include the following:

e   Returns an error from a status check of a busy port.

b   Returns a busy message from a status check of a busy port. Same as the p variable in earlier versions.

p   Continues retrying until printer accepts output.

r   Returns a `ready` message from a status check of a busy port.

n   Takes no retry action. This is the default.

Switches

None.

Note

❏ Use Ctrl-C to stop an infinite time-out loop.

Configuring Displays

MODE is used to establish the type of display adapter for a monitor.

Common Syntax and Examples

MODE *display-adapter, shift*,T

or

MODE *display-adapter*, N

or

MODE CON: cols=*c* lines=*l*

Display-adapter sets the category, which may be one of the following:

Display	Description
40 or 80	Sets the number of characters per line
bw40 or bw80	Disables color on a CGA and set characters per line
co40 or co80	Enables color and sets characters per line
mono	Defines a monochrome display with 80 character per line

shift moves CGA screens to the left or right. Options are L (left) and R (right).

T provides a test pattern to help you align the screen.

N specifies the number of lines on the screen.

CON: is the device name for the monitor. The colon is optional.

cols= sets the number of characters per line. Options for *c* are 40 and 80.

lines= sets the number of line displayed. Options for *l* are 25, 43, and 50.

Switches

None.

Notes

❑ Many applications use a device driver in addition to the information supplied by the MODE command for managing the display.

Setting Typematic Rate

MODE sets the rate at which MS-DOS repeats a character when a key is held down.

Common Syntax and Examples

```
MODE con: rate=r delay=d
```

con: refers to the keyboard. The colon is optional.

r sets the rate at which a character is repeated. Options are 1 to 32, which equals 2 to 30 characters per second.

d sets the amount of time you must wait before a character starts repeating. Options include:

Value	Seconds
1	0.25 second
2	0.50 second
3	0.75 second
4	1 second

The default is 2.

Switches

None.

Note

❑ A setting of 30, 1 provides the fastest repeat. A setting of 2, 4 provides the slowest repeat rate.

Assigning Device Code Pages

MODE sets the code pages to be used with a device.

Common Syntax and Examples

```
MODE device codepage prepare=((page) d:path\filename)

MODE device codepage select=page d:path\filename
```

```
MODE device codepage refresh

MODE device codepage /STATUS
```

device sets the device you want to use. Options are LPT1, LPT2, or LPT3.

page sets the code page number. Options are the following:

Code Page	Country or Language
437	United States
850	Multilingual (Latin I)
852	Slavic (Latin II)
860	Portuguese
863	Canadian-French
865	Nordic

`d:path\filename` sets the location and name of the codepage.

Switch

`/STATUS` or `/STA` displays the numbers of the current code pages or for a specific device.

Notes

❑ You must install ANSI.SYS to use the MODE CODEPAGE command.

❑ The MODE CODEPAGE command displays the status of the installed codepages.

❑ CODEPAGE PREPARE or CP PREP defines the available code page and must be run before running CODEPAGE SELECT.

❑ CODEPAGE SELECT or CP SEL sets which code page to use for the device specified.

❑ CODEPAGE REFRESH or CP REF reestablishes the code pages in the event of a hardware error or problem.

❑ CODEPAGE displays the code page numbers for the selected device.

Redirecting Printing

MODE is used to redirect output to a parallel port when an application will not recognize a serial port.

Common Syntax and Examples

```
MODE lptn:=comm:
```

lptn sets the parallel port. Options are LPT1, LPT2, or LPT3.

comm sets the serial port. Options are COM1, COM2, COM3, or COM4.

Switches

None.

Note

❑ To use this command, you must first use the MODE command to configure the serial port. Then, you can use a MODE assignment statement to direct information intended for the parallel port to the serial port.

MORE   Network, External

Purpose

Displays one screen of information at a time.

When To Use

Use MORE when you need to display long files one screen at a time.

Common Syntax and Examples

```
MORE < d:path\filename
```

or

```
command filename | MORE
```

The *d:* parameter specifies the drive where the files are located.

The *path* parameter is the path to the files to be displayed.

The *filename* parameter is the name of the file to be displayed. Wild cards are not permitted.

The *command* parameter is any DOS command which produces standard output.

If you need to list a long file named LEGAL.TXT in the current directory, the format is as follows:

```
more < legal.txt
```

or

```
TYPE LEGAL.TXT | MORE
```

The MORE command displays the first full screen of information with the following message at the bottom of the screen:

```
- MORE -
```

Pressing any key brings up the next screen and continues until the entire document has been displayed.

Switches

None.

Note

❏ The pipe (|) can be used with commands like TYPE, SORT, and DIR in conjunction with MORE to display output one full screen at a time. When the redirection character (<) is used, a file name must be used as the source.

MSHERC (MS-DOS 5)   External

Purpose

Provides support for the Hercules graphics card when running QBasic graphics programs.

When To Use

Use the MSHERC command when you want to run QBasic graphics programs on a system with a Hercules graphics card.

Common Syntax and Examples

```
MSHERC /HALF
```

To install support for a Hercules graphics card when running QBasic programs with graphics, type:

```
MSHERC
```

If you have a color adapter installed with the Hercules graphics card and you want to run QBasic programs with graphics, type:

```
MSHERC /HALF
```

Switch

/HALF   Specifies that a color adapter is present.

Note

❏ The application requires the presence of a Hercules graphics card to install.

NLSFUNC   Network, External

Purpose

Supports extended country information by starting the NLSFUNC program.

When To Use

Use NLSFUNC when you need to load extended country information.

Common Syntax and Examples

    NLSFUNC d:path\filename

The d: parameter specifies the drive where the files are located.

The path\ parameter is the path to the files to be displayed or changed.

The filename parameter is the name of the file to be displayed or changed. Wild cards are permitted.

The default information found in the COUNTRY.SYS file can be found by typing the following command:

    NLSFUNC

If the country information is contained in a file called NEWCTRY.SYS, the command would be:

    NLSFUNC NEWCTRY.SYS

Switches

None.

Note

❏ If the COUNTRY.SYS command is not found in the root directory, MS-DOS does not return an error message.

PATH   Network, Internal

Purpose

Sets the order in which directories are searched for programs and batch files.

When To Use

PATH can be used to display the current path setting at a DOS prompt or to open a new path to a directory or directories at a DOS prompt.

Common Syntax and Examples

    PATH=d1:path1;d2:path2;d3:path3;...

The $d1:path1$, $d2:path2$ and $d3:path3$ parameters specify the paths to be searched when seeking commands.

The following command creates a path to the DOS directory on drive C and to the legal subdirectory on drive D.

    PATH C:\;C:\DOS;D:\DATA\LEGAL;

Switches

None.

Notes

❏ The limit on PATH length is 127 characters. This restriction is one reason why you should keep directory names short.

❏ The PATH command can be placed in the AUTOEXEC.BAT file to initiate a search path on startup.

PAUSE   Batch, Internal

Purpose

Suspends processing until the user strikes a key.

When To Use

In batch files, the PAUSE command can be used to provide the user with more time to read a message, perform an action, or terminate the batch file by pressing Ctrl-C.

Common Syntax and Examples

```
PAUSE message
```

The *message* parameter can be used to specify a text string that displays before the standard pause prompt if ECHO is ON. Because this also will display the actual command line, it is generally preferable to turn ECHO OFF and use an ECHO statement before the PAUSE to display the message.

The PAUSE command generates the following message:

```
Press any key to continue...
```

If a Ctrl-C is encountered during the processing of a batch file (including during a pause), the following message is displayed:

```
Terminate batch job (Y/N)?
```

If the user reponds **Y** or **y**, the batch job will terminate. If the user responds **N** or **n**, the batch job will continue.

Switches

None.

Notes

❏ You can use an ECHO command before the PAUSE statement to create your own prompt message.

❏ You cannot use the at symbol (@) to suppress the PAUSE prompt. To eliminate the PAUSE prompt, redirect it into the NUL file by using PAUSE>NUL. If you do this, be sure to provide the user with instructions on an ECHO statement before the PAUSE command.

❏ See Chapter 13 for more information about batch files and the batch file commands.

PRINT   Network, External

Purpose

Prints one or more files while the computer performs other functions.

When To Use

Use PRINT when you want to print a long file from DOS and leave the computer free to perform other DOS functions.

Common Syntax and Examples

PRINT /D:*device* /B:*size* /U:*ticks1* /M:*ticks2* /S:*ticks3* /Q:*qsize* /T
d1:*path**filename* /C *d2*:*path2**filename2* /P *d3*:*path3**filename3*

The *d1*: parameter specifies the drive where the files are located.

The *path1*\\ parameter is the path to the files.

The *filename1* parameter is the name of the file to be printed. Wild cards are permitted.

The *d2*:*path2**filename2* parameter would specify files to be removed from the print queue (see the /C switch).

The *d3*:*path3**filename3* parameter would specify files to be added to the print queue (see the /P switch).

Suppose that you want to add a file on drive D called LEGAL.TXT to the print queue on LPT2. Issue the following command:

PRINT /D:lpt2 LEGAL.TXT /P

Switches

/D:*device*	Specifies the printer port to be used. Valid options are parallel ports lpt1, lpt2 and lpt3, serial ports com1, com2, com3 and com4. The default value is prn, which equals lpt1. If you use the /D switch it must be first.
/B:*size*	Determines the print buffer size if set to other than the default (512). The maximum size is 16384.
/U:*ticks1*	Sets the amount of time that the print command is to wait for the printer to be available. 18 ticks equal 1 second. The range is from 1 to 255 with a default of 1.
/M:*ticks2*	Sets the number of ticks that print can take to print a character. The range is from 1 to 255 with a default of 1.
/S:*ticks3*	Sets the number of ticks the DOS scheduler allows for background printing. The range is from 1 to 255 with a default of 8.
/Q:*qsize*	Specifies the number of files allowed in the print queue if different than the default of 10. Minimun amount is 4 and the maximum is 32.
/T	Using this switch removes all files from the print queue.

| /C | Removes any files listed before this switch and all following files until it encounters a /P switch. |
| /P | Adds any files listed before this switch and all following files until it encounters a /C switch. |

Notes

❏ Clock ticks are about 18 per second.

❏ You must restart the system to change any of the print options you previously established during a session.

PRINTER.SYS   Driver

Purpose

Enables support for code page switching for parallel ports.

When To Use

Use the PRINTER.SYS driver when you want to modify the output on a parallel port for international use by specifying an alternative code page.

Common Syntax and Examples

```
DEVICE=d:path\PRINTER.SYS LPTn=(type, page, extra)
```

or

```
DEVICEHIGH=d:path\PRINTER.SYS LPTn=(type, page, extra)
```

The *n* parameter specifies which parallel port is being configured.

The *type* parameter specifies the type of printer in use. Possible values include the following:

Code	Type of Printer
4201	IBM Proprinters II and III Model 4201
	IBM Proprinters II and III XL Model 4202
4208	IBM Proprinter X24E Model 4207
	IBM Proprinter XL24E Model 4208
5202	IBM Quietwriter III Model 5202

The *page* parameter specifies the code page to be supported. Possible values include:

Code Page	Country or Language
437	United States
850	Multilingual (Latin I)
852	Multilingual (Latin II)
860	Portuguese
863	Canadian-French
865	Nordic

The *extra* parameter specifies the number of additional code pages that can be supported. For EGA adapters, the maximum is 6. For LCD adpaters, the maximum is 1.

The *d:* parameter is the disk drive for the device driver.

The *path* parameter is the path for the device driver. If no path is specified, the root directory is assumed.

To install the Canadian-French code page on a Quietwriter attached to LPT1 using a copy of PRINTER.SYS in the root directory, type:

```
DEVICE=PRINTER.SYS LPT1=(5202,863)
```

Switches

None.

Note

❏ DISPLAY.SYS is used to enable code page switching for displays.

PROMPT   Network, Internal

Purpose

Sets the system command prompt.

When To Use

Use PROMPT when you want to customize the system prompt to include such features as the current directory, date, and time.

Common Syntax and Examples

PROMPT *text*

The following system prompt options are available for use as part of *text*:

Prompt	*Character*
$q	= (equal sign)
$$	$ (dollar sign)
$t	Current time
$d	Current date
$p	Current drive and path
$v	Version of DOS
$n	Current drive
$g	> (greater-than sign)
$l	< (less-than sign)
$b		(pipe)
$_	An underline and a carriage return
$e	ASCII escape code
$h	A backspace that erases the preceding character

The current drive and directory would be displayed following a greater-than symbol (>) by using the following prompt command:

PROMPT PG

The current drive and the time and date would be displayed by using the following command:

PROMPT NT$_$N

Switches

None.

Notes

❏ You can use ANSI commands to create more complex prompts.

❏ You can use the ANSI commands to create complex prompts using color, multiple lines, and special character formats.

QBASIC (MS-DOS 5)   Network, External

Purpose

Initiates QBasic and Interprets Basic Language computer programs.

When To Use

Use any time you want to program in the Basic language or work on a Basic program.

Common Syntax and Examples

QBASIC /B /EDITOR /G /H /MBF /NOHI /RUN *d:path\filename*

The *d:* parameter specifies the drive where the QBasic file is located.

The *path* parameter is the path to the file loaded into QBasic.

The *filename* parameter is the name of a QBasic program.

Switches

/B	Puts QBasic in a black-and-white mode on color monitors.
/EDITOR	Automatically starts the DOS editor.
/G	Increases update speed on a CGA monitor.
/H	Displays the maximum number of lines your monitor can display.
/MBF	Causes conversion of built-in functions MK\$\$, CVS, MKD4 and CVD to MKSMBF\$, CVSMBF, MKDMBF\$ and CVDMBF.
/NOHI	Supports monitors that do not support high-intensity video. This switch cannot be used with COMPAQ laptop systems.
/RUN	Runs a Basic program when followed by the program's file name.

Notes

❑ QBasic must be present in order to use the EDIT command.

❑ To use graphics from a QBasic program on a system with a Hercules Graphics card, you must use the MSHERC command.

RAMDRIVE.SYS (MS-DOS 5) — Driver

Purpose

Used to create a logical disk in memory instead of on a physical drive.

When To Use

Use the RAMDRIVE.SYS driver when you have memory that is not being used effectively by your system and an application has reduced performance because of the time required to access a physical disk drive.

Common Syntax and Examples

```
DEVICE=d:path\RAMDRIVE.SYS size sectors entries /E /A
```

or

```
DEVICEHIGH=d:path\RAMDRIVE.SYS size sectors entries /E /A
```

The *size* parameter specifies the size of RAM disk to be created. The default is 64K. The permissible values range from 16K through 4096K.

The *sectors* parameter specifies the size of each sector. Permissible values are 128, 256, and 512. If you use the *sectors* parameter, you must specify the *size* parameter as well.

The *entries* parameter specifies the number of file and directories entries that can be established on the RAM disk. The *entries* parameter can be specified only if both the *size* and *sectors* parameters are also included. Permissible values are 2 through 1024 and the default is 64. The value specified for *entries* should not be greater than the *size* divided by *sectors*.

The *d:* parameter is the disk drive for the device driver.

The *path* parameter is the path for the device driver. If no path is specified, the root directory is assumed.

Switches

/A Uses expanded memory for the RAM disk.

/E Uses extended memory for the RAM disk.

Notes

❑ If you specify none of the switches, the RAM disk is created in conventional memory.

❏ The actual driver must be loaded into either conventional memory or the Upper Memory Area.

❏ See Chapter 10 for a discussion of optimizing data transfer and memory management when using RAM disks.

RECOVER   External

Purpose

Recovers a file with bad sectors or a file from a disk with a damaged directory.

When To Use

Use RECOVER when you must recover data that is stored in a bad or defective location on the disk.

Common Syntax and Examples

```
RECOVER d1:path\filename
```

The `d:` parameter specifies the drive where the files to be recovered are located.

The `path\` parameter is the path to the files to be recovered.

The `filename` parameter is the name of the file to be recovered. Wild cards are not permitted.

To recover everything on drive D with an unusable directory, the format is as follows:

```
RECOVER D:
```

To recover an erased file called LEGAL.TXT in the current directory, the command is as follows:

```
RECOVER LEGAL.TXT
```

Switches

None.

Notes

❏ Wild cards cannot be used with this command.

❏ All recovered data is restored in the root directory.

❏ RECOVER will not work on a networked drive.

❏ RECOVER will not work on a file that has been deleted.

❏ You must specify a drive or a file.

REM   Batch, Internal

Purpose

Used to insert a remark or comment into a command file. The text is not displayed during execution of the file. If ECHO is ON, the actual REM command line is displayed.

When To Use

The REM command should be used to notate the purpose of a command line in CONFIG.SYS or in a batch file.

Common Syntax and Examples

```
REM message
```

The *message* parameter is any text string. It is not displayed if ECHO is set to OFF.

Suppose that a batch file contains the following lines:

```
@ECHO OFF
ECHO Line 1
REM Line 2
ECHO Line 3
```

It will produce the following output:

```
Line 1
Line 3
```

If the @ECHO OFF line is not included, the batch file contains the lines:

```
ECHO Line 1
REM Line 2
ECHO Line 3
```

The output would display the command lines and the following:

```
C:\>ECHO Line 1
Line 1
C:\>REM Line 2
C:\>ECHO Line 3
Line 3
```

Switches

None.

Notes

❏ You can use the REM statement within CONFIG.SYS files.

❏ You do not need to use the REM command on a blank line in a batch file. Blank lines are automatically ignored.

❏ See Chapter 13 for more information about batch files and the batch file commands.

RENAME (REN)   Network, Internal

Purpose

Changes the name of one or more files.

When To Use

Use REM any time you want to give a file a new name or a new extension.

Common Syntax and Examples

RENAME *d:path\old-filename new-filename*

d: is the drive the file is on.

path is the directory the file is in.

old-filename is the current name of the file.

new-filename is the new name of the file.

Suppose that you need to rename a file called OLDFILE.DOC on drive D in the data directory to NEWFILE.DOC, the command is as follows:

RENAME D:\DATA\OLDFILE.DOC NEWFILE.DOC

To rename the extensions on a group of files with the extension of ASC to DOC, type the following command:

REN *.ASC *.DOC

Switches

None.

Notes

❏ Wild cards can be used.

❏ The new file name must be unique.

REPLACE   Network, External

Purpose

Replaces and adds files from one directory to another.

When To Use

Use REPLACE to replace old files in a directory with updated files of the same name from another directory. It can also be used to add unique files from one directory to another directory.

Common Syntax and Examples

REPLACE *d1:path1\filename d2:path2* /A /P /R /W

or

REPLACE *d1:path1\filename d2:path2* /P /R /S /W /U

The *d1:path1* parameter is the path to the files to be copied.

The *filename* parameter is the name of the files to be copied. Wild cards are permitted.

The *d2:path2* parameter specifies the new location for the files.

Suppose that you want to copy a new version of a word processing form to each users directory on network drive F. The format is as follows:

REPLACE a:\newform.doc f:\ /s

Switches

/A   Adds new files to the destination directory, but does not replace current files. Cannot be used with /S or /U.

/P   Forces you to confirm replacement of the destination file.

/R   Allows replacement of read-only files and unprotected files.

/S   Searches through all subdirectories belonging to the destination directory for matching files to replace. Cannot be used with the /A switch.

/W   Waits for a disk to be inserted before completing the command.

/U   Uses the new file's date and time to replace older files in the destination directory.

Notes

The REPLACE command returns the following exit codes:

Exit Code	Description
0	Operation successful
2	Unable to find source files
3	Unable to find source or destination path
5	Access to the destination files denied
8	Not enough memory to perform operation
11	Command syntax is incorrect

RESTORE   Network, External

Purpose

Restores backup files created with the BACKUP command from one disk to another.

When To Use

Use RESTORE to load files from an old system to a new system or to restore program or data files after an accidental deletion.

Common Syntax and Examples

```
RESTORE d1: d2:path\filename /S /P /B:date1 /A:date2 /E:time1
   /L:time2 /M /N /D
```

The `d1:` parameter specifies the drive where the backup files are located.

The `d2:path2\` parameter is the location where the files are to be placed.

The `filename` parameter is the name of the file to be restored. Wild cards are permitted.

To restore all files from drive A to drive C, including subdirectories, type the following:

```
RESTORE A: C: /S
```

To restore all files backed up after 02/14/91 from drive A, including subdirectories, type the following:

```
RESTORE A: C: /S /A:02/14/91
```

Switches

/S	Restores all subdirectories
/P	Prompts on files that are read only for restoration
/B:*date1*	Restores only files modified on or before specified date
/A:*date2*	Restores only files modified on or after specified date
/E:*time1*	Restores only files modified on or earlier than a certain time
/L:*time2*	Restores only files modified on or after a certain time
/M	Restores only files modified since last backup
/N	Restores only files that are no longer on disk
/D	Displays a list of files on the backup disk that match the files on the destination disk

Notes

❑ You cannot use RESTORE to restore system files.

❑ MS-DOS version 5.0 RESTORE can restore files that are backed up using any other version of MS-DOS.

❑ The /D switch does not allow any files to be restored, but it does list files that meet the RESTORE specifications.

RMDIR (RD)   Network, Internal

Purpose

Removes an empty directory from a disk.

When To Use

This command is used to remove a directory or subdirectory that is no longer needed.

Common Syntax and Examples

```
RMDIR d:path
```

The *d*: parameter specifies the drive where the directory to be removed is located.

The *path* identifies the directory to remove.

Switches

None.

Notes

❏ A directory must be empty of all files and subdirectories before this command can remove it.

❏ You cannot delete the current directory; you first must change to another directory.

SET   Network, Internal

Purpose

Displays, sets, or removes the system environment variables.

When To Use

Use this command to control environment variables of batch files and programs. SET can be used in the AUTOEXEC.BAT file.

Common Syntax and Examples

```
SET variable=string
```

variable is the variable you want to set.

string is the string associated with the variable.

To list the current environment of your system type the following:

```
SET
```

Switches

None.

Notes

❏ When you type both a variable and string values for the SET command, DOS adds the variable to the environment and relates the string to the variable.

❏ When you use a variable in a batch file, enclose the value with percent signs (%), as in %PATH%.

SETUP (MS-DOS 5)   Installation, External

Purpose

Used to install DOS 5.

When To Use

Use SETUP when you want to install DOS 5.

Common Syntax and Examples

A:SETUP /B /F /U /M

The INSTALL command is designed to execute from drive A.

Switches

/B   Forces SETUP to use a monochrome (black-and-white) color scheme for its display.

/F   Configures SETUP to install DOS 5 onto floppy disks rather than a hard disk.

/U   Configures SETUP to ignore disk partitions that are incompatible with MS-DOS 5.

/M   Specifies that only the minimum number of files required to boot DOS be installed on the hard drive.

Notes

❑ If you need to install DOS 5 from a drive other than A, use the AS-SIGN command to map A to the appropriate drive.

❑ Each time you run the INSTALL command, it creates a new OLD_DOS directory and an UNINSTALL disk. These files are used to return you to the configuration you had prior to the INSTALL. Be sure to mark each disk with the date and time they were created.

❑ If you run INSTALL twice and decide to return to your original version of DOS, you will have to run both UNINSTALL procedures. Always UNINSTALL the most recent version.

SETVER (MS-DOS 5)   Network, External

Purpose

Sets the DOS version number that DOS reports to a program.

When To Use

Use SETVER to set old versions of programs to work with MS-DOS version 5.0 and to verify what version of DOS a program was set up to work with.

Common Syntax and Examples

    SETVER d:path\ filename n.nn

or

    SETVER d:path\ filename /DELETE /QUIET

d:path\ is the location of the SETVER.EXE program.

filename refers to the name of the program that you want to add to the version table.

n.nn is the MS-DOS version number that is to be reported to the program.

Switches

/DELETE or /D   Deletes a program entry from the version table.

/QUIET   Suppresses the message that is normally displayed during deletion.

SETVER displays the following exit codes:

Code	Description
0	Task successfully completed
1	Invalid switch specified
2	Invalid filename specified
3	Insufficient memory
4	Invalid version number
5	The entry could not be found
6	SETVER.EXE could not be found
7	The drive specified is invalid
8	Too many command-line parameters
9	Missing command-line parameters
10	Error occurred while reading SETVER.EXE

Code	Description
11	SETVER.EXE is a corrupt file
12	SETVER.EXE file does not support version table
13	Insufficient space in version table for entry
14	Error detected while writing to SETVER.EXE

Notes

❑ To use the SETVER command, the version table must be loaded by the command `DEVICE=C:\DOS\SETVER.EXE` in the CONFIG.SYS file

❑ When you make changes in the version table, you must restart your system to have them take effect.

❑ New entries for an existing program in the table will replace the old version.

SETVER.EXE (MS-DOS 5)   Driver

Purpose

Loads the version table into memory.

When To Use

Use this driver when one of your applications requires an earlier version of DOS.

Common Syntax and Examples

```
DEVICE=d:path\SETVER.EXE
```

or

```
DEVICEHIGH=d:path\SETVER.EXE
```

The `d:` parameter is the disk drive for the device driver.

The `path\` parameter is the path for the device driver. If no path is specified, the root directory is assumed.

To load the SETVER table from the \DOS directory into conventional memory, type:

```
DEVICE=\DOS\SETVER.EXE
```

Switches

None.

Note

❏ The SETVER.EXE driver must be loaded into memory to enable the version table. The version table contains information about reporting earlier versions of DOS to specific applications.

SHARE   Network, External

Purpose

Runs the SHARE program to allow file and record locking.

When To Use

SHARE is used primarily on a network or other multitasking environment to prevent unauthorized reading and writing of a file.

Common Syntax and Examples

```
SHARE /F:space /L:locks
```

To use SHARE in the CONFIG.SYS file, use the following syntax:

```
INSTALL=d:path\SHARE.EXE /F:space /L:locks
```

To set up SHARE in the CONFIG.SYS file with its default values, type the following:

```
INSTALL=C:\DOS\SHARE.EXE
```

To set up SHARE in the CONFIG.SYS file with a space of 4096 and locks of 50, use the following command:

```
INSTALL=C:\DOS\SHARE.EXE /F:4096 /L:50
```

Switches

/F:*space*   Sets up the amount of file space to be used for storage of file-sharing information. The default is 2048, which is enough for about 100 entries.

/L:*locks*   Allocates the number of files that can be locked at one time. The default is 20. The average path and file name is 20 characters.

Note

❏ Allow enough space in the /F switch for the full path and file name of each file to be stored.

SHELL=   Config

Purpose

Establishes and configures the command processor to be used.

When To Use

Use the SHELL= statement to create the environment that will be used with the command processor. The SHELL= statement should be used to install COMMAND.COM if it is in a directory other than the root directory or if you are configuring it with the COMMAND.COM parameters.

Common Syntax and Examples

```
SHELL=command-processor command-params
```

The *command-processor* is the processor that is to be used as the command environment. The default is COMMAND.COM.

The *command-params* are parameters that are to be passed to the command-processor to configure its performance.

To use COMMAND.COM (and make it permanent using the /P parameter) in your C:\DOS directory rather than the root directory, type:

```
SHELL=C:\DOS\COMMAND.COM /P
```

To add environment space to COMMAND.COM (using the /E parameter), use the following command:

```
SHELL=COMMAND.COM /E512 /P
```

Switches

None.

Note

❑ Moving COMMAND.COM to the \DOS subdirectory helps prevent you from accidentally deleting it or having it replaced by older version when copying files.

SHIFT   Batch, Internal

Purpose

Move the contents of replaceable parameters down one in the series (i.e., the contents of %5 are moved to %4).

When To Use

The SHIFT command is used in batch files to enable the user to enter more than nine replaceable parameters and for the processing of a series of values with the same code.

Common Syntax and Examples

```
SHIFT
```

The SHIFT command is entered with no parameters.

If you want to process a series of files that have been entered as parameters to a batch file, you would use the following structure within the batch file:

```
:LOOP
IF "%1"=="" GOTO EXIT
TYPE %1 | MORE
SHIFT
GOTO LOOP
:EXIT
```

This batch file shifts the values entered after the batch file name down through the replaceable parameters until no further values are available.

Switches

None.

Notes

❏ If more than nine parameters are entered by the user, only the first nine are assigned to variables (%1 through %9). The other parameters are stored and can be moved into the existing variables with the SHIFT command.

❏ See Chapter 13 for more information about batch files and the batch file commands.

SMARTDRV.SYS (MS-DOS 5)   Driver, External

Purpose

Provides intelligent disk caching.

When To Use

The SMARTDRV.SYS driver should be used whenever there is extended or expanded memory that is not needed by applications or when disk performance is crucial.

Common Syntax and Examples

DEVICE=*d:path*\SMARTDRV.SYS *maxsize MINSIZE* /A

or

DEVICEHIGH=*d:path*\SMARTDRV.SYS *maxsize minsize* /A

The *maxsize* parameter specifies the size of cache that is to be initially created by SMARTDrive.

The *minsize* parameter is used to control programs that can dynamically alter the size of the SMARTDrive cache. The cache will never be smaller than the value specified for *minsize*.

The *d:* parameter is the disk drive for the device driver.

The *path*\ parameter is the path for the device driver. If no path is specified, the root directory is assumed.

To create a cache with a maximum size of 1024K (1M) and a minimum of 256K, type the following command:

DEVICE=SMARTDRV.SYS 1024 256

Switch

/A   Specifies that the cache should be created in expanded memory rather than extended memory.

Notes

❏ By default, the cache is created in extended memory. The cache management is located in either conventional memory (DEVICE=) or the Upper Memory Area (DEVICEHIGH=).

❏ See Chapter 10 for additional information about managing memory and using SMARTDrive.

SORT   Network, External

Purpose

Reads, sorts, and writes lines from standard input to standard output.

When To Use

Use this to sort a DOS file and send the results to the display, a file, or a printer.

Common Syntax and Examples

> **SORT** /R /+n < *d1:path1\filename1* > *d2:path2\filename2*

or

> ***command*** | **SORT** /R /+n > *d2:path2 filename2*

or

> **SORT** /R /+n

d1:path1\filename1 designates the location and name of the file that needs to be sorted.

d2:path2\filename2 designates the output location of the sorted file.

To sort the NAMES.TXT file, for example, in reverse order, the command would be:

> **SORT /R < NAMES.TXT**

Switches

/R   Sorts a file in reverse order from Z to A and 0 to 9.

/+n   Sorts on a particular column in the file.

Notes

❑ Upper- or lower-case in not important to the SORT command.

❑ You cannot sort a file larger than 64K.

❑ The pipe (|) will work with SORT to redirect the output.

STACKS= Config

Purpose

Used to determine the number and size of stacks available for interrupt processing.

When To Use

Change the STACKS= setting only if you are experiencing problems with your applications and a new setting is recommended by the documentation or technical support.

Common Syntax and Examples

```
STACKS=number, size
```

The *number* parameter specifies the number of stacks that should be created.

The *size* parameter specifies the size for each stack.

To eliminate the stacks from memory, enter the following line in the CONFIG.SYS file:

```
STACKS=0,0
```

Switches

None.

Notes

❏ For most systems, the default is STACKS=9,128, which creates 9 stacks, each with 128 bytes of memory. The exceptions are the IBM PC, the IBM PC/XT and the IBM Portable, which default to 0,0 (no stacks).

❏ Some software applications (including Microsoft Windows 3) recommend setting STACKS=0,0 if you experience software problems. In some cases, this causes problems with other software, so be sure to record the value of the STACKS= setting before changing it.

❏ See Chapter 10 for a discussion of optimizing data transfer and improving system performance.

SUBST   External

Purpose

Substitutes an alias drive letter for a path name.

When To Use

SUBST speeds up the process of moving around in your computer system. It enables you to assign an unused drive letter to a complicated path, which simplifies moving through directories. The drive you assign is called a *logical drive*.

Common Syntax and Examples

SUBST *d1*: *d2:path*

or

SUBST *d1*: /D

d1: is the virtual drive that you want to assign or delete the existing assignment.

d2: is the physical drive that contains the path you want to assign.

path is the path that you want to assign.

If you want to make the directory C:\LOTUS\DATA\Q1\SOUTH the logical drive M, the format is as follows:

SUBST M: C:\LOTUS\DATA\Q1\SOUTH

If you type M:, DOS calls up the logical drive M, which is the directory C:\LOTUS\DATA\Q1\SOUTH. This is much simpler that typing the entire path.

Switch

/D deletes the virtual drive indicated.

Notes

❏ SUBST works best if the line LASTDRIVE=Z is in the CONFIG.SYS file.

❏ Do not use the following commands with a drive using SUBST:

ASSIGN	DISKCOPY	MIRROR
BACKUP	FDISKf	RECOVER
CHKDSK	FORMAT	RESTORE
DISKCOMP	LABEL	SYS

SWITCHES= | Config

Purpose

Causes DOS to interpret the keystrokes from an 101-key extended keyboard as though they were keystrokes from a conventional keyboard.

When To Use

Use this command if you are experiencing problems with programs incorrectly interpreting commands from the keyboard.

Common Syntax and Examples

```
SWITCHES=switch
```

The *switch* parameter determines what conversions are to be made by the command processor.

To have the extended keys from the 101-key extended keyboard interpreted with the same codes as the equivalent key on the standard keyboard, enter the following line in the CONFIG.SYS file:

```
SWITCHES=/K
```

Switch

/K   Converts the codes sent by the extended keys on an extended keyboard (101 key) to the standard keyboard equivalent (for example, makes both Insert keys have the same code).

Note

❏ The /K switch is the only setting supported for this statement.

SYS | External

Purpose

Copies the MS-DOS system files to the specified disk.

When To Use

Use SYS when you want to make a hard disk or floppy disk a bootable disk.

Common Syntax and Examples

> `SYS` *d1:path* **d2:**

d1:path states where the system files can be found.

d2: states where the system files should be copied to. System files can be copied only to a disk.

Switches

None.

TIME   Network, Internal

Purpose

Displays or sets the current system time.

When To Use

The TIME command can be used to display, set, or reset the current system time.

Common Syntax and Examples

> `TIME` *hours:minutes:seconds.hundredths* a or p

hours specifies the hour. Entries range from 0 to 23.

minutes specifies the minutes. Entries range from 0 to 59.

seconds specifies the seconds. Entries range from 0 to 59.

hundredths specifies hundredths of a second. Entries range from 0 to 99.

a or p stands for A.M. or P.M. The default is A.M.

To display the current system time or to enter a new time, simply type:

> `TIME`

To set your system's time to 10:40 P.M., for example, enter the following:

> `TIME 10:40P`

Switches

None.

Notes

❑ Add the TIME command to the AUTOEXEC.BAT file if you want your system to prompt you for the correct time at startup.

❑ The time format can be changed by changing the country setting in the CONFIG.SYS file.

TREE   Network, External

Purpose

Displays a graphic representation of the system's directory structure.

When To Use

TREE lists the system's directory and subdirectory structure and the files that they contain.

Common Syntax and Examples

```
TREE d1:path /F /A
```

The `d:` parameter specifies the drive that contains the directory to be displayed.

The `path` parameter is the starting location for the tree to be displayed.

Switches

/F   Displays the files associated with each directory.

/A   Uses text characters to show lines on printers that do not support graphics.

Note

❑ If you specify no path, the current directory is used as the default.

TYPE   Network, Internal

Purpose

Displays the contents of a file.

When To Use

TYPE can be used to view the contents of a file without the danger of changing the file.

Common Syntax and Examples

> TYPE d1:path**filename**

The d: parameter specifies the drive where the files are located.

The path\ parameter is the path to the files to be displayed.

The filename parameter is the name of the file to be displayed. Wild cards are not permitted.

To view the contents of a file called NAMES.TXT on drive D, use the following:

> TYPE D:\NAMES.TXT

Switches

None.

Notes

- ❑ The TYPE command does not work well with binary files.
- ❑ TYPE can be used with the MORE command.

UNDELETE (MS-DOS 5)   External

Purpose

Restores one or more previously deleted files.

When To Use

The UNDELETE command restores a file that has been deleted using the DELETE command.

Common Syntax and Examples

> UNDELETE d:path**filename** /LIST or /ALL /DOS or /DT

The d: parameter specifies the drive where the files were located.

The path\ parameter is the path to the files.

The filename parameter is the name of the file to be recovered. Wild cards are permitted.

To undelete all deleted files in the current directory, simply type:

> UNDELETE

To undelete all deleted files in the data directory with a TXT extension:

```
UNDELETE C:\DATA\*.TXT
```

Switches

/LIST   Lists the deleted files that can be recovered.

/ALL   Recovers deleted files without asking for confirmation.

/DOS   Only recovers those files shown to be deleted by DOS that are internally listed.

/DT   Restores only those files listed by the MIRROR command in the deletion-tracking file.

Notes

❑ You will have greater success using UNDELETE if you are also using the MIRROR command. MIRROR creates a deletion-tracking file that makes it easier to undelete files.

❑ If duplicate file names exist, UNDELETE replaces the missing first character with another character to create a unique file name.

❑ UNDELETE can work only if no other information has been written to the area where the deleted file was stored. For this reason, it is important to try to recover the deleted file as soon as possible after deleting it.

UNFORMAT (MS-DOS 5)   External

Purpose

Restores a disk erased or restructured by the FORMAT or RECOVER commands.

When To Use

This command is used any time your system has been formatted or the system's root directory has been erased.

Common Syntax and Examples

```
UNFORMAT d: /J
```

or

```
UNFORMAT d: /U /L /TEST /P
```

or

```
UNFORMAT /PARTN /L
```

The $d:$ parameter specifies the disk drive containing the disk to be unformatted.

To determine if UNFORMAT can recover a formatted drive C that MIRROR had previously recorded, type the following command:

```
UNFORMAT C: /J
```

To restore the formatted drive C that MIRROR had recorded and to send error messages to the printer, type the following command:

```
UNFORMAT C: /PARTN /L /P
```

Switches

/J	Checks for the file created by the MIRROR command. This switch does not actually recover anything and must be used by itself.
/U	Used when the MIRROR command has not been used.
/L	Recovers the file created by MIRROR. The MIRROR file may not be a current representation of your system's files.
/TEST	Tells you how UNFORMAT would recover the information on your system. This switch does not actually recover anything.
/P	Sends all messages to the printer port LPT1.
/PARTN	Recovers the hard disks partition table.

Notes

❏ UNFORMAT will not work on network drives.

❏ UNFORMAT cannot restore a disk that was formatted with the /U command.

❏ UNFORMAT works best on systems that are using the MS-DOS MIRROR command. MIRROR creates a file that contains information on the root directory and file allocation table. If you use MIRROR, UNFORMAT only restores to the point MIRROR was last run. Set up MIRROR in the AUTOEXEC.BAT file to update the table each time you start the system.

❏ UNFORMAT cannot recover a fragmented file, but it may try by recovering the first portion it comes to and consider the file complete.

UNINSTALL (MS-DOS 5)   Installation, External

Purpose

Restores a previous installation of DOS.

When To Use

Use UNINSTALL when you have problems with DOS 5 that were not present with an earlier DOS version.

Common Syntax and Examples

To use the UNINSTALL feature, insert the UNINSTALL #1 disk created during the INSTALLATION procedure and reboot your system.

Switches

None.

Note

❑ If you have performed multiple installations of DOS 5, each one must be uninstalled individually. If your disks are not marked with the date and time, use the DIR command to determine the creation date for each disk. Use the most recent UNINSTALL disk first.

VER   Network, Internal

Purpose

Displays the DOS version number.

When To Use

Use when you need to see what version of MS-DOS you are using.

Common Syntax and Examples

```
VER
```

To display the MS-DOS version number, type:

```
VER
```

Switches

None.

Note

❏ See the SETVER command for information about reporting earlier version of DOS to applications.

VERIFY   Network, Internal

Purpose

Sets or displays disk verification switch.

When To Use

Use this command when you want DOS to verify that no data is written to any bad sectors as defined in the DOS environment.

Common Syntax and Examples

    VERIFY ON or OFF

VERIFY ON turns the VERIFY feature on.

VERIFY OFF turns off the VERIFY feature.

Switches

None.

Notes

❏ Setting VERIFY to ON can drastically slow disk-intensive applications.

❏ See the SETVER command for information about reporting earlier versions of DOS to applications.

VOL   Network, Internal

Purpose

Displays the volume label and serial number of a disk.

When To Use

Use VOL when you need to see the disk's volume label and serial number.

Common Syntax and Examples

VOL *d1*:

d1 is the drive that contains the disk whose label and serial number you want to view.

Switches

None.

Note

❏ The name reported by the VOL command is set using the LABEL command.

XCOPY   Network, External

Purpose

Copies files, directories and subdirectories, and subdirectories.

When To Use

Use XCOPY when you want to copy all files except system files in a directory and any subdirectories and their files.

Common Syntax and Examples

XCOPY *source* *destination* /A /M /D:*date* /P /S /E /V /W

The *d1:path1* parameter is the location of the original files and subdirectories to be copied.

The *d2:path2* parameter is the new location for the copies of the original files and subdirectories.

The following command copies to drive D the WPDATA directory and any subdirectories, even if they are empty:

XCOPY C:\WPDATA D: /S /E

The following command copies every file from drive A that has a date that falls on or after 04/25/90:

XCOPY A: C: /D:04/25/90

Switches

/A	Copies only those files that have their archive file attribute set without modifying the attributes of the files to be copied.
/M	Copies only those files that have their archive file attribute set but then turns off the attributes in the files to be copied.
/D:*date*	Copies all files on or after the entered date.
/P	Asks if you want destination files created.
/S	Copies all subdirectories that have files in them.
/E	Works with the /S switch to copy even empty subdirectories.
/V	Verifies that each file copied to the destination matches the same file at the source.
/W	Displays the message `Press any key to begin copying file(s)` and waits for your action.

Notes

❏ XCOPY displays the following exit codes:

Code	Description
0	Files were copied without error.
1	No files were found to copy.
2	The user pressed Ctrl-C to terminate XCOPY.
4	Initialization error occurred. There is not enough memory or disk space, or you entered an invalid drive name or invalid syntax on the command line.
5	Disk write error occurred.

❏ The MS-DOS version 5.0 of XCOPY does not copy hidden or system files.

❏ The main differences between XCOPY and DISKCOPY are that XCOPY will copy to disks with a different format, and XCOPY will not format a disk as it copies (unlike DISKCOPY).

A

DOS 5 and Windows 3

This appendix will show you how to configure DOS 5 for use with the Windows environment. If you have already modified your CONFIG.SYS and AUTOEXEC.BAT files to configure your previous version of DOS for the Windows environment, the following sections provide you with information about the additional changes you may need to make to your system. If you have not configured your DOS environment for Windows (that is, if you either have not yet installed Windows or have been using the default configuration created by Windows), this appendix provides an overview of the changes you need to make to get the best performance out of your Windows environment. For more detailed information about configuring DOS for Windows and about tailoring the Windows environment, see *Maximizing Windows 3*, by New Riders Publishing.

If you use standard DOS applications within the Windows environment on a 386- or 486-based machine, DOS' improved memory management makes more conventional memory available within each DOS window. Memory management is discussed in detail in Chapter 11; this appendix focuses on those aspects of DOS configuration that are relevant to the Windows user.

Configuring DOS for Windows

If you are a Windows user who is upgrading to DOS 5, the most significant changes you will notice are the operating system's improved memory management and enhanced performance. Because these improvements are the result of changes in DOS, you do not need to make any changes to Windows in or-

681

der to realize their benefits. You do need to install DOS correctly, however, if you want to take advantage of its enhanced features.

Before you begin the DOS 5 installation, it is a good idea to obtain a printout of your old AUTOEXEC.BAT and CONFIG.SYS files. You can use the printout to check the settings created by the installation procedure against the customized settings you made in your previous DOS configuration.

Using the Correct Memory Drivers

After you install DOS 5, make sure that you are using the current versions of the memory managers. DOS 5 includes versions of HIMEM.SYS and EMM386.EXE (formerly EMM386.SYS), which supercede the memory managers that accompany Windows 3 and DOS 4.01. If you used the standard Windows installation, the DOS 5 installation procedure modifies the current CONFIG.SYS to reference the new drivers in the \DOS subdirectory.

If you use a different memory manager, the installation process leaves the references to the old memory manager intact. You may want to experiment with the new drivers included with DOS 5 to compare their performance against the memory manager you are currently using.

If you use multiple-configuration files, the best solution is to replace any existing memory managers with the new versions. This avoids any possible confusion about which version should be referenced.

You also need to check the hard disk for obsolete drivers. One of the improved file-management tools available within DOS 5 is its capability to search for a file across directories. You can search for a file by issuing the **DIR** command with the /S parameter from your root directory. This procedure enables you to make sure that you have only one copy of the drivers on your system. To check for copies of the Microsoft Expanded-Memory Manager (EMM386), switch to the root directory, and enter the following command:

```
DIR EMM386.* /S
```

The wild card (*) is necessary because the file's name has changed from EMM386.SYS (Windows 3 and DOS 4.01) to EMM386.EXE (DOS 5). When DOS produces a list of the instances of EMM386, it also displays the creation date for each. The one with the newest creation date is the one that should be referenced in your CONFIG.SYS file. If you want to place the memory manager in a directory other than \DOS, you should copy the version of the driver with the latest creation date to the new location. Once you have confirmed that you are loading the proper version of EMM386, go through the same steps and make sure that you are using the current version of HIMEM.SYS.

If you installed Windows (or used DOS 4.01) before you upgraded to DOS 5, you should have copies of the old drivers in your OLD_DOS directory. Leave these copies where they are; you will need them if you decide to uninstall DOS 5. If your disk contains other versions of the drivers, back up the older versions and remove them from the disk. Even if you leave them on your system, the extra files will not cause any problems as long as your CONFIG.SYS points to the current version. Still, it is a good idea to avoid any confusion by eliminating outdated versions of the drivers. Once you are confident that you want to continue with DOS 5, you can run the CLEANUP command to delete the files in the OLD_DOS directory.

Avoiding Conflicts in High Memory

If your system uses extended memory, you need to determine whether any of your programs require the High Memory Area (HMA). DOS 5 needs access to the HMA in order to free the maximum amount of conventional memory. If one of your applications uses the HMA, you cannot move DOS out of conventional memory. To find out whether an application uses the HMA, check the program's manual. To be sure that DOS and your applications do not compete for the HMA, first verify that all your applications work with DOS in conventional memory. Then load DOS into the HMA by placing the DOS=HIGH command in your CONFIG.SYS file. Use the MEM command to confirm DOS' presence in the High Memory Area.

After loading DOS into the HMA, start Windows and check each of your applications. If an application fails to work (but worked with DOS in conventional memory), you know that it requires the HMA and that you will not be able to both move DOS out of conventional memory and use that application. If you discover a conflict between DOS and an application in the HMA, you can choose one of three options:

1. Leave DOS in conventional memory.
2. Discard the application.
3. Create two sets of configuration files.

By creating two sets of configuration files, you can switch between the environments—one with DOS in the HMA, the other for running the application that requires the HMA. Chapter 12 shows you one way to automatically switch between these environments.

Memory Configurations

The settings for HIMEM.SYS are established by the DOS 5 installation procedure. If you are able to load DOS into the HMA, then the HIMEM.SYS file is installed correctly. If you configured your DOS environment to maximize Windows' performance, the DOS 5 installation procedure maintained your customized settings. This includes your configuration for SMARTDrive and RAMDrive. There are, however, some additional changes you should make to EMM386. If you are using the standard environment installed by Windows, you are probably not getting the most from your system.

The first thing to adjust is EMM386.EXE. EMM386.EXE (previously EMM386.SYS) is responsible for controlling the region of memory between 640K and 1M on 80386 and 80486 machines. This area is called the Upper Memory Area (UMA). EMM386.SYS was used only to emulate expanded memory for DOS applications. The current version (EMM386.EXE, included with DOS 5) has the additional capability of managing Upper Memory Blocks.

An Upper Memory Block (UMB) is a region of memory that is normally under the control of the operating system. These regions are not part of the conventional memory used by standard DOS applications, but they can be used to hold device drivers and small applications that do require much memory. By moving device drivers and small applications into the Upper Memory Area (UMA), you increase the amount of conventional memory available for standard DOS applications.

Even if you do not need expanded-memory emulation, it is worthwhile to install EMM386 to take advantage of its capability to move device drivers out of conventional memory. If you do not need expanded-memory emulation, you should use the NOEMS switch on EMM386. In order to enable both expanded-memory emulation and management of the UMA, use the RAM switch on EMM386.

Chapter 10 discusses the process for loading device drivers and utilities into the UMA. The basic steps are to determine how much memory the specific device driver requires, use the DEVICEHIGH= command (rather than the DEVICE= command) to load the driver into a UMB, and then make sure that the driver functions properly. Some drivers do not work in the UMA, so be systematic in how you rearrange them and only move one driver at a time, making sure to test it after it is relocated. If you use a disk cache (such as SMARTDRV.SYS) or a RAM disk (such as RAMDRIVE.SYS), you can relocate these drivers into the UMA. You cannot relocate the EMM386.EXE or HIMEM.SYS drivers into the UMA.

If you are using the settings established by the standard Windows installation procedures, you should consider making some modifications. First, make sure that the FILES= setting in your CONFIG.SYS file is at least 30. Then make sure that your BUFFERS= setting is no more than 20 (assuming that you are using SMARTDrive). Next, make sure that you are getting the best possible performance from SMARTDrive and RAMDrive.

You should use RAMDrive only if you have expanded memory physically installed in your system. If you do, use the /A parameter to create the RAM disk in expanded memory. Modify your AUTOEXEC.BAT file to create a directory called TEMP on the RAM disk and set the TEMP variable to point to that TEMP directory. For more information, read the section in Chapter 10 on using RAMDrive.

If you have sufficient memory, Windows uses a default value of 2048K (2M) as the initial cache size for SMARTDrive. For most people, a more reasonable setting is 1024K (1M) as the initial cache size. This is the cache's maximum size. The second number on the SMARTDRV.SYS line is the minimum cache size. For most purposes, this can be reduced to 256K. If necessary, Windows can dynamically adjust the cache's size. Do not use a figure smaller than 256K because there will be no performance improvement. For more information about SMARTDrive, see Chapter 10.

Finally, if you use a 386 or 486 machine and work in 386-enhanced mode, establish a permanent swap file for your Windows environment. To do this, start Windows in real mode by using the WIN /R command. Once you are within Windows, close all your applications except for the Program Manager. Be sure to close your applications (exit from them) rather than simply minimizing the windows. Activate the SWAPFILE program by using the Run command under the File menu. You are prompted with a dialog with a suggested swap file size. Unless this would take up a significant portion of your hard disk (more than 10 percent), you should accept the recommended configuration. Finally, exit from Windows and restart it in 386-enhanced mode. You should see an improvement in performance when moving between applications.

Using DOS 5 File-Management Features under Windows

File Manager features that rely on an underlying DOS command (such as FORMAT) are automatically upgraded as part of the DOS 5 installation process. Windows simply refers to these DOS commands as necessary, and any changes in the commands are transparent to the user. The DOS 5 environment includes several new file-management features, however, that are not reflected within File Manager. For example, the new UNDELETE and UNFORMAT features are not available in the current version of the Windows File Manager.

Unfortunately, if you want to incorporate the new file-management features into the Windows File Manager, you must upgrade the Windows environment. The best solution at this point is to create PIFs for those DOS file utilities you will use regularly and use the DOS Prompt window for those you use less frequently. If you have trouble running commands in the DOS Prompt window, try creating a new PIF with a larger environment space to use in place of the standard DOS prompt. To do this, enter **COMMAND** as the program title and use the /E flag to increase the environment space. You can then associate the PIF with an icon and use it in place of the standard DOS prompt icon to start a DOS window.

Using the DOS Shell and Windows 3

You need to remember two major points when running the DOS Shell from within Windows. First, you need to decide whether or not you want to run the shell as a Windows application or as a full-screen application. If you want to use the DOS Shell within a window, you must first configure its display as text. If you want to run the shell in graphics mode, you must run it as a full-screen application. To use a mouse with the DOS Shell, you must first start a full-screen DOS window and load MOUSE.COM before starting the DOS Shell. If you use the mouse in all of your applications within Windows, load the MOUSE.SYS driver in your CONFIG.SYS file.

The second point concerns the DOS Shell's task-swapping features versus Windows' multitasking capabilities. Within the DOS Shell, only the current application is processing; all others are suspended. Within Windows' 386-enhanced mode, each application, whether in the foreground or the background, continues to process. Further, the Windows environment gives you much greater control over your applications through the creation of PIFs. Because the Windows environment is more powerful and provides greater control than DOS, there is no advantage to starting applications from within the DOS Shell.

Do not use the DOS Shell (under Windows) to start applications if you want to avoid creating multiple levels of operating systems. If you are not careful, you can activate Windows on top of DOS, start the DOS Shell, then go to the command prompt and activate a second occurrence of Windows. You would then be within one incidence of Windows, which was within a DOS command Shell, which was within the DOS Shell within Windows, all of which was on top of the standard DOS operating system. Obviously, the complexity of your environment at this point increases the chances of program errors and system crashes. Never start applications from within the DOS Shell when running under Windows.

In general, you should use the DOS Shell within Windows for file management only. The best approach is to use the Dual File view within DOS Shell, which gives the maximum amount of file management control while minimizing the risk of running an application from the DOS Shell within Windows rather than from Windows directly.

Summary

The improvement in performance that can be gained from DOS 5 does not require any changes to the Windows environment. Because of the way Windows uses memory, you get the best results from your system if you configure DOS to provide the maximum amount of conventional memory. The system configurations that provided the best environment for Windows in previous versions of DOS still work with DOS 5. You need only to make sure that you are using the current drivers. If you use a permanent swap file and are forced to delete it in order to install DOS, be sure to recreate the file from within Windows when DOS is installed.

Many of the improvements in DOS' file-management capabilities are transparently added to File Manager when you upgrade DOS. An example of this is the modifications in the FORMAT command, which store the information required by UNFORMAT. Some features, such as UNFORMAT, UNDELETE, and the search capabilities of ATTRIB, are available only from within Windows via the DOS Prompt window. If you use these features often, consider creating a separate PIF for each command. If you have trouble executing a DOS command (or series of commands) from within the DOS window, consider creating a new PIF using COMMAND as the program name and expanding the environmental space with the /E parameter.

The DOS Shell has many benefits that are not currently available in the Windows File Manager. If you want to take advantage of these new features, create a PIF for the DOSSHELL command. For the most efficient file management, use the Dual File view within the DOS Shell. If you want to run the DOS Shell within a window, you must set the Display type (within DOS Shell) to Text. Otherwise, the DOS Shell must run as a full-screen application.

B

NetWare Considerations

Novell NetWare provides you with many choices. By providing multiple server platforms, NetWare gives its users the ability to choose from a range of network servers, workstations, and operating systems.

Novell has two basic classes, or families, of its popular NetWare network operating system. The first is NetWare 286, which includes ELS, Advanced, and SFT NetWare. The second is NetWare 386, which emphasizes Novell's open systems focus. Novell enjoys much popularity with over six million users worldwide.

Novell first provided solutions at the workgroup level, allowing groups of DOS users to share resources and data. Now, DOS users find that their familiar operating environment has been extended into NetWare.

Although you simplify support by upgrading all your workstations to the same version of DOS, NetWare supports multiple versions of DOS, including 3.30, 4.01, and 5.0. This appendix shows you which versions of NetWare support DOS 5 and guides you through the steps you must take to upgrade your workstations and servers to DOS 5.

Ensuring Compatibility

Before upgrading your Novell LAN workstations to DOS 5, make sure that you are using one of the following versions of NetWare, which supports DOS 5:

689

NetWare Package	Version Supporting DOS 5
ELS I	2.1x
ELS II	2.1x
Advanced	2.1x
SFT	2.1x
NetWare	2.2
NetWare 386	All versions

If your version of NetWare does not support DOS 5, contact your nearest vendor for an upgrade, or contact Novell.

Make sure that your IPX is version 3.02a or later. You can do this by changing to the directory that contains the file IPX.COM and typing IPX I. Be sure to put a blank space between the x and the I. Your system should return information about your current IPX version as well as the interrupt, DMA, and memory settings. If you do not have IPX version 3.02a, continue to operate your workstations on the older version of DOS until you can get a new copy of IPX.OBJ from NETWIRE on CompuServe or from your Novell vendor.

Running Networked Applications with DOS 5

Certain applications that you have loaded on your network may have trouble operating under DOS 5. Applications that have been designed to look for a specific version of DOS or look for a version range may not work at all, or may report errors. You can use the DOS SETVER command to trick these applications into working with DOS 5, or you can upgrade your application to a later version that specifically supports DOS 5. You may have difficulty, for example, running Central Point Software's PCFORMAT program with DOS 5. You can use the SETVER command to report a DOS version number that PCFORMAT recognizes, by issuing the following command:

```
SETVER C: PCFORMAT.EXE 4.00
```

Use the SETVER command to report DOS version 4.00 to PSPrint, as follows:

```
SETVER C: PSPRINT.EXE 4.00
```

A Note on SETVER

SETVER should be in your CONFIG.SYS file before you attempt these recommendations. The command might appear in your CONFIG.SYS file like this:

```
DEVICE=C:\DOS\SETVER.EXE
```

You need to reboot your machine in order for these changes to take effect. If these recommendations do not fix you particular problem, contact your software vendor for information regarding that application and its support of DOS 5.

Installing DOS 5 on a NetWare LAN

When you install DOS 5 on a NetWare LAN, you should take some time and think through your system. The following is a list of items you should keep in mind as you design your LAN:

❏ Should you upgrade all the workstations on your LAN to DOS 5?

❏ How should you install your dedicated server or nondedicated server, if you use one?

❏ Are there any special considerations or exceptions that have to be taken into account when using DOS 5 on a Novell LAN?

These are all valid questions. In the following pages are some helpful hints, tips, and procedures for using DOS 5 and Novell NetWare. These procedures and tips are not difficult to implement, but do require careful attention and planning.

A Note on Backing Up Your Files

Always make a complete backup of all your data before beginning any modifications to your system. You can use your current DOS BACKUP command to back up your files, or you can use a commercially available backup utility.

If you have any memory-resident programs that automatically load when your system is booted, you need to modify your AUTOEXEC.BAT file so that the programs will not load. Then reboot your machine by pressing Ctrl-Alt-Del.

Installing DOS 5 on a Floppy Disk-Based Workstation

When installing DOS 5 on a floppy-only workstation, take the following steps:

1. Start the computer, using your current version of DOS. Use a backup copy of your original DOS disks to boot the workstation. Do not attach to the server or log in.

2. If you are installing DOS from 5 1/4-inch disks, you need seven disks. Label them as follows:

   ❏ Startup

   ❏ Support

   ❏ Shell

   ❏ Help

   ❏ Basic/Edit

   ❏ Utility

   ❏ Supplemental

   If you are installing DOS from 3 1/2-inch disks, you need four disks. Label them as follows:

   ❏ Startup/Support

   ❏ Shell/Help

   ❏ Basic/Edit/Utility

   ❏ Supplemental

3. Insert Disk 1 into drive A. (If you use a different drive, simply substitute the appropriate drive letter as you follow these steps.)

4. Type `A:SETUP/F` and follow the instructions on your screen. This procedure decompresses the DOS files found on your distribution disks and copies them to the blank disks that you have previously labeled. These disks serve as backup versions of DOS 5 in a decompressed, usable form.

5. The working disks that are created during the setup process are the ones that run DOS 5. Use your original Startup disk to boot your system with DOS.

6. After using the Startup disk to boot the system, make a system disk by typing `SYS A:`. You will need a blank, formatted disk for this procedure. This will be your new workstation boot disk.

7. Your original boot disk (from the previous version of DOS) should contain a number of network files. Copy all the network files (such as IPX.COM, NETBIOS.EXE, SHELL.CFG, or NET.CFG) to your new

boot disk. Do not copy NET3.COM or NET4.COM. Also, do not use NET3.COM or NET4.COM in your AUTOEXEC.BAT or network startup file because they are used for DOS 3.x and DOS 4.x, respectively.

8. Copy NET5.COM to the new boot disk.

9. Copy CONFIG.SYS and AUTOEXEC.BAT from your Startup disk to the new boot disk. Be sure to copy all files that are called for in the CONFIG.SYS or AUTOEXEC.BAT, as well as those that are loaded during system startup, such as EMM386.EXE, HIMEM.SYS, and so on.

10. Edit your AUTOEXEC.BAT file to load IPX.COM and NET5.COM, as well as any other support files you may need.

11. Reboot your machine by pressing Ctrl-Alt-Del. Make sure that your boot disk is in drive A.

12. You now should be ready to log in to your network. You log in by typing LOGIN *username* at the F> prompt.

Installing DOS 5 on a Diskless Workstation

If you must install DOS 5 on a diskless system, take the following steps:

1. Create a boot disk as outlined in the preceding section on floppy-based setup.

2. Add the statement LASTDRIVE=E to your CONFIG.SYS file.

3. Add F: as the last line in your AUTOEXEC.BAT file. Your AUTOEXEC.BAT file should look similar to the following:

```
ECHO OFF
PROMPT $P$G
PATH=;
IPX
NET5
F:
```

4. Create a boot image for the diskless workstation. To create a boot image, you should have supervisor or equivalent access rights. Type DOSGEN at the F: prompt.

5. Copy the file created by DOSGEN (NET$DOS.SYS) to the F:\LOGIN directory along with a new copy of your AUTOEXEC.BAT file.

6. Boot the workstation to test the installation.

If this does not work, you will have to update your network adapter remote boot prom. For more information, contact your network adapter card supplier.

Installing DOS 5 on a Hard Disk-Based Workstation

To install DOS 5 on a workstation with a hard disk, take the following steps:

1. Boot the system using your current version of DOS.

2. Insert Disk 1 into drive A and type `A:SETUP`. If you use a different disk drive, simply substitute the appropriate driver letter when following these steps. Follow the instructions on the screen.

3. Copy NET5.COM to the directory that contains your network files. Replace the command that loads your network shell (typically in your AUTOEXEC.BAT) with NET5.COM.

4. Reboot your machine by pressing Ctrl-Alt-Del.

5. Verify that IPX.COM and NET5.COM have been loaded properly by typing `F:` and pressing Enter.

6. At this point, you should be ready to log in to your network. You log in by typing `LOGIN username` at the `F>` prompt.

If your workstation has multiple partitions, you do not necessarily need to repartition your hard disk before installing DOS 5. You will need to repartition your hard disk, however, if your primary DOS partition is less than 2.8M in size, or if your partition is incompatible with DOS 5.

Even if it is not necessary, you might want to repartition your hard disk to take advantage of the large partitions available under DOS 5. DOS 5 can support a partition as large as 2G.

Installing DOS 5 on a Dedicated Server

To install DOS 5 on a dedicated network file server, take the following steps:

1. Make a set of working floppies for DOS 5, as outlined in the earlier section on floppy-based workstations.

2. Log in as system supervisor.

3. Change directories to SYS:PUBLIC.

4. Make a directory for the particular computer you have. If you use an IBM PS/2, for example, create the directory by typing `MD\PUBLIC\IBM_PC`.

   To change to that directory, for example, type the following command:

   ```
   CD\PUBLIC\IBM_PC
   ```

5. Make a directory for the type of DOS that you have. For example:

   `MD\PUBLIC\IBM_PC\MSDOS`

   To change to that directory, for example, type the following:

   `CD\PUBLIC\IBM_PC\MSDOS`

6. Make a directory for the version of DOS that you have. For example:

   `MD\PUBLIC\IBM_PC\MSDOS\V5.00`

   Note that `5.00` is correct; 5.0 will not work. To change to this directory, type the following:

   `CD\PUBLIC\IBM_PC\MSDOS\V5.00`

7. Copy all files from the set of working disks that you made. For example:

   `COPY A:*.* F:\PUBLIC\IBM_PC\MSDOS\V5.00`

   Repeat this procedure for all disks—seven 5 1/4-inch disks, or four 3 1/2-inch disks.

8. Mark the DOS files as shareable and read-only, such as the following:

   `TYPE: FLAG *.* SRO`

Installing DOS 5 on a Nondedicated Server

To install DOS 5 on a nondedicated network file server, take the following steps:

1. Follow the procedures to create a DOS 5 boot disk as outlined in the preceding section on floppy disk-based systems.

2. Copy NET$OS.* and any other required files (AUTOEXEC.BAT, CONFIG.SYS, and so on) from your existing Server boot disk. (If you have not yet installed a nondedicated Novell server, follow the instructions supplied in the Novell manuals to create the necessary files. Do not use any of the Extended memory features—such as HIMEM.SYS, EMM386.EXE, or DOS=HIGH—of DOS 5 because Novell NetWare requires this memory for its exclusive use.)

3. Boot the server to check the installation.

4. Try logging in from an existing workstation.

5. Install DOS 5 for workstation access by following the instructions given in the preceding section on dedicated servers.

6. Log in to the server from a workstation that has been upgraded to DOS 5, then type **MAP** and press Enter at the F: prompt. Check to see that a search drive is properly mapped to your newly installed DOS 5. (If you do not know how to access DOS from the server, refer to the Novell installation manuals' discussion of the default login script.)

Installing DOS 5 on a NetWare 386 Server

Installing DOS 5 on a NetWare 386 server is essentially the same as installing DOS 5 on a nondedicated server, with the following differences:

❑ NetWare 386 requires a DOS partition, as well as a Novell partition on the servers' hard disk. For this reason, it is critical that you use SETUP /U when installing DOS 5 on a NetWare 386 server. Never use SETUP /H when installing DOS 5.

❑ NetWare 386 also unloads DOS from the server's RAM when it loads up. For this reason, do not load any DOS 5-specific devices or shells.

❑ NetWare 386 servers operate only in dedicated mode.

With these things in mind, here are the steps you should take to upgrade your NetWare 386 server:

1. Install DOS 5 onto the server's DOS partition as outlined in the preceding section on hard disk-based workstations. Do not use any of the extended memory features, such as HIMEM.SYS, EMM386.EXE, or DOS=HIGH of DOS 5; NetWare requires this memory for its exclusive use.

2. Boot the server to check the installation.

3. Try logging in from an existing workstation.

4. Install DOS 5 for workstation access by following the instructions outlined previously for dedicated servers.

5. Log in to the server from a workstation that has been upgraded to DOS 5 and type **MAP** and press Enter at the F: prompt. Make sure that a search drive is properly mapped to your newly installed DOS 5. (If you do not know how to access DOS from the server, refer to the Novell installation manuals' discussion of the default login script.)

Optimizing Your System

This section covers two editable system startup files: CONFIG.SYS and AUTOEXEC.BAT. You will see how you can maximize the amount of conventional memory available on your workstation without sacrificing performance.

Modifying CONFIG.SYS for DOS 5

You will want to make some modifications to your CONFIG.SYS file in order to optimize the configuration. DOS 5 offers configuration capabilities that were not available in previous versions. While your current configuration may be operational, you should make any changes outlined in the following sections that pertain to your specific situation.

Setting the FILES Statement

Follow the standards listed in Chapter 10 for modifying your system's FILES setting, based on the number of simultaneous files that will be used on the workstation's local drives. Use the Novell SHELL.CFG setting FILE HANDLES = *XX* to configure for the number of files that will be accessed at any one time on the server. Because the FILES and FILE HANDLES settings require little memory, you should be able to set them a little high without any negative effects.

Setting the BUFFERS Statement

The BUFFERS statement is a bit tougher to set than the FILES statement. Follow the procedures in Chapter 10 for setting buffers. Remember, however, that less spare memory is available when the workstation shells are loaded; it probably would not be wise to use the secondary cache setting.

Setting DEVICE=HIMEM.SYS

If you use a 286, 386, or 486 system with at least 256K of extended memory, add a DEVICE=HIMEM.SYS statement to your CONFIG.SYS file. Be sure to use the version of HIMEM.SYS supplied with DOS 5.

Setting DOS=HIGH

When added to your CONFIG.SYS file, the DOS=HIGH statement causes DOS to be loaded above the normal area, freeing up additional workstation RAM.

Because NET5.COM is available in a standard memory-only version (no XMSNET5.EXE or EMSNET5.EXE), it would be wise to load DOS=HIGH whenever possible to offset the memory loss. Remember to have DEVICE=HIMEM.SYS in the CONFIG.SYS to allow DOS 5 to be loaded high.

Setting SHELL=

Because most Novell LANs make extensive use of the DOS environment space, you probably will want to increase it. On a hard disk-based workstation, for example, you probably would add the following statement to CONFIG.SYS:

```
SHELL=C:\DOS\COMMAND.COM /E:2048 /P
```

On a floppy disk-based workstation, you might use the following statement:

```
SHELL=A:\COMMAND.COM /E:2048 /P
```

If your system displays error messages such as ?OUT OF ENVIRONMENT SPACE, increase the number. Refer to Chapter 7 for more information on setting the environment space. If every byte counts, then you might consider setting your environment space with 1KB by replacing 2048 with 1024 in the above syntax line.

Modifying AUTOEXEC.BAT for DOS 5

The AUTOEXEC.BAT file is the last file DOS reads when a workstation is booted. It further defines your operating environment. You can configure your serial or parallel ports for printing, set an environment variable for a program to use or define how your DOS prompt will appear. The following section will give you some basic guidelines for this file as related to networks.

Setting the PATH Statement

Because NetWare automatically inserts its own drive letters in a part of the PATH variable each time you log in, you probably should delete the existing PATH yourself as part of your login procedure. You can do this by placing a PATH=; command in the batch file you use to access the LAN.

Setting the PROMPT Statement

To better navigate the subdirectory structure on your server when you are not using the DOS shell, add the **PROMPT PG** statement to your AUTOEXEC.BAT file. This statement causes the operating system to display the current drive and directory path as the DOS prompt.

Loading Terminate-and-Stay-Resident (TSR) Programs

Because workstation RAM is at a premium, load TSR software into the UMA, or in expanded or extended memory whenever possible. Note that some existing TSRs may not behave properly with DOS 5 and NET5.COM. Contact your TSR vendor for specific compatibility information.

Using DOS 5 and Windows 3 on a NetWare Server

Be sure that you do not attempt to place the Windows swap file (SWAPFILE) on the file server. When placed on the server, the swap file can create excessive cable traffic, resulting in problems with both server and Windows performance. If you want to use Windows on the network, you should place the swap file on a local diskette over a server-based drive. Preferably, the swap file should be placed on a local hard drive or in a RAM disk in expanded memory.

For a complete discussion of DOS 5 and Windows, see Appendix A.

C

LAN Manager Considerations

Memory is a precious computer resource. With Microsoft LAN Manager, as with any program, you want to conserve memory to allow space for other programs. Programs run more quickly with more memory, because they do not have to compete with other programs by swapping data in and out of memory.

LAN Manager 2.0 provides the same two *memory managers* as Windows 3 to help use memory to best advantage on a computer running the MS-DOS operating system. These memory managers, however, are replaced by the drivers included with DOS 5.

This appendix describes how you can use memory most efficiently with the two memory managers provided with LAN Manager. You also will find information about third-party memory managers (not provided with LAN Manager) and tips for further reducing LAN Manager's memory use. For a more in-depth discussion of memory management, see Chapter 10.

The discussion begins with an explanation of conventional, extended, and expanded memory. If you already know about these types of memory, skip to the section titled "Using LAN Manager with Memory Managers."

701

For the purpose of discussing LAN Manager, computer memory can be divided into the following areas:

- ❏ **Expanded memory** (as much as 32M), which is memory configured for the Lotus /Intel /Microsoft (LIM) 4.0 expanded-memory specification (EMS). Physical expanded memory on an 8086-based (or higher) computer comes in the form of a card installed in the computer. If an 80386-based computer has only extended memory, an *expanded-memory emulator* memory manager can make some or all of the extended memory act like expanded memory.

- ❏ **Extended memory**, which is memory from 1088K to 16M on 80286-based computers, or to 4G on 80386-based (and higher) computers. Utilities such as Windows 3 SMARTDrive and RAMDrive use extended memory to make extra memory available to programs.

- ❏ The **High Memory Area** (HMA), which is the 64K between 1024K and 1088K. Only one program at a time can use the HMA.

- ❏ The **Upper Memory Area** (UMA), which is the 384K between 640K and 1024K (1M).

- ❏ **Conventional memory**, which is the first 640K. This area holds a portion of the MS-DOS operating system and programs.

The goal of memory management is to balance the use of these memory areas. Some programs require one or another of the areas, affecting your decision about how to plan memory use. For example, DOS 5 can load 50K of its program into the HMA; LAN Manager can load 40K. In most environments, loading DOS into the HMA is the better choice. If you have physical expanded memory, move LAN Manager to the expanded memory region. If you are emulating expanded memory, you will need to balance your programs' extended memory requirements.

Adjusting Memory Managers

In general, to adjust the configuration of memory managers:

- ❏ Decide which memory managers you want to use. This decision is usually based on the computer hardware. For example, an 80286-based computer cannot use an 80386-based expanded memory emulator.

- ❏ Install the memory managers with default options.

- ❏ Measure the memory use (described in the following section).

- ❏ Adjust options for the memory managers by modifying the CONFIG.SYS, AUTOEXEC.BAT, and LANMAN.INI files.

Measuring Memory Use

To get a good balance of memory use, you have to examine the memory configuration and adjust it. Often the only way to know whether a configuration will work is to try it.

To examine how a computer is using its memory, use the MS-DOS MEM command. The /DEBUG option of the MEM command displays a complete description of conventional memory use and a summary of expanded memory use. The /CLASSIFY option displays a listing of the programs loaded into conventional memory and the UMA and summarizes total and free conventional memory. You can also watch for messages when you start the computer. As they start, most memory managers print a message about how much memory they use and in what way they are using it.

In Microsoft Windows 3, choose About from the Help menu in either the Program Manager or the File Manager. A dialog box that contains memory information appears. The "Amount of memory free" field represents conventional memory in real mode, conventional plus extended memory in standard mode, and conventional plus virtual memory in 386 enhanced mode. For information about Windows 3 modes and virtual memory, see *Maximizing Windows 3,* by New Riders Publishing.

Using LAN Manager with Memory Managers

LAN Manager 2.0 includes two memory managers: HIMEM.DOS and EMM386.DOS. These are the same memory managers that are included with Windows 3, although they are named HIMEM.SYS and EMM386.SYS in Windows (and in other programs, such as Microsoft C). These are replaced by newer versions in DOS 5. In addition, the capabilities of EMM386.SYS have been expanded and the name changed to EMM386.EXE.

The HIMEM.DOS memory manager controls use of the HMA. The advantage of this is that access to the HMA is fast. The disadvantage is that only one program can use the HMA at a time.

The EMM386.EXE memory manager emulates expanded memory by making some of the extended memory act like expanded memory. Use EMM386.EXE when an 80386-based computer has only extended memory and you want to use expanded memory with LAN Manager. EMM386.EXE requires that HIMEM.DOS be installed as well, regardless of whether the HMA is being used.

The advantages of this are that LAN Manager does not monopolize expanded memory and that other programs can also use expanded memory. Loading LAN Manager in expanded memory saves more conventional memory than does loading only in the HMA.

The disadvantage is that access to emulated expanded memory is often slower than is access to the HMA. Speed of access to physical expanded memory depends on the manufacturer's device driver that controls the expanded memory card. Access is usually slower than is access to the HMA.

The EMM386.EXE memory manager also controls the UMA. Portions of the UMA are available to hold device drivers and small applications. DOS 5 adds DEVICEHIGH= (for device drivers) and LOADHIGH= (for applications) for freeing conventional memory by relocating program code into the UMA. In addition, some third-party extended memory managers, such as 386MAX and QEMM386, can load drivers or programs into the Upper Memory Area. Although the LAN Manager redirector cannot be loaded high, you might be able to load some components, such as network device drivers, into the upper memory area. The NetBEUI protocol, for example, can be loaded into the UMA. For information about the syntax of EMM386.EXE and HIMEM.SYS and about using the HMA and UMA, see Chapter 10.

You can install memory managers either when you install LAN Manager or anytime afterward. The *Microsoft LAN Manager Installation Guide* explains both procedures.

Loading LAN Manager in Memory

LAN Manager Enhanced can load most of the *redirector* (its core workstation software, about 45K) in the HMA or in expanded memory (EMS). LAN Manager Enhanced also loads most of the Netpopup service (about 12K) in expanded memory whenever expanded memory is available (there is no option to prevent this). LAN Manager Basic can load its redirector (about 32K) only in the HMA or conventional memory.

The memory savings gained from loading the redirector outside conventional memory are offset by the amount of conventional memory used in loading the memory managers themselves.

The following table shows LAN Manager components and the memory areas (other than conventional memory) in which they can be loaded.

Component	LAN Manager Enhanced	LAN Manager Basic
Redirector	HMA OR expanded	HMA
Netpopup Service	EMS or UMA	N/A
Messenger Service	UMA	N/A
Encrypt Service	UMA	N/A
Protocol Manager	None[1]	None[1]
Protocol	UMA	UMA
Network Adapter Drivers	UMA	UMA

For LAN Manager Enhanced, commenting out the LANMAN.INI HIMEM and LIM entries (that is, putting a semicolon at the beginning of the line) is the equivalent of giving the entry a YES value. Note, however, that if the operation does not work, LAN Manager does not display an error message. The HIMEM and LIM entries are in the [workstation] section of LANMAN.INI.

LAN Manager Enhanced loads the redirector in memory according to the following steps:

1. If LIM=YES or if it is commented out, LAN Manager loads the redirector in expanded memory (or emulated expanded memory). If LIM=NO, LAN Manager continues to step 2.

   If LIM=YES and expanded memory is not available, LAN Manager prints an error message and continues to step 2.

   If LIM is commented out and expanded memory is not available, LAN Manager continues to step 2 without printing an error message.

2. If HIMEM=YES or if it is commented out, LAN Manager loads the redirector in the HMA. If HIMEM=NO, LAN Manager continues to step 3.

   If HIMEM=YES and the HMA is not available, LAN Manager prints an error message and continues to step 3.

   If HIMEM is commented out and the HMA is not available, LAN Manager continues to step 3 without printing an error message.

3. LAN Manager loads the redirector in conventional memory.

---

[1]The Protocol Manager must remain in conventional memory.

LAN Manager Basic loads the redirector in the HMA only if the HMA is available and the LANMAN.INI REDIR line does not include a /HIMEM:NO option. You cannot load both DOS and LAN Manager into the HMA.

Recommendations

The first consideration is to free as much conventional memory as possible. Load DOS into the HMA using a DOS=HIGH, UMB in your CONFIG.SYS file. Then, load as many device drivers and utilities into the UMA as is possible using DEVICEHIGH= and LOADHIGH= commands. Finally, decide whether to run LAN Manager in conventional memory or in emulated-expanded memory.

EMM386.EXE is necessary if you want to load LAN Manager in emulated-expanded memory because LAN Manager runs outside Windows. If LAN Manager is the only program to use expanded memory outside Windows 3, you can set a small amount of expanded memory (128K is recommended) by using an option on the EMM386.DOS line in CONFIG.SYS.

Using Other Memory Managers

Only one extended memory manager and one expanded-memory manager can be loaded at a time. You can, however, use other third-party memory managers instead of the ones included with LAN Manager:

❏ For extended memory: use Qualitas 386MAX, Quarterdeck's QEMM386 or any other memory manager compatible with XMS 2.0.

❏ For emulating expanded memory on an 80386-based computer: use Qualitas 386MAX, Compaq CEMM, Quarterdeck QEMM, or any other memory manager compatible with LIM.EMS 4.0.

❏ For physical expanded memory: use the memory manager that accompanies the expanded memory card. Any such memory manager should be compatible with LAN Manager.

❏ For emulating expanded memory on an 80286-based PS/2 computer with an IBM expanded-memory adapter (XMA) installed: use the IBM DOS XMA2EMS.SYS device driver. For more information about XMA2EMS.SYS, see the IBM PC-DOS documentation.

An original equipment manufacturer (OEM) might supply a memory manager with its version of MS-DOS. This memory manager might or might not work with LAN Manager; read the OEM documentation for information about compatibility with the XMS 2.0 and LIM EMS 4.0 specifications.

LAN Manager does not take advantage of virtual control program interface (VCPI) and DOS protected mode interface (DPMI) memory for loading components, but LAN Manager is compatible with programs that use these types of memory.

Recommendations

If a third-party manager offers the benefits of HIMEM.DOS and/or EMM386.DOS and uses less conventional memory itself, use it.

If the memory manager can load any portion of LAN Manager in upper memory and load the redirector in the HMA or expanded memory, use it.

For XMA memory, use the IBM PC-DOS XMAS2EMS.SYS driver.

Other Ways to Save Conventional Memory

An advanced LAN Manager user can save even more conventional memory in the following ways:

❑ Adjust CONFIG.SYS entries so that MS-DOS uses less memory:

CONFIG.SYS Entry	Adjustment To Save Memory
BUFFERS	Reduce the number of buffers to the minimum needed for application programs. LAN Manager does not use these buffers. You can usually use as few as five buffers, or fewer if you also use a disk cache. Each buffer uses 512 bytes of memory.
FILES	Reduce the number of file handles. If you receive an error message about insufficient file handles, increase the number, restart the computer, and try again. Each file handle uses 120 bytes of memory (50 bytes for MS-DOS and 70 bytes for LAN Manager).
LASTDRIVE	Set a drive letter limit low in the alphabet. For example, if you set **LASTDRIVE=H** you can use only letters up to H as drive letters when connecting to network resources. Each drive letter uses 140 bytes of memory (70 bytes for MS-DOS and 70 bytes for LAN Manager). Therefore, LASTDRIVE=H uses 2.5K less memory than LASTDRIVE=Z.

❏ Don't run the LAN Manager Messenger and Netpopup services unless you need them. If you don't expect to send or receive messages, use the Setup program to turn off the services. Choose "View/ modify" from the Actions menu, then remove the check marks for the services in the "Workstation Primary Parameters" dialog box.

❏ Reinstall LAN Manager, using the Setup program to trim LAN Manager size by stripping away functions you might not need. After the installation sequence of dialog boxes and before restarting the computer, choose "Workstation" from the Options menu. In the "Workstation Parameters 3" dialog box, select the level of functions you want. See the *Microsoft LAN Manager Installation Guide* for a description of the options.

❏ Adjust LANMAN.INI buffer entries to use smaller and fewer buffers. Doing so can affect performance; the default values are selected for optimum performance on most networks. The *Microsoft LAN Manager Administrator's Reference* defines ranges and default values for LANMAN.INI entries. The following entries have the greatest effect on memory:

LANMAN.INI Entry	*Adjustment To Save Memory*
NUMBIGBUF	The default is 0 big buffers; do not change setting.
SIZBIGBUF	Unchanged. If you do use big buffers, do not change this setting.
NUMWORKBUF	Reduce the values of these entries.

❏ Adjust other LANMAN.INI entries that consume memory, such as NUMVIEWEDSERVERS and WRKSERVICES. Doing so, however, has little effect—often less than 1K is saved.

❏ Use a protocol and/or network adapter driver that can take advantage of upper memory (and a memory manager that makes upper memory available).

A   B   C

D

Menu Map of the DOS 5 Editor

The new MS-DOS 5 Editor is a full-screen text editor that provides better functionality and is much easier to learn and use than the DOS EDLIN command.

The editor's cursor-handling and editing features are easy to master and are a vast improvement over EDLIN's somewhat cryptic commands. This is because the editor uses cursor-movement and editing commands that are common to many popular word processors, such as Microsoft Word 5.5 for DOS and Word for Windows.

The editor supports a mouse, scroll bars, and the PgUp, PgDn, Home, End, and other standard cursor control keys. The editor also lets you take advantage of pull-down menus and dialog boxes. These features make it easy to perform search-and-replace or cut-and-paste operations that require EDLIN users to memorize constantly changing line numbers and single-letter commands.

You also can customize the editor's screen colors and tab stops. Tabs are particularity useful for creating complex batch files because the editor's Tab creates a temporary left margin. This feature keeps lines aligned under the first Tab stop until you press the Backspace key.

The new editor is useful as a file viewer, as well. Rather than using the TYPE command to view ASCII files, you can simply enter the editor to take advantage of its more flexible file-viewing capabilities.

The following menu map displays the various options available under the editor's five pull-down menus.

709

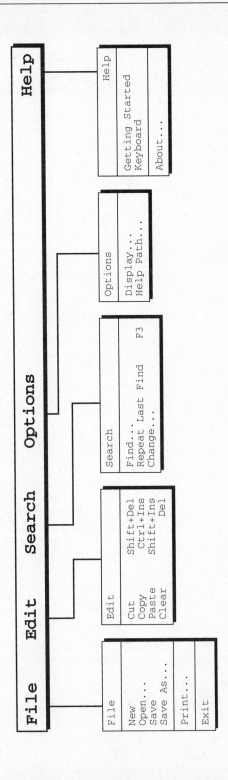

Index

N

Add to Your New Riders Library Today
with the Best Books for the Best Software

To order: Fill in the reverse side, fold, and mail